THE GENESIS OF CZECHOSLOVAKIA

JOSEF KALVODA

EAST EUROPEAN MONOGRAPHS, BOULDER
DISTRIBUTED BY COLUMBIA UNIVERSITY PRESS, NEW YORK

1986

EAST EUROPEAN MONOGRAPHS, NO. CCIX

Copyright ©1986 by Josef Kalvoda
Library of Congress Catalog Card Number 86-80731
ISBN 0-88033-106-2

Printed in the United States of America

TO THOSE
WHO SEARCH FOR TRUTH,
LOVE FREEDOM AND
FIGHT FOR JUSTICE

CONTENTS

Preface	vii
Introduction	1

CHAPTER

I. The Czechs and Slovaks and Their Leaders on the Eve of the War	10
II. The Russian and British Connections	35
III. The Emergence of the Independence Movement	60
IV. The Organization of the Czech Independence Movement by Émigrés Abroad, and Setbacks at Home	75
V. Plans for the Future of Central Europe, and the Struggle for Control of the Independence Movement	110
VI. The Spring and Early Summer of 1917, At Home and Abroad	159
VII. Peace Overtures, Propaganda, and the Building of the Czechoslovak Army	180
VIII. The Bolshevik Revolution	207
IX. The Czech Bolshevik Attempt to Control the Army Corps, the Retreat from the Ukraine, and the Peace of Brest-Litovsk	235
X. The Home Front, Congresses in Rome and Prague, and the Increasing Importance of the Army Abroad	251
XI. Masaryk's Journey to America	271
XII. The Origins of the Conflict Between the Czechoslovak Army and the Bolsheviks	304
XIII. Czechoslovak Resistance to the Bolsheviks, and the Decision to Intervene	339

XIV. The Quest for Recognition, the Fight with the Bolsheviks,
and the Limited Extent of Allied Help   377
XV. The Declaration of Independence   417
XVI. The New State at the Paris Peace Conference   435
XVII. Those Who Fought in Russia and Siberia   466
XVIII. Reflection, Recapitulation, and Aftermath 487

Notes   507
Bibliography   611
Index   649

PREFACE

In preparing this work, I have drawn heavily on my very large collection of documents and materials on Czechoslovak foreign policy (up to 1948), as well as on sources that have come to my attention during research related to other projects. In the attached bibliography, I have translated Czech or Slovak titles in order to indicate the contents of the books or articles for the benefit of those who do not read the language(s). If diacritical marks were not used in the quoted documents, I have left them out. I have not changed the spelling of names, places, or countries, either; therefore, Yugoslavia may be spelled with a Y or J and Czechoslovakia with or without a hyphen (Czecho-Slovakia), etc. In this respect I have been inconsistent in order to be more accurate.

Although I have never subscribed to the concept of a "Czechoslovak nation"–there are Czechs and Slovaks, but no "Czechoslovaks"–the term "Czechoslovaks," as well as the hyphenated terms "Czecho-Slovaks" and "Czecho-Slovakia," will be used occasionally in quoted sources, including the documents presented by the Czecho-Slovak delegation at the Paris Peace Conference in 1919. After the adoption of the 1920 constitution, Czechoslovakia became a unitary and centralized state, and the hyphen was omitted from its name. The unhyphenated terms will be used most often.

It is well known that preconceived notions die hard, that fixed opinions are seldom changed, that one man's objectivity may be another man's bias, and that in the search for truth one may, and sometimes must, destroy old myths and legends. Since reasonable people may disagree and there may be more than one correct (or wrong) interpretation of an historical event, on occasions I have referred in notes to two or three more sources that give different, opposing, or personal points of view or interpretations of the event. History, indeed, is an inexact science. Yet I hope that "The Truth Shall Prevail," as is written in the Czechoslovak coat of arms.

I am greatly indebted to those who have inspired me to write the present study, and my special thanks go to my friends, librarians, and archivists in Prague; Vienna; Washington, D.C.; Stanford, California; Lincoln, Nebraska; Hartford and New Haven, Connecticut; Munich; Marburg; Frankfurt; and elsewhere, who have helped me to secure some of the materials for this book. I am also grateful to those who have commented on drafts of the manuscript at its various stages of development. Since some of those whose kind help I would most like to acknowledge might not want to be named, for reasons of their own, I refrain from the ritual of naming individuals whose help I deeply appreciate. The only exception I make is to name Professors Béla K. Király and Stephen Fischer-Galati, without whose encouragement and help this book would not have been published at this time, and Nancy D. Mann, to thank her for copy-editing the manuscript.

Finally, for any possible error by omission or commission the responsibility is mine. In order to make the book marketable, I have shortened the original manuscript by more than one-third. Since there are several studies on the rise of the modern Czech and Slovak nations, detailed description and analysis of their history and political, social, economic, cultural, and religious developments before World War I have been omitted. Notes and the attached bibliography may serve as a guide for further study.

Avon, Connecticut   Josef Kalvoda
December 15, 19185

INTRODUCTION

The French historian Ernest Denis referred to the Czechs as the conscience of Europe; and Tomáš G. Masaryk, Czechoslovakia's first president, once stated that the Czechoslovak question is both a European and a world question. Indeed, the history of the Czech and Slovak peoples has been intimately linked with the history of all Europe, and all the upheavals that have affected this small country in the heart of Europe have had international repercussions. The Munich crisis of 1938, the events of February 1948, and the Soviet invasion of Czechoslovakia in 1968 provide proof of the above observations which have been valid in the past, are valid today, and will remain valid in the future.

Although historical events are unique, they are brought about and conditioned by series of interrelated events. Therefore, the mind of one who is searching for answers gravitates toward the past, to the beginnings of all things human, to origins and relationships. It is a truism that the key to understanding the present and the future lies in the past, that later results may be understood and explained by what preceded. Thus, this work will undertake to describe and analyze events connected with the rise of Czechoslovakia, proceeding from the assumption that *historia est magistra vitae*—that through understanding the past we may gain a better understanding of the present; that by learning from past mistakes, we may avoid making similar mistakes in the future.

The Czechoslovak Republic came into being in the years 1918 and 1919 by the amalgamation of two groups of territories: Bohemia and Moravia-Silesia, known as the Czech or historical lands, which up til then had formed a part of Cisleithanian Austria, and Slovakia and Ruthenia, which had hitherto been part of the old Hungarian kingdom. When the new state appeared on the map of Europe, the Czechs and Slovaks had a long history. Their Slavic ancestors had lived in the area since the seventh or sixth century, and possibly even earlier.[1] In the ninth century Bohemia became a part of the Frankish empire, and later a part of the subsequently established Holy Roman Empire. The prince of Bohemia became, in the twelfth century, a king and eventually one of the electors of the Holy Roman Empire.

For a time the Czechs, Slovaks, and other western Slavic tribes were unified in the Greater Moravian Empire, whose inhabitants were converted to Christianity in the first half of the ninth century. The Magyar invasion (903-907), however, brought about the breakup of the empire. The Slovaks became subjects of the Crown of St. Stephen (Hungary), while other Western Slavs lived in Bohemia, Moravia, Silesia, Serb (Sorb) Lusatia (in modern Saxony), and other such principalities.

The medieval kingdom of Bohemia, ruling also some adjacent provinces, at one time stretched from the Baltic to the Mediterranean. Occasionally, Czech (Bohemian) kings were also Holy Roman Emperors; and the lands of St. Wenceslas's Crown (Bohemia) were a part of that medieval arrangement until its termination in 1806. Thus the Czech national state existed long before Germany, Italy, and even France and Spain became united.

In the fourteenth century the kingdom had its "golden age" under the rule of Charles IV (I), who was also the Holy Roman Emperor. The fifteenth-century Hussite Wars, however, had long-range repercussions. On the one hand they served as the basis for a variety of interpretations, usually emphasizing the Czech self-image of a small but stubborn nation that was able to take on the whole of Europe. On the other hand, the country was devastated by the religious wars, and, in the long run, internally and externally weakened by the religious divisions in the nation. The process was completed by the extremely destructive Thirty Years' War (1618-1648), which reduced Bohemia's population to about one-fifth of its prewar size. The outcome of the war reaffirmed the rule of the Habsburgs over the kingdom, and the latter remained a part of their domain until 1918.[2]

In the fourteenth and fifteenth centuries the Czech (Bohemian) kings called German craftsmen and miners to settle in Bohemia and Moravia in

Introduction 3

order to develop industries and crafts. After that time Czechs and Germans lived side by side in the Czech lands. The Germans were concentrated largely in the border regions of the historical lands and in some of the larger cities. The Habsburgs' policies, especially in the eighteenth century, resulted in considerable Germanization of the population, especially in the cities and border regions. The Czech language, however, was maintained by the peasants living in the countryside.[3]

The national reawakening in the nineteenth century and the Pan-Slav agitation were manifest among both the Czechs and the Slovaks. Although there were some contacts between the Czechs and Slovaks over the centuries of their separation, the Slovak history, mentality, and culture evolved along different lines from those of the Czechs. In the nineteenth century Slovak written language was adopted by the educated Slovaks. The Slovak Catholics used in their schools one of the dialects as literary language, but it was a central Slovak dialect promoted by Ľudovít Štúr (1815-56) as the Slovak literary language that gradually gained general acceptance among the Slovaks. The language reform, Štúr's political leadership, and his emphasis on a separate Slovak national identity had a lasting impact. They created a permanent schism between the Slovaks as a whole and the Czechs. Only a small group of educated Slovaks, the Hlasists, promoted the idea of Czech-Slovak national unity before World War I.[4] They established the basis for the later concept of a "Czechoslovak" nation, adopted mostly by Czechs (and some Slovaks) during the existence of the first Czechoslovak Republic (1918-1938).

The Czech national reawakening (or renascence) in the nineteenth century reinstilled a sense of national identity and national pride among the Czechs.[5] Thus before World War I the hard-working Czechs were well organized in political parties that reflected the whole spectrum of economic and ideological interests. Their schools produced capable intelligentsia, political leaders, and technically skilled persons who built and developed Czech economic and financial institutions. The growing middle class was prosperous, and cultural life in the historical lands was flourishing. The Czechs, however, had valid political, national, and economic grievances, which their representatives in the Vienna parliament and the provincial diets did not hesitate to voice. In particular, the bulk of the prewar Czech political parties had in their programs the restoration of the historical "state rights" of the Bohemian Crown; that is, they demanded a tripartite arrangement in the Austro-Hungarian empire, in which the St. Wenceslas (Bohemian) Crown would have a position similar to that of St. Stephen (Hungary). Only the Social Democrats and Tomáš Garrigue Masaryk, the only deputy of the Realist party in the Vienna parliament, advocated autonomy for national groups on the basis of "natural right." (There were 107 Czech deputies in the Vienna parliament.) Only one small Czech Progressive State Rights Party had in its prewar program independence for the Bohemian kingdom. But the war created a new situation in which the maximalist demands of the Czech resistance at home and abroad were realized, and the Czechoslovak state was established.[6]

According to the Austro-Hungarian census of 1910, some six million Czechs and two million Slovaks lived in the empire.[7] It may be noted that, in contrast to the Czechs, whose national survival in the Habsburg empire was not in doubt on the eve of the war, the politically and nationally conscious Slovaks were reduced, through the conscious policy of Magyarization, to some one thousand families. The bulk of the Slovak nation consisted of peasants living in the mountainous regions of "Upper Hungary," deeply religious, apolitical, and resigned to their fate. While the Czechs had a full range of well-organized political parties reflecting class and ideological divisions within the nation, the Slovak National party was a loose political organization of leaders without a mass following. The party's representation in the Budapest parliament consisted of three deputies before World War I, and it shrank to just one after the declaration of war. (One deputy was called to military service and the other one resigned his mandate.) Although the policy of Magyarization affected all the national minorities living in Hungary, the nationally and politically conscious Slovaks, in particular, were on the verge of extinction when the war began.[8]

In May 1918, the leaders of the Slovak National party decided to cooperate with the Czechs, as did the Slovaks in the United States. Eventually, on October 30, 1918, political leaders of all political factions, assembled at Turčiansky Sv. Martin, formally established the Slovak National Council and issued a declaration demanding the right of national self-determination. Two days earlier, on October 28, 1918, the Czech National Committee, formed in the summer of 1918, proclaimed Czechoslovak independence in Prague. The delegates from the Slovak National Council, dispatched to Prague, cooperated with the Czechs in the latter's efforts to gain control over the area that became known as Slovakia.

Introduction 5

The Czecho-Slovak National Council in Paris, an exile group led by Tomáš G. Masaryk, Eduard Beneš, and Milan R. Štefánik, issued a declaration of independence, dated October 18, 1918, and announced the formation of a government-in-exile. The Czech National Committee proclaimed independence on October 28, and, in cooperation with the exiles, became the *de facto* government in the Czech lands.[9] Its first task was to secure the borderlands of the historical lands, inhabited predominantly by Germans, and to occupy Slovakia. The Germans were opposed to the establishment of Czech rule and to their becoming a minority in the newly proclaimed state. But the Czechs crushed their resistance and by military force occupied the borderlands during November and December 1918. The governments established by the Germans in several districts were unable to enforce their authority.

In general, three theories of the origins of Czechoslovakia have been advanced by historians and other writers. The first credits the émigrés, notably Masaryk, for winning independence; the second claims that it was the consequence of the Bolshevik revolution in Russia; and the third emphasizes the work of the resisters at home, and their assumption of power on October 28, 1918, as the decisive factor.

After World War I, the most commonly spread version of the story of the origins of Czechoslovakia proceeded from the premises that the plan originally conceived by Tomáš G. Masaryk in 1914 was realized, with some minor changes, in 1918; that eventually all Czech and Slovak political groups began to support this plan; and that, after considerable hesitation, the western powers accepted the idea of the independent state. Thus the victorious powers, most notably France, Great Britain, and the United States, made possible the realization of Czechoslovak independence. This interpretation usually glorifies the unselfishness of the western powers and ascribes idealistic motives to them. Masaryk himself was responsible, in part, for creating the legend that he almost singlehandedly succeeded in creating an independent political unit in the center of Europe. For example, he asserted that during his stay in the United States in 1918, he "was able, step by step, to persuade" the president of the United States, Woodrow Wilson, and the secretary of state, Robert Lansing, to accept his program,[10] and in 1925 he insisted that he had brought the Czechs "independence on a plate."[11] Thus the "Masaryk legend" and the cult of his personality were cultivated not merely by Masaryk's uncritical admirers but also by the "true founder" of Czechoslovakia, who, in his diplomatic efforts, was aided by Beneš, Štefánik, and others.

This version of the story tends to deemphasize the fact that the plans originally conceived by Masaryk and others underwent considerable changes, and that the great powers changed their attitudes toward the Czechoslovak independence movement in accordance with their own interests and plans for the organization of central Europe. It also downgrades the importance of the independence movement at home (led by leaders of prewar political parties, notably Dr. Karel Kramář and Dr. Alois Rašín) and the significance of the actions taken by the "men of the 28th of October," who confronted the world with a *fait accompli* by proclaiming Czechoslovak independence, assuming political power on October 28, 1918, and using the power of the state to secure the boundaries of their new country.[12] Furthermore, it must be pointed out that several historical accidents played into the hands of Masaryk, Beneš, and Štefánik, who, undoubtedly, were quick to take advantage of them.

One of these historical accidents was the Russian Revolution, a turning point in the history of Europe and the world. Interpretations of this event's relationship to Czechoslovak independence gave rise to another school of thought prevalent among Czechoslovak (communist) historiographers and writers after World War II. According to this school of thought, as stated by a Czech Communist Party official, "the realization of the Czechoslovak state independence and the founding of the Czechoslovak Republic on October 28, 1918, was the work of the revolutionary national-liberation movement of the Czechoslovak people, of the national-liberation movement which in the whole Austria-Hungary was inspired by the victory of the Great October Socialist Revolution on November 7, 1917."[13] The implication of this interpretation is that the idea of independence was raised by the followers of Lenin, who emphasized the principle of national self-determination, as if there were no Czech independence movement in existence before November 7, 1917, and as if there were no earlier programs for the establishment of an independent Czechoslovak state. The role of Masaryk is minimized, Kramář and his co-workers are largely ignored, and the role of the "working class" is magnified out of proportion, suggesting that the Czech and Slovak middle classes were against independence while the working class was for it. This view overlooks the facts that the great western powers granted recognition to the provisional government headed by Masaryk *before* the end of the war and that the anti-Bolshevik action of the Czechoslovak army in Russia and Siberia played a prominent role in the west's decision to extend that recognition.

As such and in itself, the legal act of *de facto* recognition by the western powers of the belligerency status of the Masaryk-led committee did not free the Czechs and Slovaks. It did, however, together with Wilsonian rhetoric, over-optimistic messages sent home by Beneš from abroad, and the rapidly deteriorating situation in Austria-Hungary, encourage the leaders of the resistance at home to seize political power on October 28, 1918. But the Marxist-Leninist historians have tried to prove that the collapse of Austria-Hungary and the rise of the Czechoslovak state resulted from an internal social and political revolution that was an "echo" of the October Revolution in Russia. They deny that the western powers were responsible in any way for Czechoslovak independence: "Not the star-spangled banner but the red star of the Great October Socialist Revolution... guided the struggle of the Czech people against Austria."[14] They neglect to mention the acts of Czech and Slovak politicians, and emphasize "mass action"—acts of defiance—of the Czech and Slovak peoples, such as the *švejkovina* of soldiers (an allusion to a satire by Jaroslav Hašek, *The Good Soldier Schweik*), blackmarketeering by civilians, desertions from the army, and general grumbling against the bad economic conditions in Austria-Hungary. Undoubtedly, the Bolshevik Revolution was a contributing factor in the disintegration of the Habsburg empire, but it did not engender the movement for Czechoslovak independence. The movement began long before that event.

The first interpretation has failed to explain the relationship of the October Revolution in Russia, followed by the Peace of Brest-Litovsk and its consequences (e.g., the military encounter of the Czechoslovak army with the Soviets, and the reaction to it by the oppressed peoples in Austria-Hungary) with the establishment of Czechoslovakia in 1918. The second interpretation, as well as the quest for truth, makes it necessary to describe and analyze the various plans and phases in the development of the Czechoslovak independence movement during World War I in order to determine how valid is the claim that "without the October Revolution in Russia there would be no October Revolution in Austria-Hungary."[15]

The views held by Dr. Karel Kramář, the leader of the Czech National Democratic party, journalist Jiří Stříbrný, and others represent a third school of thought. As has been mentioned in note 12, during the period between the two wars critics of Masaryk and Beneš emphasized the importance of the anti-Habsburg struggle at home and asserted that the empire was not broken up from without but broke up from within. This argument began to play a role in domestic politics in Czechoslovakia after the establishment in 1926 of the "middle-class (gentlemen) coalition" (*občanská, panská,* or *černo-zelená koalice*), which consisted of nonsocialist political parties, including the Slovak People's party led by Father Andrej Hlinka. Masaryk and Beneš were bitterly opposed to the exclusion of the socialist parties from the government. Since their supporters did not dare to attack directly Prime Minister Antonín Švehla, who was also the leader of the strongest party (Agrarian or Republican), their attacks were aimed at Dr. Kramář and the Slovak Agrarian, Dr. Milan Hodža, who was charged with opportunism and keeping "two irons in the fire."[16] In 1929 the National Socialist party and the Social Democratic party rejoined the government coalition,[17] but the polemics related to the origins of Czechoslovakia went on, and their bitterness even increased when Kramář and Stříbrný found themselves in opposition in the 1930s.

As Kramář pointed out, the Allies declared themselves in favor of the creation of an independent Polish state at their Versailles Conference held at the beginning of June 1918, but they expressed merely an earnest sympathy for the nationalistic aspirations toward freedom of the Czecho-Slovak peoples.[18] Thus, Kramář argued, Czechoslovak independence neither was given to the Czechs and Slovaks by the Allies, nor resulted from the actions taken by Masaryk and Beneš abroad; it was achieved by the nation itself. As Kramář put it, "At the right historical moment the Czech people, steadied and armed by hundreds of years of hard work, stood up and made *unum necessarium:* the people as a nation demanded its freedom, took it with its own power on October 28, restored the Czech independent state in its historical boundaries, adding Slovakia to it on the basis of the right of self-determination, and from the Allied powers [the nation] did not have to demand anything except the international recognition of its existence."[19]

This thesis was little known outside Czechoslovakia before World War II as well as after it. The successful usually write history; in Czechoslovakia

Introduction

these were Masaryk, Beneš, and their followers during the period between the two wars, and, after they seized power, the communists. Kramář and Stříbrany had no access to the government funds allotted for publicity abroad and could not pay subsidies to foreign journalists and publishers for making their views known;[20] and the foreign public as such had no particular interest in the arguments mentioned above. In contrast, those who tended to give undue credit to Masaryk and those who overemphasized the importance of the October Revolution have been able to bring their views to the attention of Western scholars and publicists. One may add that much of what has been said by some members of both schools of thought—the pro-Masaryk and pro-communist—belongs to the category of legend and semi-legend; the legendary heroes of one school become the legendary villains of the other.

It is not the purpose of this work to argue or to indulge in hair-splitting with this or that writer in order to discredit him or her. Members of all schools, as well as the more detached historians, have made contributions to our knowledge of the subject matter. Their opinions and assertions are here identified as such, and should not be confused with the views of this writer, who has tried to separate the essential from the nonessential, truth from half-truth, and realities from myths, and to avoid lengthy analyses, in order to keep the work within space limitations.

CHAPTER ONE

THE CZECHS AND SLOVAKS AND THEIR LEADERS ON THE EVE OF THE WAR

Before World War I all significant political groups in the Czech lands and Slovakia saw no other more satisfactory and realistic alternative to the existing Austro-Hungarian state.[1] Although they had grievances against the government of the Danubian monarchy, and legitimate demands that they hoped would be met in time, they considered the existing state as the most efficient basis for fulfilling their economic, social, and national desires. There was no Czech or Slovak irredenta in Austria-Hungary, and no significant group of either Czechs or Slovaks living in neighboring countries that could influence the attitudes of the two nations, as the Germans, Poles, Romanians, Italians, and Serbians influenced those who shared their languages within the Habsburg monarchy. The western powers also accepted the existence of the monarchy as a natural barrier against possible German or Russian expansion in the direction of the Balkans and the Near East, and as a viable economic unit in the Danubian area. In fact, the Habsburg monarchy was seen as a guarantor of the European balance against both Germany and Russia.

Although the Czechs and Slovaks cooperated to some extent, especially in the cultural sphere, they had different traditions and histories—and they were at different levels of economic, social, political, and cultural development. Some of the Czechs were free-thinking rationalists, while the Catholic

Eve of the War

majority of the Slovaks was deeply religious. However, the Slovak Protestant minority produced the majority of the Slovak intelligentsia, which shared, to a great degree, the outlook of the free-thinking Czechs. Most of the Slovaks were apolitical; they were not concerned with politics and their national future. On the other hand, the Czechs were highly literate people and their political life was very intense. Although a large part of their intelligentsia was somewhat religiously indifferent, the bulk of the Czechs, especially in the countryside, in Moravia, the mountainous regions, and the small towns, was deeply religious. Among the outer manifestations of this religious sentiment were mass pilgrimages to famous shrines. Indeed, the Czech culture was Catholic, despite the fact that the Roman Catholic church was losing its influence toward the end of the nineteenth and the beginning of the twentieth century.

The Czech and Slovak societies were pluralistic, and so were their nationalisms. In addition to the traditional local and regional attachments and loyalties, the Czechs and Slovaks were divided along economic lines. Indeed, there were class differences in both the two nations, and the various groups within them had their own aspirations. With a few exceptions, the status quo was accepted by the Czechs and Slovaks as a historical and practical necessity, and the proposed reforms and changes were to be carried out within the framework of the body politic. There were among the Slovaks some Russophiles such as Svetozár Hurban Vajanský, while others, like Dr. Milan Hodža, a member of the younger generation of Slovak politicians, sought a better place for the Slovaks within the Danubian empire. Although a few intellectuals, such as Professor Masaryk on the Czech side and Dr. Vavro Šrobár on the Slovak side, believed in "Czechoslovak" cultural unity, there was no plan for the formation of a "Czechoslovak" state.[2]

The pluralism of Czech society and Czech nationalism was reflected in the multiparty system that existed before the war, despite the electoral system which was what is known as single-member district, with two ballots employed in the election of deputies to the Vienna parliament. (In less ideologically divided societies this electoral system tends to produce a two-party system.) After the last prewar election in 1911, the representation of the Czech political groups (fractions) in the Vienna parliament was as follows: the Agrarian party had 36 deputies, the Social Democrats had 26 deputies, the Young Czechs had 14, the National Socials had 13, the

Catholics had 7, a bloc of Progressives had 5, the State Rightists had 4, the Old Czechs had 1, and the Realists had 1, for a total of 107 Czech deputies in Vienna.[3]

Professor Masaryk was elected in a Moravian electoral district as a candidate of the Realist party, with the help of several smaller parties and the Social Democrats who voted for him in the second (runoff) election in order to prevent the election of his opponent, a Catholic party candidate. There were no residency requirements for the candidates. The Realist party was the smallest of the Czech parties, receiving 0.6 percent (less than 5,000) of the total vote cast for the Czech parties in the election.

In contrast to the Slovaks and Ukrainians in Hungary, whose ethnic educational facilities were the most unsatisfactory among the Slavs, the Czechs had the most advanced school system and the lowest illiteracy rate—4.3 percent, as compared with 40.8 percent for Poles and 75.8 percent for Ruthenians. During the seventeenth century, as a result of the Catholic reformation, the Czechs became an overwhelmingly Catholic nation again. Before the war only 2.44 percent of the Czechs belonged to non-Roman Catholic religious denominations (largely Protestant), while the Protestant minority among the strongly religious Slovaks in Hungary amounted to 23.1 percent, in addition to a 5.5 percent minority of Greek Catholics.[4]

Although the Czechs were not as oppressed as the Slovaks, and despite their political organization and their rapidly growing economic power, they did not have equal political rights in the Habsburg monarchy because the electoral system gave a preponderance of political power to the Austrian German aristocracy and middle class. The Czechs who gained prominent positions in the diplomatic service, the government (e.g., Dr. Josef Kaizl), and the army, or who maintained contacts with foreign ambassadors in Vienna (e.g., Dr. Karel Kramář), were few, and their success was due to their exceptional talents and not to equality of opportunity. Therefore, the Czechs continuously struggled for political change within the monarchy, as did the other non-German and non-Hungarian nationalities of the Empire.[5]

It should be pointed out that in contrast to the situation of the Slovaks, who did not have political institutions of their own within the Hungarian Crown, which was dominated by the Magyars, the Czech national movement in the political sphere was strengthened by the permanent existence of the Bohemian and Moravian estates and provincial institutions —the Bohemian and Moravian diets. Thus the Czech leaders had platforms from which they could wage a struggle for the autonomy of the Bohemian Crown and against the state's alliance with Germany.

In the forefront of this national struggle for the equality of the Czech middle class with the Austrian German middle class and for the reconstruction of the monarchy was the Young Czech party.[6] The aim of this party and of many other Czechs was to bring about federalization of the empire. The Czechs found support for this cause among several French and British publicists, for whom the federalized and liberalized monarchy would be the best guarantee aagainst German expansionism. Such a solution was, presumably, also in the best interest of Russia. Therefore, those who were influenced by nationalism and Pan-Slavism (later Neo-Slavism) demanded more autonomy for the Czechs and the transformation of the dual monarchy into a federal state.

Dr. Karel Kramář (1860-1937), who gradually developed his Neo-Slavism and who evolved from Realist to Young Czech leader in 1897, was one of the Czechs who tried to push Vienna out of the Triple Alliance of 1882 and into line with France and Russia.[7] He brought the Czech question to the attention of the European public by writing two articles about it, one published in the *Revue de Paris* (February 1, 1899) and the other in the English *National Review* (October 1902).[8] Both articles provoked many international commentaries. In both of them Kramář stressed the need for a strong and independent Austria in the European balance of power, and pointed out that this could be attained only by a change of Austrian external policy. In the first article Kramář discussed the possibility of a Franco-Austro-Russian alliance; in the other he described the importance of the Czech struggle within Austria and its relationship to the Pan-German plans of Berlin, which were threatening British interests. He suggested the possibility of a change in the pro-German orientation of Austrian policy, asserting that "a strong, internally vigorous Austria, remorselessly antagonistic to the Pan-German designs, is a European necessity—indeed, a condition on which the continued existence of the Europe of to-day depends." Kramář claimed that the idea of a centralized Austria was derived from the Prussian model and that it was not suitable for an empire with many nationalities at different stages of political, social, and economic development. This centralism was strengthened by the dualistic arrangement of 1867, and the Czechs and other Slavic peoples in the Habsburg domain, "more loyal to the Emperor, taken in the mass, than his German subjects, are fighting desperately against the Germanizing and centralizing ideas which are still dominant in the policy of the really ruling power, the bureaucracy of Vienna."[9]

As one would expect, Kramář's article in the *Revue de Paris* attracted the attention of the governments at Vienna and Berlin,[10] while the other article on "Europe and the Bohemian Question," after being reprinted in the London *Times*,[11] was widely commented upon in the international press. Henry Wickham Steed, a correspondent for the *Times* in Berlin and Rome, who began his eleven years' stay in Vienna in 1902, arranged for the reprinting of Kramář's artilce and called it in his commentary "the first authoritative exposition of this aspect of a very important European controversy that has yet been laid before the British public." He also described Kramář as a man loyal to Austria who made a "dispassionate analysis of the situation" and pointed to a "danger to the future of the Austro-Hungarian Empire."[12] At this time Kramář favored a strong and independent Austria-Hungary as a barrier against German imperialism, and he hoped that it would be possible to detach the monarchy from its alliance with Germany and bring about its rapprochement with France and Russia. As he saw it, the best Czech policy was to see to it that Austria-Hungary became internally stronger and thus able to free itself from external German influence.

Kramář was born on December 27, 1860, attended universities at Berlin and Strassburg, earned the degree of Doctor of Laws at Charles University at Prague in April 1884, studied in London, and was the first Czech to enroll at the *École libre des sciences politiques* in Paris.[13] In 1896 Kramář was reelected to the Austrian parliament in Vienna; one year later he became its second vice-president, and between November 17, 1897, and March 1898 he was its first vice-president. After his election as chairman of his party, he became the Czech political leader in Vienna. There he insisted firmly on Bohemian state rights, disagreeing with the Social Democrats and Professor Masaryk in their opposition to state rights and their endorsement of the "natural rights" theory.[14]

Although Kramář made a strenuous effort to make Austria into a state that would be just to all its nationalities, in 1906 he warned that if it became a bastion of Germandom, the Slavic peoples in the empire would lose their interest in the preservation of the monarchy. He quoted František Palacký's words on the need to preserve Austria, as well as those in which the famous historian expressed his confidence in the future of the Czech nation. Kramář fought against centralizing tendencies in the state and hoped that Austria would become a federal, democratic, and predominatly Slavic state.[15] (The majority of the inhabitants of the empire were of Slavic nationality.)

As a prominent Czech political leader, Kramář maintained contacts with known politicians, journalists, and other personalities in Germany, France, Russia, and Great Britain. He tried to reconcile Russia with Austria before 1908, and in 1910 in Sophia he strove for an agreement between Bulgaria and Serbia. Kramář's political program was based on his faith in Slavdom. Its aim was the spiritual unification of all Slavic nations into one "great, strong, indestructible union, guaranteeing independence and a free development to all of its members and, simultaneously, guaranteeing by its strength and spiritual substance peace to Europe and the world."[16] He believed in the coming of the Slavic era in history. After the historical period of the Slavic peoples' sufferings, Kramář prophesied, they would become the guarantors of peace and tranquility to the whole world.[17] He rejected the oppression of one nation by another one, especially of one Slavic nation by another Slavic nation, maintaining that whoever oppresses another nation is not truly a Slav.

Kramář's Neo-Slavism emphasized the cultural links between all Slavic peoples (he, incidentally, was married to a Russian). He maintained contacts with influential Slavic political leaders within the empire, and in Serbia, Bulgaria, and Russia. Among these were Peter Stolypin, then prime minister of Russia, Roman Dmowski, the leader of the Poles, and many others.[18] Kramář rejected Russian political Pan-Slavism and in no way endorsed the weaknesses and excesses of the tsarist regime in Russia. Against the old Russian trinity—autocracy, orthodoxy, and nationalism— he erected a new Neo-Slavic trinity—freedom, equality, and brotherhood. In 1907, at a joint meeting of all Slavic deputies in Vienna, Kramář presented his Neo-Slavic program: Slavdom, as a protection against Germandom and Magyarism, must become a guarantor of European peace. The fundamental principle of Slavic policy was, Kramář emphasized, that it did not want to become either Austrian or Russian, but strictly Slavic. As he saw it, Slavic unity could not be achieved without the active participation of the Russians and the Poles. In an attempt to reconcile Poles with Russians, and with the consent of the Polish political leaders in Austria, he went to St. Petersburg in 1908.[19] To his great joy, Kramář won for the Neo-Slavic idea the whole Russian government, headed by Prime Minister Stolypin, as well as the leaders of the Poles, Roman Dmowski and Count Dzieduszycky, thus achieving, he thought, a Russo-Polish reconciliation. Stolypin made Kramář's negotiations with the Poles easier by agreeing to the restoration of self-government in the Polish kingdom. While at St. Petersburg, Kramář and other Slavic leaders decided to call a Slavic congress at Prague in the same year. In order to implement the decision, a Slavic committee was established at Prague with Kramář as its chairman. However, as it turned out, it was not possible to call an all-Slavic Congress on such short notice. Therefore, in July of 1908, only a preparatory congress was held at Prague, with Kramář presiding over it.

In his opening address Kramář stated the reasons for which the congress had been called—the promotion of Slavic mutuality and cooperation among the Slavs—and he enumerated the principles of Neo-Slavism—equality of all Slavic nations, freedom for each one, economic and cultural development of all, and the demonstration of true brotherhood not merely by words but by deeds. Kramář believed that the fate of each of the Slavic nations was inseparable from the fate of all of them, and that the weakening of one meant opening the way to the common enemy of all. All Slavic nations, Kramář contended, had a common and real interest; the purpose of the congress, then, as well as of Neo-Slavism, was to bring this concept to the attention of all Slavic peoples.[20]

As an anti-German and a pro-Russian monarchist, Kramář held ideas on the future of the Czech lands that reflected his idealistic realism (realistic idealism), Czech nationalism, and Neo-Slavism.[21] The annexation of Bosnia-Herzegovina by Austria-Hungary in 1908 was a "catastrophe" for Kramář's lifetime politics. In his words, "Berlin, not we, will make Austrian policy."[22] The event was for him a foreboding of worldwide conflict. The annexation of Bosnia-Herzegovina violated the Treaty of Berlin of 1878, since its signatories were not consulted in advance of the arbitrary Austro-Hungarian action. One of the signatories was Russia. Believing that Russia was deceived, he severed relations with Berlin's political personalities and parted for good with Austria. The annexation crisis terminated Kramář's efforts to bring about the Austro-Russian rapprochement which he had pursued for years.[23]

Kramář opposed the efforts of Professor Masaryk and the Social Democrats, who attempted to invoke the natural right theory to justify the Czechs' claim to independence, and he consistently supported the historical right to statehood of the Czech lands by pointing out the need to preserve, for economic, military, and other reasons, the unity of the Bohemain Crown, inhabited also by a German minority.[24] After 1908, he began to think seriously about a new arrangement for the Czech nation living in the Habsburg monarchy; however, being a realistic politician, he knew that only a war could bring about the separation of the Bohemian Crown from the Danubian empire. Yet he did not want war, and he feared for the Serbs. In 1909 Stolypin told him that Russia would not be ready for war for another eight or ten years, and that Russia did not want war and needed peace in order to carry out internal reforms and reorganization.[25]

Different from Kramář in outlook, philosphy, and background, Tomáš G. Masaryk (1850-1937) held his position in Czech society by virtue of his strong personality rather than as a leader of a political party. He was the only deputy of the Realist party elected to the Vienna parliament in 1911; he was known abroad as a university professor rather than as a politician. Since a large body of literature about Masaryk is available, there is no need to dwell at length here upon his pre-World War I activities.[26]

Unlike Kramář, who was in the mainstream of Czech politics, Masaryk represented its fringe and was involved in many controversies. Even his true paternity has been a subject of speculation, because of the circumstances of his birth and "a certain family resemblance between Masaryk and Josef Redlich—presumably Masaryk's half-brother, who became a distinguished Austrian politician."[27] Despite his Austrian citizenship, the latter was favored by Masaryk for the office of Czechoslovakia's minister of finances after the war.[28]

Masaryk's mother was a German, born in Moravia. She married a Slovak, ten years her junior, who hardly knew how to read and write. Less than seven months after the wedding, on March 7, 1850, Tomáš was born in a house belonging to a well-to-do Jewish entrepreneur. (Josef Redlich was born there almost two decades later.)[29] Masaryk's mother ran the family and, with her encouragement, he attended German language secondary schools. Later he went to study philosophy at the University of Vienna. He was strongly impressed with Plato, because the Greek philosopher had interests in religion, ethics, and politics; his doctoral thesis (1876)—which, like several of his other manuscripts, Masaryk burned—dealt with Plato's teaching on the immortality of the soul.[30]

Masaryk, a mediocre student, supported himself largely by tutorial work, and as a tutor, he came into contact with well-to-do Jewish families in Vienna. When one of Masaryk's students successfully completed his secondary education, his father sent both of them to Leipzig, where Masaryk studied religion and philosophy.[31] There he met his future wife, the American-born Charlotte Garrigue, whose father had migrated to the United States, where he made good. While Masaryk, supported by his Viennese benefactor, worked toward his "habilitation," Charlotte went back to the United States. Upon having an accident—she fell off a carriage—her father brought Masaryk from Germany to the United States, where he and Charlotte were to be married.[32]

Masaryk was a rather practical man in financial matters, and was not bashful about asking for money before performing any service. While discussing the wedding arrangements, Masaryk asked his future father-in-law to give the couple enough money to live on for three years, until he could support his family. Mr. Garrigue, who expected his future son-in-law to be the provider, drove a hard bargain at first; but since he wanted his daugther to get married, he gave the couple 3,000 German marks and tickets for the trip back to Europe, and sent them some financial help for a few years afterwards.[33] Upon getting married, Masaryk did something that was not usual in his native country: he adopted his wife's former surname—Garrigue—as his own middle name. (Incidentally, Masaryk had made a concession to his German-speaking environment: he changed his original name, Masárik, in Czech Masařík, to Masaryk, in order to make it easier for his fellow students to pronounce.)

Back in Europe, Masaryk continued his work on a manuscript that he wanted to use as the basis for a new application for a lectureship in philosophy. His previous habilitation work on the principles of sociology, submitted to the University of Vienna together with his application, had been rejected. One of the reasons for the rejection was that sociology had no academic status at the university. Furthermore, the university faculty was of the opinion that sociology was not in the area of philosophy either, and did not fit into any of the university's faculties (departments). However, after some delay, two of his former professors accepted it, more because of the capabilities Masaryk had demonstrated as a student than because of the quality of the monograph.³⁴ One of the two professors who accepted the dissertation was Franz Brentano, a former Catholic priest who had left the priesthood and the church.

Before his work on suicide was published in a revised form in 1881, under the title *Suicide as a Social Mass Phenomenon of Modern Civilization,* Masaryk underwent a religious crisis that caused him to leave the church of his childhood and become a Bohemian Brother, joining the Reformed Church in 1880. From then on Masaryk attacked his former religion, with which he had, informally, parted much earlier, during his student years. The struggle against the Catholic church became an obsession for him. He was impressed with *Kulturkampf,* and tried to proselytize for Protestantism among his Catholic acquaintances and students. His preoccupation with religion was already evident in *Suicide,* in which he blamed Liberalism, lacking in religious convictions, for the increase in suicides. In the preface of his monograph he stated that the purpose of his work was to show how suicide as a mass phenomenon developed out of and as a part of modern culture. He believed that suicide as a mass phenomenon occurs periodically; its sudden upsurge was due to the "sickness of our century." In the conclusion of his work he stated that "we need a religion; we need to be religious."³⁵ Fight for religion characterizes most of Masaryk's works; it is, however, *his* religion that he is fighting for, and the Catholic religion that he is fighting against.

In 1879 Masaryk became a *privatdozent* (lecturer) in Vienna, and when a separate university was set up in Prague in which all lectures were to be given in Czech, Masaryk applied for a position as assistant professor of philosophy, an appointment he received in 1883. Since his *Suicide* had been published in German, and since he had to demonstrate that he could give instruction in Czech, Masaryk published an article in Czech with the help of one of his Jewish students at Vienna, Josef Penížek.³⁶ Upon Penížek's initiative, Masaryk gave a lecture on hypnotism that was later put into grammatical and idiomatic Czech by Penížek, who prepared the article for publication. (Masaryk had attended German language schools.) According to one of Masaryk's admirers, Oskar Donath, Penížek could rightfully claim to have prepared Masaryk's way to the University of Prague by helping him to get a publication in Czech and urging him to apply for the position.³⁷

Masaryk's establishment in life was also assisted by another of his students, who committed suicide in Berlin in 1884, naming Masaryk as his sole heir. The inheritance of this fortune (60,000 florins) solved at once Masaryk's financial problems. Now he was able to pay off all his debts, to give financial help to his parents, to found a printing house for his brother, and to found a periodical (*Athenaeum*) for himself.[38] Having material security, he was able to write, publish, travel, and get involved in public affairs. His financial independence made it less risky to take stands on controversial issues of the day. He became an ardent supporter of the movement known as *"Los von Rom!"* (Away from Rome!), a slogan of the anti-Catholic agitation in Germany and Austria.

He received great publicity (a mixed blessing) for the first time during the controversy over the authenticity of two manuscripts (*Rukopisy*) on early Czech history that had been discovered in 1817-18. While the Czech nationalists considered the two manuscripts as evidence of the existence of Czech national consciousness and Czech cultural identity at an early period, Masaryk denounced them as forgeries. Masaryk was neither the first nor the last to question their authenticity. However, the manuscripts have had staunch defenders and the controversy continues.[39]

Masaryk's thinking was strongly influenced by Plato's conception of the philosopher king. Since he came to believe that sociology enables people to recognize the laws that determine the life of nations and states, Masaryk modified the Platonic dictum that kings should be philosophers into the idea of "the rule of sociologists." He was convinced that Plato was right in suggesting that "the unlawful rule of a wise man is not so bad."[40] Here is a clue to Masaryk's wartime political activity and his actions in postwar Czechoslovakia, when he became, indeed, the philospher king.

It has been noted that Masaryk's political thought and his political program included the concept of "an intensive interrelation between culture and politics" with a strong emphasis on education, and that this mode of thought resembles modern totalitarian ideologies or a totalitarian kind of democracy.[41] Thus Masaryk was out of step with the traditional Czech pluralism when he linked education and politics in a Platonic-monistic scheme of things. It is, therefore, hardly surprising that his political party conceived itself as an organization of zealous educators whose task was to bring about the desired changes in the political attitudes of the people. Indeed, the Realist party was merely an organizational backing for Masaryk, and its organ, *Čas*, merely a press agency that claimed that Masaryk was its program, that "Realism is Masaryk"[42] According to the editor of

Čas, Jan Herben, the paper's slogan was "Smash, smash, smash."[43] If Čas had any positive program, it was propaganda and adoration of Masaryk. The latter was hailed as someone able to found not merely a party, "but even a new religion," who "will be praised by future generations;" the latter "will glorify his name...."[44]

Masaryk's preoccupation with religion is well known; what is less known is the nature of his own religion. At one point in his life he wanted to become a Protestant minister and even to establish his own church. The Realist party was often called "the Masaryk sect," and its members called their leader "the Shepherd." He rejected existing churches, Christian doctines, and theological teachings.[45] His *American Lectures* makes, among others, the following statement: "We must separate our lives from churches... we must separate from the church all politics and, above all, morality and religion itself. Religion must be separated from the church, and, I am certain, from all churches. We must overcome Catholicism internally, not externally...." Masaryk called for the creation of "a new religion" that would overcome "all forms of church religion," adding that "this religion cannot be anything else than non-revealed religion, for we search for a non-revealed God, [and] this is our religious aim for which we work."[46]

Among his uncommon views was his concept of history, which was just a step away from the modern totalitarian notion that history is the present reflected in the past. In his own words, "History is not a science and knowledge about what was, and what was a long time ago, but it is knowledge and a science about what is and what will be."[47] For him history was not only the past, "but also the most recent past—that is the present." As he put it, "Also I am history with my conscience and consciousness."[48] Masaryk's concept of history helps one to understand his motivation, his subjective approach to politics and to pursuing personal objectives, his will to power, and his determination to assure for himself a place in history. Masaryk was a persistent critic for whom historical knowledge existed to serve a particular political aim. Similarly, many of his undocumented allegations were politically motivated. For example, in his book *Russland und Europa,* whose first two volumes were published in Germany in 1913, he asserts that "peoples who have remained in the Catholic fold lie more than do the Protestants."[49] Although he submitted no proof of his allegations, it was for him "the fact" that "the Pole does lie more than the Russian...."[50] He assumed what he wanted to prove.

While Kramář and most Czech politicians were Aristotelian pragmatists who accepted the pluralist nature of Czech society and for whom politics was the art of the possible, Masaryk was a Platonic monistic ideologue who wanted to change society and to give a prominent role in politics to the expert or experts—the philosopher king or kings.

After he parted with his original fellow Realists and left the Young Czech party, Masaryk formulated his political-religious-philosophical program in *The Czech Question*[51] and *The Social Question*.[52] In order to carry it out, he established his own political party in 1900. Originally, Masaryk intended to found a new church rather than just a political party. At the founding congress of the Realist party he still preferred the name Alliance of Brethren (*Jednota bratrská*), which would direct the attention of the Czech public to the religious issue, to which he ascribed the foremost importance.

Although the Realist party had few members—"all, or almost all, knew one another"—they made their presence felt in such a way that the party was called "the Masaryk sect."[53] This nickname reflected the strong commitment of its members to their leader, their intolerant attitude, and a zeal possessed usually by religious fanatics. For most members of the Czech intellectual community Masaryk was a rarity; he was an extremist inclined toward religious fanaticism, belligerently anti-Catholic; he was stimulating but not convincing. Among the Czech politicians he had few followers and many opponents, of whom the most prominent was Karel Kramář, though Masaryk was at various times involved in conflicts with Social Democrats, National Socials, Liberals, Conservatives, Catholics (all the time), and atheists. His writings reflected his special interest in philosophy and religion, but he also ventured into sociology and history.

Masaryk taught philosophy at Charles University in Prague, was keenly interested in the Slavic nationalities within the Austro-Hungarian monarchy, and liked to talk about South Slavic national unity, but at no time before the general mobilization in 1914 did he entertain the idea of the dismemberment of the Danubian monarchy or the creation of an all-Slavic empire dominated by Russia. Like the Social Democrats, with whom he had many clashes but who in 1911 made possible his election as a deputy to the Vienna parliament, he was critical of the tsarist regime, and his sympathies had been with the west ever since his student days. He had many personal contacts in France and England; his wife, born in

Brooklyn, New York, helped him to find influential friends and benefactors in the United States. Masaryk visited this country three times before the war. His acquaintance with the situation among the Czechs and Slovaks in American became very useful to him during the war. Helpful, also, was the reputation he enjoyed for his public defense of a Jew who had been tried for murder. Masaryk wrote about it, "The stand I had made in 1899 on behalf of the Jewish tramp, Leopold Hilsner, who had been falsely accused of ritual murder, was also accounted to me for righteousness."[54]

Ever since his public defense of Hilsner, Jews had considered Masaryk to be a philosemite.[55] "As early as 1907," writes Masaryk, "the New York Jews had given me a gigantic reception."[56] His reputation among Jews helped Masaryk in America and elsewhere during the war. As Masaryk recalled later, "the Jews stood by me," and he appreciated the help of both Orthodox Jews and Zionists, especially Louis D. Brandeis of the U.S. Supreme Court, who "came originally from Bohemia and enjoyed President Wilson's confidence."[57] When in 1918 Masaryk was able to obtain a loan of ten million dollars on Wall Street for the then nonexisting Czechoslovakia, he made a note for himself: "Finally, I have been able to sell my Hilsner well!"[58]

The direction of Masaryk's political development and idea underwent considerable change between *The Czech Question* (1895) and *The New Europe* (1918). First he deplored "revolutionary tactics" as obsolete; then he became a revolutionary himself. He did not expect a "world catastrophe" and "realistically took the existence of Austria for granted;" then he played a prominent role in the war and in the dismemberment of Austria-Hungary. But of greatest interest is Masaryk's description of revolution and revolutionaries in *The Social Question*. "Today revolution is narrow-mindedness.... I am against revolution-making because I believe in evolution and progress through work.... A revolutionary is Rosseau's savage, afraid of the growing complexity of society. A revolutionary negates evolution and progress, negates true civilization. Revolution is gross political primitivism.... Naturally, what I am saying here is valid about revolution in general, not merely about a political revolution, a revolution in which men hold weapons in their arms. The same ethical rules apply to economic revolution (e.g., strike), to literary revolution, and to every revolution."[59]

During World War I Masaryk, quite obviously, repudiated the Masaryk of prewar days; now he was describing the war as a "world revolution" (his war memoirs were entitled *Světová revoluce* [World Revolution], and called himself proudly "a revolutionary." He also parted with the view that Germany and Austria-Hungary were constitutional regimes guaranteeing civil rights to individuals, and began to denounce them as "theocracies" with which "the democracies" were fighting in order to reestablish the rights of the small nations (a highly dubious allegation). The "incorrigible pacifist and idealist"[60] of prewar days became a militant antipacifist propagandist during the war.

Any attempt at categorizing Masaryk is likely to stir a controversy, because, as a Czech philosopher sympathetic to Masaryk, Milan Machovec, pointed out, "quite serious people have considered him [Masaryk] to be both a proponent and an opponent of positivism, a Christian and a non-Christian, a theist and an atheist, a friend as well as a passionate enemy of Marxism. None of this is nonsense: all of this *is* contained in his work...."[61] It is possible to quote Masaryk himself either to contradict or to disprove him or his interpreters. On at least one occasion he stated that though he had taught the history of philosophy, the philosophy of history, and sociology, and though he had incorporated his own philosophy and metaphysics into them, he did not lecture or write on philosophy in any systematic manner, and therefore, he "never claimed to be a philosopher, let alone a metaphysician." Masaryk also said that some very intelligent people did not understand him, and that even he "did not understand himself."[62]

In *Tomáš G. Masaryk,* published during the "Prague Spring" in 1968, Machovec asks whether Masaryk was, "in deepest foundations, a *philosopher* or a *politician,* a *scientist* or a *religious moralist.*" Though he himself sees Masaryk as an early existentialist, Machovec answers the question by summarizing what has been written about Masaryk by his admirers and detractors:

> Whereas many Christians and many atheists found in him an almost stereotype Christian—alas, even an untimely personification of the outlived medieval piety in a epoch that was already predominantly non-religious—some theologians and even initiated atheists ascertained that there were not bare elementary foundations for acknowledging his Christianity at all....

> To some he was justifiably one of the most remarkable philosophers of all times, others asserted with no less justification that he was not a philosopher at all.... To professional expert philosophers he was more a moralist or a politician, and, eventually, something between an essayist and a preacher; alas, he neither created a philosophical system nor placed himself within a certain 'school,' and this the expert philosophers could not forgive him. To politicians he was, again, rather a philosopher, a utopian, something between a harmless dreamer and a dangerous rebel, with alternate tendencies running hither and thither; only his stern life success forced them to take him, outwardly, seriously—but even then always with reservations. But not even then did they agree on anything: to some he was, as a philosopher, rather a positivist, while to others he was an opponent of posivitism. Some have discovered in him the most remarkable depths, and others have not found in him, except for a few aphorisms, not a single regular idea that was his own. The expert scholars hesitated even to recognize his elementary university qualification —in their eyes he was merely something between a journalist and a demagogue—and, according to their professional standards, he never pursued 'real scholarship.' As far as his expertise was concerned, every professional specialist—either from the 'left' or from the 'right'—could, in one way or another, underwrite Pekař's condemnatory statements....[63]

Josef Pekař was a distinguished member of the Czech historical fraternity before World War I and a member of the historical school of Jaroslav Goll that revised romanticists' interpretations of the meaning of Czech history. In 1900 Goll, the authoritative Czech historian, questioned Masaryk's claim that churches have a determining influence on modern man; in 1910 Pekař replied to attacks on Goll and his students by one of Masaryk's supporters, J. Vančura, who made unfounded charges against them and questioned their integrity in an article eulogizing Masaryk on the occasion of his sixtieth birthday. In the scholarly Czech historical journal, *Český časopis historický*, Pekař refuted, point by point, Vančura's contentions and noted, at the same time, Masaryk's preoccupation with the anti-Catholic agitation characterized by the slogan "Away from Rome!" He further noted that he and all the other members of the historical school of Goll had escaped Masaryk's influence because their teacher had taught them how to think scientifically, i.e., critically. "We have not been taken in by Masaryk's theories and have not become his followers for the simple reason that Masaryk, as a scholar, does not impress us. . . . When we became mature scholars," writes Pekař, "we have come to realize that whenever Professor Masaryk delves into a historical question, his treatment of it and his judgement passed upon it is one-sided and doctrinaire." As a consequence, Pekař continues, he and the other members of the historical school of Goll "have had a total lack of confidence in the whole work of Masaryk, because where is no solid heuristic and careful criticism, there cannot be scholarship."[64]

Although Pekař did not deny that Masaryk had made a contribution to the cultural development of the Czech nation, and, on the contrary, credited him with enriching public life with several healthy proposals and excellent ideas, he did not want to belong to the group of people who uncritically glorified Masaryk. The Vančura article, Pekař writes, "can be explained and comprehended only if one proceeds from the assumption that it was written by an enthusiastic sectarian whose one-sided concentration of his spiritual attention to a few maxims of his party has deprived him of an ability to see things and people in a normal perspective. We defend freedom of research, which is a precondition of sound science; however, we will not permit that our freedom be limited by party prejudice and church dogmas. The spirit that speaks from Vančura's tracts is the spirit of a sect in which the first duty is the adoration of a domestic pope, and to enter which means, obviously, *sacrificare intellectum.*"[65]

Jan Herben, editor of the Realist party's paper, *Čas,* reacted to Pekař's criticism of Vančura in a series of polemical and, to Goll and Pekař, insulting articles under the title "Masaryk's Sect and the School of Goll," later published in pamphlet form. The unprecedented attack on leading members of the Czech intellectual community by a partisan of Masaryk required a longer and more detailed answer, which was given in the next issue of the *Český časopis historický* by Pekař. Under the title "Masaryk's Czech Philosophy,"[66] he made a broad indictment of the whole thesis of Vančura and other partisans of Masaryk.

Pekař points out, first, that seventeen years "have passed since the publication of *The Czech Question.* During all this long period of time no one submitted it to a factual analysis. "It would seem to me," writes Pekař, "that the fact itself testifies against the claim of direct influence of Masaryk's teaching on Czech historical science." Earlier, in 1898, Pekař had merely stated in *Český časopis historický* that he did not agree with the fundamental ideas of Masaryk's philosophy; but now he submitted the latter to a devastating criticism. Pekař regretted that an analysis of Masaryk's theories in *Český časopis historický* had led to the polemics and belligerent statements of Vančura. But this would not prevent him from submitting Masaryk's positions to an objective and calm criticism. In his endeavor he would follow Masaryk's own advice that we must be interested in finding and spreading the truth. Such an effort, writes Pekař, requires not merely toleration, but also fortitude not to accept uncritically even the most widely spread view. If he made a mistake, he would be glad to stand corrected.

First, Pekař analyzes Masaryk's philosophy of humanity. He notes that Masaryk uses the term without defining it, talks in generalities, makes sweeping generalizations, is vague, and fails to explain what he means by humanism. Masaryk has failed to notice the vast difference between the humanism of the German philosopher Johann W. Herder and the humanism of the Bohemian Brethren, a religious sect founded by Peter Chelčický in the fifteenth century. Pekař gives a series of examples of Masaryk's making equations between contradictory concepts, his manufacturing artificial constructs which have no foundation in facts, his lack of ability to see the structure of reality, and his inconsistencies and contradictions. Pekař points out that Masaryk tries to downgrade those people who preach the ideas of Sts. Cyril and Methodius by saying that whatever they have to say had already been preached by German pastors one hundred years earlier. Yet, Pekař says, although Masaryk takes such an overbearing attitude, he has certainly forgotten that the Czech humanitarian ideal has also come from a German pastor, and that that particular ideal has nothing in common with the Christian humanity of the Bohemian Brethren. One philosopher wrote, "There is no particular national ethics. Morality—humanity must be the aim of every nation." Who was the author of this quotation?, asks Pekař. "T. G. Masaryk in *The Czech Question,* on p. 69," he answers.

Second, Pekař discusses Masaryk's thesis that the Czech question is primarily a religious question, and he shows that the contention is not borne out by a critical examination of the facts. He demolishes Masaryk by Masaryk, who stated in *The Czech Question* that a Czech tries to solve a mystery by reason, while a Russian and a Pole try to solve it by emotion, i.e., religion. Pekař points at Masaryk's using pious platitudes and words without defining their meanings.

Thus, Masaryk's view of the national question is erroneous. On the one hand, Masaryk wants to give the nation a special Czech philosophy and Czech religion, and proceeds from a Czech idea of humanism; on the other, he says that there is no specific national morality or national humanity. Masaryk's analysis of the chain of development by which the Czech national consciousness became what it is now—that is, first humanity, then Slavdom, and finally Czechism—reflects his periodization of history, which has no foundation in fact, but is merely a product of his presumptive mind. The development of the Czech consciousness did not proceed from humanity to Czechism, but, on the contrary, from Czechism to humanity. Furthermore, Masaryk mistakenly asserts that the Czech national consciousness and national character are products of the reformation. If this were true, then the nation would not have outlived the counterreformation. Though its intensity has varied, the Czech national consciousness is as old as Czech history itself, and it reflects the historical continuity of the nation. Its existence did not depend on sudden changes in culture or differences in creeds and churches. The Jesuit Balbin's defense of the Czech language in the seventeenth century, or the consciously nationalistic Catholic Vavák in the late eighteenth century, represent the Czech national feeling as much as those Czechs who lived before and after them. A contemporary Czech atheist is as much a Czech as was a Czech mystic living in the middle ages. It is interesting to note, writes Pekař, that when Joseph II proclaimed the toleration of non-Catholics in 1781, none of the Czech publicists converted to Protestantism.

At the end of the eighteenth century there was no witness of a conscious Czech nationalism among the members of the Evangelical Church comparable to that of the Catholic Vavák. Undoubtedly, national consciousness existed among the Czechs before and after the proclamation of toleration by Joseph II. While it is true that at times in Czech history, e.g., in the sixteenth and seventeenth centuries, the religious idea was stronger than the national idea, nationalism was not always an unmixed blessing. "Violent nationalism, nationalism of blood and iron led primarily the Czech arm at the beginning of the Hussite revolution. At that time some German cities were set on fire... and whole communities were murdered. According to Masaryk's logic, this was the consequence of the religious idea of reformation...."

Four, Masaryk misunderstood the nature of the Czech revival and appropriated the romantic concept of Czech history, as it was worked out in Palacký's time, to his own sociological purposes. Palacký accepted the concept under the influence of Rousseau's theory of the perfectness of man in the state of nature, and, especially, under the influence of Herder and the claim that the ancient Slavs were mild, meek, obedient, democratic, thrifty, and peaceloving—in contrast to the aggressive Germans. Yet a critical investigation of the history of the Slavs and Germans shows that the theory is false. It cannot be squared with the martial spirit of the Hussites and Taborites, and it entails the demonstrably false conclusion that the Russians and Poles are nonbelligerent and thus humane and can easily be subdued.

Fifth, Masaryk, in accordance with Comte, subordinates history to sociology, to sociological preconceptions. In contrast, the historical method investigates the facts and events first and then analyzes them. Masaryk pays no attention to objective reality, and draws conclusions without doing research first; he selects from history whatever fits his preconceived notions and ignores the rest. Pekař draws the conclusion that "Masaryk's methodological approach is not compatible with unprejudiced science. It is a *reactionary* approach."

Sixth, Masaryk's "realism" is in reality quite unrealistic, and he is, in fact, an idealist who selects whatever facts, ideas, and events he judges to be opportune for his prejudgments. "An apostle, or, if you wish, a prophet envelopes and overcomes in Masaryk the scientist," writes Pekař. The violence that Masaryk does to historical science, his inadequate knowledge of the historical method, his ignorance of the strict requirements that a researcher is bound in conscience to follow, make it impossible to go along with Masaryk. Masaryk is not on guard against himself. "The obvious gap in Masaryk's philosophy," says Pekař, "does a damage to what Masaryk wants to achieve. How could we have confidence in such kind of humanity, in such a religion, that backs up its truth by such prohibited means?"

Seventh, there is a gap between Masaryk's theory and his practice. On the one hand, Masaryk strives to attain for himself and his surroundings a life *sub specie aeterni,* a moral life that calls for loving one's own neighbor as one loves oneself, believing that all evil can be eliminated only by everybody's loving everybody. But in all his critical and historical work Masaryk's love is *sub specie humani*. "His love and his hatred appear to be very one-sided, similarly as in all strong individuals who are led by theological instincts, because it does not have enough corrective in a critically calm reason." If Masaryk wrote Czech history, says Pekař, it would be a "work of sacrifice to *his* God;" from the sacrificial altars would "run blood of all those who transgressed *his* law of love and truth." This characteristic is developed even more strongly in Herben, "the principal knight of Masaryk's law of humanity." Masaryk's love appears as a hatred of anyone who disagrees with him. "What is the difference between the violence of the sword and the violence of spirit?" asks Pekař. Masaryk's followers, in their fanaticism, are not able to make a distinction between morality and immorality, truth and lie, and do not hesitate to use the most objectionable methods and calumnies if this use promises an immediate success and if it helps the community of believers to keep their faith in Masaryk's power. They do not hesitate to call those who do not agree with them opportunists and people lacking in moral strength, make wild accusations, and, at the same time, preach "Masaryk's law of love.... The new church, obviously, has her own heaven and hell."

The partisans of Masaryk, Pekař continues, have been able to present a case against the members of the school of Goll only by falsifying the writings of Pekař and others. When Pekař wrote in the previous issue of the historical journal that the state in which he and others live is sufficiently free to make it possible to search for and defend the truth without any hindrance, Dr. Herben twisted the statement and wrote that "a Czech professor kowtows Austrian freedom." Yet Masaryk wrote along the same lines in *The Czech Question:* "Our nation has in our constitutionalism, though the latter is imperfect, so much freedom that it has no reason to use violent tactics. Therefore, today the call for work, small work is so much justified.... Where does the government and police bar our teachers, our priests, our advocates and all others to work and to promote advancement of the people?" Not in vain did Masaryk raise the question, "Should it be so that a lie, in its different forms, would become directly a national weapon?" Falsification of facts and disregard for truth have been common among the members of the sect, writes Pekař. On the one hand Masaryk denounces demagogues, and on the other he and his followers use demagoguery. When Pekař wrote of Professor Vančura that "this Czech Brother behaves as a Jesuit," Dr. Herben twisted his remark by saying that for Pekař the name "Czech Brother" is name calling. The Masaryk partisans speak with a forked tongue; they charge their opponents with what they themselves are actually doing.

It seems to Pekař that Masaryk's overbearing attitude, his lack of tact and of the manners generally accepted in the scholarly community, may be the result of his having grown up in the environment of a foreign culture that was very little affected by the Czech tradition; and that he "came among us with the self-confidence of one who had been brought up in a higher civilization and to whom everything appeared small and petty."

Eighth, science and agitation do not mix. Ever since Goll and some of his older students turned away from Masaryk's "realism" so that they could remain realists and carry on truly cultural and scholarly work, they have become exposed to hateful and unfounded criticism by *Čas* any time they stood on the platform of objective scholarship and presented historical development in a different way than that required by the Czech mythology of Masaryk. "The Masaryk sect has denounced us," writes Pekař, "for not recognizing the historical-philosophical structures of Masaryk and their practical consequences (Away from Rome!), and went as far as charging us with being eager beavers who, for material benefits, have given up their own convictions." When Pekař rejected the smear and false charges, he was denounced on the ground that he rejected Masaryk's theories and practice more from lack of moral character than from lack of intellect; and the whole school of Goll was featured as the "allies of reaction." The spokesmen for today's "realists," Pekař continues, "stand in the anti-scientific camp and attempt to overcome science by journalism. They attack us because we do not want to join their own party's political agitation; they do not notice that we cannot accept their pseudo-scientific program . . . nor can we accept their *method* of struggle." *Čas* mounts personal attacks on anyone "who in defense of scientific conviction and conscience stands up against the mystical and mythical ideology of Masaryk. . . . The question is raised again whether a brutal power will suppress the idea. . . ."

Pekař concludes that he is aware of the need for moral courage "on the part of anyone who wants to say what has been no secret for a long time, but what even brave friends avoided saying for fear of terror of the daily press and the whole sect. I am not sorry for what I have done," writes Pekař. "I have contempt for their insults. I believe that I will make a certain contribution if I point at the untenable orthodoxy that has been changed into a sacred dogma and that has been the more dangerous because it has dressed itself deceitfully in a scientific garb." Here ends Pekař's criticism of Masaryk's theories and his rejection of the character-assassination techniques used by his followers. The publication of the foregoing analysis, unprecedented in the gentlemanly, tolerant, and scholarly atmosphere of Czech intellectual life, reflected Masaryk's isolation from its mainstream. His isolation was even greater in the political arena.

In contrast to the Realist party, which was merely a sect, the Czech Social Democratic party was a mass party, internationalist and Marxian in its outlook; it polled more votes than any other Czech party in the 1907 and 1911 elections. It opposed the radical Czech nationalism that was looking beyond the boundary of the state to tsarist Russia. The Social Democratic party, antitsarist and antimilitarist, as were the other European Social Democratic parties, stood for the preservation of the Danubian empire, demanding its transformation into a federation in which all the nations would have autonomy, and for the neutralization of the state in international politics. The party and its leader, Bohumír Šmeral, took the existence of Austria-Hungary, a viable economic unit in the center of Europe, for granted. A resolution passed by the party's congress in 1913 stated, "Czech Social Democracy declares openly and with no reservation whatever that the Czech question, being that of the future of a nation with no consanguine people beyond the boundaries of this state to which it could attach itself, can be solved only within the framework of Austria."[67]

Slavic deputies in the Austrian parliament, under Czech guidance and apart from the Poles, formed a loose coalition of parties to protect and promote the welfare of all the Slavic nations of the empire. The Czech Agrarian deputy, František Udržal, indicated what their aim was when he went one step beyond the position of the Czech Social Democrats and declared in an address to parliament, "We wish to save the Austrian parliament from utter ruin, but we wish to save it for the Slavs of Austria, who form two-thirds of the population. The empire is ours by right. The Slav question must be solved in favor of the Slavs in the north, in the south, and in the east of the empire. The present government must be done away with."[68] Thus the Agrarians and Social Democrats, the largest political parties representing the majority of the Czechs before the war, operated within the status quo of the Habsburg monarchy; so did the Catholic parties, which, moreover, expressly endorsed the ruling dynasty.

Although all leading Czech politicians had reckoned with the possibility of a European war since 1912, only the State Rights party, led by Deputy Antonín Kalina, supported publicly and openly the idea of an independent Czech state in the Czech historical boundaries. In May 1914, the party held its congress, which issued a manifesto in Czech, French, and Russian calling upon the Czech nation to be prepared for the possibility of a world catastrophe and to adopt a belief in the necessity of an independent Czech state. The manifesto, drafted largely by Deputy Antonín Kalina, Dr. Vítězslav Štěpánek, and Dr. Lev Borský, declared the Czech question to be not merely an internal affair of the Habsburg monarchy but an international question. It rejected the foreign policy of Austria-Hungary; it stated that both Europe and Germany knew that the restoration of a Czech state would mean the collapse of the policy of the Triple Alliance (the Central Powers), for which the Czechs were not responsible and which they opposed.[69] The manifesto, however, was ignored by all the other Czech political parties, because of the State Rights party's isolation (Kalina was a fiery orator, direct, uncompromising, undiplomatic, and much too honest for a politician), and the other parties' preoccupation with bread-and-butter issues, intraparty conflicts, and scandals, especially the "Šviha affair."[70]

The National Social party, which consistently opposed the Young Czech activist policy in Vienna, was anti-Austrian in its outlook, but the "Šviha affair" weakened it internally and externally. In December 1913, the chairman of the Club of the Deputies of the Czech National Social party in the Vienna parliament and vice-chairman of the party, Dr. Karel Šviha, made a secret offer to the Austrian government that he would deliver, for a monetary payoff, his party's vote on a measure pertaining to national defense. During the ensuing controversy over the role of Dr. Šviha in the incident, Masaryk fervently defended his colleague and the National Social party in court as well as outside it. Eventually, conclusive evidence was presented in court showing that, despite Šviha's denials and Masaryk's defense of his innocence, Šviha was a police informer who received regular monetary payments for services rendered to the director of police in Prague. The controversy was fought bitterly; as a consequence of it, both Masaryk's reputation and the credibility of the National Social party were shattered.[71]

The Slovaks, despite their oppression, continued to develop and assert their national identity. Among their leaders were a member of the older generation, the Russophile poet and political writer Svetozár Hurban Vajanský (1847-1916), and a Catholic priest, Andrej Hlinka (1864-1938). Both of them had experienced Magyar injustice, spending some time in the Magyar prison of Szeged, and both of them believed in the future of their nation. Both of them considered the Czechs as their brothers, but neither ever contemplated a fusion of the Slovaks with the Czechs, whose history, development, and culture were different. Vajanský had a faith in the historical mission of the Slovaks, whom he saw as "a nationality and a nation recognized by the throne and the law, a nation having not only its duties but also its rights."[72] His belief in Slovak nationhood, and in the Slovaks' being a separate entity in Slavdom, was shared by the Slovaks in Russia, organized in the Russo-Slovak L'. Štúr Society, and by the Russian government. In view of the fact that Vienna acquiesced in the Magyarization policies and the discrimination against Slovaks in the Hungarian-dominated half of the empire, Vajanský expected help for the Slovak nation from its powerful Russian brother. On the other hand, Dr. Milan Hodža, a younger Slovak politician, hoped and strove for federalization of the Danubian empire. Some Slovaks, the Hlasists,[73] subscribed to cultural mutuality with the Czechs and, being Czechophiles, hoped for the fusion of the Slovaks with the Czechs. Most importantly, however, the number of politically aware Slovaks was small.

Before the war the idea of one "Czechoslovak" nation and a political program for the establishment of an independent "Czechoslovak" state did not arise among the Slovaks. Therefore, the Slovaks did not expressly reject it. The Slovak politicians did not foresee the probability of such an independent state and of the dismemberment of the Austro-Hungarian empire, any more than did the vast majority of their Czech colleagues.

CHAPTER TWO

THE RUSSIAN AND BRITISH CONNECTIONS

Since Russia and Great Britian were great powers whose interests often conflicted in the Far East, the Near and Middle East, and the Balkans, their governments closely followed political, economic, and military developments in Austria-Hungary and were well acquainted with nationality problems in the multinational empire. Their observers and diplomats reported on events and personalities in the Habsburg domain, including Neo-Slav agitation.[1] It was no secret that the Czechs and Slovaks had strong pro-Russian sympathies and that traditional hostilities between the Poles and the Russians were a barrier to close political cooperation between the latter and the Western Slavs.

Among the Czech politicians who cultivated contacts with Russian, Serbian, and Bulgarian politicians was the leader of the National Social party, Václav Klofáč. He often spoke about Slavic socialism. In January 1914, he went to St. Petersburg to meet the Russian minister of foreign affairs, Sergei Sazonov, who, in turn, arranged for Klofáč a meeting with the chief of the general staff, General Zhilinsky. In their discussion Klofáč offered to organize a spy network that would work for Russia and that would conduct sabotage in the event of war. Officers and workers of the National Social party would cooperate with this network, especially in eastern Moravia and Austrian Silesia, since these regions would be especially important for Russia in a prospective invasion of Galicia and the following entry of Russian trops into the Czech lands.[2] Upon his return to

Prague, Klofáč prepared a secret memorandum on the subject that was sent through the Russian consulate in Prague to Sazonov in February 1914. Klofáč wrote that the mood of the Czechs was pro-Slavic and Russophile, and that Russian policy ought to ensure that the intensity of this attitude did not diminish. The Russian policymakers, he felt, should realize what this particular tendency among the Czechs would mean in the event of war. He proposed the establishment of offices, especially in eastern Moravia and Austrian Silesia, that would prepare the population for eventual invasion by Russian troops and that would have a list of reliable individuals to whom the Russian army could turn. The conclusion of this secret memorandum mentioned the need for 10,000 rubles annually to cover the project's expenses, including newspaper publication.[3]

The views of the National Socials were not shared by the other, more significant, Czech political groups; nor did the Russian government expect the war to come before 1917. Foreign Minister Sazonov informed Klofáč and the leader of the Czech gymnastic organization, *Sokol*, Dr. Josef Scheiner (who was in sympathy with Klofáč's views and who visited St. Petersburg in February 1914), that the Russian government could not consider Klofáč's propositions. Sazonov told Scheiner, "You are an interesting nation, but we have no interest in you. Do not rely on us; we do not have you in our military plans."[4] A careful scrutiny of the entire incident leads one to believe, however, that Sazonov was a cautious diplomat who was concerned about the possibility of an indiscretion. Had Russia had the Czechs in her warplans, Sazonov would not have revealed the fact to any foreigner, not even to Klofáč or Scheiner. There is overwhelming evidence that Sazonov was interested in the Czechs and Slovaks, though at that time he would hardly have proposed to anyone, including the tsar, their incorporation into the Russian empire. As Kramář pointed out after the war, a great power "cannot make foreign policy in the street."[5]

The Neo-Slav Kramář was pushed further into the arms of Russia by the Pan-Germanism of some Austrian Germans, who expressed contempt for all Slavic peoples, insisted on their own superiority, and looked to Germany for leadership. Also, during the Balkan Wars, in a speech in the German Reichstag on April 7, 1913, Chancellor Theobald von Bethmann-Hollweg used the unfortunate phrase, "struggle between Germandom and Slavdom"—a strong wind for the Russophile sails. In the spring of 1914,

Kramář, sensing an approaching crisis, began to realize that, in the event of war with Russia, the activist policy of the Young Czech party would have undesirable consequences. Therefore, in May 1914, before the outbreak of war, he drew up an outline for a federation of Slavic nations to be established under Russia's leadership and headed by the Russian tsar. This plan, which Kramář called the Constitution of the Slavic Empire, was based on his faith in Russia and reflected his Neo-Slavic feelings.[6] It was given personally by Kramář to Sazonov in Bucharest on June 16, 1914. (Although Kramář's plan was meant to be a secret, Masaryk learned about it from Vsevolod Svatkovsky, a Russian journalist and intelligence officer whom he met in Italy in December 1914.)[7]

In the event of war and Russian victory, Kramář proposed to resolve the problem not only of the Czechs but of all the small nations in the area between Germany and Russia.[8] The plan called for the establishment of an empire in which the tsar of Russia would also be the Polish and Czech king (tsar), and to which the tsardom of Bulgaria, the kingdom of Serbia, and the kingdom of Montenegro would also belong. The Russian tsar would represent the empire in international relations; he would have the right to appoint ministers of foreign affairs, war, and navy, common to the whole empire; and he would have the power to call the Imperial Council and the imperial *Duma* into session. The composition of the two legislative chambers, with Russia having the largest representation, would guarantee Russia's hegemony in the federation. The proposal called, furthermore, for compulsory teaching of the Russian language in non-Russian parts of the empire, and a common army and navy in which Russian would be the language of command. This project would also solve the problem of Slovakia, the latter being incorporated into the Czech lands already enlarged by Kladsko (Gladstein) and Serb Lusatia in Saxony. The Serbian kingdom would be enlarged by incorporating into it all the territories inhabited by Slavs in southern Austria-Hungary and merging Istria with Trieste and western Hungary, so that Serbia would border on the Czech kingdom.

Both Kramář's concepts, the one that had advocated the federalization of Austria-Hungary before 1908, and now the one proposing a Slavic empire, had one thing in common: neither one of them anticipated the possibility of a completely independent Czech or Czechoslovak state. For geographical, economic, and military reasons, in both of them the Czech lands were a part of a larger political unit. Kramář was aware (as was Masaryk) of the geographical factor: the Czechs were surrounded by Germans in the west, south, and north. Indeed, in one of his political speeches, on January 13, 1913, Kramář expressed his disbelief in the feasibility and advisability of a completely independent state: "Only immature political children can think of an independent Czech sthat that could be established in the center of Europe, on the line of Germany's political and economic expansion.... Because of its geographic location and economic importance, the Kingdom of Bohemia is predestined to be a cornerstone of a great power, its own or foreign...."[9] It may be noted that Kramář's proposed Slavic empire was intended to unify the Slavic countries in a similar way that the Geman empire created by Bismarck had unified the German states. The constitution of the German federation was used as a model. Prussia's leading role and her privileged position were in this case assigned to Russia, and the position of the German Kaiser in the person of the King of Prussia formed the prototype for the position of "Emperor of All Slavs and All Russia" in the person of the Russian tsar.[10]

This plan indicated that Kramář expected the Czech question to be solved by a war in which Russia would be the victor and would expand its holdings into the center of Europe. Kramář's plan also served as a conceptual framework for political action abroad at the beginning of the war. (After the war, Masaryk wrote that "the Allies expected Russians to arrive in the Czech Lands and provide arms for our people.")[11] It must be added, however, that this conceptual framework became the program for a concrete political action only after the war started. Until then, not even Kramář believed in the possibility of an "independent" Czech state affiliated with Russia.

After the beginning of the war, the majority of the Young Czech party politicians followed a pro-Austrian course, hoping for an Austrian solution of the Czech question. Furthermore, the National Socials were not uniformly behind Klofáč; a significant group of them pointed at the reactionary outlook of the tsarist regime and the unrealistic nature of the expectations that this regime could bring freedom to the oppressed nations of the Habsburg monarchy. The prevailing opinions within the Agrarian party was that Austria-Hungary was going to win the war and that a revolutionary action would be mere adventurism.[12] The Social Democratic party continued to pursue its pro-Austrian orientation; and Masaryk, who used to be called the "defender of Jews" or "traitor of the nation" by the National Socials, stood apart from the radical nationalists because of their enthusiasm for Russia and the tsar.

Although he was sympathetic to the Russian people, Masaryk's criticism of tsarism was expressed in his largest and best known work, *Russia and Europe*. In contrast to Klofáč's conspiratorial alliance with tsarist officials and Kramář's Neo-Slavism, Masaryk's ideas attempted to connect the Czech question with the problem of all small nations in Europe; he wanted to solve it through political and social progress and the peaceful development of European society. He found support for this idea from several journalists, university professors, and politicians in various European countries, including Henry Wickham Steed and R. W. Seton-Watson of England, Paul Miliukov of Russia, Baerenreither of Austria, Oscar Jaszi of Hungary, and Vandervelde of Belgium. To propagate their ideas, the *European Review,* under the editorship of Seton-Waton, was to be founded; however, the outbreak of war destroyed the whole project.[13]

When the war started, the vast majority of Czech politicians shared the belief that the breakup of the Austro-Hungarian state was not practicable, and that its political existence could not be terminated. The Social Democrats held tenaciously to their program of transforming the Austro-Hungarian empire into a socialist state, and rejected all attacks upon the territorial integrity of the unit as manifestations of nationalistic policy and class-oriented attempts to destroy the unity of the working class, playing into the hands of reactionary Russian tsarism. The majority of the Young Czech party (despite Kramář's secret contacts with the Russians) pursued the activist policy, as did the Agrarian party and a part of the National Social party. The Czech (Bohemian and Moravian) Catholic parties were not only pro-Austrian but also pro-Habsburg. This situation was a reality that had to be borne in mind by the individuals who undertook political action abroad; they had to try to win over to their program this majority of Czech politicians and the Czech people.

Kramář's first clandestine wartime contact abroad was Vladimír Sís, a correspondent of *Národní Listy*. Sís, stationed at Sophia, could not return home because of an article written by him before the war but published after its outbreak. As the Austrian police had issued a warrant for his arrest, he remained abroad and supplied Kramář, through his brother, František Sís, secretary general of the Young Czech party, with confidential information written in invisible ink and dispatched by special couriers to Prague. Rudolf Kepl, in Paris, was another of Kramář's confidants. On December 25, 1914, one of Kramář's followers, Dr. Vítězslav Štěpánek, arrived in Switzerland, where he became one of the closest collaborators of Svatopluk Koníček-Horský, a Czech-Russian emissary in Western Europe. (His activities will be discussed later.) Through these contacts abroad Kramář was kept well informed about international developments as well as about specifically Czech matters, e.g., the establishment of the *Družina* in Russia, discussed in the next chapter, which seemed to confirm Lois Tuček's prewar dreams that the Czechs would be liberated by a joint effort of Russians and Czechs. The people who maintained contact with Kramář were also eager to find out what the Czech (Kramář's) program was and what contingency plans were being made by the Czech political leaders with respect to Austria-Hungary.[14]

Kramář's activity at home was twofold. First, until he was arrested, the leader of the Young Czech party tried with some success to restrain the other leaders of his party, as well as politicians belonging to other political parties, in their manifestations of loyalty to Austria-Hungary. Second, he saw the need to keep the Allied governments informed about his plans for the future of the Czechs. Therefore, Kramář's political program to which he added new demands, in addition to those contained in the proposed "Constitution of the Slavic Empire," was transmitted by the Russian correspondent Vsevolod Svatkovsky, who became an intelligence officer of the Russian ministry of war and who was in Switzerland at that time, to Russian Foreign Minister Sazonov before the end of 1914. The Russian government was the first of the Allied governments to know of Kramář's plan, according to which the territory of the kingdom of Bohemia was to be enlarged to include upper and lower Austria north of the Danube, though without Vienna. Kramář's program was also sent by a special courier to Vladimír Sís at Sophia, where Sís prepared a memorandum based on Kramář's demands that was handed, together with a map of the proposed Czech state to the Entente ambassadors at Sophia in March 1915. This memorandum, in contrast to Kramář's original proposal, called for an *independent* Czech state including the kingdom of Bohemia, Lusatia and Slovakia. Thus the Entente powes knew of Kramář's proposal and his demands.

In view of Kramář's prominent position among the Czech leaders, one may assume that Sazonov was pleased with the proposal; he could reasonably have considered it to be a definition of Czech interests and aspirations, which the Russian government would support "against any outside interference hostile to their [Czechs] national aims," to use Sazonov's own words.[15] While Kramář's proposal in no way conflicted with Russian national interests at that point, the British, traditionally concerned with the maintenance of the balance of power in Europe, could hardly have favored it. In 1907, Sir Eyre Crowe, a permanent undersecretary in the British Foreign Office, wrote a now-famous memorandum on the wisdom of the balance. (The memorandum was secret when it was written, but was later published.)[16] Crowe argued that the primary interest of every state is the preservation of its national independence. Furthermore, he said, England had an interest in the independence of states on the continent of Europe, and was the natural ally of the smaller powers, because England is endangered if Europe comes under the dominance of one larger power or of a combination of powers. So long as Europe is divided against herself, England is safe. England, therefore, has historically entered alliances to oppose those who would concentrate hegemony over Europe in the hands of a single state or group of states.

In accordance with this principle, one week before the British declaration of war on Austria-Hungary, Crowe advocated surrounding the Central Powers with a ring of states connected to the Allied cause, a "fence shutting off Germany and Austria from the rest of the world."[17] In order to accomplish this objective, he proposed to offer arms, money, and some of the territories of the Central Powers to these states. But, his proposal counted upon the continued existence of Austria-Hungary in the European balance; and the establishment of Kramář's proposed Czech state, allied with Russia, would hardly be compatible with such a policy. The implementation of Kramář's plan would require either the complete dismemberment of Austria-Hungary or her reduction to a rump that would cease to be a viable political, economic, and military unit in Central Europe. In the existing situation the British national interest demanded the preservation of a weakened, but not powerless, Austria-Hungary, and her separation from Germany. The time was yet to come when an alternative to Kramář's proposed Czech state would be offered to the British government by Masaryk.

After Great Britain declared war on Germany on August 4, Masaryk came to believe that the conflict was motivated by the economic and political interests of the great powers. It was a contest for supremacy between England and Germany, whom he saw as the two principal rivals in the imperialistic struggle.[17] Masaryk was well known among the Czechs in the United States, just as Kramář was known in Russia. At the beginning of September 1914, a group of Czech-Americans passed through London, returning from Bohemia to the United States. Among them was Emanuel Victor Voska, a self-made businessman, who had come to America as a youth and who had already been cooperating with Masaryk before the war. In August, Voska visited Masaryk in Prague; the latter gave him documents and information for Henry Wickham Steed, political editor of the *Times* (London), who for years had been a correspondent of the paper in Rome and Vienna.[19] Steed left Vienna in 1913, and as the British expert on Austria-Hungary and the foreign editor of the *Times*, he had "much to do with the Foreign Office." It was he "who had first introduced" Robert W. Seton-Watson "into that building."[20]

Masaryk had been intimate with Steed, had known historian Seton-Watson, at least since the so-called Zagreb treason trial in 1909;[21] now he asked the British journalist, who had great clout in British government circles, for information about the war aims of the Entente Powers. Among the documents that Masaryk sent to Steed were detailed statistics on the military and financial situation of the Austro-Hungarian empire, which the British foreign policy expert forwarded immediately to Lord Kitchener in the War Office.

According to Masaryk, the sending of Voska to Steed in August 1914, with state secrets hidden in the soles of his shoes and in his daughter's corset, was "the beginning." Steed found a reliable intermediary between himself and Masaryk and introduced him also to Voska. Through him, before leaving London, Voska notified Masaryk that he was going to organize a secret network of confidants in England, France, Russia, and America, and a courier service to and from Prague. This was the beginning of Masaryk's "private" intelligence service headed by Voska, who, after its establishment, used the Bohemian National Alliance in the United States as a cover for his operations. Soon Masaryk had his own informers, especially in Vienna's central offices, who furnished him with military, industrial, economic, financial, and political intelligence data that he transmitted to Steed; the payments for it arrived through third parties in America. At this stage Masaryk was involved in "secret" work, while some Czechs abroad were preoccupied with organization and propaganda.[22]

From the information on war aims for which he had asked through Voska, dictated in the presence of the latter by Steed early in September 1914, and delivered to Masaryk by a special courier, the Czech politician learned that the Entente plans called for Russian occupation of the Czech lands and the separation of Austria from Germany. The Russian troops would bring along weapons to arm the Czechs; the Czech press was expected to place itself fully in the service of the Entente. The situation on the French front was bad, and Paris was expected to fall. According to Lord Kitchener, the war would be long—two or three years—as long as would be necessary for the Entente to win it. Finally, the message said that the war would make it possible for the Czechs to gain independence, and such an opportunity would not rise again. Masaryk was asked to convey the information to "others"; Steed thus gave him a signal to part with Austria and to embrace the idea of national independence. Indeed, the message "had a decisive influence upon Masaryk's activities,"[23] as he afterwards told Steed. (After the war Masaryk wrote to Steed about the volume relating his wartime activities, adding, "It starts in September, 1914, when I sent Voska to you. That was the beginning.")

Masaryk learned about the steps taken by spokesmen for the Czech associations in Russia, led by Dr. Vácslav Vondrák, and about the tsar's granting them an audience. The expected coming of the Russians posed a problem for him: he was known as an opponent of tsarism, and, at the same time, he was fully aware of the pro-Russian sentiment of the Czech population waiting enthusiastically for the arrival of the Russians. He told his prewar political friends that, in the even of German defeat, he could not agree to the "Russian" solution of the Czech problem. Needless to say, for the British such a solution would have meant Russian hegemony in central Europe; from their point of view, should Germany be defeated, the creation of an independent Czech state along the lines proposed by Sir Eyre Crowe would be the only acceptable alternative.

As has been mentioned above, in August 1914, Masaryk sent Voska with secret documents and other information relating to Austria-Hungary to Steed, "an evil genius" of the House of Habsburg, whom Voska called "a kind of ambassador without portfolio for the British Empire." In that month Masaryk told Voska that he himself would eventually go abroad, and he contacted politicians from other political parties in order to solicit information from them. He tried in vain to use Social Democratic party officials as his informants, in the hope that their prewar contacts with the Socialist International would be of some value to his cause. The Social Democrats were not interested in Masaryk's schemes; they were concerned with their own safety, and hoped for the transformation of the empire into a genuine federation. Since the "Šviha affair" had made him look like a defender of a police informer, Masaryk capitalized on it when he applied for the validation of his passport, and he was able to make a trip to Holland that September.[24] His British friends signaled his arrival in Holland to his prewar American "benefactor," Charles R. Crane, a multimillionaire who had manifold interests, from revolution in Albania to icons and church music in Russia, and Crane cabled to Masaryk 200 pounds sterling. (The British were already keeping in touch with Crane before the war. Masaryk was receiving payments for procuring and delivering military information. Indeed, "laundering money" was practiced long before the term for it was popularized during the U.S. Watergate scandals.) Much more money was to come from America and through America later, and, as Masaryk relates it, "with Mr. Steed's help these transactions were carried out by cable."[25] (The British government controlled the cables.)

On September 11, 1914, Masaryk wrote from Rotterdam to Voska that the latter would "not be surprised" about the former's coming there, and that the purpose of his trip was to get in touch with his English and Russian acquaintances. He pointed out that the story appearing in American newspapers that he had escaped from Prague and was on his way to America was false, and that the probable cause for its appearance was that his British friends had sent a telegram to Mr. Crane about his arrival in Holland in the company of his sister-in-law, who was going home to America. "I must remain in Europe in order to work," wrote Masaryk; "in America I would be of no help;" and he added, "I organize intelligence work, etc., as we spoke about it. It is very difficult. Our people are inexperienced in these things as yet. In spite of it, I hope that I will succeed . . . . I am away from Prague already for the second week. . . . After some time I will go away from Prague [again] and then always in two or three weeks intervals; you can figure out where [I shall go] . . . do

Russian and British Connections 45

not get confused by news about me, should they appear again. Should something happen [to me], you will receive information from England. What we discussed orally, I will not repeat; everything stands."[26] (In future letters Masaryk urged Voska to pursue intelligence work, as had been agreed between them.)

From Rotterdam Masaryk also wrote to Ernest Denis, the historian in Paris, and to Steed and Seton-Watson in London. Voska first learned about Masaryk's visit to Holland through a telegram from Steed stating that the Czech politician "did not travel to England;" however, if everything was all right, Steed hoped that Masaryk would return to Holland "around October 15," and would then come to England. Steed had already made arrangements so that Masaryk could, with the permission of police officials, land at Dover; and he told Voska that Masaryk "wishes to have consultation with responsible representatives of the Russian government and some outstanding personalities in England. This I have already arranged. As soon as he arrives, I will let you know. Simultaneously I write to Mr. Crane."

After his return from Holland, Masaryk attempted to meet politicians with whom he could communicate without telling them about his contacts abroad. On October 1 he met with five deputies of the National Social party and made a record of the meeting. (About a year later these notes were found by the Austrian police and were used as evidence against the five National Socials during their treason trial.) At the meeting Masaryk said that though the Czech deputation to the tsar (discussed in the next chapter) was very significant, the Czechs must not rely only on the Russians and must have their own program. Later in October Masaryk met with some officials of the Moravian People's Progressive party and the State Rights party. Those whom he met he tried to persuade that the "Russian" solution of the Czech question was impossible; should Germany and Austria be defeated, he suggested, the Czechs must establish their own state. Furthermore, it was necessary to work for it and to have an irredenta abroad. He was prepared to lead the action abroad; however, in order to succeed in this endeavor, he needed a mandate from home. In the existing circumstances he could not get it from the executive committess of the Czech political parties, he said, but only from individual politicians.

Before going to Holland for the second time, Masaryk discussed the question of an independent Czech state with some National Social and State Rights politicians, none of whom believed in the feasiblility of a state that would disregard historical boundaries and that would be based on ethnography. These discussions clearly indicated to Masaryk that any proposal for an independent state whose boundaries did not follow those of the Bohemian Crown would be rejected by responsible Czech politicians.

On October 2, 1914, Masaryk visited with the emperor's viceroy at Prague, Count Franz von Thun-Hohenstein, and made a record of the meeting. He told Thun that all Czech political parties had the Slavic program and Slavic sentiments. However, his book had been banned in Russia, and he could not now support tsarism and the tsarist police in Prague.[27] (Masaryk mentioned his conversation with Thun to Seton-Watson when they met in Holland.) In mid-October Masaryk received $1,000 from Voska; on October 21, 1914, Steed wired Voska to cable money in German currency through a Dutch bank to Masaryk, who was again in Rotterdam.[28] This Voska did immediately.

During his second visit to Holland Masaryk established there "a provisional propaganda center with the help of the correspondent of the 'Times'," and made arrangements for the transfer of information from England, America, and Russia through neutral Holland. Steed could not come, and therefore sent Seton-Watson to meet with Masaryk. During conversations lasting for two days, Masaryk communicated to Seton-Watson many of his views on military and political matters, saying "The role of Britain in the future settlement" should be "the Brain policy," and that Britain should have a plan so that it would be able to "give direction to the evolution of events." Furthermore, Masaryk gave Seton-Watson "a lot of secret information, some of sensenational kind"—secret information about submarines and plans of mobilization, and Romanian mobilization plans that had been procured by Austrian intelligence from a Romanian staff officer and that Masaryk had obtained from informers inside the war ministry in Vienna. Seton-Watson brought along a draft of a proposal for an independent Czech state with its boundaries drawn on the basis of ethnography, and he was surprised when Masaryk argued in favor of the historical state rights program. (Seton-Watson's proposal was adjusted to Masaryk's known prewar views on the subject.) Upon his return to England, on the basis of discussions with Masaryk, Seton-Watson drafted a memorandum that was forwarded to the governments of Britain, France, and Russia.[29]

Masaryk's program called for an independent Bohemian state that could be realized only if Germany were smashed. As far as the extent of the state was concerned, his stance was somewhat more modest than that of Kramář; he advocated the retention of the historical Czech lands, with the addition of Slovakia. (It may be noted that before the war Masaryk had been a staunch fighter against Bohemia's historical state rights; now he based his program on Bohemia's state rights, called for the retention of historical boundaries, and forgot his advocacy of the right of self-determination. He also extended the rights of the Czech state to include a claim to Slovakia, although the latter had never belonged to the St. Wenceslas Crown. Thus, Masaryk adopted the views of Kramář on this issue, though he had disagreed with them before the war.) Carpatho-Russia (Ruthenia), he further proposed, would be attached to the Russian empire. The territories in the Czech lands inhabited by Germans, with minor adjustments in the southwest and on the Austrian border, would be retained for economic reasons. Considering the existence of the German minority and relations with Germany, Masaryk believed it to be necessary that the new state border on Russia. In his view, the new state could be a kingdom, not a republic, for he considered a monarchy to be the wish of the vast majority of the nation. But he cautioned against placing a Russian grand duke on the Czech throne, believing that "a significant minority of 3 to 4 million Germans" would accept, for example, a Danish but "never a Russian" prince. Seton-Watson introduced this memorandum to several influential people in Great Britain, including Steed, who transmitted it to the French foreign minister; Ronald Burrows, principal of King's College; and George R. Clerk (later Sir George), in the Foreign Office. Through Professor Paul Vinogradov of Oxford University, who left for Petrograd, the memorandum was also transmitted to Russian Foreign Minister Sazonov. Thus Russia knew of Masaryk's program as well as Kramář's.

After his return from his second visit to Holland, Masaryk continued to talk with other Czech politicians. Through Edvard Beneš, who before the war had studied in France and was a correspondent of a Social Democratic daily in Prague, he attempted anew to find common ground with the leader of the Czech Social Democratic party, Bohumír Šmeral, but without success. As Beneš wrote about it, Šmeral told Beneš that he and his group were "crazy"; that Masaryk wanted to lead the nation to the White Mountain (an allusion to the defeat of the troops of the Bohemian estates, Czech and German Protestants, in Bohemia, on November 8, 1620)—to another national catastrophe; that he could not pursue such an irresponsible policy; and that the plans of the Masaryk-Beneš group were simply a fantasy. Šmeral inquired whether either Beneš or Masaryk had any guarantee from the Entente powers that would justify the pursuit of such policy.[30] Naturally, they had no such assurance. Furthermore, Masaryk's record of inconsistencies, shifting alliances, and "the Šviha affair" did not generate confidence in him on he part of leading Czech politicians.

Although Masaryk traveled abroad to transmit intelligence information to Seton-Watson and received funds for organizing an action at home, he kept "two irons in the fire" by maintaining contacts with the Austrian government officials in Prague and Vienna. When in December 1914, Masaryk decided to take his daughter for medical treatment to Capri, Italy, he looked up the emperor's viceroy in Prague, Count Franz von Thun-Hohenstein, and the former prime minister, E. von Körber, in Vienna, and had very friendly conversations with them. Masaryk assured Körber of his loyalty to the state in words, writing, and handshakes; and Austrian authorities, knowing Masaryk's prewar pro-German and pro-Austrian stand—he had praised the constitutionalism of the two powers—as well as his role in the "Šviha affair," made no effort to prevent him from leaving the country. (After the war Masaryk explained his assurances of loyalty to Körber as a military deception intended to throw off any suspicion that his trips abroad might have provoked.)[31] But his trip to Italy and his carelessness in handling his "clandestine" activity aroused the suspicion of Austrian police, and Masaryk, after being warned by Beneš and Steed not to return to Austria, decided to stay abroad.

Beneš stated in his message that he would contact Masaryk personally in Switzerland, where the former arrived on February 1, 1915.[32] Now Masaryk was an émigré and Beneš was his main contact at home. Masaryk charged Beneš with the responsibility of explaining his views to the politicians with whom Masaryk had dealt in the fall of 1914, making other politicians and journalists go abroad, and, finally, establishing a secret committee that would both maintain contacts with the center of the independence movement abroad and influence domestic politics. In a special message, Masaryk and Svatkovsky urged Kramář to go abroad. Although Kramář, at the meeting with Beneš, agreed to the formation of the secret committee, he did not want to emigrate, believing that he would be needed in Prague when the Russian troops arrived.[33]

In March 1915, a secret committee, the *Maffie*,[34] was established in Prague, and it maintained contacts with political émigrés abroad. The five principal leaders of the *Maffie* were Dr. Přemysl Šámal, Dr. Edvard Beneš, Dr. Josef Scheiner, Dr. Karel Kramář, and Dr. Alois Rašín. Since Masaryk was against the representation of Catholics in the secret committee, and the Young Czech party was opposed to the representation of the National Socials and the State Rights party, these groups were not admitted. The *Maffie*, however, maintained contacts with some Social Democrats (through Beneš) and with the Agrarians, without including them in planning and activity. Acting upon Masaryk's instructions, Beneš was also in touch with the leader of the State Rights party, deputy Kalina. This organization temporarily joined, but did not permanently merge, the two streams of the anti-Austrian Czech movement represented by Kramář and Masaryk.

When Masaryk arrived in Rome toward the end of December 1914, he looked up a number of people there. Among them were the Russian journalist Vsevolod Svatkovsky, who became the principal Russian intelligence officer in Bern, Paris, and Rome, and who transmitted information directly to Petrograd, maintaining direct communications with the military, incluidng the ministry of war; the Russian ambassador to Montenegro, who was visiting Rome at that time; the Serbian minister Ljubo Mihajlovič; several South Slavic politicians and émigrés in Rome; Ante Trumbić, a former member of the Vienna parliament and the future president of the Yugoslav committee in London; the Russian ambassador, and many others. Masaryk asked for an audience with the German ambassador in Rome, who, however, refused to see him. Trumbić noted in his diary that Masaryk talked to him about the need for "territorial continuity" between Yugoslavia and Bohemia, and pointed out that in the event of Bohemia's becoming independent, the state would be "a monarchy with a dynasty from the British ruling house." But, according to the report sent by the Russian ambassador in Rome to Petrograd, Masaryk told the ambassador that the Czechs wished to have a Russian king and that they would reject a ruler from a German dynasty.[35] Masaryk's conduct may be described either as "diplomatic"—keeping several options open—or as telling the people with whom he spoke what they wanted to hear, without much concern for consistency. In contrast to Masaryk, Kramář was consistently pro-Russian.

While Kramář expected an early Russian victory and a Russian solution of the Czech problem, Masaryk believed that it was also necessary to gain the sympathies of the British, French, and other governments for the Czech independence movement. Masaryk's views were expressed in the messages he was sending to Prague through Beneš and other emissaries. In his message of February 18, 1915, Masaryk stated that he expected the Russians to occupy the Czech lands. As soon as this happened, he contended, it must be exploited as a justification for action, and demands must be made for political concessions to Vienna. In another message, however, Masaryk expressed his conviction that the Czechs should not rely exclusively on the Russians; the English and the French were also important, because at the peace conference their voices would be heard and their votes would count.[36]

Masaryk's urgent messages asking for another prominent politician to join him abroad were not answered for a long time. Kramář refused to leave his homeland and was convinced that his departure would be useless, because he had "everything agreed in Russia." (His confidence in Russia, however, was not shared by all his friends.) Furthermore, it was very difficult for any Austrian national to obtain a passport for travel abroad. However, early in 1915, an Agrarian party deputy, Josef Dürich, a former member of the Old Czech party and a supporter of Kramář's Neo-Slavic political orientation, was able to obtain a passport. After conferences with Antonín Švehla (leader of the Agrarians) and Kramář, he agreed to go abroad and to remain there until the end of the war. Kramář gave him some money and asked him to "work for the great Slavic empire." Thus, in May 1915, Dürich, at the age of sixty-eight, left for Switzerland to represent abroad the home movement for independence, sent there with the knowledge of the leaders of the *Maffie* (Kramář, Šámal, and Scheiner) and the leaders of the Agrarian party (Švehla), the Old Czech party (Mattuš), and the State Rights party (Kalina).[37]

Although the person Masaryk most called for was Kramář, other politicians were also urged to go into exile. A Social Democratic deputy, Gustav Habrman, visited Masaryk in Switzerland on March 11, 1915. He promised Masaryk to come back and stay abroad, "if it will be possible." He never did.³⁸ Among the reasons why leading politicians hesitated to go abroad were the financial difficulties in which the émigrés found themselves. If the émigrés wanted to work for the cause, they had to be financially independent. Thus, leaving his homeland was for the aging Dürich a personal sacrifice that the other politicians were unwilling to make. Only Masaryk had no financial problems; he was financially secure, for he had made financial arrangements with Voska and some British personalities before he decided to stay abroad. His financial demands were not modest; in December 1914, he requested that the Czechs in America deliver to him $10,000; and in May 1915, he asked for $50,000.³⁹ The quota he demanded for 1915 was not met by the Bohemian National Alliance; at the end of the year Masaryk confirmed the receipt of $37,841. The request for 1916, however, was surpassed.⁴⁰

In addition to receiving funds from the Czechs in America, Masaryk received money from Drs. Šámal and Scheiner, Beneš, and the *Sokol* organization; and he also benefited from intelligence activities conducted by the secret organization built by Voska, who eventually had confidants in neutral, Allied, and enemy countries. His principal informer was a mail clerk at the Austro-Hungarian consulate general in New York, who was able to obtain documents; Austrian passports to be used by Voska's, Masaryk's, and Allied agents traveling in enemy countries; and other valuable material, including information on certain Austrian spies and agents of the Central Powers operating in the United States. Through clandestine or British diplomatic channels, Masaryk and Voska transmitted intelligence data that they received from New York, Vienna, and their confidants elsewhere to the British Secret Service; and the latter used some of the information in its propaganda and its effort to bring the United States into the war.⁴¹

Masaryk and Voska received instructions from Steed; the latter arranged that some funds channelled to Masaryk should not be traceable to their original source. (Indeed, the British intelligence service was known for its professionalism.) Steed acted as an intermediary between Masaryk and Crane, to whom he wrote about Masaryk as early as September 1914. However, on February 3, 1915, Masaryk wrote from Switzerland to Crane directly, asking him for funds needed for procuring valuable information, the nature of which could not be discussed in correspondence. Masaryk assumed that Steed had explained to Crane the nature of his activity. Since Crane did not cable a large sum of money immediately to Masaryk, the latter wrote to Voska on February 19, 1915, that the amounts of money that had been sent to him by Crane were insufficient for his needs, and that he hoped that his friends in London (Steed, Seton-Watson) would explain better to Crane that the Czech politician expected to get a much bigger "gift." Indeed, the American multimillionaire "gave 80,000 dollars on the Albanian revolution;" and Masaryk's cause "required no less money than Albania," and "probably more." Masaryk, therefore, asked that Voska or another member of the secret organization speak discretely about the matter with Crane. Voska, however, found out that Crane was being groomed for something much bigger, and therefore could "not act the way he would like to." Voska was able to speak only with Crane's attorney, Roger H. Williams, with whom he kept constantly in touch. On March 23, 1915, Voska wrote to Masaryk that since Crane was now an advisor to President Wilson, he was "almost constantly" in Washington, D.C., and that Masaryk's friend "will have considerable influence on the conclusion of this great epoch and, therefore, he must be very cautious." Masaryk was advised not to write to Crane directly, but to forward his letters, marked with a "W"(Wiliams), to Voska, who would thus know for whom the letters were meant. To console Masaryk, Voska assured him that he would receive all the money collected in America, and that he could count on at least $30,000 during the next six months. In addition, Masaryk would be able to draw as much money as he needed from an account that would be opened for him by Crane's attorney, Williams. (Till the end of the war Masaryk drew tens of thousands of dollars from that bank account for himself, his daughter, and, presumably, Beneš.) Voska also indicated that Williams would send funds to Masaryk's daughter Alice, then living in Prague, who had also asked Crane for money, and that Masaryk, his family, and his cause would be well provided for. In turn, Masaryk later wrote to Voska, "Your expenses should be paid by those who benefit from your activities,"[42] that is, the British Secret Service, as it eventually happened.

Since he had more than sufficient funds, it was easy for Masaryk to insist that the Czechoslovak independence movement must remain financially, and thus politically, independent. In contrast, in the summer of 1915, František Sís of the Kramář group wrote in a long memorandum for his brother in Sophia that the Entente powers (including Russia) should establish a war fund from which they would finance Czech journalism, information gathering, and agitation abroad, including the publishing of a Czech newspaper. In another communication Sís asked his brother to bring to the Russians' attention the fact that Kramář had been arrested because of reports that the Austrian general staff had received from Germany and that the latter, in turn, had received from its spies in Russia, who had penetrated the army and political offices. Sís suggested that though it was possible that Masaryk might agree with Kramář's program, Masaryk "will probably be in favor of an independent republic." This would not be a happy solution, Sís wrote, "because we are not even ready to direct ourselves—not to mention economic consequences" of such an arrangement. For this reason, Vladimír Sís should oppose Masaryk.[43]

Masaryk, indeed, proved to be a practical politician who knew the value of connections, funds, and propaganda. His principal residence was London, where he arrived in September 1915, carrying a Serbian passport issued to him by the Royal Serbian Legation at Paris on September 22, 1915.[44] He was brought to England by Seton-Watson, who believed that he could be useful in Czech and Yugoslav matters and who had plans for the Czechs. Seton-Watson saw the Czechs as sympathetic admirers of Russia who could become for the west a door upon the Slavic world.[45]

Seton-Watson wrote that Masaryk's arrival in London was connected wiht a plan for establishing a school of Slavonic and East European studies at King's College, and that "the initiative for the foundation of the School and for its original policy and aims lay with Ronald Burrows, the Principal of King's College." Early in 1915 Burrows organized a course of lectures on "The Spirit of the Allies," afterwards published in book form, in which Seton-Watson found "the first written record of a scheme which was already evolving in his mind." On March 15, 1915, Seton-Watson wrote to Burrows that he had "said just a few words" in their casual conversation "which showed that his mind was moving in the direction of a scheme" which Seton-Watson had long been thinking of, "even before the war made it 'actuel' or political." Slavonic and East European studies had been completely neglected in England, and Seton-Watson asked whether it might not be practicable to organize some kind of "Slavonic School": that, "if properly run, it could from the first form a focus for all students of any Slavonic race in London, and act as a medium between them and people interested in Slavonic studies." Seton-Watson believed that "it should be possible to get a good deal of practical support for such a scheme in wartime."

When Burrows agreed with the idea, Seton-Watson suggested to him that Masaryk might be enlisted as a prominent Slav scholar at the school. Burrows had never heard of him, but "it only took a few minutes to bring to him the great possibilities which co-operation with Masaryk might offer." As Seton-Watson noted, for the first two years of the war he was the possessor of "the only copy in England of Masaryk's great work on Russia —*Russland und Europa.*" After the war he "learned from a German acquaintance that during the same period certain high officials of the German Foreign Office kept the book for permanent reference on their table. It is quite likely that they first learned from it of a little-known revolutionary named Lenin."

Shortly after Masaryk's arrival in England, on October 5, 1915, Seton-Watson introduced him to two officers of British army intelligence. They requested, and Masaryk gave them, data on the size of the Austro-Hungarian and German armies,[46] and other information in which they were interested. Thus he established his contacts with the British ministry of war, principally through Seton-Watson and Steed, through whom he transmitted intelligence information he received from the *Maffie,* and Voska, though the latter also gave some intelligence data directly to Steed.[47]

While in England, Masaryk had the support of the Czech colony in London. On the day that the war broke out, František Kopecký and Jan Sýkora founded the London Czech Committee, which issued identity cards to Czechs living in England. Those with cards were not deported as enemy aliens. Kopecký and other Czechs in England cooperated closely with the British police and intelligence, and kept in touch with Steed. On December 4, 1915, Seton-Watson met Sir William Wiseman, the head of British intelligence in America, and Major John Baird, an intelligence officer working in London.[48] On the next day he told Masaryk that a memorandum written by Voska, which had been forwarded to Seton-Watson by Masaryk earlier, "had made a *very big* impression on our military friends," and that another colleague of the two intelligence officers whom Masaryk had already met, "a very intelligent fellow, called Sir William Wiseman," was going to America and would like to meet Masaryk before he went. Wiseman "might really be able to help the cause."[49] Seton-Watson arranged for a meeting for the two on December 31, and from then on till the end of the war Masaryk kept in touch with Wiseman.[50]

Since Voska's reports from America were of great interest to the British War Office, Masaryk encouraged Voska in his activity and tried to get financial rewards for him. He prepared a memorandum entitled "In the Eleventh Hour" for the War Office; the latter was sent personally to the newly appointed chief of the general staff, Sir William Robertson, by Ronald Burrows. Burrows also arranged for a meeting between the chief of the general staff and Seton-Watson, Masaryk, and himself. Masaryk submitted to the War Office a budget proposed by Voska, and discussed with high military officials Voska's financial needs in connection with his activities on behalf of the British. On December 31, 1915, he visited with several high political and military officials of the War Office, met Baird, and held a meeting with Wiseman. According to Masaryk's own record, Wiseman "accepted everything."[51]

Apparently the political and military officials whom Masaryk met in December 1915, agreed to finance Voska's operation in the United States. Masaryk then notified Voska that an arrangement had been made for a British officer "who knows America well" and who had already worked in intelligence to look him up in New York and identify himself with a letter from Masaryk. This officer, whom Voska "could fully trust," was Robert F. Young. The two met in February 1916. Among the questions they discussed was, first of all, the selection of couriers to Austria-Hungary. Voska used several people from different parts of America, who, as citizens of a non-belligerent country, had no difficulty in traveling to Austria-Hungary and Germany, where they could contact Voska's agents and informers. Another topic of discussion was Voska's activity in New York habor, where he tried to prevent sabotages, largely fires, on ships loaded with sugar and other goods destined for England. During these efforts to prevent sabotages, Voska's men uncovered an organization headed by Irish-Americans that was responsible for most of the fires in the harbor.[52]

It appears from the available evidence that Masaryk's being accepted by the French prime minister, Briand, early in February 1916, made a great impression on his friends in England, who wanted him to continue his propaganda and intelligence work. Sir William Robertson, who had received Masaryk's memorandum and the request that the British finance Voska's operations in America, asked Ronald Burrows to contact the director of British military intelligence, General Sir George McDonogh, and arrange for a meeting between the latter and Masaryk as soon as Masaryk returned from Paris.[53] Seemingly, Masaryk was not in a hurry to get back to London. When he returned, toward the end of February 1916, Burrows sent him a copy of a letter from General McDonogh, who was eager to see him.[54] Burrows was one of the four founders of the *New Europe*, the others being Seton-Watson, Steed, and Frederick Whyte, a liberal member of the British parliament. Burrow's arranging for Masaryk to meet the head of the British intelligence indicates that the principal of King's College knew the real reason why Masaryk was in England, and that Masaryk's professorial appointment was merely a cover for his propaganda and intelligence activity. Burrows also tried to help Masaryk obtain funding for Voska's activities in America and on the Continent, since Wiseman had not yet contacted Voska directly.[55]

In March 1916, Masaryk met the highest intelligence officers, and his own records of these meetings indicate that the British wanted to use Masaryk's contacts in France to get information on matters the French government kept from them as confidential.[56] But Masaryk was most interested in securing British financing for Voska's intelligence network. Voska's expenses were piling up and he was urging Masaryk to settle the matter. On April 22, Voska informed Masaryk that he was already in debt. Mr. Young, Voska wrote, was going back to England and would also report to Masaryk on Voska's work. Since the Voska organization in America consisted of sixty-eight people, and "so much good work" had already been done, "it would be a crime to stop now." Voska also sent Masaryk the original of a letter that he had received from the British naval attaché in the United States, Captain Guy Gaunt, highly praising Voska and promising that when the war progressed further, he would testify to Voska's "magnificent work" and the latter's great contribution to "our ultimate success. . . ."[57] Masaryk forwarded a copy of Gaunt's letter to Seton-Watson, and another one to Beneš in Paris. Undoubtedly, he also complained to Seton-Watson that the Voska matter did not proceed as it should. Replying to Masaryk's communication, Seton-Watson stated in a letter dated May 6, 1916, that he "was disgusted to learn that next to nothing had been done" in Voska's case. He blamed this inaction on the lack of coordination between the embassy and the representative of the War Office in the United States—Sir William Wiseman. The latter, Seton-Watson wrote, was already working on the problem, as was evidenced by his sending Young back to England. Seton-Watson also contacted Major

Baird of British military intelligence in the hope of getting the matter "cleared up at once."[58] Two days later, on May 8, 1916, the Voska matter was settled in accordance with what had been agreed upon between Seton-Watson and Masaryk.[59] Although the details of the arrangement were conveyed to Masaryk by Seton-Watson in private conversation, Seton-Watson's letter shows that "instructions *by cable* for his [Voska's] payment" were sent to Wiseman. Thus in May 1916, Sir William Wiseman assumed control and financing of Masaryk's "private intelligence service" headed by Voska.

Voska was a very resourceful man who went after Masaryk's real, potential, or suspected enemies mercilessly. A naturalized American citizen, he was the secretary of the Bohemian National Alliance and he used that organization as his cover. His activities in the United States were manifold, including supplying derogatory materials about those Czechs in America who did not favor the dismemberment of Austria-Hungary to the other leaders of the Bohemian National Alliance, who used the information (true or false) in their attacks on their opponents. However, his main work was intelligence, propaganda, and helping Great Britain in her efforts to bring the United States into the war with Germany.

Given the nature of the business, there is not much specific information about the operations of the British Secret Service, especially about what it did in the United States before the latter entered World War I. However, a few works on the British Secret Service are available.[60] The following data have been extracted largely from the restricted file in the William Wiseman Collection at Yale University. The documents show that William Wiseman, an army captain, was the head of British intelligence operations in the United States. His activity was kept separate from that of the British naval attaché, Commander (later Admiral) Guy Gaunt. In November 1915, "C" (Sir Mansfield Cummings, the chief of the British Secret Service during World War I, called also "chief") sent Wiseman to New York to organize an American branch of M.I.1.c (the Secret Service). In January 1916, Wiseman took charge of the American operation, which was disguised as part of the American Transport Department of the Ministry of Munitions, and conducted the Secret Service work "to the satisfaction of all [British] authorities."

A large part of his work was counterespionage and the obtaining of political information—political intelligence. Tens of thousands of cases were investigated, according to Wiseman, and, until the U.S. entry into the war, the Wiseman organization remained a secret from the U.S. authorities. "The details and extent of our organization they have never known, and don't know to this day," wrote Wiseman in a memorandum for his "chief" on September 6, 1918. Before the U.S. entry into the war and the arrival of the Balfour mission in May 1917, the activity of Wiseman's office included counterespionage; the investigation of suspects about whom the British authorities required information; the prevention of sabotage on ships loading ammunition, sugar, and other commodities in American harbors; "Irish Sedition: A general watch on the Irish movement in the United States, and investigation of suspects;" and "Investigation into Hindu Sedition in America." After the U.S. entry into the war, Wiseman's work "developed on political lines" and he acted as liaison officer between the War Cabinet and Lord Reading, "his chief duty being to keep open channel of communication between the Foreign Office and Colonel House."

Wiseman intimated that he was a special emissary for the Foreign Office in the United States, gained House's confidence, and relayed the "Colonel's" views to his superiors in London. House was so much impressed with him that he confided to him much information and never seemed to feel duped. In the course of the war Wiseman's office was reorganized. It became the office of the military attaché, which, eventually, combined "Military Intelligence 5–Adjutant Provost Marshall–Department of Irish Affairs–Department of India Affairs–Information Bureau–Intelligence and Military Control." (The Secret Service is largely responsible for espionage overseas and reports to the Foreign Office; its agents operate either from the British embassies or in a variety of other disguises, for instance as journalists and businessmen. Security [M.I.5] is responsible for counterespionage and internal security at home.)

It has been necessary to present his background information in order to place in perspective Masaryk's cooperation with Wiseman and other intelligence officers, including the director of military intelligence, Sir George Macdonogh, Burrows, Seton-Watson, and Steed, as well as the clandestine operations of Voska in America, Russia, and western and central Europe. Early in the game Masaryk and Voska discovered that intelligence agencies are financed with unvouchered funds and that in clandestine operations documentation is seldom preserved and proofs are seldom requested. From the meagre beginnings in 1914-1915, when Masaryk was in contact with Crane through Steed, whom he informed about the secret sources of the valuable information the Czech leader was able to procure, the Masaryk-Voska operation became a big enterprise. There is in the Voska papers at Prague a record of weekly expenses from December 23, 1915 (when Masaryk submitted Voska's budget to the War Office), to June 14, 1916, in the total sum of $19,956.24. In June 1916, Voska notified Masaryk that financial matters had been settled to his satisfaction. Later, apparently, Voska became more "professional" and kept no records of receipts and expenditures. Voska and Masaryk also discovered very early that through the process of "laundering," "dirty" money may become "clean" money; funds may be received through a third party—an individual, an institution, or a compatriotic organization sponsoring bazaars—so that they cannot be traced to their original giver. When on May 28, 1918, Masaryk spoke at a large meeting of Czechs and Slovaks in Chicago, he was asked whether it would be correct for the Bohemian National Alliance to publish data on its income and expenses. (This question had been asked by the Czechs and Slovaks in Chicago as well as in other Czech and Slovak settlements.) Masaryk answered, "Revolution, during which accounts would be submitted, would be for children and not for sensible people."[61] (It may be noted that after the war Voska's superior, Sir William Wiseman, became a multimillionaire and a partner in Kuhn, Loeb & Co., New York, and did not go back to Great Britain.)

Members of the Czech delegation received by the tsar in September 1914. From left to right: Jan Orszagh, Jiří Klecanda, Otakar Červený, and Svatopluk Koníček

The first two pages of Masaryk's passport. He left the country in December 1914. The Austro-Hungarian Consul General in Geneva, Switzerland, validated his passport for return home on January 28, 1915.

CHAPTER THREE

THE EMERGENCE OF THE INDEPENDENCE MOVEMENT

The anti-Austrian movement for Czechoslovak independence emerged first where its views could be freely expressed—that is, among the Czech and Slovak settlers and emigrants in Russia, France, and the United States. Czechs and Slovaks living abroad had left the monarchy largely for economic reasons, and only a small minority of them maintained contacts with home, cultivating a national consciousness in Czech and Slovak clubs. Some of the emigrants, who were still Austro-Hungarian citizens, faced the alternatives of returning home to fulfill their military obligation, or being interned as citizens of an enemy country. This problem became particularly acute in Russia, where many Czech emigrants applied for Russian citizenship and tried to prove their loyalty by enlisting in the Russian army.

The largest concentration of Czechs was in the Volhynia province (*gubernia*), and the center of Czech national life was Kiev. After the declaration of war there the Czech cultural leaders, upon the initiative of Dr. Vácslav Vondrák, a well-to-do owner of the hotel Praha and a land estate, and Otakar V. Červený, owner of a musical instrument factory, decided to send a delegation to the tsar, requesting the establishment of a Czech military unit within the tsarist army. These Czechs considered that Russia was fighting for all Slavic peoples and for the freedom of the Czech lands; therefore, they wanted to organize a Czech military force that would fight shoulder to shoulder with the Russian army against Austria-Hungary.[1]

A Czech delegation succeeded in obtaining an audience with the tsar on August 20, 1914, and submitted to him its memorandum advocating the Czechs' propagation of all-Slavic unity, praying that the tsar would succeed in ushering the "Czechoslovak" nation into the family of Slavic nations, and hoping that the independent Crown of St. Wenceslas would "shine in the rays of the Crown of Romanovs."[2] The delegation assured the tsarist government of the complete loyalty of the Czechs in Russia and requested legal protection. The Russian minister of foreign affairs, Sazonov, recommended that the delegation formulate its views and demands in writing. Accordingly, "The Memorial Script on the Czechoslovak Question," written by Jiří Klecanda, a young Czech historian employed in the Slavic division of the library of the Academy of Sciences at St. Petersburg was submitted to the tsar and then distributed in printed form to members of the Duma, members of the government, and other political and military people.

This document emphasized that it was issued at a time of historical struggle between Germandom and Slavdom, and that it expressed the "blessed dream of the Czech nation, that is, the independence of the Czech state that is attainable only with the help of the Russian Gosudar [Sovereign] and Emperor, his Government and the great Russian nation." It also stressed the unity of the "Czechoslovak" nation, sharply criticizing the Austro-Hungarian dualism by which two million Slovaks were deprived of all help from the Czech nation. It demanded the establishment of a Czech state that would be connected with the Yugoslav state at the Danube. It would consist of the kingdom of Bohemia and Slovakia, with Serb (Sorb) Lusatia belonging as an autonomous unit. The new state would be the western outpost and guardian of Slavdom; since it was therefore in the all-Slavic interest, the tsar should support its creation. The document reiterated the need for the political independence of the proposed state and urged the tsarist government to turn to the only spokesman competent to represent the wishes of the nation—the Czech politicians in Prague.

The tsarist government accepted the memorandum without making any commitment. However, the request for the establishment of a Czech military unit was looked upon favorably by the Russian ministry of war, since it would give the Russian army a psychological weapon against the Slavic, and especially Czech, elements in the Austrian army. Shortly afterward, in August 1914, the proposal to establish a Czech *Družina,* submitted to the Russian ministry of foreign affairs and ministry of war by Vondrák on behalf of the Czech colony in Russia, was approved.[3] Its commanders were to be Russian officers, and at least one-third of the lower and non-commissioned officers had to be Russians. Only Czechs who could prove that they had applied for Russian citizenship would be accepted into the *Družina.*

On September 17 representatives of Czechs from Kiev, Moscow, Petrograd, and Warsaw (the Alliance of Czech Associations in Russia, henceforth the Alliance) were received by the tsar,[4] and on September 28, the day of St. Wenceslas, patron saint of the Czechs, the first battalion, consisting of more than 700 Czechs and 16 Slovaks, was sworn in on St. Sophia Square in Kiev. On this occasion, Vondrák declared that the Czech and Slovak nations had decided to fight for their liberty and independence and to part company with Austria-Hungary. He expressed the belief that the "Lands of St. Wenceslas Crown" would be free and independent. The commander of the *Družina* recalled that the Czech nation had chosen St. Wenceslas, martyr and knight prince, for its patron: "Today the first flag, decorated by the Crown of the patron of the Czech nation, St. Wenceslas, has been blessed. With this flag you will go bravely to fight for a better future of your fatherland. And St. Wenceslas, according to the Czech poetic legend, waiting in Mount Blaník together with his knights for the last hour of liberation of the Czech nation, will come forward to you and will help you to break the centuries old irons...."[5]

The St. Wenceslas crown on the flag of the *Družina* implied that the liberated homeland was to follow thousand-year-old Christian traditions. Needless to say, this first Czech military unit was established when Masaryk was at home and still held an Austrian passport that enabled him to travel abroad and back to Austria-Hungary. In no way did he influence the formation of the independence movement in Russia or elsewhere at this time. In his dealings with Austrian government officials he still professed to be a loyal Austrian subject.

The *Družina* was dispatched to the front on October 22, 1914. At first it was seen by the Russian general staff as a group of propagandists rather than a fighting military unit that would incite an uprising among the Czechs in Austria-Hungary. Therefore, during the *Družina's* travel to the front

Emergence of Independence Movement 63

several emissaries were dispatched to Bohemia and Moravia. These individuals crossed the front line disguised as Austrian soldiers, made it to their points of destination, and informed some of the Czech political leaders at home about the establishment of the military unit, its purpose, and its expectations,[6] as well as about the independence movement in Russia.

The Czech *Družina* was attached to the Third Army on the front. Its commander, General Radko Dimitriev, was highly sympathetic to the cause of these soldiers and held in high esteem their military qualities. He therefore assigned them to reconnaissance duties, attaching companies or even smaller units to the divisional staffs and making them into divisional intelligence groups. Since the intelligence and bravery of these soldiers became very evident wherever they were deployed, the supreme command of the Russian armies authorized recruiting into the *Družina* those Czechs and Slovak prisoners of war in the sector of the Third Army who applied for membership in it. Thus some 250 prisoners of war (POWs) joined the *Družina* in December 1914, and January 1915.[7]

In order to conduct the propaganda mentioned above, Louis Tuček, Zdeněk Rejman, and a Slovak, Jozef Orszag, were appointed as political assistants to the commander of the *Družina*. When, later, the unit was assigned other duties, they became intermediaries between its command and the Czechoslovak community in Russia.[8] The latter began to collect contributions for the Fund of the Czech *Družina*, which supported the sick, military invalids, and the families of the volunteers. After its establishment, the Alliance of the Czecho-Slovak Associations was largely responsible for collecting the money.

Since applying for Russian citizenship was a condition for admission into the *Družina*, the Russian government avoided possible charges that it was arming citizens of an enemy state in contravention of the Hague Convention. The *Družina* gradually expanded and was renamed an infantry regiment in January 1916. Early, in August 1915, the general staff of the Russian army had given official consent for Czech and Slovak POWs to enter the *Družina*. The latter had several military successes, especially on the parts of its second company, which induced parts of the Austrian 28th Regiment composed of Czech soldiers to go over to the Russians near the Dukla pass, and the first company, which captured several units of Czech regiments. These activities helped the Russian army to achieve temporary local victories.

There were differences of opinion among the Czechs in Russia as to what the structure and orientation of the new state ought to be. Some went so far as to demand the establishment of a kingdom, with a Romanov as its king and an Orthodox state religion; it would have two autonomous units with separate administrations—Czech and Slovak—unified by a common ruler, army, ministry of finance, and ministry of foreign affairs. Others, such as Vondrák, favored complete independence for the Czech lands and Slovakia, the latter having political and linguistic autonomy and its own diet.

Like the Czechs, the Slovaks in Russia were divided among themselves on the issue of Slovakia's future. On the one hand, the Slovaks organized in the Czechoslovak Club at Warsaw favored Slovak autonomy within a joint state of Czechs and Slovaks; on the other the Russo-Slovak L. Štúr Society, headed by Chamberlain Savjolov, advocated attaching Slovakia to Russia. Savjolov rejected the idea of either Slovak or Czech independence and favored the union of both Slovakia and "Czechia," as autonomous units, with Russia. Since the view that the new state should be an independent political unit prevailed within the Alliance of Czech Associations in Russia, the question of Slovakia's status within that state had to be spelled out when the organization decided to change its name to the Alliance of Czecho-Slovak Associations in Russia (ASCAR). The organization's congress, held in May 1915, therefore adopted a resolution proclaiming "a complete equality of the Czech and Slovak languages," and stipulating that it was "a self-evident political principle that in the future Kingdom of Czecho-Slovakia, in addition to the main Parliament for joint matters, a separate Land Parliament for the management of Slovak specific affairs will be established, and that Slovakia is to be autonomous in the political and lingual point of view."[9]

At the second congress of the Alliance of Czecho-Slovak Associations in Russia (ACSAR) in Kiev, held in April 1916, Dr. Václav Vondrák was elected its president. The congress also decreed a war tax for its members and working POWs, and adopted a resolution demanding the freeing of POWs and their admission into the Czechoslovak military unit. The political program was expressed in the demand for a complete political liberation of the Czechs and Slovaks and the establishment of an independent state. The immediate demand was to establish a Czechoslovak army composed of POWs.[10]

Emergence of Independence Movement 65

Though many POWs volunteered for service, the admission process was slow. Therefore, about 700 soldiers and 330 officers left the camps for Odessa with the Serbian recruiters; from those about 80 officers and 200 soldiers were placed in the First Serbian Division, with which they took part in the fighting in Dobrudza in September 1916.[11] Among the officers was Radola Gajda (originally Rudolf Gejdl), who was destined to play a prominent role in the Czech military force in Russia and Siberia.

Russia was the first of the Entente powers to have to deal with plans and proposals related to the future of the Czech lands and Slovakia submitted to it by leaders of the emerging Czechoslovak independence movement. If Sazonov gave a negative answer to inquiries made by Scheiner, the leader of the Czech gymnastic association, in February 1914, it was because, in his official capacity, he "could not have answered Scheiner in any other way," said Kramář, "even if we [the Czechs] had been his one and only thought."[12] Kramář, as the reader may recall, knew the Russian government officials well and had held many private conversations with them before the war. Also, according to Sazonov's memoirs, Russia left all details concerning Czech independence "to the decision of the Czech people themselves, whose political maturity she did not call in question, reserving for herself, when the moment came, the privilege of actively helping them to realize their desires...."[13] The Russian government," writes Sazonov, "knew little about the desires and needs of the population. It seems to me, therefore, that Russia was right in adopting the attitude she did. The Russian government had decided to confine itself to energetically supporting the aspirations of the Czech people and safeguarding their interests as defined by the Czechs themselves, against any outside interference hostile to their national aims."[14]

Although sympatheic to the national aspirations of the Czechs, the Russian government had to consider the issue in its broad European setting and not in isolation. There were at least two aspects of the situation: one, the British wanted to keep Russia out of central Europe; and two, the disposition of the Czech lands and Slovakia was the pivot on which the future of Austria-Hungary turned. Undoubtedly, the establishment of a Czech state with or without Slovakia was necessarily prejudical to the maintenance of a viable Danubian empire; if the Czech state were ruled directly by, or associated closely with, the Russian empire, the Russians would have a hegemonic position on the continent of Europe that would disrupt the balance of power in the area. The destruction of one of the two empires in central Europe was not desirable, though the western allies of Russia wished to weaken both of them by tearing several provinces from them. Germany, without Alsace-Lorraine, Silesia, and the Polish or Mazzurian provinces, would still be an empire. If Austria-Hungary lost Galicia, Bukovina, Transylvania, the South Slavic provinces, and the Italian irredenta, she would still remain the strongest power between Russia and Germany. Since the Habsburg empire had been a part of the European balance of power system for some four centuries, France and Great Britain did not wish to see it disappear for fear that the power vacuum would be filled, most likely, by Russia or her satellites. Having vested interests in the preservation of the Danubian monarchy, the French and British statesmen opposed the dismemberment of the empire; and so, at least officially, did Russia.

Being aware of this situation, the Russians were cautious whenever they were confronted with the question of the war aims with respect to Austria-Hungary. In August 1914, when Russian armies were advancing through Galicia and were expected to reach the Czech lands before the end of the year, an ambiguous manifesto addressed to the "Peoples of Austria-Hungary" was issued in nine languages over the signature of the commander-in-chief, Grand Duke Nicholas Nikolaevich, uncle of the tsar.[15] This manifesto was spread among Austro-Hungarian soldiers on the front and among the peoples behind the front. It proclaimed that Russia, "which more than once in the past has shed her blood for the deliverance of peoples from an alien yoke, seeks nothing other than re-establishment of right and justice." To the peoples of Austria-Hungary Russia "brings freedom and the realization of national aspirations." The Slavic peoples of Austria-Hungary were urged to help the Russians to attain the objective and to welcome the Russian soldiers as "their own brothers and fighters" for their ideals. Russia, the proclamation said, "seeks only one goal: that each of you be able to develop and prosper, while preserving the precious heritage—language and faith—of your fathers, and that each one of you, united with your brothers, may live in peace and harmony with your neighbor, respecting their independence."[16]

Although the manifesto was well received by many members of dissatisfied national groups within the empire, it was vague and said nothing concrete about war aims and political plans with respect to Austria-Hungary.

Emergence of Independence Movement

The document was a piece of propaganda in the psychological warfare conducted by the Russian army against the enemy forces. (For that matter, the Czech *Družina* was considered by the Russian general staff as an assembly of propagandists working for the Russian army.) The mention of "language and faith" and "right and justice" was merely a pious sentiment, not a concrete political program. Indeed, independence for any of the Slavic nations in the Habsburg domain was not even mentioned. The manifesto served its purpose well, despite the fact that it dealt only with generalities.[17] In the realm of diplomacy, however, Russia had to be more specific.

On September 14, 1914, in a discussion with Maurice Paleologue and Sir George Buchanan (the French and British ambassadors), Russian forein minister Sergei Sazonov presented a war aims program of thirteen points. Among its provisions were the recognition of Serbia's claim to Bosnia, Herzegovina, and Dalmatia; the annexation by Russia of the lower course of the Niemen and the eastern part of Galicia, and the addition to the kingdom of Poland of eastern Poznan (Posen), Silesia, and the western part of Galicia; the reconstitution of Austria as a tripartite monarchy, composed of the empire of Austria, the kingdom of Bohemia, and the kingdom of Hungary. The kingdom of Hungary would have to come to terms with Romania in regard to Transylvania, and with the kingdom of Bohemia in regard to Slovakia, which would belong to the latter.[18] This political program did not suggest that Sazonov intended to dismember Austria-Hungary, although point two of his exposition stated that "territorial modifications ought to be determined according to the principle of nationality," whose implementation could easily produce that result. Yet the terms Sazonov used in September 1914, were flexible: the principle of nationality and Sazonov's mention to Paleologue one month earlier, of the need "to free Bohemia,"[19] could have been interpreted as entailing autonomy for the Czechs within the Habsburg domain, or the separation of the Bohemian Crown, enlarged by Slovakia, from it. The Russian government, no doubt, was trying to get along with the other Allies on the issue of war aims, and, at the same time, reserve to itself the freedom to act in accordance with the situation as it might develop in the future. In this respect Russia was no different from her allies.

Russia's allies considered several options in their confidential discussions of war aims, made public pronouncements on war aims, and made promises to each other, without making definite commitments until the conclusion of the secret treaties of 1915. The future of the Danubian empire was an object of Entente diplomacy, but hardly any of the Allied statesmen believed it possible or desirable to wipe the empire off the map of Europe. The Allies found it necessary to promise territorial gains at the expense of the Habsburgs in order to win new allies, especially Italy. Thus, as early as August 6, 1914, the French ambassador at St. Petersburg stated that the French government would agree to Italy's gaining considerable territories, including Trieste, from the Danubian empire. The British government agreed, and so notified Rome.[20] Also, on August 9, 1914, Sir Edward Grey, British secretary of foreign affairs, promised his diplomatic support for Romanian territorial demands on Hungary, and had "no objection to Russia obtaining those advantages" for Romania.[21] Promises of territorial gains were also made to Serbia and even Bulgaria. The British supported the view that the Southern Slavs should be strengthened in order to offer effective resistance to Germanic pressures in the Balkans, since the German threat to the British position in the Middle East and India, as exemplified in the phrase "Berlin-Bagdad," appeared a real danger.[22] Yet the British promises lacked concreteness, and only on September 1, 1915, did the Foreign Office notify Serbia that, if the latter agreed, Bosnia, Herzegovina, South Dalmatia, Slavonia, and Croatia should be permitted to decide their own fate.[23] This promise, however, did not imply the dismantling of Austria-Hungary; and it would not necessarily affect the status of the Czech lands and Slovakia. The British feared Russian hegemony in Europe; therefore, they favored the continued existence of an internationally weakened and internally reorganized Habsburg empire. The tsarist government was thus the best hope for the Czechoslovak independence movement abroad, and its spokesmen in Russia attempted to influence Russian policy in regard to Austria-Hungary.

The largest concentration of Czechs and Slovaks outside the Habsburg monarchy was in the United States; in 1910, some 500,000 Czechs and 280,000 Slovaks lived there. The number of Slovaks increased rapidly during the years before the war. Thus in 1920 there were in the United States some 1,200,000, Czechs and Slovaks, among whom the latter were already in the majority.[24] It was not feasible for these people to organize military action, since any such effort would constitute a violation of America's neutrality and its own laws.

Like those in Russia and elsewhere, Czechs and Slovaks living in the United States had no uniform ideological, religious, and political outlook. In particular, there were divisions among the Czech clubs that had been established in many settlements between the so-called free-thinkers and the Catholics. The gymnastic organization *Sokol* was not united; there was a National *Sokol* Society, a Workers *Sokol* in New York, and a Catholic *Sokol.* Early in September 1914, several groups of anti-Habsburg free-thinking Czechs merged into the Bohemian National Alliance, with Dr. L. Fisher as its chairman; this organization became the main protagonist of the Czech independence movement in the United States. Though for different reasons, Czech Catholics, Protestants, and Socialists were all opposed to the "anti-Austrian action." At the beginning of the war the Socialists followed the Social Democratic party line, believing that an independent Bohemian state could not survive if it were established. However, in the spring of 1915 Charles Pergler and J. Novák of the Bohemian branch of the American Socialist party, and some Bohemian Protestants, joined the Bohemian National Alliance. The Czech Catholics, except as a few individuals, did not participate in the independence movement until 1917, when on May 16 some Catholic groups formed the National Alliance of Bohemian Catholics. Through the efforts of Rev. Oldřich Zlámal of Cleveland, those Catholics were brought into the fold with the Bohemian National Alliance and the Slovak League of America.[25]

The Slovak League of America represented the Slovaks, who were organized independently and separately from the Czech (Bohemian and Moravian) clubs. The Slovaks were convinced of the need for Slovak autonomy, be it within Hungary or within a Czech state. Eventually, most of the leaders of the Slovak League agreed to a common political action with the Bohemian National Alliance on the basis of Slovak autonomy within the Czechoslovak state. In April 1915, with this in mind, a joint consultation of some Czechs and Slovaks living in Chicago was conducted under the chairmanship of Štefan Osuský, a young attorney of Slovak origin. Then, at a congress held at Cleveland, Ohio, on October 25, 1915, the Bohemian National Alliance and the Slovak League of America agreed to become the spokesmen of the Czecho-Slovak independence movement in the United States. Their so-called Cleveland Agreement stipulated that the objective of the movement was "the union of Czech and Slovak peoples in a federal union of states." The executive committee of the new joint organization of Czechs and Slovaks in America fostered the program of Czecho-Slovak independence; and the Czech-Slav Press Bureau was established in order to bring it to the attention of the American public. Both the Czechs and the Slovaks were to have autonomy in the federative state to be established after the war.[26]

Unlike those in Russia and the United States, Czech and Slovak emigrants in west European countries were not concentrated into numerous settlements. There were some Czech clubs in France, England, and Switzerland. Among these the most important role was played by the Czechs who settled in Paris at the beginning of the war.[27] Since the French government announced that German and Austrian citizens who did not return home would be interned in concentration camps, some Czechs left France for Switzerland. Others, upon the appeal of a Czech committee established in August 1914, reported for military duty: about 300 of them were placed in the Foreign Legion "for the duration of the war." The Czechs living in Paris were enthusiastically for France and Russia, and against Austria-Hungary. They hoped that the Russians would liberate the Czech lands, and their committee assumed the role of their spokesmen. They were aided by several French Slavists, amon whom the most prominent was the historian Ernest Denis.

At the end of January 1915, a relatively small group of "delegates" from various Czech organizations abroad met in Paris with the intention of establishing an organization that would represent the independence movement abroad, on the international scene. The meeting was called upon the initiative of a Czech from Moscow, Svatopluk Koníček, whom the Russian ministry of war had sent on a special mission abroad. His task was to organize individual Czechs and Czech colonies abroad for an anti-Austro-Hungarian action that could be used by the Russian ministry of war in its psychological warfare. Koníček, under the name of Štěpán Horský, had left Petrograd on October 12, 1914, and had traveled via Moscow, Kiev, and Odessa (where he contacted Czech organizations) to Romania and then to Bulgaria and Serbia. There he held conferences with political leaders and propagated the ideas contained in Nikolaevich's manifesto on the liberation of Slavic nations living in Austria-Hungary. In his unofficial capacity he could and did interpret that vague document in such a way as to make it more appealing to anti-Habsburg Slavs. From Serbia he went to Greece, Italy, France, England, and Switzerland and appealed to Czechs living abroad, including those in the United States, to send delegates to the Paris congress in January 1915.[28]

As a result of the Paris consultations, a National Council was established, with Ernest Denis as its honorary chairman, Koníček-Horský was elected first vice-chairman. He had arrived earlier from Switzerland and talked enthusiastically about the success of the Czechs in Russia and their having been accepted in an audience by the tsar himself. (He was one of those who had met the tsar.) Josef Čapek became second vice-chairman. Antonín Veselý was secretary, František Jackl treasurer, and Viluš Crkal the editor of *L'Independance tschèque,* a newspaper published in Paris that propagated pro-Allied views and the idea of Czech independence. With the exception of Koníček-Horský, who was from Russia, all the members of this committee were from Paris. However, the congress never established a formal organization of Czechs for independence abroad. The London Czechs did not take part in the election, and left Paris with some doubts about the wisdom of the protsarist orientation of *L'Independance tschèque* under Koníček's and Crkal's management. In fact, Crkal's uncritical admiration for the tsar and his regime, if not resented, was certainly not shared by the majority of Czechs in the three centers —Paris, London, and Switzerland. The Swiss Czechs even demanded that Ernest Denis be asked to assume the direction of the periodical and that the leadership of the National Council be changed.[29]

Thus, the first groups that began to propagate the idea of Czech independence were Czech emigrant colonies, and their movement for independence was rather spontaneous. In contrast to it, the anti-Austrian movement at home developed very slowly. One reason for this was the suspension of civil rights, including freedom of speech, press, assembly, and organization, on July 25, 1914, even before the declaration of mobilization.[30] On September 18, 1914, the parliamentary immunity of the deputies was abolished, and censorship of the press and even of private correspondence was initiated. All opposition activity thus became illegal.

Despite the unfavorable climate of opinion created by the controlled press and the measures taken by the government, Kramář declared in an article published in *Národní Listy* on August 4, 1914, that the war was a struggle between Germandom and Slavdom (as the Pan-Germanists also were saying), and expressed his belief that the future of the Czechs depended on who won.[31] What kind of future Austria-Hungary would have in the event of victory by the Central Powers was indicated in an article published in *Národní Listy* on August 24, 1914. This article suggested cautiously that the proposed customs union with Germany would bring about a German-dominated central Europe. From Hamburg to Salonica, from the North Sea to the Mediterranean Sea, "German labor and German capital would have a free field for their activity."[32]

Kramář's stand was not endorsed by all Czech political parties; in fact, most of the latter did not share his views at all. The Czech Catholic and the Slovak National parties were the first to proclaim their loyalty to the empre and its monarch; the other parties followed suit with more or less enthusiasm. Neither the Agrarians nor the Social Democrats believed in an Allied victory and the breakup of Austria-Hungary. The Social Democratic party, led by Bohumír Šmeral, upheld its 1913 program and the Marxist view according to which the implementation of economic and social reforms requires a large territory. The party saw the Czech national interest as firmly in accord with the idea of the Austrian state. Šmeral remained true to his prewar (1913) view that "the winning of Bohemian state right during the world crisis" would be "for the Czechs as a nation and their land the worst possibility."[33]

The Social Democrats also rejected Kramář's concept of the war as a "racial" struggle between Germandom and Slavdom. Even Masaryk rejected this view as one-sided; however, he did not share the Social Democrats' belief that the war was a just struggle against Russian tsarism. In fact, as long as the tsarist government was in power, Masaryk did not denounce it publicly, realizing fully that it was one of the Allied governments, and, as far as the Czechs were concerned, the most important one.[34]

The Slovak National and Populist parties endorsed the idea of the integrity and indivisibility of St. Stephen's Crown, and their activities were directed toward winning autonomy for the Slovak nation within Hungary. The lone Slovak deputy in the Budapest parliament, Rev. Ferdinand Juriga, wrote in a Slovak newspaper on August 21, 1914, that the Slovaks stood by the principle already stated by Palacký, who had suggestted that "had there been no Austro-Hungarian monarchy, it would

Emergence of Independence Movement 73

be necessary to create it."[35] Only a few Slovaks, such as the editors Bohdan Pavlů (a Moravian Slovak), Anton Štefánik, and František Votruba, who published a Slovak periodical in Prague, shared the views of Kramář and Rašín. All Czech and Slovak political parties believed in monarchy, none supporting the idea of establishing a Czechoslovak state with a republican form of government.[36]

The Czech newspapers officially endorsed the war effort, but most of them rejected the proposal for a customs union with Germany that was made by the president of the Austrian parliament in the middle of September 1914. The publications of the National Social party were suspended for ten days, and the leader of the party, deputy Václav Klofáč, was arrested on September 4, 1914. His arrest was an arbitrary violation of his parliamentary immunity and a preventive measure ordered by the supreme military headquarters.[37]

The Austrian police arrested several individuals suspected of distributing pro-Russian leaflets and of organizing groups that would cooperate with the Russians after their troops entered Czech territory. Various police investigations led to eleven trials in which over twenty death sentences were pronounced; one of the sentences was carried out in November 1914.[38] The anti-Austrian and pro-Russian mood of a considerable segment of the Czech population became most manifest among the Czech soldiers. One the eve of the departure of the 36th Regiment from Mladá Boleslav, the soldiers sang a parody of the national song that included the phrase, "The Russian is with us, and who is against us will be smashed by the Frenchman." For singing this and other parodies many soldiers were arrested. This and similar "subversive" activities were used as a pretext for the arrest of the antimilitaristic leaders of the youth of the National Social party. On October 26, 1914, six companies of the 36th Regiment, as well as other units of Czech regiments, surrendered to the Russians,[39] beginning a "movement" that became widespread in the spring of 1915 in most of those units of the Austro-Hungarian army that were composed predominantly of Czech recruits.

In April 1915, the Austro-Hungarian army was alarmed; on April 3 Prague's 28th Infantry Regiment went over to the Russians in the region northwest of Zborov, and one month later, two battalions of the 36th Regiment followed suit.[40] These defections of whole military units were the first concrete manifestations of massive Czech resistance. They led to attempts to establish military rule in some of the provinces inhabited by Slavs in Austria-Hungary. The government, to counteract the defections and demonstrate its power, decided to strike a direct blow at the Czech independence movement at home by arresting Dr. Karel Kramář on May 21, 1915.[41] As will be shown later, this event strengthened the independence movement abroad by giving it a concrete evidence of the Czech's defiance of the Habsburg state and the state's persecution of them. At the same time, it paralyzed the Czech independence movement at home for almost three years.

CHAPTER FOUR

THE ORGANIZATION OF THE CZECH INDEPENDENCE MOVEMENT BY EMIGRES ABROAD, AND SETBACKS AT HOME

Dr. Lev Sychrava of the State Rights party, who was close to the National Socials, was the first among many political emigrants from the Czech lands who left home intending to work for Czech independence. He had been rejected by the draft board, and since he did not have to serve in the army, he easily obtained a passport for travel abroad. He left Prague on September 21, 1914, and arrived in Geneva early in October. Before his departure for Switzerland, he met some of the National Socials' leaders, and, therefore, was aware that Klofáč expected "everything from the speedy arrival of the Russians."[1] Sychrava received some money from the State Rights party, and more was to come later. Dr. Josef Scheiner, the leader of the *Sokol* (the gymnastic organization), advised Sychrava to contact the Russian embassy in Bern, and to use Scheiner's name as a reference. After arriving in Switzerland, Sychrava succeeded in placing a few articles in Swiss periodicals; however, since he was alone and not a prominent politician, his propaganda for Czech independence was ineffective and was greeted with skepticism. Yet Sychrava established contacts with Czech emigrant clubs abroad, maintained contacts with his friends in Prague, and during the war, edited *Československá samostatnost,* an exile periodical.[2]

After Masaryk decided not to return home, he became a political émigré; and, as it turned out, the most important one. Before he came out publicly against Austria-Hungary in July 1915, he went to England upon the invitation of Seton-Watson. On April 20, 1915, the British historian, whose ambition was to work for British intelligence (as he eventually did),[3] introduced Masaryk to George R. Clerk, head of a special war department in the British Foreign Office, who was in constant touch with Sir Edward Grey, secretary of foreign affairs. Clerk asked Masaryk to prepare a short memorandum for his chiefs. The result was the memorandum "Independent Bohemia," received in the Foreign Office on May 3, and copies of which were printed as "confidential material."[4] The document claimed to represent the views of "all political parties except the Catholic Clericals," and to be a "program for the restoration of Bohemia as an independent state." It may be noted that the views expressed here by Masaryk assumed that the Russians would enter Bohemia and, in general, followed the tenets of the *Maffie*.

The memorandum was very lengthy, covering many subjects related to war and the postwar rearrangement of the map of Europe. It called for the renaissance of Europe on the basis of the modern principle of nationality and, at the same time, for giving Istanbul and the straits to Russia. It claimed that this concession would satisfy Russia's desires. Since Russia had no vital interests in the Gulf of Persia, the Russo-British rivalry would be resolved. The memorandum also called for the establishment of Polish, Serbo-Croat, and Bohemian states. Here Masaryk expressed his conviction that Austria-Hungary was unable to protect and administer the Czechs and other small nations, and that they must, therefore, take care of themselves. The Czechs were Slavophiles, and from the beginning of the war they had expressly sympathized with Russia, Serbia, and the Allies. Claiming that the Czechs abroad had declared themselves in favor of political independence for Bohemia, Masaryk named *La Nation tchèque*, which had been launched by him and whose first issue came out on May 1, 1915, as the official organ of "political Czechs abroad."

At this time Masaryk projected the Czech state as a monarchy, because "the majority of the Czechs" were monarchists. The ruler could be a prince from one of the Allied countries, and there could be a personal union between Serbia and the Czech state if a Czecho-Serbian corridor could be arranged. He added, however, that "the Czech people . . . are completely Russophile. A Russian dynasty in any form would be the most popular one. In any case, the Czech politicians wish to establish the Kingdom of Bohemia in complete accord with Russia. The wishes and intentions of Russia will be of determining influence."[5]

This program assumed the occupation of Germany and its defeat in the war. After the war the liberated Czechs would always act in agreement with the Entente and would always be its loyal allies. Now, the memorandum said, they wished that their Russian brethren would occupy their country; they ardently and sincerely hoped for that event. In the program formulated in "Independent Bohemia," and in *La Nation tchèque*,[6] the Czech political emigration, strengthened by the arrival of the Agrarian deputy Josef Dürich, had a basis for its action abroad.

The memorandum was submitted while Kramář was still the unquestioned leader of the independence movement at home, before his arrest, and it indicates that, on the whole, Masaryk was in accord with the views held by the *Maffie,* especially Kramář, who also expected the liberation of the Czech lands by the Russians. Masaryk's claims to territories inhabited by Germans and to a corridor through western Hungary were not compatible the principle of national self-determination, of which Masaryk was a spokesman. Also, his assertions about the number of Slovaks in Hungary were exaggerations. (Masaryk carried a map showing the extent of the projected state.) His statement that he was not one of the radicals who wished for a republic might have pleased the British, but the views that the Bohemian kingdom was to be established "in a complete accord with Russia," and that "wishes and intentions of Russia will be of determining influence" were hardly well received. His proposal was seen as premature and was accepted with skepticism in the British Foreign Office. George R. Clerk commented on it, "The Allies have a long way to go before the points of this Memo. can come up for their practical consideration."[7]

As it happened, the memorandum was never considered by the Allies. To the great disappointment of those who had expected the early arrival of the Russians, the latter never made it to Bohemia. At the beginning of May 1915, the German offensive on the Eastern Front forced the Russians to retreat; the military situation was not much changed by the Italian entry into the war. In October, a joint Austro-German-Bulgarian offensive smashed Serbia, and the Central Powers acquired a direct contact with Turkey. The space for a German-dominated central Europe was won.

At that time, also, the anti-Austrian group of Czech politicians was weakened by the Austrian government's persecution and was reduced to a small handful of people without any influence. Now the forces anticipating the preservation of the empire came to the fore. Distribution of pro-Russian manifestos and leaflets became meaningless. The 36th Regiment, a part of which had gone over to the Russians, was dissolved; and the Grand Duke Joseph, commander of two army groups, called the Czech soldiers who defected to the Russians "destructive elements." He denounced the "dishonest guys who betrayed the Kaiser and the Empire." For this "throwing dirt on the flag of the glorious and brave army," he promised either a bullet or a hangman's noose.[8] Eventually, the last wave of resistance among the Czech soldiers ended with the defection of some units to the Russians in September 1915; and the anti-Austrian spirit in the army was broken. A pro-Austrian sentiment, however, was not created.

The temporary changes on the fronts were accepted without being critically assessed and placed in proper perspective, as had happened earlier after the temporary successes of the Russian army. Depression overcame those who had been unduly optimistic some months before. In May 1915, Kramář and Scheiner were arrested on the order of the supreme commander, largely because Kramář had persuaded the leaders of the Czech parties not to dispatch a delegation of politicians to the headquarters to extend congratulations for military victories on the Russian front.[9] Scheiner was released one month later for lack of evidence, but Dr. Alois Rašín, a Young Czech deputy in Vienna, close to Kramář, was arrested on July 12, 1915. In August, indictments were initiated against Masaryk by the government, and the newspaper of the Realist party was banned. At the beginning of September 1915, in danger of being arrested, Beneš escaped abroad. Censorship was strengthened; some books were confiscated from libraries; some Czech songs were prohibited; and the activities of *Sokol* and other Czech societies were stopped.[10]

At the beginning of May 1915, before Kramář's arrest, the *Maffie* was able to prevent a public manifestation of loyalty to the regime by Czech politicians; in June, however, a series of loyalty statements appeared in the press. Pro-Austrian activism was pursued by the Agrarians, the Young Czechs (under new leadership) and the Social Democrats, led by Šmeral. The activists, in accordance with their prewar policy, endorsed the monarchy, assuming that the future of the Czech nation would continued to be bound up with that of the Austro-Hungarian state.

Before his escape from Prague, Beneš reported to Masaryk that the *Maffie* had agreed that Masaryk and Dürich could consider themselves the spokesmen of the political parties represented in the secret committee, plus the National Socials. But the Young Czechs, after the arrest of Kramář and Rašín, agreed to collaborate with the Agrarians and Social Democrats, on the assumption that Austria-Hungary would continue to exist even after the war. Thus, after Beneš's escape, of the original five in the *Maffie,* only Dr. Šámal remained. He and his coworkers continued to maintain contacts in Switzerland.[11] In August a "delegate" of the *Maffie,* Vojta Beneš, arrived in the United States and established contacts with the Bohemian National Alliance of America in Chicago. In October 1915, the Bohemian National Alliance and the Slovak League of America agreed on a programmatic goal—uniting the Czech and the Slovak nations within a federation of states (with complete autonomy for Slovakia)—and declared that the Bohemian National Alliance and the Slovak League should be considered the only representative of the two nations in the United States.[12]

While the independence movement was well established abroad toward the end of 1915, it suffered great setbacks at home from the Austrian government's actions. Most notable was the trial of Kramář and Rašín, who were charged with high treason and crimes against the war powers of the state, together with two other defendants charged with espionage. This one judicial process, with four defendants, was the most spectacular of the series of trials conducted "behind closed doors." It lasted from December 6, 1915, until June 3, 1916, when all four of the accused were sentenced to death by hanging. After an appeal by the defendants, the verdict was confirmed by the Supreme Court of Justice on November 20. The execution of the sentences was prevented only by the emperor's private physician, who did not permit the verdict to be submitted for the ruling monarch's signature. Franz-Joseph was at the time already in agony and died shortly afterwards.[13]

The next great trial involved deputies of the National Social party who were charged with having met with Professor Masaryk on October 1, 1914. On leaving the country, Masaryk had left among his papers the minutes of the meeting, which showed that the discussion had dwelt on the expected arrival of Russian troops in Bohemia and Moravia, the attitude the nation should take in that event, and the course of action that should be followed.[14] However, it was the trial of Kramář and his death sentence that aroused great interest abroad and helped to win new friends to the Czech cause. In his speeches, articles, and interviews, Masaryk argued that Kramář had represented the thinking and feeling of the Czech people, and that the other pro-Vienna politicians were forced to issue their statements of loyalty to the monarchy.[15]

The death sentences of Kramář and Rašín, and of the other two Czechs, who were unknown abroad, constituted the greatest blow to the resistance movement at home since it had started. On the other hand, in the Allied and neutral countries, the event was interpreted as a visible sign of the Czech struggle against the Habsburg state.[16] If the principle representative of Czech politics was condemned to death, the Allies reasoned, the aims of the Czechs must have been incompatible with those of Austria-Hungary; therefore, the contradictions between the Czechs and the Austro-Hungarian state could not be solved peacefully—only force could decide the outcome.

Prominent politicians, journalists, and historians in France, including Prime Minister Georges Clemenceau, Senator Stephen Pichon, who later, as minister of foreign affairs, signed a declaration recognizing the Czecho-Slovak government in exile, Ernest Denis, Louis Leger, and many others condemned the death sentence in French newspapers. Beneš, in the conclusion that he added to his pamphlet *Destroy Austria-Hungary!* capitalized on the trial of Kramář, and in the light of the verdict was able to win new friends to the cause of Czechoslovak independence. On July 9, 1916, the *Times* (London) featured a detailed story on the trial and Kramář's prewar political activity. The British director of war propaganda on the continent, Lewis B. Namier, wrote a long and informative article about Kramář and his trial in *The New Statesman.* Namier evaluated Kramář's prewar efforts to prevent Austria-Hungary from becoming a vassal of Germany in the Triple Alliance and thus serving as a bridge for German expansion into the East, the Balkans, and Asia Minor. Seton-Watson, Steed, and other British friends of Czechoslovak independence seized upon the Kramář trial as an opportunity to tell the British political public that Austrian foreign policy stood upon German foundations, that the Germans would never agree to any change in that policy, and that the Czech nation had a great mission in central Europe.[17] A similar situation existed in Italy, where the Kramář trial popularized the Czech question

Organization Abroad and Setbacks at Home 81

and brought it to the attention of the Italian masses. In America it strengthened the case of those Czechs and Slovaks who campaigned against Austria-Hungary; in fact, the Kramář affair was the first great political event that the Czechs and Slovaks abroad were able to exploit. For a long time this event was the only proof of the anti-Habsburg attitude of the Czechs at home that the Czechoslovak independence movement abroad was able to furnish to foreign publics.[18]

The trial had its strongest impact in Slavic states, especially in Russia, where Kramář had been best known. A professor of the University of Petrograd, N. J. Jastrebov, wrote in *Birzhevie Vedomosti* that the name of Kramář was known to "all educated Slavdom and, above all, to Russia. Kramář is known to all political Europe. Hated by the Germans and Hungarians and their satellites, Turkey and Bulgaria, this leader of the Czech nation has become a person dear to all those who now fight for right, freedom, and culture."[19] All Russian newspapers insisted that it was the duty of Russian policy to prevent the annihilation of the Czech nation by Austria. All of them, pro-government, opposition, conservative, or socialist, aruged that the key issue in the trial of Kramář was not his person, but the whole Czech nation and the cause of Russia. They took over from the French newspapers the thesis that the death sentence of Kramář meant "the chopping off the head" of the Czech nation. At no other time had the Czech issue been brought to light as prominently in the Russian and Allied press as on the occasion of Kramář's death sentence. The Czech question was brought into focus of international attention for the first time since the war started.[20]

For the Czechs and Slovaks abroad Kramář became the symbol of the national struggle. The Czech soldiers of the *Družina* (now enlarged into a brigade) in Russia proclaimed their determination to change the death sentence of Kramář into the death sentence of Austria-Hungary. Vengeance was on the minds of the soldiers, who began to use the slogan "For Kramář! For Rašín!" when faced with new tasks at the front. The name of Kramář was now a challenge to Czechs and Slovaks abroad—a call to struggle for the liberation of the Czech and Slovak nations, no matter how long it took.[21]

It did take much longer than most people anticipated. In December 1914, before making his final trip abroad, Masaryk expected an early arrival of the Russians into the Czech lands and believed that the war would end with an Entente victory in 1915.[22] Toward the end of that year, however, the end of the war was still not in sight; therefore, he and his coworkers had to prepare themselves for a long exile. In Septembe 1915, Masaryk accepted a lecturership at King's College, London University. In order to give him prestige and, ostensibly, material security, the college created a new position for him.[23] In reality, more important than the honorarium attached to this position was the moral, political, and financial support that Masaryk was given by the Bohemian National Alliance in the United States.

In October 1915, some 70,000 Czechs were organized in twenty-eight branches of the Bohemian National Alliance, headed by its chairman, Dr. Ludvík Fischer. A monthly, *The Bohemian Review,* edited by Dr. J. F. Smetánka, was published in Chicago; and the Slav Press Bureau, directed by Charles Pergler, was established in New York by this organization. Earlier in the year (1915), Koníček tried to rally support for his National Council at Paris; however, he met strong opposition while touring the United States. In a letter to a friend dated May 7, 1915, Koníček complained that "Sychrava and Kepl aroused the whole of America" against him. The Bohemian National Alliance supported Masaryk and refused to cooperate with him because he "travelled for Russian money."[24] The National Council was losing support even in western Europe, and it ceased to function in August 1915. In a letter to Masaryk dated July 21, 1915, Koníček wrote that he yielded to the Czech leader, to Masaryk's "pressure, terror of the Realist-Social Democrats, and the power of American dollars"[25] —an allusion to the work of the Voska-led secret society, which included some Social Democrats. Koníček retired to Switzerland, where he had the support of Dr. Vítězslav Štěpánek, who was anti-Masaryk and pro-Russian. The two continued to oppose Masaryk and "the Social Democrat demagoguery against tsarism." However, the defeat of the Koníček group and the rapprochement between the Bohemian National Alliance on the one hand, and the London and Paris Czech groups on the other, fundamentally strengthened Masaryk's position among Czech emigrants in western Europe and America.[26]

In addition to the Czech Catholics, some of the free-thinking Czechs in America did not share the anti-Austrian and Anglophile orientation of the Bohemian National Alliance. They opposed pro-Masaryk propaganda on the grounds that it lied about Austrian atrocities and oppression of the Czechs in Austria. Indeed, when in the summer of 1916 Congressman Adolph J. Sabath of Chicago inquired, through the U.S. minister at Vienna and the U.S. consul at Prague, about claims made by the pro-Masaryk propagandists, according to which one thousand persons had been executed and one hundred thousand (or even several hundred thousand) had been imprisoned in Bohemia, he was assured that there was not truth in those allegations. The exaggerations and falsehoods of the pro-Masaryk propaganda were exposed by a free-thinking Czech-American, Dr. František Iška, editor and publisher of *Vesmír* in Chicago, who, in turn, was denounced by the same propaganda as an Austrian agent. Iška wondered how Masaryk could reject all that he had stood for before the war; he hoped that one day a simple explanation would be found for this reversal. Iška believed that an independence achieved with lies could not last. The Voska group eventually silenced Iška by publishing forged documents purporting to show that he had been receiving payments from the Austrian consultate in New York.[27]

Masaryk also benefited greatly from the cooperation between the Bohemian National Alliance and the Slovak League in America, headed by Albert Mamatey, that resulted from the so-called Cleveland Agreement of October 22, 1915. As has been mentioned earlier, the two organizations agreed at Cleveland to work for the establishment of a state in which the Czechs and Slovaks would be equal partners. In February 1916, the Slovak League decided to send a delegate to Europe to meet Professor Masaryk and to explain the Slovak program to the British and French foreign ministries. Since Osuský, a Protestant, was selected to be this delegate, the league decided to send another delegate, Gustav Košík, a Catholic, to Russia. Both of them departed in May 1916, and arrived in London on June 4, 1916. As "ambassadors" of the league, their task was to promote acceptance of the Cleveland Agreement, which called for "independence of the Czech Lands and Slovakia, the uniting of the Czech and Slovak nations in a federation of states, with a complete national autonomy of Slovakia that would have its own Diet, its own schools, its own state administration, cultural freedom, and the use of the Slovak language as the official language of the State."[28] Osuský remained in Europe in charge of the Czechoslovak information office at Geneva; Košík went to Russia.

There had to be a division of tasks among the émigrés. Masaryk worked in London, Beneš in Paris, and, after his arrival, Dürich stayed in Switzerland, waiting there for an invitation to Russia. In Switzerland Dürich met with Masaryk (July 1915), led discussions with Yugoslav, Czech, and Russian politicians, established contacts through Svatkovsky with the Russian government, and secretly communicated with Prague through Sychrava and Baráček. The second half of 1915 and the early months of 1916 were the most difficult time for the independence movement abroad. The leaders of the western European governments did not then realize how important central European problems would be for the development and results of the war. Only after the destruction of Serbia did they begin to comprehend the German plan and the meaning of a German *Mitteleuropa;* only then could Masaryk and Beneš launch an effective propaganda campaign. Masaryk lectured in London and tried to establish more contacts with the ruling circles. Beneš, in France, tried to take advantage of his contacts in university circles, the historian Ernest Denis, the socialists, and his former teacher, Professor Louis Eisenmann, who, as an expert on Austria-Hungary, worked in the information department of the ministry of war.[29] (Beneš, who maintained excellent contacts with Prague, supplied intelligence information to the ministry and to Masaryk, who, in turn, transmitted it to Steed. Through his contacts in the ministry of war Beneš was able to establish connections in the ministry of foreign affairs.) L. Štrimpl, a painter and a friend from the days of his studies, an officer of the Franco-Czech League, introduced Beneš to the foreign editor of the *Journal des Dèbats;* thus Beneš became a contributor to this influential French periodical. Štrimpl also acquainted Beneš with a second lieutenant in the French army, Milan Rastislav Štefánik (1880-1919), a Slovak who had been living in France since 1904.[30]

During the years 1897-1904, Štefánik had studied astronomy at Prague and kept in touch with the Hlasists (Czechophile Slovak Protestants). His friend, Vavro Šrobár, recommended him to Masaryk. Štefánik migrated to France in 1904. As an astronomer he visited Turkestan (1906-07), and as a meteorologist, Algeria and Tunisia (1908), Tahiti (1910-11), Brazil (1912), Ecuador (1913), and Tunisia (1914). Štefánik worked for the French government and for the French navy. In 1912 he became a French citizen. Because of his scientific achivements and his service to France, he was made a knight of the Legion of Honor in 1914. In January 1915, he joined the French air force (army), and after September 1915, he served with an air force unit in Serbia. Since he had considerable experience abroad, and in view of his prewar service for the French government, he received political-military assignments in Serbia. Štefánik had a genuine interest in the Czech and Slovak problems and attempted unsuccessfully to meet Masaryk during his trip to London. When the first Czech declaration was made in November 1915, Beneš suggested to Masaryk that it could be signed by Štefánik on behalf of the Slovaks. At that time, however, Štefánik was in Serbia. When he returned to Paris, he met Beneš for the first time in Štrimpl's apartment on December 13, 1915.[31] Štefánik opened doors for Beneš to many influential people who later aided the Czech struggle abroad.

After Masaryk came out publicly against Austria-Hungary during the celebration of the five hundredth anniversary of the death of Jan Hus in Geneva on July 6, 1915, most of the Czech political émigrés in western Europe and the United States recognized Masaryk as their leader and worked under his directives. The situation was, however, different in Russia, where Masaryk was known as "unfriendly" toward the tsarist political system. There the ground was prepared for another Czech deputy of the Austrian parliament, Josef Dürich, who was waiting for an invitation to Petrograd from Foreign Minister Sazonov. Masaryk's and Dürich's philosophies were radically different, and so were their political objectives. Masaryk was pro-western in his outlook, and was a pragmatist or even an opportunist in his *modus operandi,* while Dürich stuck to his principles, followed a pro-Slavic course of action, and was "unsophisticated" in his political approaches, using logic and common sense. According to what Masaryk wrote about him after the war, Dürich was "for the Tsar and even for the Orthodox Church," and awaited "salvation from Russia."[32]

Masaryk's disdain of Dürich, however, should be put into perspective. During the period between the outbreak of the war and the February 1917 revolution in Russia, Masaryk scrupulously avoided making statements that could possibly have antagonized the tsar. On several occasions, moreover, he tried to please the Russian monarch by saying that a Russian Romanov dynasty would be most popular in Bohemia. As has been noted above, in his memorandum "Independent Bohemia" Masaryk stated that the Czechs were "completely Russophile" and that they wished to establish a kingdom of Bohemia "in complete accord with Russia."[33] In all fairness to both Masaryk and Dürich, it should be pointed out that Masaryk became a Protestant, largely because of the influence of his American-born wife; however, there is no evidence that Dürich was ever converted to Orthodoxy, as were many of the members of the *Družina*.[34] In any event, the differences between the two deputies were not apparent when, in the fall of 1915, Masaryk asked Dürich to sign a declaration for the "Czech Committee Abroad," issued on November 14, 1915.[35]

This manifesto, endoresed by representatives of Czech and Slovak organizations in Allied countries and by other public figures, was the first public, formal, and lengthy statement on the goals and objectives of the movement for Czech independence. The signatories of the manifesto expected from the Allied victory "total Czech independence and the reunion of Bohemia, Moravia, and Slovakia under one government." They declared "the contract" between the Czech nation and the Habsburgs "null and void because it had been systematically violated by the Habsburgs." They said that before the war the conflict "between the dynasty and the Czech nation was already sharp. War rendered impossible all attempts at repair."

The manifesto proclaimed, furthermore, that "the Czechs are certainly one of the ethnic groups in which the idea of Slav solidarity is the most universally known; it is part of them, it has been proclaimed by their poets, their historians, and their publicists. In recent years they have been the initiators and the promoters of a Neo-Slavism that, if it had succeeded, perhaps could have prevented the catastrophe which is laying waste to Europe. From the first moment the Czechs were opponents of the Triple Alliance and of Teutonic imperialism. Since the outbreak of the war they have shown by all means their ardent sympathies for the Russians, for Serbia, and for their allies from the West."

The manifesto also recalled that "before the war, the various Czech political parties pursued a policy of transforming the Austro-Hungarian dualism into a federalist monarchy that would have guaranteed to the various nations of the state an extended autonomy and respect for their essential rights." However, "today this spurious solution has become impossible. By causing our children and our brothers to march against our natural allies, by forcing us to carry arms against other Slavs, the Habsburgs have broken the last link that tied us to them. What we demand henceforth is a COMPLETELY INDEPENDENT CZECHOSLAV STATE. . . .

The Habsburgs are nothing more than the servants of the Hohenzollerns. ... The monarchy could have played the role of a fulcrum for peace in the world if it had respected the rights of its various peoples, and if it had grouped them around it in a free federation. We have tried to hold it back from the fatal slope toward which it was slipping rapidly; we have loyally warned the dynasty of the dangers that it was courting. All was in vain. The Habsburgs, gone mad, condemned themselves."

The manifesto, rich in details, ended as follows: "Thanks to the Allies, there will be an independent Bohemia grouping around her all her sons; Serbia will be finally delivered from the Hungarian menace; and there will be an element of balance, a guarantee of universal peace, and a useful worker in the great workshop of humanity."

The declaration was signed by Masaryk, Dürich, Bohmil Čermák, for the Alliance of the Czecho-Slovak Associations in Russia (ACSAR); Bohdan Pavlů, a former prisoner of war and editor of Petrograd's *Čechoslovák;* Dr. L. Fischer, E. Voska, and Charles Pergler for the Bohemian National Alliance in America; Albert Mamatey and Francis Daxner for the Slovak League of America; František Kupka for the Czech colony in Paris; Antonín Veselý for a group of Czech socialists in Paris; J. Sýkora for the Czech Committee of London, and Francis Kopecký for the Czech National Alliance in London. The signatures of the two old men, Masaryk and Dürich (sixty-six and sixty-nine, respectively), were affixed next to each other—Dürich's being the first one, indicating no subordination of the one to the other, nor any special position of the two among the signatories of the manifesto, most of whom represented Czech and Slovak colonies in the Allied countries.

Thus, while the three largest Czech political parties in Austria-Hungary declared themselves for continuation of the Habsburg monarchy, the exiles rejected it and promulgated a program calling for an independent state. At this time Masaryk rejected the idea of establishing an exile organization; also, in February 1916, when Bohdan Pavlů brought to him a proposal from the Czech group in Petrograd to form a central organization of the Czechoslovak independence movement abroad, he turned it down. At a meeting of émigrés held in Paris in February 1916, Masaryk insisted that the organizations of Czechs living abroad could serve only as auxiliary organs of the émigrés, that is, Dürich and himself, who alone represented the real will of the nation and Czech politics at home. Masaryk recognized Dürich's mandate and his independence. Dürich had told Masaryk that Kramář had selected him to represent the nation in Russia; to this Masaryk had "no objection as long as we are agreed upon a program."[36]

The principal task of the émigrés was to persuade the Entente powers that they should fight for a transformation of Europe; that the only alternative to a German-dominated central Europe was the liberation of the nations of central, southern and eastern Europe, and that the struggle against Germany could be greatly aided by those nations' struggle for national independence. It was necessary to convince the general public as well as the policymakers in Great Britain and France that the Czech demands were just and feasible, and that the movement was democratic in its outlook. At the same time, the movement had to be presented in Russian government circles as not too pro-western and democratic. It was known that in Russia Masaryk was viewed with mistrust, and Beneš was seen as a socialist.[37] Thus the person selected to represent the independence movement in Russia was Dürich, whose credentials were not questioned there and who was sent abroad by Kramář. Furthermore, it was necessary to maintain or renew contacts with politicians at home and to make certain that the concept of an independent Czechoslovak state would be accepted and endorsed by Czech and Slovak political leaders.[38] The latter were watching political and military developments closely. However, in early 1916 the prospect of an Allied victory seemed remote, and the Entente spokesmen indicated no interest in the dissolution of the Danubian empire. The task of the exiles was to change that situation.

On February 3, 1916, Masaryk had an audience with the French prime minister, Briand.[39] The main success of this audience consisted in the facts that Briand consented to issue a communiqué about the meeting, and that Masaryk was asked by the prime minister to prepare a memorandum for him, dealing with the matters they had discussed. In this memorandum, Masaryk briefly recapitulated the main themes of his earlier memorandum, "Independent Bohemia,"[40] supplementing them with a call for the formulation of a joint political program by the Entente powers. As he saw it, "against the All-German Central Europe, the Allies must build their own Central Europe."[41] Masaryk reemphasized the importance of the alliance of the west with Russia (and his view that the new Czech state could help to cement this alliance), as well as its importance in the new Europe. If a monarchical regime were established in the Czech state, there were several possible dynasties; or the Czechs might adopt the republican form of government. Should they do so, then the influence of France would be predominant in it. Independent Bohemia, plus Poland and Greater Serbia (more than 40 million people), would create a barrier against militaristic Prussia. Not only the Czechs, but also the Allies would profit politically and economically from such an arrangement. Since the organization of the three countries would require new railroads, canals, and the like, greater economic development and cooperation with France would be its natural outcome. Furthermore, the Czechoslovak state would need French protection. Although the two countries would not have common boundaries, an alliance was possible. According to Masaryk's memorandum, Bohemia was destined for a confidential alliance with France and Russia.

In France, Masaryk informed the Russian ambassador, Alexander P. Izvolsky, of his plans. He also had conversations with leading French politicians, which as Beneš reported to Prague, were a great success. However, he had not convinced the Allies that the liberation of the subjugated nations was compatible with their war aims and had not dispelled the British and French fear that tsarist Russia might move into a vacuum created in central and southeastern Europe if the Danubian monarchy were dismantled. Masaryk insisted that Pan-Russianism under the guise of Pan-Slavism was not part of his program, and that he wanted freedom and independence.[42]

Masaryk hesitated to establish a central political organ for the movement abroad, realizing that the number of political émigrés was very small and that such an organ would not be representative. He hoped that he himself would succeed in getting the support of the Czech emigrant organizations. Then, in February 1916, almost all political émigrés, including Masaryk, Dürich, Sychrava, and Plesinger, met in Paris to discuss their problems. The result of the Paris consultation was the transfer of the editorial office of *Československá samostatnost* to Paris and the establishment of the Czech National Council. The council, according to Dürich, consisted of Masaryk and himself, with Dr. E. Beneš as its secretary. (On February 5, 1916, Masaryk asked Dürich whether he would agree to have Beneš as the secretary general of their organization so that he could deal with governmental circles as an official of the Czech National Council rather than as a private individual. Dürich consented to Masaryk's request.)[43]

Masaryk's influence was weakest in Russia.[44] There the leaders of the Czech colonies, among whom were Koníček, Dr. Vondrák, and L. Tuček, believed that they would play prominent roles in the formation of the Czechoslovak state, thanks to the decisive role of Russia in the war and to the Czech *Družina,* which would be transformed into an independent Czechoslovak army when the Russian troops entered Bohemia. There were also those who believed in the importance of the Czech prisoners of war in Russia. The newspaper of the Alliance of the Czecho-Slovak Associations in Russia (ACSAR), *Čechoslovák,* was edited by a former prisoner of war, a Czechophile (Masarykophile) Slovak, Bohdan Pavlů; and at the end of 1915 two other former prisoners of war were working in the editorial office. There were power struggles, personality problems, and other conflicts within the Alliance (ACSAR). Koníček was one of the first problems. After his return from his western European trip, which displeased many in Russia as well as in western Europe and the United States, he became again the leading force in the Czech Committee in Moscow. The Koníček group, the Czech Committee in Moscow, was in conflict wit the Alliance (ACSAR) over the question of Slovakia's future. While the majority of the Czech associations seemed to favor attaching Slovakia to the future Czech state, the group around Koníček, as well as Moscow's Russo-Slovak L. Štúr Society, favored annexing Slovakia, in the spirit of tsarophile Pan-Slavism, to Russia. There were also personal and ideological frictions between the two main centers of Czech compatriots in Russia, one at Petrograd, the other at Kiev.

Masaryk was in touch with both these centers.[45] In his correspondence with them he emphasized that the political plan of the émigrés was "given by the program of the Czech nation at home," and that the Czech settlements abroad were merely executive and organizational organs. In a letter that Masaryk gave to Bohdan Pavlů in London on April 6, 1916, to deliver to the chairman of the Alliance (ACSAR) he wrote that "the Austrian government imprisoned the majority of the most influential Deputies: only we two, colleague Dürich and I, were fortunate to escape abroad where we undertook the work."[46] (This was, obviously, not true.) Masaryk thanked the Czechs in Russia for establishing the *Družina* and hoped that it could be expanded through the enlistment of Czech prisoners of war in Russia. "Your colony in Russia," wrote Masaryk to the chairman of the ACSAR, Bohumil Čermák, "has a special place among other colonies

—you are the only people who live in a Slavic state, in the state of determining importance. Not merely we, the Slavs, but also the non-Slavic western nations see Russia as the principal element in this war and in the future development after the war. This gives us, the Czechs and all Slavs, also moral, and to a certain extent even political, weight for which all of us are grateful to Russia. . . . Since we expect so much from Russia for our liberation, it is, therefore, extremely important that you have a correct attitude toward the Russian political world." Masaryk then apologized that he could not come to Russia because he had to organize propaganda in the west, where he found tremendous ignorance of Czech affairs; but "they know us much better in Russia and you are there." He added that "wherever I came there where is a Russian official delegation, I have considered it my duty to report myself to the Russian representatives abroad first and foremost, and I have asked them for brotherhly help."

There was no evidence in Masaryk's message to the Czechs in Russia that he had reservations about tsarism or that he would place himself in any way above Deputy Dürich. Moreover, leaflets that were spread behind the front lines encouraging Czech soldiers to desert and to let themselves be captured emphasized that Masaryk and Dürich were "the leaders of the Czecho-Slovak nation."[47] Also, advertisements placed in Czech-American papers asked for contributions to collections "for Masaryk and Dürich." The relationship between the two leaders, however, was an uneasy one.

The tensions and strained relations among the émigrés were often caused by their different assumptions about the mission of the émigrés abroad. This was, in part, the case of Masaryk versus Dürich. While Masaryk created a concrete ideological, political, and diplomatic program and attempted to have it accepted by the *Maffie,* Dürich considered himself to be merely the executor of the *Maffie's* will, and he identified this with Kramář's concept of the great Slavic empire. These differences, which contributed to the yet-to-come Masaryk-Dürich conflict, began to play an important role in the spring of 1916, when the European great powers indicated for the first time their interest in the Czech movement for independence.[48]

The great losses of manpower by the Allied armed forces brough into the forefront the question of utilizing Czech and Slovak prisoners of war, whose numbers ran more than two hundred thousand in Russia and, after Italy entered the war, tens of thousands in Italy. Therefore, the idea of an independent Czechoslovak volunteer army that would fight with the Entente forces against Germany, and would form a prerequisite for the recognition of the projected state, soon entered into the plans of the émigré leaders of the independence movement. Thus on May 29, 1915, shortly after his arrival abroad, Deputy Dürich wrote a letter to the Russian minister of foreign affairs, urging among other points the establishment of a Czechoslovak army in Russia. He also expressed the hope that he, as the representative of Kramář and the *Maffie,* would go to Russia soon. The expected invitation, however, did not arrive and Dürch had to wait.

The need to establish a more effective contact with the Russian government was realized by both Masaryk and Beneš. In a letter to Beneš dated April 6, 1916, Masaryk suggested that Dürich should go to Russia immediately. When, in the same letter, he pointed out the need to divide the roles between himself and Dürich, Beneš agreed. Dürich knew Russian and French; after his arrival abroad, Beneš saw in him a person "suitable and, above all, designated for work in Russia."[49] Beneš went beyond Masaryk in his evaluation of the importance of Russia, as appears from his letter of April 13 to Masaryk. Beneš suggested that an official agreement be made with Russia, so that the Czech independence movement could count on the Russians, and that they, too, would "comprehend our tactics."[50] Knowing the objectives of the Czech National Council, the Russians could be more free and noncommittal in their dealing with the western powers. As Beneš put it, "we do not know how they look upon our campaign; we are also exposed to the danger that they will not comprehend our work and action."[51] This suggestion was one of the first evidences of the "pactomania" for which Beneš later became famous.

Beneš began to mistrust Dürich after he discovered that Dürich had negotiated independently of him with the French government and the Russian embassy in Paris, and that he had had an audience with Prime Minister Briand (as did Masaryk). Furthermore, Dürich had contacts with those émigrés who did not recognize Masaryk as the leader of the movement abroad (and Masaryk maintained relations with those who did not approve of Dürich). Dürich's behavior, however, was hardly objectionable since he, officially, was on the same level as Masaryk: he too was a deputy of the Austrian parliament and had been sent abroad by the *Maffie.*

Organization Abroad and Setbacks at Home

The French officials dealt with Dürich with the understanding that the Czech political program for liberation was, in fact, a part of Russian politics, and they wanted to use Dürich in their dealings with the Russians in a very concrete manner. In April 1916, the first groups of Russian soliders were arriving in France, having been requested by the French government in order to strengthen the weakening French armed forces on the Western Front. Dürich was asked by French government officials to facilitate the enlistment of Czech prisoners of war in Russia in Russian military units that would be sent to France, and he promised to do so. He discussed this matter with officials in the ministry of foreign affairs and the ministry of war, and with members of the Russian military mission attached to the Russian embassy—especially General Lokhvicky, the commander of the Russian troops in France, who supported the idea of transporting some of the Czech prisoners of war to France. Eventually, all of the French and Russian officials authorized him to request that the Czech prisoners of war be armed and sent to France. While in Petrograd, he should specifically state that France had made a commitment to pay all the expenses connected with equipping and transporting the Czech troops.[52] In addition to that, the French minister of trade, Clementel, asked Dürich to assist the French trade mission in Russia, especially in matters of aviation. For this purpose the ministry assigned to Dürich an industrialist of Czech origin living in Paris, E. Stern. The ministry of war also assigned to him Lieutenant Ivan Štafl; and he himself took along for his personal needs a Czech journalist, Viluš Crkal.

Thus, the French government decided to send Dürich to Russia to organize a military force to be recruited from among Czech prisoners of war who were willing to fight in Russian military units in France. This kind of recruitment, however, was not consistent with the aim of the Czech independence movement. The formation of independent military units was to be a manifestation of the struggle for independence, and the first step toward the recognition of the future independent state. According to the French plan, however, the Czech prisoners of war were to fight under the Russian flag on the French front. This was a less than satisfactory situation.

Undoubtedly, the best conditions for the formation of a Czech army were in Russia; yet the efforts of the Alliance of the Czecho-Slovak Associations in Russia (ACSAR) did not make much progress in this respect.

In January 1916, the *Družina* was renamed the Czech infantry regiment,[53] but it remained a unit of two battalions whose eight companies, with some 1,600 men, were spread over the whole southwestern Russian front and whose soldiers were used largely for reconnaissance and patrol. Sometimes they were sent to the Austrian lines to bring back prisoners or intelligence, or both. The small number of troops was largely the result of the Russian government's disapproval of the idea of a general release of the Czech prisoners of war. In February 1916, all prisoners of war, regardless of their nationality, were sent to agricultural and public works projects. On April 21, 1916, the Kievan branch of ACSAR finally succeeded, thanks to the tireless activity of Dr. Vondrák and L. Tuček, in securing the approval of the tsar, "in principle," for the release of those Czech and Slovak prisoners of war whose reliability was certified by ACSAR.[54] At that time the decision was made to transform the Czech regiment into a brigade, and ACSAR hoped to act as a provisional government that would work for Czechoslovak independence.

Shortly after the establishment of the Czech brigade by the order of the chief of the general staff, Alexeev, on April 17, 1916,[55] ACSAR held its second congress at Kiev (April 25-May 1, 1916),[56] at which it elected new leadership with Dr. Vondrák at its helm, and adopted two resolutions. One resolution charged the new leaders with the task of "forming a Czecho-Slovak army" whose nucleus would be the current Czech brigade, and effecting the release of Czech prisoners of war, using them when the need arose. The second resolution levied a war tax on the properties held by members and a so-called national tax that would be paid by working prisoners of war from their wages. It was hoped that, eventually, a large military unit, perhaps an army, would be formed; this unit would be divided into smaller reconnaissance detachments in order to avoid the danger of great losses. As soon as the front approached the border of the Czech lands and Slovakia (the planned Brusilov offensive that started on June 4, 1916, brought this prospect nearer), the small detachments would merge into a larger unit that would become the core of the army of the Czechoslovak state. However, the plan for the formation of a large army fell through in August 1916, because of opposition to it in Russian government circles.[57]

ACSAR represented by far the majority of organized Czechs and Slovaks in Russia. Aside from it there were three small groups. In Kiev there was the so-called Czechoslavic Alliance, expressly Pan-Slavic in its orientation, and publicly opposed to Masaryk. In Moscow a splinter group of the Alliance was led by Koníček, who was unable to make the congress accept his view that the Czech and Slovak question could be resolved only within the framework of an all-Slavic alliance, and that it was therefore necessary for form in Russian an all-Slavic alliance of associations that would work for the attainment of this aim. The third small group was the Russo-Slovak L. Štúr Society, which held tenaciously to its program of attaching Slovakia to Russia. This society did not take part in the congress at all. Only nine Slovak delegates participated in the second congress that declared itself for a unified Czechoslovak state in the spirit of ACSAR's declaration of May 1915, recongnizing complete autonomy for Slovakia, and in the "small" congress of January 1916.

The tsarist organs closely followed all the developments and conflicts within the Czechoslovak independence movement in Russia. They knew well what position each group took. They were also well informed on the Czechoslovak independence movement in western Europe. A memorandum, dated June 1, 1916, drafted by M. Priklonsky, prewar consul in Budapest and an expert on Czech matters in the ministry of foreign affairs,[58] and addressed to the diplomatic office of military headquarters, mentions two aims that were pursued by the Czech organizations in Russia after the congress at Kiev. First, the Czech organizations tried to subjugate the Czechs in Russia to the absolutely uncontrolled, secret power of the Kiev committee, and through it, to Masaryk's London [sic] committee. Second, they hoped to subordinate to the same organization all Slovaks living in Russia, thus making it possible for Masaryk's Czechs to envelop the whole Slovak nation in the future. According to Priklonsky, this aim did not correspond to the Slovaks' ideas on the future of their nation, "especially of those 600,000 Slovaks living in America." He claimed that the Slovaks were closest to the Russians in language. Furthermore, since the London Czech committee was outside the influence of the Russian government and was headed by Masaryk, whose anti-Russian attitude was known and who was "more than probably under foreign material influence,"[59] and since the Kievan leadership of the Alliance was "a blind instrument" in his hands, Priklonsky proposed the establishment of two committees in Petrograd ("under secret supervision of the ministry of foreign affairs"), one Czech and the other Slovak, from among those who "sympathize with Russia." Concretely, he made the following requests: (a) to bring Koníček from Moscow and give him the means to live in Petrograd; (b) to telegraph Dürich to come to Russia immediately and furnish him with sufficient means; and (c) to furnish Professor Štěpánek with sufficient means to live in Petrograd. (Štěpánek believed that Masaryk agitated for himself, and that the others around him were asses and cowards.)

In order to implement his proposed plans for the organization of the Czechs in Russia, Priklonsky suggested that the ministry of foreign affairs open "credit up to 100,000 rubles;" or if this were too difficult, that it open a credit account in the amount of 10,000 rubles for the time being.[60] Thus, Dürich was asked by the Russian government to come to Russia and become the leader of the Czech independence movement, whose aims would closely correspond to those of Russia.

Not knowing of Priklonsky's memorandum, Masaryk did not share Beneš's worries that Russia would not comprehend the work and activities of the Czechoslovak émigrés. When Vondrák asked him to come to Russia, he replied on June 3, 1916, that his colleague Dürich would arrive there and he, Masaryk, would come later. Masaryk did not even go to Paris when Beneš, upset by Dürich's negotiations with French government officials and the Russian embassy, urgently called him. In this situation, upon the request of both governments, and with Masaryk's blessing, Dürich left for Russia via London on June 23, 1916, with Lieutenant Ivan Štafl and Viluš Crkal. Masaryk had given Dürich 6,000 francs when they met in London. At that time he told Dürich: "You will go to Russia, you will find out what the situation is there, and you will act as you see fit."[61] On the same occasion Masaryk warned Dürich about the situation among the Czechs in Russia saying that it was even worse than that of the Czech colony in Paris. Masaryk's statements were clear and unambiguous. When two delegates from Kiev arrived in London, Masaryk told them that the action abroad was led by "two legally elected deputies." He also accepted, basically, the view held by the new Kievan leadership of ACSAR on the question of building the Czechoslovak army in Russia.

The views that Masaryk recorded in his protocol on the July 6, 1916 conference with two delegates from Kiev (Z. Rejman and V. Vaněk) and sent to ACSAR in Kiev reflect his realization of the overriding importance of military action. As he put it, the formation of a Czechoslovak army would "confront Europe with an accomplished fact of the Czech armed revolution. Through this, *via facti,* the principle of the destruction of Austria will be erected... the establishment of an independent army is and will be the manifestation of our independence and will lead Europe to its recognition and the Quadruple Entente to its declaration."[62] He agreed with the views of ACSAR that "most important will be the task of the Czechoslovak army to help to occupy the Czech and the Slovak territories;" for that reason, it was desirable that the army be "used on the Russian front so that it could easily reach the Czecho-Slovak territory" and then be unified "into a greater tactical unit."

Masaryk also stated that he would consider it a very luckly and very promising move if the heir apparent to the Russian throne took over the command of the Czech army. This would be an excellent arrangement because, as he had said at home and reiterated abroad, "the Romanov dynasty would be the most popular one in Bohemia." Only if the Romanovs themselves opposed becoming the Czech rulers would he consider another dynasty; he added, however, that there would be also the possibility of establishing a republic. In any case, he declared, "Russian wishes will give us the direction."[63] This statement was in line with what Masaryk was telling the Czechs in Russia. According to him, they held a special position among the Czech colonies abroad; they were lucky to live in a Slavic state, a state that was of determining influence in Czech matters.

Before Dürich departed for Russia, on June 1, 1916, *La Nation tchèque* published an article announcing the division of functions in the Czecho-Slovak National Council that had been formed at the beginning of April 1916.[64] In this council Masaryk was president, Dürich was vice-president, and Beneš was secretary general. In a letter dated May 30, Beneš notified the leader of ACSAR about the composition of the council. The letter also stated that the three people formed a presidium that had the right to co-opt other members of the foreign committee, and that "all three of them" had a mandate that they had received "directly from Bohemia." "It was agreed," the letter said, "that Masaryk will be in London, I [Beneš] in Paris and Mr. Dürich will go to Petrograd."[65] (Note that Beneš put himself on the same level as Masaryk and Dürich. For Dürich, however, young Beneš, who held no elective office in Bohemia, was merely a secretary —an executive officer—of the council, which consisted of himself and

Masaryk.) Simultaneously, Paris was made the seat of the Czecho-Slovak National Council (CSNC). (From then on, the term Czecho-Slovak National Council was used in English language documents.) Relations between Beneš and Dürich became strained when Štefánik arrived in Paris from Italy at the beginning of June 1916. Štefánik, a rather hot-headed and impatient man, favored a strictly one-sided and pro-French orientation of the Czechoslovak independence movement abroad, and he strongly opposed Dürich's journey to Russia. He demanded that Masaryk intervene with Prime Minister Briand and the Russian ambassadors in western Europe so that he, Štefánik, could go to Russia. When Masaryk rejected the request, Štefánik and Beneš negotiated on their own with the Russian general Lokhvicky and the French officials.

Štefánik and Beneš took steps in order to make it possible for Štefánik to travel to Russia and there to recruit, on behalf of the French government, Czech and Slovak prisoners of war for military units to be dispatched to the Western Front. The result of these efforts was Prime Minister Briand's letter of July 4, 1916, in which he recommended that the ministry of war send Štefánik to Russia, in addition to Dürich and Štafl. In his letter to the minister of war, Briand suggested that Lieutenant Štefánik, who was "a Czech [sic], naturalized Frenchman, decorated by Military Cross," who had completed his assignment in the Serbian army and had just recently "fulfilled with a great success his propaganda mission in the Italian army on behalf of the Yugoslavs," and who "at the present time is at the disposal of the administration of air-force" should go to Russia on a special mission. Briand formulated this mission as "utilization of the Czech element abroad, especially in Russia and the United States."[66]

The reply to this letter, of which a copy dated July 26, 1916, was forwarded to the supreme commander of the French armies, General J. Joffre, and the record on "The use of Czech prisoners of war and the mission of Lieutenant Štefánik" of July 25, 1916,[67] throw light on the negotiations conducted by Štefánik and Beneš with French political and military officials. General Joffre originally believed that Štefánik's mission in Russia would be strictly military, however, he found out that Štefánik had "higher goals," that he was not concerned with purely military matters, and that he ventured into matters of high policy. In his negotiations with French official Štefánik presented his plan for the future organization of central and southeastern Europe, a plan that departed considerably from that of Masaryk, and that, Štefánik believed, would be more appealing to France.

According to Štefánik's plan, the German-speaking nations would be encircled by a chain of independent kingdoms so that Germany would be separated from the Balkans (where it planned its hegemony) and from Turkey. This would mean the establishment of several kingdoms, a kingdom of Poland, a kingdom of Bohemia, a kingdom of Serbia, and a kingdom of Hungary. The Polish kingdom would be under Russian influence; the Serbian kingdom would "include all the South Slavic nations of the present Austria-Hungary"; and the Hungarian kingdom would consist of "present Hungary, deprived of territories which would be surrendered to Rumania and Serbia." (Note: the French documents always describe Štefánik as "a Czech, naturalized Frenchman;" and the Slovak inhabited areas of Hungary are not mentioned in his plan at all.) General Joffe recorded, "In order to make possible the establishment of an independent Bohemian Kingdom, lieutenant Štefánik would like to build an independent Czech army (50,000 to 100,000 men) that would fight on the French and not on the Russian front, in order to prepare, thus early, the independence of the Czech Kingdom from Russia."[68]

The Štefánik proposal differed from the plans of Masaryk in that Štefánik's proposed kingdom of Bohemia would not border on Russia (it would not include the Slovaks), and would have a joint boundary with the kingdom of Serbia; both kingdoms, apparently would be under French influence. Štefánik also believed that a republican form of government in the new state was neither desirable nor practicable and might even be dangerous.[69] He was a rather conservative monarchist with aristocratic tendencies which he did not try to hide. On one occasion he told his superior, the French general Janin, that the coronation of a French prince as a Bohemian king would be the happiest day in his life.[70] As sometimes happens with those who convert to a new religion or adopt a new country, Štefánik was more pro-French than the French. His political ambition was to see French influence extended into the heart of Europe through the establishment of a new state system in central and southeastern Europe.

General Joffre noted that Štefánik conceived his mission to Russia as having much broader and more far-reaching goals than those proposed by the French prime minister; he concluded that if Štefánik were preoccupied with propagandizing for his objectives while on an official mission in Russia, he would provoke a fully justifiable resentment on the part of the Russian government and would thus endanger the success of his mission there. Therefore, Joffre believed, the sole purpose of Štefánik's mission in Russia should be the recruitment of Czech volunteers who would help increase the number of "our soldiers in France." The question whether these volunteers should be included in Russian units or placed in independent units could be answered only after "we would clearly know the number of these volunteers." Thus, General Joffre proposed, and military headquarters ordered, that Štefánik should go to Russia with a special mission. "His task is to recruit, under the supervision of General Janin [Chief of the French military mission in Russia] and with the consent of Russian [government] organs, volunteers from among the Austrian prisoners of war of Czech nationality who would be willing to serve in France either in the Russian detachments or in special units organized on the basis of an agreement between the Russian and the French governments."[71]

It is quite clear from the available French documents that the French government did not endorse Štefánik's plan for the reorganization of central and southeastern Europe, and that its sole concern was the possibility of getting new soldiers for the French front. Before going to Russia, on July 19, 1916, Štefánik received orders from the chief of the general staff, General Joffre, showing that he had to report himself to the military attaché at the French embassy in Petrograd.[72] However, Štefánik arrived in Russia in dual capacity: he was a representative of the French government, and also a representative, appointed by Beneš, with Masaryk's approval, of the Czecho-Slovak National Council in Paris.

It is hardly surprising that his views on the use of Czech soldiers on the French front were not shared by the leadership of the Alliance (ACSAR), and Masaryk was notified about the disagreement. As has been mentioned earlier, ACSAR wanted to use the troops exclusively in Russia so that they could liberate their homeland from the east. Trying to accommodate both parties, Masaryk took a position that represented a compromise between the two opposing views, one of which insisted that the troops be used on the Eastern Front, the other, on the Western Front. He suggested that the best solution would be to have one part of the army on the Eastern Front, "so that it could easily reach the Czecho-Slovak territory," and the other part on the Western Front. This compromise would assure both closer cooperation with the Allies and independence for the Czech military action.[73]

In spite of all the help Štefánik received from the French military and diplomatic missions in Russia,[74] and his constant emphasizing his own "Russian orientation" while dealing with Russian officers of the Russian general staff (the Stavka),[75] he fought an uphill battle for the Czech prisoners of war in Russia. He was handicapped by being a French citizen. His superior, the chief of the French military mission in Russia, General Janin, noted that it was rather strange that a French officer should come to Russia to recruit Czech and Slovak prisoners of war for the French front.[76] Furthermore, the issue of Czech prisoners of war and the fundamental ideological difference between Štefánik and Deputy Dürich led to a conflict between the two in which Dürich had a distinct advantage over the dashing young man: he had the confidence of the Russian government.

In contrast to Štefánik, who was concerned with French interests in the matter of the Czech prisoners of war and whose conceptual framework for a future central Europe was diametrically opposed to that of Dürich, the "second Deputy" abroad came to Russia as "a plenipotentiary of the Czech nation."

When Dürich arrived in Petrograd on July 5, 1916, he was welcomed with great enthusiasm, especially by those Czech groups in Russia that were in opposition to the Alliance (ACSAR). The first Czech who came to talk with him was Bohdan Pavlů, editor of *Čechoslovák,* who published Dürich's picture in his newspaper with enthusiastic welcoming words on the arrival of one of the two deputies who were leading the independence movement. Koníček's Russophile group placed great hopes in Dürich; Dr. Štěpánek introduced him to Priklonsky, and through the latter to Sazonov, the minister of foreign affairs, and eventually to Prime Minister Stürmer, who was just taking over the ministry of foreign affairs. Dürich submitted to the minister of foreign affairs a memorandum dealing with the Czech question.[77] In this memorandum he declared himself to be the representative of all the Czech political parties with nationalistic programs (Old Czechs, Young Czechs, Agrarians, National Socials, and the State Rights party), which together represented the majority of the nation. According to Dürich, this majority of the Czechs desired the establishment of an independent Czech kingdom with the Russian tsar, who would also be the Czech king, at its helm. The political parties that Dürich represented requested the appointment of a Russian grand duke as the viceroy of the tsar, and the incorporation of the kingdom of Bohemia into one realm with Russia, united with Russia by a common army, customs, and diplomacy.

The memorandum pointed out that a republican form of government would correspond to the views of the Social Democrats and groups related to them, the so-called Progressives, but that these views did not have the support of the nation. A part of the so-called progressive intelligentsia envisioned a dynasty from western Europe, and counted on Social Democratic and German support for it in the future Czech Diet. These people also expected that the western powers would endorse their plan in order to prevent the increase of Russian influence in central Europe. It was made clear in this memorandum that Dürich did not go along with the pro-western trend in the Czech independence movement abroad, as represented by Masaryk and Beneš, "and their Social Democratic allies" in western Europe and the United States.[78]

Minister Sazonov discussed briefly with Dürich the plan for a great Slavic empire, and, on that occasion, he told the Czech leader that the west European powers were jealously watchful of any possible strengthening of the Russian position in Europe and elsewhere. The Russian ministry of foreign affairs prepared a report for the tsar that was in accord with Dürich's memorandum. The tsar received Dürich in the presence of General Alexeev and another Russian general on August 18, 1916. Dürich was introduced as a plenipotentiary of all Czech political parties (except the Social Democrats and the Clericals) and as a representative of a trend among the Czechs that was much more favorable to Russia than that of Masaryk, who was then living in London. (Shortly afterwards, during their discussion of the question of shipping Czech troops to France, General Janin congratulated Dürich on his success and the great impression that he had made on the tsar.) Dürich, who now acted as "the plenipotentiary of the Czech nation," as *Čechoslovák* called him on August 5, 1916, found support among the Czechs in Russia, including Crkal, Štafl, Koníček, and František Král, who had formerly been affiliated with the Russian intelligence network in Bulgaria. Dürich's views were shared by many. Even Bohdan Pavlů, who had been publishing *Čechoslovák* since June 7, 1915, wrote in a Russian newspaper, *Birzhevie Vedomosti,* that he believed in a firm Czech unity with Russia, politically, economically, militarily, and dynastically.[79]

Many Russian newspapers, including *Novoe Vremia, Vechernoe Vremia,* and *Birzhevie Vedomosti,* applauded Dürich's arrival. ACSAR called a big rally in his honor in Kiev. This rally, attended by tens of thousands of Czechs, Slovaks, and Russian citizens and prisoners of war, adopted a resolution recognizing Dürich as "the sole and absolute leader of the Czechs and Slovaks in Russia."[80] He was confirmed in the same authority by countless letters and telegrams from various Czech officials living in Russia and abroad, and also from prisoners of war. Among these communications was a letter from the Bohemian National Alliance in the United States, dated October 5, 1916, containing the following words: "We will grant all your wishes and we will glady follow your directives; the Czech America will be at your disposal, even in financial matters should you need its services." Another letter, from Chicago's *Beseda,* wished Dürich complete success in his work, and expressed a readiness to give him material help.[81]

Shortly after his arrival in Russia, Dürich had a long conversation with an official in the Russian ministry of foreign affairs, Alexander Gerovsky, who came originally from Carpatho-Ruthenia and was a former governor of Eastern Galicia.[81] The Russian expert on Austria-Hungary, particularly on the Czechoslovak question, tried to find out details about the programs, communications, and authorizations that the two deputies, Masaryk and Dürich, received from the Czech independence movement at home. Dürich told Gerovsky that he had left home in April 1915, as a plenipotentiary of all Czech political parties except the Social Democrats and the Clericals, and that the parties he represented (Agrarian, Old Czech, Young Czech, National Social, and State Rights) had 70 percent of all Czech deputies in the Vienna parliament. When Masaryk went abroad, the secret committee did not yet exist in Prague, and Masaryk therefore could not have been authorized to speak in its name while abroad. Dürich knew for certain that the Agrarian party had not given Masaryk any right to speak in its name; in Dürich's opinion, the other political parties had not given him full powers either. The Czech political parties that had sent Dürich abroad had asked him to act in accordance with his best judgment, without placing him in any kind of relationship vis-à-vis Masaryk. The Realist party did not play any role in Bohemia, and Masaryk had been able to obtain a seat in the Vienna parliament merely as a compromise candidate of several Czech political parties. Thus, Masaryk represented less than 1 percent of the Czech nation.[82]

Dürich told Gerovsky, furthermore, that when the two deputies had met in Switzerland, Masaryk had told him of the need to place a member of the English dynasty at the helm of the future kingdom of Bohemia, and that he had replied to Dürich's objections that the Romanov dynasty was also "non-Slavic and German." Dürich believed, however, that the idea of placing an English king on the Bohemian throne existed not merely in Masaryk's head, it also was shared by the British. As evidence Dürich quoted a statement that Seton-Watson had made in their conversation about the future Bohemian kingdom: "We [English] have five princes," said Seton-Watson, hinting that one of them could become the Bohemian king. "There is no doubt," Gerovsky writes in the memorandum of this conversation, "that the idea of placing English princes (in accordance with the tried out German pattern) at the helm of states which will emerge after the war is very appealing to the English. There is no doubt that the idea of placing an English prince on the Bohemian throne is behind the agitation on behalf of the English dynasty among Czech émigrés carried on by Kopecký, a follower of Masaryk, who was sent from London to the United States on the pretext of agitating against strikes."[83] (Kopecký was one of the members of Voska's team operating in the United States.)

Dürich also told Gerovsky that he was in no way bound to Masaryk— whose work, however, he did not want to hamper—but was willing to come out against him, should it be necessary. He also confirmed the report that Masaryk had converted from Catholicism to the Anglican Church, while "the Czechs with nationalistic tendencies lean toward Orthodoxy." As far as the Czech organizations in Russia were concerned, Dürich said, followers of Masaryk, westernizers, and those who had been openly Austrophile in the past—elements that were unreliable from both the Czech and the Russian point of view—assumed power in those organizations and subordinated themselves completely to orders arriving from London. (Following the foreign ministry's line, in its report on Dürich for the tsar of August 17, 1916, the Stavka stated that Dürich represented a "trend in the Czech question that is more favorable to Russia than is that of Professor

Masaryk who lives in London. The Realist party plays an insignificant role in Bohemia; however, the leaders of the Czech organizations in Russia lean toward Masaryk.")[84] Gerovsky concluded that Dürich and Masaryk represented two contradictory streams in Czech politics that were characterized by two books, Masaryk's *Russland und Europa* and Josef Holeček's *Rusko a západ* (Russia and the West).[85] (Holeček was a Czech writer with Neo-Slavic leanings.)

Dürich was received by General Alexeev as well as by the tsar. The general was not satisfied with the progress in forming a Czech military unit in Russia, and hoped that Dürich would act more firmly, helping to overcome the conflicts within the Czech movement in Russia. At first he rejected the idea of shipping Czech soldiers to France; however, when Dürich insisted that Czech troops were needed there not so much for strategic reasons but primarily for political reasons, the general said that, if he could help the Czech nation by sending troops, he was not against doing so.[86] He suggested that the Czechs who wanted to work in Russia should form a united organization along with ACSAR.

Although General Alexeev, chief of staff of the supreme commander, favored building large Czech military units and supported the Czech cause wholeheartedly, he had some reservations about Dürich's capacity for leadership, considering him to be merely "a national flag"; he advised his government caution in making definite commitments for the future. But since political matters were within the jurisdiction of the ministry of foreign affairs, the Czechoslovak organizations in Russia were its responsibility.[87] Alexeev knew of the Alliance's objectionable practices with respect to the issuing of certificates of reliability (on the basis of which prisoners of war were released), the selection of officers from among those of "western" (pro-Masaryk) orientation, the intimidation of prisoners of war who were of other political orientations by threats that they could be deported to Siberia if they did not volunteer for service in the Czech military units, and the proposed "national tax" to be collected by ACSAR. Therefore, on August 23, 1916, Alexeev made a recommendation to the ministry of war that would eliminate the existing abuses and speed up the building of the Czechoslovak army.[88] According to this proposal, the main administration of the general staff, with the assistance of a military commission, would assume responsibility for forming new Czech military units, and the process would come under the immediate jurisdiction of the chief commander of the Kievan military district (circle). Alexeev specifically recommended that the military commission headed by a Russian major-general, Jaroslav Červinka, who was of Czech origin, spoke Czech, and was well acquainted with Czech national aspirations; who knew well the background of the building of the Czech brigade and the mistakes that had been made in the process; and who was competent to handle the whole complex problem. Alexeev suggested that the top positions in the Czechoslovak military units be filled by Russian generals and officers, while the other posts could be occupied by Czech officers and noncommissioned officers. Prisoners of war with officer rank must be accepted as officers, except for those who could not generate confidence. The collection of any kind of "national tax" from prisoners of war (the latter worked for wages in agriculture and industry) was improper. The issuing of certificates of reliability by the administration of ACSAR should be abolished, and the power to do so transferred to the military commission. Upon these conditions, Alexeev recommended a speedy approval of the formation of the Czechoslovak army.[89]

Alexeev discussed these matters also with Štefánik, who arrived at the headquarters at Mogylev on August 24; he emphasized the need for ending the discords among the Czechs in Russia as soon as possible. Subsequently, Dürich, as the vice-president of the Czecho-Slovak National Council, was recognized as its representative in Russia by an agreement that was concluded at a meeting in Kiev on August 29. This "Kievan Pact" was signed by Dürich and Štefánik on behalf of the Czecho-Slovak National Council (Paris), by Vondrák and J. Volf for ACSAR, and by G. Košík for the Slovak League of America.[90] The pact amounted to recognition of Dürich as the leader of the Czechoslovak independence movement in Russia, with all its programmatic ramifications.

In the abovementioned letter of May 29, 1915, to Sazonov, Dürich claimed that the Czechs had thus far been able to send abroad only two deputies, Masaryk being accredited for England and Dürich for Russia. However, no other deputy was dispatched abroad by the *Maffie* in 1916 or 1917. The deputies at home embarked on a different course of action than Dürich and Masaryk expected. In November 1916, in anticipation of the convening of the Austrian parliament, the Czech deputies in that legislative body decided to form one parliamentary club—the Czech Union.[91] It consisted of all the Czech deputies (including the Catholic deputies) except two deputies of the State Rights party, the two deputies abroad (Masaryk and Dürich) and seven other deputies who were in prison, including Kramář and Rašín. The chairman of the parliamentary club was an Agrarian, František Staněk; the first vice-chairman was a Social Democrat, Bohumír Šmeral; and the second vice-chairman, a Young Czech Jindřich G. Maštálka. At the same time a Czech National Committee (without Realist and State Rights parties represented in it) was established, with an Old Czech, Dr. Karel Mattuš, as its chairman. Its membership consisted of five Agrarians, three Young Czechs, three Social Democrats, three Catholics, two National Socials, and one representative of Adolf Stránský's Moravian People's Progressive party. The declaration of the establishment of these two organizations contained a statement of loyalty by the Czech parties to the dynasty and the empire, proclaiming that the historical mission of the empire consisted, above all, in the preservation of the indivisible realm, as well as in the complete equality of its component nations. The new Czech Union spoke with an authoritative voice that had to be heared in the Allied camp abroad; it represented the will of the nation and could not be easily dismissed. This declaration completed the contradiction between Czech policy in Austria-Hungary and the program of the Czech independence movement abroad.

Both organizations, the Czech Union and the Czech National Committee, sent representatives to the coronation of Emperor Charles as king of Hungary at Budapest in December 1916. The elected representatives endorsed the empire and the dynasty, believing that the security of the Czech nation could be assured only within the framework of the Danubian monarchy. Zdeněk Václav Tobolka, a Young Czech deputy in the Vienna parliament and a well-known historian, who published *Národní Listy,* and a Catholic deputy, Dr. Mořic Hruban, dissociated themselves openly and vocally from the émigrés, especially Masaryk, denying him the right to speak in the name of the Czech nation.[92] The culminating point in the split between the Masaryk-led independence movement abroad and the Czech Union was the so-called disavowal of January 24, 1917, in which the Czech deputies expressly disowned the activity of Masaryk and Beneš, and disclaimed any wish to be liberated from Austria-Hungary.[93] Undoubtedly, the political leaders at home had a legitimate claim to represent the nation; the émigrés, in the situation as it developed, led their own action of their own will and on their own responsibility. Beneš, Masaryk, and others tried to counteract this complete split between the home front and the exiles by increasing propaganda abroad.

The Masaryk-led independence movement maintained the Paris Czech Press Bureau, with its branches at Geneva, Rome, and London. The Geneva office was led by Dr. Štefan Osuský, who wrote articles for Swiss, French, British, and American newspapers. The office at Rome was established with the financial help of an officer of the *Družina,* Vladimír Vaněk, in October 1916. In winter, 1915, Vaněk had crossed the enemy lines to Bohemia to tell Kramář and Rašín about the establishment of the *Družina* in Russia, and about the tsar's granting an audience to a delegation of Russian Czechs and promising them to liberate the Czechs. He then made it safely back to Russia.[94] Now he was in western Europe on a mission for the Russian ministry of war, and gave Beneš and Štefánik some of his "surplus money" earmarked for financing intelligence activities. Among those who worked in the London, office, founded by Masaryk before the end of 1916, were Olga Masaryk-Halík, his daughter, J. Forman, and Vladimír Nosek.[95] There was also the Slav Press Bureau in New York. The long list of those who made contributions to the anti-Habsburg propaganda included Lev Sychrava, Vítězslav Štěpánek, Rudolf Kepl, Vojta Beneš, and Dürich's son-in-law, the writer Karel Horký.

In their attempts to influence public opinion in Allied countries, these Czechs and Slovaks were aided by the anti-Habsburgs in western Europe, the United States, and Russia. In addition to the many Russians, among the influential people who were committed to the idea of national independence for the Slavic nations living in the Danubian empire were Louis Eisenmann, Charles Seignobos, Ernest Denis, Auguste Gauvain, André Chéradame, and André Tardieu in France, and Henry W. Steed and Robert Seton-Watson in Great Britain. In 1916, André Chéradame, a French political writer, wrote books about a monstrous German plan to dominate the world, a plan that had long been underway and was connected with the vast Hamburg (Berlin)-Bagdad railway.[96]

It was easier for the Russian, British, and French friends of the Czechoslovak independence movement to place articles in periodicals published in their countries than for the exiles. But even they encountered opposition among those in western Europe who saw a need to preserve Austria-Hungary, fearing either the "Balkanization" of central Europe or its falling under Russian dominance. When the *Times* (London) declined to print certain articles written by Seton-Watson and Steed, Seton-Watson decided, upon strong urgings from Masaryk, to start publishing a new journal of opinion in Britain carrying the optimistic title *The New Europe*.[97] The periodical maintained that the aim of the Allies was to destroy Prussian militarism and to establish the small nations on a sure foundation. Seton-Watson wrote in November 1916, "The New Europe has been founed to provide material for a definite scheme of reconstruction, and to suggest to both the Allied peoples and their Governments the broad lines upon which the Europe of the future should be built."[98] This goal implied the destruction of Austria-Hungary and the reorganization of Europe. The anti-Habsburgs had their own periodical now, and the amount of their propaganda increased considerably. But propaganda alone could not influence military developments on the fronts, nor could it change the policies of the great powers to the extent desired by the Czech independence movement abroad.

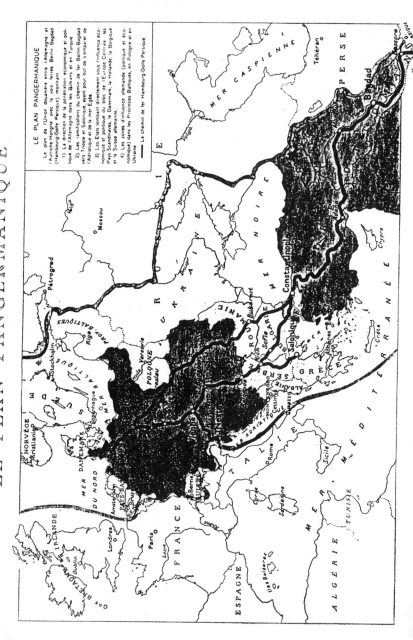

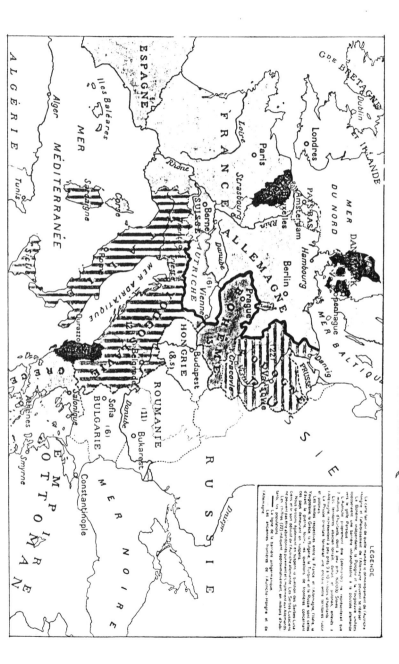

LE PLAN ANTIGERMANIQUE

Conseil National des Pays Tchèques

PARIS
18, RUE BONAPARTE

LES Tchécoslovaques habitent en masses compactes la Bohême, la Moravie, la Silésie et le nord de la Hongrie (Slovaquie).

ILS désirent s'affranchir du joug allemand et magyar et former un état indépendant sous la protection des Alliés.

LE Conseil National des Pays Tchèques veut faire connaître les aspirations de la nation tchécoslovaque, coordonner tous les efforts et préparer les dossiers qui prouvent la légitimité de ses revendications.

LE Conseil National des Pays Tchèques, seul compétent et responsable, n'agira qu'en parfaite harmonie avec les organes compétents des Puissances Alliées.

LE Secrétariat général du Conseil National des Pays Tchèques a son siège à Paris, 18, rue Bonaparte.

Représentants du Conseil National des Pays Tchèques :

T. G. MASARYK, *Professeur à l'Université de Londres, 4, Holford Road, Hampstead, London.*

J. DURICH.

MILAN STEFANIK.

E. BENÈS, *Secrétaire général, 18, Rue Bonaparte, Paris.*

CHAPTER FIVE

PLANS FOR THE FUTURE OF CENTRAL EUROPE
AND THE STRUGGLE FOR CONTROL OF
THE INDEPENDENCE MOVEMENT

From the beginning of the war till its end, the Czech question was seen by the Allies as a part of broader issues involving their national interests, such as the future of Austria-Hungary, her alliance with Germany and the latter's hegemony in Europe, the national liberation of oppressed peoples, and the postwar political and territorial settlement in general. In the initial stages of the war official pronouncements on war aims were deliberately vague, and the Allied commitment did not go beyond the famous declaration of the British prime minister, H. H. Asquith, on November 9, 1914. Although that declaration mentioned "the rights of the smaller nations of Europe," it expressly assured only the security of Belgium and, possibly, Serbia, against the aggression of powerful neighbors.[1]

The prevention of German hegemony in Europe remained the British war aim until the end of the war, an aim shared by the other Allies. On this issue, until the collapse of the regime of Alexander F. Kerensky in Russia, the interests of Great Britain, France, and Russia coincided. There was, however, much less compatibility of interests on the question of the future of Austria-Hungary. The long-standing rivalry of Russia and England subsided but was not terminated by the war, and the two powers had vested interests in many areas, including central Europe. As has been

Plans for the Future 111

mentioned earlier, France and Britain were willing to make territorial concessions at the expense of Austria-Hungary in order to bring Italy into the Allied camp. But the provisions of the Treaty of London of April 26, 1915,[2] conflicted with the interests and aspirations of a small Ally, Serbia, and thus with those of her protector, Russia. Indeed, Asquith's defense of the treaty included a statement that "Russia, after a very valiant effort, had a setback."[3]

Until her collapse, only Russia among the Allies was exposed to domestic pressure to make a public commitment to liberate the Czechs and Slovaks from a foreign yoke. Many Russians—and, especially, Czechs and Slovaks living in Russia, who numbered some 100,000 before the war[4] and increased to several hundred thousand during the war, owing to the influx of a large number of prisoners of war—believed that liberating the Czechs and Slovaks was Russia's historic mission and a Slavic duty. Also, the Russian military recognized that Czech military units fighting shoulder to shoulder with the Russians were a valuable part of their psychological warfare against enemy troops of Czech and Slovak nationality. They realized that the effectiveness of their propaganda depended, to a great extent, on public policy, since if the official policy pronouncements conflicted with those of the propagandists, the latter would lose their credibility. No similar pressures existed in either France or England, since those countries were non-Slavic and in no way related historically or politically to the Czechs and Slovaks, and the number of Czechs and Slovaks living there was negligible. However, journalists in both countries speculated about the future of Austria-Hungary and made recommendations for the future arrangement of central Europe and the Balkans. Also, foreign offices have to have a policy to follow, and it is customary to have contingency plans for future possibilities, especially if the national interest requires such plans.

The Czech issue was first brought to the attention of the Allies in September 1914. The Kramář group in Prague empowered Vladimír Sís to contact the Allied diplomats at Sophia and find out from them what they thought of the Czechs and their future, and in what way they wanted the Czechs to help the Allies in the war.[5] Sís received a direct answer from the British ambassador: British interests required saving Austria-Hungary in order to prevent the increase of Russian influence in central Europe. The French ambassador likewise insisted on the need to preserve Austria-

Hungary. He recommended, however, that the Czechs and Hungarians seize political initiative in the state, assume leadership, and jointly destroy German influence in the monarchy. In contrast to their western colleagues, the Russian diplomats in Sophia avoided giving definite answers to the questions asked by Sís, and expressed great interest in Kramář's political program. The hesitating attitude of the Russian government was undoubtedly necessitated by the firm stand taken by the western Allies on the issue of Austria-Hungary.

As early as 1915, Seton-Watson published a pamphlet entitled *What is at Stake in the War*[6] in which he outlined the "new Europe" as he saw it. Seton-Watson presupposed the dismemberment of Austria-Hungary and Turkey, because only in that way could Germany's imperialist designs be curbed. The "new Europe" of his dreams foresaw the freeing of the subjugated nations and the guaranteeing of "full linguistic and cultural liberty" to those minorities "whose separate existence" for reasons of "geography and economics" rendered impossible.[7] Naturally, the "new Europe" would have to be ruled by new governments; the orientation of the new governments was of key importance to those who proposed the dismemberment of the Habsburg monarchy.

The orientation of governmental institutions is determined by the people who operate them. The planners of the "new Europe" had therefore, to find, work with, and influence the political forces that would eventually come to power in the new states. It is a well-known sociological phenomenon that smaller groups dominate larger ones. Also, a competent, charismatic leader, if conditions are favorable, can give direction to a whole country. Seton-Watson placed high hopes in Masaryk, a pro-western leader of the Czech independence movement who, through his marriage, had ties with the Anglo-Saxon world. Seton-Watson, however, was in no position to make a definite and binding commitment on behalf of any government to Masaryk, and the latter was intelligent enough to realize that fact. It was his decision to gamble on the Allied victory and on the ability of Great Britain, should the latter so desire, to help him in his designs for a new order in central Europe. Officially, Masaryk accepted a lectureship at a salary of £200 per annum at the newly established School of Slavonic Stuies at King's College; and he delivered the inaugural lecture on "Problems of Small Nations in the European Crisis" on October 19, 1915.[8] Masaryk continued to lecture at King's College sporadically until his departure to Russia in May 1917.

Plans for the Future 113

During the first two years of the war official Russian policy on the Czechoslovak question was not always in line with Russian public opinion on the same issue. Foreign and domestic policy considerations—the possibility that the Central Powers might organize their own legions from among prisoners of war who were Rusian subjects of non-Russian nationality; the opposition of the western Allies to the idea of dismantling Austria-Hungary; the shortage of weapons and military equipment and the abundance of Russian recruits; and the need for skilled workers in military industries and farms—were among the reasons for the government's hesitation to follow popular desires and give more overt help to the Czech independence movement. The Russian government was not happy with the state of affairs among the Czechs and Slovaks in Russia, their frictions and ideological conflicts. It was fully informed on the failure of Koníček's mission in western Europe and the United States in 1914-1915, the setbacks the independence movement at home had suffered by the arrest of Kramář, and Masaryk's assumption of leadership of the Czechoslovak movement abroad. A new Russian interest in the movement was provoked by the appearance in French and British newspapers of proposals for rearranging central Europe, and by the help given by England to exiles from Austria-Hungary. Russian intelligence officers and foreign ministry experts saw a connection between those events in western Europe in mid-1916.[9]

British and French interest in the exiles and their proposals was stimulated by the reception given to Fredrich Naumann's book, *Mitteleuropa*,[10] published at the end of 1915 and quickly translated into English. Many Englishmen were soon convinced that Pan-Germanism threated British interests in the Middle East and even India. The agitation of the Pan-Germans in Germany and Austria under the leadership of Naumann, and the close collaboration of Austria-Hungary with Germany in the prosecution of the war, made the threat of a German-dominated Europe more real, especially after the collapse of Serbia. When, in the spring of 1916, the German nationalists in Austria-Hungary expressly agreed with the proposed creation of *Mitteleuropa,* the Allies came to realize that the small nations of Austria-Hungary could be very important in the effort to prevent German hegemony in Europe, André Chéradame's book, mentioned earlier, and his proposal for the formation of a "United States of Central Europe" on the ruins of Austria-Hungary, began to be taken seriously in Allied ruling circles. Assuming that the Central Powers would be defeated, Chéradame proposed to build a federation that would become a barrier against the German attempt to penetrate the Balkans and the Middle East. By implication, the proposed federation would also keep Russian influence out of the area.

The Russian intelligence officers, most notably Svatkovsky, noticed how the British and French were using Czech émigrés in their intelligence operations, assuming that those exiles might eventually become political leaders in a Czech state after the war. In a report from Paris dated April 17, 1916, Svatkovsky informed Sazonov about these new developments. Svatkovsky recommended that the Russian government pay more attention to Czech and Slovak matters, lest after the war, the central European problem be resolved "against the Russian interests."[11] Earlier in the year, in February 1916, an expert on central Europe in the Russian ministry of foreign affairs, Alexander Gerovsky, had submitted a memorandum to the Russian government in which he pointed out the great importance of the Czech and Slovak nations to the postwar settlement in Central Europe.[12] Gerovsky proposed (as Svatkovsky would do two months later) that the Russian government intervene in the Czech independence movement; otherwise, the Czech question might be settled against Russia's best interests at the end of the war. Gerovsky pointed out that the Czech independence movement was led by Masaryk, who was known to be anti-Russian and who was "more than likely under foreign financial influence." Therefore, Gerovsky recommended the formation of a pro-Russian center of the Czechoslovak exile independence movement to offset Masaryk's activities in England and France and protect Russian interests. The vast majority of Czechs and Slovaks, Gerovsky stated, were Russophiles; yet the organization of the Czech exiles was under the influence of Masaryk, an enemy of Russia. In contrast to France and England, where there were very few Czechs, Russia had a large Czech colony and should take advantage of that fact. It would be easy to form a pro-Russian exile organization in Russia; Gerovsky named Josef Dürich, deputy in the Vienna parliament, as the best representative of those Czech émigrés who were fully dedicated to Russia. He proposed to the Russian ministry of foreign affairs to bring Dürich to Russia as soon as possible, so that the deputy could assume leadership of this new central organization. Gerovsky emphasized, however, that Dürich must arrive in Russia not as a representative of Masaryk, but as a representative of the Czech and Slovak

Plans for the Future   115

nations. To be sure, Dürich was not well-known abroad; it was therefore necessary, Gerovsky wrote, "to make him known." If, as Masaryk's followers claimed, Dürich did not have an authoritative personality, it would be necessary to build him up, to make him into the leading personality. To do so would be "in the interest of Russia and Slavdom."[13] This memorandum speeded Dürich's arrival in Russia.

Proceeding on the assumption that Dürich would be a counterweight to Masaryk, Beneš, and their followers in Russia and western Europe, M. Priklonsky, an expert on Austria-Hungarian matters in the ministry of foreign affairs, proposed to establish, under the ministry's secret supervision, two committees in Russia—one Czech and the other Slovak. (Incidentally, Priklonsky proposed the formation of other committees, Galician-Russian, Slovenian, Serbian, and Croatian, under similar conditions.) Since Dürich had no money and lived in exile in poverty, the committee to be headed by him would have to be secretly financed by the Russian government. Thus, just as the "most important Czech secret society" and its Slovak counterpart in the United States had been financed by the British government since May 1916,[14] Priklonsky's proposed central organ for the Czech and Slovak exiles in Russia would be financed by the Russian government.[15]

As the British minister of munitions, E. S. Montagu, noted in August 1916, the great powers had "different and unconnected" claims and interests in many areas, including central Europe.[16] In the autumn of 1916 the prime minister of Great Britain, therefore instructed the Foreign Office to prepare a memorandum suggesting a basis for a territorial settlement in Europe. The prospective war settlement was also discussed in the British cabinet, and members of the War Committee were asked to prepare position papers on the same subject.[17]

The Foreign Office's memorandum, drawn up by Sir Ralph Paget and Sir William Tyrrell, was prepared on two alternative assumptions: "One was an Allied victory—the other a stalemate."[18] That part of the document dealing with the second alternative was brief; it merely suggested that not all war aims could be achieved in such a situation and that the government would have to decide what price to pay for peace. In contrast, the document based on the first assumption was lengthy, and was, according to Lloyd George, "the first official pronouncement in which what came to be known as self-determination constituted the principle of readjustment of national boundaries."[19] In fact, however, the memorandum says that although the principle of nationality should be one of the governing factors in territorial arrangements after the war, in concrete applications of this principle the British attitude "should be guided by circumstances generally and British interests in particular."

The portion of the memorandum drafted on the supposition of a total Allied victory assumes the end of Austria-Hungary, and is the most exhaustive treatment of territorial settlement. With respect to Poland, it makes three alternative suggestions, but finally favors the "creation of a Polish kingdom under a Russian Grand Duke." Since this kingdom would be connected with Russia merely by the personal link of its ruler, it would be "one of the most powerful units among the independent countries which are expected to come into existence upon the dissolution of the Danubian monarchy. From the point of view of England and France, this conglomeration of states would prove an efficient barrier against Russian preponderance in Europe and German extension towards the Near East." The memorandum also discusses the future Yugoslav state and the breakup of Austria-Hungary, suggesting that whether or not the Central Powers are victorious, "Austria-Hungary will remain, to all intents and purposes, subservient to its ally." Its continued existence therefore, is not desirable.

As to Bohemia, three different alternatives are considered: "first, the formation of an independent state; secondly, the linking of Bohemia with a Southern-Slav state; and thirdly, tacking it on to the Kingdom of Poland." Paget and Tyrrell are of the opinion that the third solution—attaching Bohemia to a larger Poland—"is desired both by farseeing Czechs and Poles." The union of Bohemia and Poland "would afford and promote very considerably the economic development of Poland," and the Czechs, on the other hand, "fully appreciate that they would benefit by the superior culture and civilization of the Poles."

Emphasizing that they have tried "to work out a scheme that promises permanency," the two officials present in the next portion of the memorandum a very searching study of the question of armament. They discuss the reduction of armaments in conjunction with "the creation of a League of Nations, that will be prepared to use force against any nation that breaks away from the observance of international law." Paget and Tyrrell were under no illusion "that such an instrument will become really effective until nations have learnt to subordinate their personal and individual ambitions and dreams for the benefit of the community of nations." Their memorandum was circulated to the cabinet without any recommendation or comment from Sir Edward Grey; it was not considered by the cabinet until after the War Cabinet and the Imperial Cabinet were set up in 1917.[20] Members of the British cabinet, it may be pointed out, differed in their views on what to do with Austria-Hungary, and by no means all of them had an optimistic view of the outcome of the war. For example, Lord Lansdowne warned that the responsibility of those who needlessly prolonged the war was no less than that of those who had needlessly provoked it;[21] and the secretary of the Committee of Imperial Defense, Colonel Sir Maurice Hankey, who was soon to become secretary to the War Cabinet, pointed out that nearly the whole of the territorial objective the Allies expected to attain as a result of the war "are still in the actual occupation of the enemy." On the other hand, "the territorial objectives, which the enemy seeks to attain in the war are all or nearly all at this moment in his occupation."[22]

The Russian ministry of foreign affairs, like the British Foreign Office, was preparing a confidential memoranda dealing with the future settlement of Europe. Three memoranda, drawn up between September 19 and October 30, 1916, by M. Priklonsky in the political section of the ministry, and sent to its representatives at the Stavka (military headquarters of the Russian general staff), dealt specifically with the Czech problem. The September 19, 1916, memorandum was entitled "Confidential Memorandum of the Ministry of Foreign Affairs on the Czecho-Slovak Question"; the October 3, 1916, memorandum was called "Addendum to the Secret Note on the Czecho-Slovak question"; and the October 30, 1916, memorandum was an addendum to the first one under the heading "Russia, England, and the Question of a Czechoslovak State. Conditions for a Genesis of This State."[23]

The first section of the first memorandum deals with the importance of the Czechs and Slovaks to Russia by presenting a brief history of the seven and a half million Czechs and the two and a half million Slovaks, in the context of European history. It points at the scientific, literary, and political contributions of the Czechs, whose characteristics are perserverance and firmness, and who live in extraordinarily favorable conditions. Bohemia and Moravia are one of the most important economic centers of the Habsburg monarchy. The Slovaks, on the other hand, live in much less favorable conditions. They are less energetic than the Czechs; in contrast to the area inhabited by the Czechs, Slovakia is not very suitable for a broad development of industry. Although the Slovaks do not play any significant role in the political life of Hungary, if united with the Czechs, they could become a very important factor in the establishment of a Czechoslovak state, which is hoped for by both groups as a consequence of the war.

Furthermore, the memorandum suggests influential figures in all the Entente countries hope to found "on the ruins of Austria-Hungary . . . organism of such nature that it would furnish a solid barrier against the advance of Germanism toward the East." Priklonsky points out that André Chéradame gave the clearest exposition of the German plan to set up an "economic protectorship of all Central Europe, the Balkan peninsula and the Turkish East—a plan which had begun to take shape in the form of the vast 'Hamburg-Bagdad' railway." Chéradame believed that a "United States of Central Europe" would prevent such a development. Whether the German plan or Chéradame's plan is implemented, the Czech territories, for reasons of geography, will be of crucial importance. The political system in the Czech lands is very important for the fate of the whole of Europe, as was stressed in Bismarck's dictum that whoever controls Bohemia controls Europe. These provinces are now dominated by Austria-Hungary, which is merely Germany's "vanguard in its march towards the Balkans and towards the East."

"It is hardly surprising," the memorandum continues, "that France and Britain have shown an interest in the independence movements within Austria-Hungary and among the emigrés." It is apparent to Priklonsky that these two countries wish to direct the Czechoslovak movement in a manner favorable to their own objectives. "It would be very difficult to explain this unprecedented good will through any sentiment or sympathy for the Czech nation which has been struggling for its independence for such a long time already." England has founded a professorial chair for Masaryk; and the British government seems to be striving to make London the center of the Czech national movement. It is quite apparent that there is "no serious reasons for concentrating Czech exile's political activity in London; there are very few Czechs and Slovaks in England, and the English have no ties with the Czechs and Slovaks." Furthermore, Masaryk's control of the

Plans for the Future 119

Czechoslovak organizations is hardly warranted. Although he is known as a professor in his fatherland, "in the Vienna parliament he was the lonely representative of the smallest of the Czech political groups, the Czech Realist party, the only one among all Czech political parties that was anti-Russian in its attitudes and rejected the Russian state system." (This is not quite true: the Social Democrats did not approve of tsarism either.) "His personal political views are expressed in his two volume work, *Russland und Europa,* published in Leipzig in 1913." In this work, "written in a highly unsympathetic tone toward Russia, prohibited here, Masaryk contrasts Europe with Russia, calling her a backward country which is unable to reach the European culture."

It would be no less disadvantageous to Russia, "if the center of the Czech independence movement would be brought to France," where, as in England, "there are very few Czechs and Slovaks, and where there is no tradition of close contacts with the Slavic world." It is necessary, Priklonsky writes, to keep in mind the hidden purpose of Chéradame, whose proposed "United States of Central Europe" are designed to curb the great increase of Russian influence that, "the Allies do not doubt, would follow given a favorable end of the war." Therefore, Priklonsky says, Russia "must take into her own hands the direction of the Czecho-Slovak question—as events have defined it—without going as far as to prejudge the exact form which the Czecho-Slovak government will have." In any case, the direction of Czech affairs by Russia would, "at least prevent the manifestations of anti-Russian tendencies in the area." Russia is, necessarily, more interested in the Czech question than the other Allies, because the Czech lands are "the western vanguard of Slavdom and could become, should favorable circumstances allow it, a bastion against the militant Germanism striving for control of the areas in which, in the course of history, the influence of Russia has been dominant."

In Priklonsky's analysis, the most compelling reasons for Russia to become involved in the Czech question are: first, the fact that the Czechs are a Slavic nation and are indispensable in any anti-German arrangement; second, that Bohemia, "because of her geographic location and the composition of her population, is of primary interest to us in connection with the Polish and Ukrainian questions;" and third, that "the Czech territory would also present for us a serious economic interest because of the important development of industry and agricultural techniques there." (Bohemia was the most industrialized province of Austria-Hungary.) Priklonsky concludes that it is merely natural that Russia "should deem it necessary to exercise a decisive influence on the future organization" of the Czech lands, and that the means to this end are at hand in the persons of Czech and Slovak prisoners of war, who represent a considerable proportion of the people of working age in those provinces of all social classes and occupations. He does not doubt that the prisoners of war, so much desired by France, can play a great role in the liberation of the Czech lands and Slovakia, as well as influence the orientation of the future state. Therefore, it is desirable that Russia should influence them and that foreigners should not.

The second part of the memorandum deals with the "Czecho-Slovak organizations in Russia." It begins with a brief description of the origins of the Czech independence movement at home and abroad. At the beginning of the war, a secret committee, consisting of leaders of the most important Czech political parties represented in the Vienna parliament, was established in Prague; it decided to organize political action at home and abroad. The result of this activity has been passive resistance toward Austro-Hungarian governmental institutions and the mass surrender of Czech elements in the Austrian army to the Russian armies. Although many of the Czechs had earlier fought valiantly at the front, they surrendered to the Russians when the latter were retreating; this act alone reflects the pro-Russian and Slavic orientation of the nation.

As far as action abroad is concerned, it is known to the ministry of foreign affairs that "Professor Masaryk left the country with the consent of the Austrian officials shortly after the beginning of the war, and, most likely, was not authorized by the secret committee at Prague to act in its name." At first, Masaryk lived in Switzerland and was politically inactive. However, "as soon as the Russian troops appeared in the Carpathian Mountains, he publicly raised the flag of Czech independence and went to Paris and London to work for it." In London he was give a chair of Slavic studies; "in this way the British government provides him with means." Masaryk then founded a Czech committee dedicated to propagandizing the Czech cause in western Europe. "At first, the committee was composed of two persons, Masaryk and Beneš, the latter being a Social Democrat, who became its secretary. Masaryk remained in London and Beneš established his headquarters in Paris, which, later became the official

Plans for the Future

seat of the committee." (Priklonsky admits that the information in the possession of the ministry may not always be exact and that its accuracy cannot be verified.)

"The influence of Masaryk," the memorandum continues, "has reached also into Russia where an Alliance of the Czecho-Slovak Associations in Russia was established from among the existing Czech and Slovak welfare organizations in December 1914." From the very beginning of its existence, the few people who "directed the Alliance—Čermák, Vondrák, Klecanda, Pavlů, and Pučálka-sympathized with Masaryk and followed his directives; thus the Alliance became the executor of Masaryk's influence on the Czechs and Slovaks living in Russia." The first act of the Alliance was to form a Czech army and seek financial means. On the pretext of not wanting to burden the Russian government, the means were to be obtained through a loan in France and England. This was, "most likely, Masaryk's idea. In this way he had hoped to create, and get under his control, the fundamental elements of the future Czech state —army and finances." As a basis for this army, "he used the volunteer Czech *Družina* established upon the initiative of Koníček and composed of Czechs and Slovaks [living] in Russia, Russian subjects, who had never come under an influence from Masaryk's political agitation." First, the Alliance requested that the Czech and Slovak prisoners of war be placed in the *Družina;* only afterwards did it come out with a plan to create a greater Czechoslovak army. Simultaneously, it requested the freeing of "those prisoners of war for whose reliability the Alliance would vouch." The plan was discussed in the ministerial council on June 15, 1915, but the matter was not definitely decided. "However, at the beginning of April 1916, Vondrák had the luck and the honor of being received in an audience with His Imperial Majesty, who agreed, in principle, to free captured soldiers of Slavic nationality." Shortly afterwards, on April 26, 1916 (the date is given in accordance with the Russian calendar), the Alliance organized a congress of Czecho-Slovak associations in order to discuss further developments, "in accordance with Masaryk's instructions, which had just arrived." The ministry was unable to establish the content of those instructions and of some confidential discussions at the congress, "since there is no record of these confidential meetings in the minutes of the congress." The congress decided to transfer the administration of the Alliance from Petrograd to Kiev, because "a Russian subject of Czech nationality, a Volhynia-landowner and a *zemstvo* deputy, [Vácslav] Vondrák, was elected president of the Alliance." The fact that "this personality, known for his Ukrainophile orientation and left tendencies—leaving aside his being an obvious supporter of Masaryk—has become the leading force in the Alliance makes it difficult to defend Russian state interests during the future evolution of the Czech question. The difficulty has increased even more by the transfer of the administration of the Alliance to Kiev—far away from the central Russian government."

Priklonsky notes that the authority granted to the Alliance to register prisoners of war and to issue certificates on the basis of which they may be freed has tended to give the Alliance a direct quasi-governmental power over the prisoners of war. The Alliance has used this power to increase the number of its followers and terrorize its adversaries, threatening the latter with deportation to Siberia on the grounds of suspected Austrian loyalties. The same quasi-governmental power has made it possible for the Alliance to levy a "national tax, projected to consist of 25 percent of net earnings, on Czechs and Slovaks living in Russia, prisoners of war, and even Russian citizens. Part of those proceeds, according to the secret protocol signed by Masaryk and a representative of the Alliance on July 6 and August 6, 1916 (texts of these documents are in the files of the Ministry of Foreign Affairs), is to be sent to Masaryk's council in London." Although the leaders of the Alliance have no influence on the homeland (Bohemia), their "present activity is characterized by their attempting to get influence there through their exploitation of the situation created by the power of the Russian government in Russia, though they are, in substance, enemies of our statehood and are hiding behind their pretended loyalty to our fatherland only because they take into consideration the present situation."

Furthermore, "there is an inherent danger" in the Alliance's practice of sending "experienced agents" to prisoner-of-war camps to recruit new troops. These "experienced agents," in the process of selecting officers for the Czech military units, can easily "create a cadre of agents obedient to Masaryk not only during the war but also in peacetime after the war." For the same reason, "it is no less important to define exactly what role that organization should play in the process of selecting workers from among prisoners of war for defense industries in order to eliminate the influence of undesirable elements there." This matter, Prikonsky proposes, should be placed in the hands of the ministry of war, because, should current practices continue, all the leaders of the Czech political movement in Russia might easily become merely followers of Masaryk. "Therefore, it is important to take advantage of the recent arrival of a plenipotentiary of the secret committee at Prague, Dürich, well-known for his loyalty to Russia," says Priklonsky. "He has arrived at the time when the negative aspects of the Czecho-Slovak organization existing in Russia have become apparent." In contrast to Masaryk, who has pursued his activities in England and France without being authorized to do so by the committee at Prague, "Dürich was sent abroad by the said committee; and Kramář, who is known for his dedication to Russia, took part in that decision." Dürich "is a deputy of the Czech largest, Agrarian party in the parliament at Vienna." For a long time he has been known as a friend of Russia and "an admirer of her spiritual, national, and state culture." After his departure from home, he lived in Switzerland and France, "where he found the organization already established by Masaryk. Appealing to national unity, Masaryk persuaded Dürich to participate in his organization. When Dürich arrived in Russia, he presented his program to the Ministry of Foreign Affairs and expressed his complete willingness to follow the wishes of the Russian government. Dürich was received by the tsar on August 18, 1916, and by General Alexeev, with whom he discussed his future activity in Russia."

Recognizing that Dürich enjoys great authority in Bohemia, "the Alliance called a rally in Kiev, where its activity is concentrated, with the consent of military officials, for the sole purpose of welcoming him to Russia." This rally, attended by several thousand Czechs living in the area, accepted Dürich enthusiastically and declared him "the sole and absolute" representative of all Czechs and Slovaks in Russia. Vondrák, the leader of the Alliance, could not prevent this development. Realizing that it could not remove Dürich from the leading position in Russia, the administration of the Alliance, with the help of Štefánik, a new member of Masaryk's National Council, who arrived from abroad with specific instructions from Masaryk, offered to recognize Dürich as the representative of the Czech nation in Russia on condition that Dürich recognize the National Council. "Since Dürich did not want to cause any trouble, he considered it possible to accept, temporarily, this offer."

From all this Priklonsky concludes that the Czechoslovak organizations in Russia, originally designed as welfare societies, have assumed a politico-military authority. The unhealthy environment in which they operate has led to the formation of a disciplined, foreign-based political unit that obediently follows orders from foreign organizations, which can use the Alliance for purposes incompatible with Russian state interests. The third part of the memorandum, therefore, deals with the need to bring the activity of the Czechoslovak organizations in Russia into accord with the political goals of Russia.

In this respect, says Prikonsky, the first and foremost task is "to make an effort to remove any dependence of the organizations in question on external influences, and create conditions in which activity would procede under the supervision and direction of the Russian government, so that the Czechs and Slovaks after the war, no matter what its concrete results may be, will become bearers of Russian influence in their fatherland." It is further desirable that the main center of the whole Czechoslovak national movement, now dispersed throughout Russia and other Entente countries, should be in Russia, where, as a consequence of the war, tremendous masses of Czechs and Slovaks are concentrated, and not in countries "where there are only a few agitators who do not lean on the will of the nation."

In the second memorandum, dated October 3, 1916, Priklonsky discusses the future political organization of Bohemia and Slovakia, pointing out that a more detailed and definite solution of the problem will be possible only after the war. He envisions three possibilities: one, Bohemia and Slovakia would remain under the Austro-Hungarian monarchy; two, they would be attached to Russia as an autonomous unit headed by a Russian viceroy (the project of Dr. Kramář); and three, they would form an independent state.

After a brief consideration of the first possibility, which he does not believe can be a permanent solution of the Czech and Slovak question, he delves into two other alternatives. Priklonsky believes that attaching Bohemia and Slovakia to Russia would be difficult to accomplish in the existing situation, because it would be opposed by France and Great Britain. He points out that the adherents of Chéradame propose to build against Russia a "United States of Central Europe" on the ruins of Austria-Hungary, and that the English are attempting to form a center not only for

Plans for the Future 125

the Czechoslovak independence movement, but also for similar movements among other oppressed nationalities in Austria-Hungary, for instance, the Yugoslav committee. The British have shown a particular interest in Hungary, which, in the event of the collapse of the Habsburg monarchy, could join the United States of Central Europe. In this regard one should especially note "the agitation of an influential British newspaper, the *Morning Post,* which is a significant symptomatic reflection of views on the fate of Hungary held by British political circles." The paper has periodically "urged the British to study the question of the future role and boundaries of Hungary and of the states surrounding it." Also, Italy has begun to show an interest in Hungary. "All this leads us to believe that the Western powers would see in the implementation of the second possibility with respect to the Czecho-Slovak countries, holding a pivotal position in Central Europe, a danger for the European balance which they are striving to conserve." And anyway, Priklonsky concludes, annexing Bohemia and Slovakia to Russia would not work to Russia's advantage, "at least in the present political situation," because attaching nationalities which are Slavic, to be sure, "but Catholic, raised in German culture, and never before connected with the Russian state itself, would make the task of the state administration, already complicated even without it, even more complicated."

Therefore, Priklonsky suggests the third possibility—creation of an independent state—would "suit Russia's realistic political interests much better." The majority of Czech and Slovak political leaders are striving toward this end, which is, for many reasons, desired also by Russia's allies.[24] Should conditions favor the realization of an independent Czechoslovak state, its form of government could be either monarchical or republican. It would be "most natural to leave the selection of the form of government to the Czechs and Slovaks themselves, provided that all outside pressure were excluded." According to Priklonsky, "that part of the Czech political circles which is inclined toward the republican form of government sees the foundations of the state form in close political and economic unity with republican France. However, the vast majority of the Czech nation and intelligentsia dream of the restoration of the historical Crown of St. Wenceslas," in which case, "the crucial question becomes what dynasty will be seated on the Czech throne, because historical experience shows that a dynasty can direct political development of small nations (e.g., Bulgaria, Rumania, Greece and Norway)."

There are four possibilities, as Priklonsky sees it, in the selection of a Czechoslovakian dynasty: national, South Slavic, Russian, and western European. The first would engender struggles between the aristocratic families desiring the honor, and then between the one chosen and the "democratic spirit of the Czechs." The South Slavic ruling families are extremely unpopular in the Slavic world, including their own countries —a circumstance that helps explain why the Czech and Slovak politicians favor forming either an autonomous province under the mace of an all-Russian emperor, or a kingdom under one member of the Russian imperial house.

According to Priklonsky, "a tiny majority" of Czech politicians, led by Masaryk, who lives in London, wishes to establish a Czech kingdom under a prince from the English royal house.[25] These individuals are influenced, most likely, by the role that Britain has played in Europe and by the assistance she has given not merely to the Czechoslovak, but also to other national liberation movements among oppressed peoples in Austria-Hungary. Although at first glance such a solution—the placing of a member of the English dynasty on the Czech throne—does not represent any threat to Russia, "a closer and more detailed analysis shows that this solution could produce highly undesirable consequences for us." Should it happen, Masaryk would immediately and automatically start playing the leading political role, because he has the support of British political circles and controls the Czech political movement in England and her colonies. Priklonsky says that Masaryk, who has been characterized in detail in the previous memorandum, "till now has not enjoyed any particular popularity as a politician;" however, as a professor he would be quite influential in preaching a western orientation for the Czechs. He would be able to foster among university youths alienation from and contempt for Russia, which has, according to him, a backward state system. It is obvious "that in this case he would be a powerful indoctrinator of extremist Western ideas." A school system modeled on the British schools, and journeys to England for the purpose of finishing studies there, would alienate from Russia the Czech youths who would become lost to the political and spiritual influence of Russia. The antipathy toward Russia now limited to Masaryk's group would become widespread, since the author of *Russland und Europa* and his ideological followers would gradually generate hostility toward Russia among the Czech intelligentsia.

Plans for the Future

Although Russia is benevolent toward Slavic politicians who have different political views, "she cannot extend such a benevolence to those whose activity is directed against Russia, and, in the final analysis, against their own Slavic fatherland." It is true, says the memorandum, that the German milieu was never able to eradicate Slavic ideas among the Czechs; but the effects of German culture were counterbalanced by the Czechs' hatred for their political oppressors, whereas there would be no grounds whatsoever for serious friction between the Czech state and Britain. Should the Masaryk-oriented group of politicians come to power in the liberated Czechoslovak state, the progressive withdrawal of Bohemia from Russia might lead to frictions between that state and Russia. It would also promote the separatist movement in the Ukraine, since that movement will not cease even if its principal instigator, Austria-Hungary, collapses. Czechoslovakia could become one of the hotbeds of Ukrainian propaganda, if the followers of Masaryk were permitted to direct that state. "In our own state," says Priklonsky, "they have already demonstrated their pro-Ukrainian sympathies." The state frontiers that Masaryk's followers have indicated reflect this intention. These frontiers go "well beyond the ethnic line where the Slovaks leave off, and that is to the detriment of Russians by ancestry; this would likewise have the effect of enlarging the possible sphere of action of Ukrainian agitation in a manner unacceptable to us."

Even if Masaryk does not impose his anti-Russian ideology on the Czech nation, Priklonsky is convinced that Russia "must object to an English dynasty at the helm of the Czech state on the grounds of Russian political interests." Since any federation of central European states would have enormous political importance, and since Czechoslovakia "occupies a central position among the other states which might join such a federation," it would not be in Russia's interest to let a great power such as England "have predominance of influence in Czecho-Slovakia, an influence that would, inevitably, go hand in hand with the enthroning of the English dynasty. Granted that the present rapprochement between England and Russia will, in the near future, lead to even closer cooperation, a direct influence of England on one of the named Slavic states in the area of Russian political interests could always lead to unfavorable or even dangerous consequences for Russia. Giving England a weapon such as the predominance of influence in Czecho-Slovakia, and through the latter, perhaps, in other neighboring Slavic and other states in Central Europe close to Russia, could lead to highly unprofitable and undesirable frictions between Russia and England." All these apprehensions increase in importance, Priklonsky believes, in view of the tendencies "already now" apparent, that is, "the English attempt to concentrate in their own hands influence on Czecho-Slovaks, Yugo-Slavs and Magyars in an anticipation that these nations will become parts of the Central European federation as a barrier against Germany, a barrier that could, eventually, be used against Russia." For all these reasons, "it is desirable to prevent the placing of an English dynasty at the helm of a Czecho-Slovak state, should destiny decree that there would be such a state."

Since seating in Czechoslovakia a western dynasty other than English would be either impractical or dangerous for Russia, Priklonsky concluded that "a Russian dynasty would be most fully in accord with the Russian state interests." Also, the Czech nation wishes that its old dream of seeing "the Crown of St. Wenceslas on the temple of a related Slavic prince would come true; it is highly likely that the Czechs and Slovaks would select such a prince" if they were free to make that choice. "It is reasonable to believe that such will be the choice of all Czechs and Slovaks" if they are free to express their political ideals at the moment when the decision about the form of their government is made. "The holding of such a plebiscite could hardly be objected to, if Russia guaranteed that she would not get mixed up in Czech matters." However, should opposition from the great powers make it impossible to place a Russian prince on the Bohemian throne, "every effort should be made to prevent the inauguration of a ruler from a dynasty of any oher great power and to enthrone a dynasty from some small state, such as Belgium, which ordinarily has no concern with Slavic affairs."

Priklonsky concludes that, with respect to the Czechoslovak question, Russia's main task consists in preventing the exercise of "all external influences which would not be in accord with the national aspirations of the Czechs themselves and the interests of Russia and thus also of Slavdom." This objective can be attained if the center of the Czechoslovak independence movement is in Russia, and if "at the helm of it is a personality who sincerely believes that a unity with Russia would benefit Bohemia. As far as the foreign agitation led by Masaryk and his followers in Russia is concerned, nothing should be done to bring about a schism

Plans for the Future

in the Czech national movement, and only measures aiming at terminating governmental assistance that they have had till now and that they have abused should be taken. We will not, however, hamper their activities directed toward the national rebirth of Bohemia. Under the stated conditions their activity may develop along parallel lines, and in accord with the Czechoslovak organizations directed by us in Russia."

In the third memorandum, dated October 30, 1916, Priklonsky reiterates the danger of English predominance in a future Czechoslovak state, since the latter could easily become the nucleus of a federation of small states in central Europe. Such an influence would, no doubt, lead to the development of a state orientation unfriendly toward Russia, an orientation fostered "now by Professor Masaryk who lives in London and who enjoys a special patronage of British political circles and uses this patronage in order to concentrate in his hands the whole Czecho-Slovak independence movement." Even if there were no Masaryk, any kind of English influence in the prospective state would be undesirable, says Priklonsky, since "Russia and England had been, until recently, rivals, and there is always a possibility of conflicts of interests between them in the future." He lists three sources of such potential conflict.

First, the postwar reorganization of central Europe on a new foundation. France and England may attempt to form a central European (Western Slavic) federation independent of, and opposed to, Russia, especially if the latter is strengthened by a victory in the war. Such a federation could cause a lot of trouble in the future, especially if it included parts of Poland liberated from the domination of Austria and Russia, or the whole of a united Poland. Priklonsky notes that Polish independence has become a dream of all Polish political parties in Russia and elsewhere. Second, the settlement of the Balkan problems, especially if Russia gains power over Istanbul and the Straits, as she has been promised by the Allies. To be sure, France and Britain are secure in Egypt and Suez and have sufficiently protected their interests in the eastern Mediterranean. However, there may be misunderstandings with England if and when Russia wants to exercise her rights, granted by the Allies, over Istanbul and the Straits. Third, the long-standing conflict of interest in the Near and Far East.

In the existing situation, Priklonsky believes, "it would be to our utmost disadvantage if we surrendered to England—without any pressing need for it and without any compensation—the possibility of obtaining predominant influence in the Czecho-Slovak state that may emerge if Austria-Hungary falls apart." Such a British influence would

> make our political tasks more difficult in the future, and, more so, because of the fact that, due to its pivotal position, a free Czecho-Slovakia would become the nucleus of the federation of European states discussed in the memorandum dealing with the Czech question, whose creation would be, most likely, fostered by our Allies, should the war end with the victory of powers belonging to our side. Therefore, before the Entente Powers come to the task of dismemberment of Austria-Hungary and the formation of new state organisms in her place, it is necessary for the imperial government to make arrangements for the prevention of foreign influence, especially the influence of such a powerful world power as England is, in Czecho-Slovakia and also, as much as possible, in other states, especially Slavic, which may emerge on the ruins of Austria-Hungary.

Priklonsky writes that the "foremost joint Allied objective now is to paralyze the aggressive power of Germany in the future." The most effective means to that end is to dismember Austria-Hungary, since only thus can Germany be deprived of the use of the Austro-Hungarian armed forces. In his conclusion Priklonsky says that the noble aim sought by Russia and its allies is to deliver from the authority of Vienna the peoples of Slavic nationality, the majority of the population of the empire, whose dismemberment has a special significance for two states, Russia and England. "In short, the foregoing considerations show clearly that it is necessary to dismember Austria-Hungary and to organize new national states with what remains of her territory after the Allies have set apart the territories which they claim."

Although this seems to be the memorandum's most important recommendation, the main purpose of all three documents was to develop means by which Russia could keep England out of the vital space of central Europe after the war, assuming that new states would emerge there. How to go about building the new states, what boundaries they should have, whether they should be completely independent or interdependent, whether they should be united in one or several federations, were questions Priklonsky proposed to answer in the next memorandum. No evidence is available to show whether or not such a memorandum was ever written. Between October 1916, and the collapse of tsarist Russia in February (March) 1917, the Russian ministry of foreign affairs acted upon Priklonsky's recommendations pertaining to the Czechoslovak independence movement in Russia. The Russian government, however, had to deal with the most pressing problem of the day—prosecuting the war; the same problem preoccupied the western Allies. All of them had vested interests in the outcome of the struggle, which lasted much longer than any of them had anticipated.

Responding to a request made by the president of the United States on December 18, 1916, that the belligerents state their war aims, the Allies made the first public declaration of war aims on January 10, 1917. The joint reply of the Allies to President Wilson was more specific than the original vague goal of a "reorganization of Europe on a basis of respect for nationalities." In order to enlist the support of the oppressed nationalities in Austria-Hungary and to win to their side the political leaders of the exile movements for independence, the Allies called, among other things, for "the liberation of Italians, Slavs, Roumanians, and of Czecho-Slovaks from foreign domination."[26] The phrase "liberation from foreign domination," however, is subject to interpretation as meaning either autonomy or independence. If autonomy were granted to the Czechs and Slovaks within the Austro-Hungarian state, that state would be preserved. But if the Czechs and Slovaks were given independence, or if, by some twist of history, they were able to seize governmental power in their homelands, Austria-Hungary would be doomed. In that case the political orientation of the new state would become important, as Priklonsky repeatedly pointed out in his memorandum dealing with the Czech question.

Staunch allies in the war, Britain and Russia emphasized publicly and officially the unity of their war aims, even while their foreign offices and intelligence services were scheming to keep each other out of central Europe after the war. Although the evidence available is not very great, it seems that the Masaryk-Voska group was considered the nucleus of the future governing organ in Bohemia by Sir William Wiseman, the head of British intelligence in the United States.[27] There is, however, much more direct evidence on the Russian plans involving Dürich.[28] Since the principal leader of the Czech independence movement, Kramář, was imprisoned and his future was uncertain, the Russian government officials worked with Dürich. Needless to say, neither Priklonsky, Gerovsky, and Neratov (deputy foreign minister), nor Seton-Watson, Steed, and Wiseman should be confused with their respective governments. Yet government officials carry a certain weight, and their influence—the extent of which is difficult to determine—is felt. It is possible to document that Wiseman had assumed (or pretended to assume) that Voska, and the group financed by him and operating under cover of the Bohemian National Alliance, expected to be recognized by the Allied governments. He realized that he "was rather mistaken abut their [i.e., the Bohemian National Alliance] position" in January 1918, when Voska told him that he had no such ambition and that Masaryk was the leader.[29] As far as Dürich was concerned, his case is rather easy to document. Tsarist Russia collapsed long before the end of the war, and the Russian plans involving him became public, as will be shown later. The schemes pertaining to Dürich and Masaryk, which were originally top secret, later came to light and they document the covert, behind-the-scenes struggle for control of people's minds and, thus political control of the future of central Europe. Both England and Russia wanted to win the peace and protect their interests in postwar Europe by planning its organization and cultivating some of the leaders of the independence movements within Austria-Hungary.

The struggle for control of central Europe became most manifest among the Czechs and Slovaks in Russia. However, the vast majority of them were preoccupied with other matters, did not realize what was at stake, had no idea that someone might have been pulling the strings behind the screen, and were not even aware of what was going on. Most of the leaders of the Czechoslovak independence movement ascribed too great an importance to themselves, and thus did not realize that they might have been either witting or unwitting tools in the hands of professionals promoting the interests of the great powers. The real issue—the orientation of the future Czechoslovak state and thus who was to have predominance of influence in central Europe—was buried in petty arguments and personality conflicts. The principal actors in this unfolding drama were Professor Masaryk, cultivated by the British and living in a "far-away" London; young Beneš, residing in a less "far-away" Paris; a strong-willed, passionate, and impulsive Štefánik, promoting the interests of his adopted country, France, and believing that they coincided with those of his compatriots; and an old, compromising, and accommodating Dürich, the last of the innocents, dedicated to Russia. In the conflict that developed within the Czechoslovak independence movement in Russia only the tip of the iceberg was apparent to the observers; its main body was hidden. Demagoguery, quarrels, insinuations, allegations, personal attacks, struggle for personal power, and phony issues were visible; the real issues were hidden in the secret documents of foreign offices and/or in the heads of people working for or with the intelligence services of the great powers.

As has been noted in chapter 4, the Dürich-Štefánik differences were temporarily settled at the meeting in Kiev.[30] According to the agreement stated in the "Kievan pact" of August 29, 1916, the Czecho-Slovak National Council (CSNC) (that "was approved by all competent leaders of the nation in the old country") was recognized as "responsible and competent" to speak for the nation. Therefore, "military matters and matters pertaining to prisoners of war, as inseparable parts of the diplomatic-political action," were within its jurisdiction. The representative of the CSNC in Russia was its vice-president, Dürich, who leaned on a "group of expert co-workers selected with his consent by the Czecho-Slovak National Council." As the representative of the CSNC in Russia, Dürich was entitled to speak in its name, and, furthermore, he was recognized as the representative of the Czechoslovak nation in Russia.[31]

The programmatic aspects of the agreement reflected Štefánik's idea of the formation of a "politically indivisible and free" Czechoslovak nation whose independent life was "possible under the sponsorship and protection of the Four Power Alliance." This nation had "an absolute confidence in Russia," and also believed in the "sincere and effective sympathies" that had already been demonstrated by France, England, and Italy.[32] As Štefánik stated in his letter to Masaryk of September 11, 1916, the phrase "protection of the Four Power Alliance" reflected his view of the need for "complete independence," and this point was not clearly stated in the agreement. The emphasis on "Slavic feelings toward Russia" was merely his "tactics which the French Embassy comprehended and approved.... This method was inevitable, since due to Dürich's undiplomatic conduct, talks about French intrigues began to appear in

Russian circles."[33] For Štefánik the agreement was merely a compromise, the best one that he could get; but his chief, General Janin, was not satisfied with it, because in the document France was placed on an equal footing with the other Entente powers, Janin reproached Štefánik for not sufficiently promoting French interests during the negotiations in Kiev. Štefánik defended himself by pointing out that his activity had already provoked mistrust toward him on the part of the Russian government, and he promised to correct his mistake as soon as possible.[34]

The Kievan pact was publicly repudiated by the Slovak League of America on October 25, 1916, on the grounds that it contained the term "Czechoslovak nation," which, by implication, reflected a program that could not correspond to the Slovak demand for an independent development of the Slovak nation in the future independent state. The Slovak question was a burning problem within the Czechoslovak independence movement in Russia, and thus within the independence movement abroad in general. Štefan Osuský, who as an "ambassador" of the Slovak League was concerned with the issue, wrote to Masaryk that the Slovak League might "back up our separatists in Moscow,"[35] —allusion to to the Slovak L. Štúr Society's unwillingness to cooperate with the Czechs. The society's idea was the union of "all autonomous Slovak holdings... in the womb of a great Slavia in which the idea of unity would be implemented along the model of to-days Germany. Russia in Slavia would play the role of Prussia, Poland the role of Bavaria, Bohemia and Slovakia the role of Saxony, etc.... Each unit of the mentioned Slavia would have its autonomy, its language, but the 'official' language, i.e., the diplomatic language, would be the All-Slavic, i.e., Russian language."[36]

Although Štefánik was one of the signatories of the Kievan pact, he attempted to change its recognition of Dürich's leading position in the Czechoslovak independence movement in Russia, and to interpret the agreement in favor of the Paris leadership of the National Council and its policy. In order to accomplish that, he attempted to downgrade Dürich by denouncing him at Stavka as a person of dubious morals, completely lacking in leadership qualities, and associating with individuals of questionable character. This way he tried, at first to isolate him, and then to make him completely ineffective as a political leader. Štefánik also asked for the recall of Lieutenant Štafl, Dürich's "military attaché," to France; the French military mission in Russia granted the request. Using the propaganda techniques known as "guilt by association," appeal to prejudice, and anti-Semitism, Štefánik told General Alexeev that "an Israelite Stern," who had arrived with Dürich from France and had also come with him to the Stavka, "most likely" had Dürich under his "complete domination, especially financial."[37] In Štefánik's view, Dürich was not competent to be in a leading position within the Czechoslovak independence movement in Russia. He handed General V. Gurka of the general staff a copy of the Kievan pact and suggested that an organ be created in Russia that would represent the Czecho-Slovak National Council at Paris. As its members he recommended Čermák, Klecanda, and Pavlů from the Petrograd group opposing the leadership of ACSAR, (all three cooperated with Voska's secret organization in Russia and received financial assistance from it), Dr. Vondrák, chairman of ACSAR, and Lieutenant Ferdinand Písecký and others. Štefánik did not tell General Gurka that these people were followers of Masaryk, that they would, most likely, favor Masaryk's leadership and his policies, and that Dürich would be isolated in the group. Without realizing the hidden purpose behind Štefánik's propsal, and seemingly impressed with the erudition of the dashing young officer, General Gurka approved it.[38] Subsequently, E. Stern and Lieutenant Štafl were recalled to France. After this victory Štefánik left for Petrograd to negotiate with Dürich, in the presence of Vondrák, on September 7.

But Štefánik's success was shortlived. By pretending to be a Russophile dedicated to tsarist Russia, and by his self-confident behavior, he could win the support of the director of the diplomatic office at the Stavka, Basili, and he could outwit the apolitical and unsophisticated General Gurka at the Stavka, but not the Russian ministry of foreign affairs. The latter understood quite well the meaning of Štefánik's arrangements, and it took countermeasures to reverse them. On September 9, the ministry of foreign affairs notified General Alexeev that Dürich had explained the recall of Lieutenant Štafl as an intrigue of "Masaryk and his agent Štefánik." Should Štefánik present the August 29 agreement to the general, Alexeev should keep in mind that the agreement (pact) had not been officially submitted to the ministry and that it "cannot be either adopted or approved." In further communications to headquarters, dated September 11 and 12, the ministry of foreign affairs emphasized the necessity of unifying the Czech elements devoted to Russia and assuring Dürich's leading role in the Czech movement, under the supervision and direction of the government.[39]

According to the September 11 communication, the Kievan agreement had been "forced upon Dürich one hour before his departure from Kiev by the committee dominated by Masaryk and his agents in Russia," especially Štefánik, who wanted to use Dürich as "political window dressing." While Dürich might be somewhat weak, the communication said, and might benefit from having some coworkers, the latter would have to be selected from among politically dependable Czechs. Therefore, "Štafl should remain in Russia, as Dürich is beseeching, at least until the whole affair is clarified." Dürich informed the ministry, furthermore, that Štefánik had threatened to use the utmost measures against Štafl. Štefánik's role in these events, and the danger that he might do something of the same nature again, forced the ministry of foreign affairs to "wish that he would not be allowed to have anything to do with Czech matters in Russia, even though he might be most useful in strictly military matters."[40]

"According to documentary evidence which is at our disposal," the second communication says, the ministry "is convinced that the nature of activity of the Alliance is developing into an intolerable international agitation." In accordance with the secret protocol of the

> London committee of July 6, of which text is in our hands, all negotiations pertaining to political system in Bohemia are concentrated in the hands of Masaryk, while Dürich's activity is exclusively limited to agitation among Czech prisoners of war in Russia under close supervision of Masaryk's agents, the principal of whom is Štefánik, arbitrarily co-opted by the London committee. It was decided to send to London, at the disposal of Masaryk, a large part of the proceeds from the pending taxation of Czechs and Slovaks in Russia, including the prisoners of war, those liable to military service, and even Russian citizens. Under no circumstances could we allow that the center of gravity of the Czecho-Slovak matters be transferred outside the boundaries of Russia and, at the same time, to send abroad the proceeds of the tax collected from the Czechs and Slovaks living in Russia as well as Russians. On the contrary, the state Russian interest requires that all this be concentrated here with us.

Therefore, the communication says, it is necessary to limit the sphere of influence of ACSAR as it is presently constituted, and to secure for Dürich the leading role in it. "Dürich begins to worry that he might have to cease political activity here, if the present trends continue. This would be to our great disadvantage. It is urgent, therefore, that the decision about recalling Štafl, the only person whom Dürich can trust, be rescinded."[41]

Since Štafl had been assigned to Dürich by the French government and served in the French army, all the attempts made by Russian officials to prevent his leaving for France were in vain. But, although Štafl had to leave for France, Štefánik's position at the Stavka was undermined. He lost the first round in his attempt to force upon Dürich the arrangement he had made, and was himself placed under police surveillance. He wrote to Beneš that "enemies here work against Masaryk, you, and naturally, mainly against me. Dürich is completely against us. . . . I am expelling Dürich quietly from the National Council."[42] Štefánik left Russia temporarily, upon orders to go to the French military mission in Bucharest, on October 13, 1916. There he continued his efforts to recruit volunteers for the French Foreign Legion. (Czechs in France served in the Foreign Legion; the first 300 Czechs who had volunteered in 1914 were placed in a separate Czech company, *Na zdar*. During its deployment on the front the company was decimated and all its outstanding members were killed.) The chief of the French military mission in Romania, General H. M. Berthelot, now Štefánik's superior, secured for the latter a promotion to captain, and later to major, though this ranks was limited to the duration of his stay in Romania.[43]

It may well be that Štefánik, an astronomer by profession, did not even realize that the Kievan pact attempted to violate Russian state sovereignty, and no government would tolerate that. The Russian government vetoed the pact on the grounds that it could not agree to a foreign organization making decisions about internal affairs in Russia, especially in military matters. After all, the Russian government was legally responsible for the Czech prisoners of war, who were Austro-Hungarian nationals. It would have violated international law had it allowed a self-appointed committee, not recognized by anyone as a government in exile, to decide military matters and matters pertaining to prisoners of war in Russia. Dürich was told formally that if he insisted on the pact, the Russian government could no longer deal with him. When Dürich told Štefánik about it, Štefánik admited that Dürich's position was "really tragic." Štefánik told Dürich, according to the latter, "If you will insist on the Kievan Pact, you will not be able to work on behalf of our nation, and if you want to work for the nation, you cannot keep your word. *Force majeure* is with the second alternative. We, then, will be forced to come out against you in a statement; however, you can be sure that we will do nothing that could frustrate your work."[44] The methods which Štefánik and Beneš used against Dürich later on, however, were not in line with this statement.

Dürich responded to the request of the Russian government and repudiated the Kievan pact.[45] The government was willing to permit, and did permit, the establishment of Czech military units in Russia; however, the latter had to remain under its control. (In 1916, the French government was not prepared to go even that far; when it did permit the establishment of Czechoslovak military units in France by a presidential decree more than one year later in December 1917, the armed unit was an integral part of the French army, and thus completely under French control.) The Russian ministry of foreign affairs was determined to keep the upper hand: while it favored building a Czechoslovak army, it insisted on Deputy Dürich's leading position in the Czech independence movement in Russia. It also began to foster the idea of a separate national council headed by Dürich; the latter would be aided by two Russian advisors, Alexander Gerovsky and the Neo-Slav Count Vladimír Alexeev Bobrinsky.[46]

According to Štefánik's letter to Beneš, the Russian government did not want to recognize the existence of the Czecho-Slovak National Council in Paris, for three reasons: (1) it was a non-Slavic institution, since it was led by Masaryk and Beneš; (2) it was a foreign institution; and (3) the Czech question was a Russian internal matter. Moreover, the Russian embassy at Paris reported to the Russian ministry of foreign affairs that Beneš was anti-Russian and a fanatical socialist.[47] (On October 30, Beneš sent the Štefánik letter to Masaryk. However, no action was taken on Štefánik's expelling Dürich from the CSNC.)

Realizing that Dürich was backed by the Russian government, the leadership of the ACSAR began a rapprochment with him, inviting his secretary, Crkal, to a conference in Kiev and subsequently, making an agreement with him. The conference took place early in October 1916. Crkal told his hosts that the Alliance must reach an understanding with Dürich; otherwise, it would be dissolved. The leadership of ACSAR was

Plans for the Future 139

indeed willing to make an agreement with Dürich; but it insisted on continuing its coopeation with the CSNC at Paris. But, as Crkal put it, the government "cannot tolerate that an organization existing in Russia would be directed from abroad."[48] The leadership of the Alliance then decided to send Dr. Vondrák and others to negotiate with Dürich. The agreement reached with Dürich and signed by him was rejected by the ministry of foreign affairs; Dürich retracted his signature. Now he demanded that the organ to be established contain several of his co-workers, that he be its president, and that ACSAR also nominate delegates to that organ. Since Dürich had the backing of the Russian government, his wishes were respected by ACSAR's leaders. Even Bohdan Pavlů of the Petrograd opposition to ACSAR wrote in *Čechoslovák* (October 30) that only evil tongues would bring into the Czech lines slogans such as "Masaryk contra Dürich!"[49] Dürich followed the wishes of the Russian government and had its support; for this reason most of the Czech leaders in Russia were unwilling to take a decisive stand against him. Although they might have been jealous of his leading position, they recognized him as a deputy send abroad by the *Maffie* and a spokesman of the nation in Russia.

Undoubtedly, the CSNC was not considered a representative body by all Czechs and Slovaks in Russia, as indeed, it was not. It held a weak position especially among the Slovaks. The Slovak L. Štúr Society tenaciously fostered its plan to attach Slovakia to Russia. Gustav Košík, a delegate of the Slovak League of America who had come to Russia, resented this idea and urged the Slovaks in Russia to endorse the program of the Slovak League, which called for political unity with the Czechs. The president of the Slovak L. Štúr Society, Chamberlain Savjolov, rejected the pleas made by some Slovaks in Russia to cooperate with the Czechs, and in November 1916, he stated that he did not trust the Czechs and ventured the opinion that "whoever is with the Czechs is against Russia."[50]

Mistrust, parochialism, subjectivity, and the like were very common among the Czechs and Slovaks in Russia who had aspirations toward leading positions in the exile organizations. For example, one leading Slovak émigré in Russia, I. Markovič, cooperated with Pavlů, Jiří Klencanda, and Bohumil Čermák, and others connected with *Čechoslovák,* and was, therefore, a target for the Slovaks supporting the L. Štúr Society. Markovič wrote about his "most ugly impressions" of the situation among émigrés to Vladimír Hurban, another pro-Masaryk Slovak in Russia and an intelligence officer in the Russian army attached to the Stavka, on October 28, 1916. Markovič could not comprehend where the Slovaks got their "sickly ambitiousness and megalomania," and who had grafted "arrogance and stupidity" onto people with the greatest ambition. "Here in Moscow," he wrote, "everyone feels that he has the power to send anybody else to Siberia." The situation was desperate, because "all are that way, without any exception."[51]

Propaganda and counterpropaganda created chaos in the organizations of prisoners of war and associations affiliated with the Alliance, in which "nobody trusted anybody." Recriminations were sent to the tsarist government in which people mutually accused each other of disloyalty to that government. Suspicions thrived in the sickly environment; one of the leading officials of the Alliance wrote to a friend, "I will relate to you briefly the facts: Masaryk labeled Dürich, in writing, as an Austrian agent. Beneš was accused of having connections with the Austrian government by Král who is a confidant of the general staff, etc."[52] In such a situation the people who had control of or access to the media could, and always did, maintain the upper hand. They could make or refute charges, while those who had no access to the media had to take all the abuse. In this situation Dürich was at a disadvantage, because most Czech newspapers in Russia were in pro-Masaryk hands.

In order to give Dürich his own information office, his supporters, Dr. Vítězslav Štěpánek and Viluš Crkal, founded the Czecho-Slovak Press Office. On December 14, 1916, the office issued a statement saying, "Deputy Dürich, who was sent abroad by official political leaders in the fatherland in order to take over and direct the Czech action, is establishing now, with the Government's consent, the Czechoslovak National Council in Russia. Half of the members will be appointed by him and half will be delegated by the Alliance of the Czecho-Slovak Associations in Russia." According to the statutes of the new council,[53] its president was to be appointed by the Russian ministry of the interior in agreement with the ministries of foreign affairs and war. Dürich was nominated as president. The statutes stipulated that the president "appoints 6 members and proposes that the leadership of the Alliance of the Czecho-Slovak Associations appoints the other 6 members." All twelve members had to be approved by the ministry of the interior. All official business had to be conducted in Russian; the records of the meetings (minutes) and financial matters of the council had to be under the control of the three ministries named above, which could, at any time, dissolve the council.[54]

The repetitious mention of the three ministries in the statutes indicates that the council was intended to be a working organ, acting largely in an advisory capacity to the three ministries. Under their supervision, it was to have jurisdiction in all Czech matters inside and outsie of Russia—that is, political-diplomatic affairs as well as matters pertaining to Czech prisoners of war and the formation of a Czechoslovak army in Russia. The tsarist government apparently decided to go ahead with building a Czechoslovak army in Russia, despite oppositin from many quarters, especially from those who believed that the Czechs would be more useful as workers in factories. The formation of the national council would speed up the realization of this army.

The rationale behind the provision that six members of the council would be appointed by the Czechs living in Russia and the other six by its chairman was that, since an election could be held in Russia, the principle of representation could be implemented there. However, no election could possibly be held in the Czech lands, and, therefore, the other six members, representing the nation at home, had to be appointed by the recognized spokesman of the nation in Russia—Dürich.[55] The "recognized spokesman," however, had a difficult task to satisfy the many aspirants for seats in his council. These individuals believed that the organization would be more than just an advisory organ of the Russian government; they assumed that the council would have jurisdiction over the Czechoslovak army and would serve as a provisional government of the future Czechoslovak state. Dürich could not possibly satisfy that demand. He therefore had to cope with strong opposition from those whose ambition and thirst for power he could not satiate, and also from those who opposed him for other—political, ideological, or personal—reasons. These people were now saying that the council was undemocratic and unrepresentative, and that all of its members should have been elected. Dürich met this criticism by pointing at the Paris precedent: the CSNC had not been elected by anyone. He and Masaryk had been elected at home, but nobody had elected Beneš and Štefánik. (After the war Dürich pointed at another precedent: although the Czechoslovak Revolutionary National Assembly was not elected, it "elected" Masaryk as the first president of the republic and adopted the new state constitution.)[56]

Although the Russian government was willing to deal only with Dürich, the recognized spokesman of the Czech nation in Russia, Dürich could keep in touch with other Czech institutions outside Russia, whatever their ideological orientation.[57] These included the Paris CSNC. In view of constant quarrels and arguments among the Czechs in Russia, it was hardly surprising that some individuals were eager to promote a conflict between Masaryk and Dürich. Bohdan Pavlů made the first attempt by publishing in Čechoslovák an article entitled "Dürich contra Masaryk."[58] This highly speculative article lamented the possible consequences of a split that might occur in the CSNC; it fulfilled its purpose by creating a climate of opinion in which polarization began to take place among the Czechs in Russia. As usually happens in emotionally charged situations, slander and gossip began to spread, people began to take sides, and charges and countercharges were made by both sides. On several occasions Dürich was approached by government officials who asked him for his opinion on charges made against Masaryk by the latter's opponents in Russia. Although he risked losing the government's confidence, Dürich defended Masaryk and his honor.[59] (Dürich never learned about Masaryk's connections with British intelligence; he dismissed all statements about them as mere gossip.)

Dürich appointed as members of his council Captain-Major (*štábní kapitán*) V. Klecanda, S. Koníček, F. Král, General J. Červinka, V. Švihovský, and O. Šmitt.[60] The leadership of ACSAR protested against the nondemocratic selection of the members of the council, but did appoint delegates to it. Dürich's council was endorsed by the Czech Committee in Moscow, whose chairman was one of ACSAR's delegates to it. With some reservations, the council was accepted by the Slovak L. Štúr Society; it was also endorsed by the officers of the Czech brigade, in the hope that the establishment of this organ would lead, finally, to unity within the Czechoslovak independence movement in Russia. It was further hoped that the council would prompt official permission to form a larger Czechoslovak military body in Russia. The council was, however, resisted by the Petrograd opposition group and was rejected by the newspaper *Čechoslovák*, which editorialized that Dürich's council had organizationally nothing in common with the Masaryk-led CSNC in Paris.[61] A few other small groups and individuals also came out against the council and against the complete separation of the Czechoslovak independence movement in

Plans for the Future   143

Russia from the Paris council. The dissenting groups and individuals invoked in their arguments the authority of the Paris council and Masaryk. Masaryk, in turn, received several invitations to come to Russia in order to settle the discord within the movement there.

This was a rather delicate situation for Masaryk, who was aware of his shaky position in Russia and of the possible long-range implications of Dürich's chairmanship in the newly established organization in Russia. Instead of denouncing Dürich, as some did, he tried to please the Russian government. A few weeks before the fall of Russia's ruling dynasty, he wrote an article printed in January 1917, in *Ruskaia Volia,* a newspaper published by a member of the tsarist government, A. D. Protopopov, interior minister since September 1916, who had been selected for the post by Rasputin, and was one of the gravediggers of Russia.[62] In the article, entitled "Delenda est Austria," Masaryk wrote, "The form of independence [of the Bohemian kingdom] may be different. Dynasty of Russian origin would be most popular. It may be that a personal union with Russia would do."[63] In the latter part of the article Masaryk expressed ideas similar to those contained in Dürich's "memorial script" submitted to the tsar some months earlier. Masaryk wrote,

> In any case I have to emphasize that all our political parties are Russophile through and through. I emphasize this because it was declared publicly that my book might have been directed against Russia. Nothing is further from the truth: my book is directed against absolutism in general, but now is not the time to ignite a quarrel about internal causes of the Russian problems; and if people such as Kropotkin, Plekhanov, Burcev and others are defending Russia, we may join them with an open heart. In any case we plan to leave the initiative in all Slavic matters to Russia. Should Russia recognize that giving Bohemia a non-Russian dynasty would be more desirable, then, at the end, we would have to insist only that the dynasty be a non-German one. It might also be possible to form a personal union with Serbia . . . .

This article was solicited from Masaryk by a Russian journalist, A. V. Amfiteatrov, who called Protopopov's periodical "radical-liberal." It was known in Russia that the Rasputin-selected interior minister was at that time in a deteriorated mental state bordering on insanity; and Masaryk received fair warning against any collaboration with Protopopov's paper. On December 9, 1916, B. Pavlů sent a telegram to Masaryk informing him that "the public announcement" of Masaryk's name among the collaborators with Protopopov's paper "provoked unpleasant reaction in the public opinion. It is absolutely essential that you wire your resignation immediately." Professor Vinogradov similarly warned Masaryk on December 8, 1916, having learned from newspaper advertisements, published for several weeks, that Masaryk was listed among the contributors to the new periodical. Masaryk thanked Vinogradov for the letter in a telegram of December 21, 1916, but was not moved by his warnings. Despite them, the article was published on January 4, 1917; and it was reprinted in a Czech translation in *Československá samostatnost,* Paris, on January 25, 1917.[64]

Dürich's critics who were affiliated with *Čechoslovák* likewise sent Dürich a letter dated December 9, 1916, containing, among other points, the following line: "We, who have always wished the Crown of St. Wenceslas would shine on the temples of king from the Romanov dynasty...." The letter was signed by V. Müller, V. Štíbner, Bohdan Pavlů, Ferdinand Písecký, B. Čermák, and Jiří Klecanda (the last four were members of the *Čechoslovák* editorial board).[65]

Beneš, who kept in close touch with Štefánik, calculated the pros and cons, and mapped his strategy for an attack on Dürich. On December 31, 1916, Beneš notified the leadership of ACSAR at Kiev that, under the existing circumstances, the Paris council did not consider denouncing Dürich to be good tactics. The situation would, Beneš felt, eventually develop in such a way that Dürich himself would have to repudiate the Paris council. In order to make him take that stand, it would be better tactics, he wrote, for ACSAR to come out publicly against Dürich and his coworkers.[66] Beneš apparently tried to avoid taking any action that could bring him into a confrontation with the Russian government, which stood behind Dürich; he tried to get at Dürich by using ACSAR instead. Masaryk acted even more cautiously; he merely rejected the rumors published in the Austrian press, according to which the Czechoslovak independence movement abroad was financially dependent on foreign powers. Masaryk self-righteously declared that "the Czech political action is financially completely independent;" that if an individual should, on his own, accept from anyone any kind of financial help, "we would consider it to be a transgression of our program."[67] Masaryk sent this declaration to Russia also. It was the impatient and hot-headed Štefánik, who returned with the rank of major from Romania to Russia in January 1917, who launched a campaign against Dürich and his council.[68] He struck at Dürich publicly and openly.

Although Štefánik's personal attacks on Dürich may have influenced opinion among some Czechs and Slovaks in Russia, the Russian government was not impressed with them, realizing that Štefánik, as a member of the French military mission in Russia who was under orders from General Janin, promoted French national interests. The Russian council of ministers discussed the Czechoslovak question on January 16, 1917. The proposal submitted by the ministry of foreign affairs and endorsed by the ministry of war called for the establishment of a Czecho-Slovak National Council and a new Czech pro-Russian newspaper in Russia. Both the national council and the newspaper were to be financed by the Russian government. The council of ministers approved the proposal.[69]

As it happened, the text of the proposal and the minutes of the meeting of the council of ministers fell into the hands of Štefánik, who handed them to General Janin, head of the French military mission in Russia, on February 8, 1917.[70] Štefánik obtained the documents from an intelligence network that had been organized by Voska among the followers of Masaryk in Russia. ("Voska built a whole system of espionage.... It is important to note that in 1916 our secret service established contacts with the Russian secret service," wrote Masaryk; and as Wiseman noted, Voska had "plenty of his people" in Russia.[71] At this time Voska's immediate superior was Wiseman, and his intelligence organization cooperated closely with representatives of British and French intelligence in Russia.) Štefánik now took a victorious and indignant stand toward Dürich; Janin was also indignant.

Among the points mentioned in the proposal of the Russian foreign ministry was the ministry's previously discussed concern about French and British interest in Slavic matters in general and Czech matters in particular, which "provokes hostile tendencies toward Russia on the part of Slavs in Austria." These tendencies were fed by representatives of national political organizations in the west, "such as the Yugoslav Committee in London and the Czecho-Slovak National Council in Paris. Since a group hostile in character exists in Russia... and in view of the fact that the Czechoslovak activities are supported financially by foreign states... and in view of the fact that it is absolutely necessary to protect the prisoners of war against the activities of this group, it is inevitable to secure the leadership of the Czechoslovak organization in Russia."[72] What the "captured" document said about the interests of the western powers in the Czech exiles was true, but the Russian government could not prove it; the documents obtained by Štefánik therefore gave the French government a weapon against the Russian government, which it could charge with disloyalty to an ally.

The French and the British could document the intentions and plans of the Russian government, because their intelligence services were able to obtain copies of official documents through Czech agents operating in Russia. At the same time, they were able to keep secret their own plan not to keep the promises they had made to Russia in the 1915 secret treaties, and to force a constitutional change in Russia. On January 15, 1917, Wiseman told Colonel House confidentially that Great Britain would probably try to "force Russia into a constitutional monarchy when peace was made." Wiseman believed that such constraint would be possible if the western powers declared themselves unwilling "to give a warm seaport or other concessions to a government which was not responsible to the people," because to do so would be dangerous to democracy. In this respect, Wiseman counted upon active American cooperation.[73]

In contrast to their western allies, the Russians did not have similar documentation at their disposal. (In fact, such documentation became available only in the 1960s; and some of the key documents of British intelligence are still not accessible to scholars even at the time of this writing.) Despite Štefánik's agitation, his repeated attempts to ingratiate himself with the Russian government, his audience with the tsar (who incidentially, sent friendly greetings to Masaryk through Štefánik after the latter assured him of the Czech leader's loyalty to Russia), and his emphasis on the need for a committee composed of people whom he had recommended to the ministry of war,[74] the Russian government continued to support Dürich.

In January 1917, the Russian government offically and publicly approved the creation of Dürich's council as an organ that would "paralyze" the elements within the Czechoslovak independence movement that were

Plans for the Future 147

"harmful to Russia." The government also allocated subsidies for this organization: a lump sum to cover expenses during the previous year (including a payment to Dürich of 5,000 rubles), 8,000 rubles for expenses related to the council's establishment, a monthly subvention of 4,500 rubles, and 3,500 rubles monthly for publishing a newspaper, as the document "captured" by Štefánik showed.[75]

Štefánik used this information about subsidies as evidence that Dürich's council was dependent on the government, at a meeting of delegates of all Czechoslovak organizations in Russia held in Petrograd on February 7, 1917. At this meeting Štefánik proposed to expel Dürich from the CSNC, and he so informed Beneš at Paris. This action prompted Dürich to telegraph Masaryk that Štefánik and Pavlů, claiming to speak in Masaryk's name, were disloyally working against him. He asked Masaryk to disavow the two; otherwise, Dürich would be forced to resign from the Paris council.[76] In answer, Masaryk stated that the acceptance of financial support disqualified Dürich for political work, and requested that Dürich come to London immediately so that the case could be resolved without discrediting the Paris council.

Dürich replied that Masaryk had been misinformed, and that circumstances did not allow him to travel to London. Dürich then received two letters from Štefánik, indicating clearly that the French officer was the cause of Dürich's expulsion from the CSNC and that he had also denounced and sent derogatory material against Dürich to the Russian government. Štefánik personally told Nicolai N. Pokrovsky, the Russian minister of foreign affairs, that Dürich had been expelled from the CSNC and that Štefánik was the sole representative of the Paris council in Russia.[77] Štefánik promised Dürich a copy of the charges that were to be forwarded to the Russian government, but the latter never received it. (Dürich learned from other people that the script denouncing him consisted of some thirty pages. The character of this letter is indicated by the fact that Papoušek, Masaryk's secretary while the latter was in Russia in 1917, specially excluded this letter from the documentary collection without giving any reason.) Despite continuous denunciation of Dürich by Štefánik, the Russian government, in an official letter by Pokrovsky, dated February 11, 1917, confirmed the statutes of Dürich's national council in Russia; and Dürich was asked to send the three ministries concerned a complete list of its members for confirmation.[78]

Dürich also issued a public statement on February 19, 1917, saying that he had been sent to Russia as a representative of the nation directly from the fatherland and that he was completely independent of any influence outside Russia. In the meantime, Beneš approved, by telegram, Štefánik's decision to expell Dürich from the CSNC.[79] He notified the leadership of ACSAR in Kiev that the Paris leadership stood behind Štefánik, and he requested the Kiev leadership to do likewise. (Dürich was never officially notified of his expulsion from the CSNC.) By this time, however, the leadership of ACSAR had definitely decided to endorse Dürich's council and had appointed representatives to it. Štefánik's reaction to this development was expressed in his telegram to Beneš, saying that "Priklonsky and the Black Hundreds compelled the Alliance to submit, cynically, to the pressure."[80] In his struggle for power with Dürich, Štefánik lost another round, despite the intervention of General Janin on his behalf.

In a letter to Russian military headquarters dated February 21, 1917, General Janin fully endorsed Štefánik, approved of Dürich's expulsion from the CSNC, and added that the Paris industrialist, Stern, "may be Dürich's creditor," and that General Alexeev had placed Stern under police surveillance as a consequence of Janin's denunciation of the Frenchman, "who has no official mission" in Russia and who "has property and high contacts in Paris."[81] Janin also expressed happiness that the Russian government had decorated Štefánik with the Order of St. Vladimir, considering the decoration a sign that Štefánik was appreciated in Russia, "the country toward which he had always expressed his most loyal sentiments."[82] The Russian government was moved neither by Janin's intervention on behalf of Štefánik nor by the latter's memorial script on Dürich, submitted to Pokrovsky on February 25, 1917.[83]

The seventy-year-old Dürich was puzzled by Štefánik's behavior and, needless to say, saw the situation differently from Štefánik. It was difficult for him to understand that Beneš, who had become the secretary of the CSNC only with his own consent on February 5, 1916, could expel him from that organization a year later and urge Czechs in Russia to "support Milan," as Beneš did in his telegram of February 6, 1917.[84] It was incredible to Dürich that he could be condemned for maintaining contacts with the Russian government, while Masaryk, Beneš, and Štefánik did the same. The only difference he saw was that the Russian government recognized him as the spokesman of the Czechs and not the others, who tried in vain to replace him in the confidence of the Russian government. (As has been noted in chapter 4, in April 1916, Beneš proposed to make an agreement with Russia so that the Russians—the tsarist government—"would comprehend our tactics."[85] He agreed with Masaryk's suggestion that Dürich should go to Russia.)[86] Dürich was appalled at the double-standards used by his opponents. They charged that his council was not representative, while "their" (and also Dürich's) CSNC in Paris was equally so. Dürich was charged with receiving subsidies from a foreign government, while his accusers were also receiving subsidies from foreign governments. Dürich did not see much, if any, difference between the subsidy paid by the British to Masaryk in the form of a professorial honorarium and the subsidy that he received from the Russian government.[87] (Beneš, in article 5 of the "Constitution and Federal Laws" of the CSNC, "adopted February 6, 1916," never seen by Dürich but forwarded to the U.S. government in October 1918, listed "national contributions voluntarily accepted by our compatriots" and "loans concluded in Allied countries and the United States" among the financial resources that would "enable the National Council to work politically, diplomatically and militarily for the liberation of the Czecho-Slovak countries.")[88]

Masaryk, Beneš, and Štefánik never repudiated the soldiers of the Czech brigade, officered largely by Russians, who also "took money" from the tsarist government and who, moreover, swore allegiance to the Russian tsar. Voska was paid by the English (and in 1917-1918 also by the Americans), and so were his agents. Sychrava and Baráček worked for Svatkovsky and received payments for their work; several of Masaryk's agents in Russia worked for the Russian government (e.g., Hurban); and neither Beneš nor Štefánik objected to the use of "Russian money," obtained from Vladimír Vaněk, an officer of the *Družina* who later embarked on an intelligence mission in western Europe, to establish an office in Rome that became a branch of the Czech Paris Bureau of the CSNC. Furthermore, Dürich never received any funds from the Masaryk-controlled collections among Czechs and Slovaks in America, despite the fact that his name was also used in the appeals for contributions, except for the small sum that Masaryk gave him before he went to Russia and except 9,000 rubles that he received during his most critical time in Kiev.[89] Dürich refused to accept subsidies from the French government and to take money from two gentlemen in Moscow. When in the summer of 1916 Štefánik promised Dürich plenty of money, without saying where it would come from, if the latter would "be obedient," Dürich rejected it because he wanted to remain independent of any party.[90]

Despite Štefánik's perseverance, Dürich's national council was recognized by the Russian government on March 6, 1917, and Dürich notified Masaryk about it by telegram.[91] On the same day Štefánik came to see General Alexeev at the Stavka for the last time, still trying to undermine Dürich by emphasizing his expulsion from CSNC, and demanding that a control commission, whose members (proposed by him) included some of Voska's people in Russia,[92] should supervise Dürich's national council and be directly subordinated to the chief of the general staff of the supreme command—Alexeev. This commission would deal specifically with military matters—hardly surprising in view of Štefánik's interest in the recruitment of Czech prisoners of war for France.

General Alexeev and the other highest Russian military officials were interested in the speedy building of a Czechoslovak army, but it would have to be used in Russia, on the Eastern Front, and not in France; this view was also shared by the Russian ministry of foreign affairs. As Alexeev put it, in his own handwriting, the army was to be built with the help and cooperation of the national council headed by Dürich and an executive committee headed by General Červinka.[93] The council would consist of Czechs only, while the executive committee would be composed only of Russians. The plan for building a Czechoslovak army from among Czech and Slovak prisoners of war was prepared by General Jaroslav Červinka in cooperation with the Stavka, and the Russian war council approved it on April 6, 1917.[94]

Štefánik's failure to recruit troops for the French front resulted in his being recalled to France on orders from General Janin. He had to report on his missions in Russia and Romania to the French ministries of war and foreign affairs, as well as to military headquarters. The order also indicated that he would, eventually, go to the United States to recruit volunteers for service in France.[95] Before he left Russia on March 21, 1917, the government that had recognized Dürich's national council collapsed. The overthrow of the tsarist government brought about a completely new situation as far as Dürich's future was concerned. It also started a chain of events that proved fatal to the old Russia; the Czechoslovak

Plans for the Future

independence movement in Russia and elsewhere were directly affected by the turmoil that followed.

On March 17, 1917, the day after he became minister of foreign affairs in the newly established Provisional Government, Masaryk's friend, Paul N. Miliukov, was asked by Štefánik to recognize the Czecho-Slovak National Council in Paris as the only representative of the Czechoslovak independence movement abroad.[96] Štefánik also submitted a proposal for the composition of that council's branch in Russia. Then he appointed Bohumil Čermák as the plenipotentiay of the CSNC and left Russia for London and Paris. Beneš also made a request to Miliukov similar to the one that Štefánik had made earlier. On March 16, 1917, Dr. Vondrák, president of the ACSAR, sent a telegram to Prince George E. Lvov, head of the First Provisional Government in Russia, informing him that the Alliance of the Czecho-Slovak Associations in Russia recognized Masaryk (not the CSNC) as the leader of the movement. Vondrák requested that ACSAR be recognized by the Russian government as "the representative and the organizer of the Czech nation in Russia;" then on March 17, Vondrák notified Masaryk of his action. But Štefánik had already established a Russian branch of the CSNC and appointed Čermák as its head.[97]

The leadership of ACSAR recalled its representative to Dürich's council. Now both the opposition group in Petrograd (B. Čermák, Pavlů, et al.) and the leaders of ACSAR courted the favor of the new government. Dürich still continued to pursue his activity, not immediately realizing the meaning and consequences of the radical changes in the Russian government. For that matter, the bureaucrats in the government did not realize it either: as late as March 20, 1917, the Russian ministry of foreign affairs prepared a memorandum on the establishment of Dürich's national council.[98] However, with the main base of his support—the tsarist government—gone, he was no longer treated with respect by many of those who had, shortly before, sought his favor and had recognized him as the spokesman of the nation, of the 250,000 Czech and Slovak prisoners of war in Russia and the president of the national council.

Priklonsky—who, according to Dürich, symphazied with socialist revolutionaries—remained in the ministry of foreign affairs after the revolution (governments come and go; bureaucrats remain), and asked him to sign a statement that he no longer considered himself the spokesman for the Czechoslovak independence movement in Russia. Dürich refused to sign it and continued his work even after the government cancelled all the subsidies to his council. Therefore, in mid-April 1917, the Provisional Government dissolved the Dürich-led national council.[99]

The pressures put on Dürich by government officials and bureaucrats were in line with the program of the new Provisional Government and of the Soviet of Workers' and Soldiers' Deputies in Russia, both of which rejected as a war aim the previous government's goal of increasing Russia's influence abroad. The policy "peace without annexations and indemnities" was incompatible with the establishment of an independent pro-Russian kingdom, with or without a Russian prince at its helm. Organizations of Czech prisoners of war became more active after the revolution, and they came out against Dürich and the current leadership of ACSAR. Most of them endorsed Masaryk and the Paris council instead.[100]

Masaryk never answered Dürich's telegram informing him about the establishment of the Dürich-led council in Russia, and after the revolution he agreed with the expulsion of Dürich from the CSNC. Now Dürich was under attack from many sides and was not able to answer the charges made against him because he had no newspaper at his dispoal. The anti-Dürich campaign was conducted viciously: insinuations, inuendos, demagoguery, name-calling, double standards, false charges, guilt by association, mud-slinging, smear, character assassination, appeal to ignorance, and appeal to prejudice—all these methods of gutter politics could be detected in it. In Russia Dürich was attacked most violently for his contacts with the former tsarist government by those who, before the revolution, printed the words "Gosudar" and "His Imperial Highness" in the largest and thickest letters. As an example of the slanderous attacks upon him outside of Russia, Dürich quotes a letter that Edvard Beneš sent to his brother, Vojta Beneš, who at that time was helping to organize the Bohemian National Alliance in America.[101] In the letter Beneš charged that Dürich had accused Masaryk of being "unfriendly to Russia," and had behaved so despicably that "even the greatest contempt for him cannot do justice." According to Beneš, Dürich

> committed real crimes, because he allied himself with the blackest reactionaries against us, cooperated politically with Koníček... and with Priklonsky, an official of the ministry of foreign affairs and Protopopov's monster, who favored Hungarians and who exploited

conflicts among our people against our cause. [Here Beneš is referring to the same Protopopov in whose periodical Masaryk wrote, a few weeks before the revolution, that a king from the Romanov dynasty on the Bohemian throne would be most popular. Masaryk was also listed in advertisements of Protopopov's periodical as one of its contributors.] And the old ass (and also a bad lot) was using it for his own aims. . . . In Paris I have handed a memorandum to Izvolsky in which I requested that Dürich no longer be considered our representative. Taking money from the Russian government—that is something absolutely inadmissible for us—it is the last blow to Dürich. . . . He also lied to Cardinal Amett, a politically important person. . . . Here in Paris he was spreading [gossip] about me and Sychrava that we were Austrian spies. . . . In Petrograd he allied himself with our worst enemies, and was spreading gossip that Masaryk is taking money from the Jew, Stern. He himself established a National Council, an establishment competing with the National Council at Paris, and thus was destroying unity. . . .

In April 1917, Masaryk also sent a letter to the same Vojta Beneš, expressing a hope that the Dürich problem would be resolved by the February Revolution in Russia.[102] Dürich had been expelled from the CSNC, Masaryk wrote, and would no longer be listed as vice-president. According to Masaryk, Dürich was an "unwitting victim" of Austrian and Hungarian intrigues: "he took money from a very suspicious businessman of Austrian origin [Stern?], and he took money from the Russian Ministry of Foreign Affairs. The officer who was handing him the money . . . kept a part of it for himself. He was the man who was before the war a consul at Budapest [Priklonsky] for several years. Who can guarantee that he was not paid by Austria?"[103] This letter is an example of Masaryk's use of propaganda by innuendo.

In another letter written at the beginning of 1918 Masaryk asserted that Dürich could not remain in the leadership of the independence movement because "he placed himself into service of a reactionary government, obviously Austrophile and Germanophile, and [moreover] he was against the Allies and the rest of us. *The revolution buried absolutism, its Slavic policy, and thereby also our colleague Dürich.*"[104] The two sentences are hardly consistent; and the charge was not supported by any evidence. Had the Russian government been "obviously Austrophile and Germanophile," it would hardly have entered the war in defense of a small Slavic state, Serbia. Consistency and truth are often the first casualties in struggles for power.

Attacks upon Dürich by less prominent people were conducted on much lower levels than that of the quoted examples, and Dürich was appalled by their wickedness. What was most frustrating from him was that he could not defend his honor, since all newspapers were in the hands of the opposition. He could issue only a leaflet in his defense. His accusers used double standards. On the one hand, Dürich was charged with accepting money from a Jew, Stern, who, incidentally, assured Dürich that he was not Jewish, while Masaryk a few years later even boasted about the help that he had received from the Jewish community, especially from Zionists in the United States.[105] Since the opposition to ACSAR's leaders and to Dürich came out on top after the revolution, Dürich was isolated, with only a few of his former friends remaining loyal to him.

The majority of Czechs in Russia did not take seriously the charge that had been made before the revolution that Masaryk was pro-Western, and assumed that his policy was also a Slavic policy. The officers and soldiers of the Czech brigade, who had taken an oath of loyalty to the tsar and who had endorsed Dürich's council just before the revolution, decided to make a political pronouncement on March 20 (March 7), 1917. They proclaimed the lands of the Bohemian Crown—Bohemia, Moravia, Silesia, and Slovakia [sic]—"to be a united and independent state, leaving the peace conference the exact definition of boundaries and the state system." (Slovakia never belonged to the Bohemian Crown.) They "recognized" Masaryk as the "temporary dictator of the Czechoslovak state," and the CSNC under his chairmanship as the "provisional government" to which they took an oath of allegiance. They asked their "brethren" in Bohemia and Slovakia to wait patiently for their arrival.[106] (From then on the Czech military often used the term "dictator" in referring to Masaryk.)[107] The declaration indicates that its authors had little understanding of politics and even less of international law.

It was a paradox that the officers, who were Russian citizens, largely Orthodox, proclaimed the independence of a new Slavic state, assuming that the Russian army would liberate all the named provinces, and that they declared in favor of Masaryk, a self-professed democrat, as a "temporary dictator," and in favor of the pro-Western CSNC, dominated by Masaryk, Beneš, and Štefánik, as the provisional government of the new state. A Russian officer named M. P. Mamontov, commander of the Third Regiment, had a great deal to do with preparing the pronouncement. It was the same Mamontov whose outcry against a Catholic priest launched the campaign for "mass conversion" of members of the old *Družina* to Orthodoxy.[108] Now he issued orders to his soldiers to go to Petrograd to arrest Dürich on the most ridiculous charges, including "the crime of slander" of the president of the Czechoslovak republic. Dürich was not arrested, largely because of the intervention of the editors of *Čechoslovák*, to whom such violent methods were obnoxious. Mamontov's behavior—acting upon emotional impulse and jumping from one extreme to another—was called by the Czech soldiers "mamontovshchina."[109]

In a climate of great enthusiasm for Masaryk, and overt hostility toward Dürich and his friends, the third congress of the Alliance of Czecho-Slovak Associations in Russia was called; it was convened on May 6, 1917, in Kiev. Dürich was not admitted to it. His associate, František Král, came to Kiev to take a part in the congress, but disappeared suddenly; only later did Dürich learn that Král had been imprisoned on false charges, to be released after the congress with apologies that "everything had been a mistake." The first meeting of the congress approved a resolution stating that "the Czecho-Slovak National Council, with T. G. Masaryk at its helm, is the highest organ of the Czecho-Slovak national political struggle, and, therefore, it is the duty of every Czech and Slovak to submit to its leadership." The congress prepared statutes for the Russian branch of the Czecho-Slovak National Council and approved its members. The chairman of the branch was always to be the member of the CSNC who happened to be in Russia; the vice-chairman was Bohumil Čermák, and the two secretaries, a Czech, Jiří Klecanda, and a Slovak, Dr. Jan Markovič. Thus the congress brought about a complete victory for the most radical supporters of Masaryk and a defeat for Dürich and the former leadership of ACSAR. At the Kievan congress the leadership of the Czechoslovak independence movement in Russia passed from the hands of Czech-Russians to the revolutionary émigrés from the Habsburg monarchy. After May 6, 1917, the Paris CSNC was the only recognized representative of the movement, and its branch was seated in Petrograd. After Dürich's short-lived prominence, Masaryk was called upon to assume the leadership of the movement for Czechoslovak independence in Russia.[110]

As a point of interest, one of the metamorphoses of the future author of *The Good Soldier Schweik* may be mentioned here. Because of space limitations, it has not been possible to dwell here on the Club of Confidants, an organization of soldiers and prisoners of war that advised the Alliance on matters concerning its interests. One group of the Confidants, nicknamed the "Black Hand," decided to take drastic measures to assure the victory of Masaryk and the Petrograd opposition at the congress. Several members of the Czech brigade who were known to cooperate closely with the Kiev leadership of the Alliance, including the satirist Jaroslav Hašek, a contributor to the Czech periodical *Čechoslovan*, were forced to leave Kiev during the preparations for the congress. In response, Hašek wrote a satire entitled "The Czech Pickwick Club" for a Kiev paper called *Revoluce,* which expressed the views of the former leadership of ACSAR. Hašek was arrested and tried by a "court" composed of members of the First Regiment's committee, which made him recant the content of the article, apologize publicly to all those mentioned in it, terminate his cooperation with *Revoluce,* and go to the front. In addition, he was sentenced to one week in prison. The editorial board of *Revoluce* commented on Hašek's recanting his views and pledging allegiance to the new leaders of the Russian branch of the CSNC by declaring him a traitor, and parted with him, saying that he had killed himself politically.[111]

Since Dürich had ceased to be a member of the CSNC, the latter now consisted of only three people: Masaryk, its president, Beneš, its secretary general, and Štefánik, its vice-president. Beneš described their competence in Rome in April 1918, at the last meeting of the Congress of Oppressed Nationalities from Austria-Hungary, saying, "Whenever one of us acts, he speaks with full and complete authority of all of us."[112] The Russian revolution made it possible for this self-appointed triumvirate to oust Dürich from a leading position within the Czechoslovak independence movement, and the three people now directed it in accordance with their ideological preferences.

Masaryk welcomed the revolution in Russia with enthusiasm; he believed that it would strengthen the forces among the Allies that were committeed to advancing the cause of democracy, to the destruction of Austria-Hungary, and to the establishment of a free Czechoslovakia. In his telegram to the new Russian foreign minister, historian Paul N. Miliukov, on March 18, 1917, Masaryk predicted that the revolution would bring Russia order and victory in the war, and would achieve for Russia and the Slavic peoples a position of influence in international politics. As he put it, "a free Russia meant the overthrow of Austria-Hungary and the just solution of peace questions together with other great powers."[113] Miliukov replied, "I fully agree with your thoughts as to the perspectives that free Russia opens to the family of civilized nations for the eventual reshaping of Central and Southeastern Europe." At a press conference held on March 23, 1917, the Russian foreign minister stated that among the war aims of the Allies was "the reorganization of Austria-Hungary with the liberation of the nationalities she oppresses." In particular the task of the Allies included "the solution of the Czecho-Slovak question —the creation of an independent Czecho-Slovakian state that will act as a barrier against the advance of the Germans toward countries with a non-Slavic [sic] population."[114] Thus Miliukov was the first Russian (Allied) statesman who came out openly in favor of the creation of an independent Czechoslovak state, at a time when the British favored merely equality for the Bohemian Crown with that of Hungary in the Habsburg empire, but not yet Czechoslovak unity and independence. Masaryk could not have been more pleased.

In addition to the telegram to Miliukov, Masaryk sent, simultaneously, the following telegram to M. V. Rodzianko, chairman of the Russian state Duma: "The Czechs and Slovaks have joy over your revolution that means order and victory. Ideals of the most outstanding Slavs are being realized. Slavdom will be great not merely in the geographical sense, but it also will become great spiritually. We have always loved the Russian nation and we have stood in this war on the side of our Slavic brethren against our common enemy. Thousands and thousands of dead, the victims of severe Austro-Hungarian vengeance, are also martyrs of the Russian freedom now. By giving freedom and equality to Russia, to the whole one-eight of the entire mankind, you have solved the Slavic questions. We are deeply grateful to Duma and its energetic chairman for your and our liberation."[115]

Masaryk expressed his joy over the new government's guarantee of freedom and equality to all nations in Russia; and he believed that the Entente coalition would be consolidated by the emergence of a free (democratic) Russia. The March 22, 1917 issue of *New Europe* carried Masaryk's article characteristically entitled, "Russia: From Theocracy to Democracy," in which he suggested that the new Russia was no longer a barrier to a real democracy. It thus became possible to coin and use a new slogan, "theocracy versus democracy,"[116] in order to differentiate between the Allies on the one hand and the Central Powers on the others. But Masaryk's contention that the revolution would strengthen Russia's war effort on the side of the Allies proved to be unfounded, as was his prediction that it would bring Russia order and victory in the war. He himself parted with that view after he arrived in Petrograd, where Masaryk went on a special mission for the British ministry of war, carrying an English passport (dated May 3, 1917) issued to him by the British Foreign Office under the name Thomas George Marsden, on May 16, 1917,[117] two days after Miliukov's resignation. In Russia, Masaryk's enthusiasm for the revolution evaporated. He realized that his assumptions about it were merely wishful thinking.

CHAPTER SIX

THE SPRING AND EARLY SUMMER OF 1917, AT HOME AND ABROAD

At the beginning of 1917, the Czech independence movement reached a new impasse. In contrast to the hard-line German policy, that of the new monarch of Austria-Hungary, Emperor Charles (who succeeded Franz-Joseph's sixty-four-year rule), was more moderate. At home he declared an amnesty for political offenders, pardoned Kramář and Rašín, who had been sentenced to death, and ended the persecution of the Czechs in the hope of winning them over to his side. The persecution had been exploited abroad for propaganda purposes by the Czech independence movement, which was now confronted with a new situation. Count Otakar Czernin, the emperor's minister of foreign affairs, indicated Austria's willingness to enter peace negotiations on February 5, 1917; Charles had already in his inaugural manifesto,[1] announced his desire to end the war as soon as possible. While the Allies welcomed the change and placed high hopes in the new ruler's willingness to negotiate a separate peace, the Czech independence movement, and especially Masaryk and Beneš, were horrified of the prospect.

The preservation of Austria-Hungary was favored by many British public opinion makers, on the following grounds. First, there was the great fear that an insistence on the destruction of Austria-Hungary might prolong the war, with consequent suffering for all the belligerent nations.

Second, Austria-Hungary was no worse than any other great power controlling subject nations. Although the Hungarians behaved much worse than the Austrians, the situation in the empire was hardly worse than Unionist coercion in Ireland. Third, if Austria-Hungary were partitioned, the succession states would be too small economically and militarily to be able to survive politically, and their independence would be illusory. Finally, it would be more desirable to come to terms with the enemy, once Austria-Hungary reconized that it had done wrong and showed the will to reform. It was known that Austria-Hungary was reforming, it was hoped that the subject nationalities would receive a sufficient amout of autonomy.[2]

The leaders of the Czech independence movement fully realized the gravity of the situation. Their hopes had risen in December 1916, when Lloyd George's cabinet, pledged to prosecute the war with greater energy, replaced Asquith's coalition government, and when on January 10, 1917, the Allied powers published their note to President Wilson mentioning the liberation of the several subject nationalities in the monarchy as one of their war aims. The Czech leaders hoped that the word "liberation" meant the dismemberment of Austria-Hungary, but the British and French governments *knew* that liberation is not necessarily the same thing as independence.[3] Although the statement had great propaganda value, it did not bind the Allies to dismember Austria-Hungary, should dismemberment become possible. The Allies' most immediate and most pressing need was to win the war, and if Austria-Hungary, Bulgaria, and Turkey could be detached from Germany, to defeat Germany would be much easier. Furthermore, the war had become very burdensome to all the belligerents; and on December 12, 1916, the Entente powers were invited to enter peace negotiations by the four governments of the Central Alliance.[4]

The British government was interested in receiving a formal offer of peace from Austria, and it established informal contacts with Austria-Hungarian diplomats and emissaries in Scandinavia and Switzerland.[5] In its efforts to separate Austria-Hungary from Germany, the British government also used the U.S. government as an intermediary between the Entente and Austria-Hungary, assuring the latter that the Entente did not desire its dismemberment. Czernin was notified through diplomatic channels that the president of the United States and his secretary of state,

Robert Lansing, hoped that Austria was interested in a separate peace; if the Austrian government were willing to conclude an early peace, the U.S. government could secure a definite assurance from the Entente powers against the separation of Bohemia and Hungary from Austria.[6] But the main stumbling block in any attempt to separate Austria from Germany lay in the promises that the Allies had made to Italy, Romania, and Serbia, and in Russia's claims, which the latter country could not press hard in view of the situation on the front. It was clear to British government officials that if the terms offered to Austria were harsh, they might "prove a stumbling block in way of peace."[7]

In the spring of 1917 the British views of the objectives of the war were stated in the "Balfour Memorandum," which consisted of the minutes of a March 22 meeting of the War Council of the empire at which Balfour made a sweeping review of foreign policy.[8] With respect to central Europe, Balfour proposed to attach Poland to Russia and to change the dual monarchy into a fourfold monarchy. Since separating Russia from the west by an independent Poland would have meant excluding Russia from the councils of the west, Balfour favored merely autonomy for Poland within the Russian empire. As for Bohemia, he was not certain whether the Czechs would be satisfied with autonomous status within the fourfold Habsburg empire. But Lord Robert Cecil, under secretary in the Foreign Office, as well as the prime minister, denied that they wished to break up Austria-Hungary, and insisted that they wanted the empire to become a federal state. To Cecil, national self-determination was "the pirnciple upon which our own Empire is based."[9] Cecil agreed with Sir Eric Drummond, secretary of the new foreign secretary, A. J. Balfour, and Lord Hardinge, the permanent under secretary in the Foreign Office, that there was an inherent danger of balkanization in any plan to dismember Austria-Hungary, and believed that the balance of power would be titled in the direction of Russia. A federated Austria-Hungary "would be better for the future peace of Europe than the creation of a new confederation of Slav states."[10]

In the course of discussions about the future of Austria-Hungary, Austen Chamberlain and Lord Milner agreed with the prime minister's March 22 review of foreign policy, according to which the greatest danger confronting the allies was Germany's "unbroken avenue of influence from the North Sea to the Persian Gulf."[11] This danger could be forestalled, the two gentlemen believed, by a federation of newly established states independent of Germany that would create a barrier to German expansion in east central Europe. But all the British policymakers agreed that Germany's road to the East and Middle East should be effectively blocked, and that the reorganization of central Europe was a secondary consideration for the British empire.[12] For Masaryk, in contrast, the settlement of territorial questions in the area was of foremost importance.

In the February 22, 1917, issue of *New Europe,* Masaryk wrote that while he would not assert that the liberation of Bohemia was the most vital question of the war, the war aims of the Allies could not be attained without the liberation of Bohemia. Masaryk knew well that Bohemia's liberation could not be achieved without direct Czech participation in the war against Austria-Hungary and Germany. The fact was that, till then, the Czechoslovak military contribution to the armed struggle of the Allies had amounted to very little, if anything. In Russia there were many Czech and Slovak prisoners of war, but very little progress had been made in the building of a large Czechoslovak army that could be deployed at the front. In France the Czech company in the First Regiment of the French Foreign Legion had been almost demolished. In Italy military participation by the Czechs had not even started, and there was very little hope that it could be greater in other countries, where there were few Czechs and where governments were reluctant to set new precedents by allowing the formation of an exile-directed army, thus making far-reaching political commitments concerning the future settlement in central Europe.

On the political scene the situation was no better than on the military front. Although Masaryk attempted to build around himself a center for action abroad and be its spokesman, his authority was not universally accepted among the Czechs, especially in Russia. It was even weaker at home, where his influence had never been great and had declined considerably since the early days of the war. When the Entente powers, responding to Beneš's request of December 29, 1916, included the liberation of the "Czecho-Slovaks" in the statement of their war aims on January 10, 1917,[13] the Czech deputies disavowed the Masaryk-led independence movement and rejected the proposition. On January 31, 1917, the presidium of the Union of Czech Deputies gave Czernin a vote of confidence and placed in his hands a declaration rejecting the Entente powers' call for the liberation of "Czecho-Slovaks" and proclaiming that "the

Czech nation, as in the past, now, and in the future, sees its future and conditions for its development only under the Habsburg mace."[14] Thus, in January 1917, the activist policy of the Czech political leaders reached its peak; it openly disavowed the independence movement abroad. The split between Masaryk and the Czech leaders at home was complete. Yet the year 1917 was destined to bring about a drastic change in the attitude of the politicians at home and the situation in which the independence movement found itself abroad. The main cause of these changes was the Russian Revolution and its consequences.

The fall of tsarism in Russia strengthened the Czech struggle in the west by removing the fears of the west European powers that the liberated nations of central and southeast Europe would become an easy prey of tsarist Russia. It was sugested that the Entente could now win over these nations as allies during and after the war. The February Revolution in Russia also strengthened the Czech struggle by making it possible to enlist democratic forces at home and abroad in the Czech cause and to present the war as a struggle of democracy against reaction.[15]

Although the leaders of political parties at home rejected the idea of Czech independence early in 1917, the Russian Revolution made an indelible impact on their attitude toward the issue; it also brought about a profound change in the ideo-political thrust of the exile movement. The January 10, 1917, declaration of the Entente on war aims, which included a statement on the liberation of the "Czecho-Slovaks," was a great diplomatic success abroad;[16] its disavowal by the Czech Union (the club of the Czech deputies in the Austrian parliament) was a tremendous blow to the independence movement both at home and abroad. Masaryk "explained the disavowal as an acknowledgement of the pardon granted to Dr. Kramář and his comrades."[17]

Dr. Šámal and Dr. Scheiner, leaders of the secret committee since the arrest of Kramář, in a message to Beneš early in March 1917, claimed that the statement issued by the Czech Union was the work of the individuals who signed it. Those signatories must not be regarded as the defenders of Czech rights and must be barred from all future negotiations regarding the independence of the Czech lands.[18] In another message sent from Prague in February and transmitted to Beneš on March 30, 1917,[19] those who remained from the former *Maffie* reacted to the possibility of a separate peace with Austria. In this case, the message stated, it should be made possible for the Czech nation to express its will freely. The exiles, as spokesman for the nation, should insist on the occupation of the Czech lands by the Allied armies, and on the release of all political prisoners, especially Kramář and Rašín. These stipulations reflected the writers' wishful thinking, as well as their misjudgment of political reality in the Allied countries.

Though the political leaders of the Czech nation at home disavowed the independence movement, it began to pick up some grass roots support in the Czech lands. Early in March 1917, two groups—*Národ* and *Česká demokracie*—[20] consisting of people who had been, more or less, connected with the *Maffie* in 1915, began to publish newspapers. New, smaller groups sprang up in opposition to the official leadership of the various Czech national parties. The Agrarian party continued to "keep two irons in the fire;" its daily, *Venkov,* wrote in a reserved manner while the evening newspaper, *Večerník,* followed the nationalist and more radical line. Undoubtedly, the climate of opinion at home began to change in favor of independence after the February Revolution in Russia. The first reports abut the fall of tsarism arrived in the middle of March 1917, acting as a catalyst for the activities of the Czech opposition groups and some workers and intellectuals. *Česká demokracie,* one of the two opposition groups established earlier, which published a newspaper of the same name, increased its influence. Its collaborators now included the right-wing Social Democrats Hudec and Modráček, the National Social Jiří Stříbrný, and the anarcho-communist Dr. Vrbensky.

Czernin took a public stand toward the Russian Revolution on March 31, in a special interview carried in *Fremdenblatt.* He said, in essence, that the war could be ended if Russia really wished peace, and that Austria-Hungary still adhered to its peace offer of December 12, 1916.[21] But no response came from Russia; the Provisional Government had committed itself to continuing the war on the side of the Entente. Czernin and Emperor Charles well knew how desperate the empire's situation was, both internally and externally. There was a food shortage in the cities, the population was becoming restive, the war was unpopular, and the morale of the troops was rapidly declining. At the beginning of April, the two statesmen jointly prepared a memorandum designed primarily for Kaiser Wilhelm II of Germany (although it bore only Czernin's signature and was addressed to Charles). The memorandum suggested that the war must end late in the summer or in the fall, in view of the fact that the empire faced "a collapse." It was absolutely essential to begin peace negotiations before the Entente realized that Austria-Hungary was dying.[22] Also, Czernin made another peace offer when the Provisional Government issued its declaration of April 9, saying that the aim of free Russia was not "domination of other nations...but building a firm peace based on the right of self-determination of nations."[23] In his April 14, 1917, statement, Czernin said that since Russia did not intend to occupy foreign territory and since it wanted a lasting peace in accordance with the right of nations to determine their own destiny, the aims of the Provisional Government were the same as those of the empire, as he had already pointed out on March 31. Czernin's statement ended by noting that both the Austrian and the Russian (provisional) governments "equally strive for peace with honor for both sides."[24]

Under the impact of the Russian Revolution and Czernin's pronouncements, the Czech Union adopted three basic Czech demands: democratic government, parliamentarianism, and revision of the constitution in the direction of self-determination of nations.[25] These demands were incorporated into the Union's proclamation of April 14, which reached the exiles toward the end of the month, considerably raising their hopes.[26] One cannot know what the majority of members of the Czech Union understood by the concept of "constitutional revision in the direction of self-determination"; however, constitutional revision began to be discussed within the emperor's intimate circle at about the same time —April 11.[27]

The exiles, Masaryk and Beneš in particular, were alarmed at the prospect of an early peace that might materialize as a result of negotiations conducted by Prince Sixtus of Bourbon-Parma.[28] (Although they were not apprised of the details, they did know about Austria's peace overtures and attempts to bring about a separate peace.) Their instructions to the *Maffie* in April 1917, reflected their pessimism. They asserted that only resistance at home could save the independence movement, for Austria-Hungary was making a frantic effort to save itself, and against its intrigues they were "almost helpless."[29] The politicians at home were instructed to demand "historical state right without prejudice for acquisition of Slovakia and without prejudice for the existence of Austria."[30] The exiles also directed how the Czech deputies should behave if parliament were called into session (as was announced in April), and how they should conduct themselves in parliament. The main demands of the exiles were that the Czech deputies should insist on "state right," that under no circumstances should they disavow the exiles and their program, and that they should launch a vocal and determined opposition to the government.[31]

As it happened, the government's calling the first wartime session of the Austrian parliament in May 1917, brought to the attention of the Czech intelligentsia the orientation and attitude of the Czech deputies in Vienna. On this occasion some Czech intellectuals and writes issued a statement, "The Manifesto of the Czech Writers," which was prepared by a writer, Jaroslav Kvapil, and signed by 222 artists and writers.[32] The manifesto was not intended for publication. It was handed to the chairman of the Czech Union on May 17, in order to inform him of the views of the Czech intellectual community. Two days later, however, an Agrarian newspaper, *Večernik,* published it with the first 150 signatures attached to it. The manifesto called upon the Czech deputies to be "truthful spokesmen of their nation," and asked them to stand up for "the Czech rights and Czech demands in the most decisive and dedicated manner," because these rights were gaining new support and new emphasis as Europe became more democratic. It asserted that this "democratic Europe, Europe of free and independent nations" was "the Europe of tomorrow and the future!"[33]

This demand, no doubt, influenced the thinking of some of the Czech deputies. After considerable discussion of the manifesto in the club of the Czech deputies, in which a wide range of views was expressed—from the extreme demand for national self-determination and the breakup of Austria-Hungary to the views held by the activists—a compromise was reached and the Švehla proposal was adopted. Thus, at the opening session of parliament on May 30, 1917, the Czech deputies came forward with a declaration demanding "the transformation of the monarchy into a federal state of free and equal national states," and within the realm of this federation, "the unification of all branches of the Czechoslovak nation into a democratic Czech state, including also the Slovak branch of the nation."[34] The latter provision was incorporated into the declaration on the insistence of a Slovak, Vavro Šrobár, who brought it to Prague, and in order to satisfy the demands of the writers. The idea of preserving the monarchy was included in the declaration (Beneš exhorted against it in vain) in order to satisfy the loyal Young Czechs and the Catholics; it also corresponded to the federalization plans of the Social Democrats. Although falling short of the maximum demands of the exiles, the "Manifesto of the Czech Writers" and the declaration of the Czech deputies at Vienna stood on the basis of historical "state rights" and demanded union with the Slovaks.[35] (The claim to Slovakia was not compatible with the idea of Bohemia's historical "state rights," since Slovakia had never belonged to the Crown of St. Wenceslas.) Only one deputy, State Rightist Antonín Kalina, presented his own declaration in the parliament, demanding the establishment of an independent Czech state with "all attributes of complete state sovereignty." Kalina's declaration was rejected by the Social Democratic paper, *Právo Lidu;* it was also in conflict with the "state rights" declaration of the National Alliance and the Czech deputies. While Kalina's statement endorsed the independence movement abroad, the Czech deputies' declaration rejected it.[36]

On the opening day of the parliament, the metal workers of Prague and Pilsen began a strike that, on May 31, developed into a political demonstration in Prague. The people who assembled in Old Town Square shouted, for the first time during the war, "Long Live Masaryk!" Early in June, a committee of confidants who had organized the strike drafted and accepted a resolution incorporating a demand for the establishment of an independent Czechoslovak state, in accordance with "the great idea of the Russian revolution and self-determination of European nations." The resolution disapproved the behavior of the leaders of the Social Democratic party, most notably B. Šmeral.[37]

Although the declaration of the Czech deputies of May 30, 1917, was still in conflict with the aims of the Czech independence movement abroad because it counted on the continuation of the Habsburg monarchy, it was a step forward. The forces calling for the establishment of an independent Czech state were growing; the amnesty and the return of political prisoners in the summer of 1917 strengthened these tendencies. At the same time, however, the Czech political forces began to differentiate. The group clustered around the periodical *Národ* was gradually developing into a right-wing middle class, strongly nationalistic political party that was "for Kramář"; the group *Česká demokracie* was moving closer to the

National Socials, workers, and the emerging opposition group within the Social Democratic party represented by Hudec and Modráček. However, the vast majority of active politicians wished to preserve a federalized Austria-Hungary.³⁸ Despite all these qualifications, the spring of 1917 represented a turning point in the relations between the home front and the émigrés. It became obvious that every success of the émigrés would noticeably influence Czech policy in Austria. Several such successes were in the offing, largely, because of the internal developments in Russia.³⁹

The First Provisional Government in Russia, headed by Prince George E. Lvov, was committed to continuing the war on the side of the Allies; and its foreign policy included the "liberation of Slavic nations living in Austria-Hungary, unification of Italian and Romanian territories, creation of Czechoslovak and Serbo-Croat states, unification of the Ukranian lands of Austria-Hungary with Russia." These matters were to be discussed and settled at the postwar peace conference.⁴⁰ In March and early April 1917, there was not much apparent difference between this program of the government, in which Miliukov was the minister of foreign affairs, and the program (and slogan) of the Soviets, "peace without annexations and indemnities." (Parts of Russia were occupied by foreign armies.) The Petrograd Soviet, dominated by Mensheviks and Social Revolutionaries, endorsed continuing the war to defend the revolution; this defensive attitude was also endorsed by *Izvestia,* the organ of the Bolsheviks. However, war-weariness progressed. After Lenin's return to Russia, when he proclaimed his "April Theses," the gulf between the Soviets and the Provisional Government began to deepen.⁴¹

For Masaryk the revolution meant strengthening the Entente in its struggle against the Central Powers; and after his arrival in Russia, he rejected outright the slogan of the Soviets, "peace without annexation and indemnities."⁴² As he saw it, peace without annexation meant the *status quo ante bellum,* peace based on the situation as it had existed before the war, and to him this situation was not acceptable. This slogan overlooked the German plan for the reorganization of central Europe and the French demand for the return of Alsace-Lorraine. It also threatened Russia by leaving a large part of Poland in German hands. Thus, at the first of his public appearances on May 29, 1917, Masaryk repudiated the pacificism of Tolstoy and pacifist propaganda, and came out for the continuation and energetic conduct of the war—a war that was "not the greatest evil" thought it was evil. For Masaryk, the real evil was militarism, especially Prussian militarism; thus, he reasoned, the war against the Central Powers was a defensive one, and was both morally justified and politically necessary. Only an Allied victory could force "German-Austrian tsarism" to consent to a peaceful Europe, reorganized on a democratic basis.

Masaryk's arrival in Russia was announced to the Russian public in an article written by Professor N. Jastrebov and published in *Birzheviia Vedomosti* on May 19, 1917. (Jastrebov had translated the fifth part of Masaryk's book, *The Social Question,* published in Russia in 1906. In connection with that publication Masaryk indicated for the first time that he was working on a book dealing with the Russian question, which was, according to him, above all a religious question.[43] The result of this work was his book *Russland und Europa.*) While in Russia, Masaryk was not concerned with religious developments, but was deeply involved in politics. Shortly after his arrival in Petrograd, Masaryk placed himself in charge of a propaganda commission attached to the Russian branch of the CSNC. The main purpose of the commission was to help to propagate pro-Allied views and thus to strengthen the war effort of the Allies.[44]

British agents in Russia kept in touch with Masaryk so that he could transmit "political intelligence" through them to the British government. As he had agreed with Steed in England, Masaryk dictated to a correspondent of the *Times* (London) a report of the situation in Russia, published on June 5, 1917; it reflected Masaryk's disillusionment with the revolution. According to Masaryk, there were no strong personalities in the Provisional Government, which was speaking with many, often contradictory, voices.

In order to carry out his propaganda assignment, Masaryk personally contacted the editors of several Russian papers. Among them were *Rech'* and *Russkia Vedomosti* (organs of the Cadet party), *Birzheviia Vedomosti*, the daily *Viecherniie Vremiia, Volia Naroda* (of the right-wing Social Revolutionary party), and Plekhanov's paper, *Edinstvo.* Later Masaryk cooperated with the "radical-liberal" daily of A. V. Amfiteatrov, *Volnost*, and was listed among its permanent collaborators. On May 24, 1917, under a headline "The Slogan 'without annexation,'" *Viecherniia Vremiia* carried an interview in which Masaryk stated that "peace without annexation means, in fact, status quo ante," and that this would mean that

Alsace-Lorraine and a part of Poland would remain German, not to mention the "German annexation of Austria-Hungary, Bulgaria and Turkey." Should the slogan be implemented, it would mean a German victory; and Germany would then, undoubtedly, reestablish tsarism in Russia.

On June 1, 1917, the Cadet paper, *Rech'*, reported on Masaryk's public speech at Petrograd under the headline, "Socialistic Tolstoyism." On this occasion Masaryk argued against "peace without annexations" and against fraternizing with the enemy on the front, claiming that the moral originator these pacifistic phenomena was Leo N. Tolstoy; he declared that the propagators of peace were actually advocates of Tolstoy's teaching according to which one should not resist evil by force. Masaryk said that the propagandists of this Tolstoy quietism did not know Prussian militarism, and that such a pacifism, though calling ostensibly for humanism, is, in fact, inhuman. Needless to say, Lenin's followers were anything but followers of Tolstoy.

On June 6, 1917, *Birzheviia Vedomosti* carried Masaryk's analysis of the national question, "The Problems of Small Nations and the War." In this article, he declared that there were twenty-seven independent states in Europe, of which only five could be called great. He claimed that the English and French statesmen, as well as President Wilson, had come out in favor of the rights of small nations, and that the aim of the Allies was the "reorganization of Europe on national foundations." But concretely Masaryk named only Poles, Czechoslovaks, and South Slavs as nations that had already been independent and that were bigh enough and had sufficiently "high culture" (especially Czechoslovakia)," to survive: "nations which in all respects—economic, political, cultural—can live in independent states." He also said that the belt of nations in east central Europe had to perform a specific and great role. Since the area represented a danger for European peace, "its reorganization is, in fact, the political aim of this war." He reproached the socialists for not supporting the rights of small nations. Although the socialists had always claimed that they were fighting for the interests of "the little man," wrote Masaryk, they did not seem able to grasp the importance of the national principle in the question of small nations. He claimed that the Allies were defending the equality of small nations, that they were fighting for democracy and progress; and that the Austrians and Germans, on the other hand, were defending imperialistic monarchism and absolutism.

In the June 9, 1917, issue of Plekhanov's *Edinstvo*, under the title "German-Austrian Tsarism for Russian Tsarism," Masaryk associated Austria and Germany with absolutism, claiming that their absolutism was worse than that which had existed in Russia before the revolution. (Before the war Masaryk had held just the opposite viewpoint.) *Vecherniie Vremiia*, on June 16, 1917, carried another interview with Masaryk in which he rejected the idea that the Allies, especially Russia, should discuss peace conditions with Austria-Hungary and Germany. He advocated the most resolute conduct of the war by Russia and a new offensive on the Eastern Front. The same paper carried another interview with Masaryk after the July events in Russia—the Bolshevik rebellion ("a dress rehersal for the big show," as Lenin later called it)—on July 19. Masaryk denounced the demonstrators and stated that "the people who hesitate to fight against Austrians and Germans and who, being fully armed, attack Russian citizens and shoot into them, demonstrate best in whose service they actually are." On August 23, he urged the continuation of the struggle against the Central Powers, in *Kievskaiia Mysl* and in the Romanian monarchistic paper *Romania mare;* and in another Romanian paper, *Miscarea*, on October 11, he called for the dismemberment of Austria-Hungary.

In *Birzheviia Vedomosti*, on October 7, 1917, Masaryk rejected the peace offer of Count Czernin to the Entente Powers and the Pope's offer to act as a mediator in peace negotiations. He connected the two actions and claimed that the Central Powers were instruments of the Pope of Rome, that theocracy was at war with the Entente's democracy. In another interview with the editor of *Vecherniie Vremiia*, reprinted in a French daily at Petrograd, *L'Entente*, September 30, 1917, he also rejected the peace offers and said that the aim of the war must be the dismemberment of Austria-Hungary and a new organization of Europe in which Germany would be encircled by Allied states. As an example of a possible new order in Europe he suggested the possibility of a Bohemian-Polish federation.

According to one of Wiseman's agents in Russia who cooperated closely with Masaryk, W. Somerset Maugham, Masaryk's "original purpose" in going to Russia in May 1917, on behalf of the British ministry of war was "propaganda working through some 12,000 Czech agents in Russia."[45] In fact, Masaryk acted in a dual role: first, as the leader of the Czechoslovak independence movement, and second, as a pro-British propagandist whose mission was to help to keep Russia in the war, that is, to counteract the pacifist propaganda. His role as a British propagandist remained secret for several decades, but his intent to establish a pro-western Czechoslovak state became manifest when such a state materialized in 1918. In both capacities—as a "clandestinte" propagandist and as the apparent leader of the Czechoslovak independence movement—Masaryk pursued what he conceived to be his own interests, not identifying the latter with either British national interests or the cause of Russia. When questioned by Czechs in Russia on his attitude toward Russia, Masaryk said that the Czechs must look for sympathy and support to all the Allies. He stated, "If we had bet on a single card, we would have lost everything, because France and the West would have been against us and for Austria. As far as Russia is concerned, I am a Russophile such as there are few. But I am not a tsarophile and I am not blind. I appreciate what Russia is doing for us." Masaryk expressed his pragmatism when he said, "If I say that we must not bet everything on one card, it is because Russia herself is weak, and perhaps others will decide her fate."[46]

Masaryk, furthermore, tried to separate the Czechoslovak independence movement from the problems created by the Russian Revolution. He was, to be sure, concerned with the decline of military discipline in the Russian army and the growing fraternization with enemy soldiers. Yet he instructed the Czech and Slovak soldiers and prisoners of war in Russia "under no circumstances to interfere with conditions in the Russian army," emphasizing that it was not their task to try to set the Russian army straight.[47] Raising the question "What is our task now?" he answered that the first task was to recruit as many troops as possible in order to be able to build a Czechoslovak army as large as possible. A large army would demonstrate to the whole world that the Czechs and the Slovaks were against the continuation of Austria-Hungary. In order to build a large army, it was necessary to take care of the prisoners of war and induce them to join the army. The second task was "to take care of ourselves;" this meant noninvolvement in Russian domestic affairs. This attitude did not imply any lack of sympathy for the revolution; it meant only that the Czechoslovak troops' mission was not to get mixed up in Russian internal developments. This meant that the Czechoslovak army could not be used for restoring order in Russia; that had to be handled by the Russian themselves.

Masaryk placed first priority on building a large army over which he could exercise as much control as possible. However, he did not have to start from scratch. When he arrived in Russia the Czechoslovak brigade consisted of some 9,000 men and officers, and there were plans to recruit an additional 25,000.[48] The prisoners of war who were admitted into the brigade had to apply, simultaneously, for Russian citizenship, and some of them even converted to the Orthodox religion. However, the names of the regiments—St. Wenceslas and Saints Cyril and Methodius— reflected the Russian government's realization that the Czechs and Slovaks were predominantly Catholics, and products of Catholic culture and tradition. The tsarist government did not intend to change the religious situation in the liberated Czechoslovakia. Consequently, the leaders of the Czech Catholic gymnastic association *Orel* (The Eagle), which competed (not very successfully) with *Sokol,* appealed on February 16, 1916, to the members of their association in Russia to join the brigade, and relatively large numbers of them did so.[49] As has been noted, on March 6, 1917, before the collapse of the tsarist government, the Russian war council approved General Červinka's project for building a large Czechoslovak army from among Czech and Slovak prisoners of war in Russia. The Russian Revolution, however, changed the whole situation.

The First Provisional Government in Russia was much less enthusiastic about recruiting Czech and Slovak prisoners of war into the Czech military formations than the tsarist government had been. Alexander I. Guchkov, minister of war, believed that the prisoners of war were more useful to Russia in factories than in military formations (the Russians did not have a shortage of military manpower; they did have a shortage of labor); and the only reason his proposal to bar the formation of Czechoslovak military units in Russia was not accepted by the government was Miliukov's intervention. The military staff, however, endorsed forming Czechoslovak military units even more strongly than it had before the revolution. When a compromise between the military and the government was reached on the issue of Czechoslovak military units, the government was reorganized and the new minister of war, Alexander Kerensky, stopped the recruitment and came out against the formation of Czechoslovak or any other national (non-Russian) military units.[50] Kerensky, leader of the Labor (*Trud*) party that was close to the Socialist Revolutionaries, and a member of the Petrograd Soviet, condemned the Czechoslovak independence movement in Russia for its prerevolutionary collaboration with the tsarist government. He charged it also with national chauvinism. For Kerensky, the members of the Czechoslovak brigade who were former prisoners of war were traitors to their own country, a bunch of cowards who did not have the courage to fight against the Habsburgs, overthrowing their rule from within as the Russians had done to the Romanovs. He bluntly told Dr. Vácslav Vondrák, "I cannot in any way get enthusiastic about the manner in which your countrymen carry out resistance against their government. After all... they had a possibility to start a revolution at home and overthrow the hated government, but to go to the front and then betray their country and surrender to the enemy—excuse me, but I cannot have any sympathy for such unchivalrous behavior."[51] This attitude was shared by most socialists in Russia; and the leaders of the Czechoslovak independence movement in Russia, including Masaryk, consequently cooled off in their enthusiasm for the Russian Revolution. Masaryk especially resented the high-handedness of the Russian socialists' equation of nationalism with chauvinism, charging them with being simpleminded Marxists, divorced from reality, who were using slogans and phrases that demonstrated their ignorance of real political, national, and social life in the Habsburg empire.[52]

In addition to ideological considerations, Kerensky had practical reasons for his hostility toward the Czechoslovak brigade. He feared, as did the new commander of the Kievan circle, that the Czechoslovak example would lead to the formation of other national military units, such as Polish, Finnish, Estonian, and, especially Ukrainian units. The matter was further complicated by the attempt to transfer thousands of Czechoslovak soldiers and prisoners of war to the Western Front, as had been negotiated by Štefánik in 1916, and again by Masaryk in 1917. Thus, Kerensky discontinued recruitment for the Czechoslovak brigade; he even ordered its disbanding,[53] which however, was not immediately carried out.

The turning point in the process of building the Czechoslovak armed forces in Russia was the battle at Zborov, during the July 1917, offensive. This offensive was officially described as an action that had to be taken in order to defend the revolution and to bolster the morale of the Russian troops. It was opposed by the Bolsheviks and the Petrograd Soviet, now led by the Bolsheviks. Although the offensive was a failure, the

Czechoslovak brigade was cited by headquarters for its bravery and achievement. The Czechoslovak brigade broke through three lines of trenches and captured fortified enemy positions west and southwest of the small town of Zborov. The unit captured 62 enemy officers, 3,150 soldiers, 15 pieces of artillery, and many machine guns, most of which were turned against the enemy. Kerensky, who visited the front, was very much impressed with the performance of the Czechoslovak brigade. He promoted its commander to general and promised to give full support to the efforts to organize a Czechoslovak army in Russia. General Červinka, who was of Czech origin, was then told by his superiors that he should organize as many Czech troops as he possibly could.[54]

The participation of the Czechoslovak brigade in the July offensive made it possible to organize recruitment of prisoners of war into the Czechoslovak army. The battle of Zborov was a great victory for the Czechs; at the same time, it indicated the beginning of political stratification within the military units. On the one hand, one segment of the unit followed the Bolshevik line, opposed to the offensive, refusing to take part in the battle; on the other hand a company of Czech former prisoners of war was established and attached to the staff of the Eighth Army of General Lavr Kornilov.[55] This company of shock troopers, fighting under the black Kornilov flag, was commanded by a Czech officer. Meanwhile, Masaryk and his council tried to build an army that would support neither the revolutionary Bolsheviks nor the counterrevolutionary (or any other) forces in Russia, an army loyal to the CSNC, i.e., to him. It soon became apparent, however, that the vast majority of Czech and Slovak prisoners of war, who had been drafted into the Austro-Hungarian armies, were not interested in serving in Masaryk's army or any other army.

Permission to organize a second division of the Czechoslovak army was granted on July 13, 1917,[56] but the number of recruits was not as great as Masaryk and his agents had expected. Despite the recruiting commissars' exaggerations about the glory and military significance of the battle of Zborov, and despite Masaryk's emotional, pious, and patriotic appeals, the recruitment campaign had limited success. Between May and September 1917 recruiting officers (commissars) visited 180 places where they were able to locate a total of 13,652 Czech and Slovak prisoners of war, among whom they recruited 1,500 volunteers, or eleven and a half percent. Approximately five percent of the prisoners of war proclaimed their loyalty to the Habsburg monarchy and were openly hostile to the recruiting officers; of the rest, about half were indifferent and the other half, although sympathetic to the cause of Czechoslovak independence, lacked the courage to join the Legion, as the Czechoslovak army was now often called. Also, about 150 of Masaryk's "agents" attempted to recruit Czechs and Slovaks for membership in the Russian branch of the CSNC, and the result of the drive was reported at a Moscow conference on August 30, 1917. Among the 47,271 Czechs and Slovaks contacted, only 13,518 (12,598 Czechs and 920 Slovaks) joined the organization.[57]

Although very few Czechs and Slovaks in Russia dared to challenge Masaryk's authority, the majority of them stood aloof from the action led by him. Some of those who joined the Legin were unsure of the correctness of their decision and sensed the unreality of the situation. Suspicions and fears were apparent; despite the ostracism of Dürich, personal attacks and ideological disputes still went on within the Czechoslovak independence movement in Russia. The "old Russia" was gone, and the "new Russia" did not generate much confidence. There was a lack of trust everywhere; Masaryk was suspected by some to be in foreign employ, and, in turn, he tried to silence his critics by insinuating that they might be German or Austrian agents. The polarization of political opinion among the soldiers promoted uncertainty and fear. The deep-seated subconscious fear was described by a Legionnaire, František Langer, in *Čechoslovák* on June 23, 1917. "We are afraid of all that is going on around us," he wrote. "We are afraid for our freedom, because it seems to us that Russia is weakening and falling apart.... Why were we not afraid... before the Russian revolution?... Now... everything that is happening appears to us to be subversive and destructive. It is so because we do not have enough faith in the competence of democracy, we do not believe that the democratic government is able to come to grips with the schism that is threatening... [if there is to be a hope for us] we have to transform our efforts into a heroic deed...."[58]

A newspaper published in Kiev in 1917, *Revoluce,* was more blunt. It openly protested against the "terror" to which Dürich and Král were exposed; and on September 17, 1917, it wrote, "The Russian revolution disappointed the Czechs." In its last issue, on October 13, 1917, the paper proclaimed that" in contrast to what some Russians saw, "we have not seen here tyranny before the revolution, and freedom after the revolution."[59] These were danger signals reflecting the fear within.

Masaryk did not share these fears and apprehensions. He saw in the army to be built in Russia the foundation of the future Czechoslovak state and a lever of power for the movement that he led. Since the state was to be pro-western, part of the army had to fight on the Western Front. When he and the secretary of the Russian branch of the CSNC, Jiří Klecanda, negotiated the formation of the Czechoslovak army corps in the headquarters of General Alexis Brusilov, they demanded the transfer of some of the soldiers and prisoners of war to France. They also demanded that the Czechoslovak army in Russia be subordinated to the political leadership of the Russian branch of the CSNC and that it be used only on the front against Austria-Hungary and Germany, not in internal fights in Russia. Finally, they demanded the enlargement of the Czechoslovak brigade into a division, to be united with a second division that was being formed in the rear.[60]

In his efforts to build a strong Czechoslovak army in Russia, Masaryk had the support and cooperation of the Russian branch of the CSNC, which also approved his political program, embodied in the slogan "war till the victorious end." The army was to demonstrate the Czech and Slovak participation in the war on the side of the Entente. Its recognition as a separate army was to prepare for the eventual recognition of the Czechoslovak state. It was to be the CSNC's main weapon in the effort to achieve diplomatic recognition of Czechoslovak independence.[61]

In the summer of 1917 such an independence was not in sight, and the prospect of it was bleak. On August 30, 1917, Masaryk admitted at a conference of the Russian branch of the CSNC that he could not guarantee that his organization would be "represented at the peace conferences."[62] He was aware that Austria-Hungary was making peace moves behind the scenes and that the Allies were interested in making a separate peace with the new young emperor.

On April 11, 1917, Lloyd George learned from the French prime minister, Alexander Ribot, about the letter the French president had received from Emperor Charles, through the mediation of Prince Sixtus of Bourbon-Parma.[63] An era of secret negotiations and high hopes began. In July and August 1917, the public pronouncements of British cabinet members took a conciliatory stand on Austria-Hungary that marked a very definite withdrawal from the war aims stated in the Allied note to President Wilson in January. The British now pointed out that the Allied had not pledged themselves to any particular form of liberation for the oppressed nationalities of the Habsburg empire. When at the end of the year Drummond of the Foreign Office was asked to draft a new memorandum on Austria-Hungary, he noted that since he had drafted his report in February, the situation had changed for the worse because of the collapse of Russia and the defeats suffered by Italy. Influenced by suggestions made by Count Michael Karolyi to British agents, Drummond proposed the creation of a federated Austria consisting of four parts: German Austria, Hungary, Poland, and a Yugoslav state. The Habsburg empire in his project was to be built along the same lines as the Hohenzollern empire. The Serbian dynasty, ruling the south Slav state, would "be placed somewhat in the same position towards the Emperor of Austria as the Kings of Bavaria and Saxony are towards the German Emperor."[64] According to this proposal, the Czechs would remain under direct Habsburg rule, and the position of the Slovaks in Hungary would not change, either.

In this situation Masaryk demonstrated a great deal of stubbornness, determination, and faith in his own mission. In Great Britain he was supported in his efforts by R. Seton-Watson, who, in 1917 and for the duration of the war, was employed in the Political Intelligence Department and wrote regular commentaries on Austria-Hungary.[65] Seton-Watson, Steed, and others proposed that Masaryk be appointed as a Russian expert at the Supreme War Council at Paris; formally, they did not succeed, but Masaryk was considered by some influential people in and out of the Allied governments as an expert on Russia, and his opinions were solicited.[66]

In Russia Masaryk carried on his propaganda campaign, denouncing international capitalism and the Vatican as the two principal enemies of the Czechoslovak independence movement,[67] and urging Czech and Slovak prisoners of war to volunteer for service in the Legion. On August 6, 1917, Masaryk embarked on a journey to prison camps to agitate anew for the prisoners' enlistment in the Czechoslovak army; and during August 17-21, he visited the units of the Czech brigade in the company of its commander, Colonel Mamontov. In his speeches to the troops, Masaryk claimed that the Entente powers were fighting for the right of self-determination of small nations. He called his action abroad a revolution against Austrian and German imperialism, and the war a struggle of Slavdom against Germandom; the war of the Allies he called a struggle of the republican principle with the monarchistic principle (and he left Great Britain, Italy, and Romania out of the picture); he emphasized the duty of the whole of Slavdom to stand up against Germandom. In one breath he called himself a pacifist and appealed to humanitarian principles, and, at the same time, asserted that there was no possibility of peace with the German nation. "It is necessary to fight [the Germans] with knife, with knife; yes, with knife, knife, up to the end; and this is not inhuman!"[68]

On this occasion, at Velka Berezna, Mamontov, confirmed by Masaryk as "Czechoslovak Colonel" and commander of the brigade, stood up and as "a representative of the Hussite god's troopers of the twentieth century"—as he called himself—proclaimed Czechoslovakia a republic and Masaryk its president and dictator.[69] Needless to say, most of the Legionnaires saw Masaryk as a symbol of the Czech and Slovak revolutionary democratic movement for independence, and the charismatic Czech leader impressed them so much that they followed his orders unquestioningly. Thus, Masaryk was not too much discouraged by the peace overtures; he continued to build an army, hoping that he would, one day, become its real commander-in-chief, and would be able to induce the Allied powers to recognize him as the leader of a new Czechoslovak state, thus sanctioning a new order in east central Europe. Despite the hopelessness of the situation in the summer and fall of 1917, internal developments in Russia and Austria-Hungary in 1918 resolved Masaryk's problems.

CHAPTER SEVEN

PEACE OVERTURES, PROPAGANDA, AND THE BUILDING OF THE CZECHOSLOVAK ARMY

In order to weaken their principal enemy, Germany, the Entente powers were prepared to conclude a separate peace with Austria-Hungary. In March 1917, Emperor Charles contacted the French president through his brother-in-law Sixtus of Bourbon-Parma. By the beginning of August 1917, the Austrian minister of foreign affairs, Czernin, was willing to entertain English or French proposals for a separate peace. In August 1917, Pope Benedict XV came out with his peace proposals. One month earlier a peace resolution had been passed by majority vote in the German Reichstag. The slogan adopted by the Provisional Government in Russia was "peace without annexation and indemnities;" and the American president, Woodrow Wilson, used the phrase "peace without victors and vanquished," when he declared war on Germany on April 5, 1917. The Allies wished to isolate Germany, and were prepared to agree to the preservation of the Habsburg monarchy in order to attain a separate peace with it. Such an agreement would have frustrated Masaryk's objectives and hopes.[1]

The secret Austro-Allied negotiations and the attempts made by the western allies to separate Austria-Hungary from Germany were well-known. Much less known are the Allies apprehensions and concerns about peace agitation and "German intrigues in Russia." The story of Vladimir

Peace Overtures 181

Illich Ullanov, alias N. Lenin, his trip across Germany in a sealed train car, and his subsequent arrival at the Finland station at Petrograd via Scandinavia, his "April Theses," his slogan "Peace, Bread and Land!" and his efforts to make Russia leave the war, need not be retold here. But the British response to the German-Bolshevik agitation in Russia and the Czech involvement in it has to be mentioned, since it is still little known, and most of the evidence is, unfortunately, still locked in the secret files of the British intelligence service. Yet the Wiseman Papers and other documents in the Colonel House collectin throw some light on the less than successful clandestine operations of British intelligence in Russia, and explain, to some extent, the mysterious behavior of Masaryk in Russia before and after the Bolshevik Revolution. History has shown conclusively that Thomas Garrigue Masaryk, alias Thomas G. Marsden, was no match for Lenin, if he ever had been intended as an antidote to the Bolshevik leader.

According to a report entitled "Russia," by William Wiseman, written in mid-May 1917,[2] it was "a common knowledge that the Germans are counting on their propaganda to bring about a separate peace with Russia," but the details of "their intrigues are not so well-known." The British intelligence had "reliable information that the Germans are organizing from every neutral country parties of Russian refugees, largely Jewish socialists. These parties are sent to Petrograd where they are organized by German agents posing as advanced Socialists." German agents "have already been at work in the United States, and are sending Russian-Jewish Socialists back to Petrograd who are either knowingly or unknowingly working in the German cause." There was a great need to combat this propaganda, Wiseman said, but the counterpropaganda would have to be "entirely unofficial, and very secretly organized, as any idea of Government support would ruin the scheme." The United States "is the best situated country from which to organize a counter-propaganda," since the Germans have been able to make the Russian people "somewhat suspicious of the aims of the French and English."

The scheme that Wiseman designed called for organizing the counterpropaganda "under one head in America," who would be the only person knowing the details. It involved sending six or seven different missions to Petrograd, each entirely unknown to the others, and all working along distinct lines toward a common object. None of these parties would attempt to interfere in any way with Russian domestic questions. The whole object of the scheme was first, "to expose present German intrigues and their undoubted connection with the late [i.e., tsarist] reactionary government;" and, second, "to persuade the Russians to attack the Germans with all their might, and thus accomplish the overthrow of the Hohenzollern dynasty and autocracy in Berlin."

Among the people who had brought the situation in Russia to Wiseman's attention was Emanuel Victor Voska, whose "friends" had arrived from there and had urged sending telegrams to Russia from America, since "all foreign cables have a tremendous effect on the people especially if they emanate from America."[3] Voska also suggested sendin about twelve men from the Bohemian National Alliance and the Slovak Leage to Russia, at the expense of the British and American governments, to talk to the people "and work among the Slavic elements in Russia, and explain to them the danger of the German propaganda. At least two of these people should be dependable socialists who would work among the socialists. Of course, all of them would speak Russian." Also, Wiseman believed, individuals from Polish, Russian, and Lithuanian organizations should be dispatched to Russia. Each of these missions would act separately and independently of the others; no mission would know the identity of members of the other missions. The assure the secrecy of the project, only one person would know the whole scheme.

In describing these missions, Wiseman begins with his favorite agent, Victor (Voska), whom he calls "the leader of the most important CZECH secret society in America," and who would go "with the object of organizing the Czechs and Bohemians [sic] in Russia." According to the leader of that "secret Society," Voska, there are "220,000 Bohemian prisoners of war who surrendered to Russia early in the war, about 50 percent of whom are skilled mechanics, and almost all of them entirely reliable from the Allied point of view. If these prisoners could be released they, with the other Czechs now in Russia, would form the nucleus of one of the most important and most bitterly anti-German societies. It should be remembered that the Germans have managed to secure control of the most important secret societies in Russia, and it is necessary that this German influence should be exposed and counter-Societies organized, if necessary." The other missions would be leaders from Slovak and Polish secret societies in America, an unnamed "Nihilist" leader, and a fiery, demagogic orator and anti-German Russian monk, Illiador. Altogether six or seven different missions would be sent to Petrograd. Officially, they would be sent to Russia by different philanthropic Americans who were eager to assist the new Russia; all of them would be separately given "the name of some American millionaire who would help them with funds," although in fact the financing would be done, preferably, by the American government. Wiseman also hoped to use large numbers of "intelligent Russians" for the same propaganda purposes.[4] (In *Spy and Counter-Spy* Voska *never even mentions* William Wiseman; he does, however, emphasize his own cooperation with Charles R. Crane, whom he credits with serving as liaison between his organization and the U.S. government. According to Voska, it was Crane who urged him to go to Russia. Voska claims that Crane believed that the Czechs in Russia could be organized for the purpose of counteracting German influence "just as we had organized the Czechs in the United States.")

Voska was sounded out "with regard to his going to Russia to organize a system similar to that" which he had in America. Although he would be inconvenienced "from a business point of view," he realized "the urgency of the case" and was "quite keen on going." Voska, the Wiseman report says, "would be able to obtain ample assistance in Russia as there are plenty of his people there. He hopes that his suggestion as to sending twelve delegates from the Bohemian National Alliance and Slovak League would be carried out, as he regards it as highly important and apart from that it would furnish an excuse for his visiting Russia." Among the other people who were considered for similar missions in Russia were B. K. Balutis, editor of the Chicago *Lietuva*, a Lithuanian whose wife was Russian and who spoke "Russian better than Lithuanian;" and a Pole, V. K. Raczkowski.[5]

Wiseman discussed his proposal unofficially with U.S. government officials. Since the war situation required gathering political intelligence, "The Inquiry," headed by Colonel Edward M. House, distinct from the State Department and reporting directly to the president, was established. In the interchange of political intelligence, Wiseman dealt largely with the American colonel. Now the British wanted the U.S. government to finance the "counter-propaganda against the Jewish-Socialists pacifists" in Russia, since the United States was "the best country" in which such a campaign could be organized.[6]

Wiseman's scheme was presented to Colonel House as an authoritative British proposal, and to the British Foreign Office as an authoritative American proposal.[7] The British approved the proposal in principle, but they preferred to have the American government handle the matter, because they had already spent large sums of money on propaganda and intelligence in Russia. President Wilson, influenced by reports on "Germany's intrigues in Russia," was "anxious to try the scheme as soon as possible." The U.S. government paid $75,000 to Wiseman, who requested an equal amount from the British government. Wiseman was to be the only agent who would not have to "report to House or anyone as to methods employed but only as to results."[8]

Although the British hoped that the U.S. government would sponsor (finance) the project, Colonel House insisted on implementing the counter propaganda scheme in Russia jointly with the British, "since the scheme depends on help of certain Slavic societies for dealing with whom Wiseman is necessary."[9] Since Wiseman knew House's position, he was skeptical about the U.S. government's willingness to underwrite the whole project, and the Foreign Office therefore agreed to cosponsor the venture by placing $75,000 to Wiseman's credit at J. P. Morgan & Co. Thus, in the second half of June 1917, the project would proceed as planned, with the details yet to be worked out.

Toward the end of June 1917, a bogus "Committee, of Slav Origin, for Russia" was established in the United States, consisting of six Czechs and Slovaks, headed by Emanuel V. Voska, secretary of the Bohemian National Alliance and director of the Slav Press Bureau in New York. The members of the committee gave the following reasons for their proposed undertaking:[10] (1) No element can influence the present Russian government and the Russian people as well as men representing American citizens who are the nationals of small Slavic nations oppressed by the Austro-Hungarian government. (2) The small nations, especially the Czechs, Slovaks, and South Slavs, have more interest than any other racial group in helping to stabilize conditions in Russia, and can impress this fact upon the Russian people more forcefully than anybody else. (3) Because of their racial kinship, they understand best the nature and character of the Russian people, can speak Russian, and are loved by the Russians. (4) The present Russian government has authorized the formation of an independent Czecho-Slovak army that probably will number about 250,000 men. This army consists of Czecho-Slovak prisoners who originally were drafted into the Austrian army, but surrendered to the Russians. The permission to organize an independent army is tantamount to a recognition of Bohemian independence, which at least implicitly is "also recognized in the Flag Day speech of President Wilson." (5) Immediately upon the outbreak of the world war, American citizens of Slav origin frustrated German attempts to organize strikes in munition factories, and prevented many criminal attempts aimed at the interests of the United States. (6) The government of the United States has proclaimed the right of small nations to govern themselves. (7) It is in the interest of the United States and the Allies that the influence of the Slavic element and its knowledge of Russian conditions be employed to further the common cause of all the nations opposed to German militarism and German aggression. (8) The suggested members of the Committee of Six are among "the best and ablest citizens of the United States, whose judgment and reliability is known also in important official American circles."

It is hardly surprising that Wiseman was most impressed with the statement, repeated in the document, that the "Russian Government has already agreed to the formation of a Czecho-Slovak Army which will probably number 250,000 men from among the Czechs and Slovaks now serving in the Russian Army and the Czech officers who have surrendered from the Austrians to the Russians. This means to say that the Russian Government recognize these people as a political force and are anxious to help them."[11] This statement by Wiseman, however, was based on information received from Voska, who, like Masaryk, was a propagandist and who liked to exaggerate. The truth of the matter was that on June 30, 1917, when the report was written, the future of the Czechoslovak army in Russia was uncertain, because Kerensky had ordered that the Czech brigade be disbanded, as the preceding chapter has noted.

While it is true that there were some 250,000 Czech and Slovak prisoners of war in Russia toward the end of 1916,[12] not quite 4,000 of them had served in the Czech brigade.[13] The tsarist war council, to be sure, had approved the formation of a Czechoslovak army on March 6, 1917, but the First Provisional Government, especially Guchkov and Kerensky, opposed it. Kerensky approved the formation of the Second Division only after the battle of Zborov in July. But even when the Russian government gave permission to form an army, it was unrealistic to expect that all the Czech and Slovak prisoners of war in Russia would volunteer for service in it, or in any army. These prisoners had been conscripted into the Austro-Hungarian armies, and most of them had no desire to fight their compatriots as the Czechs did in the battle of Zborov, where they fought against Czech regiments of the Austrian army. Although Masaryk, in accordance with his plans and the wishes of the British War Office, tried to recruit as many volunteers as possible, between May 1917, when he arrived in Russia, and September 1917, only 21,760 prisoners were persuaded to join the Legion.[14] (This meant that approximately ten percent of the Czech and Slovak prisoners of war joined the Czechoslovak army.) In September and October 1917, when the situation in Russia became chaotic, a new recruiting drive was launched, with the result that toward the end of 1917 there were some 40,000 volunteers (including Czecho-Russians and Russian officers) who formed the hard core of the Legion.[15] This was a far cry from the 250,000 man army. But though Wiseman's scheme emphasized propaganda, his interest in the Czechoslovak troops was understandable: there are situations in which even the best propaganda is no substitute for a military force.

On July 12, 1917, Wiseman had worked out the details of the Voska mission. In order to have a credible cover, Voska "will write a letter to the Secretary of State, announcing his departure in the company of other members of the Committee of American Citizens of Slav Origin to Petrograd for the purpose of studying conditions in Russia. In his letter he will offer services of his Committee, as American citizens, to the State Department." The State Department would approve the mission, and would issue passports to Voska and his fellow travellers.[16] The same document discussed the "perfecting of arrangements for the forwarding of M[augham]'s reports and cables through the U.S. Embassy;" and listed the names and addresses of the members of Voska's group. (W. Somerset Maugham, one of Wiseman's agents currently in Switzerland, was also to be dispatched to Petrograd, but his work would be independent of Voska's four-member group.)

On July 19, 1917, a list of code names for the clandestine Maugham-Voska expedition was completed. Voska was "Victor"; Ven Švarc, assistant city attorney of Cleveland, Ohio, was "Arnold"; Reverend A. B. Koukol, president of the Slavonic Emigration Institute, New York, was "Bennett"; and Joseph Martínek, editor of the socialist paper, *Dělnické listy*, Cleveland, Ohio, was "Smith." Among the other code names were "Marcus" for Masaryk, "Long" for Štefánik, "Davis" for Lenin, "Cole" for Trotsky, "Warring Co." for the Russian government, etc. The password was "Friend of Mr. King of New York," and "should V[ictor] have occasion to wire about W. S. M[augham], he will call him IVAN."[17] The main purpose of the operation, in addition to the espionage and counterespionage that were Voska's speciality, was to combat the German-financed peace propaganda of the Bolsheviks in order to keep Russia in the war.

Before his departure for Russia, Voska was instructed to go to Petrograd to establish there "a branch of the Slav Press Bureau," and to "organize the Czechs and Slovaks of the Empire to keep Russia in the war." He was guaranteed the reimbursement of "any reasonable expense;" he had "the greatest freedom of action;" but he had to cooperate with "the Inter-Allied Committee in Petrograd," and, above all, he had to hurry.[18] Before he left the United States, Voska received two checks amounting to $4,000.[19] Voska and his companions also had to act as liaison officers between Masaryk and Maugham. The British writer came to Petrograd with instructions "to get in touch with parties hostile to the government and devise a scheme that would keep Russia in the war and prevent the Bolsheviks, supported by the Central Powers, from seizing power."[20]

When Voska arrived in Petrograd at the beginning of September, Masaryk helped him to establish a branch of the Slav Press Bureau, which was to make use of the Masaryk-led CSNC and its 1,200 branches with some 70,000 members, and "the 89,000 Czech soldiers in the Russian army" who were "also practically under his [Masaryk's] control."[21] (It is apparent that these figures were given to Maugham by Masaryk and that they were highly inflated.) The British agents were able to use the services of Czechs who crossed the Austro-German lines and then returned to the Russian lines. (As Maugham put it, "some Czechs are reported to have made four or five such trips. Czech agents have been used for trips to Germany....")[22]

Voska met in Russia many members of the Allied intelligence service with whom he had collaborated in the United States. They included professors, writers, and even "a few prominent politicians," all of whom came to work against German "separate peace" propaganda and against German espionage. Among agents with this mission Voska lists Masaryk,

Madame Pankhurst, V. Burtsev, and Crane. The latter came to Russia as a member of the Root mission dispatched there by the U.S. government; Masaryk and Voska were in close contact with him. Some of Voska's people, e.g., Čermák, Klecanda and Pavlů, were put in touch with the Second Bureau—the inter-Allied committee coordinating the intelligence activities of western Allied agents in Russia. Although Masaryk asked Voska and the other members of his team "to keep hands off the Legion," since the latter was, according to Masaryk, "a guest in the country," the Czech-American intelligence officer was able to utilize Masaryk's own military intelligence in Russia, and his "boys acted with ruthlessness which the situation demanded."[23] Voska claims that Koukol and Švarc rounded up "twelve hundred good men, available for either secret service or propaganda." In Petrograd Voska met "for the first time W. Somerset Maugham, English novelist," who acted as his "liaison with the British."[24]

Voska liked to boast and exaggerate. Although he stayed in Russia for only a few weeks—he left Russia for Sweden and London at the end of September—he claims that he was able to train so many propagandists that he would have been able "to flood the streets and squares with orators of Czech blood and Russian by birth," but he was prevented from doing so by the inter-Allied committee.[25] According to Voska, the order that he received said that "the people are tired of speeches and are no longer influenced by them;" only written material should be used in propaganda. But, Voska says, the use of pamphlets was meaningless, because "only 4 percent of the Russian people could read—and of these at least half couldn't do it without moving their lips."[26] (Before the war at least 40 percent of the Russians were literate.) Voska's description of the mission is not very accurate; however, one of the members of his team, Reverend Koukol, gives a more sober and more contemporary account of its experience in Russia, details of which will be given later. He says that the mission arrived in Petrograd on September 2, "that is only two weeks before Korniloff's attempted coup d'etat, which was practically the last desperate attempt to establish order in Russia and to preserve her as a fighting power;" and that the turmoil that followed hampered its activity.[27]

Late in September 1917, Voska left Russia for Stockholm and London to work on a "Report and Suggestions on Propaganda Work in Russia," submitted to His Excellency Sir Edward Carson, member of the War

Cabinet, and the Honorable Colonel E. M. House, on November 6, 1917, the day before the Kerensky government was toppled.[28] In this long document Voska says that there is "a need of propaganda in a great style" in Russia, "in conjunction with an extensive propaganda in the Northern countries" where the Germans "after their successful game in the Balkans, begin to use the same tactics." The German government "gives millions at the disposal of their organizations, and agents in Russia and Scandinavia. Besides the organization of Lenin and Trotsky in Russia, there is also the organization of Furstenberg and K. Radek in Sweden." The Germans "have always had strong organizations among their numerous colonists in Russia," says Voska they had agents there under the old regime and were not surprised by the revolution in March. Voska believes that "it is imperative for us to speak louder than the German agents, to do more and better work than they are doing, and at the same time paralyze, frustrate and destroy their propaganda." He describes the Russian people as "endowed with all the virtues of a good child. They are trustful, soft in their nature and kind-hearted." Therefore, it has been rather easy for the Germans "to gain the faith of the Russian people, who, moreover, through sudden events became naively highly-strung and easily accessible to inconsistent and contradictory theories which lead them astray."

Hitherto the Russian people "have listened only to the apostles of hatred toward England," says the report. "Now it is necessary that they should listen to acknowledged English spokesmen of affection to Russia and world democracy." Such spokesmen must make themselves heard in Russia, not merely in Petrograd. English and American action in Russia "should be united and conducted by a *single organization* with common funds," because work done by many organizations cannot be so successful. Voska proposes three kinds of activities: (1) film propaganda; (2) lectures; and (3) other means, including distribution of books and journals. He proposes to use the Czechoslovak organizations in Russia to distribute propaganda, and he urges support of the Slav Press Bureau, which has branches in the United States, Russia, and other countries. The Czechoslovak organizations, Voska says, maintain friendly connections with other Slav organizations, and they alone, represent over 34,000 members, organized in more than 1,200 branches" in Russia. In addition to these branches, there are also 300 representatives in places where there are no branches, "so that they have centers in some 1,500 places." Furthermore, there is the Czechoslovak army," through which the other Czecho-Slovak organizations can keep in contact with the Russian army." Since the Czechoslovaks are friendly with Russia as well as the western Allies, and since they know that the destruction of German imperialism is "a necessary condition for the future development of the Czecho-Slovak nation," their organizations would be glad to "carry out the work of anti-German propaganda."

Among the means to be used in this propaganda Voska lists "systematically following the press and polemically replying to every pro-German article that may appear in the Russian press; attending lectures, meetings, and sermons in Churches (where also German propaganda is active) and by skilfully arguing with the speakers' views and opinions; supply, through special bureaus established for that purpose, material to German colonists and their organizations in Russia, German and Magyar prisoners of war, their organizations and press." Furthermore, Voska recommends infiltrating "the secret organizations of German agents, and by frustrating the criminal German spy activities by means of information thus obtained just as it was done by the Bohemian organizations in America." Finally, there is the field of hard intelligence. Voska proposes to use "the Czech volunteers who are well-organized and who are scattered as interpreters along the whole Russian front, for cross examination of German and Magyar prisoners of war, on which grounds systematic reports about the military and economic situation may be obtained."

Voska points out that part of this work "is already being carried out and will be financed exclusively by the Czecho-Slovak organizations." Since the regular income of these organizations is not sufficient to meet all expenses, "the Czecho-Slovak National Council issued a Czecho-Slovak Revolutionary Loan of 20 million francs which will be subscribed by the Czechs and Slovaks in America, Russia, England, France and Italy, and the Czecho-Slovak National Council earnestly hopes that the Governments of those countries will not put any obstacles in the way of this loan."

In the conclusion of his report Voska urges that the work must be done "rapidly so that results may be noticeable before the forthcoming elections in Russia at which the future fate of Russia and her attitude toward the Allies will be decided." He recommends giving full support to the "Centre Party" composed of "Cossacks and the patriotic elements which will have the support of the strongest men in Russia" and which can bridge the gap between extreme left and right. (It is not clear what he means by the "Centre Party"; however, his mention of Kaledin, Savinkov, and Plekhanov indicates that he meant the Cossacks, the Socialist Revolutionary party, right-wing Mensheviks, and similar groups.) He recommends supporting this party, "military help not excepting," but "only in return for a compensation." The Allies have "ample time" to grasp "the reigns of the Russian situation," but now they must act immediately and decisively to combat the activity of "the army of German agents." In order to do so, he proposes to establish a joint Anglo-American committee composed of "the most eminent English and American people acquainted with Russia, led by the chief Government representatives. This body would form the central organization of all propaganda work in Russia and Scandinavia, and would work in conjunction with the Czecho-Slovak and other small Slav nations organizations. The selection of workers should be made so that the same people can work in Russia after the war in different branches of trade and industries in the interest of Great Britain and America respectively." However, his praise for "the results of the work" obtained by himself and his Czechoslovak compatriots as "the best proofs and guarantee that the British and American Government can with the entire confidence entrust the organization of this work in Russia" to him—modesty was not one of his virtues—must have fallen upon deaf ears: the Bolsheviks seized power at Petrograd before anyone could have acted upon Voska's recommendations.

Voska's scheme of large-scale propaganda under his direction, aimed at preventing a Bolshevik takeover, now became meaningless. Since he was of no use to the British in Russia, Voska was sent by his superior, Wiseman, to the United States, though his coworkers stayed in Russia for another few months. Rev. Koukol wrote about their experience:[29]

> ...we arrived in Russia at a time when it was becoming clear that Russian matters were approaching their crisis...and...these conditions nearly paralyzed our entire activity. The very fact that after the fall of Riga the Czecho-Slovak National Council, on whose cooperation we principally counted, began to take steps for removal from Petrograd to Moscow caused us considerable difficulties in collecting the preliminary data concerning our local organizations

and in preparing a correct list of them. It also prevented our workers in Russia, especially those in the Petrograd offices of our organization—in spite of their desire to do so—to give us that cooperation which was absolutely necessary to us and upon which we had to depend to successfully prosecute our undertaking. Thus, e.g., the investigations of several cases, such as that of Mme. Sumenson, Mme de Cramme, Baron Rosen, Posse, etc., in which we started to get some evidence, had to be given up because the men detailed to follow them had to leave Petrograd.

In spite of the uncertain prospects, we continued our preparations for the establishment of a centre from which to conduct a systematic propaganda. As you know already from Mr. Voska's report, our intention was to establish a branch of our Slav Press Bureau in Petrograd and use it as a means in conducting a pro-Ally propaganda in Russia. Besides our own workers, we planned to have an advisory committee composed of some of the most prominent Russian journalists and political leaders. I had already secured the cooperation of the following men: Professor Yastreboff, of Petrograd University, Nicholas Sokoloff, a close friend of Prof. Miliukoff and co-editor of the *Rietch,* Pitirin Sorokin, a prominent Social Revolutionist and member of the editorial staff of the *Volia Naroda,* Vladimir Burtseff, and Professor Adrianoff. The last named was to act as the Russian Director of the Bureau, for which position he was eminently qualified by his experience and his wide connections in the journalistic world. Professor Adrianoff used to be the assistant editor of the *Russkaya Volia* and acted as Petrograd correspondent of the Moscow *Russkoye Slovo.*

Along with these preparations we were also getting ready some of the literature for the proposed propaganda. To start with, we intended to publish a series of short pamphlets and a series of picture postal cards. These were to be distributed among the soldiers as well as among the people in cities and villages. For this purpose we had already assured the cooperation of a Russian organization which was engaged in the work of supplying reading matter to the soldiers at the front. Besides this work, the Bureau was to maintain a journalistic propaganda by furnishing articles and information to newspapers and other periodicals.

Peace Overtures

We also planned to organize a clearing house for information regarding the activities of German agents in Russia, as well as, regarding conditions in Germany and Austria. This information was to be gathered: (1) through our organizations in Russia, through which we would have been able to reach more than 1200 different localities scattered in all parts of Russia; (2) through a correspondence bureau in Stockholm, or some other neutral European city, in charge of our men; (3) through the foreign branch of the official intelligence bureau (kontra razviedka) which at that time—end of October—was being reorganized and in which we had already made arrangements to have one or more of our men; (4) through the military intelligence bureau at the front, in which a great number of our men were employed as interpreters and in other capacities. Considerable correspondence had been conducted and many conferences had been held in preparation of this work. In order to establish personal contact with some of the people whom we wanted to enlist in this work, I made a trip to Moscow, Kieff and to the headquarters of our army in Volhynia. In this connection, in order to make my report complete, I beg to state that my colleagues, Mr. Svarc and Mr. Martinek, made trips, one to Helsingfors and the other to Stockholm, of which they made reports to Mr. M[augham].

The Bolshevik revolution upset our plans not only because it disconcerted the people on whose cooperation we counted so that, for a time at least, they were not able to decide upon any action, but principally because it disturbed the material conditions of life in Russia to such an extent as to make it extremely difficult to maintain any regular communication. The only thing that remained for us to do was to watch the course of events and the activities of the Bolshevik leaders. These observations led us to the conclusion that Bolsheviks were being used—to say the least—as tools of the German government for the purpose of destroying the Russian army and navy. This conclusion was sustained especially by the fact that among the men closest to the Bolshevik leaders were many Germans, notably such well known German agents as Karl Radek and Parvus (Hoelflund) [sic]. Another fact worth noting was the presence among the Bolsheviks of many persons who used to be identified with the most reactionary activities of the autocratic regime. This tended to create a strong suspicion that the monarchistic forces also hoped to profit by the havoc resulting from the clumsy experiments of the radical revolutionaries.

During the latter part of December we succeeded in getting one of our men, Frank Stilip, into the Bureau of Propaganda which the Bolsheviks organized in their Commissariat of Foreign Affairs. Arrangements were also made that all important information gathered by our organization should be reported to Lt. Commander McLaren or his representative through Mr. Vladimir Hurban. Mr. Hurban has resided in Russia for ten years, had served in the Russian army from the beginning of the present war and had behind him an excellent record as officer of the intelligence department in the General Staff.

As to the situation in general, it is my opinion that no matter how bad things in Russia may appear, it should not be given up as entirely lost to the cause of the Allies. One of the principal causes of the Bolshevik success was the ignorance of the Russian people as to the aims of the Allies in the present war, their ability and their determination to carry it to a victorious issue. This ignorance was not limited to the illiterate masses, but was quite prevalent even among the officers and the bourgeois intelligentzia [sic]. This opinion was quite common that through the withdrawal of Russia from the war the Allies will be forced to give up the struggle and conclude peace. Another common belief was that the Allies were letting Russia do all the hard fighting, while they were taking it easy and making money out of the war, scheming at the same time how to make peace at the expense of Russia. To counteract this ignorance, it seems to me, some way should be found in which to conduct a campaign of education. Judging by my own experience, as well as, by the success of the propaganda conducted by the American Committee, the work could be best done quite openly, without in any way disguising its source, motives or aims.

It is quite doubtful whether Russia will be able to organize any effective resistance to German invasion without outside help. At the time I left, the question was rather as to Russia's willingness to oppose Germany. The yearning for peace and order was so great and so universal that the Russians [were] quite ready to submit to German domination, if it had come in a form less humiliating to the Russian self-esteem. I believe that the Germans made another of their many psychological mistakes when they began to coerce Russia to make peace.

In this connection permit me to say a few words regarding the proposed Japanese intervention [Koukol, apparently, knew of the Masaryk proposal.] I believe that any intervention, even the best intentioned one—unless it comes under conditions which I shall presently state—would be resented by all classes of the Russian people, and most of all, of course, the intervention of Japan or China. It is perfectly wrong to suppose that the Russian people are lacking in self-respect and pride; on the contrary, I am firmly convinced that they are in some respects more sensitive than any other nation.

Besides this, all Russians, for reasons upon which it is not necessary to dwell [i.e., the memory of the Russo-Japanese war and the fear of the 'yellow peril' prevalent in Russia ever since the days of the Tatar occupation], fear and suspect the Japanese more than any other people. If, therefore, it is found necessary to intervene in order to establish order in Russia and to save her from German domination, it should be done only under the following conditions: (1) The intervention should come only after a formal request by some recognized authority in Russia. (2) It should be under the joined auspices and responsibility of the Allies, even though Japanese troops principally might be used. It would be well if the chief command of such expedition were in the hands of the Allies, especially of Americans, as the latter are more trusted by the Russians than any other of the Allies. (3) The objects of the intervention should be strictly defined and made known among the Russian people as widely as possible.

In spite of the apparently meager results of our trip to Russia, it is not entirely without a certain value. In the first place, it served to bring about a closer contact between the Czecho-Slovak organizations and the Allied representatives in Russia, making a further cooperation between them possible. In the second place, it gave the members of our mission the opportunity to see the baneful effect of the combined socialistic, pacifist and pro-German propaganda, and this knowledge not only enables us to counteract similar agitation going on in this country, but will give considerable weight to our warnings against this kind of propaganda among our people.

Despite all the propaganda and talk about peace by statesman and plain folks, the war went on and soldiers continued to be killed. The greatest lack of human reserves was in France; anybody who offered troops was welcome there. Since very few Czech and Slovak prisoners of war could be found in French prison camps, it would have been necessary to bring soldiers and prisoners of war from other countries in order to build a Czechoslovak army there. After the entry of the United States into the war, it became possible to recruit Czech and Slovak volunteers from America, where Štefánik was dispatched in the spring of 1917, after the failure of his mission in Russia in 1916-1917. He arrived in the United States on behalf of the French government and the CSNC on June 15, 1917, to recruit soldiers for the French Foreign Legion. But the number of those who volunteered for service was much smaller than Beneš and Štefánik had anticipated.[30] (The total number of volunteers who reached the Western Front before the end of the war was 2,300.[31] Some 30,000 additional men of Czech and Slovak origin served in the U.S. Army.)[32] The reason for the small number of volunteers was that the U.S. government registered men between the ages of twenty and thirty, and Štefánik was allowed to enlist only those over thirty and those below that age who were not American citizens. Furthermore, the volunteers were to become soldiers in the French armed forces, where material conditions were considerably worse than those in the U.S. army. The largest number of volunteers was therefore expected to come from Russia, where Masaryk negotiated for the transfer of some 30,000 Czechs and Slovaks to France on the basis of an agreement reached with the French government on June 13, 1917.[33]

Expecting the arrival of volunteers from the United States, Russia, and Italy, Beneš conducted negotiations with the French government officials for the establishment of the Czechoslovak army. In the French ministry of war a section was organized to deal with the question of "national armies" —Polish, Czechoslovak, and, at the beginning, even Romanian. The Polish committee in France agreed to the formation of Polish military units within the French army, commanded by French officers, but Beneš, Sychrava, and Osusky, the spokesmen of the CSNC, refused to agree to a similar arrangement with respect to Czech troops. Beneš wanted an autonomous Czechoslovak national army under the supreme political command of the CSNC (representing the "Czechoslovak" nation). The enlistment of the troops would be handled by the council, which would have to approve the appointment of commanders; Czechs and Slovaks would have a preferential claim to these positions. The army would be financed through a loan to be repaid by the future Czechoslovak state.[34]

The last demand was not acceptable to the French ministry of foreign affairs, which pointed out in its reply that such a loan would entail the assumption of a far-reaching political obligation by the French government, an obligation that France was not then prepared to assume. To agree to the demand that the debt should be taken over by the Czechoslovak state after the war would imply the acceptance of the establishment of a future independent Czechoslovak state as a part of the war aim, and a definite commitment to this end by the French government.[35]

Even though he did not achieve this ultimate objective—a definite commitment by the French government to work for the establishment of a independent Czechoslovak state—Beneš was satisfied with the French government's consent to form a separate Czechoslovak army within the French armed forces and to recognize the CSNC as the spokesman for the independence movement. This was a great success, indeed. The main problem now was to find enough troops so that the army could, in fact, be built.

Although Masaryk received tens of thousands of dollars from various collections among Czechs in the United States, the recruitment of volunteers in this country had a slow start. As a result of Štefánik's campaign, a training center for Czech-American volunteers was established at Stamford, Connecticut, under the direction of Charles Pergler. Early in November 1917, the first one hundred volunteers arrived in France.[36] This was hardly enough to build an army.

In Italy the number of Czech prisoners of war was much greater than in France; thus, early in September 1917, Beneš went there to negotiate with the Italian government for their transfer to France. On September 6, he was accepted by Baron Sonnino, the Italian minister of foreign affairs, who suggested to Beneš that it would be easier to form Czechoslovak military units in Italy. Sonnino rejected Beneš's request that Italy release those Czechs and Slovak prisoners of war who volunteered for service in the Czechoslovak army in France. Beneš quickly reacted by preparing a memorandum for the Italian ministry of foreign affairs, in which he requested the formation of military units in Italy that would be part of the independence movement of the Czechoslovak nation. He proposed that the CSNC have the exclusive right to conduct recruitment. The CSNC would be the supreme organ controlling these troops from the political and national point of view. The troops would take an oath to the "Czechoslovak nation of which the Czecho-Slovak National Council is its representative," the officers would be of "Czechoslovak" nationality, the army would be considered as a national army; only from the miltiary-technical point of view would it be under Italian command. Expenses for the army would be covered by the Italian government from a loan that would be paid either by the future Czechoslovak state, or by someone whose duty it would be, in accordance with the decision made about it at the peace conference. The last point in Beneš's memorandum was that the troops would not be used on the Italian front. Where and how the army was to be used would have to be decided jointly by the Italian government and the CSNC.[37]

The reply that Beneš received from the Italian ministry of war[38] was ambiguous. It consented to the proposal to form Czechoslovak military units in Italy, it officially took notice of the CSNC and its office at Rome, and it agreed to free Czech prisoners of war from the camps. The soldiers had to take an oath of allegiance to "the Czechoslovak cause," not to the CSNC. The Italian government did not want to recognize the CSNC, as Beneš had requested. Beneš made some comments on the reply, but did not reject it. He hoped that after the formation of the Czechoslovak army in France, it might be possible either to move the Czechoslovak units from Italy to France, or to negotiate about forming Czechoslovak units on the Italian front.

In view of the small number of volunteers from the United States and the qualified success of negotiations in Italy, it was obvious that the best chance to build a large, strong army lay in Russia. The Russian military favored such an army, but political developments and changes in the military leadership of the Russian army were barriers to a speedy buildup of the Czechoslovak army corps. Masaryk described the difficulties at a conference of the members and coworkers of the Russian branch of the CSNC on September 12, 1917. He pointed out that first

"Brusilov promised everything," but then, when Masaryk arrived in Kiev, Brusilov was gone. Masaryk had to start new negotiations with Generals Kornilov, Denikin, and Markov; and when everything was settled with them, they were "locked up." He stressed, however, that he would never give up; that he was going to contact the new military commander in Russia, to whom he would repeat that the Czechoslovak troops must never be used inside Russia. The army was to be used only against the external enemy. Yet, Masaryk told his audience, as he always told the soldiers, Czechoslovaks must be "loyal to Russia." Russia had become a problem for all mankind; and, as Masaryk put it, from the point of view of the Czechoslovak national interest it was "necessary that Russia is strong." In view of the world situation, he said, "what would a weak Russian mean to us if we obtain independence and not have enough support?"[39]

This rhetoric appealed to the pro-Russian, Slavic feelings of the Czechs in Russia, especially of those who served in the Czechoslovak army, rather than expressing a real concern for a strong Russia. "Every morning, Masaryk "drank of cup of chocolate" with the British private agent, Maugham, at the Hotel Europa in Petrograd, and "discussed with him how best to make use of his devoted Czechs." A confidential statement that Masaryk made for Maugham on September 1, 1917, better represents his real feelings about Russia than his rhetoric does. Since Masaryk himself reviewed the statement before Maugham dispatched it to his superiors, there cannot be any doubt that it reflects his views. Masaryk said,

> The internal and external weakening of Russia means eo ipso the strengthening of the Central Powers, which makes it more necessary to form independent Bohemian, Polish and South-Slav states as a natural barrier against Pangermanism. The dismemberment of Austria-Hungary is the real object of the war; Germany must be prevented from using Austria-Hungary with its population of 51 millions for her imperialistic aims. Austria-Hungary is the Prussian bridge to the nearer and to the farther East.[40]

Masaryk wanted a weak Russia. If the western Allies were not worried about the possible increase of Russian influence in central Europe, his own chances for getting their support in his efforts to bring about the establishment of an independent Czech state, and thus a new order in central Europe, would be enhanced.

In the same report Masaryk made a statement that makes him sound like a false prophet: "Nothing can be awaited from Russia," he said, "except that she will not make a separate peace, and will continue to hold a certain number of German troops on the Eastern front. There is no danger of a separate peace, because Russia realizes that she can get nothing from Germany except a certain amount of money. She can get neither railways nor the bread which at the moment she chiefly lacks; and peace with the Central Powers would leave her internal condition unchanged."

It is interesting to note that on the one hand Masaryk tried to get the Czechoslovak troops out of Russia, and on June 13 concluded an agreement on the transfer of 30,000 of them to France; on the other hand, on September 1, 1917, he recommended that the Allies send "a Japanese army of at least 300,000 men," which would "serve to restore the moral [sic] of the Russian troops."

Although Masaryk believed that it was to the Allied advantage to help Russia, he insisted that such help would have to be merely financial, "in moderation and only on explicit conditions." Furthermore, Masaryk insisted "on the need of a definite *quid pro quo* for all money advanced." Maugham quoted him directly as saying, "If you give them all they ask without conditions, they will spend it like children, and you will get nothing in return."

It was well-known that the Japanese had been unpopular in Russia ever since the Russo-Japanese war of 1904-1905, and that the Russians had never forgotten the two hundred years of Tatar-Mongol occupation of their country. Nevertheless, Masaryk further suggested that "Japanese intervention might be paid for, if money would not be accepted, by the cession of a part of Manchuria, which in fact is already under Japanese influence." He also thought that "Russia would be willing to cede to China some part of Central Asia; faced with the alternative of losing a part of Asia and falling into complete political and economic dependence on Germany, Russia could be induced to choose the former." (The suggestion again indicates Masaryk's desire for a weak Russia.) Finally, Masaryk "insisted repeatedly on the fact that now the war could be won only by victories on the Western front, and urged the necessity of a large American army being placed in the field with as little delay as possible."[41]

Apparently, Masaryk wanted to have his troops in the west when the day of victory arrived, believing that "being there" would be advantageous to his cause. It would seem that the main reason for his insistence on the transfer of the Czechoslovak troops to France was that he wanted to come home as the "liberator" from the west and not from the east, and thus assure for himself the leading role in a pro-western Czechoslovak state. Furthermore, the more Russia was humiliated and weakened, the better chance he would have for the realization of his secret plan.

Maugham did not quite agree with Masaryk's views on the situation in Russia, and he even contradicted them in his own report, pointing out that the Allies (including the Japanese) were unpopular in Russia. On about September 23, Maugham reported that Kerensky was losing favor and probably would not last.[42] On the other hand, according to *Utro Rosiji* of September 1, 1917, Masaryk was optimistic. He said that the current (Kornilov) crisis would be "happily resolved," and that the main task of Russia was to form a new administration. Asserting that tsarism was rotten to the core and that its fall represented the first half of the revolution, he explained that he expected the second half of the revolution—the positive and constructive one—to arrive soon. The revolution in Russia was an evolutionary process, and Masaryk expressed his conviction that it "will overcome extremes." In the same interview Masaryk demanded independence for the Czechs and Slovaks, but rejected the Finns' demand for independence from Russia.

Maugham and many others did not share Masaryk's optimism. The Allied diplomats could not fail to notice the approaching crisis. On October 9, 1917, Allied ambassadors in Russia protested jointly to Prime Minister Kerensky against the disintegration of the Russian army and the chaos in the rear.[43] The Russian government, however, needed and expected help, not protests. Such help was contemplated for the future, but the need for it was imminent. On October 30, Kerensky himself told Maugham that he did not believe that his government could continue, in view of the German peace offer, the coming winter, and the efforts made by Allied diplomats to keep Russia down. Kerensky asked Maugham to convey his views to the British prime minister, Lloyd George, as Maugham indeed did when he arrived in London in early November, acting upon Wiseman's instructions.[44] On November 6, U.S. Ambassador Francis proposed sending two U.S. divisions to Russia to improve public morale;[45] at this time, however, the Revolution was already at the threshold. Russia had needed help much earlier.

Although Masaryk was a westerner in his thoughts and deeds, he presented himself as a Slavophile or even a Russophile in his public pronouncements to the troops. In contrast, the soldiers and offiers of the Legion were genuinely concerned with the fate of Russia and felt a responsibility toward her. Before the battle of Zborov, some officers of the Legion attempted to include the whole Czech brigade in the "battalions of death." A Czech company joined the shock troops called *Kornilovci*,[46] who were personally loyal to General Lavr Kornilov, comannder-in-chief after the July offensive failed, in the hope that he would restore order on the front and the morale of the troops.

General Kornilov had become a national hero when he managed to escape from Austrian captivity. Toward the end of April 1915, Kornilov was very seriously wounded and captured. A Czech soldier, František Mrňák, helped the general to make it back to Russia in August 1915. Kornilov erroneously believed that Mrňák had been either killed or executed for helping him escape, and therefore had a sentimental attachment to him and the Czech cause.[47] (As it happened, the soldier outlived the general.) He was so much impressed with the Czechs that he included the Czech *Kornilovci* in his personal guards at Stavka. When he became commander-in-chief of the Russian armies, Masaryk sent him a congratulatory telegram that alluded to Kornilov's captivity in Austria, saying that the new generalissimo had had the opportunity to see with his own eyes the situation in Austria-Hungary and notice the "firm will of the Czechoslovak nation and its willingness to bring all necessary sacrifices for its own liberation from the German-Hungarian yoke." Masaryk expressed a conviction that Kornilov would give the Czechoslovaks "the opportunity to fight for independence and freedom." He also wished "from the bottom of his heart" that Kornilov would organize "all elements of Free Russia and lead her to victory that would benefit democracy and Slavdom."[48]

According to V. Sidorin, one of the close coworkers of General Kornilov, the general was fond of the Czechs and placed high hopes in the Czechoslovak army when he approved its formation.[49] Early in August 1917, he turned to the Czech organizations and committees within the Czech military units with a request for help against the Bolsheviks. Acting upon his instructions, a Czech officer in his general staff, Vladimír Klecanda called a meeting of chairmen of the regimental committees, representing the troops, and informed them that Kornilov intended to occupy Moscow and Petrograd in order to prevent a Bolshevik seizure of power.[50] Officers of the Czech regiments rallied immediately to Kornilov's side and conducted secret meetings at which they discussed preparations for the project and the ways in which Czech troops could take part in it. The rank and file soldiers, represented by the committees, and the officers of the army endorsed fully Kornilov's plan to take measures to prevent the Bolsheviks from assuming political power in Russia.[51]

While the Czech army fully supported Kornilov and took at face value Masaryk's words about the need for a strong Russia, the Czech leader was closely affiliated with the British propaganda teams in Russia, all of which followed the principles enumerated by Wiseman in his May 15, 1917, propaganda scheme for Russia. One of these principles was that none of the propaganda groups "would attempt to interfere in any way with Russian domestic questions."[52] Masaryk stated that principle as "non-interference in affairs in the Russian army" in his first address to the Czechoslovak army and prisoners of war at Petrograd on May 28, 1917,[53] and repeated the principle of "non-interference with domestic matters" on many other occasions. He told the soldiers that it was not their task to establish order in the Russian army. In accordance with his principle, during the first days of the Kornilov incident, Masaryk notifed Russian headquarters that the Czech units must not be used in internal political struggles; this was the first time that the proclaimed neutrality was applied in practice.

In contrast to Masrryk, who in his heart was a westerner and for whom Russia was merely a place where he could recruit troops for another war theater, the soldiers and officers of the Legion were genuinely interested in preventing the collapse of Russia, believing that this was both their Slavic duty and the best long-range interest of the Czechs, the Slovaks, and the rest of the European nations. On the one hand, Masaryk and the Soviets opposed Kornilov's attempt to restore order in Russia and eliminate the Bolshevik threat; on the other, most of the Czech political leaders and the military took the side of the Russian general who had helped them build the Czechoslovak army corps. Even after the end of the incident, on September 15, 1917, Bohdan Pavlů, an ardent Masaryk supporter, published an editorial in the official organ of the Russian branch of the CSNC, *Čechoslovák,* asserting that the Kornilov action was "inevitable and necessary for the reorganization of Russia."[54] Pavlů wrote that the number of the Bolsheviks was very small, and he exhorted the troops to resist Bolshevik agitation. Along similar lines, the official organ of the Czechoslovak army, *Československý voják,* in its first issue on October 11, 1917 defended the Kornilov's "shock troops," calling them "conscious democrats" and "native brothers" of the Czech soldiers.[55] Even the leaders of the Czech Social Democratic party organizations in Kiev, Houska, Richter, Kysela, and others published an appeal to Social Democrats in the Czechoslovak military units, beseeching their comrades not to trust the Czech-Bolshevik agitators in Kiev, and to go hand in hand with the rest of the nation, since "all comrades and the whole Czecho-Slovak nation stands on the platform of the Czecho-Slovak National Council headed by Professor Masaryk."[56] The latter's authority was such that his public statements were not questioned and his orders were followed by the Czech Legion.

At the beginning of October 1917, a new memorandum by Masaryk was submitted to headquarters.[57] In it he requested the formation of a separate Czechoslovak army corps with General V. N. Shokorov as its commander, General Červinka as the "Chief of all Czecho-Slovak reserve units," and Jiří Klecanda and Prokop Maxa as plenipotentiaries (commissars) of the Russian branch of the CSNC. (Eventually, these two Masaryk confidants, Klecanda and Maxa, became Masaryk's representatives with the commander of the army corps.) Finally, Masaryk stipulated that the appropriate military officers should be notified that the Czechoslovak army could be used only against external enemies of Russia, that is against Austria-Hungary and Germany.

General Dukhonin, the chief of staff of the new supreme commander, Kerensky, met all these demands in his order of October 9, 1917. Two days later a new monthly, *Československý voják,* began to be published for the soldiers of the army corps. Its editor was the writer Rudolf Medek. Also, in the middle of October, the first transport of Czechoslovak soldiers and officers (about 1,200) sailed from Archangel with France as its destination. The second transport departed in November, but was delayed by the severe winter. It arrived in France in March 1918.

In order to facilitate the buildup of the army units in both Russia and France, Masaryk issued a new proclamation to the Czech and Slovak prisoners of war in September 1917, urging them to join the Czechoslovak army, made possibe by the new, free Russia which also made possible the formation of an army in France. Masaryk proclaimed the army's determination to fight side by side with the Allies for the liberation of Europe from Prussian militarism, for the democratic principle of self-determination of nations, and for the liberation of "our nation," which had been solemnly promised by the Allies.[58]

Since the Russian army was falling apart, and a complete collapse on the Russian front could be predicted, Masaryk was concerned about the use of the growing Czechoslovak army corps, which already consisted of almost 40,000 men. The French military mission in Russia believed that the simplest solution of the problem would be to transfer the Czechoslovak units to the Romanian front, where Romania, defending herself on about one-third of her territory, would welcome the Czech troops. Therefore, Masaryk went to Jassy, the center of Romania at that time,[59] to discuss the matter with the Romanian government, the diplomatic representatives of the Entente, the chief of the French military mission in Romania, General Henri M. Berthelot, and the commander of the Russian troops on the Romanian front, General Dimitri G. Shcherbachev. Masaryk agreed to send the Czechoslovak army corps to Romania, and several Romanian newspapers announced the agreement, which, in the event, was never kept. Masaryk returned to Petrograd via Kiev on November 5, 1917, on the eve of the Bolshevik Revolution, and he watched the event that profoundly changed the situation in Russia. He then explained his refusal to send the Czech troops to Romania by pointing at the possibility of collapse on the Romanian front, in which case Romania would be able neither to continue her defense nor to supply the Czechoslovak army corps. Notwithstanding French wishes to the contrary, Masaryk decided that the Czechoslovak army would not go to help the Romanians fight the Central Powers.[60]

In Romania Masaryk was received with the honors given to heads of independent states, a sign of the growing recognition of the importance of the Czechoslovak independence movement and of the growing Czechoslovak army.[61] That army, in view of the decaying Russian front, had an increasing military significance. Masaryk's standing as president of the CSNC also improved because of developments in international politics. First of all, Austrian secret overtures for peace did not bring any results, largely because Czernin's insisted on preserving the prewar boundaries of the Habsburg monarchy and because the Germans intervened against his attempts to reach an understanding with the Entente powers. Also, Emperor Charles gave up his effort to reach a separate peace. He accepted instead the German proposal to launch a new fight for "peace with victory" on the Italian front. This agreement led to a successful offensive, the defeat of the Italians at Caporeto, the fall of the Italian government, and the arrival of a new prime minister, Vittorio E. Orlando. Early in November 1917, France got a new prime minister and minister of war, Georges Clemenceau, who presented his cabinet to parliament as one committed to "unlimited war." The arrival in France of the first transport of volunteers from Russia, and three transports of volunteers from the United States, brought about the promulgation of a decree by the president of the French Republic on December 16, 1917, establishing an autonomous Czechoslovak army. From the military point of view, the new army recognized the supreme authority of the French military command, and legally it was under the jurisdiction of the French government. However, it would fight against the Central Powers under its own flag.[62] After the U.S. declaration of war on Austria-Hungary on December 7, 1917, the enlistment of Czech and Slovak volunteers from America increased, though not substantially, and the number of troops who arrived from the United States was totally insufficient to build up the Czechoslovak army in France.

Thus, only in Russia was there a real chance of recruiting troops, and it was in Russia that the Czechoslovak army corps was, in fact, established. However, the seizure of power by the Bolsheviks in Petrograd opened a new chapter in the corps' history and influenced developments in the independence movement.

CHAPTER EIGHT

THE BOLSHEVIK REVOLUTION

After the "Kornilov affair," events in Russia proceeded rapidly toward their culmination. The situation became chaotic when Kornilov and Denikin were placed under arrest and when the Bolsheviks gained, for the first time, a majority in the Petrograd Soviet in September 1917. Kerensky proclaimed a republic and became a virtual dictator within his government, but the latter was losing the support of the masses and could no longer count on the support of the armed forces. Kerensky was becoming a general without an army; his releasing the previously detained Bolsheviks, including Trotsky, and their formation of the Red Guard, ostensibly to fight the "counter-revolution," made the Boleshevik party into a political factor that proved fatal not only to Kerensky but also to Russia. While most of the commanders in the Russian army believed that their first duty was to hold the front inasmuch as it was possible, the Bolsheviks demonstrated their "gratitude" to Kerensky, who released their leaders and imprisoned their enemies, by attempting to wrest political power from him; on November 7 (October 25), 1917, they seized power in Petrograd.[1]

The Bolshevik victory came as a big surprise to Masaryk as he admitted on December 14, 1917, when he declared in Kiev that "nobody could have expected that Russia would undergo such a crisis."[2] Whether or not Masaryk could have prevented the Bolshevik's coming to power is a matter of conjecture. Ten days before the Bolsheviks struck, Masaryk told the members of the Russian branch of the CSNC at their meeting at Petrograd that he had assured Kerensky's minister of war that the Czechoslovak army was willing to fight against the internal enemy led by the Bolsheviks;[3] and at another meeting of the same group at Kiev, on December 1, 1917, he stated publicly (and his speech was printed in *Čechoslovák*, No. 117) that before October 27 he had ordered the army not to get mixed up in internal conflicts in Russia. On this and many other occasions he assumed full responsibility for the neutral stand taken by the Czechoslovak army during the Bolshevik Revolution as well as during Kornilov's attempt to restore order in Russia. He demonstrated that he meant business and was prepared to enforce neutrality by removing from their positions in the Czechoslovak army several Russian officers who had followed the orders of their Russian superiors (the Czechoslovak army corps was a part of the Russian army) and had taken action on November 12, 1917, against the Bolsheviks, when the latter tried to capture political power in Kiev.[4]

Masaryk was a stubborn man; sometimes he tried to make the world safe for his theories rather than adjust himself to the reality in which he lived. For him, as for Kerensky, the enemy was on the right, not on the left, even though he did, verbally, denounce the Bolsheviks as German agents. The crux of the matter was that Masaryk had little real interest in a strong Russia; on the contrary, the weaker Russia was, the better chance there was that Great Britain would approve the dismemberment of Austria-Hungary and would permit the establishment of an independent Czechoslovak state. For that reason he tried to get the Czechoslovak troops to the western war theater. Voska, who never questioned anything that his master did, writes that Masaryk "with horror repelled the idea" of the Czechoslovak army corps marching on Petrograd and seizing power on behalf of the Russian republic, because the Legionnaires were merely guests in the country and he "would not tolerate the idea that the liberal Czechoslovak Republic which he had envisioned should begin its career with an act of conquest." Nevertheless, Voska believed that "the Legion could have taken and held Petrograd."[5]

It probably could. The untrained and poorly armed Bolsheviks, whose only heavy weapons were provided by the ship *Aurora* were not match for the Czechoslovak army corps, consisting of two divisions with some 40,000 well-trained troops, now largely former prisoners of war, equipped with artillery and commanded by Russian and Czech officers, some of whom had considerable combat experience. Was the Legion willing to fight? The troops, as well as other Czechs and Slovaks in Russia, had been exposed to the Masaryk-Voska propaganda according to which the Bolsheviks, especially Lenin and Trotsky, were German agents. Masaryk himself said that he could not visualize how a Czech prisoner of war who was a Social Democrat could possibly acknowledge Lenin as his comrade, agree with his defeatism, and become his follower.[6] For the restless soldiers and officers of the Legion the march on Petrograd would have been the long-awaited opportunity to redeem themselves by a heroic act and free themselves from their subconscious fears, as the Legionnaire writer, František Langer, wrote.[7] The heroes of Zborov, who had demonstrated their ability to defeat an enemy three times their number, would have had a bonanza with the half-armed Bolshevik rabble in Petrograd. But they followed the orders of their "dictator"—Masaryk, who, some thirteen months later, told the Czechoslovak ministerial council that through the Czechoslovak soldiers he could have saved Russia from Bolshevism.[8]

Masaryk's attitude toward the Soviets was ambivalent and opportunistic. He denounced them for their peace propaganda before the Revolution, and cooperated with them after they assumed political power, in parts of Russia where the Czechoslovak army corps happened to be in Soviet-controlled territory. In the summer and fall of 1917, Masaryk and his agents propagated pro-Allied views aimed at making Russia stay in the war. (Apparently, he did not consider this an involvement in Russian domestic affairs.) He asserted that despite the Bolsheviks' professed desire for peace, they prolonged the war by their agitation. Masaryk did not believe, as the Bolsheviks did, that the German proletariat would come to their help. He protested against the instructions drawn up by the Central Executive Committee of the Soviets for the Soviet delegate to the Allied conference, published in *Izvestia* on October 7, 1917.[9]

Masaryk's protesting telegram was printed in *Russkiia Vedomosti* on October 30 (17), 1917;[10] it was a masterpiece of propaganda. According to the telegram, the instructions "sin[ned] against the principle of self-determination of peoples as adopted by the Russian revolution, and against democracy." Although they "adhere to the principle of the self-determination of peoples," they "are silent about the Czechs and Slovaks, who number ten million. The people of Huss and Comenius, a people no less than their oppressors, are forgotten!" Charging that the instructions "protect Austria-Hungary," he accused their authors of not knowing several critically important facts. First, "during the war Austria-Hungary executed from 30,000 to 40,000 people." (This was a gross exaggeration. On several other occasions Masaryk used the figure "from 30,000 to 60,000" or merely 60,000.)[11] Second, Masaryk asserted that "all political leaders and deputies in the parliament from the Czech, Italian, and other peoples were imprisoned and sentenced to death." (This was not true. Masaryk's argument was an appeal to ignorance. Out of 107 Czech deputies in the Vienna parliament only Kramář and Rašín were sentenced to death, and they were amnestied by the new emperor and then released from prison on July 10, 1917, three months *before* Masaryk wrote the protest. Masaryk knew it; the event was commented upon in the world press and also in the Czech exile publications.) Third, Masaryk said that "the Germans and the Magyars maintain their domination in elections and in the government by means of brazenly unconcealed force." (This was not true in the Austrian portion of the empire.) Furthermore, "the peoples of Austria and Hungary have for centuries been fighting for freedom and independence." (We have noticed that even Masaryk favored the continuation of Austria-Hungary in 1909.)[12] Masaryk also charged that the instructions "defend this medieval artificial state"—Austria-Hungary—and "a dynasty which holds seven millions in slavery with the aid of an army and militarism, in alliance with the exploiting aristocracy, with Germans and Magyars." He asserted that the committee, given the opportunity to choose between "a degenerated dynasty and the freedom of seven peoples, numbering over 30 million," "took the side of the dynasty." Needless to say, propaganda statements must be accepted, not analyzed, if they are to be effective and if the big lie is to succeed.

Even after the Bolshevik victory in November, Masaryk wrote to Plekhanov, a Russian Menshevik (father of Russian Marxism), that the revolution was "illegal," an act without moral and political justification in view of the establishment of the republic and the introduction of a parliament and civil freedoms.[13] On November 10 (October 28), 1917, in his paper *Edinstvo*, Plekhanov condemned the Bolshevik uprising, called it madness, and was bitter about the "uncultured" Bolsheviks who called him an imperialist for his stand on the war. Masaryk responded to Plekhanov's outcry with a letter published under the title "Impressions from Moscow," in *Edinstvo,* November 28 (15), 1917. Masaryk related his experience with the revolution in Moscow and rejected the Bolshevik violence. He asked, "Why could they not wait for the Constituent Assembly? Why now, in winter, make haste with a radical agrarian program? Is it even thinkable that the solution of the peasant crisis lies in allotments of small strips of land?" (This was Masaryk's comment on Lenin's "Decree on Land.") Masaryk continued:

> I repeat the bloody revolution was not inevitable, and, therefore, it is without justification. The direct objective of politics is the saving human life and the correct use of human resources; the degree of barbarism and the degree of real culture can be demonstrated on how personalities and nations can spare human life.... Every movement has to be judged on the basis of what consequences if produces. I admit that all the consequences of the Bolshevik revolution cannot be assessed as yet, but it is clear to me already now that their politics lack realism. Their foremost wish is peace, but, in reality, they prolong the war. A decisive offensive in June [July] would have brought peace closer, because it would have weakened Germans and Austrians. The Bolsheviks agitate against the war, but they protect Germans and are not sorry for the blood of their brethren. The Bolsheviks expect help mostly from the German Socialists, but the German armies, composed of German Socialists, are marching on Petrograd and occupy Russian land.

Masaryk ends this long letter with the sentence, "No, comrades, Russia needs a revolution of brains and hearts."

In this letter Masaryk expressed his conviction that he Bolsheviks, who did not even know what to do with the 600 people who were in his Moscow hotel, were incapable of governing 170 million people. He believed that the establishment of the Soviet government was merely a passing phase in the Russian Revolution. Yet he cooperated with the Soviet government as long as he stayed in Russia, never publicly questioning its legitimacy. He claimed to have had an influence on the Bolsheviks;[14] professed his "absolute loyalty" to Russia and correct attitude toward the

Soviet government;[15] signed an agreement with the Bolshevik government;[16] and advocated its recognition as a *de facto* government of Russia by the Allies.[17]

But no matter what he said about the Bolsheviks before and after the Bolshevik Revolution, on one issue Masaryk remained consistent: he always proclaimed his policy of noninvolvement in Russian domestic affairs, and, at the same time, expressed the Czechs' and Slovaks' loyalty and willingness to help Russia. Thus, on August 31, 1917, he and the Russian branch of the CSNC published a resolution, addressed to the Czechoslovak public, containing the phrase, "The faith in Russia and the love for the great Russian nation which re-enforced our nation during the time of its struggle against a powerful enemy, has stayed with us and we shall demonstrate it now during this time so difficult for Russia."[18] On September 18, 1917, Masaryk declared, "Free Russia has made possible for us the formation of our first independent army, and we are grateful to her!"[19] Early in December 1917, the Russian branch of the CSNC, of which he was the president, passed a resolution proclaiming, "It is a fatal error to expect that Germany could have a democratic revolution. Therefore, in the interest of peace and democracy, we reject categorically any compromise [with respect to the continuation of the war] . . . . We will remain loyal to Russia even in the most difficult times, firmly believing that she, correctly understanding her democratic tasks and her mission as an organic whole. . . will never betray the just and truly democratic aims of her Allies."[20] Leaving aside the contradictions between Masaryk's public pronouncements and the policy that he actually pursued, and the contradition between his professed love for Russia and duty to help her, and his policy of noninvolvement and nonintervention in her domestic affairs, the events that followed the Bolshevik Revolution confronted the Czechoslovak independence movement with the question: Whose Russia?

The emergence of Bolshevik power in Russia, which polarized Russian society and led to a civil struggle, brought about differentiations within the Czechoslovak independence movement in Russia as well. In the situation as it developed, Masaryk's principle of noninvolvement in Russian domestic affairs became an unattainable proposition. On the one hand, there were the left-wing Social Democrats who sympathized with the Bolshevik Revolution and, in an attempt to "help Russia" by fighting "capitalist enemies" of the Revolution, did their best to destroy the unity of the Czechoslovak independence movement. On the other hand, the right-wing elements within the Czechoslovak independence movement, especially those individuals who appreciated the help that they had received from the former tsarist government, threw their lot in with the counter-revolution; in order to "help Russia," they joined the Volunteer Aarmy on the Don. Masaryk was asked by both camps to "save Russia." However, he placed his idea of the Czechoslovak state and his own role in it above anything else, and he pursued this idea relentlessly. Eventually, the Czechoslovak army had to fight the Bolsheviks, but this outcome was not due to Masaryk's designs; on the contrary, he worked as hard as he could to prevent it from happening. The fight was forced on the army by the Bolsheviks, who proved that neutrality and Masaryk's basic principle of non-involvement in Russian internal conflicts had become obsolete, unworkable, and unrealistic propositions in the age of totalitarian ideologies inaugurated by the October Revolution.

His ambivalent attitude toward the Bolshevik party and the Soviet government notwithstanding, Masaryk did not change his views on the task and mission of the Czechoslovak army in Russia. On November 9, 1917, before his departure from Petrograd for Moscow and Kiev, Masaryk sent a message to all military officers and commanders, and to the plenipotentiaries of the Russian branch of the CSNC at headquarters and in the staff of the army corps, in which he insisted that the Czechoslovak troops must not be used "in any way" in the current intraparty political struggle.[21] After his arrival in Kiev he repeated, "We will not get mixed up in political conflicts among the Russian political parties. We are soldiers, not cops and gendarmes."[22] This statement, he insisted, did not imply that he regarded all political parties in Russia with an equal affection. Although he was against Bolshevism and considered it to be merely a passing phenomenon, he stated at Kiev that he would deal with whatever political parties were in power in Russia. He further contended that it was in the interest of the army corps not to provoke or alienate any of the political groups competing for power in Russia. On November 9, 1917, General V. N. Shokorov, the commander of the Czechoslovak army corps, issued an order corresponding to Masaryk's instructions, stating that any Czechoslovak intervention in internal struggles and any participation in them on behalf of any political party was intolerable. At the same time, he urged the units to support those who were maintaining order, to stay where they were, to prevent robberies and violence, and not to permit damage to railroads and munition depots by anyone. The order was also signed by Prokop Maxa, who rejected the request made by a commissar in the Russian army (Kirilenko) and his assistant, Nicholas Grigoriev, that some of the Czechoslovak troops be used in Kiev for guarding purposes.[23]

The commander of Kiev's military circles (the Eleventh Army of the South Western Front, to which the two divisions of the Czechoslovak army corps belonged) General Kwiecinski, and the commissar of the Provisional Government, Kirilenko, ordered the Russian Republican army to occupy key points in the city as soon as the first reports arrived on the Bolshevik uprising in Petrograd. Although Maxa refused to consent to the use of the Czechoslovak army's Second Divison, located close to Kiev, to guard some strategic points in Kiev, the commander of the First Division, Colonel Mamontov, instructed the commanders of the First Regiment and the First Artillery Brigade of his division to go to Kiev. He notified them that they, together with the shock regiment of *Kornilovci* (the First Slovonic Regiment) were henceforth placed under the jurisdiction of the assistant commissar of the front, Grigoriev. After being told by Mamontov "to beat, kill, not spare anyone,"[24] the Czech Second Regiment reached Kiev during the night of November 10-11; its commander immediately notified the chairman of the military commission of the Russian branch of the CSNC about the arrival of the regiment. When in the morning of November 11 Maxa inquired about the decision to bring those troops to Kiev, pointing at Shokorov's order of November 9, he was told by the spokesman for headquarters that the Czech units would not be used in street fighting, should it occur. Maxa then personally assured the representative of the Ukrainian Central Council (Rada) that the presence of the Czechoslovak troops was not directed against it and that the troops would not be used in possible clashes in the streets.[25]

However, representatives of the executive committee of the Czechoslovak Social Democratic party organization in Kiev, among whom were A. Hais and A. Můna, looked up Maxa on November 11. They requested the withdrawal of the Czechoslovak units from Kiev, claiming that there was a danger that the troops would be dragged, eventually, into street fighting in the city. Maxa denied the request, assuring the spokesman that such a danger did not exist. The socialists, however, rejected his contention. They notified the Rada on the next day that the arrival of the Czechoslovak regiments in Kiev was "an unpleasant surprise to them," and that the army whad not been built for the purpose of intervening in Russian internal affairs. The socialists demanded the removal of the troops. They also published a leaflet, distributed to the troops, which recalled that the Czechoslovaks had maintained strict neutrality during the Kornilov affair. The soldiers should remember that they were guests in Russia and that they must not allow their arms to be soiled by "Slavic and proletarian blood."[26]

While these left-wing socialists demanded complete neutrality on the part of the Czechoslovak troops in the turmoil and in possible clashes with the Bolsheviks, who had been reported moving southward toward Kiev, the commander of Kiev's military circle, General Kwiecinski, was counting on the Czechs' help in the defense of the city. His orders were to maintain peace and order and to keep the city in Russian hands. He was in touch with Dürich, who had arrived in Kiev earlier and who took part in consultations held there by the Cossacks. Expecting the arrival of Russian, Cossack, and Czech units that were needed to strengthen the city's defenses against the Bolsheviks—who were forming an army and who also had supporters in the city—General Kwiecinski told Dürich, "I beseech you, Czechs, do not forske Russia at this difficult time." Dürich's reply was that the Czech soldiers sympathized with Russia; and judging by enthusiasm of the soldiers of the Second Regiment who came to Kiev, they were eager to fight the Bolsheviks. However, Dürich believed, one Czech regiment was not sufficient for any major military operation. Since Kwiecinski had the authority to do so, Dürich advised the general to bring the whole Czechoslovak army to Kiev. The army, together with the Russian and Cossack troops, Dürich believed, would be a firm barrier against the coming danger of Bolshevism. Dürich then addressed the soldiers of two companies belonging to the Czech regiment, who were assigned to guard the headquarters of the commander of Kiev's military cirile (the Eleventh Army).[27]

On the night of November 11 there were clashes in the streets of Kiev between Russian cadets and units that proclaimed their allegiance to the Bolshevik party. On the next day some of the Czech units took part in the fighting; two Czechs were killed and three wounded. This involvement prompted the Czechoslovak left-wing Social Democrats to make a new protest to Maxa; the latter then requested the commander of the military circle to withdraw all Czech military units from the streets of Kiev and ensure their speedy departure from the city. The commander of the Czech Second Regiment was instructed by Maxa to maintain "strict neutrality," and to comply only with those military orders that had been expressly endorsed by him. On the morning of November 13, the resigning Kwiecinski informed Dürich that Maxa had barred any further arrival of Czechoslovak troops—troops that, as Dürich put it, would be a great help to the Russian military units against the coming danger of Bolshevism.[28] When Dürich, and a representative of a Czech organization in Kiev, František Dědina, attempted to change Maxa's course of action (or, rather, non-action) by taking up the matter directly with the military comission of the Russian branch of the CSNC, they were unsuccessful.

Maxa, as political commissar in the Czechoslovak army, issued on November 14 a proclamation that justified his own conduct and rejected all attempts to involve Czechoslovak troops in the street fighting in Kiev. He insisted on complete neutrality; and to assure this, Masaryk's instructions ordered some personnel changes in the command of the Czechoslovak units, including the replacement of Colonel Mamontov as commander of the First Division by General Kolomenski on November 18.[29] (On January 9 [December 27, 1918], Masaryk dismissed Mamontov altogether from the Czechoslovak army because he had advocated joining the Kaledin forces on the Don.)

After his arrival in Kiev, Masaryk issued a new proclamation on November 22,[30] that reiterated his policy of noninvolvement in political struggles in Russia and condemned the attempts of "irresponsible people to use our troops for police and gendarme services." On November 28, he and Maxa issued a "Manifesto" condemning the spread of "reactinary political statements" directed against individual nations and Russian political parties (that is, against the Ukrainians and the Bolshevik party) in which promises were made, in the name of Czechs, concerning the use of Czechoslovak troops. Masaryk condemned this agitation and repeatedly emphasized the principle of neutrality. He fully endorsed Maxa's barring the bringing of Czech troops to Kiev during the events of November 9-11, proclaiming that the one Czech regiment that had arrived in Kiev came there "without our knowledge and against our will," and "thanks to our efforts, the regiment was speedily recalled."[31] Both Masaryk and Maxa condemned the "Slavic dilettantes" who did not even know that "the official Russia" (i.e., the Soviet government) had recognized the special standing of the Ukraine and negotiated with the Ukrainians about their legal status.[32]

One of those "Slavic dilettantes," Dürich, saw the situation differently. He believed that Maxa's refusal, in the name of Masaryk, to let Czech troops reinforce Kwiecinski at Kiev, in the long run helped the Bolsheviks. The commander of the Kievan garrison of the Russian Republican army, realizing his inability to defend the city with the small number of troops at his command, placed the administration of Kiev in the hands of the Ukrainian Rada, headed by the historian Michael Hrushevsky, and departed with his troops southward. (Until then the authority of the Rada was only nominal—it had practically no troops at its disposal.) As Dürich put it, "the consequences of the Czech defection were fatal, even catastrophic."[33] The accuracy of his evaluation of the events in Kiev, their importance, and their long-range consequences, however, were realized by the Czech soldiers and officers only after the Bolsheviks captured the city on February 8, 1918.

The chairman of the Ukrainian Rada, Hrushevsky, and other officials of the new Ukrainian government received from Masaryk a memorandum prepared by Maxa, denouncing Dürich's connections with the former tsarist government, for which he had been expelled from the Czecho-Slovak National Council. The memorandum stated that Dürich was alleged to have proposed the use of Czechoslovak troops in Kiev during the tumultous days in that city, and that he was under the influence of irresponsible individuals who would like to come back to power in the Czechoslovak independence movement in Russia. At Kiev, those individuals included F. Král, V. Crkal, F. Dědina, and G. A. Zíval. In Moscow, similar aims wre pursued by Svatopluk Koníček-Horský and Dr. Vít Štěpánek. These were the main spokesmen for the Czech "political reaction" in Russia; the former deputy Dürich was under their influence.[34]

Although Masaryk prevented the use of the Czechoslovak units in Russia's internal political struggle at that time, he did not solve the problem of their future use in the war. The Bolshevik seizure of power in Petrograd and Moscow brought about the establishment of Soviet rule in a large part of Russia. Outside the Soviet influence were the Ukraine, where the Central Council held little political power and was recognized by the Lenin government; some parts of southern Russia, where General A. M. Kaledin established a military Don government seated at Novocherkask; the southern Urals, under the rule of General A. J. Dutov, and some territories inhabited by non-Russian (and non-Slavic) peoples. The Soviet's (Lenin's) rule was not generally accepted as legitimate even by many Russian socialists, including some Bolsheviks. Attempts were made to form an all-socialist government that would consist of Socialist Revolutionaries (SRs), Bolsheviks, and Mensheviks, with a Socialist Revolutionary, Victor M. Chernov, as its president. Chernov appeared at the headquarters of the Russian army on November 22, 1917. There General Dukhonin, who had been ordered by the Soviet government to initiate peace talks two days earlier but had refused to do so, was dismissed and replaced by a member of the Soviet government, Ensign Nicholas V. Krylenko. Kryleno instructed military units to initiate armistice negotiations directly, each in its own sector. The Entente powers protested against the armistice negotiations to General Dukhonin, who then ordered the army to continue the war, because a new government was in the process of being formed. However, Krylenko made contacts with the German units, and announced that negotiations would begin on December 2, 1917.

In this fluctuating situation Masaryk had to decide what to do. He had several options: (1) go to the Romanian front; (2) to go to France. This would be the best solution, in his view. But was it practicable to transfer the whole army there when Russia was in flux? Would it be fair to Russia, which had given the Czechs the opportunity to form their own army, to desert her in her gravest hour? (3) to join the Volunteer army on the Don. One of Dürich's men, F. Král, left for the Don and beginning at the end of November 1917, organized there, with Captain Němeček, a unit composed of Czech volunteers (POWs) that fought on the side of the Russian Volunteer Army. (4) to join the Bolsheviks. The last alternative was advocated by a few left-wing Social Democrats. František Beneš and Karel Knoflíček, former Social Democrats, who were employed in the printing shop of *Čechoslovák* in Petrograd in the summer of 1917, established contacts with Leo Bronstein Trotsky's group, which merged with the Bolsheviks in August 1917. In July 1917, they participated in the antiwar demonstrations in Petrograd, were dismissed from the printing shop, and were later arrested. Once released from prison after the Bolshevik Revolution, with the help of Trotsky they published articles in *Pravda, Izvestia,* and *Armia i flot,* claiming to represent the "Social Democratic organization of Czech prisoners of war in Petrograd." They also had contacts with another leading Bolshevik, Karl Radek, and they parroted the slogans of the Bolshevik party coined for Russian soldiers. They urged the members of the Czechoslovak army corps to lay down their arms, and to drive out "all agents of capitalism who are campaigning for war" (i.e., Masaryk).[35] Since Bolshevik Russia was struggling for "peace without annexation and indemnities" on the basis of self-determination of nations, they claimed, Russia was also assuring the Czechs of their national rights. However, the agitation of Beneš and Knoflíček was ineffective, largely because they used very abstract arguments and because the army corps was located on the territory of the Ukrainian Republic, where there was another center of an independent Czech Social Democratic party. Although they did not directly support the Bolsheviks, these Social Democrats also gave Masaryk many problems.

The Bolshevik Revolution and Lenin's call for peace created an explosive situation in Russia. At first, the Allied diplomats in Moscow tended to agree with the many anti-Bolshevik Russians that the Bolsheviks were too weak to survive as the government of Russia.[36] Because Kerensky was unpopular in the country and was disliked by a great many foreign diplomats and military attachés, the Allies made no effort to save his regime. Although the Bolshevik coup was a Russian internal affair, its implication with respect to the conduct of the war was of vital concern to the Allies. The Bolshevik "Decree on Peace" and the subsequent peace moves made by the Lenin government forced the Allies to take a stand toward the Bolsheviks. Thus, the British War Office informed the War Cabinet that a separate peace by Russia would prolong the war.[37] But at this juncture neither the British nor the French were prepared to intervene against the Bolsheviks, to suppress them and restore Kerensky. Fundamentally, the Allies adopted a dual policy vis-à-vis the Bolsheviks, keeing in touch with them and, at the same time, aiding their opposition through military missions. The main Allied concern was to hold the front against the Germans, and the nature of the government in Russia was of secondary importance. Therefore, the military mission of the western

Allies attempted to enlist the support of all Russians who were willing to continue the war.

In order to discuss the new situation in Russia, Allied, Russian, Romanian, and Czech representatives met at a conference at Jassy, Romania, toward the end of November 1917. It was known that the Cossack General A. M. Kaledin, who had broken with Kerensky after the Kornilov affair, had several thousand troops under his command at Novocherkask, on the Don, and had proclaimed his opposition to the Bolsheviks and his loyalty to the Allies. Also, the king of Romania had told the British and French ambassadors at Jassy that, in view of the collapse of Russia and despite it, if his government continued to receive support from the Allies, he would try to force a passage through Russia with a portion of his troops in an effort to effect a junction with the Cossacks on the Don. However, if he did not receive the necessary assurances from the Allies, he would abdicate or even come to terms with the Central Powers.[38] Thus, from the Allied point of view, it was highly desirable to prevent the collapse of the Romanian front and to keep the lines of communication open between the Romanian army and the Cossacks on the Don. The representative of the Czechoslovak army in Russia, officer Čeřensky, was therefore asked whether the Czechoslovak army would be able and willing to take upon itself occupation of the territory between Bessarabia and the Don region. In his response to the question, Čeřenský explained why the Czechoslovak army was prevented from "intervening in internal affairs of Russia;" the reason was Masaryk's neutrality policy. Čeřenský said that "without an express order of the dictator of our nation, Masaryk, the army will not undertake anything." He suggested, furthermore, that if the Allies desired the participation of the Czech Legion in any of their actions, they should first transfer it completely into their service and furnish it with all necessities, and, especially, secure it financially. Should the Allies extend credits to the Legion, then it would be possible to consider the plan presented by the Allied spokesmen and General Alexeev, who wanted the Legion to occupy the main railroad centers between Bessarabia and the Don. Miliukov wrote about the plan directly to Masaryk. Alexeev was convinced that he, with the Czech Legion, could save the Don region and, eventually, the whole of Russia from Bolshevism.[39]

While the Allied representatives at Jassy tried to prevent the withdrawal of Romania from the war and attempted to enlist the help of the Czechoslovak army corps, Maugham, Masaryk's fellow chocolate drinker at the

The Bolshevik Revolution

Hotel Europa in Petrograd, was back in London conferring with government officials. As we noted earlier, Voska was also in London, but his recommendations about Anglo-American propaganda in Russia on a grand scale became of historical interest only. Maugham knew that propaganda could not salvage the situation in Russia. He and a Polish journalist, Jan Horodyski, proposed that the Allies, in order to achieve victory, make a bold decision to keep the Eastern Front active. The only way to prevent the front from collapsing completely was to contact immediately the leader of the Don Cossacks, General Kaledin, commanding troops loyal to the Allies, who could restore order and carry on the war. Maugham and Horodyski recommended that Kaledin be given financial support by the western Allies, and that he assume dictatorial powers and command over his own Cossacks, 100,000 men to be furnished by the Allies, and the Czech and Polish armies (estimated at 80,000 each) already in existence in southern Russia. Since the leftist anti-Bolshevik Boris V. Savinkov, a former terrorist, had made a good impression on Maugham, the latter recommended Savinkov as Kaledin's political advisor. It was hoped that Kaledin would attract loyal troops from other parts of Russia and that he would form an army about a million strong. The Maugham proposal was drafted by Wiseman, and the draft, in a revised form, was first discussed by Balfour with Colonel House and others, and then submitted to the British War Cabinet.[40]

The Allies, especially the British, wanted to keep the Romanian army on their side and to keep Russia from making a separate pace. Therefore, on December 3, 1917, the British War Cabinet decided to underwrite financially the Russian elements genuinely friendly to the Entente, of whom the chief were General Kaledin, Alexeev, and their supporters.[41] The cabinet was of the opinion that it would be possible to form a reasonably stable government in southern Russia (the Caucasus, the Cossack regions, and the Ukraine). This government, together with Romania, would be able to hold the front against the Central Powers, and would, through its command of coal, oil, and corn, effectively control the whole of Russia. Subsequently, the British military attaché in Jassy was instructed to go, possibly with his French colleague, to Kaledin. He was authorized to grant Kaledin "financial support up to any figure necessary."[42] In this British plan to reinvigorate the Eastern Front, endorsed by the French and U.S. governments, the Czechoslovak army corps, because of its strategic location, would play a key role. The British assumed that the Czechs were committed to the struggle against the Germans, and that they would be eager to fight on the front; however, they were bound to be disappointed, as the French had been earlier when Masaryk refused to leave the Ukraine an to take the army to the Romanian front.[43] Again as then, Masaryk insisted on neutrality, which he seemingly interpreted to mean a refusal to participate in any Allied action on the Eastern Front.

In contrast to Masaryk's position, Dürich's views on the need to resist the Bolsheviks were more in accord with those of the Allies and many of the Czech military and political leaders. The latter, however, did not challenge Masaryk's decisions and followed his leadership. Dürich was convinced that Maxa's and Masaryk's "neutrality" policy actually played into the hands of the Bolsheviks. Dürich contended that had the Czechs given help to General Kwiecinski when the latter requested it, Kiev would not have fallen into either Ukrainian or Bolshevik hands. He pointed out that, after the departure of the Russian troops from Kiev, the weak Ukrainian Rada was not able to cope with the agitation of the Bolsheviks and their military threat. Some two and a half months after the city was placed in the hands of the Rada, the Bolsheviks overran the Ukraine on the pretext that the Ukrainian government was giving aid to "counter-revolutionaries." Dürich offered testimony, confirmed by impartial experts, that neither the Ukrainian Rada nor the Bolsheviks had a proper and efficient military organization; both of them proved ignorant of military matters and had "a panicky fear of the Czechs."[44] The Czechs, together with the Russian army, could have prevented southern Russia's falling into the hands of either the Bolsheviks or the Germans. Even before the Bolshevik occupation of Kiev, Dürich asserted that the slogan of "non-involvement in Russia's internal affairs" entailed "a real interention on behalf of the Bolsheviks who were not 'an internal Russian affair' but a European affair.[45] The Bolshevik attempts to conquer Russia and to take the country out of the war were of great concern to the Allies. Bolshevism was therefore a Czech business, and it had to be opposed with all means. Not only Dürich, but many people in Russia, Europe, and America believed that the leaders of the Russian Bolshevik party were "agents of Berlin," as Jaroslav Hašek maintained in an article published in the *Čechoslovan* (Kiev) on January 6, 1918. Dürich was also critical of the other slogan used in Kiev by some Czechs: that it was necessary "to spare the Czech blood." It was his view that had the Czechs cooperated with General Kwiecinski and the Russian army, their losses would have been minimal and Czech blood would not have had to be shed "thousand times more" in the Ukraine, Russia, and Siberia later on.[46]

At this time Masaryk and Maxa were criticized by the aging Dürich, who was defeated but not destroyed. More than one year later, in January, 1919, Bohdan Pavlů, M. R. Štefánik (now already a general and minister of war in the Czechoslovak government), and General Janin would condemn Maxa for what he had done in Kiev, whose "logical consequence was the liquidation" of the Czech action in the Ukraine and Russia. They would reproach him with having been willing to "negoatiate with the Ukrainians, allies of Germans," during the departure from Kiev, and with other follies.[47] Though Masaryk had publicly taken responsibility for all this on several occasions, Pavlů, Štefánik, and Janin did not dare to criticize any of his decisions openly; instead, when Maxa traveled to Czechoslovakia in January 1919, on behalf of the Bolshevik regime, they blamed him for all that had happened.

The events in Kiev were significant for several reasons. First, Masaryk proved again that he and not Dürich or anybody else was in charge. Second, the Czechoslovak army corps, which was a part of the Eleventh Army of the South Western Front, followed the orders of its political commissar, Prokop Maxa, and his superior, Masaryk, and not those of the commanding officer of the Russian Eleventh Army. Third, those Russian officers who took orders from their superiors, agreed with them, and were willing to implement them were removed from the Czechoslovak army. This fact amply demonstrated to all parties concerned that Masaryk was the "dictator" of the army corps both in name and in reality. From then on, he was commander in chief of the Czechoslovak army; the situation did not change when the army became, technically, a part of the French army. Now Masaryk acted as a sovereign, deciding what policy the army should follow.

The army was the foundation of the future state to be created in accordance with Masaryk's philosophy. Masaryk therefore proceeded subtly to assure its pro-western and Hussite orientation by introducing a new military decoration and renaming the regiments. On August 31 (September 13), 1917, the division's order announced that Masaryk had approved a "Hussite Cross" to replace the Russian St. George Cross with which 267 members of the First Brigade had been decorated before January 1917.

(Also, 201 St. George medals had been awarded till then.) In order to break with the Catholic tradition and to show the Hussite outlook of the army for anyone to see in the future, the First Regiment of St. Wenceslas became the regiment of Master John Huss, the regiment of Sts. Cyril and Methodius was renamed the regiment of George of Podiebrady, the Third Regiment and the artillery brigade were assigned to John Žižka, etc.; and the whole First Division was called "Hussite."[48] The patron saints of the heroes of Zborov—Saints Wenceslas and Cyril and Methodius—were replaced by those in whose name the struggle against the Catholic Church would be bitterly fought in postwar Czechoslovakia. Masaryk never mentioned these things in his public pronouncements to the soldiers. His plan remained secret; his rhetoric contained phrases such as "we will be completely loyal to the Bolsheviks,"[49] and "we, the Czechoslovaks, love Russia, and we wish her to become a strong and free democracy."[50]

In his confidential and public discussions of what was to be done in the existing situation late in November and early in December 1917,[51] Masaryk pointed out that the Czechoslovak army was equipped and supplied by the Provisional Government and that its duty was to fight on the front. Furthermore, an agreement with France made it possible to send some 30,000 or more soldiers to France. The Bolsheviks, who claimed that they were the government of Russia, could not prevent the transfer of troops to France. They could not be recognized by the Czechoslovaks as the Russian government, nor would they be recognized as such by any government, said Masaryk. The Czechoslovaks could not follow the wishes of the Bolsheviks, because the latter could not conclude peace with anyone (since no government would recognize them). If the anarchy prevalent in Russia continued, the army would not consider itself bound by the promises that had been made and would not go to the front. In any case, it would take another month or two to complete the formation of the corps; in the meantime the French would take care of all the Czech troops. Furthermore, Masaryk stated, General Dukhonin was to be informed about whatever course of action was followed.

Should the Bolsheviks become the government and conclude a peace after all, Masaryk said, then they could merely disband the Czechoslovak military formations, but they could not hand the Czechoslovaks over to Austria-Hungary or Germany. In this extreme case, the Czechoslovaks would appeal to the Bolsheviks as fellow-revolutionaries; and since every peace agreement makes possible the insertion of an amnesty clause, the Bolsheviks would have to do at least that much for the Czechoslovaks. After all, the Czechoslovak attitude toward the Bolsheviks was governed by the principle of noninvolvement in internal political conflicts in Russia, and the Bolsheviks "will not be provoked" so that they could not interfere with "our work."

If peace were concluded by a government headed by Chernov—a government "recognized by the whole nation"—then the Czechoslovaks would demand the shipment of the whole army corps to France. Finally, the Allies might declare war on Russia and Japan might come out against Russia. In that case there would be no other alternative except "to go with the Allies." The army would not fight against Russia, indeed, but the Czechs would demand that the whole army corps be transferred to France.

For Masaryk, the main task of the Czechoslovak independence movement was to save the army corps. This task was related to the fundamental question of whether the Russian army could be restored and whether the Czechoslovaks could help in this restoration. As has been mentioned earlier, toward the end of November 1917, the French and English military missions and the Romanian government suggested transfering the army corps to the Romanian front, but Masaryk rejected this idea; he favored transferring the army corps to France. However, there were technical difficulties. First of all, the capacity of the railroads to Archangel and Murmansk was limited; furthermore, such a move would have required shipping the troops over territory controlled by the Bolsheviks, and Masaryk had ruled out going to France via Siberia because of the high costs involved. It should be repeated, however, that Masaryk's policy of noninvolvement in Russian internal affairs was not generally accepted and that it was challenged by the political left and right within the Czechoslovak independence movement as well as by internal political developments in Russia.

As Masaryk stated after the war, "our army had been formed in agreement with Rusia; our soldiers had sworn allegiance to Russia; we were devoted to Russia."[52] But this statement once again begged the questions: what kind of Russia? whose Russia? who represented the "real Russia"? Masaryk's assumption that the Bolsheviks could not conclude peace with the Central Powers, and that peace could be concluded only by a government that would represent the "whole Russia," proved to be wrong. Masaryk misjudged the Bolsheviks when he thought that they were amateurs, and he underestimated their will to power and their ability to hold power once they seized it. Polarization was taking place in Russia, and the Bolshevik power was challenged by the "Whites." As it happened, before his own dismissal on December 1, 1917, General Dukhonin released the arrested Russian generals, including Kornilov and Denikin. These officers sped to General Kaledin in the Don region, where they joined Generals M. V. Alexeev and P. N. Krasnov. On the same day Dukhonin appointed General Shcherbachev as the commander of the Russian troops on the Romanian front. (After the Bolshevik takeover of the headquarters, Dukhonin was murdered by drunken soldiers.)

On December 3, 1917, the Bolsheviks sued for peace. General Max Hoffmann, the German commander on the Eastern Front, granted them a ten-day armistice beginning December 7. Masaryk's assumptions notwithstanding, for reasons of their own, the Central Powers were willing to recognize the Bolshevik Council of People's Commissars as the government of Russia. In view of these developments, Masaryk began to consider another possible course of action. He negotiated with the government of the Ukrainian Republic for recognition of the Czecho-Slovak National Council as the only representative of the Czechoslovak nation, and he requested that that government furnish the Czechoslovak army corps with arms and supplies. Finally, Masaryk requested that if the Ukrainian government concluded peace with Austria-Hungary and Germany, it would allow the Czechoslovak troops to leave the Ukraine. For obvious reasons Masaryk's immediate concern was his relationship with the Ukrainian government. However, events proceeded faster than Masaryk had anticipated.

When in the middle of December 1917, the Ukrainian Rada disbanded the small Bolshevik garrison in the Ukraine and assumed full governmental powers, Masaryk ceased to recognize the Bolshevik government. He no longer needed it, since the Ukrainian government now assumed responsibility for holding the southern sector of the front and supplying the Czechoslovak army corps. Earlier in December, Masaryk had organized a consultative committee of nationalities oppressed by German and Austro-Hungarian imperialism, and at one of its public meetings on December 12, 1917, held under the sponsorship of the Ukrainian Central

Council in the Kievan circus, Masaryk, as the main speaker, called for the dismemberment of Austria-Hungary and the formation of a belt of independent states in central Europe, including an independent Ukraine. (One should not look for consistency in Masaryk's pronouncements.) In his conversations he approved of the Ukrainian action, justifying it on the grounds that "Russia is not able to establish order."⁵³ The overthrow of the Soviet power in the Ukraine and the establishment of the nationalist regime was hailed by the Czech newspaper, *Čechoslovan*, published in Kiev, while the official organ of Masaryk, *Československý deník*, was more reserved, emphasizing Czech neutrality in Russian internal affairs.

Masaryk launched *Československý deník* as the central organ of the CSNC and the Alliance of the Czecho-Slovak Associations in Russia after his arrival in Kiev, where he also moved the central office of the Russian branch of the CSNC. (Until then it had been in Petrograd.) In the first issue of the paper, on December 12, 1917, Masaryk published a letter to President Wilson, thanking him for the U.S. declaration of war on Austria-Hungary on December 7. In his letter Masaryk called Wilson a defender of the "principle of nationality" and a supporter of dismembering Austria-Hungary, though, at that time, Wilson held just the opposite views. (When he asked the U.S. Congress to declare war on Austria-Hungary, he emphasized that the United States did not intend to impair or destroy the Habsburg empire; and in his Fourteen Points he called merely for autonomy for the nationalities within Austria-Hungary.)

In these uncertain times, from December 13 to December 20, 1917, the second plenary meeting of the members of the Russian branch of the CSNC was held in Kiev. In his main report to the plenary session of the branch Masaryk reiterated some of the views that he had stated at the November meeting of the branch. He again expressed his doubt that the Bolsheviks could conclude peace, because the Germans would not recognize as the government a group that did not represent the whole country. However, he believed, the new government that would follow the downfall of the Bolsheviks, a government "recognized by the whole nation," might conclude peace.* In that case, it would be necessary to

---

* Masaryk was a victim of his own misjudgment of the Bolsheviks as "just another political party," as were many of his contemporaries and those

place the Czechoslovak army under the protection of the Allies, and to transfer it either to France or to another front: Turkish or Romanian. Masaryk held that the Ukrainian government had to be taken into account, since the Czech army corps was on Ukrainian territory. However, he wished the Czechoslovak independence movement to assume a different attitude toward Russia than toward the Ukrainian government. Now Masaryk disapproved of separating the Ukraine from Russia. He rejected cooperation with the Cossacks, and he dissociated himself from Captain Němeček and F. Král, who organized the Czech military unit at Rostov on the Don. At the end of his report he declared, "One thing I must emphasize: *our neutrality under all circumstances.*" Although he had no sympathies toward the Bolsheviks, he felt that "we should not send our corps against them. We do not want to spill Russian blood and we will not spill it."[54]

This was a declaration of intentions, well meant but difficult to implement. The Czechoslovak army corps was confronted with situations that changed from day to day as a result of a chain of events that was put into motion by the Ukrainian government's attempt to assert its authority and resist the Bolsheviks.[55] On December 17, when a six-day armistice was concluded, all armies on the "Ukrainian" front were placed under the command of General Shcherbachev. Then, during the negotiations at Brest-Litovsk, the armistice was extended for another twenty-eight days. During this time the Ukrainian government was responsible for holding the Ukrainian front; it allowed the Don Cossacks to return home from the front through the Ukraine, while not permitting the passage of the Bolshevik detachments across the country to the Don to fight the

who came after him. His contention was that since the Bolsheviks permitted an election to the Constituent Assembly, they would follow the practices generally used in parliamentary democracies and would resign after convening the assembly. The preliminary results of that election were known on December 8. On the basis of these preliminary results the Czech Social Democratic newspaper *Svoboda* predicted that the Socialist Revolutionaries would get 50 to 55 percent the deputies, the Bolsheviks 20 to 30 percent, and the Kadets 12 to 15 percent. When the Constituent Assembly met in January 1918, Lenin, realizing that he could not control it, ordered it disbanded.

Cossack army there. Accusing the Ukrainian government of counterrevolutionary activity, of an alliance with Kaledin, and of cooperation with other reactionary factions, the Bolsheviks delivered to it an ultimatum demanding permission for their forces to cross the country, joint action against the Don Cossacks, and recognition of the soviet form of government in the Ukraine. Since acceptance of these demands would have destroyed Ukrainian autonomy and delivered the country to the Bolsheviks, the Ukrainian government refused to comply, whereupon the Soviet government decided to send Russian troops to the Ukraine to disband the Central Council. Simultaneously, the Congress of Ukrainian Soviets, at its meeting at Kharkov on December 24 and 25, proclaimed the establishment of the Ukrainian Soviet Republic, prompting the Ukrainian government to seek a rapprochement with Germany.[56]

The French military mission at Kiev attempted to prevent the Ukrainian-German understanding by offering the Ukrainian state financial help and the use of military organizations representing national groups within Austria-Hungary, especially the Czechoslovak army corps. Notwithstanding these promises, the Ukrainian government, realizing its own weakness and knowing that it had no military supplies with which to oppose the Central Powers, that it was threatened by the Bolsheviks, and that, in view of Masaryk's disapproval of Ukrainian independence and his strict neutrality toward the Bolsheviks, it could not count on any help from the Czech army corps, decided to take part in peace negotiations and settle its problems in a different manner than that proposed by the French.[57]

The French interest in the Ukrainian situation becomes clear if it is placed in perspective. After the November Jassy conference, on December 23, 1917, the military representatives of the Supreme War Council, believing that the reconstruction of the Eastern Front and the withholding of Russian supplies from the Central Powers were vital to winning the war, recommended that "all national troops in Russia who were determined to continue the war should be supported by every means in our power."[58] Also, an Anglo-French convention of December 23, 1917, regulating the future action of France and Britain in southern Russia, contemplated the support of General Alexeev, and divided the spheres of action of the two powers along geographical lines, placing the Ukraine (and thus the Czech army corps) in the French zone of responsibility.[59]

French and British military missions were also attached to the armies organized by General Alexeev at Rostov on the Don (and financed the Czech unit organized there by Colonel Král and Captain Němeček). Toward the end of December 1917, General Alexeev asked Masaryk, in the name of these missions, to agree to the transfer of the Czechoslovak army to the Don. Masaryk was thus asked to make common cause with Generals Kornilov and Alexeev and his friend Miliukov against the Bolsheviks. He declined.[60]

When Masaryk was forced to deal with the question of the Russian Volunteer Army on the Don, he was evasive. He said that he was not fundamentally against it, but requested detailed information about the political program of General Alexeev, his attitudes toward the Constituent Assembly, the "temporary" (Lenin's) government, and the Ukraine. He insisted on the need to inform Alexeev, and the French representative with Alexeev, about Dürich, Král, and others, and the "behind the scene monarchical influences." He also explained his feeling that if the Don opposed the Ukraine, the latter would be forced into German arms. This reaction was, however, merely stalling tactics and a rationalization of Masaryk's unwillingness to commit the Czechoslovak army to any action in Russia. Publicly and openly he did not rule out the possibility of coming over to the Don at some future time. However, according to him, there was no unity of views on the part of the representatives of the Allies as to where the Czech army corps should go. As he put it, "Alexeev requests, in the name of the Allies, that we come to the Don. Berthelot [General Berthelot headed the French military mission in Romania] wants us, in the name of the Allies, in Romania. Finally, Tabouis [General Tabouis was the head of the French mission at Kiev, maintaining liaison with the Ukrainian government] recognizes our importance in the Ukraine."[61]

The preceding statement is one of Masaryk's casuistries. He himself contributed most to the confusion on the part of the Allied representatives, by refusing to permit the two Czech divisions to occupy Bessarabia and southern Russia (Ukraine), when such a request was made by the chiefs of the Allied military missions at their conference at Jassy, toward the end of November 1917. Now, to go to the Romanian front, to remain in the Ukraine, and to join the Cossacks on the Don amounted to one and the same thing: to make a definite commitment to the Allied cause. The

Czechoslovak army corps was to form the connecting link between the Romanian army, concentrated on a small part of Romanian territory, and the pro-Allied forces on the Don.[62] Indeed, the Czechoslovak army corps was declared by Masaryk a part of the French armed forces (after the establishment of the Czechoslovak army in France by the presidential decree of December 16, 1917), and was located in the area of French responsibility (in accordance with the Anglo-French agreement of December 23, 1917). The request that the Czechoslovak troops establish a junction with the Romanian army and the army of General Kaledin, made by the French government on December 29, 1917, reflected the Allied concern with the Romanian front and the need to prevent its collapse. The Romanian king notified the Allies on December 12, 1917, of his loyalty to the Allied cause and his willingness to retreat to southern Russia with his army.[63] Since the Czech army was at hand, it could have served as a junction with the Kaledin-Kornilov troops at the Don, and thus it could have made such a retreat possible. But Masaryk refused to cooperate, and everything collapsed.

As late as January 16, 1918, the French government attempted to prevent Romania's signing a separate peace by indicating that Romania's demands at the peace conference would be fulfilled only if the Romanian army retreated to southern Russia and remained loyal to the Allies till the end of the war.[65] However, Masaryk's refusal to provide the necessary cover for the Romanian army's retreat forced the king to conclude a separate peace. Also, on January 25, 1918, the Ukrainian Rada proclaimed Ukrainian independence and sent its delegate to Brest-Litovsk to sue for peace. Undoubtedly, the collapse of the Romanian-Ukrainian front was a setback for the Allies, and Masaryk was justifiably blamed for it.[66]

The decision made by the Ukrainian Rada to take part in peace negotiations at Brest-Litovsk early in January 1918, and the uprising against the Kaledin government on the Don at Yekaterinoslav on January 6, 1918, bringing about the establishment of a Soviet regime there on January 11, resulted in separating the Ukraine from the territories controlled by the Volunteer Army. This separation placed the Czechoslovak army corps in an awkward position. The Russian branch of the CSNC decided definitely to make the army corps into a part of the Czechoslovak army in France, so that its material security would be provided for by the

Entente powers and its transfer to France could be hastened.[67] (Until March 1918, the Czechoslovak army, as a part of the Russian army, was supplied by the Russian and Ukrainian governments.) All proposals for cooperation with General Alexeev were rejected. When Alexeev asked Czech prisoners of war in Tagangrod to join his army, the prisoners' organizations sent a delegation to the Russian branch of the CSNC to inquire how they should reply to the general's offer. The branch (Masaryk), on January 20, 1918, instructed the Czech prisoners of war not to enter the Volunteer Army, nor cooperate with it in any way, not even by working in military factories, since, according to the branch, such work would also constitute a kind of military service.[68]

On January 25 (February 7), the Ukraine declared its independence; and on the next day Masaryk renounced the agreement of January 2, 1918, that he had signed with the Ukrainian government. He said that he could "not recognize an independent Ukraine, outside the framework of Russia, as a legal body politics. This goes completely against my grains."[69] However, the Ukrainian declaration of independence was merely a pretext for Masaryk's repudiation of the agreement; he had known since January 10 that the Allies would assume financing the Legion and, therefore, he no longer needed the Ukrainian government.[70] He demanded, however, that the Ukraine honor the last point of the agreement: the free departure of the Czechoslovak troops from the Ukraine in the event that the government conclude peace. Also, as a result of protracted negotiations with representatives of the Allies, Masaryk was able to notify General Shokorov, the commander of the Czechoslovak army corps, that the French government had agreed to consider the Czechoslovak army in all parts of the former Russian state as a part of the Czechoslovak army under French command, and that from then on, all activity of the army corps would take place in close cooperation with the Allies.[71] The cooperation, however, meant that Masaryk would call the shots and the Allies would pay the bills.

Realizing the weakness of the Ukrainian government, and knowing that it could not count on any support from the 42,000 troops organized in the Czechoslovak army corps, the Bolsheviks began their advance toward Kiev a few days after Masaryk renounced the agreement with the Ukraine. The Czechs living in Kiev urged Masaryk to take a public stand against the Bolsheviks and their attempt to conquer the city, and, if necessary, to order the army to take a part in its defense, believing that a statement to that effect would be sufficient to scare the poorly trained and poorly equipped Red Guards off, and that the latter would not dare to attack the Czech army corps. But Masaryk refused, claiming that the individuals who asked him to fight the Bolsheviks were probably victims of "an Austrian intrigue."[72] When the Ukrainians asked Masaryk for help in the defense of the city, Masaryk told them, "No, gentlemen! Your Bolsheviks are a [political] party and you are fighting against your own people."[73]

Masaryk objected to the rumors, spread by some Ukranians, accordinto the which the Czechs would fight the Bolshevik invaders, calling them "a possible Austrian intrigue," and a manifestation of Ukrainian "disloyalty" toward the Czechs. The Red Guards, however, would have been easily taken care of by the Czech army, since they were poorly trained and poorly equipped. Even Masaryk called them "militarily ineffective."[74] He explained the Czech inaction: "If we gave orders to oppose the Bolesheviks, we would get in conflicts ourselves," since the army was composed of "various political parties with a relatively large number of Social Democrats." Thus, at the end, "a Czech would stand up against a Czech."[75] Acting upon Masaryk's instructions, the Second Division established a contact with the Boleshevik commander, Michael A. Muraviev, who "recognized" the Czehcs, "armed neutrality not only for the second division but also for the whole corps, and thus the whole affair was settled," as Masaryk described the incident.[76]

Despite Masaryk's orders forbidding the Czech soldiers to take part in the defense of the city, some of them joined the Ukrainians in their struggle against the invaders and about a dozen of them lost their lives during the fighting in Kiev. There was also Czechs among the invading Bolsheviks; one of them was Muraviev's chief of staff and became the commander of the city after the Bolsheviks conquered it.[77] With Kiev in Bolshevik hands, the Czech Bolsheviks began their campaign against the Czechoslovak army and the whole Masaryk-led independence movement, disregarding its neutral stand and the agreement with the French government making the Czechoslovak army a part of the French armed forces. The latter agreement resolved the legal standing of the Czechoslovak troops in Russia, but their practical standing in the Ukraine remained as uncertain as ever. It became increasingly difficult to implement the constantly proclaimed neutrality. Although many Czechs took the Bolsheviks for what they were, it took Masaryk and some others a considerable length of time to realize that they were not just "another political party" and that the party of professional revolutionaries was totally committed to revolution-making, in Russia and elsewhere.

CHAPTER NINE

THE CZECH BOLSHEVIK ATTEMPT TO CONTROL THE ARMY, THE REATREAT FROM THE UKRAINE, AND THE PEACE OF BREST-LITOVSK

Despite Masaryk's refusal to take any action that would topple the Bolshevik regime in Russia and his constant insistence on transferring the Czechoslovak Legion to France, the Czechoslovak communist historians call him an agent of French and British imperialism. While Masaryk's connections with the British and French governments can be easily documented, and while it is a matter of public record that from March 1918 on the French and British governments made substantial financial contributions to the recruitment and maintenance of the Czechoslovak Legion,[1] the communist historians go too far in their allegations. To be sure, Masaryk was a pro-western propagandist sent to Russia by the British, but this does not imply that Masaryk was a British puppet. Although he did take all the help that he could get from the British and French, he was his own agent, just as Lenin was Lenin's agent, though he was sent to Russia by the German general staff and received funds for his pacifist propaganda from the Germans. Masaryk's foremost objective was the establishment of a pro-western Czechoslovak state, headed by him and having a political system that would reflect his philosophy. He wanted to have the Czech Legion in France so that he could demonstrate that he, and not someone else, was the Czech leader, and so that he could use the Legion as a lever during the peace negotiations.

As has been noted, Masaryk did his best to prevent the engagement of the Czechoslovak army in any fighting inside Russia or on the front. While in Russia, he realized that the projection that Voska had given British intelligence in May and June 1917, on the number of potential Czechoslovak troops (250,000) was too high, and that only a fraction of the Czech and Slovak prisoners of war in Russia, fewer than 15 percent of them, had actually joined the army. One could suggest a few reasons for the reluctance of the Czech and Slovak prisoners of war to join the Czechoslovak Legion. Some of them were loyal to Austria-Hungary. Some of them did not have much confidence in Masaryk, being aware of his prewar ideology and politics. But the vast majority of them, including even some of those who volunteered for service in the Legion, did not want to fight on behalf of anybody, especially not against their own compatriots on the other side of the front. (On the Western Front, presumably, they would fight Germans.) After the Peace of Brest-Litovsk, when it became possible for some of the prisoners of war to return home, a considerable number of the Czechs and Slovaks in Russia chose not to do so for fear that they would be sent to fight on the Italian front. Undoubtedly, most of those who joined the Legion, especially those who did so before the February Revolution, were sincerely commited to the idea of an independent Czechoslovak state. However, there were those who joined the Legion for other reasons, including personal and economic ones. Those among the prisoners of war who possessed skills and worked in industries, or those who volunteered for work in agriculture, had a tolerable or even comfortable life. Those who did not have technically useful skills, who did not want to work in factories or agriculture (mainly unskilled workers and intelligentsia), found their life in captivity in Russia much more difficult. For many of them joining the Legion meant escaping the misery of prisoner of war camps.

There are no exact statistics on the social composition of the Legion. According to the estimates made by Czech Bolesheviks in Russia, almost 70 percent of the Legionnaires were workers, 10 percent petty bourgeois elements, and 10 percent kulaks.[2] The social composition of the Legion was stated in a letter by Beneš dated July 29, 1919, as follows: 20 percent farmers and agricultural workers; 20 percent students, including university students; 5 percent employees of banks and commercial businesses; 20 percent factory workers; 25 percent artisans; and 10 percent small businessmen.[3] Neither Beneš's figures nor the Communists' can be verified, and both refer to the situation as it existed in the Legion in 1919, after the establishment of the Czechoslovak state and the mobilization of the Czechs and Slovaks still in Siberia by the Czechoslovak government.

The political and socioeconomic situation among the prisoners of war was reflected in the composition of the Legion. Many of its members were Social Democrats, National Socials, or sympathizers with the socialist parties. Many of those whose motives for joining the Legion were other than anti-Habsburg Czech nationalism were more fascinated with the prospect of a long journey to France than with the fighting on the Eastern Front that was urged by the Allies and by many officers of the Legion. They agreed with Masaryk, who tried to avoid combat and save the Legion for the Western Front, where it would arrive toward the end of the war. But inaction and avoidance of contact with the enemy brought about a serious morale problem in the Legion.

Masaryk's neutrality notwithstanding, the Bolshevik commitment to revolution-making at home and abroad was evident with the Czechoslovak independence movement in Russia; the latter became a microcosm of the agitation for a world revolution. Masaryk discouraged the formation of political parties within the Legion, excepting the Social Democratic party. He assumed that the Czech socialists could have a beneficial influence on the Russian socialists. But the influence of the socialists was a two-way street. The bulk of the Legionnaires did not belong to any formally established political organization, and there are no reliable statistics on the prewar political affiliation of their families. The Social Democratic party, however, was very active within the Legion, creating problems for Masaryk and the officers, though the Czech leader professed to be favorably inclined toward the Social Democratic social and political objectives.

In addition to the two Social Democrats in Petrograd, František Beneš and Karel Knoflíček, who publicly endorsed the policy of the Bolshevik party, there were other Czech socialist and workers' groups in Russia. The one in Moscow supported the Masaryk-oriented Russian branch of the CSNC even after the October Revolution, as did the Social Democratic party organizations established within the Czechoslovak army corps. However, the Czechoslovak Social Democratic party in Kiev, and its newspaper

Svoboda, attempted to play an independent role. This independence led to friction between the so-called Central Committee of the Social Democratic party in Kiev and the soldiers, who resented the independent attitude of the newspaper and called for "unity" within the ranks. Some of the more radical soldiers even called on the Russian branch of the CSNC to close down *Svoboda.* The main bone of contention between the newspaper and the military socialists was the question of recruitment into the Czechoslovak army corps. For the soldiers, it was a sacred duty of every Czech and Slovak, regardless of political orientation, to enlist in the army, while *Svoboda* and the Social Democratic party in Kiev emphasized the voluntary nature of enlistment.[4]

Gradually the conflict sharpened. On November 22, 1917, *Svoboda* claimed that "the weapons that the capitalists put into the hands of the working people" would be turned, eventually, against their suppliers. The working people in Russia "had already done so, and the same will happen in the states of Western Europe sooner or latter." The soldiers, on the other hand, were of the opinion that the Czechoslovak army would arrive home united; that, since it would consist predominantly of workers, it would be able to defend the interests of both the workers and the young state.[5]

The friction between the army and the Social Democratic party in Kiev was also caused by uncertainty about the army's future and its mission. The Social Democrats who served in the army stood, on the whole, behind Masaryk, agreeing that the army should maintain neutrality in Russian internal affairs. They also hoped that an accommodation with the majority of the Kievan Social Democrats was possible. However, the conflict between the Social Democratic soldiers and the Social Democratic organization in Kiev came into the open at the conference of the Czech Social Democratic party in Kiev, which had opened on December 8, 1917, when the soldiers walked out and decided to hold their own conference on December 9 and 10. At the Social Democratic party's conference the main report was delivered by Alois Můna, who, referring to Masaryk's propagandistic conjectures, declared that if England was really interested in the liberation of subjugated nations, she would have to liberate the Irish, the Boers, and the peoples of India first. As he saw it, the war was not being waged for the liberation of peoples; peoples had to liberate themselves by revolution.[6]

The resolution adopted at this conference claimed that the war had been caused by the capitalist governments of both camps, and that the real liberation of all nations would take place only after the overthrow of capitalism by the proletarians of the whole world. This liberation could be achieved not by war but by a revolution such as had been accomplished by the Russian proletariat.[7] In contrast to this Bolshevik-style resolution signed by A. Hais, A. Můna, F. Novotný, and others, the resolution adopted by the Social Democratic soldiers at their own conference endorsed the revolutionary war against Austria-Hungary. Following the Marxist line, it blamed the capitalist order, especially the imperialistic expansionism of Austria-Hungary and Germany, as the main cause of the war. Still, the Social Democrats, because of their solidarity with the whole Czech nation, would voluntarily take part in the struggle for independence and the establishment of an independent Czechoslovak state. The soldiers' resolution expressed the conviction that the future independent Czechoslovak democratic republic would give workers complete social freedom, and that eventually the rule of socialism would come. It rejected, however, the Bolshevik tendency represented by *Svoboda* and the Central Committee of the Social Democratic party in Kiev, on the grounds that the attempt to reach the final goals of socialism "at the present time contains in itself the danger of doing damage to what is attainable."[8]

Masaryk called the people around *Svoboda* "our Czech Bolsheviks," who, in establishing "their own different, hostile organization,"[9] were attacking the independence movement. However, after both conferences, *Svoboda* rejected the view that it represented the "Czech Bolsheviks" and called for the formation of a coalition government in Russia that would reflect the results of the election to the Constituent Assembly. Responding to Masaryk's statement that, from the point of view of neutrality, "we cannot approve . . . of the call for an alliance with the Soviets," *Svoboda* insisted that "to go with the Soviets does not mean that the Czech Socialists should go with the Bolsheviks." It claimed that endorsement of Czech demands could be given only by the Soviets. As *Svoboda* said, the Czech socialists could not turn to Miliukov, Kornilov, and Kaledin in an effort to have their aspirations realized.

Mutual recriminations continued. The Kievan branch of the CSNC accused the Kievan Central Committee of the Social Democratic party of Bolshevism, while the Social Democrats replied by categorizing the Kievan branch with the tsarist generals. The Kievan Social Democrats insisted that, even before the establishment of the Czechoslovak state, conditions had to be created within the independence movement that would guarantee the socialist development of the future Czechoslovakia. They believed that the Czechoslovak independence movement must continue the world revolution that had started in Russia. Therefore, they did not endorse building the army corps, even if they did not fight publicly against it. They insisted on the continuation of the Social Democratic party, independent of the Russian branch of the CSNC, in order to inject the ideas of socialism into the Czechoslovak independence movement and the Czechoslovak army. The Kievan Social Democrats saw in the Russian Revolution a great help for the attainment of their objectives. They also believed that it was everyone's duty to support this revolution. As J. Hašek put it, "At first we needed Russia, and now Russia needs us."[10] They objected to the presence in the Russian branch of the CSNC of the former representatives of the Czechoslovak independence movement in tsarist Russia, especially Jiří, Bohdan Pavlu, and Prokop Maxa.

The main opponents of the Kieven Central Committee of the Social Democratic party were the soldiers, whose influence in the branch of the CSNC was increasing. (Rudolf Medek, representing the army, was the third vice-chairman of the branch.) *Československý deník,* edited by B. Pavlů, cultivated their hostility. The most radical of the Czech Social Democrats in Russia were F. Beneš and K. Knoflíček, living in Petrograd, where they published the first issue of *Pochodeň* on February 7, 1918. With the left-wing Bolsheviks, they believed that a socialist revolution in central and eastern Europe would automatically result from the electrifying influence of the socialist revolution in Russia and the peace declarations of the new Soviet government. This view was rejected by the organizations of the Czech prisoners of war, the CSNC, and even the Kievan Social Democrats. The radical Bolshevik *Pochodeň* proclaimed that "our aims can be attained *only* through the struggle of the proletariat of all nations against the international capitalist class." It denounced the Masaryk-led movement, recommended demobilizing the Czech volunteers, and labeled the CSNC a "counterrevolutionary organization."[11]

The leaders of the Russian branch of the CSNC and the army corps found themselves in Soviet-controlled territory when Soviet troops captured Kiev on February 8, 1918. The CSNC leaders and the army corps maintained complete neutrality during the fighting. The Soviet troops recognized the "armed neutrality" of the Czechoslovaks in an agreement confirmed by the supreme commander of the Soviet army in the Ukraine, Michael A. Muraviev. On this occasion, the Presidium of the Russian branch of the CSNC issued a proclamation to the "Citizens of Kiev," emphasizing that the Czechoslovak troops "always maintained, maintain, and will maintain the strictest neutrality in internal political conflicts in Russia." On the eve of the entry of Soviet soldiers into Kiev, on February 7 (January 25), 1918, Masaryk issued a proclamation to the Legionnaires saying that, despite the rumor related to the negotiations at Brest-Litovsk, "our army and our organized prisoners of war do not retreat in any way from their revolutionary struggle against Austria-Hungary and Germany." Continuing to fight for the self-determination and independence of the Czechoslovak nation, the Czechoslovak troops in the Ukraine and all parts of the former Russian state were "a part of the Czechoslovak army that is under command of the French Supreme Commander. From now on the future development and destination of our army will be decided in closest agreement with the Allies."[12]

Masaryk, Maxa, and the representatives of the French, Serbian, and British missions negotiated with Muraviev on February 10. In the agreement they reached, all the Czechoslovak troops in Russia and the Ukraine were given the status of "armed neutrality" with respect to internal politics in Russia and the Ukraine. The chief of Muraviev's staff informed Masaryk on February 16 that the supreme commander of the Soviet troops had no objection to the departure of Czechoslovak units for France or to their being transferred elsewhere.[13] (On the copy of the communication from Muraviev that was sent to Paris, Masaryk wrote by hand the following remark: "A proof that it is possible to do business with the Bolsheviks.")[14]

On February 12, 1918, the Russian branch of the CSNC issued a new proclamation "On the Further Recruitment of the Army and the Organization of Prisioners of War," whose purpose was to counteract the rumors arriving from Brest-Litovsk about a separate peace in the immediate future. It urged those Czechs and Slovaks who had not already done so to join the Legion. The appeal was followed up by Masaryk's speech at the meeting of the Russian branch of the CSNC at Kiev on February 14, 1918, which urged the branch to do anything possible to prevent the return home of prisoners of war, should peace be concluded at all. (On February 14 [February 1], 1918, the Soviets introduced a new calendar. For events after this date, there is no need to give two dates in order to prevent confusion.) According to Masaryk, Austria-Hungary and Russia would exchange prisoners of war on the following legal-military basis: "Austria will request our prisoners of war from Russia in exchange for Russian prisoners of war held in Austria. Any of our well-informed prisoners of war will tell the Bolsheviks: I do not want to go home! And the Bolshevik government is democratic and socialist: it cannot force him to return. We must be aware of it!" The soldiers of the Czechoslovak army are, according to the generally accepted international norms, deserters, said Masaryk, and as such they cannot be "extradited by any democratic government." This principle is endorsed by "all liberal states, except Germany and Austria." (This was not true.) Masaryk also discussed the social problems in the army, saying that although it was necessary to pay attention to the social welfare of prisoners of war and soldiers, any attempt "to solve the social problem, e.g., agrarian, is impossible, leaving aside the fact that most people do not understand these things in the first place." As far as the Bolsheviks were concerned, Masaryk reported that he had already received a concrete answer "from the presently ruling circles," and that "they recognize our armed neutrality." As soon as fighting began in Kiev, Masaryk said, he had told everybody, and

> especially to the representatives of the Allies publicly: I am not afraid of the Bolshevik victory. Why? Because I did consider the recent conduct of the Ukrainian government to be harmful to our Slavic cause; because of it [i.e., the Ukrainian government's declaration of independence] the Ukraine could become a German-Austro-Hungarian province. The Bolsheviks, by their re-attaching the Ukraine to Russia, are closer to our aim. This does not imply that I approve of the system of Russian Bolshevism; it is as foreign to us as was tsarism. Our army began under the tsar, existed under the Provisional government, and now exists under Bolshevism. All the

same....We are not Russians....The Bolsheviks are at home and can, therefore, solve internal Russian problems. We will be completely loyal to the Bolsheviks and honest with them; however, we will not promise any collaboration with them that would not be practicable.[15]

It seemed to Masaryk that the Soviet occupation of Kiev would make it possible for the Czechoslovak army corps to get out of a difficult situation and finally be transported to the Western Front. Matters became much more complicated, however, when the Czechoslovak left-wing socialists came out against neutrality and against the departure of the Czechoslovak armed forces from Russia.

Although *Svoboda* had endorsed neutrality during the fight for Kiev and the street fighting there, on February 14 it changed its stand and adopted the line of *Pochodeň*. Its declaration, addressed to "Comrades! Czechoslovak Workers, and Soldiers!" asserted that "the proletarian revolution goes victoriously throughout the world," and that the workers of Austria and Germany were following the example of their Russian comrades. Contrary to fact, it asserted that "the Czech proletariat sheds blood in the streets of Prague," and that the hour of revolution had come. In this "hour of struggle with the capital," the Czech proletarian could not remain neutral. An appeal was made to "organize a Czechoslovak socialist army'" and a "Czechoslovak Red Guard." Furthermore, *Svoboda* asserted, the Czechoslovak independence movement abroad must be given a new direction. At the same time, recruitment began for the Czechoslovak units of the Red Guard, organized with the consent of the Kievan Soviet and the encouragement of the Czech Bolshevik commander of the city. The Czechoslovak troops, however, were not much influenced by this agitation, though about two hundred soldiers and some prisoners of war joined the Red Guard.[16]

The Russian branch of the CSNC denounced the organizing of the Red Guard as a violation of neutrality. *Československý deník* wrote on February 16, 1918, that while a Red Guard was being organized in Kiev, a Black Guard was being organized on the Don; it rejected both. This polarization among the Czechs in Russia was called a fragmentation of forces by the representatives of the CSNC, which reprinted articles from Social Democratic newspapers in western Europe and Austria-Hungary in order to prove that there was no socialist revolution under way there, and that the Social Democratic parties there advocated not the class struggle and the struggle for socialism, but the struggle against the Central Powers and for national independence.[17]

Masaryk entered the polemics between the partisans of neutrality on the one hand and those of cooperation with the Soviets on the other, by emphasizing again and again the principle of neutrality and the need to continue the fight against Austria-Hungary. "We are not Russians," Masaryk said, and therefore "we cannot intervene in Russian economic and other conditions."[18]

The "Russian conditions," however, intervened in the Czechoslovak independence movement and the army. Masaryk did not comprehend the adverse effects of inaction, idleness, and avoiding combat on the men, especially on those soldiers who had joined the Legion because they had been inspired by heroism and the somewhat exaggerated glory of the battle of Zborov. There was a serious morale problem in the Legion. After the dismissal of most of the Russian officers and the voluntary departure of others, the officer corps of the Legion was rather young. The newly promoted regimental commanders were men in their twenties or thirties; their lack of experience and maturity made them unsure of themselves and unable to generate respect and confidence on the part of regular soldiers and noncommissioned officers. Among the youthful commanders were Lieutenant Stanislav Čeček, Lieutenant Jan Syrovy, Lieutenant-Colonel Sergei Vojtsekhovskii, Lieutenant Gajer, Captain Radola Gajda, Captain Komárek, etc.[19]

On February 17, Masaryk held a conference with General Shokorov, his commander in chief, and General Dieterichs, his chief of general staff, in the presence of political commissars Jiří Klecanda and Prokop Maxa. The sole item on the agenda was "the moral decay of the Legion." The two general were unhappy with the demoralization of the troops and the agitation from within and from without, and felt that both men and officers needed reeducation, because they did not understand their duties. On the same day the Russian branch of the CSNC held its meeting and discussed the dissatisfaction of the soldiers. According to one member of the branch, 80 percent of the troops were dissatisfied with the situation in the Legion. Under pressure from the Social Democratic members of the branch, Masaryk accepted the resignation of its two right-wing members.

His appeasement of the left-wingers, however, did not stop the pressure from the extreme left, urging that the whole army corps join the revolution.[20] A decision was therefore made to withdraw the Legion from Kiev, the hotbed of Bolshevik agitation.

At its last meeting at Kiev on February 20, the Russian branch of the CSNC ordered the Legion to leave the Ukraine, and called a military congress for March 15, 1918; on the next day the office of the branch moved out of Kiev to Piriatin. Masaryk then departed for Moscow in the company of members of the French and British missions. While the army corps prepared to leave Russia for France, a handful of Social Democrats called for the use of the corps in defense of revolutionary Russia. Petrograd's *Pochodeň* and Kiev's *Svoboda* were convinced that the world revolution had begun; they demanded the "purging" of the army's "bourgeois counter-revolutionary elements" and the entry of the corps "as one great whole into the Socialist army."[21]

In the midst of the ensuing agitation, in which the left-wing Social Democrats called for the defense of the Czechoslovak and Russian revolutions, one of them, A. Můna, proposed the establishment of a "Czechoslovak Revolutionary Council of Workers and Soldiers." At a meeting called *ad hoc* by left-wing Social Democrats, on February 24, 1918, Masaryk, who was away in Moscow, was elected chairman of this council without his knowledge. Members of this council were individuals from the socialist organizations, including the Czech Red Guard. This "new organ of power" invoked Masaryk's name in calling for the arming of all Czechs and Slovaks and their concentration in a Czechoslovak (socialist) army. A. Hais and K. Koníček claimed that the establishment of this revolutionary organ constituted, in fact, the "seizure of power" within the Czechoslovak liberation movement and the Czechoslovak army corps by the Czech Bolsheviks. The Revolutionary Council claimed to represent the whole revolutionary action in Russia. It demanded a purge of "reactionaries" in the Czechoslovak army corps, especially the dismissal of the commissar of the Czechoslovak army, Professor Maxa. In his place left wing socialist comrade Janík was to be "elected," with Vaníček as his deputy.[22]

The Czech Bolsheviks attempted to confuse and deceive their compatriots in Russia and seize control of the army. As a result of their intensive agitation, however, "only 218 men out of the whole army joined the Reds, and several of them came back the next day." According to Masaryk, this episode opened the eyes of many soldiers who, till then, were unaware of Bolshevik methods and propoganda.[23] (It was doubtful that it was an eyeopener for Masaryk, who continued on the same course,.) Many of the soldiers and officers realized that Dürich might not have been wrong, after all, and they began to question the wisdom and motives of Maxa and others who denounced him as "a reactionary" and a "Slavic dilettante."

The attempted coup d'état failed. The Czech Bolsheviks also failed in their effort to turn the Czechoslovak troops against the Germans who had invaded the Ukraine. (Being unable to cope with the Bolsheviks, who had occupied most of the Ukraine, the Ukrainian Rada had appealed to the Germans for help.) The Czech Bolsheviks formed a battalion in the Red Army and were now urging the Czechs to stop the German advance,[24] but the Czech soldiers did not forget the recent urgent call for the dissolution of the Czechoslovak army, the formation of the Red Guard, and the Bolshevik attempt to usurp the leadership of the Czechoslovak independence movement. The Czech soldiers were unwilling to listen now to the sudden cry by the same people to fight the Central Powers. Some Czech units were already withdrawing from the right (western) bank of the Dnieper River to its left (eastern) bank on February 23 and 24. *Svoboda's* appeals were of no avail; the soldiers were also skeptical about the sincerity of *Pochodeň's* sudden greetings to "the Czech revolutionary army," which it had described just two weeks earlier, on February 7, 1918, as "a shameful corpus of the bastardly Czech military action." In view of the Soviet government's subsequent acceptance of the German ultimatum to recall its troops from the Ukraine, Czechoslovak resistance to the German troops would have been much worse than just an exercise in futility; it would have been both a political and a military mistake. The only rational course of action the Czech troops could have followed was to retreat from the Ukraine in order to save the army corps. This they did.

After the collapse of Soviet power in the Ukraine, the Czechoslovak Revolutionary Council of Workers and Soldiers collapsed. This failure, and the retreat of the Czechoslovak troops from the Ukraine, considerably weakened the extreme left in the Czechoslovak independence movement. The left-wing Central Committee of the Kievan Czechoslovak Social

Democratic party moved closer to the Petrograd group of Koníček and Beneš; with a few defectors from the Russian branch of the CSNC (Skoták, Synek, Vaníček, and Koudelka) and other individuals they strengthened the emerging Czechoslovak communist movement in Russia.[25] The Czech and Slovak communists established their organization in isolation from the Czechoslovak army and the mainstream of the Czechoslovak independence movement.

In his last public speech before his departure from Russia, on February 27, 1918, Masaryk stated that the whole army corps would be transferred to France. "Our boys will be moved there in groups. . . . The whole expedition is directed by a French General. This will simplify the matter . . . we will also continue further recrutiment." As far as the prisoners of war were concerned, Masaryk said that anyone who had returned home was "immediately placed into the army," and most of the Czech returnees were "pushed into Hungarian regiments and sent to the Italian front. It is our duty to see to it that as few people as possible are permitted to go home." Masaryk said that after a lot of thinking, he had arrived at the conclusion that a well-organized army would be more beneficial to the independence movement than anything else. Therefore, "we will continue to insist on military organization and will ship soldiers to France, so that they could not go home. Thus, our task will remain the same."[26]

As long as Russia had been united and all government offices had been concentrated in Petrograd, said Masaryk, the Russian branch of the CSNC had been there also. But Russia was falling apart, and different governments, though temporary in nature, were being organized. Therefore, Masaryk believed, the recruitment and organizational structure of the military formations had to be adjusted to the existing situation. He stated that there would be "rallying points in different provinces, in Siberia, Don, etc.," and military units "will be organized there. At the present time," said Masaryk, "a soldier does not need anything but a rifle in order to defend himself not against the Bolsheviks, but against bandits."[27] (This statement demonstrates Masaryk's simplification of the recruitment problem and his lack of understanding of logistics and military science.)

Masaryk had left the Ukraine on February 22, upon the suggestion of General Tabouis, and had arrived in Moscow, where the Soviet government had relocated from Petrograd. He negotiated with the Soviet authorities, in accordance with the decision of the Supreme War Council in Paris, about the transfer of the Czechoslovak Legion to France via Vladivostok, and with the Allied representatives about the financing of the expedition. While in Moscow, Masaryk was received by Prince Eugene N. Trubeckoj, former member of the tsarist State Council, on March 1; on March 2 and 5, 1918, he conducted discussions with Boris V. Savinkov, now in the employ of the British, who had selected him as the political advisor of the "Whites" on the Don.[28] The subject of the discussions was the anti-Bolshevik action on the Don and its financial needs. Reportedly, Savinkov complained that the shortage of funds was responsible for the slow progress in building the Volunteer Army, and Masaryk arranged for Savinkov to receive through Jiří Klecanda, 200,000 rubles, for which the left-wing former terrorist was grateful.[29] Since Masaryk was not short of funds, being in constant touch with British and French agents and members of military missions, he was able to help out Savinkov.[30] (This seems to be a case of "laundering money." Later the Allied missions subsidized Savinkov directly.)

In Moscow Masaryk arranged for the financing of the Czech Legion by the western Allies from March 1918, on. On the actual amount of money spent by the Allies on the Czech Legion the communist historians quote Lenin, and he, in turn, quotes the Czech Bolshevik newspaper, *Průkopník svobody*. According to its account, on March 7, 1918, the Russian branch of the CSNC received the first payment of 3,000,000 rubles from the French consul in Moscow. The money was given to František Šíp, who was in charge of financial matters and procurement for the Legion. Altogether, the French consul gave Šíp and Bohumil Čermák of the Russian branch of the CSNC 8,000,000 rubles; other persons received some money; and the British consul contributed 80,000 pounds sterling. Thus, according to this source, the total amount received by the Legion from the French and British governments was approximately 15,000,000 rubles.[31] Lenin's claim that the French consul in Moscow, Grenard, had instructions to pay out credits to the Czech Legion in rubles is borne out by evidence obtained from French government archives; by Masaryk's book; by Šíp, who was in charge of procurement and thus, presumably, paid out most of the money, and who dealt with the Russian cooperatives in Siberia that were supplying the troops; by the final report of the liquidation commission in Czechoslovakia in 1934.[32] Naturally, since the Legion was no longer supplied by the Ukrainian government or the

Bolsheviks and was traveling to France, it had to live on credits from the western Allies.

In Moscow Masaryk appointed as his plenipotentiary for political negotiations Jiří Klecanda, for military matters Prokop Maxa, and for financial matters F. Šíp. He also gave Klecanda written instructions on how to handle all kinds of situations, including armed attack by any party in Siberia—in which case the troops were to resort to "energetic defense" —and how to use various individuals in the army and the branch of the CSNC.[33] (Klecanda died suddenly in Omsk on April 28, 1918.)

Before taking off for Vladivostok, Masaryk issued two last manifestoes: one dated March 6, 1918, addressed to the "Russian Czechs and Slovaks," announcing that a part of the army was leaving for the French front; and the other dated March 7, 1918, addressed to "Brothers Soldiers and Prisoners of War!"[34] Masaryk told the soldiers that he was leaving in order to become their "quartermaster in France, where we shall meet again." Reflecting his tendency to exaggerate, he claimed that "50,000 our beautiful, brave soldiers" were on their way to France, and that an "additional 50,000 have enlisted." When "the Russians began to make peace, I saw to it that ours would get to the French front." (The fact is that Masaryk signed an agreement with Albert Thomas, the French minister of munitions, to transfer 30,000 troops to France, shortly after his arrival in Russia, on June 13, 1917.)[35] "Even the Bolshevik government agreed to provide sufficient number of trains for the transportation of our army," said Masaryk. "Then an excellent army of 100,000 will be in France. In Italy there are more than 20,000 prisoners of war and from among these three fourths fight already shoulder to shoulder with Italy."[36]

The truth of the matter was that the Italian army had placed some Czech prisoners of war in labor battalions and used them for manual work behind the front. Alarmed at these developments, Štefánik hurried to Italy to negotiate the establishment of a Czechoslovak army in Italy to be sent to France, with not much success. He submitted a memorandum on the subject to the Italian government on March 14, 1918; on April 19, he received oral consent to the transfer of some volunteers to France, followed by an agreement between the CSNC and the Italian prime minister signed on April 21, 1918.[37] The Czechoslovak division took a larger part in Italian military operations on the front only in the summer of 1918, though individual Czechs joined the Italian army in

1917. (A Czech deserter, František Hlaváćek, became an officer in the Italian army in April 1917.)[38]

Although military decisions in World War I were destined to take place on the Western Front, the Czechoslovak army never arrived in France; it was prevented from doing so by developments in Russia. The Soviet government accepted the humiliating conditions and signed the peace treaty of Brest-Litovsk on March 3, 1917. Among the treaty provisions that affected the status of the Czechoslovak army were the Soviet commitments: (a) to stop propaganda and agitation against the governments of the public and military institutions of the Central Powers (art. 2); (b) to carry out, without delay, the full demobilization of the army (art. 5); (c) to clear Ukrainian territory (art. 6); and (d) to release and return prisoners of war (art. 8).[39]

After a protracted debate during the Fourth Congress of Soviets, Lenin brought off the ratification of the treaty against vigorous opposition, thereby provoking hostility toward his regime on the part of a great many Russians of all shades of political opinion. This created a new situation for the Allies; their agents in Russia who hoped that the Bolsheviks might invite an intervention in order to restore the Eastern Front against the Central Powers proved to be wrong. The treaty was a milestone for Lenin, an opening of a new era of Soviet-German cooperation, and a document that, he believed, would be torn up by the German proletariat after a successful socialist revolution in Germany. The treaty meant for him, above all, international recognition of his regime. Being recognized as the government of Russia by the Central Powers, the revolutionary government was the only recognized government in Russia. This made it possible for Lenin to concentrate the Bolshevik efforts on defeating those in Russia who opposed his rule. Russia was out of the war, but another war, a civil war, was to plague that country for several years to come.

CHAPTER TEN

THE HOME FRONT, CONGRESSES IN ROME AND PRAGUE, AND THE INCREASING IMPORTANCE OF THE ARMY ABROAD

In his amnesty manifesto of July 2, 1917, Emperor Charles announced the pardon of political offenders and expressed a hope that all peoples in the empire would join him in his efforts to heal the wounds of the war. A total of 719 Czechs, including many members of the *Sokol* organization, went free. Since the amnesty did not include Karel Kramář and Alois Rašín, the Czech Union urged the emperor to grant them pardon, and they were released from prison on July 10, 1917, though the Austrian authorities refused to restore their mandates on the ground that they were convicted felons. On July 3, 1917, Masaryk and Dürich lost their seats in the Vienna parliament, because they did not comply with the rules of order—they neither attended nor excused themselves for not attending the meeting of the parliament.[1]

Contrary to his expectations, the magnanimous emperor's act did not join all the nations in the empire in the effort to remedy the wounds of war. On the contrary, it was resented and denounced by some of the Czech-hating Austrian Germans on the one hand, and it strengthened the Czech resistance on the other. The radicals among the Austrian Germans called for hanging every traitor in time of war, and the Czechs gave Kramář a hero's welcome upon his return to Prague in October 1917. According to František Soukup, a Czech Social Democrat, "the Emperor's amnesty did not create in the Czech nation an atmosphere of conciliation and gratitude. Quite the contrary! It only strengthened Czech resistance."[2] Although the leader of the Czech Social Democrats declared in the Vienna parliament on June 13 that his party "stands unreservedly on the basis of the Austria state idea," he resigned the leadership of the party on September 29, 1917, and on October 4 gave up the vice-chairmanship of the Czech Union.[3] A right-wing socialist and follower of Masaryk, Gustav Habrman, succeeded him in the party post, and a National Social, Václav Klofáč, who had been released from prison in July, in the Czech Union function. The nationalistic wing on the political right began to gravitate around Kramář and Rašín.

In January 1918, a majority of the State Rights party decided to join the Young Czech party. Also, Adolf Stranský's Moravian People's Progressive party merged with the party of Kramář and Rašín. Subsequently, on February 9, 1918, the Young Czech party ceased to exist and in its place a new party was established under the name of Czech State-Right Democracy. Its chairman was Karel Kramář, who also became, formally and in fact, the leader of the national independence movement at home.[4] Another leader of the party and the movement, Alois Rašín, was the principal author of the so-called Epiphany Declaration of January 6, 1918,[5] adopted as a resolution by the "general diet" of all Czech deputies in the Austrian imperial parliament and in the Czech lands' diets. The meeting of these deputies was called for the express purpose of giving an official Czech reply to a policy statement made by the Austrian minister of foreign affairs, Czernin, on December 25, 1917.

On Christmas Day, 1917, at Brest-Litovsk, speaking for the Central Powers, Czernin accepted parts of the Bolshevik peace proposal calling for no war indemnities, no forcible annexation of territories conquered during the war, the withdrawal of troops occupying such territories, and the restoration of political independence to peoples that had lost it during the war. The Central Powers were willing to conclude, immediately, a general peace on two conditions. One, all powers participating in the war would bind themselves to the terms specified by Czernin. Two, with respect to point three of the Bolshevik proposal, the question of self-determination for national groups that before the war had not been politically independent, their cases were *not* to be solved internationally at Brest-

Litovsk, but independently and "constitutionally" by the states concerned.[6] By insisting that the question of self-determination of national minorities was an internal affair of the Habsburg state, and that it would have to be solved in accordance with the constitution of that state, Czernin implicitly rejected the request that had been made by Deputies Staněk and Klofáč, in the name of the Union of Czech Deputies, on December 4, 1917. The deputies then demanded that the Austrian delegation to the peace negotiations at Brest-Litovsk incorporate the principle of self-determination into its peace proposal, and that the composition of Austria's delegation reflect the strength of the various nationalities in the monarchy. They demanded that one-fifth of the delegation's membership be reserved for Czechs and Slovaks. The Czech deputies to the Austrian parliament were unhappy about Czernin's rejection of their demands, and their resolution reflected their disappointment.[7]

The Epiphany Declaration recalled that the Czech deputies in their memorandum of December 8, 1870, during the Franco-Prussian War, had expressed their views on general European problems and solemnly declared that "only from the recognition of the equality of all nations and from natural respect for the right of self-determination could come true equality and fraternity, and general peace and true humanity." The Czech deputies, true to the principles of their ancestors, "in the name of the Czech nation and its oppressed and forcibly silenced Slovak branch in Hungary," greeted with joy the fact that all states now accepted the right of nations to free self-determination as "a guarantee of a general and lasting peace." While the "new Russia" also accepted the principle of self-determination of nations as a fundamental condition for peace during attempts to obtain a general settlement, the Austro-Hungarian delegate declared "in the name of the Quadruple Alliance that the question of self-determination of those nations which have not hitherto enjoyed political independence should be solved in a constitutional manner within the existing state." The deputies rejected this view. The "indignantly" expressed regret that their nation was being deprived of its political independence and of the right of self-determination, and that by means of artificial electoral statutes, they were left to "the mercy of the German minority and the government of the centralized German bureaucracy."

"Our brother Slovaks became the victims of Magyar brutality," the declaration continued; and in Hungary *"constitution is nothing but a means of shameful domination by the oligarchy of a few Magyar aristocratic families."* And yet,

> Our nation longs with all the democracies of the world for a general and lasting peace. But our nation is fully aware that *no peace can be permanent except a peace which will abolish old injustice...* predominance of states and nations over other nations.... *We Deputies of the Czech nation declare that a peace which would not bring our nation full liberty could not be and would not mean a peace to us,* but would be only the beginning of a new, desperate, and continuous struggle for our political independence.... *Our nation asks for independence* on the ground of its historical rights, and is imbued with the fervent desire to contribute towards the new development of humanity on the basis of liberty and fraternity in a free competition with other free nations, which our nation hopes to accomplish in a sovereign, equal, democratic and socially just state of its own, built upon the equality of all its citizens within the historic boundaries of the Bohemian lands and of Slovakia, guaranteeing full and equal national rights to all minorities... we solemnly protest against the rejection of the right of self-determination at the peace negotiations, and *demand that, in the sense of this right, all nations, including, therefore, the Czecho-Slovaks, be guaranteed participation and full freedom of defending their rights at the Peace Conference.*

The prohibition against publishing the resolution and the government's attempt to thwart it in parliament emphasized its defiance, and led to greater harmony between the Czech political leaders at home and the exile independence movement. Statements indicating oppostion to the Austro-Hungarian regime by Czech politicians at home were very helpful to the exiles, and Beneš's messages urged continuation of the opposition tactics and defiance. The government's reaction to the resolution was reflected also in a public statement by Count Czernin on April 2, 1918, which rejected the activities of "certain leaders of the people" who pass resolutions "which have no connection with the idea of the state, find no words of reproach for Czech troops who fight criminally against their own native land and their brothers in arms." These leaders, protected by parliamentary immunity, "deliver with impunity speeches which cannot be construed otherwise than as an invitation to our enemies to continue the fight, all in order that their political aspirations may be furthered.... The wretched Masaryk is not unique in his kind. There are also Masaryks within the boundaries of the Monarchy."[8] Although Czernin made a distinction between the Czech people and "certain of their leaders" who were "committing high treason," the distinction was lost in the rhetoric that followed. As Masaryk later recalled, Czernin had helped Masaryk's cause tremendously by accusing "the whole people" of agreeing with him and by saying, "There are such fellows as Masaryk even within the frontiers of the Empire."[9] The Czech masses were becoming strongly nationalistic, and they encouraged the nationalistic policies of the Czech politicians. The peasants began to resist requisioning, food and fuel shortages provoked bitterness among workers and city dwellers, and desertions from the army at the front became frequent. The hard winter of 1917-1918 accelerated the economic difficulties in the empire and the now widespread resentment of the war.[10] The general strike that started on January 14, 1918, as a protest against the further reduction of rations of flour and bread developed into a political manifestation supporting democratization of the monarchy, peace on the basis of self-determination, and the release of political prisoners. Thus the establishment of an independent state was no longer a program embraced by only a small group of exiles; gradually, the people and their leaders came to support it as well. The Austro-Hungarian government did not realize that it was playing with fire when it decided to negotiate for peace with the Bolsheviks. The "victorious" Peace of Brest-Litovsk, with all of its moral and political ramifications, including the recognition of the Lenin government, was destined to be a pyrrhic victory for the Habsburgs.

The peace treaty was concluded at the expense of the Poles, who considered it to be a "grave injustice" perpetrated by the Austrian emperor, as Stanisław Głabiński, a Polish deputy at Vienna, stated in a letter to Charles.[11] Antoher Polish deputy, the socialist Ignacy Daszyński, declared at a session of the Vienna parliament that at Brest-Litovsk Czernin had intentionally trampled upon Polish rights, and that the Polish nation had drawn a lesson for it: never bind the national question with the interests of the dynasty. "The Habsburg star," he said, "fell from the Polish sky on February 9, 1918."[12] The Polish deputies declared war on the Brest-Litovsk treaty, and this brought them closer to the Czechs and Yugoslavs in opposition to the monarchy. It was not mere coincidence that the Czech *Maffie* was instructed on February 18, 1918, to pursue "a separatist policy if possible, in addition to Yugoslavs, together with Poles, Italians, Rumanians...."[13] This broadening of the anti-Habsburg front later proved fatal to the monarchy.

The apparent double standard adopted by Czernin at Brest-Litovsk contributed greatly to the decision of a great many Poles, Yugoslavs, and Czechs to part company with the monarchy. The Brest-Litovsk treaty was, in the short run, a great victory for Czernin, who, after his return from Brest-Litovsk, was glorified in Vienna as a "peacemaker" and savior of Austria-Hungary. Intoxicated with his success, he became intolerant of the obstructionist techniques of the representatives of the oppressed nations in the empire. His bitter attack on Masaryk and on the Czech deputies who, protected by parliamentary immunity, called on the Entente to continue the war, provoked a reaction on the part of the Czech leaders. Even the activists declared that Czernin's form of speech was "completely intolerable and hasty" and that it only gave Masaryk valuable publicity.[14] The "radical" deputies assessed the "statesmanlike qualities" of Czernin even less favorably. The reaction to his speech culminated in the so-called national oath—a manifesto read by a Czech writer, Alois Jirásek—at a Czech-Yugoslav demonstration "for the right of national self-determination" on April 13, 1918.[15]

At this rally, held at the Smetana Hall in Prague, highly emotional speeches were delivered by spokesmen for the two nations. When Jirásek read a sentence from the "national oath" saying, "we raise our hands," hundreds of hands rose to swear to fight for an independent Czechoslovak state. Speaking on behalf of the Yugoslavs, Dr. Ante Pavelić and Dr. Anton Korošec adopted this oath also for the Yugoslav nation. The culiminating point of the manifestation arrived when Dr. Kramář ended his address with a slogan that, he exhorted, must become from then on the slogan of both nations: "Loyalty for loyalty, forever!"[16] Next day, on April 14, 1918, the person most responsible for the "national oath," Czernin, left his ministerial office, accompanied by the emperor's conviction that Czernin was his misfortune.[17]

The exile independence movement now emphasized its unity of aims with the home front, and capitalized on the fact that the Czech deputies had come out into the open as supporters of independence. In the spring of 1918, however, the exile movement was confronted with a difficult task: to prevent the Allies from making a separate peace with Austria-Hungary. Should this happen, there would be no independent Czechoslovakia. In November and December 1917, a new round of confidential negotiations for a separate peace was initiated; the leaders of the Czechoslovak independence movement abroad (Masaryk, Beneš, and Štefánik) were aware of these negotiations. In December 1917, and January 1918, attempts at a separate peace with the Habsburg monarch were reflected in the public statements of leading statesmen of the Allies.

When he recommended a declaration of war on Austria-Hungary on December 4, 1917, President Wilson said that the United States did not wish "to impair or rearrange" the Austro-Hungarian empire.[18] In a speech of January 5, 1918, the British prime minister, Lloyd George, agreed with the American president, saying, "The break-up of Austria-Hungary is no part of our war aim."[19] The French premier, Clemenceau, publicly endorsed this statement. Although Lloyd George approved of the Italian and Romanian territorial demands on Austria-Hungary, he did not mention the Czechoslovak and Yugoslav questions. When Wilson proclaimed his famous "Fourteen Points" as his conditions for a general peace, he mentioned the independence of Poland. In the tenth point, however, referring to Austria-Hungary, he said merely that the nations of that political unit, "whose place among nations we wish to see protected and assured, should be given the freest opportunity of autonomous development."[20] Thus, the Allies rejected the dismemberment of Austria-Hungary and the way was still open for the empire's preservation.

The secret negotiations with Austria-Hungary and the public statements of Allied leaders were aimed at weakening Germany by breaking off Austria-Hungary from it. That Emperor Charles was interested in the peace proposals became obvious in early 1918, when he refused the German demand to send Austro-Hungarian troops to the Western Front. The broad masses of people in England agreed with the stand taken by the government; the Labor party refused to admit that the dismemberment of Austria-Hungary ought to be a war aim of Great Britain, and a very large part of the press—Liberal, Conservative, and Labor—called for a negotiated peace.[21] Thus the spokesmen for the Czechoslovak independence movement abroad had the uneasy task of campaigning both against the stand taken by the Allied governments on the question of preserving Austria-Hungary and against the prevailing public opinion. Indeed, this was the darkest hour for those who advocated the liberation of the subject nationalities of the monarchy. At this time the Czechs in England were very unpopular, and were even called foreing "Sinnfeinists." (In Irish "Sinn Fein" means "Ourselves alone." "Sin Fein" was a slogan of Irish nationalists, and also an anti-British political party founded in 1899.) Masaryk tried to counteract the implied equation of the Czech independence movement with that of the Irish by denying any similarity between the two. As he stated later, in a memorandum submitted to the U.S. State Department, "Everybody understands that an Irish committee, should there by any, cannot be recognized."[22] (This statement was typical of Masaryk: while the Czechs had the right to independence, the Irish and many other peoples, including the Ukrainians, did not.)

For tactical reasons Masaryk did not publicly protest Lloyd George's war aims speech of January 5, 1918, which called only for autonomy, not independence, for the oppressed Austro-Hungarian peoples, nor did he criticize President Wilson. The president was not moved by a letter from the Bohemian National Alliance of December 18, 1917, pointing out the inadequacy of mere autonomy for the peoples in the Habsburg monarchy,[23] and he continued to believe that Austria-Hungary, freed from German influence, performed a useful role in Europe. His "Fourteen Points" assumed the continuation of the Danubian empire. Oral and written protests by Olga Masaryk and Vladimír Nosek in England, M. Plesinger in Switzerland, and others elsewhere against the position taken by Woodrow Wilson and Lloyd George had very little impact.

The most effective instrument of the exile movement was the army organized on the basis of the decree of the president of the French Republic dated December 16, 1917. According to that decree, "the Czecho-Slovaks organized in an autonomous army" recognized "from the military standpoint the supreme authority of the French High Command," but would "fight under their own flag against the Central Powers." From the political standpoint, this national army was placed under "the direction of the Czecho-Slovak National Council with headquarters at Paris." The French government would supply its equipment and would assure its maintenance. "Provisions governing the French Army as regards organization, military ranks, administration and discipline, are applicable to the

Czecho-Slovak Army." The army would be recruited from among Czechs and Slovaks serving with the French armed forces, and among Czechs and Slovaks from other countries who were permitted to be transferred into the Czecho-Slovak army or to volunteer for service in the army for the duration of the war. General Maurice Janin, the former chief of the French military mission in Russia, responded to Štefánik's request and agreed to become the commander of the army in France. It was hoped that the transport of prisoners of war and Czechoslovak troops from Russia, with volunteers from America and Italy, would make possible the building of a large military force that would play a prominent military role in France. According to an agreement signed by Clemenceau and Beneš, the Czechoslovak army was to have a certain amount of autonomy, and its members would take an oath of loyalty to "the Czechoslovak nation whose representative is the Czecho-Slovak National Council."[24] This was a great step forward.

However, secret peace negotiations continued in February and March of 1918; the Allied governments still hoped for a separate peace with Austria-Hungary. In this situation developments on the Italian front and the attitude of the Italian government became very important for the exile movement. After the defeat the Italians suffered at Caporetto in October 1917 and the advances made on the Italian front by the German and Austrian armies, the Italian public was shocked. The Italian government was concerned about the poor performance of its troops and was seeking to remedy the situation. When the report of the establishment of the Czechoslovak army in France reached Italy, several members of the Italian parliament began to urge the establishment of a "Czech legion" in Italy. The Italian ministry also expressed interest in obtaining official permission to use Czech prisoners of war organized in military formations at the front, since according to C. Pettorelli-Finzi, a major in the Italian intelligence service, the deployment of Czech troops would encourage the desertion of Czechs in the Austro-Hungarian army. In one of his memoranda of January 23, 1918, Major Finzi proposed to the chief of the Italian general staff the establishment of a Czech legion that would have a military purpose: the weakening of the Austrian army. Moreover, as he put it in the memorandum, "the establishment of the 'independent Czechoslovak state' and its official recognition by the Allied States is an urgent necessity for Italy."[25] It was no coincidence that the

Czechoslovak information service in Italy participated in drafting this memorandum, copies of which were distributed to influential political personalities in Rome.[26]

In addition to military reasons for the favorable climate of opinion concerning an independent Czechoslovak state, there were Italian diplomatic considerations. At the beginning of 1918, the peace overtures to Austria-Hungary endangered Italian territorial ambitions, because the Austro-Hungarian government insisted on the prewar boundaries of the empire as a precondition for any separate peace. After the defeat of Serbia, Russia, and Romania, Italy was the only Allied power that had territorial demands on Austria-Hungary. Italy alone fought against the Austro-Hungarian armies, and part of her territory was occupied. Thus for Italy, the independence movement within the empire, as well as outside it, became increasingly important because it could be of immediate help. It is true that the Italian territorial demands were in conflict with those of Serbia; however, early in 1918, Serbia was in no position to press its demands. In this context the Czechoslovak exile independence movement was seen by some Italian officials as a possible mediator between Italy and Yugoslavia. All these factors together created favorable conditions for the Czechoslovak independence movement in Italy. The hopes of the Czech independence movement were shattered, however, when Italy decided to form labor battalions of Czech prisoners of war for work behind the front.[27]

The secretariat of the CSNC at Paris was alarmed. Štefánik went immediately to Rome, where he negotiated the transfer of Czechoslovak prisoners of war to France. Štefánik was primarily interested in strengthening the Czechoslovak army in France, but the Italian government was not responsive to his proposals. Eventually, at the end of March 1918, the Italian military and the prime minister, Vittorio Orlando, suggested forming Czechoslovak units within the Italian army. Štefánik did not accept this proposal and left for Paris on March 25, 1918.[28] He returned to Italy a few days later in order to take part in the Congress of Oppressed Nationalities of Austria-Hungary.

At this congress, held in Rome on April 8-9, 1918, representatives of Italians, Poles, Romanians, Yugoslavs, and Czecho-Slovaks stated the following principles to guide their common action:

1. Each of these peoples proclaims its right to constitute its own nationality and state unity or to complete this unity and to attain full political and economic independence.
2. Each of these peoples recognizes in the Austro-Hungarian Monarchy the instrument of German domination and the fundamental obstacle to the realization of its aspirations and rights.
3. The Congress recognizes the necessity of a common struggle against common oppressors in order that each of these people may attain its complete liberation and complete national unity as a single free state.[29]

Among the most important confidential documents produced at the congress was a resolution dealing with propaganda, which reflected the influence and interests of the Czecho-Slovak independence movement. The congress urged the Allied powers to look upon the military organizations of the oppressed peoples not only from a strictly military point of view but also as a moral factor, the most important one in the struggle. The resolution, moreover, expressed a wish that "elements belonging to the oppressed peoples" be used on the Austro-Italian front. Furthermore, the Allied propaganda organs should publicize in enemy countries, with the consent of the Allied governments, the fact that all the Allied states had accepted as fighting forces on their fronts armies composed of members of the nations that had expressed a wish to free themselves from the German-Hungarian yoke and to establish independent states. Soldiers of these units were under the jurisdiction of the national councils, which acted in harmony with the Entente powers. Finally, these nations had the right to establish independent states.[30]

The congress at Rome paved the way to the establishment of a Czechoslovak army in Italy. While Beneš directed the work of the Czechoslovak delegation at the congress, Štefánik negotiated with the Italian government. On April 12, 1918, the Italian prime minister, Orlando, received delegates to the congress and notified them of the steps that had already been taken in the matter of the Czechoslovak army in Italy. Shortly afterward, the recruitment of troops from among the members of the labor battalions and in the camps of prisoners of war got under way. Before the end of April, four regiments were built. What was more important, the Czechoslovak army in Italy was established not by a presidential decree, as had been the case in France, but by an agreement between the Italian government and the CSNC, signed by Orlando and Štefánik on behalf of the two parties on April 21, 1918.[31]

By this agreement the Italian government recognized the existence of a united and autonomous Czechoslovak army that was, from the national, political, and legal point of view, under the jurisdiction of the CSNC. The agreement stated that the expenses with the Czechoslovak army would be borne by the CSNC, and that Italy had assumed the obligation to furnish "all financial advancements," and means necessary for the maintenance and the operations of the Czechoslovak army in Italy in such a way that they could be converted into a Czechoslovak "national debt." This was the greatest stride in the progress toward recognition of a future state that the CSNC had made since the establishment of the army in France. Now the Italian government was a party to an international agreement signed and negotiated by the CSNC; an Allied government had committed itself to claim repayment of a "national debt" from a state that did not as yet exist. Also, the celebration of the transfer of the flag to the Czechoslovak units took place in the spring of 1918, with an official of the Italian government—the Prime Minister himself—taking part. Orlando's speech, delivered on this occasion, ended with: "Long live free Bohemia!"[32]

The Rome Congress of Oppressed Nationalities and the establishment of the Czechoslovak army in Italy had far-reaching consequences for the Czechoslovak independence movement beyond the borders of Italy. A delegation of participants in the congress was given an audience by Prime Minister Clemenceau, whose attitude had been changed by his recent conflict with Czernin. In a speech to members of the Vienna city council on April 2, 1918, Czernin had declared that the French government had initiated separate negotiations with Austria-Hungary just before launching a new German offensive on the Western Front in the spring of 1918, and that the negotiations had come to naught because of the impossibility of compromise on the question of Alsace-Lorraine. This statement was not quite true, since Austria, not France, had taken the first step in the negotiations, and it also breached the mutual secrecy of the negotiations. (Emperor Charles did not fully inform his foreing minister of the steps that he had taken to bring about a separate peace.) Clemenceau replied to Czernin that it was Vienna and not he who had asked for a separate peace, that Austria had initiated the negotiations. Czernin publicly reasserted his previous statement, and thereupon Clemenceau exposed the whole Sixtus affair;[33] he made public the so-called Sixtus letter. The controversy created by Czernin became a worldwide sensation. Some blamed Czernin, and others Clemenceau for ending the hope for a negotiated peace, making peace possible only through new negotiations or a military victory on the Western Front.[34] In his clash with Clemenceau, Czernin was at a disadvantage because he did not know the content of the letter written by Emperor Charles to Prince Sixtus of Bourbon-Parma at the beginning of the emperor's peace moves. In his March 24, 1917, letter to Sixtus, Charles had stated that he supported "France's just claim regarding Alsace-Lorraine," and that he would use all his personal influence and any other means in his power to make his allies agree to it. The prince showed the letter to President Poincaré on March 31, 1917, and gave a copy of it to Premier Alexandre Ribot.[35] A year later, Clemenceau provoked by Czernin's statement, had the letter published in Paris, thus compromising Austria-Hungary everywhere. The emperor at first denied the authenticity of the letter even to Czernin. After Clemenceau published a facsimile, the government at Vienna asserted first that the letter was a forgery, and later, under the full impact of the French revelation, that only the passage referring to France's just claims to Alsace-Lorraine was falsified. A series of accusations and denunciations of the "rotten conscience" of the Austrian emperor and his chief minister emanated from France. Emperor Charles denied making the statement regarding Alsace-Lorraine in his communication to the German Kaiser of April 11, 1918. Despite this denial, the Austrian emperor was suspected of treason in Berlin. Czernin, who felt himself betrayed by Charles, was forced to submit his resignation on April 14, 1918. He was succeeded by Count Istvan Burian.

On April 16, 1918, Ambassador Sharp in Paris telegraphed Lansing that, according to informed opinion in France, Clemenceau had made "a fatal mistake in publishing that letter," and that "all hopes for peace through Austria vanished with this fatal indiscretion."[36] Sharp and Lansing believed that the prevailing judgment in Paris and London was that the affair precluded "any possibility of future negotiations during the war with Austria" and had "in fact had the result of knitting more closely together the interests of Germany and Austria."[37] Lansing concluded that "hope of a separate peace with Austria-Hungary was abandoned, and the reasons for dealing leniently with that Empire by giving the impression that its territorial integrity was not threatened disappeared, especially as the Emperor Karl's desire, as stated by Doctor [Heinrich] Lammasch, to reorganize the existing Daul Monarchy by making it a monarchical confederation of autonomous states, could never be realized with Burian and the reactionaries in control of public affairs."[38]

In order to placate Germany, the Austrian emperor went to Canossa; on May 12, 1918, at the Geman imperial headquarters at Spaa, William II and Charles signed a political treaty tying Austria-Hungary to Germany politically, military, and economically. Before his trip to Spaa, Charles sent a telegram to the Kaiser saying that Mr. Clemenceau's accusations against him were so contemptible that he had decided "not to continue the discussions with France any longer." His answer would be given by his "cannons in the West."[39] The explosion of the Sixtus time bomb and the handling of the affair by Czernin and Charles, especially their denunciations of Clemenceau and the subsequent agreement at Spaa, destroyed Austria's chances to secure a separate peace as well as her chance for political preservation of the Danubian empire. All attempts at a separate peace with Austria-Hungary ended. The outcome of the war was to be decided by the force of arms on military fronts and by the dissatisfied peoples within Austria-Hungary.

The exposure of the Sixtus letter and the Austrian official reaction to it coincided with the Rome Congress of Oppressed Nationalities in April 1918. During the audience granted to the representatives of the congress by Clemenceau, the French prime minister spoke very encouragingly to the spokesmen for the national movements and condemned the Habsburg monarchy. The situation also improved in England and the United States. In England negotiations with the government were conducted by Beneš, who left Paris for London on May 7, 1918. After his arrival in the United States in late April 1918, Masaryk took part in action aimed at winning U.S. recognition of the CSNC. The reports on the Rome congress and on the military convention of April 21, 1918, between Italy and the CSNC by the U.S. ambassador to Italy, Nelson Page, brought these matters to the attention of the U.S. government.[40]

The Rome congress and the Sixtus affair had a strong impact on the home front. On May 10, 1918, Beneš reported from Paris on the significance of the Rome congress for the Czech independence movement in a jubilant secret message: "After our return from the Congress of Rome, Clemenceau and Pichon gave us a definite promise that they will recognize us and declare us for fully independent. Clemenceau made the same statement in the commission dealing with the letter of Emperor Charles, and he declared that they will recognize and declare independence of Austro-Hungarian nations." The situation in France and England was, Beneš stated, "excellent"; the Clemenceau-Czernin affair "definitely destroyed all bridges to Austria-Hungary." As a consequence of it, "the Allies would go resolutely and fully against Austria," Beneš's message said.[41]

After the Rome congress, *Maffie* decided to call an analogous congress of oppressed nations at Prague as a response from within Austria-Hungary to the events at Rome. It therefore turned the long-prepared celebration of the fiftieth anniversary of the laying of the foundation stone at the National Theatre (May 16, 1918) into a demonstration for national independence. Slavic politicians and journalists were welcomed on this occasion by Kramář, who had since mid-April been the principal leader of the independence movement at home. Kramář concluded his opening address by reciting the prophecy of Libuše (wife of the founder of the first Czech dynasty, the Přemyslids): "Our nation will never pass away...."[42] On the next day, May 17, a congress (conference) of the oppressed nations in Austria-Hungary took place,[43] and Slavic delegates attended confidential meetings held in Kramář's villa. The main theme of discussion at these meetings was how to bring about an effective exchange of information on political aims, programs, and prevailing moods, among people in the Czech, Yugoslav, and Polish lands.

The leaders of the Czech independence movement at home had a program for the establishment of an independent Czechoslovak state. They were not concerned at this point, with the consistency or inconsistency of invoking state historical rights as the basis for their claim to Slovakia. Nor were they worried about the prospect that the right of self-determination might be invoked by Germans living in the borderlands of Bohemia and Moravia, or by Poles, Hungarians, and, possibly, Ruthenians. In the heat generated by nationalistic passions, the Czech program appeared clear to the leaders at home. The Yugoslav program was not so clear; however, the Slavic leaders of the independence movements did not bother to solve the theoretical questions involved in their claims to independence and state sovereignty. They were concerned with aims and action, not theory. At the principal meeting in Kramář's villa a "Revolutionary Committee" was established for the purpose of directing, jointly and uniformly, the whole revolutionary movement in Austria-Hungary and organizing and coordinating the struggle for independent Czechoslovak, Polish, and Yugoslav states.[44] Kramář became the president of this committee, as well as the visible head of the Czech independence movement at home. The vast majority of politicians, one by one, began to give up their pro-Austrian orientation and accepted his leadership. By May 30, 1918, only a small minority of Czech politicians still publicly supported the transformation of the Habsburg empire into a federal union.[45]

The events in Prague captured the attention of foreign political observers. The U.S. minister in Switzerland telegraphed to the secretary of state on May 23, 1918, that he had learned from *Národní Listy* (May 16, 1918) that "great demonstrations took place at fiftieth anniversary of city theatre" on May 15 "under presidency of Kramář and that resolutions of most important character were adopted. This meeting is of unusual importance in that for the first time representatives of Yugo-Slavs, Galicians, Ukrainians and Poles met with Czechs and were united in their declarations against their common enemies, Austria and Germany. Austrian official *communiqué* speaks of serious nature of resolutions adopted and of order for several preventive measures to be taken. The abovementioned paper has been suppressed. From independent sources the gravity of this meeting is emphasized." According to the U.S minister, "it appears possible that the first step has been taken in the long-expected revolt of the oppressed nationalities against Austria." He urged giving moral assistance to the oppressed nationalities "in the way of demonstrations in the United States by the nationalities affected by this news;" and he suggested that "Professor Masaryk of Chicago, one of the Czech leaders, be advised."[46]

In Paris Beneš used the May demonstrations in Prague in order to advance the aims of the Czechoslovak independence movement abroad. On May 28, 1918, he assured the U.S diplomatic liaison officer with the Supreme War Council, Arthur A. Frazier, that the Czechoslovak, Yugoslav, and Polish movements "were essentially democratic in spirit" and that he anticipated "the formation of independent states in Bohemia, Poland and the territory occupied by Jugo-Slavs." Beneš told Frazier that the Czechs were preparing "for a revolutionary movement [revolution?] which will take place at a moment when the Allies are able to deal a successful blow on the western front;" however, "at the present time an uprising would merely mean further massacres in Bohemia." (There were no massacres in Bohemia.) Beneš expected "the final collapse of Austria" in March 1919. It would be preceded by "outbreaks of Bolshevism in Galicia, Hungary, and German Austria." Bolshevism, according to Beneš, could not make headway "amongst the Czechs as there are no illiterates amongst the people." Beneš told Frazier that he had discussed the same subject with Balfour, Lord Robert Cecil, and Clemenceau, all of whom were "in sympathy with his views and have promised support." But Beneš was "convinced that President Wilson's words would carry far greater weight than those of any European statesmen."[47]

Although the "national oath" in April and the May celebrations at Prague represented a tremendous success for the independence movement at home, the war aims of the independence movement abroad were not looked upon favorably in England in the spring of 1918. Influential British periodicals saw in Austria "a peace factor" and condemned not only the "childish and anarchistic idea of breaking-up Austria-Hungary" for which the Czech *Sinnfeinists* strove, but also the demand for a "federalization" of the Danubian monarchy that would require its dismemberment. As the *Nation* put it, the Slav extremists rejected the view that an agreement should be made with the Austrian government and they expected that the peace conference would solve their problem for them. But it was hardly conceivable that the peace conference would even consider the internal organization of Austria-Hungary, unless by some miracle the Entente could dictate the peace rather than negotiate it. Above all, the disruption of the monarchy should not be purchased by the prolongation of the war. There was a new Austria since the accession of Charles, and the country was disillusioned wit the war; furthermore, the Russian threat was gone.[48] Yet there were people in England who held just the opposite view. Among those Englishmen who advocated and defended the idea of breaking up Austria-Hungary was Seton-Watson, who publicly condemned the secret negotiations for a separate peace with the Habsburgs. It may be added, however, that after Czernin's speech of April 2, 1918, indicating Austria's dependence on Germany and taking a hard-line on Germany's continuation of the war, the position of the Czechoslovak independence movement in Britain improved somewhat.[49]

Despite the unfavorable climate of opinion in Great Britain, Beneš arrived in London to conduct negotiations for recognition of the CSNC. Accompanied by H. W. Steed, Beneš was received on May 10, 1918, by the secretary of foreign affairs, A. J. Balfour. Beneš explained to Balfour the general status of affairs related to the Czechoslovak situation: the establishment of national armies in France, Italy, and Russia; the status of the CSNC and its cooperation with the leaders of the Czech political parties at home; and the general conditions in the Czech lands. Beneš asked the British government to recognize all the national institutions and to take the same position toward the CSNC as had the French government. Reportedly, Balfour expressed his sympathy with Bohemian independence, Then, Beneš on May 10 and 11, handed him two memoranda he had written in France.[50] The first one described the Czechoslovak independence movement abroad. The second requested that the British government accord the same status to the CSNC that it had received from the French, Italian, and former Russian (Provisional) governments. He asked, furthermore, that the British government take into consideration the existence of the Czechoslovak army, agreeing to its establishment by recognizing the CSNC as its supreme political organ, and by appointing a liaison officer to it as soon as necessary.

Beneš also negotiated with the secretary of the blockade, Robert Cecil, and the British secretary of war, Alfred Milner. The immediate result of these negotiations appeared in a public pronouncement by Robert Cecil, who stated in a speech on the third anniversary of Italy's entrance into the war that he welcomed the recent Congress of Oppressed Nationalities at Rome, which had helped to cement the bonds between these peoples and the Allies; and that the problem of Austria-Hungary should not be viewed as that of its dismemberment, but as the liberation of nations under its yoke. The British desired, he said, that these nations enjoy freedom and independence, and that they form a kind of federation that would maintain in central Europe the principles on which European policy must be built, if "we are not to live to see an unheard-of disaster."[51] This was, definitely, a new note in a public pronouncement made by a British government official; more than likely, it stemmed from British interest in the Czechoslovak troops in Russia and Siberia.

In his conversation with Lord Robert Cecil on May 15, 1918, Beneš noticed that, while the French wanted to transfer the Czechoslovak troops from Russia and Siberia to the Western Front as soon as possible, the British were inclined to keep the Czechoslovak army in Russia and Siberia, primarily in order to prevent German and Bolshevik military and propaganda activities from moving to the Far East. Lord Cecil asked Beneš directly whether the Czecho-Slovak National Council would be willing to leave the troops there for those purposes. Beneš replied that the council insisted on transferring at least 30,000 troops to France, in accordance with the original agreement made with the French government; however, it would not oppose the restoration of the Eastern Front by the Czechoslovak and Allied troops against Germany "if such an allied action could be counted upon."[52]

Balfour replied to Beneš's two memoranda in a letter dated June 3, 1918, saying that the British government was willing to recognize the Czecho-Slovak National Council as the supreme organ of the Czechoslovak movement in the Allied countries, and that it also willingly recognized the Czechoslovak army as an organized unit fighting on behalf of the Allied cause. It would appoint a liaison officer to this army as soon as the need for liaison arose. Finally, the Allied governments had been informed of the foregoing decisions.[53]

The degree of recognition of the Czechoslovak independence movement implied in Balfour's letter, and the British willingness to recognize the Czechoslovak army as a unit fighting for the Allied cause, were related to the Allied decision to use the army to occupy certain strategic points along the Trans-Siberian Railway, made on May 28, 1918, three days after the successful uprising of the Czechs against the Bolsheviks.[54] The British secretary of foreign affairs already knew of the conflict of the Czechoslovak troops with the Bolsheviks in Russia and Siberia. Thus the limited recognition of the CSNC was related to a military and political decision that either had already been made by the British government or was in the process of being made: the decision to intervene in Russia and Siberia.

After returning to Paris, Beneš sent a very optimistic report to Prague describing his negotiations with the British government and the British willingness to "transport 70,000 troops from Russia to France."[55] Leaving aside Beneš's exaggerations, the transport of the troops would doubtless have strengthened the position of the CSNC in the west, but it was not destined to happen. Beneš's premature optimism was also reflected in his expectation that Czechoslovak independence would be proclaimed in the near future and a provisional Czechoslovak government would be established. As he explained in his message to Prague, this provisional government in exile would consider itself to be "a delegation" and at the same time merely "one part" of the provisional government whose "second part" would be in Bohemia.[56] The time had yet to come when that would really happen.

Beneš's "victory letter" at the end of May was followed by a sober message on June 14, 1918.[57] Beneš repeated his claim that politically "everything had been won;" however, the military situation was not very favorable. "If we want to win," the message said, "you at home also must do all that can possibly be done." Reportedly, the military situation was bad; Beneš admitted the possibility of the loss of Paris. He projected that the war would continue into 1919; the Allies would not be able to do anything of consequence before the spring of 1919. He requested sabotage and preparation for a revolution to be launched at the precise moment when the Allies would be in a position to help it by a decisive offensive. Beneš warned against acting prematurely, without coordinating the revolutionary action with the Allied offensive and without waiting for specific instructions from abroad. Although he liked to make predictions, he did not foresee the significance and the consequences of the Czechoslovak anti-Bolshevik uprising in Russia and Siberia.

CHAPTER ELEVEN

MASARYK'S JOURNEY TO AMERICA

When Masaryk left Moscow on March 8, 1918, and embarked on his long journey to the United States via Siberia and Japan, he was convinced that the future of the Czechoslovak army in Russia was settled: the army would withdraw from that unhapply land and reach the Western Front as speedily as possible. The arrangements he had made with the Soviet government provided for the transportation of the troops and the maintenance of their neutrality in the internal political turmoil in Russia. However, during his long trip across Siberia, the Allied capitals engaged in intensive diplomacy concerning intervention in Russia. Masaryk was not informed about it; neither was he able to foresee what would happen during his absence from Russia to the arrangements he had made earlier.

As early as September 1, 1917, Masaryk had proposed sending to Russia 300,000 Japanese troops, for which Japan would be compensated by some territories on the mainland of Asia in the Far East. However skeptical the British government might have been about Masaryk's idea at the time, it began to consider Japanese intervention in Siberia early in February 1918, and so notified the Allies. The British proposed Japanese occupation of the Chinese Eastern and Amur Railways, and, possibly, the whole Trans-Siberian Railway, but the Japanese government requested "a free hand in the event of intervention in Siberia." However, U.S.

Ambassador Francis reported from Russia that "all Russians" were "violently opposed to Japanese interference." The American government expressed its opposition to a Japanese intervention in Russia on the grounds that such intervention would be unpopular among the Russians and that it was in the interest of the Allies not "to estrange any considerable portion of the people of Russia." Secretary of State Lansing stated his position on Japanese intervention in his confidential memorandum of March 18, 1918, with which the president entirely agreed.[1]

Lansing noted that "the proposal to request Japan to send an expeditionary force into Siberia is urged with varying degrees of earnestness by the British, French and Italian Governments, which desire to made the Japanese Government a mandatory of the Powers." However, it appeared that the Japanese government did "not desire to act jointly with other Governments, preferring to act without cooperation other than approval." Since the burden of the military operations in Siberia would fall upon Japan, the two chief considerations involved in the proposed action by Japan were: *"First,* what would be the moral effect on the Russian people? *Second,* what would be the military benefit?

Lansing answered the first question in the negative: the moral effect would be bad, since the Russian people would receive the Japanese intervention with general disfavor. Except for a few small groups, the Russians would become bitterly hostile to Japan and to the powers that had assented to her action. "There would be the charge that Russia had been betrayed by her professed friends and delivered over to the yellow race." Russia might even turn to Germany for aid in her attempt to resist "the 'Yellow Peril' which would seem imminent." As for the second consideration, Lansing saw that Japan might prevent the transportation of supplies from Vladivostok westward; and, should Japan occupy western Siberia, Germany might not be able to obtain grain and cattle from that area. He noted, however, that the supplies stored at Vladivostok were not then being shipped westward, that the Bolsheviks were weaker in eastern Siberia than anywhere else in Russia, and that there were considerable logistical problems involved in the proposed Japanese military operation. First of all, to guard the five thousand miles of a single railway line from Vladivostok to western Siberia and European Russia would be a very formidable task in view "of the almost certain hostility of the Russian people to Japanese occupation of Siberia and the pro-German sentiment which would result."

Lansing concluded that a Japanese intervention would merely "unite the various Russian factions against this country and thereby... deliver Russia into the hands of the Germans;" he saw no likely military compensation. Therefore, he writes, "we must await new developments." Thus, the American government rejected the use of Japanese troops, realizing fully how unpopular these would be in Russia, but it did not offer an alternative, the sending of its own troops to Russia; and the Czechoslovak army was not mentioned in the Lansing memorandum at all.

While Masaryk was travelling across Siberia, on March 15, 1918, French, British, and Italian government and military officials met in London to discuss the possibility of a Japanese intervention in Russia in order to reestablish the Eastern Front. A few days after this conference a memorandum by the British military expert on Russia, Major General Knox, was circulated; in the document two Allied agents in Russia, British Bruce Lockhart and American Lieutenant Colonel Raymond Robins, were blamed for the "delay in the East."[2] Discussions continued to be held in military and political circles during which the issue of the Czech troops in Russia was brought up, especially after the news arrived in the west about the Czech military encounter with the Germans at Bakhmach railroad junction in the Ukraine. On March 21, 1918, General Foch suggested that there might be merit in the Bolshevik plan to retain the Czechoslovak army in Russia and use it as the nucleus for the new Russian army, since, in this case, the Czechs could be used on the spot and would not have to be transported to France.[3] On the same day the British Foreign Office prepared a memorandum for the War Office on the role and usefulness of the Czechoslovak army in Russia. The lengthy document was not acted upon for some time; however, on April 1, 1918, the War Office corrected some inaccuracies in the Foreign Office memorandum;[4] it was doubtful that the army consisted of some 70,000 troops, in view of the fact that there had been some 42,000 Czechs organized in it at Kiev, before the Bolsheviks took the city.

The memorandum pointed out that earlier attempts to send the Czechoslovak army to the Romanian front had been unsuccessful because Masaryk refused to move. By this time, the memorandum said, the French officers attached to the army most likely had left it. Late in March 1918, the army was moving from Kursk to Samara. According to the reports received, the troops were now, probably, without artillery and ammunition and had difficulties with their own transportation. Trotsky had asked the Czechs to become the nucleus of the new Russian army, but they refused, insisting on going to France. Since no ships were available for the troops at Vladivostok, the War Office believed that they should be kept in Russia for some time. While waiting in Russia, these troops could be used, according to the War Office, in one of three different ways: (a) they could be concentrated around Omsk (Siberia); (b) they could be rerouted to Archangel; and (c) they could be concentrated in the Trans-Bajkal region for possible assistance to Ataman Semenov. In the view of General MacDonogh, director of operations at the War Office, the first proposition was the most attractive, because the Czechs then would be able to block any action by German prisoners of war in Siberia.[5] The French did not quite agree with that proposition, for they were badly in need of new troops; the Czechs were, reportedly, already on their way to France and their morale was high. The French consul at Vladivostok expected them to arrive soon and even asked for instructions on how to deal with them.[6] The Bolsheviks, however, were suspicious of the French officers in Russia and therefore of the Czechoslovak army, which was a part of the French legions. The commissar of internal affairs told Jiří Klecanda, who represented the Czechoslovak army in Moscow, where he negotiated the transit of the troops across Soviet-held territory toward the end of March 1918, that it was not possible to let the Czechoslovak echelons move across Siberia, because the French could command them "in the Far East against the Bolsheviks."[7] When the French military attaché in Moscow, General Lavergne, was confronted with the proposition, he stated on March 27, 1918, that since the Czechs wanted to go to France, "France merely helps them."[8]

After the Japanese surprise landing on April 4, the French still believed that the Czechs would come to France but agreed to let them help Ataman Semenov while waiting for British ships to arrive for them. Only when the Czechs actually assembled in Vladivostok would the final decision be made on what to do with them.[9] However, should the Czechs moving toward Vladivostok be stopped by Trotsky on account of the Japanese landing, they should be rerouted to Archangel, according to Lavergne's suggestion of April 9.[10] The French general staff discussed the transportation of the Czechs, whose morale was reported to be excellent, with the British on April 16, and suggested that if the British were willing to evacuate the Czechs to France via Archangel, the Czechs could in the meantime be used to guard the northern harbors.[11] The British welcomed this suggestion, seeing the Czechs as the only force in Russia willing to fight the Germans. Therefore, the troops were to be rerouted from Sibera to Archangel and Murmansk, and then to France. There were no British ships available at the northern ports, but the British apparently thought that evacuating the Czechs to France was not urgent, and that they could be used to guard war material and railways in the Russian north.[12] The French general staff, however, hesitated to rerout all the Czechs who had already reached Siberia.[13] On April 26, Clemenceau requested that the French ambassador in Tokyo to get Japanese help in bringing to France those Czechs who were already in Vladivostok.[14]

The success or failure of the British and French plans concerning the Legion would depend, ultimately, on the Czechs' willingness to cooperate. Therefore, the Allies wanted to know Masaryk's views on the matter. The Czech leader reached Tokyo on April 8, 1918, and was met there by the American ambassador, Roland S. Morris. Morris had been asked by U.S. Secretary of State Lansing to look up Masaryk and inform the State Department about the latter's views on the general situation in Russia and on any possibility of organizing there effective resistance against the Central Powers. In addition, Morris was asked to send the State Department any information that Masaryk wanted to give.[15]

Lansing had a great interest in Masaryk's views because he had received information on the Czechoslovak army corps in connection with the preparations and plans for the Allied intervention in Siberia. A leading proponent of the intervention was the French ambassador in Russia, Joseph Noulens, whose recommendations were transmitted to the State Department by the French ambassador in Washington, Jusserand, on March 24, 1918. Noulens believed that only military action by Japan, taken as soon as possible in the name of and in cooperation with the Allies, could frustrate the German plans in eastern Europe. The Japanese intervention should be accompanied by the landing of inter-Allied armed forces in Murmansk and Archangel; the Czechs, who had not as yet been sent to the Far East, could be extremely useful in this matter.[16]

Like the British, the French diplomat would have preferred that the Czechs stay in Russia and Siberia rather than travel to France, and so would American diplomatic personnel in Russia. For example, on March 29, 1918, Raymond Robins, the head of the American Red Cross mission in Russia, who was an unofficial American representative with the Bolshevik government, inquired of U.S. Ambassador Francis, who was at Vologda, whether he had been informed about the policy or wishes of the American government with respect to the transportation of the Czechoslovak troops via the United States for service in France. Robins suggested that sending these detachments around the world to the French front would be a futile waste of time, money, and tonnage.[17]

On April 2, 1918, Francis telegraphed Lansing that a recruiting office for Czech prisoners of war who were willingto fight against the Germans had been opened in Moscow.[18] This was an office of the Czechoslovak army that was attempting to form another army corps from among the prisoners of war still in Russia. Naturally, Lansing was interested in Masaryk's position on the use of the Czech troops in Russia. Therefore, upon Lansing's advice, Morris asked Masaryk to write a memorandum "on the state of Russia and Bolshevism" for President Wilson. Ambassador Morris also asked Masaryk a number of questions, transmitting his answers to the U.S. State Department.[19]

Masaryk told Morris that he was strongly opposed to intervention in Russia, because he believed that the Bolshevik regime would last for some time. Eventually, he thought, it would be succeeded by a coalition government consisting of Bolsheviks, Socialists, and Liberals. In his opinion, it was possible that "the Bolsheviks, with aid and sympathy from the Allies, could organize, within a year, a substantial army to oppose German aggression."[20]

His fourteen-point memorandum, written on April 10, 1918, in Tokyo, was primarily designed to give a general view of the situation in Russia to President Wilson.[21] Although it was marked "private and confidential," the memorandum was also distributed to the representatives of other Allied powers in Tokyo, who sent it to their home offices. In this lengthy document Masaryk wrote that "the Allies should recognize the Bolshevik government" *de facto,* because "if the Allies are on good terms with the Bolshevists they can influence them, as did the Germans who had recognized them and concluded peace with them." Masaryk added that he knew the weaknesses of the Bolsheviks but that he also knew the weaknesses of the other political parties that "are neither better nor abler."

The monarchical movement was weak, he said, and "the Allies must not support it." Neither from the Cadets nor from the Social Revolutionaries who were "organizing themselves against the Bolshevists," did Masaryk expect "any considerable success." He claimed that the Allies had made a mistake in assuming that "Alexeeff and Korniloff would win a big success on the Don;" he did not believe such a success possible, and he had refused to join them, although these leaders had invited him to do so.

Masaryk was convinced that "the Bolshevists will hold power longer than their adversaries suppose." Although weakened by their failure in the peace negotiations (they accepted the humiliating conditions of the Treaty of Brest-Litovsk), "they are gaining sympathies because they are learning to work, and because the other parties are weak." However, like all the other parties, "they will die of political dilettantism [sic]" Masaryk was inclined to think that "after a time, a Coalition Government (the Socialist Parties and the Cadet Left) might meet with general approval, though there would also have to be Bolshevists in the Government." Believing that a "lasting Democratic and Republican Government in Russia" would exercise great pressure "on Prussia and Austria," he saw "this" as "one reason why the Germans and the Austrians are anti-Bolshevist."

Masaryk reiterated his conviction that "all the small peoples in the East Europe...need a strong Russia lest they be at the mercy of the Germans and Austrians. The Allies must support Russia at all costs and by all possible means. If the Germans subdue the East they will then subdue the West." Pointing out that an independent Ukraine would be "an Austrian or a German province," he hoped that a "capable Government [of Russia] could induce the Ukrainians to be satisfied with an autonomous Republic, forming part of Russia."

In the next part of the memorandum Masaryk urged the Allies to form "a common policy on the best way of supporting Russia." He made some recommendations with respect to economic assistance to Russia by the Allies, which greatly resembled the proposals Lenin made to the United States one month later. He believed that the "Allies might influence the German and Austrian prisoners who remained in Russia by means of the press and special agents;" and, as he put it, he had not seen "armed German or Austrian prisoners" in Siberia "between March 15 and April 2," though the anarchy in Siberia was "not greater than in Russia." In Masaryk's view, an army (presumably Russian) comprising "a million men could be raised in from six to nine months. The Red Guard is unimportant and the Bolshevists have called upon the officers of the old Tsarist army to join their army as instructors."

Masaryk also reported in this memorandum that he had "succeeded in organizing a corps of 50,000 men out of Czech and Slovak prisoners," and had

> agreed with the French Government to send it to France; the Allies can help to transport it. They are excellent soldiers, as they showed in the offensive last June. We can organize a second corps of the same size. This must be done to prevent our prisoners from returning to Austria, where they would be sent to oppose the Allies on the Italian or the French front. The Allies have agreed to provide us with the necessary means. . . . The significance of having the whole Czech army in France is obvious; and I must acknowledge that France understood the political importance of the matter from the outset and has supported our national movement in every way. M. Briand was the first statesmen openly to promise our people the help of the French Republic. He it was who succeeded in putting into the Allied reply to President Wilson the explicit demand that the Czechoslovaks should be liberated. The Czechoslovaks are the most westerly slav barrier against Germany and Austria. In present circumstances 100,000, nay, even 50,000 trained soldiers are very important.

The Masaryk memorandum, especially the sections dealing with the Bolshevik regime and his advice to the Allies to recognize it, was destined to do him and his cause more harm than good, as will be shown later. It reflected Masaryk's lack of understanding of the nature of Lenin's party, "the party of the new type." That incomprehension was not, unfortunately confined merely to the Czech leader. His claim that he had succeeded in organizing the Czechoslovak army gives himself more credit than he deserved; the army was organized by a joint effort of Czechs in Russia, and Masaryk had found a Czech brigade of 9,000 strong when he first arrived in Russia in May 1917. The importance of having the whole Czech army in France was "obvious" to him (i.e., to assure his leadership of the state to be established), but not to the Allies for whom the memorandum was designed. From the Allied point of view, and from the point of view of the majority of the Czechs commited to Czechoslovak independence, the Czech army could perform a much more useful service in Russia than on the Western Front. Even Beneš could not fail to notice that the memorandum caused consternation in Paris, where there prevailed "a firm belief in a new uptrun of events in Russia," and where "nobody believed in the duration of the Bolshevik regime." Beneš mentions *Echo de Paris* as one of the newspapers that were amazed by Masaryk's views.[22] Beneš understood the meaning of the unfavorable report on Masaryk that the French ambassador in Tokyo sent to the Foreign Office, and tried to counteract it by directing the attention of French officials, politicians, and journalists to the question of transporting the troops to France. For a long time he could not convince Štefánik of the correctness of Masaryk's views.[23] Rightly or wrongly, there had been some people who believed that Masaryk did his best to save the Bolshevik regime in Russia.[24]

In Tokyo, and earlier in Vladivostok, Masaryk negotiated with representatives of Allied powers and urged a speedy departure of the Czechoslovak troops from Siberia. Masaryk opposed the rumored intervention in Russia; he even advocated recognition of the Bolshevik regime. Yet, at the time he was preparing his memorandum for President Wilson, Great Britain and France were considering using the Czechoslovak army to intervene in Russia. When French government officials raised the question with Beneš on April 1, he answered it in the negative. Clemenceau reported to London that the Czechoslovak army, whose discipline and morale was excellent in the midst of the general demoralization and disorganization of the Russian army, continued to move to the Far East in order to reach France. The Czech leaders, he stated, "for moral reasons" opposed using the Czechoslovak corps in Russia.[25] Russia, however, continued to be of great interest to the Allies. Since the spring of 1918, the CSNC had consequently become "a real something among the Allies, politically and power-wise," according to Beneš.[26]

Masaryk left Japan on April 19; on April 29 he arrived in Vancouver. Before his arrival in Washington, D.C. on May 9, 1918, Albert H. Putney, of the U.S. State Department, with the help of Charles Pergler of the Bohemian National Alliance, prepared for Lansing a long memorandum entitled "Slavs of Austria-Hungary."[27] Putney suggested that historically Bohemia had been an elective and independent monarchy; that the Habsburgs, though they had attempted to suppress Czech state rights, had not destroyed them; that Bohemia had the right to terminate its dynastic relationship with Austria; and that the United States and the Allies ought to recognize those rights. In another, shorter memorandum for the president, Putney recommended that the United States issue a proclamation (1) recognizing Bohemia as an independent elective monarchy, (2) declaring that the current Habsburg government was unconstitutional and that the Czechs had the right to reject the usurper without committing treason, and (3) since there was no government in Bohemia that could be considered as a government both *de jure* and *de facto,* recognizing the CSNC as the true representative of the Czechoslovak nation.

Because of the tireless activity of the Bohemian National Alliance and the Slovak League in America before Masaryk's arrival, the U.S. government was favorably inclined toward the demands of the Czechoslovak independence movement in America. The latter was helped by two significant events in 1917: the Russian revolution and the entry of the United States into the war, especially the U.S. declaration of war on Austria-Hungary in December 1917. Its base was broadened when, because of the strenuous efforts of Rev. Oldřich Zlámal of Cleveland, the National Alliance of Bohemian Catholics joined it. A joint meeting of representatives of the Bohemian National Alliance and the National Alliance of Bohemian Catholics, held at Chicago on May 17, 1917, passed a resolution stating in part that "the foundation of the Czecho-Slovak Republic" was the aim toward which both organizations worked. At another joint meeting, on July 4, 1917, the two organizations submitted to the political and national leadership of the Czecho-Slovak National Council at Paris. The recognition of the Paris council, headed by Professor Masaryk, who was known to American Catholic Czechs as an enemy of the Catholic Church, was justified on the grounds of the higher interest of the nation, but it was not accomplished without long debates and subsequent controversies among Catholic Czechs in the United States. The National Alliance of Bohemian Catholics contributed some $600,000 to the CSNC; it sent to the Holy Sea a check for $5,000 together with a memorandum asking for the pope's support of "Czechoslovak" freedom and independence; and it took several other actions on behalf of the independence movement.[28]

Early in February 1918, the Bohemian National Alliance and the Slovak League of America called a conference of representatives of the Czechs and Slovaks in the United States. This conference agreed that the Bohemian National Alliance and the Slovak League would form a branch of the Czecho-Slovak National Council, in which each organization would be represented by an equal number of members. About a month later, on March 10, a sixteen-member branch of the CSNC in America was formed. Affiliated with it were the principal organizations of the Czechs and Slovaks in America—the Bohemian National Alliance (including the Czech Social Democrats), the Slovak League and the National Alliance of Bohemian Catholics. Like the Russian CSNC, the U.S. branch did not have a president (the office was to be exercised always by the member of the CSNC [Paris] who was present in the United States). Charles Pergler, a socialist, was elected vice-president. The American branch had its office in Washington, D.C., with Pergler in charge. The establishment of the branch did not mean the abolition of the main Czech and Slovak organizations in America; they remained active. The branch merely acted as the executive of the coalition of the Czech and Slovak organizations; it was also the representative of the Paris-based CSNC in the United States. As one of its first acts, the branch submitted a translation of the "Epiphany Declaration" to the U.S. Department of State on March 14, 1918.[29]

After the U.S. declaration of war on Austria-Hungary in December 1917, "Victor"—Voska, back from his unsuccessful mission in Russia—rediscovered his American citizenship and offered his services to his "adopted country with the solemn promise" that all his previous experiences and connections with revolutionary organizations "will be exclusively used to bringing about the downfall of militaristic imperialism of the Central Powers through a certain form of revolution in the above mentioned Empire with the help of an American-British committee of two, appointed by the United States and British authorities," to which committee he would report on the progress of the work. He suggested Charles R. Crane for the United States and William Wiseman for Great Britain as members of the committee. (It is apparent that Voska, Crane, and Wiseman worked for the same Cause.) Voska recommended that the American government "start an organized propaganda and support on behalf of the revolutionary movement in the Austro-Hungarian Empire which would eventually penetrate to Germany, Bulgaria and Turkey."

Believing that the undertaking "is a great necessity without which a complete victory is unthinkable in the near future," he made the following claim: "The Austro-Hungarian Empire is ripest for a revolution which would shorten the war as it would bring disorganization not only into Austro-Hungarian countries but to a great extent disorganization into Germany, Bulgaria and Turkey because Austria-Hungary is the connecting link between the northern and southern nations under the Prussian military control. If unified military effort from the outside is accompanied by revolutionary effort from the inside of the Austro-Hungarian Empire it would bring about the fall of this artificial state formation in 1918." To effect this, "it is essential to support all Czechoslovak, Jugoslav, Polish, Russian and Italian anti-Austrian endeavors and to form a central organization which would be connected with all the revolutionary organizations of the above-mentioned nationalities."[30]

Voska asked for a special appointment as an officer in the United States Army; for permission to select six men as his staff who would receive commissions with lieutenant's rank and salary, and at least twelve civilians; for the right to use an official channel for sending dispatches and cablegrams; and for the right to use as many agents and workers as he needed, throughout Austro-Hungarian countries or elsewhere. In addition, he wanted to have two offices, one in New York and the other close to the Franco-Swiss boundary. The work would have to be "absolutely confidential in every respect," and he would be solely responsible to the committee of the two gentlemen. His annual salary would be $10,000 (1918 dollars); and the total budget for one year he estimated at $695,000.[31]

William Wiseman, in a letter to Gordon Auchincloss of the U.S. State Department (son-in-law of Colonel House, with whom he was intimate), highly recommended Voska for intelligence and propaganda work, saying that he thought "very highly" of Voska's ability "in these sort of schemes." Since Voska and his coworkers were American citizens, Wiseman believed that "they have to work under the orders of the U[nited]. S[tates]. G[overnment]., and the necessary funds, if it was decided to provide them, would be paid out to someone you appoint to supervise their show."[32] Eventually, Voska was appointed captain in the U.S. intelligence service and was sent to Europe on a temporary assignment to the Committee on Public Information, reporting to Will Irwin for orders.[33] After having worked for Masaryk, and for the British, and after his failure in Russia,

Voska was now working officially for Uncle Sam, though he maintained contacts with Wiseman and Masaryk as before.[34] Now Wiseman had his man, Voska, in the Inquiry (and later as a member of the U.S. delegation at the Paris Peace Conference), and was able to use this additional channel to feed "information" to Colonel House and obtain desired information at the same time.

It was no accident that Voska was eager to build a propaganda and espionage center in Europe using American money, and that Wiseman was pleased that the U.S. government sent him there. While in England in October and November 1917, Voska met with Wiseman, Sir Edward Carson, member of the war cabinet; Robert F. Young, the British Intelligence Service officer who had worked with the Czechs in the United States and had been a link between the service and Masaryk; and Lord Northcliffe, chief of the British propaganda, whose propaganda material Voska had distributed in the United States since 1914. (Some 46,640 books and pamphlets were sent to all important places in America.) Now they discussed the further dissemination of pro-Allied propaganda and the combating of enemy propaganda, especially in the United States and Russia. In February 1918, the British government established an official propaganda organization, the Department of Propaganda in Enemy Countries, headed by Lord Northcliffe. Steed was placed in charge of the Austro-Hungarian section of the department, and Seton-Watson was one of his principal helpers in the propaganda efforts.[35]

The Czech propaganda in the United States was conducted by revolutionaries, with Perlger at their helm, till the spring of 1918; Masaryk, who arrived at Vancouver on April 28, 1918, was expected to become a big help in their efforts. However, after Lansing received the Tokyo memorandum on April 13, he lost interest in Masaryk. But the latter received a hero's welcome in Chicago on May 5, 1918. According to newspaper accounts, more than 100,000 people cheered him in the streets. From Chicago he went to Washington, D.C., Boston, New York, Pittsburgh, and other places. In Pittsburgh, the center of the Slovak League, representatives of that organization met with representatives of the Bohemian National Alliance and the National Alliance of Bohemian Catholics on May 30, 1918. The purpose of the meeting was to discuss the organization of the future Czechoslovak state. Since several of the Slovak spokesmen expressed their apprehension that their compatriots in the new state might not have complete equality with the Czech nation, Masaryk drafted a statement that would assure Slovakia a complete autonomy. The new state would rest on the equality of the two nations. In order to satisfy the Slovak League completely, Masaryk agreed to insert the word "Diet" into the document.[36] This agreement, as revised by Masaryk and written by him in Slovak, is known as the Pittsburgh Agreement (Pact). It approved "a political program aiming at the union of the Czechs and Slovaks in an independent state comprising of the Czech Lands and Slovakia." As regards Slovakia, the agreement stipulated that "Slovakia shall have its own administration, its own Diet, and its own courts. The Slovak language shall be the official language in the schools, in governmental offices, and in public life generally." Furthermore, "the Czecho-Slovak State shall be a republic, and its constitution a democratic one." Detailed provisions relating to the organization of the state were "left to the liberated Czechs and Slovaks and their duly elected representatives."

This document, drafted and signed by Masaryk and others, brought the Slovaks in America, constituting about one-third of the Slovak nation, into the ranks of the Czecho-Slovak [sic] independence movement. It guaranteed their countrymen in Slovakia equality and autonomous development in the state yet to be established. From then on the Slovaks in America wholeheartedly supported Masaryk, thus helping him to "prove" that the Slovaks opposed Austria-Hungary and that they favored the establishment of a "national" state of the Czechs and Slovaks. After the war, however, Masaryk disavowed the Pittsburgh Agreement, calling it "a local understanding between American Czechs and Slovaks." He wrote that he had signed the "Convention"—emphasizing that it was not a "Treaty"—in order to appease "a small Slovak faction which was dreaming of God knows what sort of independence for Slovakia, since the ideas of some Russian Slavophiles, and of Štúr and Hurban-Vajanský, had taken root even among the American Slovaks."[37] When Father Andrej Hlinka, the leader of the Slovak People's party, reminded Masaryk about his commitment to the Slovaks, Masaryk responded by attacking him personally and calling him a "liar" without saying what he was supposed to be lying about. In his letter to Father Hlinka of October 12, 1929, Masaryk called the Pittsburgh Agreement a "forgery" (a *falsum*), although he himself drafted it and signed it twice. (The second signature was affixed to a calligraphic copy of it submitted to him by Albert Mamatey, president of the Slovak League in America, on November 14, 1918, on the day of his election as president of the new Czecho-Slovak Republic and a few days before his departure from the United States).[38]

The Pittsburgh Agreement, though far-reaching in its consequences many years later, was not the main purpose of Masaryk's journey to America. He was primarily interested in the transportation of the Czechoslovak army corps from Russia to France, and in the diplomatic recognition of the CSNC and its army as a necessary prerequisite for the future recognition of the Czechoslovak state. The transfer of the troops had already been his chief concern on his way to the United States. While he tried to make the necessary arrangement in Vladivostok and Tokyo, his efforts were paralleled by those of the secretariat of the CSNC in Paris.

As Masaryk and Beneš saw it, the transfer of the troops was a precondition for the success of their action in the west. From March 1918, on, Beneš followed with great apprehension indications appearing in the military reports that suggested that it would be better to use the Czechoslovak troops in Russia. The CSNC stated its negative position on the matter very clearly on April 2, 1918, when it was asked to reply to a query from the French military attaché in London. One day earlier, the attaché had reported that the British general staff had submitted to the British Foreign Office a note related to the deployment in Russia of the Czechoslovak army corps. Reportedly, Trotsky had requested that the Czechoslovak army corps be left in Russia and become the hard core of the reorganized Russian army. However, the Russian branch of the CSNC rejected the proposition, and thus the whole corps was on its way to Vladivostok.[39] The British ministry of war strongly doubted that enough ships could be made available to transport the men to Europe, and pointed out that if this army had a real value, then it should be used in Russia or Siberia.

Beneš rejected the idea of using the troops in western Siberia; he reinterated his previous requests for the transfer of these units to France.[40] According to him, the Czech soldiers were very enthusiastic about fighting on the Western Front. The rumors that were circulating (according to which the Czechoslovak units were being deserted by the very Allies that had organized them) would mean a tremendous blow to the Czechoslovak nation's resistance to the Austro-Hungarian government. Masaryk spoke along the same lines in Vladivostok, Tokyo, and the United States.

In view of Masaryk's and Beneš's opposition to the British proposal (and for his own reasons as well), Clemenceau attempted to obtain the necessary tonnage from the British, who could not provide the ships. Therefore, in the middle of April, Clemenceau placed a request for the needed tonnage before the U.S. government. As Secretary of State Lansing stated in his cable of April 22, however, the American government could not furnish the tonnage for the transport of these troops across the Pacific.[41]

The shortage of ships made the transportation of the troops impossible within the foreseeable future. On May 2, then, the Supreme War Council approved the proposal to direct as many Czech units as possible toward Archangel and to negotiate with Japan for the transportation of the troops that were moving closer to Vladivostok. Despite Clemenceau's resistance, the British secretary of war, Milner, secured permission for the majority of the troops belonging to the Czechoslovak army corps to travel to Archangel and Murmansk.[42] In Archangel the British had a military base that was an important storage depot for war material. The Czechoslovak units that arrived there were to be used for the defense of the two harbors, Archangel and Murmansk, and the railroad to Murmansk. The units that had already reached points east of Omsk could eventually cooperate with Allied operations in Siberia.[43] The British had their plan for the use of the troops, and their view prevailed in the Supreme War Council.

Despite these developments, Beneš, the "eternal optimist," reported on May 2 to the branch of the CSNC in Washington, D.C., that the troops were already on their way from Russia to France, and that arrangements had been made for the transportation of the troops with the help of England and the United States. As Beneš stated it, this meant that "within the next three months we may have in France 50,000-60,000 soldiers," or with those who would arrive from Italy, 80,000. The nonexistent Czechoslovakia was thus "militarily stronger than Belgium, Portugal, and Serbia;" next to England, France, and the United States and Italy, Czechoslovakia was "the greatest enemy" of Germany and Austria-Hungary. "We are next after Italy," Beneš said, and added that "this is a very important thing."[44] Later, however, during his negotiations in London, on May 14, 1918, Beneš made an agreement with the War Office in which he consented to the use of the Czechoslovak troops in western Russia as part of a massive Allied intervention against the Germans, on condition that there should be no intervention in Russian internal affairs [sic] and that at least half of the 75,000 [sic] troops would be transported to France.[45] Similar optimism (and exaggeration) were shown by Masaryk upon his arrival in Chicago, where he told journalists on May 7, 1918, that it was necessary to transport from Russia to France the first Czechoslovak army corps of 50,000 men as well as 50,000 other men who, according to Masaryk, had enlisted in the second Czechoslovak army corps. "Then," he declared the next day, "within a few months we will have on the Western front an army of 100,000 to 120,000 men, all excellent soldiers, and the whole world will have to reckon seriously with us."[46] In Washington, D.C., he was welcomed by some members of the U.S. Congress. In an interview published in the *Washington Post* on May 12, 1918, Masaryk repeated almost verbatim some of the statements that he had made in his Tokyo memorandum of April 10. He also stressed the necessity for cooperation between the Entente powers and the Soviet regime in Russia, and the need to transport the Czechoslovak army corps to France. In his other public statements and speeches Masaryk repeated what he had said in Chicago about the transportation of 50,000-100,000 Czechoslovak troops to France.

The French government was displeased by Masaryk's opposition to the Allied plan that the Legion should help occupy a base in the Russian north and the railways out of Murmansk and Archangel, or the Trans-Siberian Railway and Vladivostok in the east. In his telegram of April 30, 1918, the French foreign minister, Pichon, informed the French ambassador in Washington that while "Beneš, Štefánik and all the others are ready to obey all the decisions of the Allied Supreme War Council at Versailles upon which all hopes of Bohemia depend," Masaryk was pursuing a different course of action. Pichon asked the ambassador to explain to Masaryk the need for his cooperation with the Allies. On May 12 the French ambassador thanked Pichon for his confidential telegram pertaining to Masaryk and the "quasi-Bolshevik tendencies of the leader of the Czech nation." His pro-Bolshevik views, however, would make all negotiations with him difficult and embarrassing, the ambassador believed. On May 13 the ambassador told Pichon that Masaryk constantly recommended *de facto* recognition of the Soviet government by the Allies, that he talked with contempt about the other Russian political parties, and that he emphasized the strength and relative stability of the Lenin government, and the need for attaching the Ukraine to Russia.[47] Such private and public statements by Masaryk made the idea of dismembering Austria-Hungary and establishing an independent Czechoslovak state led by him very problematic, not only in France but also in Great Britain.

On April 27, 1918, Masaryk wrote a letter to Seton-Watson in which he expressed satisfaction that the Czech soldiers were able to travel not only through Siberia, but also through Archangel and Murmansk, and concluded that it "shows that one can come to an agreement with the Bolsheviks." In 1943 Seton-Watson commented on it and the Tokyo memorandum enclosed in the letter: "Read in May 1918, this letter and memorandum were too strong meat even for his friends in London, still more for the official world for which they were intended."[48] Although before Masaryk left Russia Voska sent him several telegrams saying that Crane had "arranged everything for a conference with our President [Wilson]," the latter did not receive Masaryk upon his arrival in Washington, D.C.

Indeed, the president was urged by Charles Crane and his son, Richard Crane, secretary to Secretary of State Lansing, to receive Masaryk. Crane recommended Masaryk in the most laudatory terms: "the wisest and most influential Slav of our day." Crane believed that "only a Slav of such dimensions could fully understand and synthesize what the President was trying to do."[49] However, in May 1918, President Wilson was not interested in listening to the advice of Masaryk, who was recommending *de facto* recognition of the Lenin regime in Russia.

In mid-May 1918, the State Department transmitted to President Wilson a lengthy report written by the American military attaché in Russia (Vologda), dated May 10. It gave a detailed description of the growth of the Czechoslovak army and how the Czech prisoners of war preferred to join the Czech Legion rather than the Red Guards, despite the pressure put on them by the Bolshevik government. The main point in the report, however, was the statement that the Russian branch of the CSNC would not allow any of the Czech military units to be used for policing the railways, and, most likely, the troops could not be used in the event of a military intervention, unless Russia expressly requested it.[50] The report indicated that the U.S. government was considering the possibility of using the Czechs as a police on Russian railways. The main proponent of this plan was Butler J. Wright, chancellor of the American embassy in Russia, who believed that an inter-Allied force, 60,000 men strong (20,000 each of Americans, Japanese, and Czechs, could control the main railways in Russia. The U.S. ambassador in Japan, Morris, knew of Wright's plan of intervention, according to which the role of the Czechs would be "to maintain open the communication line in Siberia." Masaryk's refusal to take part in such an intervention must have disappointed President Wilson, who apparently saw merit in the plan to use the Czechs to police the railways and thus control the main lines of communication and transportation.

Despite the generally favorable U.S. attitude toward the national liberation movements in Austria-Hungary, Masaryk received a cool reception in official Washington because of his views on the Bolshevik regime. The U.S. State Department was receiving reports from Europe and Russia in which both the Czechoslovak army and the home resistance appeared in a highly favorable light. At the beginning of May 1918, the U.S. ambassador in Italy, Nelson Page, wrote to the secretary of state about the Rome Congress of Oppressed Nationalities and the importance of the Czech soldiers in Italy. He recommended that the U.S. government publicly endorse the Czechoslovak independence movement. On May 7, Page reported on the Czechoslovak-Italian agreement of April 21, 1918, and stated that England reportedly intended to conclude a similar agreement.[51] On May 13, the U.S. ambassador in Switzerland sent a telegram to Colonel House, received on May 15, that advocated exploiting the momentum of political crisis in Austria-Hungary by giving support to those oppressed nationalities within the Habsburg empire that desired freedom. The Austrian emperor had had plenty of time to do something in this matter; it would therefore be a politically correct move to join the Allies and work for the dismemberment of Austria-Hungary. Such a policy would bring about more success. It seemed that the time was ripe for placing Austria-Hungary in the same category as Germany and for taking steps against those irresponsible governments.[52]

On May 16, Masaryk attended a dinner in the home of Richard C. Crane, son of Charles R. Crane, whom he knew from prewar days and who was an official in the State Department (after the war he became the first U.S. minister to Czechoslovakia). Among those present were several officials of the U.S. government: Butler Wright, Joseph Grew, Julius Lay, Basil Miles, and Breckinridge Long, the third assistant secretary of state. In his memorandum of the conversation Breckinridge Long recorded Masaryk's views on the situation in Russia.[53] Masaryk believed that it was not possible for the Russians to undertake any offensive action against the Germans, and that the latter would not enter either Petrograd or Moscow, for two reasons: "first, that being political centers they would incur political opposition for having broken flagrantly the Brest-Litovsk treaty, and second, that if they are in possession of either or both places they would immediately become responsible for the feeding and supplying of the population there resident which they would be unable to do." The shortage of foodstuffs and the problem of supplying the population could not be solved by either the Bolsheviks of the Germans; and "Germany can only profit by the antagonism to the Bolshevik on the part of the remainder of the population." (Here Masaryk assumes what he wants to prove: opposition to the Bolsheviks would benefit Germany, and, therefore, his policy of neutrality is correct.)

Masaryk felt that "the spirits [sic] which are moving toward independence in various parts of the old Russian Empire, are hopeful signs but . . . there is little hope that these independent separate movements will be co-ordinated." He added that "the Red Guard are a source of great embarrassment to the Bolsheviks [sic]; that the people in other parts of Europe and in this country do not contribute to the Bolshevik any true, logical property and [he] contends that in Bolshevism there is a real thought and a real idea." He said, furthermore, that "the Red Guard are simply violent anarchists who masquerade under the cloak of Bolshevism and do the cause great harm." According to Masaryk, "the only thing on which the Russian people are united is in establishing independent governments, but, that the objects and purposes of the establishment differs in each locality. He likened Russia to a great hospital in which there were a number of sick patients—the patients, for the purpose of the analogy being the independence movements for government—in which hospital the directing genius would order the same kind of medicine for all of the patients, prescribing quinine for each on Monday and some other medicine for all of them on Tuesday."

The preceding statement reflects Masaryk's intense interest in Plato. In the *Republic* the Greek philosopher compares "the philosopher king" to a physician and people to patients. However, the movements for independence in Russia could hardly be compared to sick people in a hospital who are willing to take the medicine prescribed for them by the nonexistent "directing genius"; and, above all, both analogies—Plato's and Masaryk's—are false.

According to Long's memorandum of the conversation, Masaryk was "particularly interested in spreading propaganda amongst the Checko-Slavs [sic] and fomenting them to revolt against Austria." But Long saw the scheme as being "impractical." He writes that "there is little utility in propaganda particularly under a strongly centralized government, where most of the men are in the army, unless it is backed up by some strength and is given some force in the way of military help. Propaganda itself can do no harm, but it can lead to no tangible results."[54]

Breckinridge Long, who had to deal with concrete problems connected with the conduct of the war and the situation in Russia, was interested in the Czech troops, not in Masaryk's propaganda scheme. On May 21, Boris Miles notified Long that he had given a memorandum on the Semenov movement in the Far East to the secretary of state. Should the U.S. government decide to support Semenov, it would be most useful to take advantage of the Czech troops, of whom 6,000 were already in Vladivostok, 40,000 were ready to depart for Archangel, and, in additon, another 50,000 were being organized. (Masaryk opposed any cooperation with Semenov, Denikin, Alexeev, or any other anti-Bolshevik group. The figures that Miles received from sources close to Masaryk were inflated; and the statement that the bulk of the troops were ready to travel to Archangel was incorrect.) Miles recommended that some of the Czechoslovak troops be taken over by the American government and assisted by American officers. Colonel Emerson and three of this assistants, Miles wrote, had left Vladivostok for Vologda on May 19, "to confer with Mr. Francis as to whether anything can be done for the Railways in European Russia. Mr. Stevens with one hundred engineers are woking on the Chinese Eastern Railway; the balance of the Corps of American Railway engineers —about eighty men—are at Nagasaki waiting developments."[55] This memorandum indicates that there was an American alternative to the British-sponsored proposal that the Japanese occupy the Russian railways, a plan than anticipated, instead, that American engineers might operate the Russian railways with the assistance of the Czech troops.

Masaryk's negative stand on any Czech participation in an Allied intervention in Russia notwithstanding, the Allies continued to be interested in the Czecion Legion and the independence movement within Austria-Hungary. As a follow-up to his dispatch of May 13, the U.S. ambassador in Switzerland recommended on May 23, 1918, that the United States give public support to the independence movements, including the Czech, within Austria-Hungary.[56] On May 28, recalling the coming of the fourth anniversary of Austria-Hungary's declaration of war on Serbia, the Serbian minister in Washington, Lubo Mihailović, submitted a memorandum to the secretary of state urging that the United States publicly recognize the right of national self-determination for the nationalities of Austria-Hungary, and arguing that such a formal recognition of their demands would play a tremendous role in the prosecution of the war. He called for the unification of all Southern Slavs in one state, the establishment of an independent Bohemia and an independent Poland, and the dismemberment of Austria-Hungary as the main condition of a lasting peace.[57] The oppressed nations' efforts to obtain American recognition were rewarded on May 29, 1918, when U.S. Secretary of State Lansing public stated that "the proceedings of the Congress of Oppressed Races of Austria-Hungary, which was held in Rome in April, have been followed with great interest by the government of the United States, and that the nationalistic aspirations of the Czecho-Slovaks and Jugo-Slavs for freedom have the earnest sympathy of this Government."[58] Although Lansing's statement was not fully satisfactory to the leaders of the independence movements abroad, and they made their views known to him, the statement was endorsed in a joint declaration of England, France, and Italy on June 3, 1918.[59]

Lansing did not grant an audience to Masaryk until the day after European newspapers carried sensational news about the Czech army's uprising against the Bolsheviks (on June 3, 1918, the same day the British government indicated its willingness to recognize the CSNC, having earlier informed the U.S. secretary of state about its plans). The fact that Masaryk had to wait one month for the audience, despite his excellent contacts in the State Department and the many interventions made on his behalf by public figures in the United States,[60] was due, most likely, to the "bad press" and "silent treatment" that he received in the United States because of his views on the situation in Russia and his categorical rejection of proposals for armed intervention there. Masary was saying publicly and privately what he had stated in the "private and confidential" Tokyo memorandum, prepared for President Wilson. This document accounts for the tone of a note written by a State Department official who granted permission for Masaryk to enter the United States. According to the note of permission, the Czech leader "wishes to visit Washington in the interest of the Russian Bolshevik government." Later the same official reported the arrival of "Professor Masaryk, alias Marsden, of the Bolshevik government in Russia."[61] All Masaryk's statements to the press calling for collaboration with the Soviet government were received in official Washington with both embarrassment and rejection.

Indeed, when on May 27, 1918, all American newspapers reported Lord Cecil's announcement that the British government had no intention of recognizing the Bolshevik government in Russia, the *New York Times*[62] carried an interview in which Professor Masaryk emphasized the need for collaboration between the Allies and the Bolsheviks. The day before, the same newspaper had printed an article on Masaryk's work and the Czechoslovak independence movement. It contained a statement by Masaryk according to which the main problem of the Czechoslovaks was the transportation of the Czech Legion from Russia to France. Masaryk wished that the army would travel to France through the United States in order to inspire the Czechs living in this country. Because of his pro-Bolshevik views, when he arrived in Boston, the local daily newspapers ignored him making no mention of his visit at all.

In spite of Masaryk's neutralist policy, the Czech army in Russia found itself, involuntarily and accidentally, in the role of an interventionist force toward the end of May 1918. Acting our of self-preservation, the Czech military defied the Masaryk-appointed political leader, Maxa, disregarded Masaryk's instructions to maintain strict neutrality, and revolted against the Bolsheviks. The news of their action caused a sensation in Allied countries; suddenly the Czechs were given tremendous amounts of favorable publicity. On June 3, 1918, the *New York Times* carried an Associated Press dispatch dated June 2, claiming that a conspiracy against the Bolshevik regime extended throughout Russia, and that the Czechoslovak troops were "said to have captured important railroad junction and lines." Believing that the revolt of the Czechoslovak army might have far-reaching consequences, Lansing received Masaryk on June 3, 1918.

The State Department was considering Wrigth's plan to use the Czechs as a police force to guard railroads in Russia and keep the lines of communication open between Russia and Vladivostok.[63] But Masaryk told Lansing on June 3, as in subsequent conversations, that the Czechs did not wish to fight against Russians, and that included the Bolsheviks. He urged the United States to help transport the Czechoslovak army corps from Russia to France.[64] Masaryk apparently did not understand that the Czech troops were already in a life-and-death struggle with the Bolsheviks, that there was no way back for them. Neither did he know that some two months earlier American representatives in Russia had believed that the transfer of the Czech Legion to France would be a futile waste of time, money, and tonnage.[65] It did not occur to him that the Allies might have had their own reasons for not providing ships to transport the troops to France, and that they might have anticipated a greater use for the Czechs in Russia. While Lansing was preoccupied with the question of an Allied intervention in Russia, Masaryk asked him to provide ships for the Legionnaires and to transport at least a few regiments through the United States, in order to "greatly inspire our people here."[66]

Masaryk's anti-interventionst position, which was, rightly or wrongly, interpreted by many as reflecting a pro-Bolshevik orientation, may have delayed U.S. recognition of the CSNC. On May 30, 1918, in a memorandum for the president, Lansing stated his views on the desirability of partitioning Austria-Hungary among the nationalities of which it was composed.[67] According to Lansing, the treaty of military alliance between Austria-Hungary and Germany of May 12, 1918, reportedly placed the entire military establishment of the former under the control of the latter for a period of twenty years. The submission of the Austrian emperor, his going to the German grand headquarters in order to show his loyalty to Germany, removed "all possibility of separating the two empires." If Austria were permitted to remain in possession of the territory within her borders, "the German Emperor will control millions of people utterly hostile to the Germans, who will be in a state of servitude." When Charles "showed that a separate peace was in vain and when he became a vassal of Germany, a revision of policy became necessary. From that moment Austria-Hungary lost its right to exist as an Empire including these oppressed races." In view of the new developments, it seemed to the secretary of state that "Austria-Hungary must be practically blotted out as an empire. It should be partitioned among the nationalities of which it is composed. As a great power it should no longer exist. The Poles, Czechs and other peoples who long for independence and hate all foreign sovereignty must not be brought under the Prussian yoke by continuing them as provinces of Austria-Hungary. It would be criminal to coerce them and it would be folly for the world to permit it." Lansing believed that the United States should "encourage in every possible way the national desires of these peoples." If need be, he would "favor going so far as to promise them their independence when the Central Powers were defeated if that would induce them to revolt against German-owned Austria-Hungary." While this memorandum favored a public pronouncement to the new policy toward the Austro-Hungarian empire, in his official statements Lansing proceeded cautiously, waiting for the president's decision. He did not mention the new policy even to Masaryk during the June 3 audience, and he was, apparently, not impressed with what the Czech leader told him.

In the second half of May 1918, Masaryk's popularity in official Washington hit rock bottom; in mid-June it began to climb sky high. Throughout June newspapers in all Allied countries carried news of the exploits of the Czechoslovak army in Russia and Siberia. The *New York Times* and the *New York Herald Tribune* called for the formation of a Russian army to liberate Russia from the German yoke and the Red terror. The *New York Times* of June 9, 1918, urged the restoration of Russia with the help of an Allied force that would become the nucleus of the Russian army. On June 11 the *Washington Post* wrote that the friendly Russians were calling for a "rallying point," a center around which the dispersed Russian soldiers could be organized in order to resist the Bolshevik government which was under German influence. Ambassador Page wrote from Rome along similar lines on May 28, in a letter that reached Lansing on June 13.[68] On June 7, the Russian ambassador in Washington told Breckinridge Long that despite Masaryk's declaration that the Czechs would not fight on Russian soil against any part of the Russian population, these soldiers would, eventually, resist the Bolsheviks. They could then be used as a military expedition that would eliminate the Bolshevik influence and, under the leadership of the Allies, would restore order in Russia.[69] On the next day, June 8, Lansing received a memorandum from the British embassy in Washington, stating that Balfour was prepared to recognize the Czechoslovak army as an Allied force fighting for the interest of the Allies. The British government was also prepared to recognize the CSNC in the same way as it had been recognized by the French and Italian governments, and was willing to give it the same rights that had already been given to the Polish National Committee.[70]

On June 9 the *New York Times* published two articles pointing at the danger of German influence in Russia and suggesting that the war could be either won or lost in Russia. Moreover, since June 3, 1918, all American newspapers had been carrying news of the successes of the Czech Legion in Russia, praising the courage of the few who were accomplishing so much. The *New York Herald* featured a cartoon showing a small Czechoslovak knight with his sword drawn, leading from danger the Russian giant.[71] On June 16, the *Washington Sunday Star* wrote that the Czech victories might mean the beginning of a new era in Russia; and on the same day the *Chicago Herald-Examiner* emphasized that the success of the Czechoslovaks resolved the Allied problem and that their victories had given the long-awaited opportunity to the enemies of the Germans in Russia. On June 19, the *New York Times* quoted an article printed in *Echo de Paris*, advising the French government to capitalize on the Czech success in Siberia by launching the long-awaited intervention in Russia. In its own editorial comment the *New York Times* reproached the U.S. government for underestimating the significance of the Czech military action in Russia. It asserted that the Czechs were capable of becoming a nucleus of resistance to the Bolsheviks. Referring to the toppling of the Bolshevik rule in Siberia by the Czechs, the *Washington Post* of June 19 wrote that the new Russian government was supported by the Czechoslovak army. On June 16, the same paper carried a statement made by General Berthelot, who had come to Washington to win over President Wilson to an Allied intervention in Russia. Berthelot said that only an Allied military intervention would save Russia from being enveloped by Germany. "Those who support the Bolsheviks," the general said, "are helping the German Empire. Intervention is the only hope."[72]

"In dealing with the question of intervention in Russia, for which Great Britain and France are pressing," writes Lansing in his confidential memorandum for the president of June 12, 1918,[73] "the determination of a policy, based on the assumption that only an expedition composed of the United States, Allied Nations, and Japan would be acceptable to the Russians...depends primarily upon the ability to transport the troops." He had sounded the Japanese and examined the American shipping situation, but "there are no ships to carry troops across the Pacific." In the given situation, Lansing saw "no reason to pass upon the wisdom of intervention via Vladivostok. As to intervention via the northern ports [Murmansk and Archangel or both] I am in favor of doing as Foch wishes." When a preponderence of manpower in France was gained, then "it will be advisable to determine upon a policy." Lansing added that he proceeded from the premise "that it would be a grave error for Japan to send an expedition alone."

"There is only one other method of opposing German penetration into Siberia, *unless the Czecho-Slovaks are willing to resist Russians who ally themselves with the Germans,* and that is by some form of peaceful assistance through a commission representative of commercial, agricultural, labor, financial, and social activities." (Emphasis added; the Czechs had already been fighting the Bolsheviks since May 25, 1918.) "I believe," writes Lansing, "that a constituted body of Americans going via Vladivostok to assist the Russians would be effective in keeping the Siberians at least from German domination. It might require *an international police force* [emphasis added] to protect the commission, but I do not think that it would have to be large or would be resented."

"At present that is *the only practical plan* [emphasis added] I see, and I shall lay it before the President."

The foregoing shows, first, that the implementation of the U.S. government's "practical plan" required "an international police force to protect the commission" that would assist the Russians; and, second, that should the Czechoslovaks be willing to "resist Russians who ally themseleves with the Germans," as they already had, a new situation would arise in Russia and a new decision with respect to intervention would have to be made. The only stumbling block was Masaryk, who was not influenced by newspaper reports and held tenaciously to neutrality, who insisted on transporting the troops from Siberia to France (though ships were not available), and who urged the Allies to recognize the Bolsheviks as a *de facto* government of Russia. The Czech leader did not know that giving the Bolshevik government material and financial support in the event that it should decide to defend Russia against German aggression had already been ruled "out of the question" by the Wilson administration on February 19,

1918, that is, before the signing of the Brest-Litovsk treaty in March 1918. Furthermore, on February 23, Lansing told Assistant Secretary of State Breckinridge Long that the Bolsheviks were ultimately more dangerous to American security than was Germany, because Bolshevism denied both nationality and property rights and had threatened this country with revolution. On the previous day Wilson and Lansing had decided that the U.S. government would not recognize or deal with Lenin's regime even on a basis of wartime expediency.[74]

Ever since his arrival in the United States, Masaryk had desired to see President Wilson; the latter was reluctant to receive him, despite the many interventions on his behalf, including those of French ambassador Jusserand, the two Cranes, and Congressman Adolph J. Sabath of Chicago. The congressman, who had originally come from Bohemia, advised Masaryk on how to win the president's favor. Sabath knew that Wilson objected to a unilateral Japanese intervention, but favored the use of the Czechoslovak troops in Russia and Siberia for police purposes, guarding the Trans-Siberian Railway, and maintaining order in the Far East, where, especially in Vladivostok, there were huge amounts of stored war materials sent to Russia by the United States, for which, of course, no payment had as yet been made.[75] On Sunday, June 16, 1918, when Sabath wrote to the president asking him to grant an audience to Masaryk, the *Washington Post* featured a front-page article under the headline, "Czechs Rule Siberia." Two days later, on June 18, the *New York Times,* under the headlines "Czechs Extending Siberian Successes" and "Ex-Austrian Prisoners Control the Railroad for a Distance of 1,250 Miles," carried a telegram from London, dated June 15, according to which the Czechs, "having occupied Samara on the Volga" were continuing their advance. In his memoirs Masaryk admits that it was the Siberian "Anabasis" of the Legion that "had attracted" President Wilson's attention and "had awakened his good will."[76] Thus, on June 19, 1918, after six weeks of waiting, Masaryk was finally received by the American president.

According to his book, Masaryk discussed with Wilson the need to dismember Austria-Hungary, Clemenceau's revelation of the Austrian peace maneuvers, and the Austrian responsibility for the war, among other things.[77] Masaryk also asked the president to help transport the Czechoslovak troops from Russia to France, asserting that the troops were the best anti-Austrian propaganda among the non-German and non-Hungarian nations of Austria. Historians Kalina and Mamatey have noted that Masaryk's memoirs inaccurately describe his meeting with Wilson, and that he mixes the content of two conversations, the second of which did not take place until September 11, 1918, almost three months later.[78] As it happened, there was no meeting of minds between Masaryk and the president on the issue of intervention in Russia, and for this reason that day may have been the most crucial one in the history of the Russian Civil War.

Masaryk's own handwritten notes, and the typewritten notes about this meeting with the president,[79] show that Wilson was preoccupied with the question of how to help Russia. He explained to Masaryk the plan of Japanese intervention and "what it would mean for Russia," expressing, no doubt, his disapproval of sending a large Japanese army to Russia. His main interest was not in Austria-Hungary, but in the Czechoslovak army and its use to restore order in Russia. Masaryk's record of the audience shows that Wilson used the term "nucleus" several times in their conversation; and this word indicates that he told Masaryk about the plan advocated by several American diplomats and Lansing. This plan provided that the Czechoslovak army would become the nucleus around which an anti-Bolshevik and pro-Allied army could be built from among the Russians and other Slavic peoples in Russia. But Masaryk told Wilson that he opposed this plan, because he did not know what such "a small intervention" involving some 50,000 to 100,000 troops could accomplish. He rejected the idea that the Czechoslovak military units could form the nucleus of the Allies forces in Russia and occupy the Trans-Siberian Railway.[80] On the contrary, he insisted on their transportation to France. Needless to say, without Masaryk's cooperation the Wilson plan could not be implemented. In his notes Masaryk made a remark in English: "Exactly —I never could get more information." It shows that Masaryk did not know what was going on in Allied diplomatic circles and that his thinking was out of step with that of the Allied statesmen.

Masaryk, however, was "in favor of renewing the war upon Germany by the whole Japanese army," or, as his handwritten record states, "a war of Japan against Germany. But there are difficulties with it. The principal one is: How to pay the Japanese? This the Allies must realize." The record indicates that Wilson replied "the Allies would finance" the massive Japanese intervention Masaryk suggested. But, said Masaryk, "this is not enough, the Japanese may want territory."

Masaryk's notes, a sketchy mixture of Czech and English phrases, are intelligible only if one is aware of Masaryk's views on the question of Japanese intervention in Russia as they are reflected in a report dated September 1, 1917, and written from Petrograd by W. Somerset Maugham.[81] On this date, Masaryk proposed that the Allied send "a Japanese army, at least 300,000 men" to Russia in order to "restore the moral [sic] of the Russian troops." Since Masaryk came back to the idea of sending a large Japanese army to Russia in his second audience with Wilson on September 11, 1918, then advocated it in his official communiqués, and again mentioned it publicly in February 1919, the logical deduction is that during his first audience with Wilson Masaryk proposed sending the Japanese army to Russia to fight "Germany." But Wilson replied (on June 19, 1918) that he "knew that they have only 250,000 [troops] and the same number of reserves," and that they would hardly be able "to assemble one million men."[82]

Although in the June 19 audience Masaryk proposed sending a Japanese army to Russia, he also asked the president to provide ships to transport the Czechoslovak troops from Siberia to France. He repeated the same request to Lansing six days later. Wilson regretted that he could not accommodate Masaryk, and the audience ended on the president's comment that he considered himself bound by the Allies. "Foch is the military leader, and he, thus, subordinated himself to him," reads Masaryk's note.

As Richard Crane told Gordon Auchincloss, son-in-law of Colonel House and counselor in the State Department, and as the latter recorded in his diary on June 19, Wilson told Masaryk that "he had a plan for the coordination of the Red Cross which make for the barter and exchange of commodities in Russia; and that he intended to place under the charge of one man and that this man was not a business man." Auchincloss guessed that the president had decided to adopt the suggestion made in the letter from the secretary of state, which he himself had prepared. His ownly wish was "that he would hurry up and act."[83]

Wilson's plan probably evolved from several proposals that had been submitted to him earlier. As early as March 11, 1918, in his memorandum to Colonel House, Wiseman had advised that the United States send a commission composed of Red Cross, Y.M.C.A., propaganda, and military recruiting units to Vladivostok and Murmansk to help the Russians organize themselves against the Germans. In their conversation on May 30, Wilson told Wiseman that "his own idea was to send a Civil commission of British, French and Americans, to Russia to help organize the railroads and food supplies, and, since currency is worthless, organize a system of barter. He would send such missions to Vladivostok and Murmansk."[84] On June 5, 1918, a committee that had been appointed in May, by the chairman of the War Trade Board, and had been charged with preparing a report on Russia, submitted its findings on conditions in Russia and recommended ways of bringing about closer and more friendly relations between the two countries and opposing German commercial activities in Russia. The report made several specific recommendations, the chief of which was that the president appoint a Russian commissioner, "all matters pertaining to Russia to center in him in the future;" and that he be assisted and advised by a mission composed of various specialists. This mission "should proceed at once to Vladivostok and beginning in eastern Siberia push westward creating an organization for the distribution and exchange for domestic products of all those commodities which the Russian people most urgently require." Furthermore, the report said, "this organization should base upon the Trans-Siberian Railway and move westwardly along this line as rapidly as the country can be organized."[85]

On June 13, Auchincloss, after talking to several Democratic party officials and Colonel House, and after discussing the matter with Herbert Hoover, who headed the Food Administration, wrote a letter on the Siberian situation that Lansing singed and sent to the president. Two specific suggestions were made in it: (1) "the creation of the Commission for the Relief of Russia," and (2) an announcement by the president that would give "some tangible evidence to the world that the United States proposes to stand by Russia and to assist the Russian people in the circumstances in which they find themselves." It concluded that "armed intervention to protect the humanitarian work done by the Commission would be much preferable to armed intervention before this work had been begun."[86] The counselor worte to Mrs. Wilson asking her "to tell the President that the Colonel [House] entirely approved of the suggestion made in the letter." Auchincloss regretted that the president did not act upon the suggestion.[87] Because the Czechs already controlled most of the Trans-Siberian Railway, the plan could have been easily implemented had not Masaryk refused to cooperate.

Masaryk's and Beneš's views on the matter were not shared by all the leading members of the independence movement. While visiting Italy in February 1918, Štefánik disagreed with Masaryk's conduct in Russia. He even wanted to go to Russia and take the army "into his own hands." When a report about Masaryk's Tokyo memorandum for President Wilson arrived in France in April, Štefánik again expressed his disapproval of Masaryk's position.[88]

In June 1918, disapproval of Masaryk's policies was voiced by, among others, Dr. Lev Borský of the State Rights party, whose prewar program called for the establishment of an independent, sovereign state, and who had arrived in exile in January 1918. Borský considered the transport of the troops to France to be a fundamental mistake for two reasons: (1) if transferred to France, the army could not play the premier role it would if it remained in Siberia; and (2) the Czech policymakers should see to it that the army was out of reach of Allies who could disarm it at the end of the war. The army should be situated in such a way that, through military action, it could enforce independence. When Borský brought up the matter with Beneš and protested against the transfer of the army, Beneš stated that both he and Masaryk wanted to have as large an army in France as possible. Borský suggested that Beneš should officially request the tonnage but, in reality, try to postpone the transport as long as possible.[89] Beneš rejected the tactics of Borský, who, however, had no illusions about the motives and objectives of the independence movement's leaders.

Although Masaryk and Beneš shared the same objective and their views coincided on most issues, Beneš was more flexible and was willing to make concessions to the British and French in the matter of deployment of the Czechoslovak troops in Russia. Still, as late as July 28, 1918, he wrote from Paris to Masaryk in America as follows:

> As far as the 'intervention' in Russia is concerned, France wants to send there Janin and along with him Štefánik in order to consolidate our army, organize it and carry out the matter [intervention] in a systematic manner. It seems to me that Janin could do really a lot; and as our Generalissimo he will have an interest to do as much as possible, and to save as many soldiers for France as possible. It was agreed here that ours are staying in Siberia as a provisorium, until

they will be replaced by other [troops], or as long as it is not possible to transport them immediately. However, it has been decided that as soon as Janin will arrive there, he will start sending them [to France] on installments. I think that this is the only right, and, at the present time, the only feasible thing to do. Naturally, we will win on the European battlefield, especially in France. If we will have at least 20-25,000 of our soldiers here, we will achieve politically everything that we will want to [i.e., Masaryk and Beneš would be recognized as the political leaders of the 'Czechoslovak nation' and thus they would attain their personal objectives]. And then, at the moment of peace, I think, we must be with the army there where will be America and France.[90]

The troops, however, never arrived in France; the problem of their transportation has already been solved by the events in Russia and by the Czechoslovak army itself.

CHAPTER TWELVE

THE ORIGINS OF THE CONFLICT BETWEEN THE CZECHOSLOVAK ARMY AND THE BOLSHEVIKS

While the people on the home front who strove for Czechoslovak independence were not directly influenced by the political, economic, and social program of the October Revolution,[1] this event sharply polarized the Czechoslovak independence movement in Russia. During 1918, the Bolshevik movement did not find supporters and agitators in the Czech lands and Slovakia; there was no group of professional revolutionaries in those countries who would, as Lenin had advocated, seize political power in a violent proletarian revolution. The anti-Habsburg movement in the Czech lands was led by middle-class nationalists; by no stretch of the imagination could it be described as a class struggle of the workers against the bourgeoisie. Even workers embraced the ideas of nationalism and independence and cooperated with the middle-class political groups and their leaders. In Russia, however, the October Revolution and the arrival of Bolshevik power led to divisions within the Czechoslovak independence movement.

On one hand, the political right, represented by Josef Dürich, F. Král, Captain Němeček, and S. Koníček, joined the anti-Bolshevik forces and struggled jointly with the Whites against the "un-Russian" regime of Lenin. (As is well known, Lenin was charged with being a German spy, sent by the German general staff to Russia to conduct pacifist propaganda and demoralize Russian troops on the front;[2] also he concluded peace with the Central Powers, accepting their humiliating conditions.) On the other hand, the left-wing Social Democrats embraced the program of the Bolshevik Revolution and threw in their lot with the revolutionaries, dreaming of the world revolution and the transformation of the "imperialist war" into a class war in which the proletarians would overthrow capitalist rule. Neither group was very large, and the majority of those who favored Czechoslovak independence followed Masaryk's "neutralist" course. It should be added, however, that the right-wing elements always remained within the independence movement and did not try to harm it. They did not proselytize among the soldiers of the corps in any systematic manner, while the left-wing elements did proselytize and did cause, by their agitation and obstructionism, a great many difficulties for the Czechoslovak army corps. Eventually these elements separated themselves from the Czechoslovak independence movement altogether.

The Czechoslovak Communist Party was founded in Russia even before the establishment of the Czechoslovak state, and its activity abroad foreboded the political stratification in postwar Czechoslovakia, with all its political and class conflicts. Even before the emergence of the Czechoslovak state, a "civil war" took place among the forces that were originally committed to its establishment. The conflict started, at first, over Masaryk's noninvolvement policy. Eventually the issue between the Czechoslovak Bolsheviks on the one hand and the rest of the Czechoslovak independence movement on the other became, not the existence of the state itself, but what was to be its social, economic, and political structure, and who was to have political power in it.

Masaryk's determination to get the Czechoslovak army out of Russia as soon as possible was not shared by those Czechs and Slovaks in Russia who professed their love for Russia, a Slavic country that had made the formation of military units possible and that was in grave need of help at the most critical time of its history. These Czechs and Slovaks believed that Masaryk's policy of "noninvolvement" or "nonintervention" in Russian domestic affairs was wrong morally and politically. As has been stated earlier, the leaders of the Volunteer Army on the Don, among whom were Alexeev and Kornilov, appealed to the Czechs to join them in their struggle against the Bolsheviks; they pointed at the many German and Hungarian prisoners of war cooperating with the Bolsheviks and enlisting in the Red Guards. They appealed to the patriotism of the Czechs and Slovaks who were committed to the struggle against the Germans and Austro-Hungarians, in the hope that, after the defeat of the Lenin government, which had made peace overtures to the Central Powers just after its establishment and had eventually concluded peace with them, the Eastern Front could be restored; and in the further hope that the Czechoslovak troops could go to their liberated homeland shoulder to shoulder with their Russian brothers. Responding to this "call of duty," a small group of strongly pro-Russian Czechs, led by F. Král and Captain Němeček, formed a company in January 1918. These men fought with the Volunteer Army, despite Masaryk's protests and despite his refusal to bring the Czechoslovak army to the side of the Whites.[3] In January 1918, some of the Czech prisoners of war and a few members of the Czechoslovak army joined the Red Guards[4] in response to the appeal made to them by the Bolsheviks and their supporters among the Czech left-wing Social Democrats, National Socials, and Anarchists.

This stratification among the Czechs and Slovaks in Russia did not lead to conflict with the Bolsheviks immediately, but it was a very important factor in the clashes that occurred in May and June 1918. The rupture between the Czechoslovaks and the Bolsheviks was gradual, and was brought about by a chain of events in the spring of 1918. Early in March 1918, the Czechoslovak army corps was concentrated in the Ukraine. Since it was the only well-organized and disciplined military unit in Russia at that time, even Trotsky, who was alarmed by both the advances of the Austrian and German armies into southern Russia and the possibility of using the Czechoslovak Legion to oppose the invaders; he suggested to Captain Sadoul (French) and Bruce Lockhart (British) the possibillty of using the Czechoslovak Legion to oppose the invaders; he even welcomed the landing at Murmansk of a small British force that was sent to oppose the Germans and Finns, who were threatening the Murmansk railway.[5]

Receiving optimistic reports from their agents in Russia,[6] for a long time the Allies hoped that the Russian front could be restored and that the advancing German and Austro-Hungarian armies could be stopped, and even, perhaps, thrown back. There were, however, differences of opinion among the western powers, as well as among individuals representing

Origins of the Conflict 307

them in Russia, on how to achieve that objective. On the one hand, some Allied diplomats and members of the military missions encouraged the anti-Bolshevik groups to overthrow the Lenin government and reestablish the Eastern Front. On the other hand, some American officials and representatives of the other Allied powers conferred with Bolshevik leaders, hoping to induce them to take an anti-German stand and continue the war. Should the Bolshevik government continue the war against Germany and Austria-Hungary, they suggested, it would received assistance from the Allied countries as the Provisional Government had.[7] At first Great Britain favored intervention against the Germans, hoping that the Bolsheviks would invite it, while France and Japan advocated intervention against the Bolsheviks, and the United States opposed any intervention in the Russian Far East.[8]

In January 1918, Allied diplomats considered sending French troops to Vladivostok and Irkuts, Siberia; on January 28, 1918, the British began to entertain the idea of using Japanese troops to occupy the Trans-Siberian Railway, recommended this course to the U.S. government, and asked the latter to consent to a possible deployment of Japanese troops to guard the railway.[9] At the beginning of February 1918, the British War Office submitted to the French general staff a confidential memorandum recommending Japanese occupation of the Trans-Siberian Railway from Vladivostok to Cheliabinsk on the grounds that, if a German domination of Russia and Siberia represented a grave danger, then a German-Japanese overlordship over the whole world would be an even greater danger. Such a possibility could be eliminated only if Japan got involved in a real war with Germany, something the Japanese had been avoiding since the beginning of the war.[10] The Allies, naturally, knew of the existence of the Czech Legion and of Masaryk's unwillingness to involve it in any military action in Russia.

In March 1918, Czechoslovak troops left the Ukraine without any major difficulty and reached Soviet-held territory. While retreating, they had to engage in a few skirmishes with German troops advancing into the Zhitomir region. The largest engagement took place at the railroad junction at Bakhmach. There Captain E. Kadlec, former editor of *Revoluce*, demonstrated his ability as a military strategist when he led his troops against German pursuees and threw them back with relatively few losses.[11] Captain Kadlec was a former officers in the Belgian army in the Congo; he was the only Czech officer in the army who had previous staff experience.

According to a report prepared for Masaryk by Captain Vladimír S. Hurban,[13] at the end of March 1918, nearly 50,000 Czech troops near Kiev received a message from the Austrian emperor that they should disarmy and return home. The Legionnaires were promised an amnesty; the Czechs would receive autonomy within the Habsburg monarchy. The Legionnaires rejected the offer and retreated from Kiev to Soviet-held territory. In the "battle of Bakhmach" the Czechs lost "600 men in dead, wounded and unaccountable," while they "buried 2,000 Germans in one day." Hurban also describes the cooperation between the Czech Legion and the Bolsheviks during the retreat.

While the figure for dead Germans cannot be verified and may have been exaggerated, the "battle of Bakhmach" had a threefold significance. First, it was the first encounter of the Czechoslovak army with the Germans during the war, the first combat operation since Zborov in July 1917, and was therefore of great psychological value to the morale of the troops. Second, it was the first opportunity of the Czechs to fight side by side with the Bolsheviks and to observe their behavior. Third, the event was noticed in both Allied and Central Powers' countries. The British Foreign Office, especially, began to recognize the military potential of the army.

The fact that the German military commander asked for an armistice, though he was later overruled by his superiors, who refused to negotiate with "the rebels,"[14] made the soldiers and young officers feel important. Those of the latter who had had no combat experience since their capture by the Russians were given an opportunity to prove themselves under fire, and they gave a good account of themselves. German arrogance against the Czech "armistice negotiators," and the abrupt ending of the negotiations made the soldiers and officers aware of their status as deserters and mutineers who could not expect mercy from the Germans. The executions of captured Czechs strengthened the soldiers' realization that they had burned their bridges when they joined the Legion and that there was no way back for them, that they could not return home as other prisoners of war could, and as so many of them did, when they had the opportunity. Fear of the Germans and Hungarians, whose hostility many of them had already experienced in prison camps, kept the members of the Czechoslovak army corps together.

At Bakhmach the Czech troops had a chance to size up the "Red youth," who, although heavily armed, were ready to fly from any attack. The Red

Guards and the "army," consisting of volunteers, poorly trained and poorly disciplined, were more interested in plunder and easy loot than in fighting. Indeed, Bakhmach was a tremendous morale booster for the Czechs. After that event, both their self-confidence and their contempt for the Bolshevik rabble were on the increase.

On March 21, 1918, under the impact of Bakhmach, the British Foreign Office prepared a memorandum for the War Office on the rule and usefulness of the Czechoslovak army in Russia.[15] The British Foreign Office saw in the Legion an element that could block the spread of German-Bolshevik military action and propaganda in the Far East. (This was after the ratification of the Treaty of Brest-Litovsk by the Soviets.) The memorandum was answered by the War Office on April 1, 1918. In its communication to the Foreign Office, the War Office doubted that there were 70,000 Czechs organized in the Legion; but both the War Office and the Foreign Office realized the potential usefulness of the Czechoslovak army, which was, in March and April 1918, the only viable organized military force in Russia that could be used either against the Germans on the front or against the Bolsheviks. Therefore, early in April 1918, the British government began to publicly deal with the Czecho-Slovak National Council.[16]

At this time Russia was, militarily, a power vacuum in which the Czech Legion moved toward its destination. There were, of course, the Red Guards and the Red Army, but they were of highly dubious value in combat. Until April 22, 1918, volunteers who joined the Red Army were not bound to the service at all, and after that date the length of service was fixed for half a year. Even this arrangement proved highly unsatisfactory; therefore, on May 29, 1918, after the revolt of the Czechoslovak army corps, the Soviet government promulgated a decree concerning compulsory service in the Bolshevik armed forces.[17]

Allied diplomats on the spot who were considering an intervention were fully aware of the weaknesses of the Bolsheviks. On March 3, 1918, the possibility of Czech involvement in an intervention was privately mentioned to some of the Czech military and political leaders by French General Paris, who was attached to the Czechoslovak army corps to direct the transfer of the Czech troops to France. He said that should an intervention take place, it would come from the south, in cooperation with the Russian anti-Bolshevik forces on the Don. General Dieterichs, chief of staff of the Czechoslovak army, proposed that in that case the Legion could join the forces commanded by General Alexeev, capture the principal railways, and then march jointly with the Whites on Petrograd and Moscow.[18] Dieterich's propsal became meaningless when on March 7 Masaryk sent an explicit order to the Legion from Moscow barring any Czech action in Russia. Instead, by the terms of an agreement with the Bolsheviks, the whole army had to go to France. Though the French wished that the troops would stay in Russia as "a basis for struggle against the Bolsheviks,"[19] the Legion followed Masaryk's directives.

Before his departure from Moscow for Vladivostok, Masaryk secured credits from the Allies—some 15,000,000 rubles—and from the association of cooperatives, controlled largely by Socialist Revolutionaries. On their way to Vladivostok the troops would purchase supplies from those cooperatives, and, therefore, would no longer live on credits from the Russian (Bolshevik) government.[20] Masaryk left Moscow on March 7, and charged Jiří Klecanda and Prokop Maxa with responsibility for Czech affairs in Russia. Neither of the two young men had the necessary qualifications for handling the enormous political and military problems that confronted the Legion on its way out of Russia, nor was it a good arrangement to have two persons, rather than one, in charge of political and military matters. (Perhaps Masaryk wanted one to watch the other, so that neither could strip him of political and military leadership, as could have happened easily had he appointed a more mature person as his deputy.) Masaryk was involved in conspiratorial work, he knew the "rules of the game," and he therefore gave written instructions to only one of the two young men, Klecanda, who, however, died suddenly in April.[21]

Since the Czech army was out of the Ukraine, the two plenipotentiaries had to conduct new negotiations with the Bolsheviks for the transit of the troops to Vladivostok. The negotiations were held locally with the commander of the Southern Front, V. Antonov-Ovseyenko, largely by Maxa; in Petrograd and Moscow with the Council of People's Commissars (Sovnarkom) by Klecanda. The latter, in his negotiations with high government officials, secured Sovnarkom's permission to evacuate the whole army via Siberia on March 15, 1918. Aralov, Stalin, and others who represented Sovnarkom in these negotiations most likely were eager to see the "only disciplined army" in Russia, together with its tsarist officers, out of their sight as soon as possible, and as far away as possible from the centers of counterrevolution in the Ukraine and the Don territory.

Origins of the Conflict 311

Simultaneously with the negotiations in Moscow, Maxa negotiated with the Soviet at Kursk.[22] There the Bolsheviks saw the situation differently. They assumed that the Czechs were on the run, and that they could be made to pay a price for permission to leave Russia. They reproached the Czechs with abandoning the German front and taking along with them weapons that had been obtained from the Russian Army. Maxa was receptive to Bolshevik arguments. On March 16, the day after Sovnarkom silently approved free passage for the Czechs to Vladivostok without requiring that they surrender their arms, Maxa, without consulting Klecanda, who was in Moscow, signed a local agreement that was highly unfavorable to the Czechs and whose ambiguity was bound to cause disagreements in the future. According to this agreement, the Czechs had to surrender "excessive" artillery, machine guns, and armored cars. On March 16, 1918, V. Antonov-Ovseyenko, commander of the Soviet troops in the "Southern Republics," publicly thanked "our comrades of the Czechoslovak corps, who have fought faithfully and valiantly" and who " are now leaving the Ukraine and are returning a part of their arms."[23] Antonov-Ovseyenko declared, "The revolutionary troops will never forget the fraternal help which the Czechoslovak corps has rendered the working people of the Ukraine in their struggle against the imperialist looters. The revolutionary troops accept as a token of friendship the arms which the Czechoslovaks are leaving."[24] In the meantime, in Moscow, Klecanda was given consent to form at Omsk a second Czechoslovak army corps for which the Czechs hoped to recruit volunteers from among prisoners of war. Things appeared to be settled now. On March 21, Maxa wrote happily: "For the time being we ride on.... It is almost a miracle."[25]

The miracle, however, was short-lived. Already in Moscow Klecanda began to sense that the Bolsheviks were hatching a secret plot against the Legion, and the first difficulty came sooner than anyone expected. On March 22, 1918, the Omsk Soviet ordered that the Czechoslovak trains be halted and troops be disarmed. The chairman of the Omsk Soviet told Maxa that this was done because the army corps had failed to hand over to Ovseyenko's men some artillery material, that some of the Russian officers of the army corps had behaved in a provocative manner with respect to the Soviet organs, and that permission to stop the transports had been given to him by J. V. Stalin, a member of the Soviet government in Moscow.[26] Krutikov, Soviet commissar of war, gave the order to stop and disarm the trains carrying Czechoslovaks, claiming that it was "treason to the Soviet" to let them proceed to eastern Siberia. The Omsk Soviet suggested to the Soviet government in Moscow that the Czechoslovaks be sent out via Archangel.[27]

On March 23, Klecanda wrote from Moscow that a misunderstanding had occurred between Lenin and Trotsky. Lenin had given permission for the transfer of the Czechoslovak army to France, while Trotsky requested the French not to transport the troops to France because Russia would resume the war and he himself would organize an army around the Czechoslovak army corps.[28] As Beneš recorded it, false information arrived in France, according to which Masaryk had agreed with the Bolshevik government that the Czechoslovak army should remain in Russia; therefore, the French military mission in Russia stopped all preparations for its transportation.[29] Spreading false information was one of the weapons in the Bolshevik arsenal.

In the following days the presidium of the Russian branch of the CSNC discussed the situation that had emerged. B. Pavlů suggested that the Czechoslovaks should not disarm and that they should fight their way through to Vladivostok, but the chief of staff, General Dieterichs, rejected this proposition. (Should there be a fight, it would have to be in cooperation with the Volunteer Army, as Dieterichs had suggested at the beginning of March.) With Pavlů dissenting, Maxa, backed by Dieterichs, favored negotiations with the Soviets, and proposed, on March 25, the surrender of most of the arms held by the Czechs in return for permission to proceed to Vladivostok. The chairman of the Soviet at Penza, Kurayev, telegraphed this proposal to Moscow; and in a telegram dated March 26, 1918, Stalin agreed on the condition that the Czechoslovaks proceed immediately to Vladivostok and that the "counter-revolutionary commanders" be immediately removed. The telegram stipulated a further condition—"the Czechoslovaks shall proceed not as fighting units but as a group of free citizens, taking with them a certain quantity of arms for self-defense against the attacks of the counter-revolutionaries." Stalin, acting under the authority of Sovnarkom, ordered the Penza Soviet "to remove all the old commissars [with the Czechoslovak trains] and appoint new ones who can be depended upon to accompany and protect the Czechoslovaks as an organized unit on their way to Vladivostok and to keep the Council of People's Commissars informed of all events connected

Origins of the Conflict 313

with their movements.... The Council of People's Commissars wishes to be of assistance to the Czechoslovaks while they are on Russian territory, provided they are honest and sincerely loyal."³⁰ The March 26 agreement between the CSNC (Maxa) and the Soviets permitted the retention of 168 rifles and one machine gun for each train. The rest of the arms had to be surrendered at Penza. This order increased the importance of Penza: while the trains before Penza were armed, those that passed through the city were "disarmed;" they had only a limited number of small arms and a small amount of ammunition for them.

Maxa's agreement with the Bolsheviks was not in line with the views of Klecanda, who, on March 23, 1918, sent a danger signal to the presidial commission of the Russian branch of the CSNC: three days earlier an order to stop and disarm the trains, contrary to what had been agreed earlier, had been issued by the Bolsheviks in Moscow. Replying to the order, the Penza Soviet noted that it was not feasible to disarm the Legion, since the latter was much larger and much better armed than were the local Red Guards. Klecanda stated specifically that "the telegrams which I saw with my own eyes" confirmed "the absolute necessity to keep all weapons"; he added that the Bolshevik conduct was insincere—to put it directly, "sneaky and deceitful." After learning about Maxa's capitulation, on March 31, Klecanda urged the branch of the CSNC not to disarm the troops, because that Boleshevik government might be replaced by a new one; in that case, the Legion's presence in Siberia would be of great importance.³¹ Klecanda left Moscow to make an investigation on the spot; he then went to Omsk to organize among prisoners of war in Siberia the second army corps. Eventually, he died there. He was thus spared witnessing the failure of the Czech political leadership in dealing with the Bolsheviks. From then on Maxa was Masaryk's sole representative in Russia.

In addition to the ambiguity of Stalin's order (e.g., how one should determine who is "honest and sincerely loyal" and who is a counter-revolutionary), and the conditions made in it (e.g., the removal of the "counter-revolutionary commanders" and the appointment of new commissars), there were other factors that made this agreement precarious. First of all, there was no complete unity among the members of the Lenin government on the issue of the Czechoslovaks' leaving Russia (e.g., Trotsky, who was building a new Red Army, was in grave need of trained troops and opposed the Czech Legion's departure). Second, the Treaty of Brest-Litovsk, ratified by the Soviets on March 15, obliged the Soviet government to demobilize, exchange prisoners of war, and prohibit anti-German propaganda. Thus, the existence of an army corps that was a part of the French army, composed of former prisoners of war to whom Austria-Hungary had a legal claim, and moving on Soviet territory toward Vladivostok, was difficult to square with the conditions of the treaty and with the "neutrality" of Lenin's Russia. Third, the Soviet government had an ideological commitment to carry out Marxist-socialist revolution at home and abroad (despite the temporary "peace" with the Central Powers), while the Czechoslovaks were going to fight, ostensibly, for the capitalist French, British, American, and, ultimately, Czechoslovak states. This ideological aspect of the situation was resented, in particular, by the Czech Bolsheviks in Russia. For them, allowing the Czechoslovak army to proceed with its plans would be a betrayal of the revolution.

Maxa was denounced ten months later by Pavlů, Štefánik, and Janin for making the March 26 agreement, and was blamed for creating the Legion's "desperate situation" by consenting to the surrender of arms at Penza.[32] But Masaryk himself approved Maxa's action when he learned about it on his way to the United States. He attached to his "Tokyo Memorandum" for President Wilson, cited earlier, a note quoting the *Japan Advertiser* of April 11, 1918, as having reported, "As a result of an understanding between Trotsky and the French Ambassador, the army of Czechoslovak volunteers which was going to France surrendered its weapons to the Soviet authorities. With the exception of General Dieterichs, who was accompanying the Corps to France, the officers have been dismissed." Masaryk added to this news item his own comment: "This news is good. The corps going to France needs no weapons, as it will be armed again in France. The officers in questin are Russian officers who joined our army."[33]

The unilateral disarmament and surrender of arms to potential enemies, and the making of deals with the Bolsheviks in order to appease them, were rejected from the very beginning by those among the Czechs in Russia who favored cooperation with the Whites. For them the Bolshevik regime was, if not a creation of the Germans, than, at least, a willing and witting collaborator with the Central Powers. The most prominent among these Czechs was Dürich, who left Kiev with the retreating Czechoslovak

Origins of the Conflict

army. His anti-Bolshevism was consistent with his Slavic and pro-Russian orientation. As we may recall, he had advocated joining forces with the national Russian (Republican) army in November 1917, and had been denounced accordingly by Masaryk and others. (The charge that Dürich had been, before the Russian revolution in March 1917, "in the service of a reactionary government, apparently Austrophile and Germanophile, against the Allies and the rest of us," made by Masaryk in the spring of 1918,[34] was patently false.) While traveling with the army toward Penza, Dürich carried on conversations with soldiers and officers all of whom were friendly with him. The train by which Dürich traveled was under the command of Captain Kadlec. Acting upon the request of the Russian branch of the CSNC, Kadlec suggested that Dürich precede the unit to the staff of the Czechoslovak army at Penza. Assuming that the leaders of the Russian branch of the CSNC had had a change of heart, Dürich went to Penza.[35] The presidium of the branch there, however, did not know what to do with him. His presence was an embarrassement both to those who may have agreed with his views on the nature of the Bolshevik regime but did not want to admit their agreement publicly and to those who disagreed with him. He was therefore invited to go to Omsk, Siberia, or Gelendjik on the shores of the Black Sea. Dürich decided to go to Gelendjik.

The effort to get Dürich out of the way was related to a debate between Pavlů and Maxa on the army's stance toward the Bolsheviks; the latter, especially, knew that Dürich could provide an alternative leadership for the Legion. Pavlů was convinced that the army should fight rather than surrender its weapons at Penza, while Maxa insisted on negotiations and appeasement of the Bolsheviks. Toward the end of March, after the first clashes with the Bolsheviks, some officers and soldiers in the Czechoslovak army, as well as civilians, agreed with Dürich's criticism of Masaryk's neutralist policy, and these people, in turn, were considered by uncritical supporters of Masaryk as "unsavory elements." Later, Vladimír S. Hurban, one of Masaryk's "agents" in tsarist Russia and a tsarist intelligence officer, a member of the branch at Penza, wrote about Dürich to Masaryk in Washington:

> The presence of Dürich made our position toward the Soviets more difficult. We were negotiating with them and they wanted to find

among us some "counter-revolutionary" attitude so that they could use it as a pretext against us. The Soviets knew well that in Kiev Dürich was giving our army at the disposal of the Black Hundreds. ...Dürich also did not behave in the required restrained manner during his stay in the transport, and unsavory elements in our army have always found aid and comfort in him...his presence in our army was undesirable...therefore, it was necessary to send Dürich to a safe place....At the given time such a place was our sanatorium at Gelendjik....Captain Zajíček, along with Dürich, left Penza on March 23.[36]

The journey to Gelendjik was long and difficult for the aging Dürich, who saw destruction and Bolshevik activity along the railway in the areas through which he was passing. He described it as "a way of the cross."[37] He witnessed how the formerly mighty Russian empire was collapsing, and how desperately the few volunteers around Kornilov and Alexeev were fighting the incited masses, which had lost discipline and with it even human nature. His grief became the greater the more he realized that he could do nothing about the situation. His personality and his views were not wanted. He noticed in the eyes of many Russians a silent reproach that the Czechs, by taking a "neutralist" stand, had let loose the Bolsheviks. He felt guilty before the Russian nation, yet he could not prevent in any way the tragedy that he was witnessing. He was sent to seclusion, where he stayed until August 1918, when General Alexeev sent for him and asked him to stay at his headquarters.[38]

While the political "right" was easily taken care of by the CSNC, led by Maxa, the extreme left caused constant problems. The small group of Czech Bolsheviks in Russia consisted of "professional revolutionaries" and followers of Lenin. Although few, they helped create in Russia what Winston Churchill descibed as "a state without a nation, an army without a country, a religion without a God. The Government which claimed to be the new Russian sprang from Revolution and was fed by Terror. It had denounced the faith of treaties; it had made a separate peace; it had released a million Germans for the final onslaught in the West. It had declared that between itself and non-Communist society no good faith, public or private, could exist and no engagements need be respected...
Thus the Russian people were deprived of Victory, Honour, Freedom,

Peace and Bread...."[39] More important, the Czechoslovak Bolsheviks played a prominent role in bringing about the ensuing conflict between the Czechoslovak army and the Soviets. A look at the emerging extreme left among the Czechs in Russia is therefore in order at this point.

At the end of March 1918, a left-wing Social Democratic group from Petrograd moved to Moscow together with the Soviet government and began to publish there *Průkopník,* a propaganda organ of the Bolsheviks. Another group of socialists from Kiev also came to Moscow, where on May 18, 1918, *Svoboda* was issued, becoming the second Czechoslovak left-wing socialist periodical published in the city. Thus Moscow became the Russian center of the Czechoslovak communist movement, which was separated from the Czechoslovak independence movement by its radical Marxist ideology, though it did accept the program of an independent Czech state. That state, however, was to be a socialist republic—a part of the European Federation of Socialist Republics.[40]

The programmatic article in the first issue of *Průkopník* (March 27, 1918) entitled "Why Are We Communists?" merely repeated the thesis of the former Petrograd group: the proletariat must liberate its country through the world revolution. It rejected the view that France could give independence to the Czech nation, and asserted that "no capitalist state is interested in saving and liberating small nations.... Our liberation will come about only through the world social revolution." It simplified the issues into two possible alternatives: "either we will stand loyally behind the Russian revolution, against the bourgeoisie and capitalism, either we will become real revolutionaries and will have for our aim the building of Communist society, or we will continue to be a toy in the hands of the bourgeoisie and the capital." This kind of "either-or" argument was hardly appealing to the Czechoslovak soldiers; however, Jaroslav Hašek's article, "Why Going to France?" was a more effective piece of propaganda, for it addressed itself to the most acute issue with which the soldiers were confronted. Hašek claimed that the leaders of the Russian branch of the CSNC had fooled everybody, including Professor Masaryk, when they made him endorse the idea of going to France. Aside from the falsehood on which the argument was based, the main thrust of it was that the Czechoslovaks had to remain in Russia, take part in the restoration of the Russian army, "and participate actively in the Russian revolution and help the Russian nation to secure the Soviet republic from which originate the rays of liberation for the whole world, including our [own] nation." Here in Russia "must remain everyone of us who knows that we are the descendants of Taborites,* the first Socialists and Communists in Europe." "Our political significance is here and not in the West. We must help Russia! . . . We are the avantgarde of rebellion and we must remain here!"[41]

Meanwhile, on April 5, 1918, a small detachment of the Japanese army landed at Vladivostok. The Siberian soviets began to fear Japanese intervention, and their mistrust of the Czechoslovak troops increased. To this psychological factor were added many technical problems, such as the lack of locomotives and the slow movement of the trains. The soldiers and officers of the Czechoslovak army corps looked upon these delays as acts of obstructionism for which the Soviet government was responsible. There was no need for such obstruction, they believed, since the Czechoslovaks maintained a strict neutrality and their movement toward Vladivostok, and out of the country, was not directed against the Soviets. The nervousness of those who were eager to reach Vladivostok in the shortest possible time was aggravated by the activities of Czechoslovak Bolshevik agitation groups located at all large railroad stations in Eastern Russia, through which the Czechoslovak echelons were passing. These agitators' activities were in conflict with the agreement that the Soviet government had made with the CSNC, yet their agitation was given official blessing by the Bolsheviks.

In Penza the chairman of the local soviet, Kurayev, attempted to reach an accommodation with the army corps, and the disarmament of the troops proceeded satisfactorily under the supervision of a mixed Czechoslovak-Soviet commission. This was not to the liking of Jaroslav Štrombach, the organizer of the Czechoslovak Red Army unit at Penza, who wrote to his comrades in Moscow on April 3, 1918, that he was going to be in a "terrible fight" and that he had requested Kurayev not to let the Czechoslovak units proceed eastward "at any price." He urged the Czechoslovak communist group in Moscow to back him up and to ask the Soviet government to issue orders that would correspond to his views. He continued that the comrades in Moscow must give the Penza group more assistance, and that what was most needed at Penza was "agitators,

---

* A group of radical Hussites fighting under Žižka during the Hussite wars.

office help, everything." He pointed out that all the trains had to pass through Penza, and his group was thus in a strategic position. He continued, "After agitation and recruitment and after we grant our permission, the trains which have gone through our processing (with the remaining scrap officers and servants of capitalism) will be allowed to go further.... Slow transportation and continuous interruptions diminish enthusiasm for France and the people are becoming convinced that it is nonsense to go there.... Send us as many newspapers as possible.... Do not spare money on this. The field of agitation here is really great. We have to permeate the people with internationalism. And, above all, send us more literature. We need more authority. Arrange that the Penza Soviet is ordered to yield to us unconditionally...."[42]

Průkopník, published by the Czechoslovak communists in Moscow, also appealed to the Czechoslovak soldiers not to leave Russia, employing various tricks and arguments. Thus, the April 18, 1918, issue of *Průkopník*, under the headline "Vladivostok or Archangel," carried an article written by one of the participants at the international congress of prisoners of war, saying, "There we learned that the whole Siberia with its camps of prisoners of war... is in a complete Socialist boiling." It could not be possible for the Czechoslovak corps to go to France, because "here stand armed battalions of prisoners of war from all nationalities ready to throw back the attack of Japanese militarists. Is it possible, is it thinkable, that the Czech army would be able to cut their way through these thousands of revolutionary prisoners of war... who have taken up arms against all imperialists and who do not comprehend and cannot comprehend the problem of the Czech army, thanks to the efforts of reckless Czech patriots, in any other way than as an imperialist question? ... This merciless reality cannot be told to the Czech army," and at the last moment the troops would be told the "strategic plan was changed and that a shorter way will be taken to France, via Archangel.... Now it is not merely a flight before revolutionary Russia.... *The way via Archangel means, in addition, the flight of the Czech army before the vital revolutionary movement of the Austrian proletariat of all nationalities, as well as the proletariat of Germany,* represented by the hundreds of thousands of prisoners of war in Siberia."[43]

Not only was this argument far-fetched and based on the inaccurate assessment of the situation in Siberia; but it also worked in just the opposite way from what had been originally intended. It catalyzed the already strong natinalism of the Czech soldiers, and strengthened the argument that German and Hungarian prisoners of war were fighting on the side of the Soviets. It also stiffened the soldiers' resistance to the idea of going to France via Archangel.

In April the pressures exerted by the Czech Bolsheviks on the Czech army through the Soviet authorities, and their tireless agitation and artificial delays in moving the echelons forward, created tension within the Legion. The commanding group within the Russian branch of the CSNC, which insisted on neutrality toward the Soviets and on going to France via Vladivostok with the consent of the Soviet government, was losing support in the Legion. Rumors spread that a complete disarming was imminent and that the Czechs would be repatriated to Austria-Hungary. Counter-rumors and counter-propaganda claimed that the Bolsheviks were German puppets and that the only remedy was to shoot one's way to Vladivostok. The voices calling for going to Vladivostok by the Legion's own means and in its own way, or, as the troops were saying, "through our own order," without regard to the Soviet organs of power, were growing stronger and stronger. Certain Czech officers began to consider plans for defense, in any and every contingency.[44]

On April 7, the Czechoslovak trains were forbidden to move through Samara; two days later the same thing happened. This halt prompted the French military attaché in Russia, General Lavergne, to telegraph home that, as a consequence of the Japanese landing at Vladivostok, "Trotsky issued an order to step the movement of the Czechoslovak army corps to the Far East."[45] He requested instructions on the possibility of transporting the Czechoslovak troops via Archangel. The issuance on April 12 of two Soviet orders, one directing the local soviets to stop Czechoslovak trains, and the second one directing them to allow the trains to proceed to Vladivostok, created a great deal of confusion. To resolve the complicated situation, some officers of the First Czechoslovak Division met secretly at Kirsanov on April 14, to discuss the matter. This meeting produced the so-called Kirsanov Resolution.[46] One of its key sentences declared that "due to violation of the former agreement and attempts to disarm the Czechoslovaks by force, the Army Corps will under no condition surrender its arms before reaching Vladivostok." The resolution stated, furthermore, that the Czechoslovak experience during the past six weeks had brought the Czechs to the conclusion that it was "impossible to count upon reaching an agreement with the Soviet government." It was true that the Bolsheviks had met many of their obligations in the past, because they feared the strength of the army corps; but, "as soon as we surrender our arms their attitude toward us will change and we shall have no means of bringing pressure." Thus, the officers decided that, in the event that "irresponsible elements engage in operations against Czechoslovak units... they will be met with due resistance." The resolution reflected the prevailing mood among the soldiers, who were convinced that they had to resist, by force, if necessary, any attempt to obstruct the progress of the army corps toward its destination.[47]

The situation was further aggravated by the German protest against the reported oppression of German prisoners of war in Russia. Two days later, on April 21, 1918, the new commissar of foreign affairs, G. V. Chicherin, sent the following telegram to the Siberian soviets: "Fearing that Japan will advance to Siberia, Germany is categorically demanding that German war prisoners held in Eastern Siberia be removed at once to either Western Siberia or European Russia. Please take all necessary measures. The Czechoslovak echelons must not go further east."[48]

Already, on April 17, the Bolsheviks, alarmed by news about the advance of the anti-Bolshevik Cossack leader, Semenov, toward Karymsk in eastern Siberia, had declared martial law. Chicherin's telegram and the behavior of the local soviets led to increased bitterness on the part of the part of the Czechoslovak troops. Representatives of the Russian branch of the CSNC attempted to calm the rising passions of both sides; the Omsk office of the CSNC succeeded in obtaining the consent of the Irkutsk soviet for the echelons east of Omsk to continue on their way to Vladivostok, and it began to consider seriously the possibility that the units of the First Division might go via Archangel or Murmansk. However, the patience of the soldiers and officers of the First Division was running out; they were much more embittered than their comrades east of Omsk or those in Vladivostok.

Thus, on April 27, 1918, delegates from units of the First Division met for preliminary consultations in order to prepare themselves for the proposed congress of army delegates. The Russian branch of the CSNC disapproved of this meeting, which was called to order by the chairman of the division committee. At the meeting the CSNC was criticized by both "left" and "right." At the beginning of the meeting the main critics were the left-wingers, the former members of the Kievan Czechoslovak Council of Workers and Soldiers, who, at the end of that short-lived incident, had been glad that the army had not responded to their appeals to fight the Germans and the Ukrainians, and that they could leave Kiev under its protection. These individuals, Skoták, Vaníček, Koudelka, and Synek, demanded that the army not leave Russia; they opposed further eastward movement of the echelons. In view of the generally known mood of the troops, who demanded a speedy arrival in Vladivostok, the proposals of the leftists were rejected by the vast majority of the delegates. After that, the left-wing socialists left the conference and joined the Czechoslovak Red Army unit at Penza. At that time this unit consisted of only about 200 men; the socialists thus represented a welcome addition. As Moscow's *Svoboda* put it (May 18, 1918), the preliminary consultations at Penza caused the "comrades" to walk out of the Czechoslovak army. Following the Bolshevik line, the newspaper claimed that "in the rays of the Russian revolution, revolution in Central and Western Europe is being born. The world revolution will bring about the liberation of the Czech and Slovak peoples...."[49] According to this left-wing socialist view, it was wrong to go to France when socialist Russia was building a new army and the foundations of a new social system in Russia and the world.

The army that the Moscow Czechoslovak communists proposed to build was to be a Czechoslovak socialist army; however, its members had to adopt Soviet Russian citizenship (in order to avoid charges of violation of the Treaty of Brest-Litovsk). The acquisition of citizenship was a simple matter: three days after filing a formal application for citizenship with the local soviet, the applicant acquired citizenship in the Soviet Russian state. In accordance with the requirement that members of the Red Army must be citizens of Soviet Russia, *Průkopník,* on May 17, 1918, issued an appeal to "all Czechoslovaks in Russia," claiming that their duty was to enter the Red Army and to become Russian citizens. This appeal clearly demonstrated to the Czechoslovak soldiers the dependence of the Czechoslovak communist movement on the Soviet regime. Subsequently, the Czechoslovak Red Army units were small; the largest one, the First Czechoslovak Revolutionary Regiment, was established at Penza in April 1918.[50]

The Czechoslovak communists followed the instructions of the Russian Communist Party to which they belonged. As followers of Lenin, they were thinking in terms of world revolution. On May 9, 1918, upon Lenin's initiative, a Federation of the Foreign Groups of the Russian Communist Party was established for the purpose of (a) converting the prisoners of war to Bolshevism; (b) enlisting those prisoners of war who stayed in Russia into the fighting units of the Red Army; and (c) enlisting their aid in spreading Bolshevik revolution to their homelands. Béla Kun, who had joined the Bolsheviks before the revolution and who took part in the event, was elected chairman of the federation. One may note, parenthetically, that Hungarians represented the largest group in the federation, and that in the protracted struggle following the revolution between 80,000 and 100,000 Hungarians fought with the Bolsheviks.[51] This means that between 15 and 20 percent of the Hungarian prisoners of war, whose number was estimated to be 500,000, joined the Bolsheviks, in contrast to some 10,000 Czechs and Slovaks who did likewise, i.e., approximately 4 percent of Czech and Slovak prisoners of war in Russia.[52]

The composition of the federation's leadership and the large number of Hungarians fighting with the Bolsheviks were among the factors that helped to crystallize the anti-Bolshevik attitude of the Czechoslovak army. The Czechoslovak section of the federation was small, but its task was great: to prevent by all means the transportation of the Czechoslovak army to France. The Czechoslovak communists asserted that they could not "take upon their conscience" the fact that promising Czech boys would be "sacrificed to the capitalist-imperialist war in France."[53] Another reason for their agitation against the exodus of troops to France was that they wished to help the Soviet government in building the Red Army. After the mass exchange of prisoners of war that followed ratification of the Brest-Litovsk treaty, Czech communist agitators were sent to all centers on the railroad between Penza and Vladivostok. Their task was to recruit troops for the Red Army and to agitate against the neutralist policy of the army, which was moving eastward. On May 9, *Průkopník* claimed that "the Czechoslovak army may save Russia today; it can defeat the threatening reaction and secure freedom." Denouncing its neutrality, *Průkopník* asserted that "our work is to remain here and to save fraternal Russia." The Czechoslovaks were urged to help build a unified army and have their own corps in it; then they would be able to "make order in Russia and abroad!" Every Czech in Russia "must be a revolutionary," a soldier in the revolutionary Red Army.

Undoubtedly, these emotional appeals reflected both Trotsky's desire to use the Czechoslovak army corps as the nucleus for the newly built Red Army and the Czech communists' belief that Soviet Russia was the basis for a world revolution that was "just around the corner." At that time, however, other contingency plans for the Czechs were being made in London and Moscow.

Early in April 1918, the British War Office doubted that sufficient tonnage could be found to transport the Czechoslovak troops from Vladivostok to France. It considered three alternative uses of the Czechoslovak units in Siberia: (a) to concentrate the troops around Omsk to prevent the enemy from penetrating into Siberia; (b) to send them to Archangel to protect supplies and to attempt to establish contact with Siberia via Perm; and (c) to move the Czechs beyond the Bajkal Lake, where they could cooperate with Ataman Semenov.[54] The CSNC rejected these proposals and insisted on the transfer of the army to France.[55]

In the meantime the French military mission in Moscow and the Russian branch of the CSNC discussed with the Soviet government the plan for transporting the Czechoslovak military units west of Omsk via Archangel. The result of these negotiations was, as General Lavergne reported from Moscow to Paris, that the Soviet government, specifically Trotsky, consented to the transportation of the troops west of Omsk, and that the Soviet military commander of the northern sector counted on these units for the defense of the two harbors, Murmansk and Archangel.[56] However, the Soviet government insisted that, with regard to Germany, the operation had to remain secret. The CSNC demanded a guarantee from the French military mission that the trip to the north would really mean a shortening of the way to France and that the Czechoslovaks would not be dragged into a possible conflict in Russia.

The concern of the CSNC was understandable: there was a great deal of talk about intervention. At that time the Czechs did not know, however, that in mid-May a decision had been made in the British War Office to send General F. C. Poole with an infantry unit to Murmansk; his mission was to organize the Czechoslovaks, who, reported, were on their way there already, together with Russian units, into a force that would be under his command and at his disposal.[57] They did not know that on

May 15, 1918, Beneš had approved Lord Cecil's plan calling for leaving some of the Czech troops in Russia on condition that the Allies issue a declaration recognizing the Czechs as Allies and affirming the justice of their claims for independence.[58] While the Soviets and the British intended to use the troops for their own purposes in the Russian north, the Czechoslovaks were unwilling to change the route toward their "destination." Contrary to Bolshevik propaganda voiced in *Pochodeň* and *Svoboda*, Siberia was not "safe for Soviets." Anti-Bolshevik forces there were looking for help from the Czechoslovaks who were moving eastward. Since the Russian branch of the CSNC in Moscow had made agreements with the trading cooperatives run by Socialist Revolutionaries (SRs) for supplying the Czechoslovak troops on their way to Vladivostok, the Czechoslovaks came into contact with the SR organizations in Siberia. In fact, these organizations were contacting Czech officers by themselves and were complaining about their plight under the Soviets. Thus the Czechoslovaks found out that they had many friends and sympathizers in Siberia; the strongly anti-Bolshevik officers, especially, quickly realized that the local population could be of great help to them. Among these officers were the commander of the Seventh Regiment, Captain Radola Gajda, who had come to the Czechoslovak brigade from the Serbian volunteer division, and his deputy Captain Kadlec. On May 3, 1918, Captain Gajda sent contingency plans to the echelons belonging to the Seventh Regiment and two other companies. These plans, prepared by Kadlec, anticipated several different situations that might develop between the Czechoslovak troops and the soviets. A specific course of action was suggested to meet these contingencies, including the use of force against the Bolsheviks if necessary.[59]

Another plan involving the Czechoslovak army entailed forming on May 15, 1918, a Czechoslovak section of the People's Commissariat of Nationalities. The head of the commissariat, Stalin, made K. Knoflíček the chief of the section, with A. Hais as his deputy and Josef Beneš as secretary of the section. These Czechoslovak communists prepared a "plan" for the formation of the Czechoslovak Red Army; and they recommended to their superior the following: (1) the administrative liquidation of the Russian branch of the CSNC and the transfer of its functions to the Czechoslovak section of the People's Commissariat of Nationalities; (2) the convocation of a "congress" of delegates of the Czechoslovak army corps and the Czechoslovak units of the Red Army, which would then adopt a resolution calling for the dissolution of the Czechoslovak national military units and the formation of Czechoslovak socialist military units; (3) the placement of Czechoslovaks who were unemployed after the dissolution of the army corps in labor battalions; and (4) the abolition of *Československý deník,* the organ of the CSNC, and confiscation of its printing plant. Furthermore, the government should issue an order to dissolve the army corps and an order to the railroad workers prohibiting them from permitting the Czechoslovak units to proceed eastward. A new newspaper, *Československá rudá armáda* (Czechoslovak Red Army), which began to be published at Penza on May 12, 1918, made an emotional appeal to "comrades" in the Czechoslovak army not to leave Russia—"socialist Russia that you should love and support with all your powers, because Russia lifted up the flag of liberation of the proletariat of the whole world." The "comrades," the new paper proclaimed, should not go "to support with their blood capitalist France" and the counterrevolution, but should join the Red Army.[60]

The Czechoslovak communists acted with the determination of fanatics who had the power of the government behind them. On May 9, A. Hais, accompanied by three armed members of the Czech Red Guard, delivered the order of the Soviet Central Requisition Commission that confiscated the offices of the Russian branch of the CSNC in Moscow. He placed the offices at the disposal of the socialist publication *Svoboda.* By an order of the government, the Czechoslovak section in the People's Commissariat of Nationalities, established by the decree of May 15, was to be the only official Czechoslovak organ of power in Soviet Russia. An article of the decree stated that all contacts between Czechs and Slovaks living in Soviet Russia, on one hand, and the Soviet government, on the other, could take place only through this section. All these actions manifested the readiness of the Czech communists to take over the Czechoslovak independence (liberation) movement and to mold it in their own image, both in Soviet Russia and elsewhere. *Průkopník* described that readiness on May 17, 1918, as follows: "We have taken the leadership of the Czech political action in Russia into our own hands. We are forming here the Czechoslovak Red Army.... In the next few days the Commissariat for handling all Czechoslovak affairs will be open in Moscow and our emissaries will be sent to America [to work] among our countrymen-Socialists there...."[61]

Thus, in mid-May 1918, several plans related to the future use of the Czechoslovak troops were made: (1) to ship the troops to the French front; (2) to get rid of the army corps as soon as possible, as some of the Soviet government leaders wished; (3) to use the army to intervene against the Bolsheviks; (4) to bring it to the side of the White Army; (5) to use it in northern Russia as the British wished; (6) to bring it to the side of the revolution as the Czechoslovak communists wished. All these plans became past history in the second half of May, when the Czechoslovak soldiers and officers decided to take another course of action not previously planned by anyone.

In the middle of May an election of delegates to the Czechoslovak congress was held in an atmosphere of excitement, nervousness, and irritability. The Russian branch of the CSNC attempted to calm the soldiers, who were alarmed by rumors that a part of the army corps would be diverted to Archangel instead of proceeding to Vladivostok. Officials of the CSNC, however, stated openly that it was not possible to transport the troops speedily to Vladivostok, and the official newspaper suggested that if it were necessary, then the other way (via Archangel) should be taken. On May 22, 1918, Československý deník carried an article saying that the French government had decided that a part of the army corps should go via Archangel. However, rumors got into circulation that the story was merely a Bolshevik trick, and that the transport would never arrive at the northern harbor. The soldiers' resentment against the idea of going via Archangel was growing stronger and stronger. They mistrusted the Bolsheviks and even those who dealt with them. It was hoped that the congress would dispel all the fears and suspicions. However, the congress brought about an unexpected result.

The proposition to go to France via Archangel had already been rejected by the delegates at the preliminary conference on May 15, 1918, at Cheliabinsk. In that city, just the day before, there had occurred an event that later became known as "the incident," and was believed to have sparked the conflict between the Czechoslovaks and the Bolsheviks. It was one of a series of incidents between the Czechoslovak troops and the Soviet-sponsored Red Guards, which included individuals with varied motives for joining the Bolshevik instrument of force, among whom were some Hungarian and German prisoners of war. On the morning of May 14, a train carrying Austro-Hungarian prisoners of war was passing through the railroad station. Somebody from one of the wagons threw a piece of iron into a small group of soldiers of the Sixth Czechoslovak Regiment, and one Czech soldier was seriously injured. The soldiers stopped the train, ordered out the prisoners of war, and killed a Hungarian prisoner who was believed to be the culprit. The local soviet at Cheliabinsk, dominated by Hungarian "internationalists" who had hindered the eastbound trains carrying Czech soldiers on previous occasions, arrested the guard of the Sixth Regiment that had stopped the train, the Czechs who had been called by the Bolshevik authority as witnesses, and the delegation of Czech soldiers who were sent to the soviet to demand the release of their compatriots. This arrogant behavior and the treatment accorded the Czech soldiers enraged the Czechs; they disarmed the Red Guards at the railway station and occupied it; then they went to the city, where they released the imprisoned Czechs, seized the arsenals, and armed themselves.

The incident was settled by the local disputants and part of the seized weapons were returned. The Czech newspaper, *Československý deník*, published at that time at Omsk, mentioned this event on May 21 on page four, and pointed out that such accidents do happen when people are irritated and embittered by the situation they are in. It warned against repetition of similar incidents and pointed out that such conflicts might sometimes be staged to create hindrances on the way out of Russia. The report about the incident sent by telegraph to Moscow by the circuit military commissar at Cheliabinsk, Sadlucki, described the event and stated that he had released the imprisoned Czechs in order to "forestall bloodshed," since he fully realized how well-disciplined the Czechs were and how unprepared the Red Army was. The machine guns and rifles had already been returned by the Czechs on May 18, and the Czechs assured the commissar that the other weapons would be returned soon. The Czech masses were becoming restive, Sadlucki wired to Moscow; they refused to obey the leaders of the armed units because they mistrusted the guarantees given to them by the Soviet government that they would be transported to Vladivostok. "We wanted to disarm them [i.e., the Czechs]," the report said, "but we were not strong enough." After this action, the Czechs posted a declaration that they were not against the Soviet government.[62]

The incident was settled, but the Bolsheviks in Moscow had already decided to pursue a tough policy against the Czechoslovak army corps. The Soviet commissar of war, Trotsky, and his deputy, P. V. Aralov, knew that the agreement ratified by Stalin was being carried out inefficiently, that the movement of Czechoslovak troops eastward was extremely slow, and that many echelons, fully armed, still had not reached Penza. The German government pressured the Soviets not to permit the exit of the Czechoslovak troops and urged the transportation of their own prisoners of war still in Siberia and Russia. As has been pointed out earlier, the Peace of Brest-Litovsk bound the Lenin government not to tolerate amred anti-German forces in Russia. Also, the Czechoslovak army corps came out strongly against the shipment of some of its units to Archangel, as had been agreed between the Soviet and the French governments.[63] Trotsky and Aralov were in contact with the representatives of the Russian branch of the CSNC, P. Maxa and B. Čermák, who promised speedy departure of the troops in both directions—to Vladivostok and Archangel—and who were willing to have the troops disarmed. Apparently, they were not able to make the army accept this solution of the problem. In their momentous decision, however, Trotsky and Aralov acted upon the advice of the Czechoslovak communists in Moscow, who had promised to win over at least a part of the army corps for the Red Army, with the rest to be placed in labor units after the dissolution of the army corps.[64] Thus Trotsky decided to disarm the troops and dismantle the Czechoslovak army. The dice were cast.

The Czech Legionnaires were not taken by surprise in the events that were gaining momentum. Since May 17, 1918, they had controlled the telegraph office at Cheliabinsk and were able to intercept messages sent from Moscow to local soviets in Siberia.[65] On the night of May 20-21, Maxa and Čermák were arrested in Moscow. They were told that they would be released only after the complete settlement of the Cheliabinsk incident and after the complete disarming of the Czechoslovak troops. They were compelled to sign an order to the Czechoslovak troops to surrender their arms, unconditionally, to local Soviet representatives. The Siberian soviets received a telegram from Trotsky's deputy, Aralov, on May 20, 1918, stating that "by the order of the Chairman of the Commissariat of War, Comrade Trotsky, you are to detrain the Czechslovaks and organize them into labor units or draft them into the Soviet Red

Army. Do everything in your power to assist the Czechoslovak Communists...."[66] The Maxa-Čermák order, issued in the name of the Russian branch of the CSNC and dated May 21, 1918, in addition to ordering complete disarming of the Czechoslovak troops, stated that "the protection of the trains devolves completely upon the Soviet organs of the Russian Federated Republic. Anyone not complying with this order will be considered a traitor and declared outside the law."[67] This was an inglorious end ot the political leadership that Masaryk left in charge of the army in Russia. The declaration completed the split between the Russian branch of the CSNC, represented by commissar (plenipotentiary) Maxa, and the Czechoslovak army.

Following the practice of their Russian comrades, the Czechoslovak communists attempted "to legitimize" the attempted coup d'état in the Czechoslovak independence movement by calling a congress, assuming that the latter would merely "ratify" an accomplished fact.[68] In preparation for the congress, on May 24, 1918, *Průkopník* carried an article under the headline: "The Czech White Guards," which placed the whole Czechoslovak army corps in the ranks of the enemies of Soviet power. It said, in part, "The Czech White Guard is going to France. Now we know clearly and definitely why it does not stay in Russia.... We do not object to it. But we cannot remain silent with respect to what the White Guard did along the way.... With the Czech White Guard and its representatives [the branch of the CSNC] ... we have finished.... In Moscow the leaders of this Guard have been arrested." On the next day, May 25, at the same time when Trotsky's telegram made a final, definitive end to all negotiations and demanded the unconditional surrender of all arms by the Czechoslovaks, the preliminary consultations of the delegates were taking place in the Hotel Europa in Moscow. The congress was called jointly by the "Central Committee of the Czechoslovan Social Democratic Workers party at Kiev (now in Moscow) and the Czechslovak Communist party in Moscow." According to the Czech communist newspaper, *Československá rudá armáda,* published at Penza, the main purpose of the congress was to bring about the merger of the two workers' parties. Assuming that Aralov's and Trotsky's orders had finally resolved the question of the transportation of Czechoslovak troops to France and had dissolved the army corps, the Czechoslovak communists and their allies decided, with great self-assuredness, to form a "united" political party.*

The congress was attended by 79 delegates claiming to represent 5,600 members of the two groups and 22 delegates representing the 1,850 Czechoslovaks in the Red Guards and the Red Army. Its resolution reflected the dependence of the Czechoslovak communists on the Soviet government and the influence of their Russian comrades. The congress fully endorsed the Marxist-Leninist concept of the war and the revolution as they were understood by the Russian Communist Party and proclaimed in the emerging Third International. One of the statements made by the congress was as follows: "We fully approve the program and tactics of the Russian Communist Party of Bolsheviks, we accept the name Czechoslovak Communist party, and we enter into contact with the international union of workers under the Third International. By this we emphasize the necessity and the duty of workers of all states and nations to stand shoulder to shoulder with the Russian social revolution." The three principal resolutions passed by the congress also reflected this basic conceptual framework.

In the first resolution the congress declared that "the Czechoslovak socialist proletariat will always loyally defend Russian freedom as well as the Russian proletarian republic," and it expressed its "firm conviction that the Russian proletariat can throw back the wild attacks by the reaction and will defend its liberty until the time [when] the proletariat of Western Europe will come to help." The second resolution was directed to the "Czechoslovak workers within the boundaries of Austria-Hungary," urging them "to throw off any compromise with the bourgeoisie who, at the first opportune moment, would betray the interest of the working class, and prepare, together with all socialistically conscious workers of all nations of Austria, the great day of European social revolution." Promising to come to their aid "in the hour of the decisive clash with capitalistic imperialism," the resolution declared that the Czechoslovak communists in Russia formed "the auxiliary movement of the Czechoslovak workers

---

* Some thirty years later, in 1948, this precedent was followed much more successfully when the Social Democrat and Communist parties "merged" in one—the Communist Party of Czechoslovakia—as a manifestation of complete seizure of power in Czechoslovakia.

for the social revolution in the west of Europe.... Long live the Czechoslovak Socialist Republic in the Federative Union of the Socialist Republics of Europe!"

This program of the Czechoslovak communists in Russia was in accord with the strategic planning of the Bolsheviks and the Third International, which was then being formed (although it was referred to as if it already existed) and which was influenced in its strategic and tactical approaches by the Marxist-Leninist ideology. The Czechoslovak communists expected a political and social revolution to take place in central and western Europe, and they considered themselves its vanguard. Their strategy for liberation was based on the assumption that the proletariat in central and western Europe would rise against the existing governments, and that the socialist revolution in Europe was a precondition for the liberation of the Czechoslovaks. The Czechoslovak communists discarded the prewar Social Democratic party line according to which the strategic aim of the socialists was to transform the Danubian empire into a socialist state. They now adopted the ideas of a *Czechoslovak* state and one *Czechoslovak* nation; however, the socialist republic, if and when it was established, would have to be a part of the federation of European socialist republics. They rejected the view that an independent Czechoslovak state could emerge as a result of the military victories of the Entente powes over Germany. Blinded by their ideology, they could not imagine that the Entente powers could or would help establish a Czechoslovak state. One of the reports delivered at the congress stated quite clearly that the Entente powers, "without regard whether in the mother country or in colonies, keep nations in subjugation and have made them into an object of merciless exploitation." As the Czechoslovak communists saw matters, the only guarantee of national liberation was the survival and strengthening of the base and center of the European socialist revolution—Soviet Russia.

The strategic program of the Czechoslovak communists in Russia was not, however, accepted by the Czech and Slovak socialit movements at home, who did not share their hopes, or, more accurately, their illusions. The socialists at home were not under the influence of the Czechoslovak communists in "remote" Russia; they were coming closer and closer to the program of the national movement for independence led by the middle-class prewar politicians, especially Kramář and Rašín, and the Masaryk-

Beneš-Štefánik triumvirate (and others) abroad. The wartime program of the Czechoslovak communists in Russia, however, had a strong impact on the fundamental orientation of the future Communist Party of Czechoslovakia and its attitude toward the Czechoslovak Republic. The emergence of the bourgeois republic was neither expected nor believed possible by the Czechoslovak communists. When it became a reality, they saw the new republic as an instrument of capitalist-imperialist France and its domestic lackeys. The communists then concluded that the instrument of capitalist-imperialist oppression had to be smashed, and a new "instrument of oppression" (state), the dictatorship of the proletariat, had to be erected in its place. This was indeed to happen some thirty years later.

The third resolution of the congress was related to the immediate tasks of the Czechoslovak Communist movement in Russia, in particular to the situation in the Czechoslovak army corps and the Russian branch of the CSNC. The resolution stated that "the so-called branch of the Czecho-Slovak National Council in Russia has never been the representative and the spokesman of the Czechoslovak proletariat." It called upon the proletarians "who still serve in the army created by the National Council" to leave the ranks of those "who are wittingly betraying the Russian revolution and are selling the proletarians in the Czechoslovak army to the French bourgeoisie." It asserted that "whoever at this hour leaves the Russian Socialist Republic will become the traitor to the international socialist proletariat." The congress, then, appealed to the Social Democrats in the Czechoslovak army corps to join "the Czechoslovak Red Army that is a part of the Red Army of the Russian Federated Republic."

The congress also elected a twenty-member Central Executive Committee and decided that the two newspapers, *Svoboda* and *Průkopník,* would merge into one official organ of the Czechoslovak Communist Party, *Průkopník svobody* (Pioneer of Freedom). While the congress was still in session, the delegates were notified about the growing spirit of rebellion in the Czechoslovak army. Shortly after the congress adjourned, the remaining delegates were informed that the Czechoslovak army corps had revolted against the Soviet government. The delegates then appealed to the soldiers of the corps to refuse to take part in the "counter-revolutionary struggle" and to comply with the order of the Soviet government to lay down all arms. Můna, Koza, Synek, and other delegates were invited to confer with Lenin, Trotsky, Stalin, and Aralov in the Kremlin. At this conference the Czechoslovak Communist Party was asked to share in the liquidation of the conflict between the Soviets and the Czechoslovak army corps. The Party did its share, indeed, in all attempts to demoralize the troops, to make the army ineffective, and, if possible, to destroy it altogether.

Amid these developments, the delegates of the army congress were arriving at Cheliabinsk. During the preliminary consultations on May 20, 1918, a Temporary Executive Committee (TEC) was elected. It was composed of the current members of the Russian branch of the CSNC, and the commanders of regiments (Lieutenant Colonel Sergei Vojsekhovskii, Captain Gajda, and Lieutenant Čeček), with Bohdan Pavlů as its chairman. During the discussions over the next two days the delegates decided to disregard the orders that had arrived from Moscow and not to surrender weapons to the local soviets. With Maxa under arrest in Moscow and the army's highest command in Vladivostok, Bohdan Pavlů and the insurgent young officers assumed command of the troops. The elected committee (TEC) was placed in charge of the operations connected with the transportation of the troops to Vladivostok and the three officers in the TEC were given complete jurisdiction over the units of the Czechoslovak army corps that had not yet arrived in Vladivostok. Thus Čeček became the commander of the Penza group of echelons in European Russia, Vojtsekhovskii of the Cheliabinsk group in western Siberia, and Gajda of the echelons between Omsk and Irkutsk.[69]

On May 22 the congress sent the following resolution to the Russian branch of the CSNC in Moscow, the French military mission at Vologda, and the soviets along the Trans-Siberian Railway: "The Congress of the Czechoslovak Revolutionary Army, assembled at Cheliabinsk, declares in the presence of War Commissar Sadlutsky its feeling of sympathy with the Russian revolutionary people in their difficult struggle for the consolidation of the revolution. However, the Congress is convinced that the Soviet government is powerless to guarantee our troops free and safe passage to Vladivostok and, therefore, has unanimously decided not to surrender its arms until it receives assurance that the Corps will be allowed to depart and will be protected against counter-revolutionary trains."[70]

Although the resolution's semantics reflected the terminology used by the CSNC, its effect was a complete break with the Soviets. The army had decided to go to Vladivostok by its own means and in its own way.

Origins of the Conflict   335

The decision to place the army outside the political control of the Russian branch of the CSNC (a part of which was imprisoned in Moscow, another part was in Omsk, and still another part in Vladivostok), and outside the jurisdiction of the army commander (General Shokorov was in Omsk and the chief of staff, General Dieterichs, in Vladivostok), was the result of the mood of the troops, who had become angered by unkept promises, and who had long advocated taking matters into their own hands. From the point of view of the leaders of the CSNC and the Bolsheviks, this was a mutiny and a complete break with Masaryk's neutralist policy. Although no public statement was ever issued suggesting that the military leadership of the Czechoslovak army corps—Generals Shokorov and Dieterichs—had been deposed together with the political leadership represented by Maxa and Čermák, Pavlů and the young officers acted as if this had happened.

On May 23, 1918, the first unit charged with enforcing its own order and armed with machine guns placed on locomotives was dispatched from Cheliabinsk to Omsk. At the afternoon meeting, the congress decided to remove the transportation of the troops from the jurisdiction of the Russian branch of the CSNC and to give it to the TEC; future "eventual directives" of the branch were declared invalid.[71] On the same day a new telegram was sent by Aralov to the Siberian soviets, directing them to proceed immediately with "the disarming and disbanding of all echelons and units of the Czechoslovak Army Corps." In accord with the wishes of the Czechoslovak communists in Moscow, Aralov ordered that "from the present Army Corps you are to form Red Army units and labor detachments. If you need the help of Czechoslovak commissars, you are to turn to the Czechoslovak Social-Democratic committees at Penza, Samara, Petropavlovsk, and Omsk." To encourage the Soviet interest in carrying out the order, the last sentence of the telegram said: "I bring to your attention that in the echelons are supplies of alcohol."[72]

The decisions of the congress were communicated to the Soviet government on May 23, 1918, in a telegram that stated, in part:

> The Congress of Representatives of the Czechoslovak Corps at Cheliabinsk has resolved to delegate exclusive charge of the transportation of Czechoslovak troops to the Temporary Executive Committee chosen by the Congress. Orders issued by representatives of

any other Czechoslovak organization are invalid. With the reference to the order to surrender arms, issued by the representatives of the Czecho-Slovak National Council, Maxa and War Commissar [sic] Aralov, the Congress has unanimously decided not to surrender arms before reaching Vladivostok, considering them a guarantee of safe travel. The assurances of safe transportation from the authorities of the Federal Soviet Republic cannot satisfy us.... The Congress protests against the repeated attempts to disarm and stop Czechoslovak echelons.... Although taking certain precautionary measures, the Czechoslovak [Temporary] Executive Committee entertains the hope that the Soviet government will place no obstacles in the way of the departing Czechoslovak revolutionary troops.... Our hope for a peaceful settlement of this involved situation is the greater since every conflict would only prejudice the position of the local Soviet organs in Siberia. [Signed] Bohdan Pavlů, Chairman of the Czechoslovak Executive Committee.[73]

Members of the Russian branch of the CSNC at Omsk attempted to prevent a complete break with the Bolsheviks by telegraphing Captain Gajda, on the morning of May 25, no to take any action in his capacity as commander of troops east of Omsk. He was informed that General Foch had "ordered one of our divisions to go to Archangel," and that the army must obey orders. It was necessary "to comply with the Russian government and direct ourselves by its dispositions. Of course, it is possible to negotiate with it!" In the name of members of the Russian branch of the CSNC at Omsk, Gajda was urged to remain calm and not to start any fights. "We do not want and we cannot fight the Bolsheviks. That would destroy us! ..." the order said. In the same telegram, signed by Dr. Kudela, Major Guinet, and General Shokorov, the commander-in-chief threatened Gajda with a court martial if he did not obey the order.[74] Also, the newspaper published by the Russian branch of the CSNC, *Československý deník,* carried, on May 25, an interview with Major A. Guinet, who insisted that the First Czechoslovak Division would go to Archangel. The editorial repeated that this interview was intended to dispel "doubts that arise in our midst because of the ignorance and the lack of understanding, and as a consequence of dastardly agitation."[75]

Origins of the Conflict 337

But these steps could no longer stop the chain of events that led to the open clash with the Bolsheviks. On the afternoon of May 25, Captain Kadlec, acting upon Gajda's instructions, occupied Mariinsk, east of Nikolaevsk; at about the same time, west of this town, an anti-Soviet uprising took place at Chulymska. On the night of May 26, Gajda took Novonikolaevsk, where the Provisional Government of Siberia was established. The day before, on May 25, Trotsky sent telegrams to all soviets along with Penza-Omsk railway line ordering them

> to disarm Czechoslovaks immediately. Every armed Czechoslovak found on the railway is to be shot on the spot; every troop train in which even one armed man is found shall be unloaded, and its soldiers shall all be interned in a prisoners' camp. Local war commissars must proceed at once to carry out this order; every delay will be considered treason and will bring the offender severe punishment. At the same time, reliable forces entrusted with teaching the rebels a lesson are being sent to the rear of the Czechoslovaks. Honest Czechoslovaks who surrender their arms and submit to the Soviet Government will be treated as brothers and given every assistance. Inform all railway workers that not a single car of armed Czechoslovaks is to be allowed to move eastward. Those who submit to violence and assist the Czechoslovaks in their movement east will be severely punished. This order is to be read to all Czechoslovak units and to all railway workers in places where Czechoslovaks are found. War commissars will report on its execution. [Signed] L. Trotsky, People's Commissar of War.[76]

This order was the answer to the telegram sent by the Temporary Executive Committee to the Soviet government two days earlier. Nothing now could have stopped the armed clash between the Czechoslovaks and the Soviets. The Soviet for Central Siberia had directed all soviets to disarm the Czechslovak echelons in its order of May 26. As the telegram said, if local forces "are not adequate to disarm them, do everything possible to stop the echelons: sidetrack them, take their locomotives, in urgent cases tear up the railway tracks."[77] This was much easier said than done, especially when the local soviets were confronted with the not-yet disarmed Czechoslovaks west of Penza. Thus, on May 26, 1918, the Penza Soviet telegraphed Trotsky that it had held a conference "which was attended by Czechoslovak Communists" and "we arrived at the conclusion that we could not carry out the order in its full sense as you demand...." To this Trotsky replied on the same day "Comrades! Military orders ...should not be discussed but obeyed. Any representative of the War Commissariat who is so cowardly as to evade disarming the Czechoslovaks will be brought by me before the Military Tribunal. It is your duty to act immediately and energetically!"[78] The bridges were burned; there was no way back for either side.

The war between the Bolsheviks and the Czechs that began at the end of May 1918, was a historical accident leading to an almost immediate recognition of the Czechoslovak army's belligerency by the British and French governments. Ironically, the uprising of the Czechoslovak troops against the Bolsheviks was, at the smae time, a revolution "against Maxa and, thus, against Masaryk."[79] As a Russian historian and several other writers saw it, the war began against the principle of neutrality promulgated by "the dictator" Masaryk. "Had it happened a few months earlier, the Czecho-Slovak army could have easily taken care of the gangs of the Red Guards which were almost unorganized at that time as yet."[80] However, the Czechs resorted to arms in order to save themselves and to reach their destination (Vladivostok), not in an effort to destroy the Red Guards and the Bolshevik regime. The irony of the situation was that the anti-Bolshevik uprising helped Masaryk and Beneš, who were opposed to it, to obtain recognition as the *de facto* belligerent provisional government of the then nonexistent Czechoslovak state. They were thus able to assume the most prominent positions in that state when it was formed after the war.

CHAPTER THIRTEEN

CZECHOSLOVAK RESISTANCE TO THE BOLSHEVIKS, AND THE DECISION TO INTERVENE

In retrospect, it appears that the Czechoslovak military had a better insight into the actual political situation in Russia and assessed much better the nature of Soviet power than did most of the civilian members of the Russian branch of the CSNC and its local branches in Siberia.[1] In their determination to get out of Russia, the Temporary Executive Committee and the three military commanders who were charged with responsibility for the three sectors of the railway ignored protests made by the representatives of the CSNC in local branches in Omsk and Vladivostok, and their branches' insistence that negotiations with the Soviets must continue, on the assumption that accommodation with the latter was possible. Neither did the Czechoslovak military follow the instructions of General Shokorov and the French military personnel in Siberia and Moscow.

An ad hoc staff was formed from among four regimental commanders, Lieutenant Colonel Vojtsekhovskii, Lieutenant Čeček, Captain Gajda, and Lieutenant Syrový, to prepare a plan for the transportation of troops and the occupation of the Trans-Siberian Railway. According to the plan, the Penza group of trains (echelons) was to be commanded by Čeček, the Cheliabinsk group by Vojtsekhovskii, the Omsk group by Syrový, and the eastern group by Gajda. The officers hoped that the strong Vladivostok garrison under General Dieterichs would come forward to meet Gajda's group; they decided that the action would start simultaneously in all sectors, but not before the Council of People's Commissars replied to the latest Czech appeal to refrain from attempting to disarm the Czechoslovak troops.[2]

While the Czech military appealed to the Bolsheviks to let them proceed eastward, the local branch of the CSNC in Vladivostok and the Vladivostok Soviet were urging the soldiers not to fight. In their proclamation of May 29, 1918, the Vladivostok Czechs and Bolsheviks asserted that the transportation of the troops to Vladivostok was fully secured and that only technical reasons (there were no ships there) held it back. It reported that 12,000 Czechoslovak troops were already there, that they were well cared for, that the local soviet government supported them, and that they in turn were friendly and loyal to the Soviet government. Violence would only slow down the movement eastward; therefore, the joint proclamation "urgently demanded" the immediate liquidation of all conflicts along the railway.

However, armed clashes had already been occurring for several days. As early as May 25, 1918, upon Aralov's instructions, two trains carrying Soviet and internationalist Red Guards left Omsk and headed westward in order to disarm a detachment of the Sixth Czechoslovak Regiment. The attackers were thrown back to Omsk. On that day the Czechs intercepted Trotsky's telegram that gave the order to shoot every Czechoslovak apprehended in arms. On May 26, an attempt to disarm a Czechoslovak train at Irkutsk resulted in an armed clash, and when in the evening of that day two other trains carrying Czech troops arrived at Irkutsk, they were attacked by armed Austrian and German prisoners of war. In the ensuing struggle five prisoners of war were killed; and the Czechs "captured twenty-two Austrians, four Germans, and nine Russians who were members of the Red Guard."[3]

On the night of May 26-27, the Czechoslovaks occupied the most important railroad junction, Cheliabinsk. On May 28, the TEC issued a manifesto entitled "To all, to All!" which said in part:

> The Central Soviet government, after threats to disarm the Czechoslovaks, resorted on May 25 to a sneak attack on a Czechoslovak train near Omsk with the help of armed Austrians and Germans. . . .

The Czechoslovaks replied to this provocation by a short hit on the night of May 27, and as a consequence of it, they conquered all of the most important places along the railway from Cheliabinsk to Irkutsk, with the exception of the area around Omsk. We are leaving the civilian government in place. The Czechoslovaks do not want to get involved in internal affairs of the Russian nation; they only secured themselves against the attack of armed prisoners who threatened under the guise of internationalism, to take control of the great Siberian railway.... [Signed] Bohdan Pavlů, Chairman; František Richter, Secretary.[4]

The presence of a large number of Hungarian and German prisoners of war in Siberia was one of the factors that helped to crystallize the Czechoslovak soldiers' attitude toward the Soviet government. The estimated number of all prisoners of war was close to two million, about two-thirds of whom were subjects of Austria-Hungary. After the Peace of Brest-Litovsk, German and Austro-Hungarian commissions for the exchange of prisoners tried to repatriate their nationals as speedily as possible, while the Bolsheviks conducted propaganda campaigns among the prisoners of war, attempting to induce them into the international legions of the Red Army, the Red Guards, and labor detachments, in defense of the Soviet regime and the anticipated world revolution. On several occasions, the German ambassador in Moscow, Mirbach, protested against Bolshevik activities among the prisoners of war; and Trotsky therefore ordered local soviets to keep the prisoners isolated in camps.[5] The local authorities, however, paid no attention to these orders and zealously recruited prisoners of war for Soviet armed units, which were deployed in armed clashes with the Czechoslovaks.

The most serious armed clash took place at Penza on May 28, 1918. In Penza the situation was more explosive than at other places along the railway. According to the March agreement, all Czechoslovak echelons had to go through Penza, where they had to leave their arms, except for a specified small number of rifles and machine guns with which they were to protect themselves against "counterrevolutionary" forces in Siberia. Thus the trains west of Penza were fully armed. Furthermore, the city became the most important center of Czechoslovak Bolshevik agitation aimed at recruiting Czechoslovak troops into the Red Army. As has been mentioned earlier, at the beginning of May the local Czechoslovak Red Army unit was strengthened by several left-wing socialists from the Czechoslovak army corps (Vaníček, Koudelka, Skoták, and others). These former Legionnaires also took part in all the efforts to recruit more Czechs and Slovaks for the cause of the Bolshevik world revolution. On May 12, a new newspaper, *Československá rudá armáda* (Czechoslovak Red Army) began to be published at Penza. By the middle of May, the First Czechoslovak [Bolshevik] Revolutionary Regiment numbered more than 700 men. The regiment took part in fighting the anti-Bolshevik uprising at Kuzneck, and 220 men commanded by J. Štrombach were sent to suppress the anti-Soviet uprising at Saratov. From there these troops did not return, because they were sent instead to fight the units of the Cossack ataman Dutov.[6]

When Trotsky's telegram arrived at Penza, the chairman of the regional soviet, Kurayev, called a conference that included representatives of the Czechoslovak communist group—that is, those who were not at the communist congress held in Moscow at that time. The Penza conference concluded that Trotsky's directive could not be fulfilled for the simple reason that the Czechoslovak units at the Penza railway station and on the railway before Penza were full armed and clearly had the upper hand. Trotsky, as has been mentioned earlier, replied angrily to the telegram from Penza, saying that orders were not to be discussed—they must be complied with. Thus, at a large meeting of Czechoslovak troops, in the afternoon of May 27, Kurayiev tried for the last time to convince the soldiers to lay down their arms and avoid shedding brotherly Russian blood. Since the echelons that were still in European Russia were most embittered by the constant delays of their departure to Vladivostok, the tension among those troops was the greatest. Kurayev's efforts were therefore futile; the soldiers had been disappointed too many times before. Led by Lieutenant Čeček, who came back to Penza from the Cheliabinsk congress with instructions to go forward "through our own order," and to use force if necessary, the Czechsolovak troops refused to disarm, even partially, and began to move eastward. The tension culminated early on May 28, when a train from Moscow arived at the Penza railway station with reinforcements, including three armored cars, for the Soviet military units there. Czechoslovak soldiers from the echelons standing at the railway station took possession of the arms immediately, and turned down Kurayev's request for their return. On that day severe figting broke out at Penza, resulting in the Czechoslovak troops' taking the whole city on the next day. Companies of the First Czechoslovak Revolutionary Regiment (a Bolshevik unit) also participated in the battle for Penza; thus, for the first time, Czechoslovaks were fighting Czechoslovaks in this war of a "new type." This was the beginning of a "civil war" among members of armed forces who were far away from home, from their native land, from a state that did not yet even exist. During the fighting, 128 members of the Czechoslovak Red Army units were killed and three officials of the Czechoslovak communist group at Penza were taken prisoner.[7]

On May 30, posters were placed in Penza' streets bearing an announcement, signed by Lieutenant Švec, that the Czechoslovaks had no intention of changing the political regime in Russia, tha they were not taking the government of Penza into their own hands, and that they would leave the city as soon as the departure of their echelons was ensured. An agreement was reached wit the soviet at Penza that freed the way to Syzran. By June 1, all the Czechoslovak units from the Penza region were beyond the Volga River. Then, however, the troops had to fight their way to Samara. The wrath of the Czech soldiers was directed at anyone they believed to be standing in their way to Vladivostok. They overthrew local soviets that attempted to carry out the order of the Soviet government to disarm and shoot armed Czechoslovaks. As a result of the overthrow of Soviet rule along the railway, anti-Soviet organizations began to emerge; with them new anti-Soviet governments sprang up in the Ural region and in Siberia. These governments welcomed the Czechoslovak troops as their liberators from Soviet terror. Some Russian and Siberian anti-Bolshevik military units were formed in cooperation with the Czechoslovak army corps.

As soon as Captains Gajda and Kadlec took the first military actions in the sector between Omsk and Irkutsk, a new Provisional Siberian Government, composed of Socialist Revolutionaries and Mensheviks, was established at Novonikolaevsk. It began to build its own military formations from officers of the former tsarist army and student volunteers. The cooperation between the anti-Bolshevik forces and the Czechoslovak army units inevitably brought the Czechs into the Russian civil war. Some members of the Russian branch of the CSNC and members of foreign military missions attempted to stop this course of events by issuing appeals and "orders" to the three military commanders, insisting on "negotiations."

Captain Gajda rejected telegraphed appeals from French Major Arsène Vergé dated June 2 and 3. According to Vergé, the "Soviet organs enlist all their strength to make possible the speeding of the transports;" and "the Czechoslovaks have neither a right nor an interest to intervene in internal struggles." On June 3, Gajda instructed all the troops under his command that "the military collegium gave me the jurisdiction over the group east of Omsk and all the detachments of the Second division;" and without "my knowledge no agreements or armistice . . . may be concluded." If any members of the CSNC interfered with his orders, Gajda said, they should be arrested. Also at that time, the hastily established Provisional Siberian Government notified the representatives of the Entente powers in Siberia that it was giving the Czechslovak army corps a choice: either go to France, or continue to fight Germany "in the ranks of the Russian army." It also told the Entente that the military units of the Provisional Siberian Government fully agreed and cooperated with the Czechoslovaks' action.[8]

The decision made by the Czechoslovak military congress to stand up against the Bolsheviks, and the early easy Czechoslovak victories, took the Soviet government by surprise. Unable to win militarily, the Soviets tried to subdue the Czechoslovak army coprs by using treachery and appeals to negotiations. The Soviet government made the captive Maxa send messages to the TEC, and just before the battle at Lipjag, which opened the way to Samara, a Soviet airplane dropped leaflets containing messages from Maxa on the Czechoslovak echelons of the Penza group. Maxa's leaflets included the following words:

> Brethren! I appeal to you in the name of your leader, Professor Masaryk, in the name of our fatherland . . . in the name of our French friends: Wake up from this grave misunderstanding that threatens to destroy our sacred cause. . . . Immediately stop all operations . . . and send delegates to negotiations. To continue the hostile behavior would mean, inevitably, to create animosity between ourselves and the brotherly Russian people. That you must not allow to happen! We will not, indeed, permit the development of a struggle between Czechoslovak revolutionaries and Russian revolutionaries. This is the most terrible of all struggles—the fratricidal struggle. . . . Your transportation is guaranteed by the French and the English governments.

...However, there is only one way to reach this aim: stop immediately all hostile operations and start to negotiate.... Send the delegates with a white flag unarmed along the railway tracks toward Syzran....

On the back side of the leaflet, which was written in Russian, was an addendum in French: "Dear friends, in the name of General Lavergne...I request you to follow the instructions of Professor Maxa. Your transport to France is guaranteed by the French government in agreement with the Russian government. Captain [an illegible signature]."

The soldiers would no longer be taken in by this trick; they knew what kind of decision had been made in Moscow and what would await them should they agree to negotiate with those who had issued orders to shoot them on the spot. Major Guinet, who tried to comply with the order to bring the Czechoslovak units west of Omsk to the northern Russian harbors, was unable to convince the TEC to follow his instructions. Guinet charged the Czechoslovak officers with having counterrevolutionary desires and tried to send a telegram to this effect to Major Vergé in Irkutsk; however, the telegram was intercepted by the Czechs. The cooperation of railway masters and postmasters with the Czechoslovaks made it possible for them to obtain intelligence and act upon it quickly. The instructions telegraphed to the soviets along the railway by the Soviet government, as well as messages indicating the movements of the Red Army troops, fell into the hands of the Czechoslovaks.[9] Here lies one partial explanation of the fact that the Czechslovak officers had beeter information about what was going on than had their "political superiors" in the branch of the CSNC and the members of the foreign military missions.

Although it was the Soviet government that caused the Czechoslovak military to stand up against the Soviets and their "internationalist" Red Guards and Red Army units, the master propagandist Lenin, in a telegram to all soviets (July 1, 1918), blamed the ensuing bloodshed on "counter-revolutionary provocateurs" who dragged the Czechoslovaks into the uprising by using deception. At first this line was followed by *Československý deník,* in which Josef Kudela wrote, on May 28, that the Soviet government had many enemies who were trying to make the Czechoslovaks take a stand on their behalf. He declared categorically: "This is not our task!" On June 2, Kudela still asserted that the military success "must not confuse us;" that "our principle was, is and will be: not to get involved in internal matters." The changes in Russian society that resulted from the Czechoslovak action during these few days, however, made his change his mind. On June 4, he wrote, "From our attempt to force our way throught, a situation is developing which has a far-reaching, yet unassessable, international importance. The Soviet government in Siberia is falling apart.... In its place a new administration, a new government is being built, founded on the principle of universal equal suffrage with its slogans: All-Siberian Constitutional Convention and the restoration of the anti-German front." Kudela now wrote of the "tremendous task that destiny has placed before us." Two days earlier, in a more prosaic manner, Pavlů and Richter of the TEC described the situation in a letter to the editor of *Československý deník:* "Originally, we thought that the overthrow of military power [of the Soviets] would be enough; however, today we see that the liberated country must be organized anew politically and militarily. To terminate the neutrality [stand] is both in our own interest and in the interest of the country too."

This change in the attitude of *Československý deník* was caused by two factors: (1) from the practical point of view, to overthrow Soviet military power, but leave the organs of Soviet civil power intact, would have resulted in a constant need to watch the Bolsheviks and to engage in new battles with the troops that they would be able to marshal; (2) there was a spontaneous mushrooming of new governments composed of Socialist Revolutionaries and Mensheviks, who were taking political power from the soviets weakened by the Czechoslovak military victories. Thus, in the June 4, 1918, Russian edition of *Československý deník,* B. Pavlů announced, in the name of the TEC, that "in view of the constant violence used by the Soviet government against us we are ceasing to observe neutrality toward the Soviet government and we support all [political] parties whose slogan is Constituent Assembly, and [thus] we support the Provisional Siberian Government." (The Constituent Assembly had been elected in December 1917, and dissolved by Lenin in January 1918.)

In accordance with their plan, Gajda's forces were moving westward from the east, and troops under Vojtsekhovskii's command eastward from the west. Vojtsekhovskii took Omsk on June 7, 1918, and that city became the seat of the Provisional Siberian Government. One day later, Čeček's troops took Samara, where an "All-Russian" government of the

Constituent Assembly was established with the backing of Victor Chernov, the leader of the Socialist Revolutionary party.

Since the Czechoslovak army was technically a part of the Czechoslovak army in France, and thus also a part of the French army, the French military personnel attached to the Czechoslovak units represented the French army, and, indirectly, the French government. Major Guinet, as a soldier, was accustomed to following standing orders without question (even if they might have been made obsolete or unworkable by new developments). The chairman and secretary of the TEC, Pavlů and Richter realized that Guinet's directives were old, and replied to his objections accordingly in a letter dated June 2, 1918: "In accordance with certain pronouncements we believe that our taking a stand [against the Bolsheviks] corresponds to the interests of the Allies to a greater degree than, perhaps, the French representative realizes." Indeed, Major Guinet changed his attitude in accordance with the new instructions he received. On June 4, he reproached the Czechoslovaks with having "violated" neutrality, while two days later, on June 6, after receiving new directives from his superiors, he proclaimed that the French government had never even considered disarming the Legion, as demanded by the Bolsheviks, and that the French would be the first to urge the Czechs to fight, should it be necessary and should it not be possible to reach an agreement with to Soviets. However, he still advised the Czechs to negotiate with the Soviet government in the hope that an agreement could be reached.[10]

By this time the TEC had become aware of the previous French plans to take the troops out of the country via Archangel and Murmansk, as well as Vladivostok, and of Britain's reliance on some of the Czechoslovak troops to secure Allied positions in the Russian north. The TEC also knew about the shortage of tonnage to transport the troops from either the Russian north or Vladivostok. The new military and political leaders of the Czechslovak army corps in Russia understood the political significance of the action that was taken, and the nature of the situation, as it developed before and after the Trotsky order of May 25; and the efforts made by French military personnel to make the corps negotiate with the organs of Soviet power, and to accomplish the original plan of transferring at least one-half of the army corps to the north, were therefore in vain.

Also in vain were the efforts of the Russian branch of the CSNC at Vladivostok to stop the "mutiny" as late as June 16, 1918, when the whole of western Siberia was locked in a deadly struggle with the Bolsheviks. Houska, Špaček, Girsa, and General Dieterichs "strongly reminded" the troops fighting their way eastward that "the only aim" was for all to arrive "to the French front as soon as possible," and, therefore, a "complete neutrality in Russian affairs" was a necessity. The fighting units were urged to conclude agreements with the local soviets in Siberia for the transfer of the troops to Vladivostok in accordance with the agreement reached with the Soviets on March 26, 1918, the agreement that had "proved to be completely satisfactory during the shipment of the first 12 trains"—as if nothing had happened since March, and as if Trotsky had issued no order on May 25.[11]

The preceding detailed description of events refutes the charges later made by the communists that the officers fo the Legion had planned the uprising upon instructions from the Allies, and had followed their directives. The truth of the matter was that the Allied representatives on the spot were advising against any military action against the Bolsheviks. On May 26, implementing Trotsky's order of May 25, the Reds attacked a train carrying Czech troops upon its arrival at Irkutsk. When two other trains that followed this one received the news of what had happened to their comrades in arms, they stopped short of Irkutsk. The soldiers occupied two railway stations in the vicinity of Irkutsk, took possession of food and artillery depots, arrested some members of the local soviet, and began an offensive against Irkutsk in order to free their comrades there. On the next day, after capturing Irkutsk, upon the insistence of the French and American consuls general they concluded peace with the Bolsheviks and returned all captured weapons, even those that they themselves had in their trains (except thirty rifles), when the Bolsheviks promised to let them go to Vladivostok. Although making that agreement was a mistake on the part of the commanders of the trains, the incident shows that there was no joint plan to revolt against the Bolsheviks or even to capture the railway to Vladivostok. The Czech commanders followed the advice of the two Allied consuls and gave up strategically important center that they had taken with the loss of thirty dead and sixty-three wounded brethren. Six weeks later, Gajda's units had to take the same place again at a great cost and under much more difficult conditions.[12]

The senior Allied diplomats in Russia comprehended the situation and the nature of the new development between the Czechoslovak army and the Soviets much better than their military aides who were untrained in politics and lacked understanding of political problems. The uprising of anti-Soviet political forces, under the umbrella of the Czechoslovak military action, showed the weakness of the Soviets, and led the Allied diplomats in Russia to believe that Soviet rule would soon collapse. The French ambassador, J. Noulens, quickly reached the conclusion that the Czechoslovak military leaders had no other choice, that their taking a stand against the Soviets was a matter of self-defense and self-preservation and, thus, the only correct course of action. He announced his support for the Czechoslovak resistance to the Soviet decision to disarm the troops. He convinced the other representatives of the Entente powers that what the Czechoslovaks had done was right. On May 31, 1918, he telegraphed to General Lavergne, "Naturally, neither you nor any other officier who is attached to, or who will be sent to the Czech units will in any way advise or urge the disarmament of these units;" he justified his stand by "the odious speech of Trotsky's order" of May 25.[13] The same "distasteful" order by Trotsky was named by David R. Francis, U.S. ambassador in Russia, as the reason for the Czech refusal to lay down arms. In his May 31 telegram to the secretary of state, Francis also mentioned information that his attaché had received from an anti-Bolshevik employee of the Soviet government, according to which Soviet power was hanging by a thread, and at the "first manifestation of Allied intervention" the Soviet government would be overturned. This employee asked the attaché: "Why are not Allies taking a definite action?"[14]

On June 4, 1918, representatives of France, England, the United States, and Italy lodged a protest against the disarmament order with the People's Commissar of Foreign Affairs, Chicherin. The military attachés of these countries also demanded an audience with Trotsky. The Czechoslovak uprising was discussed by the Soviet government during the night of June 4-5, 1918, according to a telegram sent by General Lavergne to Paris. The general reported that the Soviet government had considered the possibility that the Allied protest against the order to disarm the Czechoslovaks could forebode intervention; in that case, it would be necessary for the Soviets to continue energetic and speedy operations against the Czechoslovaks. This view was stubbornly defended by Trotsky, while Lenin believed that intervention could not take place as yet, that Trotsky's conduct was too brutal, and that it was necessary to find a basis for agreement. Lavergne concluded in his telegram that "we cannot allow the Czechoslovaks to be disarmed."[15]

The Allied diplomats in Russia rejected the demand that the Czechoslovaks be completely disarmed. U.S. Ambassador Francis wired to the State Department on June 3, 1918, that, in his judgment, the Czechoslovaks should not be disarmed and that he had instructed the consulate general to inform the Soviet government that "the Allies would consider disarmament and severe treatment as inspired by Germany or, certainly, by hostile sentiment toward the Allies."[16] On the next day Lansing wired to Francis that "the Department is considering carefully" the ambassador's suggestion to intervene in Siberia,[17] and asked him to suggest a "more concrete form and plan of action, taking into consideration the fact that the military forces to be employed would . . . be almost wholly Japanese."[18] The U.S. minister in China, Reinsch, wired to Lansing on June 5, 1918, that "all American representatives in Siberia are agreed that Allied intervention is absolutely demanded; Siberia will be in German control unless immediate action is taken. . . . Presence of Czecho-Slovaks can be utilized. American force of 10,000 considered sufficient,[19]

On the same day, June 5, 1918, the Temporary Executive Committee informed the French mission in Russia why the Czechoslovaks had taken to arms. The document cited the following reasons:

(1) The Czechoslovak action along the Penza-Irkutsk railway was prompted by the threats of the Soviet government to break up our units, intern them as war prisoners, and shoot all armed Czechoslovaks. We had reliable information that . . . our military organization was to be completely disbanded and that its units were to be forced into service in the Red Army. This compelled us to prepare for armed defense. (2) The spark that set us into action . . . was the treacherous attack upon our echelon at Marianovka, near Omsk, on May 25. We retaliated by occupying all important stations along the line Cheliabinsk-Omsk-Irkutsk. . . . (3) At first our tactics were directed toward insuring a safe and unimpeded passage to France for ourselves. We did not what to interfere in Russian internal affairs and allowed the Soviets to remain in their places. Soon, however, we became convinced that the Cheliabinsk Soviet . . . had organized an armed strike movement against us. Thereupon we decided to

remove the Soviet authorities from their positions, especially after we received new reports... that the Soviet government was mobilizing all its forces against us. (4) Under these circumstances we decided to give up our policy of political neutrality and summon to our help all the best elements of the local population.[20]

In his telegram of June 7, 1918, Ambassador Francis reported to Washington that the Soviet order to disarm the Czechoslovaks and to disband their army had reportedly been dictated by the Germans. He pointed out that many German and Austrian prisoners of war were members of the Red Guards fighting the Czechoslovaks, that the Soviet government was spreading Bolshevik doctine among the Czechoslovaks, and that it interfered in every possible way with the departure of the army corps, claiming that the latter was a counterrevolutionary organization.[21] The situation became crystal clear when on June 11, 1918, the Council of People's Commissars published a decree dissolving the Russian branch of the CSNC "and all organizations and committees associated with it," and announcing that "property, capital, archives, etc. of the above mentioned organizations are turned over to the Czechoslovak section attached to the People's Commissariat of Nationalities."[22] As we have noted, this had actually been accomplished one month earlier. The Czechoslovaks already knew then what was in store for them and had reasons to disagree with the military aides of the Allied missions.

On June 12, Chicherin issued a note to the Allied diplomatic representatives answering their protest of June 4, "in which they declared that the disarming of the Czechoslovaks would be considered by their governments as an unfriendly act... since the Czechoslovak troops are Allied troops and are under the protection and care of the Entente Powers." Chicherin claimed that disarming the Czechoslovaks "is necessitated primarily by the fact that Russia is a neutral power and cannot tolerate the presence in her territories of armed forces not belonging to the army of the Soviet Republic." However, he said, the immediate cause of "the taking of decisive and strong measures to disarm the Czechoslovaks is to be found in their activities.... They began a rebellion in Cheliabinsk on May 26... and the subsequent spread of the rebellion led to the occupation by the Czechoslovaks of Penza, Samara, Novonikolaevsk, Omsk and other cities.... Everywhere the Czechoslovaks acted in cooperation with the White Guards and counter-revolutionary Russian officers."[23] Chicherin thus confirmed that the "rebellion in Cheliabinsk" began on May 26, that is, one day after Trotsky issued the order to shoot every armed Czechoslovak.

The intervention of Allied diplomats in Russia on behalf of the Czechoslovak army corps strengthened the position of the TEC. The editorial offices of *Československý deník* were moved west to Cheliabinsk on June 10, and on June 11, 1918, B. Pavlů called upon the Czechoslovak units in Vladivostok to come back to Siberia. As Gajda put it in his letter to Captain Kadlec on June 10, "Peace with the Bolsheviks is already ruled out and our task is to conclude the work that we have begun." He informed his deptuy that he had sent several people to Vladivostok with an order that the Fifth and Eighth Regiments, which had already arrived in Vladivostok, should go back in order to establish contact with his troops. He also mentioned that the Czechoslovak units would support, wherever possible, the Provisional Siberian Government and the formation of a Siberian army. Two days later he stated, "Any negotiation with the Bolsheviks or conclusion of peace with them is completely ruled out; we are now in a life-or-death struggle with them; we must destroy the Bolsheviks at any price. According to the reports I have received, we will, most likely, not travel to France."[24] The official position of the TEC was stated by B. Pavlů in a letter to František Langer dated June 13: "Our political position is that, at places occupied by us we support the democratic forces of the nation...and we share the principle of the new Siberian government...Constituent Assembly."[25]

The Allied representatives in Russia, Siberia, and China realized the importance of the Czechoslovak action in Siberia and eastern Russia. For example, in a telegram dated June 13, 1918, the American representative at Peking concurred with his colleagues that "it would be a serious mistake to remove the Czecho-Slovak troops from Siberia." These units, he reported, with only token support "could control all of Siberia against the Germans. They are sympathetic to the Russian population, eager to be accessories to the Allied cause;" and their "removal would greatly benefit Germany and further discourage Russia. If they were not in Siberia, it would be worthwhile to bring them there from a distance."[26] On the next day Ambassador Francis wired the State Department that he had learned through his French colleague in Moscow that the June 3 Paris conference of the Supreme War Council had decided to hold Murmansk and Archangel, if possible, and then land Allied troops there, in order to hold these harbors, as well as "to keep Czech detachments in Russia for the present."[27] Answering a query from the secretary of state about the proposed intervention in Russia, Francis cabled on June 15, 1918, to Washington, D.C., that "intervention from the east will be welcomed by great majority of Russians," and that "armed Czechs are rapidly extending domination westward, which Soviet government [is] powerless to prevent except by arming German prisoners of war which [it is] reported doing."[28]

Czechoslovak victories in Russia and Siberia caused a sensation in Allied countries, and earned the Czechoslovaks, represented by the CSNC with Masaryk at its helm, considerable military, political, and moral significance. The *de facto* French recognition of the Czecho-Slovak National Council as the lawful government of the Czecho-Slovak state on June 15, 1198,[29] was undoubtedly related to the great importance ascribed to the Czechoslovak army's action in Russia, in particular the occupation of the 5,000-mile-long Siberian railway and the cities along it up to the harbor of Vladivostok. The French government was no longer interested in the transfer of these troops to France. On the contrary, on June 20, 1918, General Lavergne received a clear directive from Paris saying, "The temporary motionlessness of the Czechoslovak divisions . . . ought to be used: (a) to broaden the centers of resistance, built by these divisions, by rallying around them the Siberian and Cossack elements that are advocating the restoration of order; (b) to complete the possession of the Siberian railway; (c) to prepare and cover the eventual Allied intervention from the east."[30]

The Czechoslovak army newspaper, *Československý deník,* printed a declaration by Major Guinet addressed to the Czechoslovak soldiers, announcing the arrival of a special telegram from the French ambassador stating that the Allies had taken steps on behalf of the Czechoslovaks in Russia. The major paid respects to those "whose views he did not always share," and wrote that to his great joy he was authorized to give thanks, on behalf of the Allies, to the Czechoslovak units for their action. On June 22, 1918, Čeček, the commander of the most westward part of the Czechoslovak army in Russia, received the following message from the French consul at Samara: "The French government notifies the Czech detachments concentrated in Samara that without expressed and authentic instructions from the authorities of the Allied armies they should not leave any of the positions held. On the contrary, they should fortify them. ...The aim of the Czech detachments is no longer to transport themselves by train via Vladivostok to France, but to prepare the eastern front on the Volga River."[31]

The governments of England and France now used the presence and successes of the Czechoslovak troops in Russia and Siberia as arguments to induce the American government to consent to intervention in Siberia and to the deployment of Japanese troops there. The British and the French argued that if intervention were not undertaken in Siberia and the Eastern Front were not restored, Germany could make eastern Europe its colony, even if the Allies won the war on the Western Front. Also, on June 22, 1918, Ambassador Francis urged armed intervention, saying that the "Russian people are expecting America to lead in intervention." He believed that "failure to intervene will prolong the war perhaps two years and cost us priceless blood and untold treasure as such failure would enable Germany to draw on Russia for supplies and perhaps to organize an army. Intervention would be opportune. Czecho-Slovaks control a great portion of the Siberian Railway and, if intervention [were] announced, would dominate its entire length.... Our Allies are all insisting upon intervention ... and may possibly ... intervene without our consent. Such a position ... would be embarrassing...."[32]

Although a detailed discussion of the decision to intervene in Russia is not practical in this volume, a brief mention of it is necessary. It has been noted earlier that the British considered Japanese intervention in Siberia in January and February 1918, and that the United States government opposed it. After prolonged discussions and diplomatic negotiations, in mid-June 1918, the British War Office marshaled in great detail its military arguments for intervention in Siberia and Russia.[33] If the war went on through 1919 and even 1920, an Allied intervention could have great effect on the military campaign in 1919, since the Germans, facing a threat in the east, would be forced to withdraw some of their divisions in the west. Should the Germans not be challenged in the east and should they be able to draw on the natural resources of Russia, the Ukraine, and other parts of the former Romanov empire, they might greatly increase their pressure in the west. Even though American troops would be arriving in large numbers in the western theater of the war, the Central Powers would still continue their military superiority there. In such a situation the Allies not only would have little chance to secure a victory in 1919 but also, most likely, would for the early part of that year be in danger of defeat.[34]

In addition to this main argument for intervention, there was another one equally important. Would the objectives for which the Allies were fighting be secured, even if Germany should be heavily defeated in the west, if the Eastern Front were not reconstituted? Should the Central Powers be driven out of France and Belgium, they would still be able to offset their losses by their gains in the east. Only an armed intervention in the east would compel the Germans to disgorge the wheat and coal, the oil and minerals, of the Ukraine and the Caucasus. To be sure, the intervention force would have to be supplied by the Allies in the first instance, the document said, but the objective would be to reconstitute the power of Russia so that when the Allied armies were withdrawn, Russia herself would be able to defend her independence, honor, and national existence from German spoliation.[35]

The British did not propose to weaken the Allied force in the west to provide an intervention force in the east. Therefore, the bulk of the troops would have to be furnished by Japan, with small detachments of British and American troops to indicate the international character of the undertaking and reassure the Russians that the Allied motives were not to humiliate Russia, but to help her restore her national existence. The Japanese forces would be deployed along the Trans-Siberian Railway from Vladivostok to the Ural. The British War Office envisaged the need for eight and a half Japanese divisions; six and a half would be needed to guard the Trans-Siberian Railway and the other two would be used to establish the forward line.[36]

The aim of the Japanese divisions should be to reach the Volga basin and control it, as well as to establish a front along the line Vologda-Samara, with detachments at Archangel and Astrakhan. The occupation of the main railways in the area would effectively block German access to Siberian wheat, cotton, and Ural minerals; and would render difficult the repatriation of German and Austro-Hungarian prisoners of war who would otherwise be used as reinforcements on the Western Front. Behind the Allied front, the Russians would rally to a government pledged to restore order and sane government in Russia. Russian forces would then carry on the westward offensive, helped by partisan warfare in western parts of Russia. Since the intervention would revive national Russia, the sections of the Russian population that desired freedom and good government would certainly rally to the forces of intervention and a national Russian government.[37]

When the astounding feats of the Czechoslovaks became known, their control of the railway and the collapse of Bolshevik power in Siberia demonstrated even to the unbelievers that the bulk of the Siberian population was not sympathetic to the Bolsheviks. While on June 19 the British War Office completed its study pointing out the military need for intervention, on June 20, the French ministry of war sent to General Lavergne in Russia the first telegraphic instructions on the subject. In view of the developments in Russia and the immobilization of the Czech regiments, the telegram urged that the Czechs not abandon positions held by them. Although no decision had as yet been made on an Allied intervention, the Czechs should be ready just in case. The instructions stipulated, furthermore, that local Russian elements wishing the restoration of order should rally around the Czechoslovak positions, and that the Trans-Siberain Railway should be occupied so that an Allied intervention could be carried out, should such an intervention be undertaken. In addition, General Alba requested that the Czechs not surrender their weapons, and that those of them who had already arrived in Vladivostok disarmed, should be given weapons again. Beneš and General Janin, the supreme commander of the Czechoslovak army, were informed about the French government action, and both of them consented to the French instructions.[38]

Although on June 4, 1918, at a meeting of the TEC at Cheliabinsk, Major Guinet denounced the Legionnaires for violating the neutralist policy of Masaryk, told them that they had gone "astray politically," and philosophized that "we do not direct events, they direct us," seventeen days later he turned around 180 degrees. At a TEC meeting on June 21, 1918, he told those present—General Shokorov, Colonel Vojtsekhovskii, Richter, Bém, Závada, David, Ježek, and Kysela—that he was happy to convey to the Czechoslovak army some very good news. "I have just received a telegram from Major Royard at Perm," he said, "according to which the Allies decided to take an action in Siberia. I have been authorized by all Allied governments to thank the Czechoslovak army for its military deeds. [No such authorization was given to him at this time.] The uprising of the Czechoslovaks, though it was somewhat premature, today is in accord with the policy of the Allies; thus, the Czechoslovak army appears to be the advanced guard of the Allied armies which will arrive in Siberia to be deployed here toward the end of this month already. Your task now is to hold the present positions, not to give them up, to take care of the occupation of the Siberian railway, and to await the arrival of the Allied armies." Guinet tried to justify his previous behavior by saying that "the Allied missions apologize to you for their taking steps against your uprising; it was due to their having exact instructions, to their having orders not to intervene in internal affairs of Russia."[39]

The decision to intervene was conveyed to the Czechoslovak army corps on June 29, 1918, a few days before it was actually made by the Allied War Council, in a message from Guinet. Guinet notified the Czech headquarters that he had received from the French ambassador a ciphered telegram informing him that the Allies would intervene in Russia, and that he had been authorized "to express the thanks of the Allies to the Czechoslovak troops for their action in Russia. The behavior of Czechoslovaks, arising out of clear understanding of the situation, is to the greater honor of the whole Czechoslovak army . . . . Only a short time ago members of the French mission were making efforts to maintain relations with the Russian Soviet government. But this government no longer deserves such consideration in the eyes of the Allies and the civilized world. We are no longer in contact with the Bolsheviks . . . . " Promising support to the Czechoslovak army, Guinet ended his message as follows: "It is to you that we owe the re-establishment of the Russian front . . . against the real enemies of Russia and of the Allies . . . . The French mission, always a faithful ally of Russia, is fighting at her side in the first trench of this new front."[40] On that day, June 29, encouraged by Allied representatives, the Czechs expelled the Soviet government from Vladivostok and took over control of the city.[41]

Earlier, on June 25, representatives of the Russian branch of the CSNC at Vladivostok met with the Allied consuls and naval commanders and told them that the Czech forces in Vladivostok (some 15,000) would have to be sent back to Siberia to establish a junction with the rest of the Czechoslovak army. The CSNC represenatives urgently requested that the Allies send to their assistance a force of at least 100,000 men and a large quantity of arms and ammunition. After the Czech take-over of the city, of which the Allied representatives heartily approved, the naval commanders of the Allied powers landed small contingents of troops in Vladivostok. On July 6, a proclaimation signed by the representatives of Britain, France, Japan, the United States, China, and the Czech army announced that the whole Vladivostok area had been taken under the temporary protection of the Allied powers, who would take all necessary measures "for its defense against both external and internal dangers."[42]

The whole month of inaction on the part of the Vladivostok garrison, while the westward units had been struggling with the Bolsheviks since May 25, was due to the Vladivostok command's following Masaryk's neutralist policy and his orders, and to its unwillingness to send any help to those who were fighting their way eastward through Siberia. This month gave the Bolsheviks a breathing spell during which they could and did build an army based on conscription and the duty to serve for an indefinite time during the civil war. The new, disciplined, conscript army proved to be a more formidable foe than the ineffective "volunteer" Red Army and the loosely organized Red Guards.[43]

Masaryk proceeded from incorrect assumption about the origins and nature of the conflict between the Czechs and the Bolsheviks. In his opinion the Czechs had responded to a Geman or Austrian provocation; the conflict was a result of an Austrian or German intrigue, and he was convinced that he could settle it peacefully. He was also convinced that he could do business with his fellow-revolutionaries, the Bolsheviks, not realizing that their objectives were diametrically opposed to his own. Masaryk saw the situation through glasses tinged with his own self-interest and wishful thinking, ignoring the existence of the Treaty of Brest-Litovsk and the coincidence of interests between the Bolsheviks and the governments of the Central Powers. The Bolsheviks needed the international recognition of the Central Powers and peace on the Eastern Front in order to accomplish their objectives in Russia; the Central Powers needed Bolshevik rule in order to keep Russia in a state of military and political impotence.

Even after the July 6, 1918, assassination of the German ambassador to Moscow, Count Mirbach-Harff, which the Germans could have used as grounds for breaking diplomatic relations with Sovnarkom, German Foreign Minister Kühlmann advised Kaiser Wilhelm II not to break with Lenin: "If at all possible, the resumption of regular warfare in the East must be avoided." His successor, Hintze, a former naval attaché in St. Petersburg, argued against the resumption of hostilities between the Germans and Soviet Russia: "Anybody but the Bolsheviks would naturally suit us more, but they cannot provide what we need most: the implementation of peace of Brest and the continued military paralysis of Russia."[44] The Bolsheviks, on the other hand, had made their choice when they ratified the peace treaty as a temporary expedient, believing in the magic of world revolution.

The Germans accepted the Bolshevik conspiritorial view of the Czech revolt, and they backed their ally, Lenin on this issue. According to Lenin, the Allied officers were behind the Czech uprising and had also directed its military operations. (In fact, the few Allied military officers who were with the Czechs before and after the uprising were advising against it and caused only confusion.) If the German or Austrian involvement in the Czech-Bolshevik conflict was grossly exaggerated by Masaryk, then the German influence on Bolshevik policy decisions was exaggerated by many Rusian Left SRs. Early in July 1918, at the Fifth All-Russian Congress of Soviets, one of them, Kamkov, thundered: "The dictatorship of the proletariat has developed into a dictatorship of Mirbach! Down with Mirbach! Away with the German butchers! Away with the hangman's noose of Brest!"[45] Ironically, while the Left SRs dared to denounce the Bolsheviks as allies of Germans and charged them with taking orders from Germans even at the Fifth All-Russian Congress of Soviets, Masaryk was recommending that the Allies recognize them as the government of Russia.

Though for different reasons, Masaryk, the Germans, and the Bolsheviks saw the Czech-Bolshevik conflict as the result of a conspiracy or an intrigue. Lenin stated the Bolshevik view on June 27, 1918, when he said that "the Czechoslovak mutiny... is obviously being supported by Anglo-French imperialism in the pursuit of overthrowing the Soviet government."[46] Although the French and British governments might have wished that someone would overthrow the Bolshevik government (Boris Savinkov's activity aimed in that direction) and, apparently, one of the aims of the proposed intervention was to replace the "internationalist" Bolshevik regime by a national Russian government, the facts in the case of the Czechoslovak revolt show that the Legionnaires rose against the Bolsheviks in order to save themselves, to reach Vladivostok, and, thus to be able to go to France. The idea of overthrowing Lenin's government was not on their mind.

The favorable publicity generated in the Allied countries (especially in the United States) by the Czechoslovak's army's stand against the Bolsheviks helped open many doors that Professor Masaryk's Tokyo memorandum had closed to him. President Wilson received him in the White House on June 19, 1918, and, as has been pointed out already, the day may have been the most crucial one in the history of the Russian civil war. Earlier, on May 30, William Wiseman reporeted to London that Wilson had told him that the U.S. government would favor military intervention in Russia if the Allies were invited "by any responsible and representative body."[47] Since then such a request had come from the leader of the All-Russian Union of Co-operative Societies, who expressed his opposition to the Bolsheviks and asked the United States to take the lead in intervention. On June 19 Wilson commented to Lansing on this request to bring social order to Russia's east and to make possible Siberian resistance to German penetration, saying that the organization might "be of very great service as instruments for what we are now planning to do in Siberia."[48] On the same day the president also asked Secretary of War Baker to prepare a campaign plan for Siberia. In his own plan the key role was to be played by the Czechs, whom he saw as Slavic kinsmen of the Russians, a strong, effective force, the kind of nucleus he had been looking for since mid-April; the president was prepared to support them in view of the fact that they were not merely anti-Bolshevik, but also anti-German if not anti-Japanese. Masaryk, however, was still insisting on transporting the Czechs to France.

Though Masaryk assured Lansing that the Czechs would not fight "against the Russians but only sought to pass via Vladivostok to the western front," and though he rejected the Wilson plan on June 19, it seemed to Lansing on June 23 that "the situation of the Czecho-Slovak forces in western Siberia" created "a new condition which should receive careful consideration." Since their efforts to reach Vladivostok were opposed by the Bolsheviks, "they are fighting the Red Guards along the Siberian line with more or less success." Lansing wanted to confer with the president on the subject, and he asked him, in advance, two questions: (1) "As these troops are most loyal to our cause and have been most unjustly treated by the various Soviets ought we not to consider whether something cannot be done to support them?" (2) "Is it not possible that in this body of capable and loyal troops may be found a nucleus for military occupation of the Siberian railway?" Two days later, Secretary Lansing sent a telegram to the U.S. consul at Vladivostok, asking him for a complete report on the organization of the Czechoslovak troops at Vladivostok, their number, morale, character and number of high officers, etc., and urging him to reply as soon as possible.[49]

On the same day, June 25, after receiving new reports for Siberia, Lansing requested Masaryk to come to see him in the State Department again, and to discuss with him "the possibility of using the Czechs in Siberia." He also saw Boris Miles about "finding out as to arms of Czechs in Siberia."[50] The fact that Lansing earlier sent an urgent telegram to Vladivostok about the Czechoslovak Legion indicates that he had already counted on the services of the Czechs in Siberia, as did the other Allied governments. During this day Lansing conferred twice with the president, on nationalities within Austria and on Siberia. On the same day he received a memorandum from Assistant Secretary of State Phillips, recommending that the United States recognize the CSNC jointly with the British and French governments. Despite pressures from the two allied governments, the recognition was not granted; most likely, Lansing was not impressed with what Masaryk told him at the meeting.

According to Masaryk's record of the audience, Lansing asked Masaryk whether the Czech troops could be used "as police for their Amer[ican] mission." Masaryk answered yes, but he stated two conditions. First, he would have to know how the U.S. government planned to get the American mission to the Bolsheviks (*sic*), and what was its purpose; and second, Czechoslovak relations with the Bolsheviks would have to be settled peacefully.[51]

Masaryk's two conditions could only have embarrassed Lansing. The secretary of state was talking about Wilson's projected economic relief commission of merchants, agricultural experts, labor advisers, Red Cross representatives, and agents of the Young Men's Christian Association. Such a commission could function only if it were protected by the Czechoslovak army, controlling the railroads and keeping open the door to Russia from the Far East. In view of the Russians' friendly attitude toward the Czechoslovak army, the latter could become a nucleus about which the Russians might rally and, possibly, become again a military factor in the war. But Masaryk was preoccupied with the question of recognition of the Bolsheviks as the government of Russia. To meet his first condition would have implied recognition of the Lenin government; and the second condition could not have been met at all. There was no way back for either side in the struggle between the Czechs and the Bolsheviks.

Masaryk also brought up the question of the Austrian Slavs and Lansing's May 29 declaration, suggesting that a more definite statement of support for the subject peoples in Austria-Hungary be issued by the U.S. government. Masaryk's criticism of U.S. policy with regard to the subject nationalities in the Habsburg empire was, however, out of date. Since the declaration of May 29, the U.S. position had already been revised in Lansing's June 24 letter of Mihajlović.[52]

At their meeting, Masaryk had an additional embarrassment for the secretary of state: he asked Lansing to forward a memorandum to Chicherin, the Soviet commissar of foreign affairs. The memorandum was sent by the State Department to Chicherin "at Dr. Masaryk's expense" and "not through American diplomatic channels" to Moscow.[53]

The communication to Chicherin was Masaryk's own reaction to an interview with the commissar by an Associated Press reporter.

> In the interview... you explain your hostile attitude towards our Czechoslovak troops in Russia by saying that they have been counter-revolutionary since the days of the Kiev Rada [Central Council], and that they even conspired against the Soviet government.... I was in Russia since May 1917 till March 1918; I organized the troops, I know every detail of their life during this period; with the full knowledge of all circumstances I must state that your assertion is incorrect, and that you are mistaken.... I can prove by incontrovertible documents that I rejected every plan directed against your government submitted to me by your political adversaries; even of such adversaries who justly could not be called counter-revolutionist. I can prove that until lately I recommended to the Allies' statesmen to be on good terms with your government. We Czecho-Slovaks love Russia, and we wish her to be a strong and free democracy....
> We have been absolutely loyal to Russia and correct in our attitude toward your government; in recognition of this loyalty Commander Muraviev granted our army free passage to France (February 16), and the same has been granted by the Soviets of Moscow. Being away from Russia three months, and having no detailed reports, I

dare not express an opinion on what is happening now. It seems that some local soviet yielded to the Austrian and German intrigue [sic] and attacked our troops, who under given circumstances have been forced to defend themselves. I would not oppose your demand for disarmament if you can guarantee us free and unmolested passage to France. I assure you our soldiers' only wish is to fight the common enemy and help, by that, Russia. I ask you in the name of democracy to keep the promise given by your own commander. Please investigate the matter, for it would be a disgraceful absurdity that a democratic and socialist government should by mistake promote the interests of its greatest enemies.[54]

This quoted document, as well as his conversation with Lansing, clearly indicates that Masaryk was inadequately informed about the situation in Russia and that he misunderstood both the nature of the Soviet regime and its objectives. He failed to take Lenin for what he really was: a professional revolutionary who was fully committed to the cause of world revolution. While Masaryk assumed that Germany was the "common enemy," Moscow did not see it that way. After all, Germany had granted international recognition to the Lenin regime and signed the peace treaty with it. (Lenin had expected a lot from Germany: a proletarian revolution that would spark off the world revolution.) Masaryk's concept of democracy was not the same as that of the Bolsheviks, who understood "democracy" to mean the dictatorship of the proletariat, which always is in reality the dictatorship of their party, the party of a "new type." At the end of June 1918, Masaryk still insisted on the transfer of the Czechoslovak army to France. One month after the life-or-death struggle started, he was still willing to agree to the disarming of the Czechoslovak army by the Soviet government. Masaryk's views on the situation were diametrically opposed to those of the TEC, which reflected the opinion of the troops in Russia. His views also differed from those of the Entente statesmen and diplomats who saw the Bolsheviks as allies and tools of Germany.

On June 25, the day Lansing conferred with Masaryk, the U.S. consul at Vladivostok sent two telegrams to the secretary of state. In one of them he reported that two principal members of the CSNC at Vladivostok had met with the Allied consuls and said that the 15,000 Czech troops in the city must return west to assist their fellows. They needed arms and ammuntion, and these they requested from the Allies, together with a supporting Allied armed force. The Czechs needed 13,000 rifles, three mounted batteries, 100 machine guns, and 1,000,000 cartridges, "and should be supported by from 50 to 100,000 Allied troops, to establish permanent front against Germany."[55] If intervention were to be undertaken, the Czechs spokesmen said, advantage should be taken of the Czechs's holding a large section of the railway; and the action "must be begun here within three weeks." In the second telegram, also received by Lansing on June 26, the U.S. consul reported that the Czechs had abandoned evacuation via Archangel, and that their force was "splendidly adequate *nucleus* [emphasis added] for a new Siberian army." With Allied support "an army of minimum 200,000 [could] be organized in Siberia" to operate against the Germans in European Russia. This might bring Russia also back into the war; and the consul "strongly urged" consideration of "this plan as conceivably offering quick and effective aid Allied cause." When, four days later, the Vladivostok Soviet decided to dispatch war material westward to be used, apparently, against their comrades, the Czechs disbanded the soviet and took over the city.

Beneš, in Paris, who, unlike Masaryk, had "no connection with the army in Russia," agreed to the use of the Legion in an intervention, should one be decided upon.[56] He did not hesitate to put the Legion at the disposal of the Allies "where it was needed most," knowing that they would, one day, make decisions about the existence or nonexistence of the Czechoslovak state and its government. For him consent to Czech participation in an intervention was "a matter of tactics; what really counts is what we shall gain by it politically."[57] Furthermore, the Legion was already "intervening;" it had made the break with Masaryk's neutralist policy anyway. Now Beneš tried to make the best of it. In his message home early in July he wrote, "We are playing the foremost part in the Siberian intervention and . . . you will see that within a short time we shall have the leading role [in it] both militarily and politically . . . ."[58]

After Beneš expressly endorsed the Czechoslovak Legion's role in the intervention, Masaryk was the only one of the triumvirate (Masaryk-Beneš-Štefánik) who was out of step. Štefánik had disapproved Masaryk's neutralist policy already in February 1918. At that time, in connection with the French plan of having the Czechoslovak army corps transferred to the Romanian front, Major Štefánik (a temporary rank) was promoted to Lieutenant Colonel (also a temporary rank), was made an aide to General Janin, the commander in chief of the Czechoslovak army, and received orders to go to Jassy, Romania, on February 11, 1918.[59] But Masaryk refused to cooperate with the Allies; the Czechoslovak army did not go to the Romanian front, and, therefore, Štefánik's mission to Romania did not materialize.

On July 1, 1918, Basil Miles notified Lansing of the arrival of a telegram from Vladivostok giving details about the equipment and condition of the Czechoslovaks there, and handed a copy of the telegram to Chief of Staff General Peyton C. March.[60] The telegram stated that the morale of the Czechoslovak forces at Vladivostok was "magnificent," but that they had only 2,500 rifles, 26 machine guns, 586,000 cartridges, 1,800 hand grenades, and no other arms or ammunition for the 14,000 men and 5,000 officers. They needed at least 13,000 rifles and other weapons, in addition to medical supplies and other equipment. If the Allies assured them of help, they would wait for its arrival; otherwise they would go back to Siberia to help their countrymen there with 2,500 men for whom arms were available. They would welcome an Allied armed force; and they especially needed the assistance of railroad engineers for repair work. General March had already informed his superiors that he could procure 13,000 Russian rilfes and one million rounds of ammunition, and, if the president decided to help the Czechoslovaks, he might "possibly find some machine guns for them." The material would be brought to Vladivostok on American naval vessels. The general, however, believed that military intervention would be "hazardous, extremely difficult, and unsound policy."[61]

The success of an Allied intervention in Russia would depend, to a great extent, on the U.S. government's endorsement and its willingness to contribute troops for that purpose. The Czechoslovak victories throughout Siberia were used by the Entente statesmen and by the Allied Supreme War Council as support for their appeals to President Wilson to endorse an Allied intervention in Siberia and Russia.

On July 3, 1918, Secretary Lansing was informed that the "Czecho-Slovaks have taken possession of Vladivostok."[62] One day earlier, on July 2, the U.S. diplomatic liaison officer wired to the secretary of state[63] that the Supreme War Council considered Allied intervention in Russia and Siberia "an urgent and imperative necessity" in view of the complete change in the situation since its last meeting. "In the first place," the telegram stated,

> the recent action of the Czecho-Slovak troops has transformed the Siberian eclipse. There is now a force of 50,000 troops, of Slav nationality, totally disinterested in internal politics of Russia... in control of the railway in western Siberia. This success of the Czechoslovak troops proves that the bulk of the Siberian population are no longer sympathetic to the Bolsheviks and must be friendly disposed to the Allied cause. It also removes the apprehension that Allied intervention will meet... serious opposition from the local population east of the Urals.... Provided intervention takes place in time, there will be a Slav army in western Siberia to which Russian patriots can rally.... This Czecho-Slovak force, however, is in grave danger of being cut off by the organization of German and Austro-Hungarian prisoners of war at Irkutsk, and an appeal for immediate military assistance has been made by the Czech National Council to the Allied consuls at Vladivostok. The Allies are under the responsibility of taking immediate action, if these gallant allies are not to be overwhelmed. To fail in bringing support to these faithful troops, now desperately fighting for the Allied cause, would not only forever discredit the Allies, but might have a disastrous effect on the Slav population both of Russia itself and of Austria-Hungary and the Balkans as proving that the Allies are unable or unwilling to exert themselves effectively to save the Slav world from falling wholly under German domination.... Intervention in Siberia, therefore, is an urgent necessity both to save the Czecho-Slovaks and to take advantage of an opportunity of gaining control of Siberia for the Allies which may never return....[64]

The Supreme War Council urged intervention for three reasons: (1) to help the Czechoslovaks, (2) "to save Russia from the establishment of autocracy supported by German bayonets," and (3) because it was "essential in order to win the war."[65] The communication of the Supreme War Council and a memorandum by the secretary of state were discussed at a White House conference on July 6, 1918. The Lansing memorandum of July 4, 1918,[66] shows clearly how the actions of the Czechoslovak army had substantially changed the situation in Siberia: "The capture of Vladivostok on June 29th by the Czecho-Slovaks and the success of their fellow-countrymen in western Siberia have materially changed the situation, by introducing a sentimental element into the question of our duty." The United States has the responsibility to render them aid, because a failure to do so might lead to their defeat and this country would be blamed for it. "This responsibility is increased and made almost imperative because they are being attacked by released Germans and Austrians."

Lansing suggested the following policy: First, immediately to aid "these loyal troops by furnishing the 15,000 at Vladivostok with arms, artillery, ammunition and supplies...so that they can proceed westward to aid the 50,000 west of Irkutsk." Second, to send troops "to assist them in policing the railroad as they advance" and to help them disarm "the Germans and Austrians who oppose them," because there is "a moral obligation to save these men from our common enemies...." Third, though most of the troops would be supplied by Japan, to include some U.S. and Allied troops also. Fourth, to announce "this intended assistance" and to notify "the Czecho-Slovaks at Vladivostok and in western Siberia" about it immediately. At the same time to issue a declaration that the Allies have "no intention to interfere with internal affairs of Russia;" that "in no event will the territory of Russia be occupied for a longer time than is necessary to prevent German domination;" and that after the expeditionary forces have accomplished their mission, "the territory and sovereignty of Russia...will be as complete and unimpaired as they were before the troops entered upon Russian soil." Fifth, to send a commission to Vladivostok "with the announced purpose of assisting...the Russian people by restoring normal conditions of trade, industry and social order....This commission should proceed westward from Vladivostok following...the Czecho-Slovaks."

Clearly, Lansing favored an intervention in Russia, urged the president to send military help to the Czechoslovaks and also Allied military forces, and proposed the pacification of Siberia as far west as possible. General March, on the other hand, opposed military intervention, and so did Masaryk. It is not possible to determine how much the Czech leader's opposition to intervene against the Bolsheviks influenced Wilson. We know, however, that at the White House conference held on July 6, 1918, proposals for restoration of the Eastern Front against the Central Powers was rejected.

According to Lansing's memorandum of the conference, the latter discussed the communication of the Supreme War Council "favoring an attempt to restore an eastern front against the Central Powers; and also a memorandum by the Secretary of State." It decided, first, "that the establishment of an eastern front through a military expedition, even if it was wise to employ a large Japanese force, is physically impossible though the front was established east of the Ural Mountains;" second, "that under present conditions any advance westward of Irkutsk does not seem possible and needs no further consideration;" third, "that the present situation of the Czecho-Slovaks requires this Government and other governments to make an effort to aid those at Vladivostok in forming a junction with their compatriots in western Siberia;" and fourth, "that in view of the inability of the United States to furnish any considerable force within a short-time to assist the Czecho-Slovaks," the Japanese government should furnish "small arms, machine guns, and ammunition to the Czecho-Slovaks at Vladivostok," provided the Japanese government agreed to cooperate. In addition, a military force of some 7,000 Americans and 7,000 Japanese should be assembled in Vladivostok to guard the lines of communication of the Czechoslovaks proceeding toward Irkutsk.

In addition, avaliable forces from the American and Allied naval vessels should land in Vladivostok, hold the city, and cooperate with the Czechoslovaks. Finally, the conference agreed, "[(d) The public announcement by this and Japansese Governments that the purpose of landing troops is to aid Czecho-Slovaks against German and Austrian prisoners, that there is no purpose to interfere with internal affairs of Russia, and that they guarantee not to impair the political or territorial sovereignty of Russia;] (e) To await further developments before taking further steps."[67]

While, on July 6, the American government decided that the establishmen of an Eastern Front was "physically impossible" and took a wait-and-see attitude toward developments in Russia, on the same day, the Penza and Cheliabinsk groups of the Czechoslovaks established a junction in the Ural mountains. As they had already established contacts with the Gajda group at Omsk on June 10, the whole Trans-Siberian Railway up to Irkutsk was thus occupied by the Czechoslovaks. On July 7, Colonel Ček received an order from Colonel Vojtsekhovskii, who, in the absence of General Dieterichs, was the chief of staff of the army corps, to defend the Volga front until the arrival of the Allied armies. On the same day

Čeček issued the following historic order of the commander of the rear guard of the Czechoslovak corps: "Notify all brothers that in conformity with the decision of the Congress of the Army Corps and our National Council, and with the concurrence of the Allies, our Corps has been made the advance guard of the Allied Forces. The instructions issued by the Staff of the Army Corps aim at the establishment of an anti-German front in Russia in conjunction with the whole Russian people and our Allies."[68] The order issued by Čeček, his superiors, and the Congress of the Army Corps was based on information and instructions from French official circles.[69] While the French and British governments favored restoring the Eastern Front, the White House had ruled it out on the grounds that it was "physically impossible." But, Čeček and his comrades in arms in Russia and Siberia did not know that.

The Czechoslovaks had reasons to be optimistic. On July 6, 1918, an anti-Soviet uprising took place at Yaroslav, and anti-Soviet governments, largely Social Revolutionary in their composition, were established in Siberia, Samara, and the Ural region. The left-wing Socialist Revolutionaries even attempted to take power in Moscow. On July 4 and 5, at the Fifth Congress of Soviets, they demanded the restoration of hostilities with Germany, and on July 6, after the assassination attempt on Count Mirbach, the German ambassador at Moscow, they captured the central telephone office and announced their assumption of power. Reacting to these developments, Commander Muraviev, whose troops were fighting units of the Czechoslovak army in the Volga region, changed the front to Moscow. On the next day, however, the left-wing Socialist Revolutionaries participating in the congress were arrested, centers of anti-Bolshevik resistance in Moscow were suppressed, and Muraviev committed suicide.[70] The Red front against the Czechs was restored. Irkutsk was taken by Gajda's units on July 11, "practically without resistance," as the U.S. consul at Irkutsk, Harris, reported to the secretary of state.[71] In his words, the city had been "completely terrorized" by anarchists, Bolsheviks, and Red Guards "until within a few hours of the time when the Czech and Cossack cavalry entered." The Czechs and Cossacks were "received with enthusiasm by the people. As if by magic, law and order were established and the streets became crowded with every class of society exceedingly happy at having been rescued from Bolshevik rule. The White Guard took over policing the city and the former local Duma assumed charge of the municipal government;" life returned to normalcy in every sense. The consul general expressed his happiness over "the passing of the Bolsheviks" and the Siberian people's "coming to themselves again." He paid tribute to a "handful of Czecho-Slovak soldiers, men of unparalleled courage, trained in the school of adversity, having always in mind the oppression of their own country, after fighting their way out of the hands of their Austro-Hungarian pursuers, after fighting their way out of the Ukraine, after being completely disarmed in the city of Penza, realizing that the time had come for action which meant to them liberty or death, they have, unaided by the assistance of the outside world, entirely dependent upon their own resources in the heart of a vast continent, and surrounded by enemies whose every act towards them means ruin, performed a deed which will live in history as long as the deeds of mankind shall be worthy of chronicling." In his view it was "absolutely necessary that the Czecho-Slovak troops should remain in Russia and not be sent to France as was originally intended," since "no one knows the frame of mind, customs, and habits of the Russian people better than the Czechs. They all speak Russian, and if their units are left unimpaired they will form the backbone of Allied intervention" and thus reestablish the Eastern Front. He pointed to Gajda's "carrying on an energetic campaign against the remaining Red Guard and Magyar prisoners of war" in order to open up the way to Vladivostok.[72]

Eventually, even Masaryk came to realize that, in the situation as it had development in Russia, the policy of noninvolvement had been abandoned by the troops and even by Beneš; and, above all, that stubborn insistence on it was a stumbling block in his efforts to obtain U.S. recognition of the CSNC. In July 1918, Masaryk received a communication from Vladivostok that made it clear to him that the whole Czechoslovak Legion was cooperating with the Allies, and that the troops sent back to Siberia were badly in need of weapons, ammunition, and other supplies. He mentioned the report of July 14 in a confidential enclosure to his July 20, 1918, request for U.S. recognition of the CSNC as "the representative of the future Government of the Czecho-Slovak free state."[73] Masaryk wrote that "this recognition has become practically necessary; I dispose of three armies (in Russia, France, and Italy), I am, as a wit said, the master of Siberia and half Russia, and yet I am in the United States formally a private man." In the first part of the "confidential" enclosure to this memorandum Masaryk described "the international position of our army," stating that the army in Russia "has been sustained first by the old regime, then by the Provisional Government, for some time by the Ukrainian Rada, and in the test phase even by the Bolshevik Government." In the second part of the enclosure he discussed how the Bolsheviks broke "the agreement" and attacked the army, "acting in bad faith against the principle of democracy," and asserted that this "explains the war between the Bolshevik Government and our army in Russia and Siberia." According to "all reports from Siberia and Russia," the Czechoslovak troops never attacked the Bolsheviks and "only defended themselves having been attacked, often in a very treacherous manner." He regretted to say that the Bolshevik government "proves to be more than weak against the German and Austrian aggression," and that he "no longer can believe in the Bolshevik Government's loyalty toward the Allies." Still paying lip service to "no interfering in the internal (administrative) affairs of the country," he pointed out that "our army, fighting the Germans and Austrians must fight those Russian troops and parties which are united with the Germans and Austrians against the Allies."

In the third part of the enclosure Masaryk asked for help for the Czechoslovak army in Russia and Siberia. In a rather lengthy and characteristic fashion, he, as "President of our National Council to whom the army in Russia has sworn allegiance," asked for arms and ammunition "in sufficient quantities for continued fighting in regular battles" without specifying their kind and numbers. In view of the long distance from the Allies countries to Siberia, Masaryk suggested that "the first supplies" could be provided by Japan. He asked that Vladivostok be occupied "by an Allied detachment" so that "a considerable part of our unit in Vladivostok can be despatched West."

Needless to say, Masaryk was several weeks behind the actual developments. The Allies had already landed at Vladivostok and the Czech troops for whom weapons were available had gone back to Siberia. As soon as the first request for weapons arrived from Vladivostok on June 29, as has been pointed out above, General March expressed his willingness to procure for the Czechs 13,000 rifles, some machine guns, and ammunition for both, if the president approved of giving the Czechs military assistance. In his communication Masaryk complained that "it is the state of indecision which we feel badly;" and that he was "prevented from giving clear and definite orders to our troops." Yet if anyone was responsible for the "indecision," it was Masaryk. The troops did not need his "clear and definite orders;" they had already rejected his neutralist policy two months earlier. The help that they needed most was denied to them by the stubborn insistence of Masaryk that they should "negotiate" with the Bolsheviks, not fight them, and by his offer to Chicherin that the Czechs would disarm if the Soviets guaranteed them a free departure to France. But even on July 20 Masaryk still wished the whole army to be sent to France; however, he conceded that "under given circumstances we wish to make the best possible use of our army to the benefit of Russia and the Allies." As "the simplest expedient" Masaryk proposed "to despatch a Japanese unit of about two divisions, to cooperate with the smaller Allied units."

It may well be argued that had Masaryk asked for Allied help for the troops at least one month earlier, rather than offering to surrender arms to the Soviets in his message to Chicherin, the help would have been already under way and the White House would have made a different decision about intervention and the use of the Czechoslovaks as a nucleus for all Allied forces in Russia and Siberia. Now, in order to maintain his political leadership and to be able to act as the spokesman for the Czechoslovak army, he endorsed and captialized on its action while asking for American recognition of his council "as the representative of the future Government of the Czecho-Slovak free state."

It is rather obvious why Masaryk injected himself into the situation; it is less obvious what his motives were for consistently urging that the Allies send Japanese troops to Siberia and transfer the Czech troops to France, and why he failed to ask for specific weapons and equipment for the Legionnaires even after the U.S. government approved credits for his council. In contrast to Masaryk, the Russian spokesmen in the United States saw a danger in sending a large Japanese force to Siberia. They insisted that the Allied troops sent to Russia and Siberia be under an Ameican supreme commander and that Japan publicly renounce any territorial claim to parts of Siberia. The American government agreed with this view; its official position on this issue was communicated to the British, French, Italian, and Chinese Allies on July 26, 1918. The U.S. government urged that all powers contributing forces for an action in Russia and Siberia assure "the people of Russia in the most public and solemn manner that none of the governments uniting in action either in Siberia or in northern Russia contemplate any interference of any kind with the political sovereignty of Russia, any intervention in her internal affairs, or any impairment of her territorial integrity either now or hereafter, but that each associate power has the single object of affording such aid as shall be acceptable, to the Russian people in their endeavour to regain control of their own affairs, their own territory, and their own destiny."[74]

Whereas the U.S. government opposed any impairment of Russia's territorial integrity, Masaryk considered "paying the Japanese" with Russian territories. Whereas the U.S. government was making available military supplies for the Czechs in Siberia, for several weeks Masaryk did not let any American official know exactly what was needed. As late as September 16, 1918, Bernard Baruch wrote to the president that he could not get "either from Professor Masaryk or anyone else accurate information as to what was desired." On the next day President Wilson notified Baruch that he had made available from a special fund $1,500,000 for the purpose of sending the Czechoslovaks all the supplies that Baruch had mentioned in his letter of the previous day. On that same day, September 17, Breckinridge Long asked Masaryk to come to his home. In their conversations he suggested that Masaryk should not talk merely to Baruch, but should deal with the proper authorities in the U.S. government, who could procure materials for the troops in Siberia, using the credits that had been made available by the U.S. government to his council. Masaryk, though he paid lip service to the needs of the troops, indicated no interest in the "nuts and bolts" aspects of the military operations of the Czechoslovak army in Siberia. He told Long, however, that the non-German population of the Central Powers was like "the negro of America, in that they were the slaves and servants of the Germans." That was hardly true. He also claimed that the establishment of an independent states, "Poland, Bohemia, Roumania, etc.—would remove all cause of war from Europe by releasing those 160,000,000 of peoples for independent and constructive work instead of keeping them repressed and under hostile influences."[75]

Because of space limitations, it is not feasible to dwell here on Masaryk's other statements; the above statements show, however, that Masaryk was not eager to get the needed weapons and reinforcements from the Allied countries on whose behalf the Czechoslovaks were fighting.

He tenaciously insisted on the army's transfer to France and the sending of a large Japanese force to Russia, and on a Japanese command over the Allied forces in Russia and Siberia.

On July 21, 1918, Masaryk sent greetings to the Czechoslovaks in Siberia and Russia, assuring them that he was "very satisfied" with their conduct and that they would get help. For the time being they had to remain in Russia and, with the help of the Allies, fight the common enemy there.[76] In this and future telegrams to the troops, Masaryk claimed that the fight was, and had to be, "against Austrians and Germans and also against those Russian troops and detachments which unite themselves with Austrians and Germans against the Allies." Warning against making political arrangements with monarchists and reactionaries, Masaryk repeatedly emphasized that "our enemies in Russia" were Hungarians, Austrians, and Germans, and from among Russians "only those individuals, fractions or parties which against the interests of Russia are joining our enemies against our friends and against us. Our army is democratic and serves democratic aims."[77]

Masaryk expressly approved the anti-Bolshevik action taken by the soldiers in his messages to them on July 21 and August 1, 1918. He also realized the tremendous political value of the valiant army that had stood up against those who had "treacherously attacked it," to whom it had been "loyal" and to whom it had done "only good."[78] In his August 1, 1918, order to the Czechoslovak army in Russia, he said, "You have done strictly your duty imposed on you by your conscience and our national program; you did go, and you are going in the life-and-death struggle for freedom and independence of your nation as well as other nations."[79] He had changed his position 180 degrees. Masaryk applauded the "heroic deeds" of the soldiers and praised their will and sharp vision," which destroyed the "plans of the enemy." He expressed his confidence in the troops and their commander, General Dieterichs, and he notified them that "in view of circumstantial developments, you will stay in Russia for the time being and you shall fight in accord with the Allies."[80]

The Czechoslovaks did fight in accord with *some* of the Allies. The launching of their offensive was undertaken on the assumption that an immediate and effective Allied intervention would take place. The Russian Socialist Revolutionaries, who cooperated with the Czechs, proceeded from the same assumption. As one of their leaders, V. I. Lebedev, noted in his diary: "The Allies (through their representatives) promised to send a landing force to Archangel and to Siberia via Vladivostok. . . . All our calculations rested on this. Briefly, our plan was as follows: insurrection in the Volga region, capture of Kazan, Simbirsk, Samara, Saratov; mobilization beyond this line; landing of an Allied force at Archangel; and movement towards Vologda to join with the Volga front. . . . Under such conditions not only anti-Bolsheviks but even those sympathizing with the Soviets wouldhave to choose between an alliance with Germany against all the Russian democratic parties and an alliance with us against Imperial Germany which had seized half of European Russia."[81] The Czechs and their Russian allies firmly believed that the Allies were coming to their aid in order to restore the Eastern Front; and the Czech move on Ekaterinburg, captured on July 25, was undertaken in expecation of speedy and effective Allied support.

Before the Czechs reached the city, Tsar Nicholas II and his family were murdered on July 16, 1918. According to Trotsky, the decision to liquidate the royal family was made by Lenin, who believed that the Bolsheviks should not "leave the Whites a live banner to rally around," especially under the Bolshevik's difficult circumstances. In the words of Trotsky, "the decision was not only expedient by necessary. The severity of this summary justice showed the world that we would continue to fight on mercilessly, stopping at nothing. The execution of the Tsar's family was needed not only in order to frighten, horrify, and dishearten the enemy but also in order to shake up our own ranks, to show them that there was no turning back, that ahead lay either complete victory or complete ruin."[82]

The Czech offensive was undertaken on the basis of three assumptions: (1) that the military action could be easily accomplished; (2) that the Czech action would be merely auxiliary to an all-Russian uprising against the Bolshevik regime; and (3) that the Allies would send massive help to build the Eastern Front.[83] Therefore, Čeček, who commanded the units farthest west, Czech and Russian, attempted to join forces with General Denikin and the Cossack armies at Tsarytsyn (today's Volgograd), so that they could launch a joint offensive aimed at the capture of Moscow.[84] One may only speculate how different the situation might have been had Masaryk agreed to join the anti-Bolshevik forces, the Volunteer Army, several months earlier, or had the Czechs in May decided to march on Moscow jointly with the Whites rather than fight their way through Siberia to Vladivostok.

July was a difficult month for the Bolsheviks. Lenin fully realized the significance of the Volga front established by the Czechoslovaks and their Russian allies, the Samara government (or *Komuch* as it came to be called from the initials of its Russian name) that had been established by a group of seventy Socialist Revolutionary members of the disbanded Constituent Assembly and headed by Viktor Chernov. This government managed to build up a People's Army that by August 1918, numbered over 10,000. (Since the *Komuch* adopted the extreme program of the Left SRs, it denied itself the support of most of the prosperous farming population in the region.) Lenin released the danger signal on August 1, 1918, when he vehemently urged his coworkers on the (Bolshevik) eastern front to defeat Čeček's forces, saying: "Now the *whole* fate of the revolution is put on one card: a speedy victory over the Czechslovaks on the Kazan-Ural-Samara front. Everything depends on that."[85] Now, indeed, the Czechoslovak army threatened the very existence of the Bolshevik regime in Russia. A few months earlier, hand in hand with the Russian anti-Bolshevik forces, it would have had a much better chance to topple it.

CHAPTER FOURTEEN

THE QUEST FOR RECOGNITION, THE FIGHT
WITH THE BOLSHEVIKS, AND THE
LIMITED EXTENT OF ALLIED HELP

In his postwar writing Beneš deemphasized the anti-Bolshevik uprising of the Czechoslovak army in Russia and emphasized his own diplomatic activity as factors in the Allied decision to recognize the CSNC as the provisional government of a future Czechoslovak state.[1] However, he himself writes about his fruitless efforts to obtain recognition of the CSNC at Paris and London in May 1918, and about his disappointment with the Versailles declaration of June 3, 1918.[2] The Allied declaration called for the establishment of an independent and united Polish state, but it expressed only sympathy for the national aspirations of Czecho-Slovaks and Yugo-Slavs.

On June 4, 1918, Beneš renewed his negotiations with Orlando and Sonnino, who came to Paris. Noticing the favorable publicity given to the anti-Bolshevik action of the Legion in Russia and sensing a genuine interest in the Czechoslovak troops on the part of the French government, Beneš asked for French recognition on June 5, 1918. The French government was receptive to the idea, but it would have preferred to grant such a recognition by a joint declaration with Great Britain and the United States. The British indicated their willingness to reward the Czechs for their work in Russia, but President Wilson refused to make such a commitment.³ In view of Beneš's denial that the action of the Czechoslovak army in Russia and Siberia was the main factor in the Allied recognition, it is useful to quote Balfour's telegram to Lord Reading of June 5, 1918, in which, for the first time, the British government indicated its willingness to recongize the CSNC: "I have informed the Representative of the Czecho-Slovak National Council that H.M.G. are prepared to recognize the Council in the same manner as has been done by the French and Italian Governments and to accord to it the same political rights concerning civil affairs of Czecho-Slovaks as has been already conceded to the Polish National Committee. I am also assuring them that we recognize the Czecho-Slovak Army as an organized Unit operating in the Allied cause and will be prepared, when the advisability arises, to attach a British Liaison Officer thereto."⁴

The second half of the telegram was sent to British diplomatic representatives at Paris, Rome, and Washington: "Please inform Government to which you are accredited and explain [that] we have been obliged to take this action in view of not only the activity and cooperation being afforded to Czecho-Slovaks on Italian and Western Fronts but also of the fact that there are some 50,000 Czecho-Slovaks in Russia composed partly of Prisoners and Deserters whom we have every hope of organizing into an effective Force to combat the enemy in the Eastern or Western Theatres of War."⁵

The Allied governments realized the value of the Czechoslovak army's startling success. Czech control of the Trans-Siberian Railway prevented or at least hampered the shipment home of Austro-Hungarian and German prisoners of war, who could have been put in uniforms again on the Western and Italian fronts. The spectacular performance of the relatively small number of Czechoslovaks increased the prestige of the CSNC and made its claim to represent the wishes and desires of the Czechs and Slovaks more credible. Furthermore, the Allies came to recognize the value of an organization of Czechoslovaks outside Austria-Hungary as a factor contributing to the decline of morale of the non-German and non-Hungarian peoples in the Austrian empire. Thus, when in the middle of June 1918, the CSNC at Paris submitted to the French government a request for recognition of the existence of a Czechoslovak state and *de facto* recognition of the Czecho-Slovak National Council as the lawful government of that state, the French government gave it serious consideration and contacted the governments of England and the United States in order to find out their views on the subject.[6]

On June 18, 1918, Secretary of State Lansing cabled the U.S. ambassador in France that the British government was prepared to recognize the CSNC in the same manner as it had been recognized by the French and Italian governments, and requested all pertinent data on the CSNC and its recognition by the various governments.[7] The requested information was cabled back to the State Department on June 22. Most of the data came from Beneš who told the ambassador (a) that the British government had promised Beneš that it would recognize the council; (b) that the council had a representative in Washington, D.C.; (c) that Masaryk was in the United States; and (d) that Congressman Sabath of Illinois, formerly the ambassador's "colleague in Congress and a Bohemian by nationality, was in hearty sympathy with the purposes of the Council." Beneš also told the ambassador that the CSNC was formulating plans for placing Czechoslovak troops in Russia at the disposal of the Allies, and that 80,000 of these might be sent to France.[8] (Beneš's figures on the number of troops were too high.)

As has been noted earlier, the U.S. State Department was very sympathetic to the Czech cause, and on May 9, 1918, Albert H. Putney, chief of the Near Eastern Division in the State Department, submitted to the secretary of state a memorandum on "Slavs of Austria-Hungary," in which he argued that Bohemia had the right to be considered an independent country.[9] When the suggestion to use the Czechoslovak army, which had already revolted against the Bolsheviks, was brought to the attention of the president on June 13, 1918, Wilson replied: "There seems to me to emerge from this suggestion the shadow of a plan that might be worked, with Japanese and other assistance. These people [i.e., the Czechs and Slovaks] are cousins of the Russians."[10] As has been noted, at their meeting on June 19, Masaryk rejected Wilson's plan and insisted on transferring the troops to France. However, on June 27 the president approved Lansing's June 24 memorandum on Austria-Hungary.[11]

In this document Lansing wrote that "as long as there was a chance of entering into a separate peace with Austria-Hungary, it was wise and expedient to do so, even though it was contrary to the just claims of the nationalists within that Empire which sought independence." When the informal negotiations "were brought to an end by the unwise publication of the Prince Sixtus letter and the resulting declaration of the Emperor Karl of his loyalty to the German alliance... a new situation was presented." Lansing suggested that the president "declare without reservation for an independent Poland, an independent Bohemia and an independent Southern Slav State, and a return of the Romanian and Italians to their natural allegiances. That would mean "in effect the dismemberment of the present Austro-Hungarian Empire into its original elements, leaving these independent nationalities for form such separate states or federal states as they might themselves decide to form, especially if the severance of Austria and Hungary resulted." Claiming, though not quite correctly, that that state had been held together "chiefly by fear of the power and greed of the Russian Empire," he said that after the tsar was overthrown, "the dread of absorption by the Muscovite power disappeared and the desire for national independence became dominant." Lansing advocated the dismemberment of Austria-Hungary: "The entire surrender of the Dual Monarchy to the German Empire should remove all sympathy and compassion for the Habsburg rulers. They are not longer entitled to merciful considerate treatment since they have become vassals of the Hohenzollerns."

The declaration is very clear, and the president did indeed endorse the idea of independent Polish, Bohemian, and South Slavic states. He was not prepared, however, to recognize the Masaryk-led Czecho-Slovak National Council, as William Phillips, assistant secretary of state, had recommended. On June 25, 1918, Phillips submitted to Lansing a memorandum on "Recognition of the Czecho-Slovak National Council"[12] reporting that the State Department had been informed by the British embassy that the British government "are prepared to recognize the Czecho-Slovak National Council in 'the same manner as it had been recognized by the French and Italian Governments.'" The memorandum pointed out athat "the French Government has submitted to us a political program, embodying: (1) The recognition of the Czecho-Slovak State; and (2) The *de facto* recognition of the National Council of the Czecho-Slovak countries as constituting the lawful government of that state, including the granting of a loan, etc. The French desire to recognize the *de facto* existence of a Czech [sic] Nation with a national entity and to permit the Czech National Council to represent in France the political and administrative interests of the Czech Nation until it is able to adopt a final constitution." Phillips recommended that the United States "recognize the *de facto* existence of the Council and so advise the British, French and Italian Governments."

Although Lansing sympathized with the independence movement and recommended the dismemberment of Austria-Hungary and the establishment of an independent Czech state, he did not endorse Phillip's recommendation, and, despite the pressure from the Allies, especially France, to extend such a recognition, the president decided "not to give formal recognition at the present time to the Czecho-Slovak National Council."[13] There is no ironclad proof that Lansing advised the president against recognition because of Masaryk's refusal to allow the use of the Czechoslovak army in an intervention in Russia, but it is highly likely that Masaryk's pro-Bolshevik stance played a role in the U.S. refusal to recognize the CSNC in June, July, and August 1918. As has been noted earlier, despite Masaryk's anti-interventionist position and his advocacy of *de facto* recognition of the Bolsheviks as the government of Russia, Lansing was eager to help the Czechoslovak troops in Siberia. Like the other Allies, he recognized their importance there and endorsed their action, as did U.S. Ambassador Francis, stationed at Vologda. From the latter Lansing received a telegram on June 23, 1918, saying in part, "If Germans take Moscow they can advance to Vologda, and if Czechs are defeated or leave Russia, Soviet Government or Germany will control [the] Siberian railway and Allied missions here will be compelled to remove to Archangel."[14] As we have already seen, on June 25 Lansing asked Masaryk to consent to the use of the Czech troops in Russia for the protection of Wilson's projected American mission there. Masaryk replied that he would have to know the purpose of the mission and that it would have to be an American mission to the Bolshevik government.[15]

Notwithstanding Masaryk's unrealistic demands, when the Czech military leaders at Vladivostok decided to send help to their comrades in Siberia and asked for American assistance, Lansing rushed the news to the president with a purple tag marked "IMPORTANT."[16] Whether or not Masaryk was the main stumbling block to U.S. recognition of the CSNC is a matter of conjecture. However, the Czech historian, Antonín S. Kalina, in the first documented study on the recognition of the CSNC, arrived at the conclusion that Lansing was not satisfied with Masaryk during their second conversation on June 25, and that he advised the president against recognition, despite the urgings of the British and French.[17] Wilson and Lansing recognized the Czechs' right to independence, but did not recognize Masaryk as their spokesman. Masaryk's later claim that he had been able "step by step, to persuade the President and Mr. Lansing to accept our program," reflects his subjective judgment, not the objective reality behind the eventual U.S. decision to recognize the CSNC. That decision was made not because of, but in spite of, Masaryk. For that matter, the Lansing declaration of June 28, 1918, was not the result of Masaryk's representations, as he claims.[18]

On June 26, 1918, Masaryk submitted a memorandum to Lansing requesting a revision of the May 29 declaration "regarding the nationalistic aspirations for freedom of the Czecho-Slovaks and Jugo-Slavs."[19] This revision had already been made, on June 24, as Lansing's reply to the June 14 letter of the Serbian minister, Mihailović, indicates. In his reply Lansing used a sentence later incorporated into the June 28 U.S. public declaration on the Slavic peoples, asserting that "all members of the Slavic race must be completely liberated from the Austrian yoke."[20] While this declaration improved considerably the position of the CSNC, the incident shows that Masaryk did not follow closely the development of American diplomacy and that he did not realize, at this time, the importance of the Czechoslovak action in Russia and Siberia. It was for that action that the U.S. government was prepared to reward his council by recognizing it as the representative of the Czech nation.

The decision not to recognize the CSNC was made on June 29, 1918. On that day Lansing wrote to Wilson that the French ambassador was "anxiously waiting" an expression of American views regarding the Czecho-Slovak National Council so that its position could be "fully established" on July 1, "when the President of France takes part in an important ceremony at which the Council will be formally recognized by the French Government."[21] In another letter of that day Lansing wrote to the president that "the Allies are constantly seeking to have us act jointly with them in political matters," but he believed that "to keep our hands free and to act independently is our best policy, since we can in that way avoid taking sides in the conflict of interests."[22] After a telephone conversation with the president, the secretary of state notified the French government that the president had not authorized recognition of the CSNC.[23]

Quest for Recognition 383

Although the French government would have preferred joint recognition, Wilson's refusal prevented that from happening. Still, on June 29, 1918, the French foreign minister, Pichon, sent Beneš a letter in which he solemnly declared, in the name of the French government, that France "considers as just and necessary to declare the right of your nation on independence and publicly and officially recognize the Czecho-Slovak National Council as the supreme organ administering the interests of the nation and as the first foundation of the future Czechosloak government." Pichon expressed his "most sincere and warmest wish" that the Czechoslovak state, by a joint effort of all the Allies and in close connection with Poland and the South Slavic state, would become "an unsurmountable barrier against German attacks and a factor for peace in Europe."[24] On the same day the president of the French republic delivered the flag to the Czechoslovak army in France and gave a lengthy and emotionally charged speech.[25] In his June 29 telegram to the secretary of state, the French foreign minister notified Lansing that France recognized the CSNC "as the supreme organization of the Czecho-Slovak movement in the Entente countries" and declared that "it will support in all earnestness the aspirations to independence for which its soldiers are fighting in the ranks of the Allies."[26]

The French recognition did not imply an Allied commitment either to dismember Austria-Hungary or to establish a Czechoslovak state, but merely reflected French appreciation of what the Czechoslovak army had done for the Allies in Russia and Siberia. The army had acted as *deux ex machina* for the projected intervention, and the troops were notified about their role in the Allied intervention, though prematurely, when Major Guinet communicated to them the thanks of Allies for "the reestablishment of the Russian front" on June 21, 1918.[27] Pichon's June 29 letter was described by Beneš in his July 8 report to Prague as "the greatest political success" that the CSNC had had till then, as "the total recognition of all our rights and demands; it is a complete victory."[28]

After his victory in France, Beneš attempted to win another one in Britian, but the Foreign Office was not very cooperative. Beneš's request for recognition of the sovereignty of the CSNC was seen as a "very novel idea,"[29] —as it was, since the new political entity that the CSNC proposed to represent had no clearly defined territory, and the territory, claimed by the CSNC was under the suzerainty of another recognized power. Lewis Namier in the Foreign Office also doubted the wisdom of establishing a new precedent by recognizing the CSNC, headed by Masaryk, since he was not sure what the Czechs at home would think about it.[30] The British knew quite well that Kramář, the leader of the home resistance, had been Masaryk's principal opponent before the war. Masaryk's recommendation that the Allies recognize the Bolshevik regime as a *de facto* government of Russia, and his refusal to consent to the use of the army in an intervention, were in accord neither with Allied policy nor with Kramář's pro-Russian and anti-Bolshevik views. While the French and British urged the United States to take part in the anti-Bolshevik intervention, and while the Czechoslovak troops, against Masaryk's publicly stated policy, were locked in a life-and-death struggle with the Bolsheviks, Masaryk still opposed Allied intervention in Russia and Siberia.

On July 1, 1918, British Secretary of Foreign Affairs Balfour wrote a letter to Minister Pichon that his government "joined fully in the sentiments so remarkably expressed in the speech of the President" at the flag ceremony (the president followed the same line as Minister Pichon).[31] Balfour not only publicly expressed sympathy with the French government's decision, but also appeared publicly with Beneš at a demonstration of Yugoslavs in London on July 25, and admitted that since Austria-Hungary had become a vassal of Germany, central European problems could no longer be solved without the help of the nations of Austria. Beneš had concrete proposals concerning how these nations could help the Allied cause and what, specifically, he and the CSNC demanded. In his lengthy memorandum to the British government[32] he proceeded from the assumption that Czechoslovak independence had been officially recognized by France and that the CSNC was considered by France to be the first foundation of the national government. As he put it, the secretary general of the CSNC, was being invited to take part in official acts in the same way as representatives of independent states. Furthermore, the council directed three armies, in France, Italy, and Russia, and exercised with respect to those armies executive powers possessed only by real governments.

In practice, however, the situation was not that simple, since the CSNC was only half-soverign with respect to the armies, and this fact was preventing the unification of the whole Czechslovak independence movement.

Quest for Recognition 385

For example, Beneš wrote, the CSNC would like to unite the Czechoslovak army in Italy with that in France, but the Italian government wanted to keep the Czechoslovak national army in Italy under its own control. The CSNC, being only half-sovereign, did not have sufficient strength and support to demand that the army should belong exclusively to it. Beneš emphasized the advantage of increased sovereignty of the CSNC with respect to the disposition of the whole army in the war with Germany. He asked that, in order to strengthen the effectiveness and the morale of the Czechslovak army in Russia for the intervention already under way, the Allies not dispose of the Czechoslovak armies in either Italy or Russia without consulting the CSNC. Although the CSNC insisted on its goal of transporting the troops from Russia to the Western Front, he wrote, it now wanted to keep them, in agreement with England and France, "temporarily in Russia." It would therefore send the supreme commander of the Czechoslovak armies, General Janin, with General Štefánik, to Russia so that they could consolidate the Czechoslovak forces there, "subordinate the whole Czechoslovak army to a systematic action," and thus prepare the "intervention in a decisive manner." After their task was completed, they could direct the transportation of the troops to western Europe. All this required, however, that the CSNC "receives a real *governing sovereignty*."[33] This was the price that Beneš asked for the CSNC's endorsement of the Czechoslovak army's "intervention" and for its becoming the advance guard of the Allied forces in Russia.

Among other reasons why the British should grant complete recognition of the CSNC, Beneš listed the following: that recognition would encourage the national liberation movements in the Austro-Hungarian monarchy; that the Czechoslovak troops had rendered a special service to England, in preventing the Germans from reaching Persia, Afghanistan, and India via Russia; that the Czechoslovak action in Siberia and Russia had created, according to the prevailing opinion in France, the possibility that both the United States and Japan could be persuaded to intervene massively in Russia; and that since there was no Czechoslovak army in England, England could take the initiative in recognizing the belligerency of the army ("exceeding 100,000" and thus no longer capable of being considered a goup of traitors and rebels) and its government.

Beneš also pointed out in this memorandum that he had asked the Czech political leaders to establish a national council there, to be part of the National Council seated at Paris. He urged this Prague council to consider itself as a provisional government of the Czech lands and as a part of the CSNC at Paris. The establishment on July 13 of the Czech National Committee at Prague (headed by Kramář) was, Beneš said in his memorandum, the fulfillment of this instruction. According to him, it would be a terrible blow to Austria if the CSNC were recognized as a government.[34]

In his memorandum to the British government Beneš overstated the strength of the Czechoslovak army; he also exaggerated its strength in his statement on political and economic conditions in the Balkans, submitted to the U.S. ambassador in Paris on July 11, 1918. Together with the statement, Beneš handed the ambassador maps showing the locations of the different peoples of Europe, the relative size of their territories, location of principal railways, etc.; on these maps he marked the areas inhabited by Slavic peoples as much larger than was true at the time. Beneš demanded complete separation of "his people" and the dismemberment of the monarchy. His estimate of the Czechoslovak troops in Russia and Siberia was too high—"from 80,000 to 90,000"; and, despite his later statement to the contrary, Beneš could not have been unaware of his exaggeration.[35] His claim, however, was believable; the ambassador pointed at the almost daily reports of the achievements of the Czech forces as "proof of his statements."[36]

The army in Russia and Siberia was the CSNC's best credential; and both Beneš and Masaryk knew it. As Masaryk wrote in his book, "Even sober-minded political and military men ascribed great military importance to our command of the railway. Ludendorff induced the German Government to protest to the Bolshevists, alleging that the march of our men had prevented the German prisoners from returning home to strengthen the Germany army."[37] Here Masaryk corroborates the testimony of General Gajda, according to whom, "the colossal, several hundred thousand-man strong army of prisoners of war, already on its way to Germany, was stopped at the exact time when the Germans, developing their utmost efforts, were throwing their last units on the French front. This deprived Germany of tremendous reserves. Also, the economic plans of the German general staff... especially the exploitation of economic and mineral riches in the Ural region and in Siberia, were suddenly frustrated. . . . Thus our military assistance to the Entente regained for us our independence."[38]

On the home front the defeats of the Central Powers in the summer of 1918 helped to shape the attitudes of the Czech political leaders. Beneš had informed the *Maffie* on June 14, 1918, that the independence movement abroad had espoused noninvolvement in Russian affairs so that Czech soldiers "would not fight against a certain group of Russians," and that the army was, on the whole, being saved for the Allied front in France.[39] The *Maffie*, however, had its own intelligence network in Galicia, built by a Slovene, Dr. Kavčić, which supplied both the Slovenian and the Czech secret committees with information on events in Russia. Through their Polish contacts, Kramář, Švehla, and Rašín, among others, learned about the Czechoslovak uprising against the Bolsheviks, their march through Siberia, and the national (White) Russian armies in Russia.[40]

In his messages home Beneš emphasized Czechoslovak diplomatic and political successes abroad and urged the Czech leaders not to denounce the Czech political leadership in France under any circumstances; he encouraged them to cooperate with it. The failure to win the war, especially the collapse of the Austrian offensive against Italy in June 1918, was interpreted by Czech politicians, as well as by politicians of other non-German and non-Hungarian natinalities in the empire, as a symptom of weakness; and they began to express publicly in the Austrian parliament their opposition to the continuation of the monarchy. Expecting the military defeat of Austria-Hungary and the victory of the Entente powers, Czech political leaders restored the National Committee on July 13, 1918. This became the official organ of the national independence movement at home. It was composed of representatives of political parties, with seats allocated according to the results of the last prewar election in 1911. In this committee the Agrarians had eight representatives; the Social Democrats, seven; Kramář's Czech State Right Democracy, five; the National Socials, four; the Catholics, four; and the Old Czechs and Realists, one each. An additional eight members were selected without regard to party affiliation, and seats in the committee were reserved for future representatives of the Slovaks. K. Kramář was the chairman, A. Švehla and V. Klofáč were vice-chairmen, and F. Soukup was the secretary. The National Committee declared its program on July 13, 1918, stating, among other things, that the "mission of the Czechoslovak National Committee at Prague is postulated by the demand of these times" which was for "the right of self-determination in a fully independent Czechoslovak State with its own administration within its own borders and under its own sovereignty."[41]

It was assumed that after the defeat of Austria-Hungary, the National Committee would be recognized by the victorious Allies as the future organ of state power. Thus, from the middle of July, there was no difference in aims between the Czechoslovak independence movements abroad and at home. Cooperation between the two committees consisted of sending and receiving messages with information and instructions. In one of them (July 8, 1918), Beneš asked the Czech political leaders to be prepared for the possibility of "the blow against Germany and Austria" in November, though it was possible that the war might go on until the following spring.[42]

Beneš was fully aware of the importance of the armed struggle, as contemporary documents show. On July 28, 1918, Beneš in Paris wrote to Masaryk in America that "in France we have achieved a total victory—by army in Italy, Russia and also in France. I have attempted to exploit the situation politically, and you have already seen the letter of Pichon and the telegram of Balfour.... The French and British had promised to issue a declaration at Versailles, but Sonnino prevented it because of the Yugoslavs...."[43] Beneš claimed that he had prepared the draft of the Pichon letter of June 29, 1918, and that all his demands had been accepted completely, "even the historical right and the right on Bohemian Germans." The CSNC, Beneš wrote, "functions officially as a government but formally and outwardly they are afraid to recognize us as a government." While he was satisfied with the situation in France, Beneš believed that the Foreign Office's reluctance to recognize the CNSC as a government of the future Czechoslovak state was caused by "fear that they would have to recognize the Committee of Dmowski [Polish] and the Yugoslav Committee, and they do not want to do that." Also, Beneš had the impression that the British saw such a recognition as being "against all the traditions of diplomacy." On the next day, Beneš wrote, he would negotiate the matter of recognition with Robert Cecil and then with Foreign Minister Balfour. Beneš believed that it would be easy to obtain French recognition of the CSNC as a provisional government of the future state if Great Britain were willing to go along.[44]

As Beneš recorded it, during his negotiations with Robert Cecil in London in July 1918, Cecil, although very much interested in the Czech army in Russia, told Beneš that the British government would hardly "discuss the new state and new government;" it would not go so far as that.[45] However, within one month, Beneš received Balfour's letter of August 9, 1918, which, Beneš believed, dealt the death blow to Austria-Hungary.

In its declaration of August 9, 1918,[46] the British government recognized the CSNC as "the supreme organ of the Czecho-Slovak national interests, and as the present trustee of the future Czechoslovak government," having the right "to exercise supreme authority" over the Czechoslovak belligerent army "waging a regular warfare against Austria-Hungary and Germany." The Balfour declaration pointed out that the Czechoslovaks had built a "considerably big army fighting on three different fronts, and it [the army] attempted in Russia and Siberia to stop the German invasion." Recognition was thus granted primarily because the Czechoslovak army had made a contribution to the Allied war effort, especially in Russia and Siberia.

Two days before issuing that declaration, Lloyd George highly praised the action of the Czech troops in Russia and Siberia. The declaration itself stated that Great Britain recognized "the Czecho-Slovaks as an Allied nation" and the "unity of the three Czecho-Slovak Armies as an Allied and Belligerent Army."[47] An editorial in *The Times* (London) of August 15, 1918, pointed out that this was the first time the British government "has officially declared a race residing in Habsburg territories to be an Ally" and that the decision "was reached after full and mature consideration. The service which the Czecho-Slovaks have rendered in Siberia has amply merited this recompense, for they have shown how Russia may yet be saved from German domination. If ever a people proved its fitness for freedom, the soldiers of this Slav democracy have done so." In a similar vein, an editorial in the *New York Times* (August 15, 1918) pointed out that "the Czechoslovaks deserve a recompense for the services they have rendered to the Allies." The consequences of this recognition must be considered, however, since it would commit the Allies to "the principle of the dismemberment of the Austro-Hungarian Empire."

The editorial comment in the *New York Times* notwithstanding, British recognition did not commit the Allies to dismember Austria-Hungary, as Cecil pointed out in his communication to Balfour of September 5, 1918. "Our recognition of the Czechs was very carefully worded," he wrote, "an although it would undoubtedly be consistent with the dismemberment of Austria it does not in fact bind us to that solution."[48] That possibility occurred to Beneš too, and it bothered him. He asked Steed, whose idea it originally was to phrase the recognition that way, what the wording "trustee for the future Czechoslovak goverment" meant. He got the following answer: "Don't ask, my dear fellow... You will never understand. 'Trustee' is a mystical word. It is legal, moral, metaphysical, anything you like, but it will do business for you."[49] It did indeed do business for Beneš.

An agreement based on the declaration of August 9, 1918, was concluded on September 3 between the British government and the Czecho-Slovak National Council, in which His Majesty's Government undertook to maintain diplomatic relations with the CSNC "until the organization of the future Czecho-Slovak Government." The British government agreed to place the Czechoslovak armies "under the general control of the Czecho-Slovak National Council." It expressed its willingness to participate on terms of equality with other Allies "in the event of a loan being advanced to the Czecho-Slovak National Council." It recognized "the right of the Czecho-Slovak National Council to be represented at any Allied conference when questions affecting the interests of the Czecho-Slovaks are under discussion." It began to recognize passports issued by the CSNC or its duly authorized representatives. Finally, it obliged itself to "treat communications passing between the Czecho-Slovak National Council and its representatives in London on the same footing as communications passing between a friendly Government and its representative in London."[50]

British recognition prepared the ground for other Allied governments to follow suit. In the United States Masaryk exerted a strong effort to obtain the U.S. government's recognition of the future Czechoslovak state and of the CSNC as a *de facto* government; however, pressures from Allied governments were more influential than his memorandum of August 31, and all his previous communications with Lansing (whose importance he overstated).[51]

The U.S. government recognized the CSNC in an announcement by the secretary of state on September 3, 1918, after protracted consideration of the matter. As we have noted earlier, Phillip's June 25 recommendation to recognize the *de facto* existence of the Czecho-Slovak National Council was not followed. On August 19, 1918, Secretary of State Lansing took up the matter in a long letter to the president, counseling against granting "full recognition to the Czecho-Slovaks as a sovereign nation."[52] He did, however, recommend two alternative limited recognitions. First, the United States might "recognize the belligerency of the Czecho-Slovak revolutionists in view of their military organization operating in Siberia and Eastern Russia... and the Czecho-Slovak Council with Masaryk as its head as a *de facto* Revolutionary Government." Second, the United States might issue a general declaration that it was "prepared to advance the cause of national freedom by assuming relations with any council or body of men truly representative of revolutionists against the Austro-Hungarian Government, who seek national independence by force of arms."

Among the attachments to this Lansing letter was a new memorandum by Albert H. Putney, entitled "Bohemia *de jure* an Independent Elective Monarchy," suggesting that "the Bohemians stand in a different position from any other subject people who are asking the assistance of the United States in securing their freedom and independence."[53] It said that "for many centuries before the election of Ferdinand of Austria as king of Bohemia in 1526, Bohemia had been an absolutely independent country and for considerable period prior to this date it had been an elective monarchy. The election of Ferdinand as king of Bohemia was for the sole purpose of uniting the forces of the two countries to resist the Turks and it was not contended that there should be any permanent union of Bohemia and Austria or that the elective character of the Bohemian kingship should be abolished." It recommended as "a very attractive war step," that the United States declare: "(1) that we regard Bohemia as an independent elective monarchy; (2) that the present Habsburg government of Bohemia is unconstitutional and an usurpation and that therefore the Bohemians have the right to resist such government without being guilty of treason; and (3) that in the absence of a government of Bohemia which is both *de facto* and *de jure* the United States recognize the Czecho-Slovak National Council as the true representative of the Czecho-Slovak race."[54]

The president answered Lansing's letter on August 22, and agreed that the time had come to take "definite action in this important matter."[55]

He also instructed Lansing to draft a public announcement and carry it out. Before doing so, on August 23, Lansing sought legal advice from L. H. Woolsey on precedents and on a suitable manner in which the recognition could be carried out. Woolsey prepared a lengthy documents analyzing the legal aspects of recognition of Czechoslovak belligerency and explaining how such a proclamation could be issued.[56] On the same day Lansing invited Masaryk to come to his office to discuss the situation in Russia and Siberia and the recognition of the CSNC.[57] At their meeting Masaryk promised to furnish the secretary of state with memoranda on both problems, as well as with a copy of the British recognition of August 9, 1918.[58]

Lansing, though determined to extend a kind of recognition to the CSNC, had legal and political reservations, which are stated in his memorandum of August 23, 1918. He points out that the press and sympathizers are exerting a stron gpressure on the U.S. government to recognize "the Czecho-Slovaks as an independent nationality" and to adopt "the course taken by Great Britain, France and Italy," since the heroic and romantic action of the Czechoslovak troops had aroused general enthusiasm. "No tale of military achievement in this war is more astounding," and the emotional "state of public opinion must be reckoned with." Lansing himself has been "deeply impressed" with "the courage and temper of men who have overcome such obstacles" and it has therefore not been an "easy matter to view the subject coldly and weigh fairly the reasons for and against recognition of the Czecho-Slovaks as a nation."

Lansing has no doubt that "the full recognition of these people as an independent state entitled to the possession of the territories included within Bohemia, Slovakia and Moravia" would "meet most fully the popular demand" and it would "undoubtedly give new courage to the Czechs and Slovaks in Russia, Siberia and even elsewhere and would bind them still more closely to the common cause." It would also "receive the unanimous approval of the American people." However, should the U.S. government made such a declaration and show such concern for oppressed nations, the Central Powers would, most likely, raise the question why "do we not take a definite stand for the independence of Ireland, Egypt, India and South Africa;" this country "would invite the charge of inconsistency and prejudice." In addition, should the United States ignore "the claims of the Irish and others under the sovereignty of the Entente

Powers," it would place itself in an embarrassing position at the peace conference, where, most likely, such subjects would be discussed. The United States should not take a position that would affect its influence or limit its freedom of action.

By recognizing the "Czecho-Slovaks as an independent nation," the British government puts itself in "an anomalous position in view of the nationalities subject to the British Crown." If Lansing were an Austrian statesman, he "would retaliate by recognizing the independence of Ireland, Egypt and India." He wondered how the British delegates to the peace conference "will explain this apparent inconsistency." As he put it, "Great Britain has already an unenviable reputation for having one rule for herself and another for other nations;" therefore, "she is charged with more or less reason with selfishness, injustice and lack of principle." Since the United States does not want to lose "the high place of influence" which it has among the nations, it "ought to be very careful not to earn the same reputation."

For these reasons Lansing is "opposed to recognizing the national independence of the Czecho-Slovaks or to accept them as a sovereign state." He believes that it would be better and safer "to recognize their belligerency as they are prosecuting open war against Austria-Hungary and her Allies. If they succeed in their revolt and are associated with the United States and the Entente in military victory, they will have established by force of arms their sovereign right to self rule and to independence." The same policy "should be followed in the case of Jugo-Slavs...."[59]

This memorandum reflects Lansing's concern about precedents, principles, double standards, and far-reaching commitments that might be difficult to follow in similar situations. In addition, Lansing did not want to foreclose the possibility of a negotiated peace, as his August 25, 1918, memorandum on the probability of peace proposals by the Central Powers demonstrates.[60] In this document Lansing expresses his conviction that, because of continued successes by Allied armies for nearly six weeks, "the Central Powers will very soon suggest peace negotiations." Should a proposal come from Vienna, it should be rejected; but Lansing was undecided what policy should be pursued should the peace proposal come from Germany. "Much will depend on the military situation and on the sincerity of Germany's overtures," he wrote. He was, however, "positive" that the Central Powers would make a peace offensive "very soon" and that the United States "must be ready to meet it in a way which will leave us in the advantageous position."[61]

Lansing studied carefully a draft declaration on the recognition of the CSNC submitted to him by Woolsey. He drafted the public pronouncement on August 25. After comparing it, most likely, with the British note recognizing the CSNC and after a conference with the president on August 30,[62] he revised his own draft. In the final version of the public declaration of August 30, 1918, which was published on September 3, Lansing omitted all reference to the geographical units of the Bohemian Crown and Slovakia, and, as the British recognition did, he referred merely to the "Czecho-Slovaks."

Although developments on the fronts, diplomatic activities, and governmental decisions were interrelated, a detailed discussion of the events on the Italian and Volga fronts, the Czechoslovak army's cooperation with the various Russian groups, and its leaders' views on the latter's political programs would greatly expand the scope of this work and, therefore, is not practical. Suffice it to say that the Czechoslovak army congress held in Omsk (Siberia) July 23-August 3, 1918, made political-military decisions about the future actions of the army. The congress issued a proclamation to "The Russian Public" stating that the Czechoslovak army could not endorse those Russian political trends that might lead to the establishment of a dictatorship or the return of the tsarist regime, and that the army wished Russia to have a firm and democratic government that would preserve for the Russian people all the precious rights and privileges achieved by the February Revolution, to which the Czechoslovak nation owed its clear statement of the principle of self-determination of nations. The congress elected the new leaders for the Russian branch of the CSNC: three vice-presidents, Bohdan Pavlů, Janko Jesenský, and Josef Patejdl; František Richtr as the secretary; and several other members.[63]

As has been noted earlier, Masaryk verbally approved the army's action in his telegram of July 21; however, the leaders of the independence movement in Russia were wondering about his past and current views and motives. Therefore, they sent one of Masaryk's early "agents" in Russia, Captain Vladimír S. Hurban, a former tsarist intelligence officer who had been attached to the Stavka to Washington to explain the situation in Russia and Siberia to Masaryk and urge him to secure help for the troops fighting the Bolsheviks. In addition to Hurban's August 6 report to Masaryk, the Russian branch of the CSNC urged Masaryk and the Allies to send help immediately. In their July 31 report on the condition of the Czech army and request for supplies and reinforcements, three members of the Russian branch of the CSNC urged their leader "to place at once before the Allies" the question of arming and equipping the troops and the need for expediting military support, "which Japan would have already given" if the Allies had obtained "the official concurrence of the United States. This point is an essential one for us." According to this report, Bolshevism seemed to be disappearing; it continued to exist "only by force of the Germans and Magyars of the International Army." The movement against the Bolsheviks "has been strengthened throughout Russia by our action, and reports have been received indicating the deposition of Soviets in Russia; and it is also stated that a coalition central government has been created in European Russia, including Miliukov and Rodzianko." The CSNC members requested Masaryk's views on whether the troops would stay in Russia and whether they could "depend upon completing our army with volunteers from the United States." Masaryk answered, in a telegram sent to Siberia on August 10, that he was sending 100,000 rifles, 4 million cartridges, and 100 machine-guns. But, though Masaryk had received American credits, these weapons never reached the Legion in Siberia; nor, indeed, were they ever procured.[64]

On August 3, 1918, the U.S. government issued a public statement on the limited extent of its military and economic action in Russia, saying that "military intervention in Russia would be more likely to add to the present sad confusion there than to cure it, and would injure Russia rather than help her out of her distress." As the U.S. government saw it, "military action is admissible in Russia now only to render such protectin and help as is possible to the Czecho-Slovaks against the armed Austrian and German prisoners who are attacking them and to steady any efforts at self-government or self-defense in which the Russians themselves may be willing to accept assistance." The statement also promised economic assistance to the Siberians. On the whole, it was ambiguous; yet it stated defintely that the U.S. and Japanese governments would send "a force of a few thousand men to Vladivostok" to safeguard the rear of the "westward moving Czecho-Slovaks."[65]

After this issuance of what was believed to be an official statement of policy, the U.S. government received many urgent requests from Allied diplomats and military personnel in Russia to dispatch troops up to Irkutsk (and perhaps as far west as Omsk), so that the Czechoslovak guard units there and along the railway up to Vladivostok could be sent to western Siberia and to the Volga front.[66] All these requests and recommendations with regard to sending U.S. troops to Siberia were taken up by the president in a While House conference with Secretary of State Lansing on August 20, 1918. It was decided that the U.S. government could not supply more troops than the number earlier agreed upon between the United States and Japan; that the U.S. government was "not in favor of proceeding west of Irkutsk in relieving the Czecho-Slovaks in western Siberia;" and that the U.S. government "favors the retirement of Czecho-Slovaks eastward from western Siberia as rapidly as safety will permit."[67]

U.S. Siberian policy, as recorded in Lansing's memorandum of this meeting, fell short of the desires of the Czechoslovak troops in Russia, who, in an attempt to restore the front against the Central Powers, were moving westward along the Siberian railway and along the Volga river. Their urgent requests for help, and his own interest in keep the troops loyal and obtaining U.S. recognition, prompted Masaryk to discuss with Lansing on August 25 the situation in Russia and Siberia and the question of recognition of the CSNC. Lansing and Masaryk agreed that the latter would furnish the former with memoranda on both problems.[68] In the first memorandum, delivered to the State Department "to be read also by the President,"[69] Masaryk stated his arguments for intervention.

This document, dated August 28, 1918, in which Masaryk "limited himself" to "the most important facts" and "briefly stated" some of his opinions, consisted of sixteen pages plus seven pages of supplementary materials, and was entitled " The Situation in Russia and the Military Help of the Allies and the United States."[70] Masaryk here interprets the declaration of August 3, 1918, as binding "the Allies and the United States to a swift aid to Russia and our Army." He suggests that "after this declaration it is not only the fate of our army, but the moral, political and military good name of the United States and the Allies that is at stake. The Austrians and Germans must not win in Russia: an Allied defeat there would have also an unfavorable influence upon the Western front . . . ." After this declaration, according to Masaryk, negotiations

Quest for Recognition 397

with the Bolsheviks had become impossible, "more so, that the Bolsheviks, led by Austrians and Germans [sic], declared a holy war against the Allies and especially against the Czechoslovak Army." The Allies must have, Masaryk says, "a definite political and military aim," and they have to formulate "a definite plan;" they "must lay most stress upon the restoration of orderly administration.... Order must be restored..." in Russia. Masaryk "gravely warns" against the often repeated slogan: "The Russian Nation must decide, THEY WILL HELP THEMSELVES[capital letters in original], etc. The Russian nation does not exist to-day, because it is disorganized [sic] ; just for that reason all capable existing organizations must be used, successively to organize the whole nation."[71]

"The aim must be one: to unite all Russia (except Poland) into a single republic, in which the nationalities which ask for it will possess a complete national autonomy. Finland will return into its pre-war union." Masaryk "personally favored" a republican form of government for Russia, because there was "no capable candidate" for the monarchy, and because "the Russian republic will be a constant pressure and political suggestion for Germany."

Masaryk then describes "the behavior of the Germans and Austrians in Russia," suggesting that they were "using the Bolsheviks, and partly also other parties, for their purposes" in a nonmilitary way, and also militarily by "using...their prisoners of war...militarily against our army and against the Allies." He points at the military and economic significance of the Czechoslovak's army's action in the Volga area and in Siberia, and urges sending military aid, including "the Allied Armies," to Russia and Siberia. He reiterates here the proposal made in his July 20 memorandum for the deployment of "two divisions" of Japanese troops in the area. He also proposes the creation of "a unified command in Siberia" with a Japanese commander in chief, "as Japan will have to furnish the strongest contingent of troops. The Allied units will be represented in a common military council, of which General Dieterichs will also be a member."

In the section of the memorandum dealing with Masaryk's relations with the Bolsheviks, the Czech leader says that he is speaking from his own experience, that he was in contact with them in the Ukraine and Moscow, that he knows "how to work with them" and that he "had a certain amount of influence over them." He "never agreed with the whole of their program," however, and he "utterly condemns their tactics." The section contains some spicy sentences, such as, "Lenin is a Jesuit... an honorable and moral object cannot be achieve by dishonorable methods. Bolshevism is clearly amateurism in all respects [sic], and cannot administer Russia and bring about order there." Referring to Norman Hapgood's quotation of Lenin as having said that "out of a hundred Bolsheviks one was responsible, the rest were fools and criminals," it repeats the story of the Czechoslovak army's early cooperation and later conflict with the Bolsheviks. When the Bolsheviks "showed themselves openly faithless, when they combined with the Germans, we were forced to take the defensive. With those 99 fools and criminals peaceful dealing is impossible; their aggression must be energetically repelled. This they understand and this only."

Masaryk did not expect "effective help" from "the Russian Army" for "a considerable period," since "the organization of Russian military units, and the return of the troops to discipline, will require several months." Therefore, it was not possible "to count on a greater Russian Army." Semenov's troops in the Far East, Masaryk suggests, should be used only "for lack of better material." He finds consolation in his belief that "the Bolsheviks...will also be without an army: they have shown their weakness in this respect." The last proposition was true a few months earlier, not at the end of August 1918. Now it was merely wishful thinking on Masaryk's part.

The next four sections of the document (eleven through fourteen) discuss the military situation of the Czechoslovak army in Russia and Siberia. The Czechoslovak army, according to Masaryk, "was forced into the fight by Bolshevik faithlessness and Austro-German aggressiveness." The army is holding the railroad from the Volga to Vladivostok and is scattered over a large territory. Masaryk predicts that "the enemy will endeavor to defeat it and, if possible, to annihilate the units on the Volga and Ural, and after that in Siberia." To that end the Bolsheviks are sending reinforcements from Russia and are also using the Austro-German prisoners. In Masaryk's view, it is essential to hold the Volga front, and the Allied reinforcements must aid the Czechoslovak troops in the area "with arms, ammunition and so on, and...reinforce them with a part of the Allied units." Masaryk also points out the difficulty in the proposed plan to evacuate the Czechoslovak units from the Volga and western Siberia to the Far East. The abandonment of the Volga region and the railroads to the Far East and Turkestan would put the Ural region with its mineral wealth, and Siberia with its stores of foodstuffs and grain, at the disposal of the Bolsheviks and their German allies. The people in the whole area, disappointed at being left to the mercy of the Bolsheviks, would turn against the Allies. The territory would be left in a state of anarchy and the opponents of the Bolsheviks would be massacred by the Red Guards. Finally, Masaryk believes, it is easier to get the Allied reiforcements to the West—to the Volga front—than it would be to move the Czechoslovak army to the East—to Vladivostok.

In Masaryk's view, it is in the interest of the Allies to hold the Volga front, so that the enemy cannot draw on the wealth of natural and human resources in the Volga region, the Urals, and Siberia. The western units of the Czechslovak army "must be reinforced with Allied troops," or it would not be possible to maintain junctions with the Perm-Vologda-Archangelsk Allied outposts. (Such a junction was never established.) The Czechoslovak army, Masaryk says, "is insufficiently armed; according to the agreement with the Bolsheviks they surrendered their arms and kept only about 10 rifles for each 100 men; now they have only what they could save in the unequal fighting in some places, and what they took from the enemy." (Note: (1) Masaryk had approved of the surrender of arms to the potential enemy; and (2) Czech units west of Penza at the time of the revolt were armed, though not with heavy weapons.) The Czechoslovak army, Masaryk says, lacks clothing, sanitary necessities, arms, and ammunition. "The Allies must, however, also help with military force." The army is spread thinly over a huge territory, which it cannot hold for much longer, Masaryk warns. "In the first place, it must not be forgotten that our troops are tired out already, not only by continuous fighting, but also by the terrible surprises of the Russian conditions. There is no unit in any of the fighting armies which would be in continuous action for only a tenth of the time that our army is in action. I am in receipt of a request to obtain rest for them by the military help of the Allies." Mas- also requests help "for eventual wintering."

In the section of the document entitled "The military and political task of the Czechoslovak Army," Masaryk states that "the military quality of our army is generally recognized." The Allies, "from the military point of view," have a duty "to make the most effective use of such a military force." Masaryk emphasizes that the army was organized for war against Austria-Hungary and Germany not only in France and Italy, but also in Russia; nevertheless, transportation of the army from Russia to France "is still our military and political aim." The army has "a great political and military significance: Austria-Hungary was considerably weakened by it, her population and her army demoralized... Austrians and the Germans have therefore endeavored to prevent our army from coming from Russia to France; to that end they forced the Bolsheviks to break their own agreements and pledges, to that end they are organizing their war prisoners against us and the Allies." (Trotsky, of course, did not have to be "forced" by Germans to order the Czech Legion dismantled; he had his own reasons for doing so.)

"It is therefore in the military and political interest of the Allies and of America that our army gets from Russia to France. The more of our soldiers will get to the Western Front, the less America will have to send there." Masaryk realizes the magnitude of the task of transporting troops over such a long distance, but he believes that it is both feasible and necessary, because the army "will have a special and very important part to play on the Western front at the moment of decisive victory: it will have to attempt an invasion of Austria-Hungary." Yet he admits that the army "can be used with advantage in Russia. Our men know Russia and Russian." In any case, what will be done with the army "depends on the further developments of the Russian situation and on the plans of the Allies in Russia. Meanwhile the army will stay in Russia (Siberia) and co-operate with the Allies."

Masaryk then proposes "that after Siberia is put into order, and that should be accomplished before winter, half of our army be transported to France; the other half could in the meantime remain in Russia." He also proposes sending one or two regiments to France via America soon, because "in general the appearance of our 'romantics' from Russia would have a beneficial effect on the American public." He again urges the Allies to send "a considerably greater force" to Russia. (At the same time, he wants to ship half the Legion to France.) The Allied policy toward "the various Russian parties and governments... should be clearer and more energetic. A precise political (and administrative) plan is also necessary for success of the military operations."[72]

This memorandum shows that Masaryk reversed himself on the role of the Czech troops in Russia. On June 19, at the White House audience with Wilson, Masaryk rejected the president's plan according to which the Czech troops would become the nucleus of the Allied forces guarding the Trans-Siberian Railway, and would protect the American mission to Siberia. On June 25, he embarrassed Secretary Lansing by asking him to forward a telegram to Chicherin offering the surrender of all weapons by the Czech Legion in exchange for a promise of free passage to Vladivostok. Now, asking for American recognition of the CSNC as a *de facto* government, Masaryk rejected his own long-held policy of noninvolvement and nonintervention in Russian affairs, approved of the Legion's action, and urged sending a much greater Allied military force to Russia. (According to the decision made at the White House conference on July 6, 1918, the number of American troops to be landed at Vladivostok was to be approximately the same as that of the Japanese, about 7,000 men each. On this occasion Auchincloss regretted that the plan he had suggested several weeks earlier was not adopted. "Assistance to the Czecho-Slovaks could have been made an additional reason for sending in troops;" and he believed that the president was right in thinking that Japanese force would not be well received by the Russians.)[73]

In accordance with the British view, Masaryk also proposed a unified military command in Siberia with a Japanese commander in chief, because Japan would have to supply "the strongest contingent of troops." He held tenaciously to this view in his audience with Wilson on September 11, 1918, on the grounds that if the Japanese contributed the largest number of troops, it would be "just that they would be in command." On this occasion President Wilson told Masaryk directly that he was afraid that the Russians would not like a Japanese supreme command over the Allied troops. Neither would the Americans; indeed, most likely, not even the Czechs would favor it. (Wilson's information was correct. As the British Political Intelligence Department reported, General Gajda voiced opinions frequently expressed in Japan when he stated that "the object of the Japanese is to weaken Russia.")[74] Wilson, furthermore, did not like the idea that the Japanese should have more troops in Russia than the Czech Legion, still favoring the latter as the hard core of the Allied forces so that the Bolsheviks could not exploit anti-Japanese sentiment in Russia. Masaryk disagreed with Wilson on this issue, claiming that "it is a German intrigue that exaggerates the tension between the Japanese and America." He asserted that the Russians would not have bad feelings about a Japanese command in Russia. Wilson, however, indicated very diplomatically to Masaryk that he might be a victim of British propoganda, saying, "Between ourselves, the English always try to exploit everything for themselves."[75]

On August 31 Masaryk submitted to the secretary of state a twenty-page memorandum entitled "The Recognition of the Czechoslovak National Council and the Czechoslovak Army,"[76] divided into ten parts with two appendices. Like other propoganda statements written by Masaryk, it was a mixture of some historical facts as he saw them, truths and half-truths, and inaccuracies.[77] It reflected his thinking, his idiosyncracies, and his ideological and political arguments for the dismemberment of Austria-Hungary and the establishment of an independent Czechoslovak state. It was delivered too late to be studied by Lansing and to influence the U.S. declaration of September 3, 1918.

On the day that Masaryk's text was delivered to the U.S. State Department, Lansing sent the president his draft of the U.S. recognition of the CSNC, making no reference to Masaryk's memorandum in the covering letter, but urging the president to publish the proclamation as soon as possible, for reasons of political expediency.[78] The U.S. recognition, based on Czechoslovak belligerency, stated:

> The Czecho-Slovak peoples, having taken up arms against the German and Austro-Hungarian Empires, and having placed organized armies in the field which are waging war against those Empires under officers of their own nationality... and the Czecho-Slovaks having, in prosecution of their independent purposes in the present war, confided supreme political authority to the Czecho-Slovak National Council. The Government of the United States recognizes that a state of belligerency exists between the Czecho-Slovaks thus organized and the German and Austro-Hungarian Empires. It also recognizes the Czecho-Slovak National Council as a *de facto* belligerent government clothed with proper authority to direct the military and political affairs of the Czecho-Slovaks. The Government of the United States further declares that it is prepared to enter formally into relations with the *de facto* government thus recognized for the purpose of prosecuting the war against the common enemy, the Empires of Germany and Austria-Hungary.

Commenting on the recognition of the CSNC by the U.S. and other Allied powers, the September 4 *New York Times* editorialized, "It follows of necessity that at the peace conference" the Czechoslovaks' "separation from Austria-Hungary will be insisted upon and their recognition as a nation will be a natural consequence."
Notwithstanding this comment, the American declaration specifically recognized the Czechoslovak belligerency and nothing more. It committed the United States to uphold the Czechoslovak peoples' independence of Austria-Hungary, but it did not say anything specific about what form that independence should have and in no sense implied the recognition of any territorial claim. It did not recognize Bohemia's historical right to independence nor the principle of self-determination. Since the revolutionary and belligerent government was not in possession of the territory that it claimed and had no effective control over that territory, it lacked the most essential element of sovereignty. Thus the American, as well as the British government, could easily have denied a place at a peace conference to the recognized CSNC if nobody seized political power on its behalf at home. Yet other recognitions followed.

On September 9, 1918, the Japanese government declared that it was "happy to regard the Czecho-Slovak army as an allied and belligerent army waging regular warfare against Austria-Hungary and Germany and to recognize the right of the Czecho-Slovak National Council to exercise the supreme control over that army." The Japanese government was "prepared to enter into communication with the duly authorized representatives of the Czecho-Slovak National Council whenever necessary on all matters of mutual interest to the Japanese and Czecho-Slovak forces in Siberia."[80]

While Beneš obtained Japanese recognition without much difficulty, Italy hesitated to extend similar recognition out of fear that by acknowledging the principle of self-determination and the right of Austro-Hungarian peoples to statehood, might establish a precedent that might prejudice Italy's claim (in accordance with the secret agreement made in 1915) to certain territories of the Habsburg empire inhabited by Southern Slavs. Beneš had to use a great deal of maneuvering and all his diplomatic skill in order to achieve Italian recognition of the CSNC as a *de facto* Czechoslovak government. Beneš emphasized the economic advantages that Italy would gain by future Czechoslovak use of Italian harbors, and

Italian access to Czechoslovak coal. He argued, in a memorandum to the Italian government (September 24, 1918), the necessity of making a political convention between the two countries even before the end of the war.[81] Yet it was not until October 3, 1918, that Prime Minister Orlando made a speech in the Italian parliament mentioning Italian recognition of the CSNC as a *de facto* government, and discussing the desired postwar Czechoslovak-Italian cooperation.[82]

After the U.S. recognition of the CSNC as a *de facto* government, Masaryk sought an audience with Wilson. In a letter to the president dated September 7, 1918, Masaryk expressed his gratitude for the U.S. government's recognition of "the justice of our struggle for independence and national unity." He believed that "America's recognition will strengthen our armies and our whole nation in their unshakable decision to sacrifice everything for the liberation of Europe and mankind."[83] In turn, at the White House audience on September 11, 1918, Wilson told Masaryk that he "did not know an example in the history of wars that an army as poorly armed as yours would behave as yours have."[84] He added that "especially by your armies, you have demonstrated that you insist on complete independence. We have merely recognized an accomplished fact."[85]

Lloyd George paid a similar tribute to the Czechoslovak army on September 11. The British prime minister, on behalf of the British War Cabinet, sent the president of the CSNC at Paris "heartiest congratulations on the striking success won by the Czechoslovak forces against armies of German and Austrian troops in Siberia. The story of the adventures and triumphs of this small army is indeed one of the freatest epics of history. It has filled us with admiration for the courage, persistence and self-control of your countrymen and shows what can be done to triumph over time, distance, and lack of material resources by those holding the spirit of freedom in their hearts. Your nation has rendered inestimable service to Russia and to the Allies in their struggle to free the world from despotism; we shall never forget it."[86]

In the meantime the Czechoslovak army and its Russian allies were under the command of General Syrový, who, in turn, was subordinated to the French General Janin. The latter was still in France, but before his departure for Siberia, on September 3, 1918, Janin received orders from the French ministry of war, issued in agreement with the Supreme War

Council. The Czechoslovak troops were to control the whole of Siberia, and to establish junctions with the Allied forces in the Russian north and with the anti-German and anti-Bolshevik groups of Russians in the Volga, Don, and Black Sea regions. In view of the limited human Czech and Slovak resources and the small number of troops in the field, this was an ambitious project, indeed.[87]

Acting upon the orders of the Allied command at Vologda, the Czechoslovaks mounted a westward offensive on the Volga front, taking Kazan (where they captured the Russian gold reserve) on August 7, and expanded their control over territories as far as Samara and Orenburg. The troops were thinly spread, and without Allied help they could not long carry on the offensive in several directions. The total number of Czechs and Slovaks in Russia had declined considerably since the conclusion of the Treaty of Brest-Litovsk. As of July 31, 1918, 522,235 prisoners of war had returned to Austria-Hungary, of whom between 65,000 and 75,000 were probably Czechs and Slovaks.[88] According to an official report submitted to the Czech military congress held at Omsk on August 21, 1918, out of 180,000 Czech and Slovak prisoners of war who were still in Russia, only 58,604 had registered for service in the Czechoslovak army, that is, less than one-third. Therefore, on August 20, 1918, the Russian branch of the CSNC issued a proclamation broadening the decreed mobilization to include all Czechoslovak civilian and military prisoners of war in Russia and all citizens of the future Czechoslovak state.[89] The attempts to "impress" prisoners of war into military service were not very successful, and, in the long run, the pressure placed on many of the Czech and Slovak prisoners of war to join the Legion became counterproductive. The involuntary "volunteers" became an easy prey for the Bolshevik propagandists, especially when things began to go from bad to worse.

The French officers on the spot, especially Captain Bordes and Major Guinet, acted with great self-confidence as "representatives of the Allies," presented their own interpretations of what they believed was Allied policy, made unauthorized promises, and thus raised the hopes and expectations of the Czechoslovaks. Contrary to rumors and propaganda, neither the Germans whom the Czechs expected to fight, nor the Allies by whom they expected to be relieved, ever arrived on the Volga front.[90] At the end of August the Bolsheviks concluded an agreement with the Germans that freed the Soviet forces to be moved eastward. Trotsky, who had succeeded in building a new, disciplined army trained largely by former tsarist officers, assumed command in person. He ruthlessly restored discipline, and the Bolsheviks began to mount their counteroffensive early in September 1918. At this time the Czechs were commanded by three youthful officers who during the three months of fighting had been promoted to generals—Gajda was 26, Čeček 32, and Syrový 33; they were supported by the more experienced Generals Dieterichs, Vojtsekhovskii, and Bogoslovskii.[91] (When the revolt started, Svrový had held the rank of lieutenant; now he was appointed the commander in chief of the Czechoslovak and Russian forces.) The young officers were still full of enthusiasm, but their troops were already tired out by constant fighting and began to show signs of exhaustion and demoralization.

On September 2, 1918, the U.S. consul general at Irkutsk, Harris, cabled to the U.S. secretary of state that the Bolsheviks had succeeded in breaking the railway line at Ufa, thus proving that "the Czechs are not strong enough to hold their grip on such a large territory and will be destroyed unless Allies hurry to their assistance. Russian army not progress as it should and cannot be depended on to materially assist Czechs." Two days later, on September 4, 1918, Harris sent a new cable to the secretary of state reporting further Bolshevik conquests on the western Volga front, and warning that Orenburg, Simbirsk, and Kazan were in danger of being retaken by the Bolsheviks. An earlier report from the American vice-consul at Samara stated that the Bolsheviks were getting stronger at the front west of the Volga, "due to the artillery which is under German direction. Unless Allies make strenuous efforts, half the results of Czech victories will be lost."[92]

An indication of the U.S. State Department's interest in extending aid to the Czechs and Russians fighting side by side may be found in the cable to Harris dated September 5, 1918, and sent via China. It inquired about the number of Russian troops cooperating with the Czechs west of Irkutsk, including European Russia; their organization, supplies, and morale; whether they were representative of the sentiment of the Siberian people; and who their leaders were.[93] But the Czechs needed immediate help, not inquiries. The only reinforcements they got on the Volga front came from their own Irkutsk garrison early in September—some 2,200 men.[94] This was a drop in the bucket. After the assassination of Uritsky at Petrograd and the August 30 attempt on Lenin's life in Moscow, the

Bolsheviks unleashed the Red Terror ("legalized" by the Council of People's Commissars on September 5, 1918), and proceeded to mass their troops against the Czechs. As Harris reported, more than 30,000 well armed Bolshevik troops (with heavy weapons and airplanes) were moving on Kazan; moreover, "according to a German order, a desperate effort is to be made against Czechs' victorious advance. It is, therefore, of great importance to come in touch with Vyatka with the Allied contingent which landed in Archangel."[95] There were only about 12,000 Czech troops on the Volga front; even together with the Russian auxiliary forces, they could not withstand the onslaught. As Harris put it in his cable of September 10, the Russians at Kazan were "afraid to identify themselves with [the anti-Bolshevik] movement," since the Bolsheviks' might return.[96] He also said that the new Russian army performed very poorly during the fighting around Kazan—"officers and men alike have deserted important positions." The Czechs, therefore, were not able to replace their losses by recruits from among the Russian population in the area. Their urgent appeals for help remained unanswered. On September 10, the Red Army recaptured Kazan, which the Czechs had evacuated the previous night.[97]

By coincidence, on September 10, the day before Lloyd George sent his congratulatory message to the CSNC in Paris, Trotsky issued a victory statement that Kazan had been taken "from the White Guards and Czecho-Slovaks. It is a turning point. The advance of the enemy has at last been stopped; his spirit is broken. After Kazan we shall recapture Ekaterinburg, Simbirsk, Samara, and the other cities on the Volga, in the Urals, and in Siberia."[98]

The Red Army offensive on the Volga front necessitated the return of the Czechoslovak troops that had fought their way through Siberia. Caldwell, the U.S. Consul at Vladivostok, reported in a telegram to Washington, D.C., on September 12, that this return movement had begun on September 9, under General Gajda, "who has been appointed commander of all Czech forces. General Dietrichs . . . assumes command and organization of Russian forces which had been cooperating with the Czechs." The Czechslovak troops retreating from Kazan were in desparate need of rifles and ammunition. Although they had received closed to 7,000 Japanese rifles, no cartridges were supplied for them. The Red Army massed "between 30,000 and 40,000 Bolshevik and Austro-German war prisoners around Ekaterinburg, commanded by an Austrian general," against "some

12,000 Czechs and Cossacks." It was doubtful, Caldwell cabled, that the Czechs and Cossacks could hold the city.[99]

The slow progress made in recruting troops for the Volunteer (People's) Army was explained by the fact that the Bolsheviks were terrorizing the population, and that there was an enormous lack of arms and equipment. Replying to the State Department's inquiry on the state of the Russian army, the U.S. representatives in China reported on September 3 that "it is claimed and believed that a much larger force can be mobilized if the Allies would be willing to supply material and trained officers." The Bolshevik party had practically ceased to exist in western Siberia and the Russian troops were directed by the Omsk government. The Czechoslovaks "report that their recent engagements in Ekaterinburg-Perm district have been against forces composed exclusively of Magyars officered by Germans and Austrians." The Czech troops were exposed to the Bolshevik propaganda according to which "Americans are willing to spend money but not to fight." The U.S. representative emphasized the need for the Allies to send troops to help the Czechs, who might otherwise come to believe the Bolshevik propaganda.[100]

After the fall of Kazan the Czechoslovak army was forced onto the defensive, under attack from the increasingly well-organized, equipped, and disciplined Red Army. Simbirsk fell on September 12, and the Czechoslovak and national Russian armies were forced to retreat to the left bank of the Volga. Fresh troops were dispatched by the Bolsheviks against the Czechs; not even the formation of a new Czechoslovak division composed of recruits from the Siberian prison camps was able to reverse the trend. After the evacuation of Kazan the possibility of establishing a junction with Archangel was lost. As Pavlů reported to Harris on September 15, "there are no arms." The lack of arms prevented the arming of Russians who might have been drafted into the national Russian army. Thus, said Pavlů, if help does not come from the east soon, "we will be forced to abandon Samara and retreat to Ufa. That means to lose the possibility of an early junction with General Alexeev, who is operating towards Tsarytsyn in conjunction with the British on the Caspian Sea."[101]

During the critical days of the struggle on the Volga front, from September 8 to 23, 1918, when the Bolsheviks succeeded in turning the trend and forcing the Czechoslovaks and their Russian allies onto the defenseive, various anti-Bolshevik groups met in a state conference at Ufa in order to form an all-Russian government. On September 12, Bohdan Pavlů, representing the Russian branch of the CSNC, delivered a passionate plea to the delegates of the various political groups "to form an all-Russian government which would have the support of all strata of the Russian people." He pointed to the gravity of the moment, which resulted from the collapse of the front north of Ufa and the fall of Kazan, a city captured by the Czechoslovaks on August 7. The Ufa meeting made a special appeal to the Allies for immediate help. The enthusiasm of the Ufa meeting was dampened by the uncertainty of the situation on the front and in the rear, and rumors "that the Allies may not recognize the all-Russian government" which would be formed at Ufa. As Pavlů reported on September 15, the plan was to place power in the hands of five or seven persons elected by the Ufa meeting; these would nominate a cabinet responsible to the Constituent Assembly, to a quorum of the conference, or to some other new assembly that might evolve from the Ufa meeting. Pavlů believed that "the maintaining of the prestige of the Constituent Assembly" would favorably influence "the psychology of the masses of the part of Russia not yet liberated from the Bolsheviks."[102] As a result of an agreement reached at this conference, the Ufa Directorate was established, the All-Russian Provisional Government was elected, and a new Constitution was adopted on September 23, 1918.

The Bolsheviks, however, could not be halted by conferences and young, unarmed governments. On September 12, Czech Major General Syrový, commander in chief of the Czech and Russian troops, telegraphed from Cheliabinsk to the U.S. Consul at Vladivostok that the Volga situation was critical, that the Czechoslovak troops, "wearied by three months' uninterrupted fighting, tire incredibly fast, and transfer of troops from east will only delay catastrophe temporarily. It is impossible to operate without immediate assistance of strong Allied force." Syrový demanded from the Allies an "immediate and categorical reply" to his questions: "(1) Is it their intention to participate in any way in operations supporting us on Volga front; (2) if so do they intend to start at once an extraordinary transfer of troops and in what numbers? . . . There is small hope of aid from Russian army in near future." Syrový requested an immediate telegraphic answer from the Allies; however, his message reached Washington only five days later, on September 17,[103] and it was another several days before Washington made a decision on this and several other similar requests.

One of the requests came from the Russian ambassador, who came to the State Department on September 17, 1918, to ask for military supplies to "the Russian people." He had received "several cables from the Omsk government indicating that they were forming an army to fight against the German and Austrian prisoners opposing the Czechs on the Volga River [and] on the Ekaterinburg front." He "wanted to know whether he could encourage them in their expectation that they will receive help." He was told, however, that "there was no government in Russia" that the State Department would recognize, and that it was therefore impossible for the United States to assist those whom he represented.[104]

Another urgent plea came from the U.S. ambassador in Japan, temporarily at Vladivostok, who cabled the secretary of state: "Reports from the Volga region all agree that the Czech forces there are seriously menaced from various directions. Their commanding officers are pleading earnestly for immediate assistance. General Gajda has come to Vladivostok for the avowed purpose of urging upon the Allies the necessity of some immediate help without which the Czechs will be compelled to fall back to a position east of the Ural Mountains, possibly to Omsk. He fears that if they thus fall back, they will leave their supporters in the evacuated towns defenseless against the general massacres which are likely to follow." The single question the Czechoslovaks wanted to have answered was whether the Allies would send them help so that they could hold the Volga region, or at least the line of the Urals, during the coming winter and thus "keep the door into European Russia open." As the ambassador cabled, it could not be done, "unless reeinforcements are sent to them promptly."[105]

The ambassador also reported that U.S. General William S. Graves felt that he should go to Omsk with a substantial portion of the troops under his command. This move would have the following advantages:

> (1) It would give much needed support to the Czech forces in the Volga region and would, therefore, be consistent with the purpose of the present expedition. (2) It would make more certain the protection of the railway, and thus secure a base from which economic and other activities might penetrate even into European Russia. (3) The presence of an Allied force, and particularly of

American troops in that part of Russia, would have a strong moral effect upon the entire population in a territory which directly affects European Russia. (4) It would have the additional advantage of giving our own forces during the winter an opportunity for more valuable service than any that will present itself in Vladivostok where there is so little direct contact with Russian opinion.

Admiral Knight was "convinced that such an expedition, far from antagonizing the Russian people, would be generally welcomed and would form a very effective center for American activities in that part of Siberia. General Graves has studied carefully the strategic situation and feels that there are no serious military difficulties or dangers involved." In the ambassador's view, "such movement would be entirely consistent with the policy which has been adopted by our Government in reference to Siberia." He expressed a fear that "our failure to come into closer contact with the Czech forces and with the Russian people in western Siberia may have serious results." He had already found that the British and French representatives at Vladivostok, "particularly General Knox and General Paris, are influencing the Czech leaders with impracticable plans to create by force a new Russian army and a new eastern front. General Gajda, who is very young, has been impressed by these schemes and misled by unauthorized suggestions of ultimate American support." The ambassador believed "that General Graves' presence in Western Siberia would steady to Czechs' leaders and make clear to them and to the Russian people our policy and purpose." The ambassador recommended that General Graves be authorized to go to Omsk with a substantial portion of his troops. He urged that whatever decision was made, it should be communicated to the Czech commanders at the earliest possible moment, because their plans for the winter were "dependent upon the character and extent of the assistance" they could count on receiving from the U.S. and other Allied governments.[106]

Three days later, on September 26, the U.S. government's answer was cabled to the U.S. ambassador in Japan. On the next day, September 27, a memorandum with essentially the same information was communicated to the representatives of Great Britain, France, Italy, Japan, the Russian ambassador, and Professor Masaryk. The ambassador's suggestion that "General Graves establish himself at Omsk or any other point in the far interior" was rejected, because it was "the unqualified judgment of our military authorities that to attempt military activities west of the Urals is to attempt the impossible," and the Czech forces "should retire to the eastern side of the Urals" where they would be able to obtain supplies from the east and where they would be in a position "to make it impossible for the Germans to draw supplies of any kind from western Siberia." The ambassador in Tokyo was also informed, confidentially, that "the ideas and purposes of the Allies with respect to military operations in Siberia and on the Volga front are ideas and purposes with which we have no sympathy."[107]

The policy decision dissociating the United States from Allied policy in Russia was made in a conference at the White House on September 25, and it contrasted sharply with Lansing's recommendations to the president. On September 9, the secretary of state told the president, "Our confidence in the Czech forces has been justified and the fact that now a Russian military force of equal strength has joined them combined with the gratifying reception given the Czechs by the civilian population of the localities occupied is strong evidence to prove that the Russians are entirely satisfied to cooperate with the Czechs in Russia and that assistance to the Czechs amounts to assistance to the Russians."[108] In late September Lansing was even more convinced than he had been in July of the need to help the Czechs, whom he saw as a shield for the anti-Bolshevik Russians. "If the Czecho-Slovaks withdraw to the east of the Ural," Lansing believed, "the Russian communities of the Volga region, which have been friendly to the Czecho-Slovaks... will be at the mercy of the Red Guards, who have committed such monstrous crimes within the past six weeks in Moscow and other cities. Lansing confessed to the president that he sympathized "with the spirit of the Czecho-Slovaks when they say that they cannot abandon their helpless friends to certain massacre and pillage;" and he believed that "the world would be disposed to condemn such a course, and that the Czecho-Slovaks with their high sense of honor would rather die on the Volga than bear the charge of such ingratitude." Furthermore, Lansing assumed that the "Czecho-Slovak force west of the Urals will remain there and do the best they can to protect the friendly Russian communities from Bolshevik excesses."[109]

In rejecting Lansing's (and Phillip's) recommendation and the Allied policy, President Wilson followed the advice of General March and Justice Brandeis, who used "every influence" to discourage him from action in Russia or Siberia. The decision was also a qualified success for Masaryk, who, after attaining the long-sought American recognition (based on Czechoslovak belligerency) was again promoting his plan to transfer the army from Russia and Siberia to France. Masaryk tried to influence President Wilson to help him attain his objective. On September 16, 1918, the president thanked the Czech leader for the latter's "counsel and guidance," which he "valued;" and on September 20, the president instructed the secretary of state "to communicate to the governments concerned his 'insistence' that the Czecho-Slovaks come eastward and ultimately be transferred to the French front." The secretary of state and his aides, however, realized that such a communication would be contrary to "the President's statement in his famous Aide Memoire of July 17th, in which he announced our position but said that this was not intended as a criticism of any independent action which the other governments might care to undertake." Therefore, on September 21 Lansing sent the president a letter drawing his attention to the fact that the United States was "not in a position to 'insist' upon any particular course of action in Russia; and asking whether he could modify his previous instructions in this respect." Even though the confidential memorandum to the Allies of September 27 reflected a modification of the president's position, the French ambassador called the State Department and expressed consternation regarding Russia and Siberia, fearing that the decision to advice the Czechoslovaks to withdraw from Russia "would lead to wholesale massacre of the Russian population and that the United States would then be obliged to take the blame. He thought it was tragic and was much excited." Phillips commented in his diary that "the President has, of course considered the possibility of massacres, but decided that there was nothing to be done. I wish, myself, that he had not made the decision."[110]

On September 27, an official memorandum to Professor Masaryk stated that the U.S. government "cannot cooperate in any effort to establish lines of operation and defense through from Siberia to Archangel." Furthermore, in view of the fact that "no gathering of any effective force by the Russians is to be hoped for," the U.S. government "will insist with the other governments, so far as United States cooperation is concerned, that all military effort in northern Russia be given up, except guarding the ports themselves." Although the United States would send supplies, no more American troops would be sent to the northern ports.[111]

Early in October the British military authorities, who disagreed with the American analysis of the situation, believed that Britain was "honourably bound" to stand by her friends in European Russia; and the British government decided not to ask the Czechs to withdraw east of the Urals. The British believed that the Czechs, if given full support by all the Allies, might still be able, in conjunction with the forces under General Alexeev, to hold the line of the Volga "against any force that is likely to be brought there by our enemies."[112] In mid-October, General Knox, chief of the British Military Mission at Vladivostok, deplored the inaction of the combined forces that the Allies kept at Vladivostok and urged that they go to the Urals, suggesting that had they done so a month earlier, they could have reached Moscow before the end of the winter. The general appealed to the American public, emphasizing the urgent need to help the Czechs for humanitarian reasons. He wondered whether "the humanitarians of all countries understood what it means for the Czechs to evacuate a city like Samara," and whether they realized "that it means that every decent citizen will get his throat cut as soon as the Czechs leave."[113]

The U.S. memorandum of September 27, 1918, put Masaryk "in a rather singular position," as he stated in his "Notes" on the memorandum for Wiseman, with whom he kept in touch and whom he asked to see on October 1. Masaryk wrote that the memorandum "radically changes the Statement of August 3rd," which Masaryk had interpreted as binding the Allies to prevent the Austrians and Germans from winning in Russia: "The question arises as to why is the Statement of August 3rd cancelled at a time when the whole situation, political and military, is changing so favourably." Although in his September 21 agreement with General Janin Masaryk himself "viewed the possibility of retiring over the Urals," the question "of retirement over the Urals is a strategical one," and should be left to the military authorities. While "the Statement of August 3rd accepts the westward move of our troops, and the strategical aid of the Allies has been planned in accordance with it," wrote Masaryk, "the Memorandum changes this one all-important point, arguing the military activities west of the Urals are impossible. In my opinion they are not quite impossible, if our troops get in time the necessary arms and ammunition and help in general; such activities will be made more possible if the Allies send some larger military assistance."[114]

Masaryk, furthermore, believed that the recent reverses of the Germans in the West and the promising developments of things on the Eastern front" had decreased the Bolsheviks' regard for Germany and Austria. He would "use this change to try to detach the Bolsheviks from the Germans and Austrians; I would try to get paid for the retirement, to put it bluntly." He "would speak even with the devil;" and it was his conviction "that the attitude of the Allies towards the Bolsheviks has been a wrong one from the beginning." Also, the memorandum representing "such a radical change from the stand of the Statement of August 3rd will have a very bad effect on the Russian people;" and he believed that "a considerable Russian force could be organized in a few months." In conclusion, Masaryk advised that the memorandum be sent to General Janin. He was sending the general his own "Notes, asking him to devote his whole attention to the suggested plan of retirement over the Urals," because the restrictions of the Murmansk and Archangel operations, and the abandonment of Russia (proper) to herself," seemed to him "to be the salient points of the Memorandum."[115]

Toward the end of September 1918, the Czechs in Russia still hoped that help would be forthcoming. The situation around Samara had become critical. As the U.S. vice-consul there reported, Czechs and Russians were tired from weeks of constant fighting an enemy "five times" their number, aided by German officers and advancing on Samara. Eight hundred Siberians had no guns; and since no weapons were available, it was useless to recruit more Russians. "Even a few hundred fresh Allies would bring sufficient encouragement," reported the vice-consul; he warned that Samara might well fall into the hands of the Red Army, and that large quantities of valuable supplies would then fall into German hands. Then, he contended, the Germans would have control of the whole Volga river valley and practically all of Russia. "Such a catastrophe would crush the hopes of the Russian people now fighting with Czechs against German domination of the whole country and relying on Allied help."[116]

A desperate appeal for Allied help was dispatched by the Russian branch of the CSNC to the Allied consuls in order to save the Volga front, but to no avail. The soldiers on the front, poorly fed, insufficiently clothed, and lacking medical supplies and ammunition, began to lose hope, and their morale began to decline. They still made strenuous efforts to defend Samara; however, on October 7, 1918, the city was captured by the Red Army. Two days later Secretary of State Lansing cabled to the U.S. consul general at Irkutsk that the U.S. government had "expressed its opinion to the Allies that the Czechs should withdraw from the Volga front."[117]

Reporting on the climate of opinion among the Czechoslovak troops, the U.S. consul detailed for special duty in Russia and Siberia, Jameson, cabled to the secretary of state on October 10, 1918, that the Czechoslovaks held the U.S. government solely responsible for the Allied failure to aid them on the Volga front. He reported that the British and Japanese "openly state that the Americans assume the responsibility for betrayal of Czechoslovak lives"; that the new Russian army was infected with the idea that the United States was a danger to the Russians, since it had prevented the Allies from helping the Czechoslovaks on the Volga front; that the Russians were already turning against the Americans and the Allies because of their constant delays in sending aid; and that "America was the most popular nation with the Czechs and the majority of Russians months ago but now reverse is true." However, there was still time to make the name of the United States respected as before by the Czechs and the Russians, by taking an immediate action; that was, "if American troops, no matter how few, arrive on the Volga front." Even two battalions of troops in American uniforms "would show that we were supporting Czech Allies, not betraying them. Even if it is decided not advisable to form a front in Russia, it is vital to send American troops to the Volga front now and afterwards to withdraw [the] Czech and American troops." Jameson believed that it was "vital to American prestige and Czechs' morale that we contradict German reports of our standpoint by actual appearance in the field."[118] No such troops ever appeared on the Volga front; and at the end of October the Japanese government refused a British request to send additional forces to Siberia to support the Czechs in the Volga region.[119]

The retreat of the Czechoslovaks from the Volga front and the Bolshevik victories could no longer influence the course of events on the political-diplomatic fronts in Washington, Paris, London, Vienna, and Prague. The soldiers had already done their part; the rest of the work had to be done by the Czechoslovak spokesmen abroad and the nation and its leaders at home.

CHAPTER FIFTEEN

THE DECLARATION OF INDEPENDENCE

From one of the messages sent by Beneš to Prague, it appears that the leaders of the Czechoslovak independence movement in exile were considering the establishment of a provisional government as early as May 27, 1918. Beneš said that, most likely, after the declaration of independence a new provisional government would be established, and the leaders of the Czech political parties should be prepared for it. Under no circumstances should they disavow it; on the contrary, they should keep in mind that the provisional government in exile would consider itself to be a delegation and, at the same time, a part of the provisional government whose second part would be in Bohemia. He reiterated the same theme in his lengthy reports of July 8 and September 11, 1918.[1] In the September message Beneš wrote that a definite decision had been made to build a state organization with a regular government and diplomatic corps, and that Masaryk was the head of this government. At that time Beneš was negotiating with the French ministry of foreign affairs about the formation of this government, whose seat was to be in Paris; in his September 18 telegram to Masaryk,[2] who was in the United States at the time, Beneš reported that the French and British governments had accepted, in principle, recognition of the Czechoslovak government, and that, in agreement with the French ministry of foreign affairs, the Czechoslovaks should build a regular central governing organ in the immediate future. Beneš suggested several individuals for diplomatic appointments to head missions in Rome, Paris, London, Washington, and Tokyo; he asked Masaryk for his view and consent. Masaryk approved the plan and recommended Charles Pergler to represent the CSNC in the United States.[3]

Preparations for the establishment of a provisional government necessitated arrangements for the transfer of power in the Czech lands at the moment of Austria-Hungary's military collapse. In his message to Prague Beneš always emphasized the need to reject proposals for collaboration with the Austro-Hungarian government, including refusal even to attend meetings of parliament. In view of the Allied victories and Beneš's optimistic messages, the National Committee at Prague and the Union of Czech Deputies adopted a resolution on September 29, 1918,[4] in line with Beneš's directives. In this resolution the Czech political leaders declared that they did "not believe any more the given and unkept promises," and that the Vienna government was unable to give them anything that they had asked for. The resolution continued: "Our nation can never expect to get its liberty from those who at all times regard it only as a subject of ruthless exploitation.... Our nation has nothing in common with those who are responsible for the horrors of this war.... The Czech nation will follow its anti-German policy whatever may happen, assured that its just cause will finally triumph, especially today when it becomes a part of the great ideals of the Entente, whose victory will be the only good product by this terrible war."[5]

The resolution and public statements of the Czech deputies in the Austrian parliament helped the cause of the exile liberation movement exactly at the time when Austria-Hungary made its last attempt to save itself. On October 5, 1918, Austria-Hungary and Germany transmitted a note to President Wilson requesting an armistice and the immediate initiation of peace negotiations, based on the president's "Fourteen Points" of January 8, 1918.[6] Wilson answered only the German note, delaying his response to the Austro-Hungarian one. On October 14, 1918, Beneš visited the French ministry of foreign affairs and was assured that Austria-Hungary was doomed, that nothing could save it, and that it was no longer possible for the Habsburg empire to survive.[7] Beneš was encouraged by these assurances, as well as by Wilson's second answer to Germany, demanding the end of the absolutist rule of the Kaiser. Late in the afternoon on the same day, Beneš handed a note to the French ministry of foreign affairs and informed the other Allied governments that a provisional Czechoslovak government had been formed on September 26, 1918.[8] (On that day Masaryk approved Beneš's proposal to form a provisional government.) The note recalled the U.S. government's declaration of September 3, the agreements with Britain (September 3) and France (September 28), and the declaration of the Italian prime minister on October 3, 1918. "In view of these successive recognitions," the Allied governments were informed that a provisional Czechoslovak government had been formed and seated, provisionally, at Paris. It consisted of the following members: "Professor Thomas G. Masaryk, President of the Provisional Government and of the Cabinet of Ministers, and Minister of Finance. Dr. Edward Beneš, Minister of Foreign Affairs and of the Interior. General Milan R. Štefánik, Minister of War." The provisional government decided to accredit Dr. Stephen Osuský to His Majesty's Government in Great Britain; Dr. Lev Sychrava to the French government; Dr. Lev Borský to the government of Italy; Charles Pergler to the government of the United States; and Bohdan Pavlů to Russia. The note stated further that the decision to form the government had been made "in agreement with political leaders at home," and that "on October 2, 1918, the Czecho-Slovak [sic] Deputy Staněk, President of the Union of Czech Deputies to the Parliament in Vienna, solemnly announced that the Czecho-Slovak National Council in Paris is to be considered as the supreme organ of the Czecho-Slovak armies and that it is entitled to represent the Czecho-Slovak nation in the Allied countries and at the Peace Conference...."[9]

In a secret message from Prague on October 11, Beneš was notified that preparations had been made for the inauguration of a provisional government that would maintain order in the Czech lands until the arrival of the Allies and Beneš.[10] Earlier, a declaration of the Czech deputies, presented by the Agrarian František Staněk at the first session of the Vienna parliament rejected the proposed autonomy and expressed confidence in an early Allied victory.[11] As soon as this happened, the Czech leaders at home would assume political power; and they made preparations for it, as did the Croats, the Slovenes, and the Poles. On October 2, 1918, Father Anton Korošec, who a few days later became the president of the Yugoslav National Council at Zagreb, speaking on behalf of Yugoslav political parties of both Austria and Hungary, declared in the Vienna parliament that the Yugoslavs intended to create a single, independent state and that the government of the empire would not have the right to speak for them at the peace conference.[12] A similar declaration was made on the same day by Polish socialist Deputy Ignacy Daszynski.[13] But the emperor still believed that, after making the peace offer to President Wilson, he could save the empire. He therefore invited spokesmen for the parliamentary clubs to meet with him and discuss the future developments in the monarchy. Four representatives of the Czech Alliance, Staněk, Tusar, Fiedler, and Hruban, visited him on October 12, and stated their demands. Three days later, during the question time in the parliament, the Czech deputies repeated the same demands. These were, (1) immediate establishment of a Czech national government in Prague; (2) its participation in deliberations at the peace conference; and (3) the transfer of all Czech regiments from Hungarian and German-Austrian territories to their fatherland. The emperor came to realize that the situation had reached a crisis and that it was worse than he had thought. Austria-Hungary was falling apart.[14]

The Czech National Committee planned to assume political power at the moment of Austria-Hungary's capitulation, but subtly and without an advance announcement. This tactic was either not comprehended or not approved by the Socialist Council, representing the Socialist parties, which, with the approval of the Social Democratic and Czech Socialist parties, decided to call a general strike on October 14. Without consulting the national committee and its secretary Dr. Soukup, a Social Democrat, who had prepared a proclamation for that occasion, two personal enemies of Kramář and Rašín added to the proclamation a paragraph calling for the establishment of a republic: "The time has come! We have cast off our chains! We have risen to independence... with the approval of the whole democratic world, we declare that we stand here today as the executive of State Sovereignty, as citizens of a free Czechoslovak Republic.... Our cause is the cause of the whole world...."[15]

The declaration urged the socialists to call meetings throughout the country; the latter, however, should not be connected in any way with boycotts of and violence against the Jews. (Most Jews in Austria-Hungary spoke German and supported the empire. The National Social party was anti-Semitic before and during the war.) The proclamation mentioned a republic, though the leaders of the Czech political parties were not certain about what form of government the new state would have; some of the socialists were prepared to accept a monarchy, it that were the price of independence.[16] They did not know that since October 13 Masaryk had been working feverishly on a declaration of independence that also called for a republican form of government in the new state. That declaration was being drafted, with the help of many Americans, in Washington, D.C.[17]

Before Masaryk completed his declaration of independence, on October 15, 1918, France recognized the Czechoslovak provisional government in a letter signed by S. Pichon, minister of foreign affairs, and addressed to Beneš. Earlier, a secret agreement between the government of France and the Czecho-Slovak National Council was concluded at Paris. Although a definitive text of the agreement was agreed upon on September 10, its effective date was September 28, 1918. The agreement began as follows: "On Saint Wenceslas day a treaty was signed...from which, it was agreed, the first four articles would be published...." In article one of the agreement the CSNC agreed to "continue giving the Government of the French Republic the co-operation of its armies for the pursuit of the present war," including the Czechoslovak army in Russia and Siberia. In article two the French government promised to support the CSNC as a *de facto* government of Czechoslovakia in its efforts to reconstitute an independent Czechoslovak state "within the limits of its ancient provinces." The most important was article three, which said: "The Government of the French Republic accords to the Czechoslovak nation the right to be represented at the inter-Allied conferences, where questions concerning the interests of the Czecho-Slovaks will be discussed."[18]

Thus, according to the secret agreement of September 28, 1918, the CSNC placed the Czechoslovak armies, most notably the Czechoslovak army fighting the Bolsheviks in Russia and Siberia, at the disposal of the French government; and the latter recognized the historical boundaries of the new state, and also by implication, the Czech claim to Slovakia, which did not belong to the historical provinces, as well as the right of the "Czechoslovak nation" to be represented at the peace conference. The U.S. government was notified about this commitment that the French government had made in this agreement.[19] The term "ancient provinces" *would have to be interpreted* as including the borderlands of the Czech provinces inhabited predominantly by Germans; and it *could be interpreted* as including Serb (Sorb) Lusatia, or even Silesia, which also used to be provinces belonging to the Crown of St. Wenceslas. Among the

Allies, France was the only power that recognized, before the end of the war, the Czech territorial claims. Since the agreement was secret, the Czechs at home did not know about it, and their leaders were wondering about international guarantees for the new state and its boundaries. (The question was raised on the floor of the Revolutionary National Assembly. Therefore, at a meeting of that assembly, on January 14, 1919, Kramář, then the prime minister of Czecho-Slovakia, read the agreement of September 28, 1918, and the Pichon letter of June 29, and used these statements as proofs that France had guaranteed Czechoslovakia its historical boundaries. After the Paris Peace Conference, on September 30, 1919, Kramář publicly acknowledged France's endorsement of all demands made by the Czecho-Slovak delegation at the conference.)[20]

On October 16, 1918, Masaryk submitted to the U.S. secretary of state the first draft of the Czechoslovak declaration of independence,[21] and Emperor Charles of Austria-Hungary issued a manifesto offering to transform the Habsburg monarchy into a league of free peoples.[22] The manifesto and the willingness to transform the Austrian part of the Danubian empire into a federation had come too late; the decisive moves leading toward dismemberment of the political and economic unit in central Europe had been made earlier, and the emperor could no longer reverse the course of events.

The imperial manifesto of October 16, announcing the intended federalization of Cisleithanian Austria (and thus not applying to Hungary) in order to solve the central problem of Austrian internal politics that had plagued that state for two generations, merely accelerated the inevitable development. The Hungarian rulers used it as a pretext for the severance of the dualistic union with Austria, claiming that even Cisleithanian Austria's projected federalization affected the basic premises of the Compromise of 1867 that had created the dual monarchy.[23] The Hungarian government's insistence on the integrity of St. Stephen's Crown and its unwillingness to grant any concession to the non-Magyar nationalities in the "Hungarian national state" made the proposal for federalization of the Habsburg empire unworkable, even if the Allies had been willing to accept it as the basis for the new order in the Danubian area. The threat made by the Hungarian prime minister, Alexander Werkerle, to cut off Hungary's food supplies to Austria, promoted insecurity and chaos; the withdrawal of Magyar Hungarian troops from the front hastened the military disaster of the army.[24] The establishment of the Provisional German Austrian National Assembly on October 21, 1918, another direct consequence of the manifesto, also speeded the disintegration of the empire. However, it was a note from President Wilson dated October 18, 1918, that brought the Habsburg monarchy to the brink of collapse.[25]

When Secretary of State Lansing received Masaryk's programmatic declaration dated October 18, 1918, he had already received from President Wilson the naswer to the government of Austria-Hungary, which was now willing to accept Wilson's "Fourteen Points" as the basis for a peace settlement. The U.S. note of October 18, 1918, which President Wilson had drafted in person, informed the Swedish minister, who had transmitted Austrian peace offers to the government of the United States, that the situation had changed since January 8, 1918, that the United States had recognized the Czecho-Slovak National Council as "a *de facto* belligerent government clothed with proper authority to direct the military and political affairs of the Czecho-Slovaks." Thus President Wilson was "no longer at liberty to accept the mere 'autonomy' of these peoples as the basis for peace," the note said, "but is obliged to insist that they, and not he, shall be the judges of what action of the Austro-Hungarian government will satisfy their aspirations and their conception of their rights and destiny as members of the family of nations."[26] Although Masaryk claimed that he "checkmated the manifesto by declaring... independence on October 18," and that the American reply was "the death sentence of the Habsburg dynasty,"[27] the Czechoslovak declaration of independence, usually called "the Washington Declaration" by Czech and Slovak writers, did not influence the content of the American note. It did, however, show Masaryk's concept of the rights and destiny of the Czechs and Slovaks. It said, in part:

> At this grave moment, when the Hohenzollerns are offering peace in order to stop the victorious advance of the Allied armies and to prevent the dismemberment of Austria-Hungary and Turkey, and when the Habsburgs are promising the federalization of the Empire and autonomy to the dissatisfied nationalities committed to their rule, we, the Czechoslovak National Council, recognized by the Allied and American Governments as the Provisional Government of the Czechoslovak State and Nation, in complete accord with the

Declaration of the Czech Deputies, made in Prague on January 6, 1918, and realizing that federalization, and still more, autonomy, mean nothing under a Habsburg dynasty, do hereby make and declare this our Declaration of Independence.[28]

"We have been an independent State since the Seventh Century," the declaration said, invoking the "historic right" to statehood. It charged that "the Habsburgs broke their compact with our nation by illegally transgressing our rights and violating the Constitution of our State which they had pledged themselves to uphold;" the Czechs, therefore, "refuse to remain a part of Austria-Hungary any longer in any form." The Czechs also "claim the right of Bohemia to be reunited with her Slovak brethren of Slovakia, once part of our national State."

The Declaration was designed to appeal to the American public (it certainly appealed more to Americans than to Czechs and Slovaks) by claiming that "the ideals of modern democracy" had been "the ideals of our [Czech] nation for centuries." It said, furthermore, that "we accept the American principles as laid down by President Wilson: the principles of liberated mankind—of the actual equality of nations—and of governments deriving all their just powers from the consent of the governed. We, the nation of Comenius, cannot but accept these principles expressed in the American Declaration of Independence, the principles of Lincoln, and of the Declaration of the Rights of Man and of the Citizen. For these principles our nation shed its blood in the memorable Hussite Wars five hundred years ago; for these same principles, beside her Allies in Russia, Italy, and France, our nation is shedding its blood today."

The declaration then outlined the main principles of the "Constitution of the Czechoslovak Nation." The Czechoslovak state was to be a representative democracy, a republic, guaranteeing all basic freedoms, with the church separated from the state. There was to be universal suffrage and equality of women with men, and the rights of minorities were to be safeguarded by proportional representation, with the stipulation that "national minorities shall enjoy equal rights." The government was to be parliamentary in form, "and shall recognize the principles of initiative and referendum." The standing army "will be replaced by militia." (Of these principles, the separation of church and state, initiative and referendum, and the replacement of the standing army by a militia were not implemented in the Czechoslovak state.)

The Declaration pledged the conduct of "far-reaching social and economic reforms," the abolishment of "patents of nobility," the acceptance of "the democratic and social principle of nationalism" and the doctrine that "all covenants and treaties shall be entered into openly and frankly without secret diplomacy." The final paragraphs expressed the belief that "democracy has defeated theocratic autocracy," that "militarism is overcome," and that "the forces of darkness have served the victory of light—the longed-for age of humanity is dawning." To the declaration were affixed the names of Masaryk, Beneš, and Štefánik, although Štefánik was not consulted on its content and later expressed disagreement with the separation of church and state, the replacement of the army by militia, and the republican form of government.[29] It may be added, parenthetically, that when the Czechoslovak Revolutionary National Assembly drafted the Czechoslovak constitution of 1920, it largely ignored Masaryk's Washington Declaration.

On October 19, 1918, Masaryk requested a loan from the U.S. government for the Czecho-Slovak National Council as a *de facto* cobelligerent government.[30] On the same day the National Committee in Prague issued a declaration rejecting "any negotiation concerning reorganization of Austrian internal affairs," and recognized the Czechoslovak independence movement abroad as an integral part of the legitimate representation of Czechoslovak wishes. The Czech question was declared to be no longer "a question of an internal reform of Austria-Hungary." And since the emperor's proclamation of federalization of the state was not acceptable to the leaders of Hungary, they, together with President Wilson's reply, completed the demoralization of the country. Now the Austro-Germans demanded the establishment of an independent German-Austrian state that would include the territories inhabited by Germans in the Czech lands; and the Czech deputies, under the chairmanship of Kramář, adopted resolutions calling for the formation of an independent state without negotiations with Vienna, regarding the situation as "an international problem to be solved together with other world problems," and "in agreement with the internationally recognized part of the nation which is outside the Czech territory."[31]

Toward the end of October, 1918, many people in Wahsington, where Masaryk's influence was at its peak, believed that the destruction of the Habsburg monarchy would not bring about a Balkanization of central

Europe, and that on the ruins of Austria-Hungary a new central European federation would emerge. Between October 23 and 26, 1918, twelve nations from central Europe were represented by seventy-two delegates at a conference of the Mid-European Democratic Union, held at Independence Hall in Philadelphia. Masaryk presided over the conference, which had some rather stormy sessions. Masaryk's views were reflected in the final resolution of the conference, called the "Declaration of Common Aims of the Independent Mid-European Nations," which was eventually read by Masaryk in front of Independence Hall. This declaration, like the Czechoslovak declaration of independence, was designed for the American public; it was hailed by the American press as something approaching a declaration of independence of a united Europe.[32]

The original of the declaration was submitted to President Wilson by Masaryk, who was the first of the twelve signatories to sign it. In the accompanying letter to Wilson, dated November 1, 1918, Masaryk wrote that the Democratic Mid-European Union "tries to replace the German plan of Mittel-Europa by a positive plan of reorganization of the many smaller nations which are located between the Germans. . .and Russians; there are about eighteen such nations, beginning with the Finns and ending with the Greeks." Masaryk asserted that the "primary aim of the war and the coming peace is the reorganization of the East, including now Russia," and that the first condition of this "reorganization of Eastern Europe and through it of Europe and mankind, is the dismemberment of Austria-Hungary composed of eight non-German nations, oppressed and exploited by a degenerate dynasty and reckless feudal aristocracy supported by the Germans and Magyars."

Claiming to represent "more than fifty million people constituting a chain of nations lying between the Baltic, the Adriatic and the Black Seas, comprising Czecho-Slovaks, Poles, Jugoslovs, Ukranians, Uhro-Rusins, Lithuanians, Roumanians and Italian Irredentists, Unredeemed Greeks, Albanians, Zionists and Armenians, wholly or partly subject to alien domination," the signatories of the declaration subscribed to six "basic principles for all free peoples." According to the first two principles, "all governments derive their just power from the consent of the governed," and "inalienable right of every people" is to "organize their own government on such principles and in such form as they believe will best promote their welfare, safety and happinness." The signatories of

Declaration of Independence 427

the declaration pledged "on behalf of their respective nations" that the principles set forth in it "shall be incorporated in the organic laws of whatever government our respective peoples may hereafter establish." As it happened, the vast majority of the Czechoslovak Revolutionary (Constituent) National Assembly, established after the war, followed Masaryk's views and paid no attention to the principles stated in the Declaration of the Common Aims of the Independent Mid-European Nations. The assembly did not derive its power from the consent of the governed; it was not elected by the peoples of Czechoslovakia; the Germans, Hungarians, Poles, and Ruthenians in Czechoslovakia were not represented in it at all; and the Germans, Hungarians, Slovaks, and Ruthenians living in the country were not allowed to "organize their own government on such principles and in such form as they believe will best promote their welfare, safety and happiness."

During the time when this declaration was promulgated in Philadelphia, delegates of the Czech National Committee at Prague were arriving in Geneva, Switzerland. In view of both internal and external developments, the Austrian government permitted the departure of several Czech political leaders abroad to discuss with the representatives of the provisional government the future conduct of Czech politics. One part of the delegation left Prague on Ocotber 22; another, headed by Kramář, on October 25. Among the members of the second group were V. Klofáč, F. Staněk, G. Habrman, and A. Kalina. Just before the scheduled departure of the delegation, Emperor Charles extended a personal invitation to Klofáč for a talk. The two met on October 22, at 8:30 P. M. During their conversation the emperor did not express any political demand or proposition; he merely made a plea that Klofáč should influence the Czechs in such a way that whatever happend should happen without bloodshed. To this Klofáč replied that the Czech nation desired and prayed for the same end.[33]

There is no evidence that Charles asked Klorać to come to see him in order to make a last effort to save the empire. The Emperor's gesture seems to have reflected his resignation and his being prepared for the worst. The new government, headed by Heinrich Lammasch, the last prime minister of Austria, assumed office on October 25, and its task was no longer to save the empire, but to oversee its peaceful and orderly liquidation.[34]

On October 28, 1918, Dr. Beneš and several other members of the independence movement abroad arrived in Geneva to meet the leaders from the homeland and to discuss current political problems with them.[35] At their joint meeting Beneš reported on the international situation and reiterated his prediction that the war would go on into 1919, and would be decided, definitely, the following spring. Neither he nor the others present at the consultations at Geneva had any idea of what was happening at that time in Prague.

Under the impact of desparate reports from the front in northern Italy, where the Austro-Hugarian army was disintegrating and thus making possible the unexpected success of the Italian offensive, the Austrian minister of foreign affairs announced in a diplomatic note of October 27 that the empire accepted all the conditions made by President Wilson on October 18, 1918. This note was published in Prague on October 28. It was understood as an unconditional capitulation by Austria-Hungary. People swarmed into the streets of Prague to demonstrate, and the Czech National Committee assumed all executive powers. The committee issued a proclamation to the "Czechoslovak People" saying that on October 28, the Czechoslovak state "entered into the ranks of the independent states of the civilized world." It appealed to the people not to forget about discipline, reminding them that as citizens they had not only rights but also duties. "Our liberators, Masaryk and Wilson," the proclamation said, "must not be deceived for having thought they had gained liberty for a people capable of self-government. The great moments in which we live must not be marred by any reprehensible acts . . . . Each of you ought to respect unreservedly what is sacred to others. Neither individual liberty nor private property must be attacked. Obey without questions the instructions of the National Committee."[36]

Following this declaration of independence, the "first law of the Czechslovak state" was promulgated. The National Committee at Prague, "in the name of the Czechoslovak people," proclaimed itself the "executive organ of the sovereign political authority." In the first three articles of the "law" it proclaimed that the national assembly would, ultimately, determine the form of the Czechoslovak state, that all existing provincial and imperial laws and ordinances remained, temporarily, in force, and that local governments were under the jurisdiction of the National Committee.[37]

The transfer of power into the hands of the new executive and administrative organ of state power was very easy, smooth, and without any serious incident.

Joyful that the war was over, the Czech population accepted the new organ of state power without any visible opposition and with a great deal of enthusiasm; but Slovakia and the areas in the Czech lands inhabited by Germans remained outside the national committee's control.

From the beginning the Czechs who worked for Czechoslovak independence had planned to include Slovakia, known as Upper Hungary, in the state to be created on the ruins of Austria-Hungary. For Kramář, Slovaks were the closest Slavic kin of the Czechs, and Slovakia was the necessary link between the Czech lands and Russia. Masaryk, on the other hand, felt that Slovaks were Czechs speaking merely with a local dialect. As one nation, the Czechs and Slovaks ought to live in one state.

At the beginning of the war, Ferdiš Juriga, a Slovak deputy in the Hungarian parliament, affirmed the loyalty of the Slovaks to the Hungarian government; however, toward the war's end he and other Slovak leaders began to voice disapproval of the existing conditions in Hungary. While the Slovak masses were largely apolitical, the leaders of the Slovak National party and the Slovak People's party held differing views on the future of the Slovaks, some favoring autonomy within Hungary and others advocating union with the Czech lands. Eventually, when toward the end of May, 1918, the leaders of the Slovak National party met at Turčiansky Sv. Martin (henceforth Martin), Father Andrej Hlinka emerged as a spokesman for cooperation with the Czechs, declaring, "We have to state definitely whether we will continue to live with the Hungarians or with the Czechs. We cannot avoid this question; let us say publicly that we are for a Czechoslovak orientation. The thousand-year marriage with the Magyars has not succeeded. We must dissolve it."[38] Yet, for the next few months the political situation remained dormant, and only in October did the Slovak leaders formally establish their National Council.

There were signs of the approaching end of the war when on October 19 the only Slovak representative in the Hungarian parliament, Juriga, read a declaration demanding for the Slovaks the right to decide their own destinies. The declaration emphasized that the Hungarian parliament and government did not have the right to speak for the Slovaks; that the Slovak representatives at the peace conference would have to be selected by their own national assembly or its organ, the Slovak National Council, and that no other person had the right to negotiate and decide on behalf of the Slovak nation. The Slovaks, Juriga declared, demanded for themselves the right of self-determination, just as they recognized the right to self-determination of the other nationalities in Hungary.[39]

Juriga's reference to the Slovak National Council indicated that the first steps toward its information had been taken; its purpose was to seek unification of all political segments of the nation in one representative body. The Slovak National Council was formally established in Martin on October 30, 1918. Its chairman was Matúš Dula and its secretary Karol A. Medvecky. The Slovak National party, the Slovak People's party, and the Slovak Social Democratic party were represented in the council.[40]

When the Slovak leaders assembled in Martin on October 30, they did not know that two days earlier the Czech National Committee in Prague had proclaimed Czechoslovak independence. They knew, however, that the new minister of foreign affairs of Austria-Hungary, Gyula Andrassy, had accepted Wilson's conditions for peace and had recognized the right of the nationalities in Austria-Hungary, more specifically the right of the Czechs, Slovaks, and Southern Slavs, to decide their future destinies.[41] Therefore, representatives of all Slovak political parties, organized as "the National Council of the Slovak branch of the united Czecho-Slovak Nation," insisted "on the right of self-determination accepted by the whole world," and, as "the National Council of the Czecho-Slovak Nation living in Hungary," they declared: "1. The Slovak Nation is part of the Czecho-Slovak Nation, united in language and in the history of its culture.... 2. For this Czecho-Slovak Nation we demand an unlimited right of self-determination on the basis of complete independence. On the basis of this principle, we express our consent with the new condition of international law accepted on October 28, 1918, by the Austro-Hungarian minister of Foreign Affairs. 3. We demand an immediate conclusion of peace based on humanitarian Christian principles, a peace which would prevent future wars and continuing armament through international safeguards...."[42] Thus Slovakia was to become a part of Czecho-Slovakia.

The Czech political leaders were surprised by the sudden collapse of Austria-Hungary; yet they assumed political power without hesitation and with the intention of keeping it. They had been preparing themselves for this contingency ever since Kramář had assumed the leadership of the

National Committee. Those members of the National Committee who arrived at Geneva held conferences with Beneš, who proposed that the National Committee issue a declaration approving the conduct of the provisional government (abroad), denouncing the Habsburg dynasty, and rejecting the further existence of Austria-Hungary. Beneš's proposal was accepted and incorporated in a declaration dated October 31, 1918. This Geneva declaration, signed by K. Kramář, V. Klofáč, S. Habrman, F. Staněk, and A. Kalina, stated, in part, that the Czecho-Slovak deputies and delegates of the Prague National Committee had met in the presence of Edvard Beneš, minister of foreign affairs of the provisional government "of the Czecho-Slovak Countries," and that they declared "solemnly in the name of the Czecho-Slovak Nation" that they fully approved the political and military actions of the provisional government; that the Czecho-Slovak nation "definitely severed all bonds with Vienna and Budapest;" that "no bond exists or shall ever exist between the Nation and the Habsburg Dynasty;" and that the peace conference was to offer "an opportunity for the Czecho-Slovak Nation to aid in establishing in Central Europe . . . a political system which will assure a just and lasting peace for the whole of Europe."[43]

Beneš left Switzerland for Paris, where he discovered that armistice negotiations with Austria-Hungary were already under way without the presence of a Czechoslovak representative. He protested immediately to the French ministry of foreign affairs, invoking the secret agreement of September 28, 1918. The French and British governments had conveniently forgotten the agreements they had signed with Beneš giving him the right to be represented at Allied conferences affecting Czecho-Slovak interests.[44] But now in view of the collapse of the Danubian monarchy and the establishment of Czech rule in Prague and Yugoslav rule in Zagreb, the foreign offices were apologetic, realizing that they had to get used to the "new diplomacy" of an unorthodox ally. Therefore, on November 2, 1918, Beneš was invited to a meeting presided over by the American delegate, Colonel House, and including delegations from France, headed by Clemenceau, Great Britain headed by Lloyd George, and Italy, headed by Orlando, as well ans representatives of Japan, Serbia, and Greece. On November 4, 1918, Beneš received a formal invitation to Versailles, and on the same day he attended for the first time an Allied conference of the chief executives. If the armistice recognized by implication the existence of Austria-Hungary, the conference of November 4, also by implication recognized the end of the Habsburg empire.[45] Czechoslovakia was the only one of the succession states of Austria-Hungary that was represented at the conference, and thus entered the forum of international politics under exceptional circumstances. Beneš's diplomatic victory was complete; he "could not even beleive it." As he expressed it, "Three years ago I was running . . . across the Czech border, sneaking deceitfully through the underbrush in order to evade the eyes of Austrian and Bavarian officials . . . and today I sit here, together with representatives of France, England, United States . . . deciding the destinies of Emperors William and Charles and signing the conditions of their capitulation."[46] Beneš remained in France to participate in the peace negotiations and the signing of the peace treaties in 1919. He returned to Prague, after four years of exile, on September 24, 1919.[47]

Toward the end of October, 1918, the Czechoslovak independence movement acheived its objective with the establishment of an indepent Czechoslovak state. The Provisionsal Constitution of the Czechoslovak Republic was promulgated on November 14, 1918. Among the contributing factors that determined the republican character of the new state were the collapse of tsarist Russia, Masaryk's own preference for a republic, and the help he and his coworkers received from the United States and France. On November 14, 1918, at the first meeting of the Revolutionary National Assembly, consisting of 249 delegates[48] (Germans, Hungarians, Poles, and Ruthenians living in the new state were not represented in the assembly), Masaryk was unanimously elected president of the republic.[49] Later, the Revolutionary National Assembly was increased to 270 members in order to "accommodate" the Slovaks. Out of 270 seats the Slovaks held officially 54 (although in accordance with their populations they should have had more than 70), but among these were some Czechs, including Alice Masaryk, the president's daughter. According to Karol Sidor, a Slovak autonomist, the Slovaks held only 40 seats (with Dr. Šrobár 41), and out of these 40 seats 30 were held by Protestants and only 10 by Catholics, although Slovakia was 80 percent Catholic.[50] Obviously, the genuine Slovaks and Catholics were discriminated against in the Revolutionary National Assembly, which became the Constituent Assembly charged with drafting a constitution. This situation gave the Slovaks, especially Father Hlinka, reason to be unhappy about

Declaration of Independence 433

the position of Slovaks in the new state. The Revolutionary (Constituent) National Assembly was dominated by pro-Masaryk Czechs. When Masaryk, now the acknowledged leader of the new state, arrived in Prague on December 21, he was welcomed as the liberator by a great demonstration in the city. Later, he was usually called by his followers "President-Liberator."

On December 22, 1918, the second day after his arrival in Prague, Masaryk delivered his first message to the Czechoslovak Revolutionary National Assembly.[51] The prewar "Realist" Masaryk proclaimed that the world had become divided into two camps, and that in the global struggle between the two camps "the idealists have won." It was a victory of "spirit over matter, right over violence, and the truth over guile." Theocratic autocracy had been subdued by democracy—it was a victory of "non-militaristic democracy defending humanitarian ideals." The Allies had declared "consistently that all nations, not only the big but also the small ones, have the right of independence: President Wilson formulated the foremost principles of democracy, contained in the American Declaration of Independence and the French Declaration of the Rights of Man and Citizen.... Revolution won over the legitimist statism.... President Wilson declared as a war aim the liberation of the whole mankind. Against the four Central Powers the whole mankind united...." Denouncing the Habsburgs and their "misuse of religion for their base materialistic aims," Masaryk praised the "national awakening led by the idea of humanity and from it stemming democracy," and declared that "the fate of our nation is directly and logically tied with the West and its modern democracy."

Masaryk's rhetoric, as usual, led him to exaggerate his own work by claiming that "we have organized all our emigrant colonies abroad," whereas, in fact, the Czech and Slovak colonies abroad were the first to organize the Czecho-Slovak independence movement abroad.[52] He also "categorically stated" that "we did not take a penny from the Allies—I emphasize that," he said, "because our opponents talk about Russian, English and other money. And, similarly, I categorically declare that during the whole time [while abroad] we did not use a single untruth against our enemies, not even one of the so-called diplomatic cunnings—such an honest political struggle, such an honest revolution, I dare to say, has hardly ever been conducted!"

The record shows otherwise. If Lansing was right in saying that "Great Britain has already an unenviable reputation of having one rule for herself and another rule for other nations. As a result she is charged with more or less reason with selfishness, injustice and lack of principle,"[53] then Masaryk was "more British" than the British themselves. Lansing warned that the United States "ought to be very careful not to earn the same reputation,"[54] Masaryk made a great stride toward, and well beyond, that unenviable goal.

CHAPTER SIXTEEN

THE NEW STATE AT
THE PARIS PEACE CONFERENCE

The Czech struggle for independence culminated in the National Committee's assuming governmental authority at Prague on October 28, 1918. The revolutionary seizure of power ensured that the victorious great powers would not go back on their promises to the Czech exiles, and that they would respect the will of the nation. Had there been no such demonstration of the nation's determination to rule its own destiny, all the work done abroad by the armies, and by Masaryk, Beneš, Štefánik, and others, would have been of little effect. A few months after that event, Kramář noticed at the Paris Peace Conference that some of the British and even French statesmen could not part with the idea of preserving a federated Austria-Hungary.[1]

Had it not been for the revolutionary act of October 28, prepared and executed by the home political leaders, the Czechs might well not have been invited to the conference at all. After the "men of the twenty-eighth of October" assumed political power and proclaimed Czechoslovak independence, the Entente powers had to contend with the new political unit in central Europe and respect it as an ally. Thus, Beneš, who was not invited to the first meeting of the conference that began on October 31, after his return from Switzerland and his protest to the French ministry of foreign affairs, was invited to the next meetings of the conference. He represented there the only succession state of Austria-Hungary granted such an honor and privilege from the beginning of the conference.

The new—revolutionary—Czechoslovak government had to cope with several problems immediately. Although it had the full support and cooperation of the Czechs, many of whom expressed their enthusiasm and joy over the newly won independence after "three hundred years of living under the Habsburg yoke," Germans living in the historical lands refused to recognize the authority of the new state. Within a few days, they established their own governments in four regions (provinces) inhabited predominantly by Germans. On October 29, 1918, Dr. Rudolph Lodgman von Auen assumed leadership of the provincial government of Deutschböhmen (German Bohemia), centered at Liberec in northern Bohemia. On the same day, the Germans of Moravia, Austrian Silesia, and eastern Bohemia proclaimed the provisional government of Sudentenland under Dr. R. Freissler.[2] The other two provincial governments were established in southern Moravia and in western Bohemia. The spokesmen for the four provincial governments demanded that those areas be attached to German Austria. Responding to the request, the Austrian National Provisional Assembly accepted German Bohemia as part of the new Austrian state at its meeting of October 30, 1918;[3] the other provinces were claimed by Austria later.

Spokesmen for Deutschböhmen and Sudetenland attempted to negotiate with the Czech National Committee at Prague as equal partners on the basis of the principle that the consent of the governed is the essential foundation of a democratic state. Also, at the invitation of the Czech Social Democrat Rudolf Bechyně, who was of the opinion that the new state should have within its borders as few Germans as possible and was willing to sacrifice the historical boundaries, Dr. Lodgman visited Prague for conversations with several members of the Czech Natinal Committee. The leader of the German Social Democrats in Bohemia, Josef Seliger, went one step further and negotiated a limited autonomy for German Bohemia. Two Czech Social Democratic leaders, František Soukup and Antonín Němec, favored such a solution and agreed with him that the question of self-determination could be postponed. However, Dr. Alois Rašín, a member of the Czech National Committee and an orginal member of the *Maffie,* made an end to these negotiations on November 9, 1918, when he told Seliger categorically, "We do not negotiate with rebels!"

Bechyně late criticized Rašín for this statement, saying that it had poisoned relations between Czechs and Germans.[4] In his report on the talks in Prague, Seliger stated that his argument that "the right of self-determination is Wilson's program," was answered, "the right of self-determination is only a phrase—today, it is force which decides."[5] After their unsuccessful attempts at negotiating directly with the Czech National Committee at Prague, the Germans in Bohemia and Moravia turned to President Wilson and the Paris Peace Conference and invoked the right of self-determination.

The provisional government of Deutschböhmen sent a note of protest against the "imperialistic encroachments of the Czech state" to President Wilson, protector of all minorities and their right of self-determination. The communication arrived in Washington on November 21, 1918. The note, drawn up by those who claimed to speak "in the name of two and one-half million Germans in Bohemia who, appealing to that right of self-determination, consider themselves a constituent part of the free German Republic," asked Wilson to protect this German minority in Bohemia and to prevent the use of force against them.[6] The Austrian government also engaged in diplomatic activity on behalf of "more than three million Germans" living in "large, coherent territories of Bohemia and Moravia." It asked that a plebiscite, supervised by neutral authorities, be held in these regions to determine the wishes of the people, since the Czechoslovak state intended to incorporate them into its territory without awaiting the decision of the peace conference.[7]

German Austria appealed to the Allied governments, including the French. Replying to communications from the government of German Austria dated December 13 and December 16, 1918, French President Pichon rejected the proposed plebiscite and arbitration. The presidential note said that the "Czecho-Slovak State," as a recognized power, "has for its boundaries, at least until the decision of the Peace Conference is reached, the boundaries of the historic provinces of Bohemia, Moravia and of Austrian Silesia."[8] General Franchet d'Esperey, commander of the French Balkan armies, asked Austria to withdraw its forces from Slovakia. The French government took the side of the Czechs.

At Paris, Beneš, the principal negotiator of the Czechoslovak government, used his wartime contacts in the war and foreign offices to further his cause. Masaryk was still in the United States, whence he sent

Beneš instructions on November 7, 1918.⁹ His nineteen-point letter covers a large variety of subjects. First, Masaryk asks Beneš about the material needs of the new state, and informs him that President Wilson "wants to help us in any possible way." Second, Masaryk is organizing the Mid-European Union "on economic foundation," and "a corporation that will take care of the reconstruction of the zone of small nations." Third, the "Little Russians" from Hungary want a union with the Czechoslovak state, but are opposed to the "Carpathorussians" and the "Ukrainians." Carpatho-Russia would be Czechoslovak's connecting link with Romania, and Masaryk urges Beneš "to cultivate the Rumanians." In the sixth point Masaryk delves into the Russian problem, urging help for Russia and arms and "military reenforcement" for the Czech army in Russia. "The Allies," Masaryk writes, "must have the courage to come out against the Bolsheviks who are incompetent administrators." The Allies erred "by supporting everybody" in Russia. Since the Romanovs are incompetent, it is necessary to create a coalition government in a federalized Russia. The best solution would be to keep Russia as she was before the war, with the possible exception of granting independence to Finland on condition that she "not go with Germany" and that she conclude an economic agreement with Russia. The Baltic nations and the Ukraine will have to remain within Russia as federal republics. Since it is not possible to establish order in Russia without an army, "the Allies (with us) must organize a Russian army." However, its political leadership must be Russian.

Masaryk points out that the Prussians are "brutal" but "not as base and false" as the Austrians are. He directs Beneš to stand on "the historical right" and on the claim that "we have created the state" and that Germans were merely invited by the Czech kings to settle in the Bohemian Crown lands. As "the culmination of political recognition" Masaryk wants to obtain a ten-million-dollar loan from the United States and he asks Beneš to convey to the French that this action is not directed "against them." He also informs Beneš that "Colonel House is a pacifist in his soul [sic], but believes honestly in democracy and 'liberalism' and is open to suggestions." In addition, Beneš is advised that "Sir Wiseman is intimate with him [House]; and you can influence him through Wiseman." But Beneš must watch Voska so that the latter would "not spoil something because of his ignorance." At this time Voska, a captain in the

U.S. military intelligence, was working for "The Inquiry" in Europe and was attached to the U.S. delegation at the peace conference. As has been noted earlier, Wiseman had succeeded in placing Voska in "The Inquiry," and considered his agent to be reliable and dedicated to the British cause. It seems that Masaryk was not certain that Voska was smart enough to play successfully the role of a triple agent. (In a letter to Beneš, dated January 5, 1919, Masaryk urged his protégé "to exploit" two British architects of the "New Europe," Seton-Watson and Steed.)[10] In November 1918, Masaryk conveyed to Beneš that "tactics are now important —tactics—political and social tact."

Masaryk wrote, furthermore, that he would remain in the United States "until Wilson will decide all that he has to decide," and that he was also working on his book *Nová Europa* (*The New Europe*), parts of which had already been published in *Čechoslovák* earlier in 1918. In the last part of the book, entitled "The Democratic Peace and Its Conditions," Masaryk declared that there would be "only three new states in Europe, Poland, Czechoslovakia and Finland"; that Russia would become a federation of nations including the Estonians, the Letts, the Lithuanians, the Ukrainians, and the nations of the Caucasus, who would have autonomy within Russia; and that the English and French parts of Asia would remain under English and French rule. Theocracy "must be abolished everywhere," says Masaryk; and "nations which have the right of self-determination will be admitted to the peace congress." (Obviously, the right of self-determination did not belong to the national groups whom Masaryk assigned to the great powers, to Czechoslovakia, and to Russia.) The congress would agree on "a law [that would be] internationally guaranteed and [that would] secure national minorities cultural and national equality." The law would also state other rules, for instance, that "alcoholism must be internationally suppressed." He ends the book on a biblical note: even democracy "hopes that there will be one sheepfold and one shepherd"; and the slogan of democratic Europe is "Jesus, not Caesar."[11] This slogan notwithstanding, neither Masaryk nor Beneš was an other-worldly follower of Jesus seeking the kingdom of God; both of them amply demonstrated their commitment to the kingdom of this world.

Beneš was not satisfied with the prospect that the territorial questions concerning Czechoslovakia would be decided by the conference. Therefore, he initiated a policy of *faits accomplis* in order to secure the territories claimed by the new state. In addition to the German-inhabited areas in the historical lands, there were the questions of Slovakia and Teschen. These territories had to be occupied militarily, and this could be done only with the help of at least one great power. The power on which Czechoslovakia would lean was France, which was interested in both weakening Germany and promoting its own hegemony in central Europe. Czechoslovakia also wanted to build its own hegemony in the area; it could do so only with the consent and cooperation of France. Thus, in view of the compatibility of French and Czechoslovak interests in foreign affairs, plans were made for building a new order in central Europe that would be acceptable to both countries.

Beneš expressed his views on the relationship between the two countries in a letter of November 9, 1918, to the National Committee, in which he asked the committee for approval of his plan to bring a French military-political mission to Prague: "(a) I take the position that our future military organization must be under French influence for political reasons, because France will have tremendous influence and will always support us in all respects. (b) Our location in Central Europe endows us with unusually great importance; France is aware of it. The French want to establish closer factual contacts with us, and we, in turn, can derive from it unusally great political, diplomatic and economic benefits. At the present time there is no Russian influence, and we will need foreign assistance in organizing our armed forces anyway...."[12] The government at Prague agreed with Beneš's proposal, and the relationship between the two countries was established by the subordination of the Czechoslovak army to the French army. France sent military officers to Czechoslovakia to help to build the country's armed forces. On January 20, 1919, the situation was legalized in the first treaty concerning a French military mission to Czechoslovakia. The extent and effectiveness of the arrangement was more exactly defined by the treaty of August 1, 1920.[13] This treaty was visible evidence of Czechoslovakia's one-sided foreign policy orientation toward France, which apparently benefited the country in the short run, during the occupation of the territories claimed by the new state and at the Paris Peace Conference.

Before Beneš asked the Kramář government at Prague to endorse his plan for bringing French military advisers to Czechoslovakia, he had tried to convince the Allies, especially France, of the importance of Czechoslovakia's strategic location for the domination of central Europe. In his memorandum of November 3, 1918, to the Allies, Beneš pointed at the possibility of exercising influence, from the Czechoslovak base, on Austria, Hungary, Italy, and Poland, and also, by implication, on Russia and the Ukraine. In addition, Czechoslovakia was not far from Berlin. At the same time Beneš emphasized that Czechoslovakia was a country of peace, while "in this situation the danger of Bolshevism in Vienna is especially threatening, and, for specific reasons, even more so than in Budapest. Only the Czechs can stop this movement."[14] Beneš also pointed at the danger of Bolshevism in a letter to Clemenceau dated December 16, 1918, in which he requested the subordination of the Czechoslovak army to the supreme commander of the French forces, Marshal Foch. Beneš suggested that the Czech military forces could be used, "should it be necessary, for the maintenance of order and stopping the tide of Bolshevism in the neighboring countries."[15]

Since Austria-Hungary and Germany had lost the war, they were not represented at the Paris Peace Conference, where Beneš was rallying support for his government's proposed new, reconstructed central Europe, which would be "neither German nor Russian," and in which Czechoslovakia would hold a pivotal position. The Czechoslovak delegation at Paris, led at first by Beneš and later by Kramář' prepared an elaborate justification of its territorial claims.[16] These claims were summarized in *Mémoire* No. 2 in seven points, including demands for the inclusion in Czecho-Slovakia of the three principal countries of "the ancient Crown of Bohemia" (Bohemia, Moravia, and Silesia); rectification of the borderlands of the three "historical countries" at the expense of Germany and Austria; the further inclusion of Slovakia, Subcarpathian Ruthenia, the corridor to Yugoslavia, and Serb Lusatia; the internationalization of several rivers and railroads; and the protection of the Czech minority in Vienna.[17] The *Mémoires* claimed that the "Czecho-Slovaks" numbered ten million,[18] and that their territorial claims were based on "historic tradition," since Bohemia, Moravia, Silesia, Slovakia, and Lusatia "formed the bases of the first Czecho-Slovak State."[19] The Czecho-Slovak Republic also asked for the inclusion of three small regions that actually belonged to Prussian Silesia and Lower Austria; these claims were "based on the Principle of Nationality." The incorporation of these regions into the new state, it was claimed, "would in no way injure the vital interests of the neighboring States."[20] The Czecho-Slovaks also claimed the Slovak territory, including certain regions "partly inhabited by a popularion of Magyars," on the grounds that the territory claimed formed a geographical unit, and that it was needed for economic and political reasons, in addition to the grounds that the peace conference ought to apply "the same principle of reparations to the Magyars as those applied to the Germans."[21]

The inclusion into the new state of Serb Lusatia and a corridor to Yugoslavia would have meant the inclusion of territories inhabited mostly, if not exclusively, by non-Slavic peoples: Germans and Magyars. The Czecho-Slovak claim to these territories was based on the following argument: "In order to establish in Central Europe a new political system which would assure a lasting peace, it is necessary to separate the Germans and the Magyars one from the other, and to bring together the Czecho-Slovaks and the Jugoslavs. It is not a local problem for the Czechs or the Jugoslavs; it is a European problem."[22] The Serbs of Lusatia, who were divided between Prussia and Saxony, "must be united into a single territory" and "must be assured a direct contact with the Czechs in order to facilitate intellectual and economic relations between those two nations."[23] The whole problem of Lusatia was presented also in a separate memorandum.[24]

The *Mémoires* contained many statistics and maps supporting the claims made by the new state. These statistics challenged the prewar census in Austria-Hungary, asserting that the official figures resulted from "systematic falsification of the Austrian census and the pressure exercised on the Czecho-Slovak population."[25] It was also claimed that the Germans had been "artificially installed in Bohemia as colonists, or officials or bureaucrats."[26] However, the new republic would "in no way oppress the Gemans;" on the contrary, they would "enjoy an order of justice and liberty."[27] An appendix dealt specifically with "Oppresion of the Slovaks by the Magyar Government, Expressed in Official Figures."[28] Here again, the *Mémoire* asserted that the Hungarians were falsifying the official census.

Mémoire No. 6 dealt with the Ruthenians of Hungary, concluding that they were "a nation closely related to the Slovaks, live under the same conditions as the Slovaks, that they are in very intimate relations with them, that their union to the Czecho-Slovak Republic would cause no difficulty whatever." Furthermore, this solution "would best respond to political reality and to the principles of justice." It was pointed out that "certain representatives of the Ruthenians of Hungary" had already expressed their preference for this resolution of their situation.[29]

The Czechoslovak delegates to the peace conference tried to win support for their position by contacting other delegates privately and informally, as well as officially. Thus, even before Czechoslovakia presented her case to the Council of Ten on February 5, 1919, the peacemakers were asked to accept boundaries for the new state that went well beyond the territories inhabited predominantly by Czechs and Slovaks, on the grounds that the new order in central Europe required a strategically defensible and economically strong Czechoslovakia to help the Allies replace German and Austrian influence in the area. The argument was appealing, especially to the French, who were interested in building a circle of states separating Germany from her eastern ally—Lenin's Russia.[30] In the actual presentation of the Czechoslovak position before the Council of Ten, the foreign minister of Czechoslovakia emphasized the strategic importance of his state—"the advanced guard of Slavdom in the West"—in curbing the "Germanic mass" of eighty million. If a strong Czechoslovakia blocked their way, the Germans would never again attempt forcible invasion of southern and eastern Europe. The Czechs, Beneš argued, had always considered it their special mission to resist the Teutonic flood; as "protectors of democracy against Germanism... it was their duty at all times to fight the Germans."[31] Another aspect of the special mission of the Czechoslovaks was to serve as a connecting link between Russia and the west.[32]

In his conferences with members of Allied delegations, Beneš attempted to win over the latter to his position, trying to capitalize on their sympathy towards the Czechoslovak troops operating in Russia. Thus, on February 7, 1919, he told Doctors Day and Seymour and Major Douglas Johnson of the U.S. delegation that "between 40 per cent and 45 per cent of these troops had already been lost;" but he added that

> despite the fact that the remainder must also be sacrificed, it was not possible for his government to withdraw them. They have been co-operating with the anti-Bolshevik element in an effort to overcome the menace of Bolshevism in Russia and could not desert their

Russian friends in this critical emergency. The Czecho-Slovaks were practically the only support upon which the better elements of the Russian people could count. Bolshevism in Russia must ultimately disappear and it was in the highest degree important that a regenerated Russia should be able to say that the Czecho-Slovaks had not left them to the mercy of Bolshevism, but had remained loyal friends even at the cost of the practical destruction of their small army, the Czecho-Slovaks would constitute a small nation and it was important for them to have the great Russian people their steadfast friends."[33]

Beneš also "lightly touched upon the difficulty of maintaining a good morale in the Czecho-Slovak army when they were fighting against such heavy odds and without adequate support from the Allies." Major Johnson inferred that Beneš "felt much disappointed that the Allies were not rendering effective assistance to the Czecho-Slovak army in their difficult task." Despite the "difficulty he was enountering in representing the more immoderate elements among this people," Beneš stated that it was his ambition "in as much as the Czechs had made war with the Allies, that they should also make peace with the Allies and in accordance with their friendly advice; and that where opinions differed, the Czechs should present their case fully and frankly and then loyally abide by the decisions reached by the great Powers to whom they were so deeply indebted."[34]

Major Johnson's testimony shows that Beneš was using the Russian situation in order to gain Allied support for the Czechoslovak cause. But a few years later, Beneš claimed, "The Allies tried to use our soldiers in Russia, but this we opposed.... Our Army participated in the fighting against the Bolsheviks contrary to its will and that of its leaders; the first phase of its military action was devoted exclusively to the struggle against the Central Powers; and only in the second phase was the Russian conflict forced upon us; but even then our Army was solely on the defensive.... The only correct attitude of our Army in Russia was one of non-interference in Russian internal affairs...." According to Beneš, the fundamental standpoint of the Czechoslovak parliament was as follows: "As early as the spring of 1919, all our political parties without execption took a stand against an interventionist policy in Russia, even though we were opposed to the methods of Bolshevism and did not agree with its foreign propaganda and its efforts for a World Revolution...."[35] (Beneš's statement was not accurate; Kramář and his party favored intervention.) Privately and publicly Beneš assured the conference that Czechoslovakia had no intention of oppressing the Germans or other minorities, and would grant them minority rights.[36] In view of what was to happen later, especially during the Sudeten crisis in 1938, it may be useful to quote from *Mémoire* No. 3 parts of the section entitled "The lot of the Germans in the Czecho-Slovak Republic":

> it is absolutely necessary to know how the Germans are treated in the Czecho-Slovak Republic. Not only is the Czecho-Slovak Republic ready to accept, if need be, any international order of things in favour of minorities established by the Peace Conference, but it is, moreover, ready to forestall such provisions and given the Germans the rights due them.
>
> The Czecho-Slovak Republic will be purely democratic State. The electoral law will be based on universal and equal suffrage; all offices will be accessible to every citizen; the tongue spoken by minorities will be everywhere admitted. No minorities will be refused right of having their own schools, their judges and their tribunals It should be added that although the Czechs are aware that the Germans were excessively privileged under the old regime, they have no intention of suppressing either the schools or universities or technical schools belonging to the Germans, which institutions however had but a small number of students before the war.
>
> In fine, the Germans in Bohemia [sic] would have the same rights as the Czecho-Slovaks themselves. The German tongue would be the second tongue of the land and no vexatious measures would be taken against the German population. *The regime adopted would be similar to that of Switzerland* [emphasis added].[37]

Beneš elaborated on this point in his note of May 20, 1919, in which he announced the intention of the Czechoslovak state to apply the principles of the Swiss Republic in creating the organs of the new state; this would make Czechoslovakia "a sort of Switzerland." In the conclusion of his memorandum Beneš promised "an extremely liberal regime, which will very much resemble that of Switzerland."[38]

"This regime," *Memoire* No. 3 continues,

> would be instituted in Bohemia [*sic*], not only because the Czechs are and always have been imbued with the profoundest sentiment of democracy, law and justice, and recognize those rights even to the adversaries, but also for the reason that the Czechs consider that solution, favourable to the Germans, to be in the political interest of their own country and nation.
>
> They have, throughout the whole of the XIXth century given proofs of great practical sense and chiefly political sense. They are too 'realistic' and have too much good sense not to see that violence and injustice were the cause of the disaster of Austria-Hungary, and that a similar policy could be but detrimental to their own State and nation. The Germans themselves know and avow the truth of this.

These were, however, merely promises of rights to be granted the Germans in Czechoslovakia.

The same *Mémoire* claimed, without offering any proof, that "(1) the Germans of Bohemia do not represent united element, properly organized and led towards a definite aim; (2) they have no leaders enjoying the confidence of the people, and that there is in Bohemia no really strong popular movement entitled to invoke the principle of the right of nations to decide their own fate; (3) on the contrary, those among the Germans of Bohemia who are at present capable of clearly expressing a political idea, declare, willy-nilly, that their economic interests urge the Germans of Bohemia to prefer the Czecho-Slovak State to a great Germany; and that the union of German Bohemia to Germany is an illusion." This was hardly true; the Germans of Bohemia did object to being incorporated into the new Czechoslovak state.

No attempt was made at the peace conference to dispute the fact that there was a large German minority in the Czech lands. How many Germans lived there was, however, a matter of controversy. On the one hand, the Austrian government claimed at St. Germain to be pleading on behalf of some four million Sudeten Germans, and thus added on about a million. On the other hand, Beneš lowered the number by about the same figure. The Germans asserted that Beneš was deliberately misleading the conference in his *Mémoires*. He denied this.[39] The *Mémoires* were, no doubt, propaganda statements. The municipal elections of 1919 and the census of 1921 showed that both the Austrian government and Beneš exaggerated, and that the truth was somewhere between the two positions. According to the census of 1921, 8.8 million (65.5 percent) of the people living in the new state were Czechs and Slovaks. (The statistics recorded merely "Czechoslovak" nationality. According to a rough estimate, there were 6.8 million Czechs and 2 million Slovaks.) In addition, 3.1 million (23.4 percent) were Germans, 0.75 million (5.6 percent) Hungarians, 0.46 million (3.4 percent) Ukrainians, and 75,000 (0.6 percent) Poles.[40]

In answer to a question from David Lloyd George, Beneš, who did not want a plebiscite, admitted that the Germans living in the Czech historical provinces would vote against the Czechoslovak state. But he played on the antisocialist orientation of the statesmen at Paris, claiming that the Germans would vote against the Czechoslovak state and for inclusion in Germany because of the influence of the German Social Democratic party, "which thought that Germany would henceforth have a Social Democratic regime. The Czech government was a coalition government and was regarded by them as bourgeois," wrote Lloyd George.[41] But, said Beneš, had the Germans in the Czech lands been allowed to have their will and to have the territories inhabited by them attached to Austria (which, on November 12, had declared its wish "to form part of the Great German Republic")[42] the German regions of Bohemia, Moravia, and Silesia would, in effect, become part of Germany. Since the atmosphere at the conference was anti-German, the expert advice available to the victors was mostly that of well-known critics of the Habsburg monarchy, and since the French government especially wanted to weaken Germany, the Allies tacitly tolerated Czech military occupation of the German borderlands.

It was essential for the new state to present itself to the world as an orderly one. Therefore, on November 5, 1918, Beneš warned Kramář from Paris to "avoid all struggles and bloody riots in the German parts of Bohemia." At the same time he emphasized the need to place by a *fait accompli* those districts under firm Czech control, so that no news would arrive from those areas indicating the formation of independent political organizations expressing an uncompromising attitude toward the Czechs.[43] The truth of the matter was that the Germans could not fight the Czech army, which was being built under the leadership of the French mission, and which was, technically, under the command of the supreme military commander of the Allied troops, Marshal Foch. As an Allied force, the Czech army could participate in carrying out the terms of the armistice, which included the right to occupy strategic positions within the Austro-Hungarian territories.[44] Thus, in a relatively short time during November and December 1918, Czech troops penetrated the borderlands without any major incident and established effective control over the German-inhabited regions in the historical lands. German leaders, however, continued to protest the Czech presence, and the Germans in the Czech lands stood behind them. When on March 4, 1919, the German Social Democratic party organized a demonstration of workers demanding the right of the Germans in the Czech lands to take part in election of the Viennese parliament, the demand was endorsed by all German political parties. On that occasion, however, the Czechoslovak government did not hesitate to use its armed might. Shots were fired into the crowd of demonstrators, and fifty-four people were killed.[45]

The Czech military occupation of the German-inhabited borderlands solved only one of the territorial problems facing the new state. The annexation of Slovakia was no less important to the Kramář government than was securing the historical boundaries of the Czech lands. Although the representatives of all Slovak political parties assembled at Martin on October 30, 1918, had declared themselves in favor of Slovakia's becoming a part of Czechoslovakia, the Slovak-inhabited territory was under the control of the Hungarian state administration. The new Hungarian government of Count Michael Károlyi attempted to ingratiate itself with the Slovaks (and Hungarians) by announcing liberal policies, promising land reform, and adopting popular social measures such as increased wages and employment for demobilized soldiers. Károlyi negotiated with France with considerable success. Article 17 of the armistice agreement between the Allies and Hungary, signed at Belgrade on November 13, 1918, stated explicitly that all Hungarian territory, with the exception of Croatia and Slavonia, was to remain under Hungarian administration and that the Allies would not interfere with internal administration in Hungary.[46] No provision was made for evacuation of the Slovak-inhabited area. The Károlyi government interpreted this omission as meaning that Slovakia would remain part of Hungary. The Czechs did not see it that way.

The Kramář government at Prague launched a struggle for Slovakia: diplomatic (at Paris, through Beneš) and military (in Slovakia itself,

The New State

whither Kramář dispatched military units). The government also appointed Dr. Vavro Šrobár, a Slovak subscribing to the "Czechoslovak" concept, as minister for Slovakia. His task was to force the Hungarian state apparatus out of Slovakia, occupy the country, and maintain order there. The Hungarian government, however, invoked the armistice agreement between Budapest and General Franchet d'Esperey, concluded at Belgrade on November 13, 1918, and insisted on its claim to Slovakia as an integral part of the Hungarian state. In his communication to Kramář's government at Prague, the Hungarian prime minister, Count Michael Károlyi, proposed that a Slovak National Council be established on condition that it recognize Hungarian sovereignty over the province. Kramář replied as follows, in a telegram sent to Károlyi on November 14, 1918:

> I take the liberty to point out that our Republic has been recognized by the Entente as an Allied power and that our Minister, Dr. Beneš, as a regular member of the military council of Allied powers, takes part in proceedings at Versailles. As a consequence of this we have, according to article three of the concluded armistice, the right to occupy all places regarded as important for the preservation of order. It is not our intention to occupy any territory by the force of arms, because, just as the Hungarian government does, we wait for the final decision of the peace conference.
>
> We came to Slovakia for no other reason than to prevent violence and anarchy, as we had been requested to do, since the administrative officials and the Hungarian gendarmerie left their posts.
>
> If the Hungarian army would attempt to use violence in order to force out our security detachments now, we would be forced to turn to the Entente with a request for military action, and we would be also forced to make the Hungarian government responsible for all insults and violence perpetrated on the Slovak people.
>
> We cannot agree with your proposal that the Slovak National Council alone administers the Slovak territory on the condition that it recognizes Hungarian sovereignty, because you and your government had recognized the right of self-determination for the Slovaks and their National Council on October 29, and, as a consequence of it, on October 30, the National Council solemnly proclaimed, in accordance with the principle of self-determination of nations, its

uniting with the Czech nation in the Czechoslovak state. Therefore, I request your government to issue, without any delay, orders to its army to refrain from any attack on our patrol detachments.[47]

There were in fact some armed clashes with Hungarian troops when the Czechoslovak government tried to establish its authority in Slovakia, with the help of the Italian military mission led by General Luigi Piccione, which arrived with the Czech Italian Legion in December 1918, and that of the French mission, which arrived in February 1919. The French military mission, headed by General Maurice Pellé, aimed chiefly to assist in organizing the new Czechoslovak general staff; its political adviser was a man for whom Beneš had worked during the war, an expert on Austria-Hungary in the French ministry of war, Louis Eisenmann.[48] In the contest for influence in Czechoslovakia between Italy and France the latter won; the regulations, organization, and structure of the Czechoslovak army were based on the French model.

The situation in Slovakia became complicated with the establishment of the rule of Béla Kun in Hungary in March 1919.[49] Béla Kun, who had earlier returned home from Soviet Russia, attempted to spread Soviet power into central Europe, thus creating a clear and present danger to the very existence of the Czechoslovak state. His action reflected the internationalist nature of the communist movement. While the Czechoslovak troops were struggling against the Hungarian Red Guards in Siberia, the Hungarian Bolsheviks were challenging the new order in central Europe, the new order that had been made possible by the Czechoslovak anti-Bolshevik action; now the Reds were threatening to seize power in their own homeland. The close link between the Bolshevik regime in Hungary and the Soviet power in Russia was clearly stated by Béla Kun in his appeal to the "Hungarian Internationalists" in Russia on April 23, 1919:

> May you be inspired by the profound knowledge that the Russian Soviet Republic is joined in the closest alliance with the Hungarian Soviet Republic.... Today you, Hungarian Red fighters battling the bands of Kolchak and the counter-revolutionaries on Russian soil, are fighting no less for the Hungarian Soviet Republic than if you were at home, for Hungary and Russia today are as one body had soul. The Hungarian proletariat has taken up arms against the

counter-revolution wherever this is necessary, and former Russian prisoners of war in Hungary have also formed Red detachments there to defend the Hungarian front of the international revolution.... The orders of the Hungarian Soviet Republic are: no one must leave the battlefield!

Lenin fully endorsed this appeal, adding, "I trust the Hungarian comrades will cherish the interests of the international cause above all."[51] To demonstrate the unity of aims of the international Bolshevik movement, the Soviets supported the Béla Kun regime militarily when the troops of Romania moved against it on April 16, 1919. On April 23, 1919, the command of the Ukrainian front was instructed "to establish uninterrupted contact with Hungary." On May 1, the Soviet government sent a note to the Romanian government demanding an end to the military action. Shortly afterwards the Soviets launched an offensive in order to link-up with the Soviet-Hungarian forces.[52] These forces had been taken by surprise in April when Czech military units led by French and Italian officers, together with the Romanian army, conducted a successful military campaign against the Soviets in Hungary. In April, the Soviet-Hungarian troops were forced to retreat. However, encouraged by the prospect of Soviet assistance, they took the offensive in May. In June 1919, the Czechoslovak units were forced out of Hungarian territory and the Hungarian Red Army reached the Polish boundaries in eastern Slovakia. In order to gain some support from the local Slovak population for Soviet power, "Czechoslovak Internationalists" called a meeting at Prešov, where, on June 16, 1919, the Slovak Soviet Republic was proclaimed.[53] This was the first attempt to establish a dictatorship of the proletariat on the territory of the Czechoslovak state. From this base the "Czechoslovak Internationalists" called upon the proletariat of the whole country to raise the banner of socialist revolution. Symbolically, the group that proclaimed the establishment of Soviet Slovakia was led by a Czech communist, Antonín Janoušek, who on June 20 assumed the chairmanship of the short-lived revolutionary government. As usual, the Bolsheviks operated on two levels: on the one hand, the agitators called upon the proletarians to destroy the "imperialists," and on the other hand, the leader of the group, Janoušek, telegraphed the Czechoslovak government on June 16 that "it remains our supreme desire to live in an undivided state united with the Czech proletariat, our blood brothers." As he put it, the leaders of the revolution wished to work in the closest alliance with the Czech proletariat "for universal peace, for the establishment of a proletarian state of all peoples...."[54] The Slovak Republic of Soviets called a meeting at Prešov at which it announced its position in international relations. In an appeal to the world proletariat, "the newly born Slovak Republic of Soviets" announced that it "considers its victorious brothers—Soviet Russia and the Hungarian Republic of Soviets—to be its natural allies, and places itself under the protection of the entire international proletariat, under the protection of the united workers' International...." In a telegram to Lenin, the Slovak revolutionary Soviet government acknowledged him as "the leader of the international proletariat."[55] The fate of Soviet Slovakia, however, was closely tied to the fate of its main protector—Soviet Hungary. It lasted less than three weeks. When the Hungarian Republic of Soviets collapsed, it ceased to exist.[56]

Although the Czechoslovak government's policy of creating accomplished facts succeeded in the case of Slovakia and in the case of the historical boundaries of the Czech lands, it was not fully successful in the case of the Duchy of Teschen, where it met strong opposition from Poland. The coal-rich territory was believed to be vitally important for the new state. In January 1919, Czech troops were dispatched into Teschen, a province in which the Poles were in the majority. Warsaw, refusing to withdraw from Teschen, ordered its troops to answer "violence with violence."[57] After a weeks' fighting, the conflict was terminated on orders from the Entente; this was not, however, the end of the controversy. In the summer of 1920, when the Poles were in a very difficult situation, negotiations concerning Teschen were renewed, and Czechoslovakia was able to gain a part of this territory.[58] Thus, while territories claimed by the new state were being secured by force of arms, the Paris conference had to take into account these *faits accomplis*.

At the peace conference, wherever self-determination would have played into the hands of Austria, the Czechoslovak delegate advanced arguments based on defensible frontiers, economic viability, and historic continuity of the historial lands. In the case of Slovakia he invoked the principle of nationality. Furthermore, Beneš pointed out that Czechoslovakia "was an element of order and democracy constituting a barrier against the spread of Bolshevism into Central Europe, and should therefore be supported by the West."⁵⁹ The threat of Bolshevism (and a real threat indeed) was used by Beneš in order to advance the cause of the Czechoslovak state—an island of peace, order, and democracy amid the turmoil of the rest of central Europe. When the Czechoslovak government planned to occupy the whole Teschen area, Beneš wrote a letter to Pichon dated January 10, 1919, claiming that Bolshevism was threatening the industrial district, which should therefore be occupied. "If we were masters of those regions," the letter said, "it would be the only means to stop the Bolshevik invasion."⁶⁰

In early 1919, events in Hungary focused the attention of the Entente statesmen on the area again. Negotiators at the Paris Peace Conference had a possible Allied intervention in Russia constantly in mind. Kramář's proposal to establish military units composed of Russian exiles and prisoners of war and to train them in Czechoslovakia for combat in Russia, was under serious consideration. When the Bolshevik revolution occurred in Hungary, and when the Soviets attempted to establish a junction with the troops of Béla Kun, Marshal Foch worked out a plan for military action against the Hungarian Soviet Republic.⁶¹ This brought into focus the strategic importance of Slovakia and Subcarpathian Ruthenia. Marshal Foch, the main French proponent of intervention, proposed launching a campaign against the Bolshevik regime in Hungary. After the liquidation of the Hungarian Bolsheviks, he advocated continuing the campaign against the Soviet regime in Russia, which had instigated the Bolshevik seizure of power in Hungary. The first part of the plan was put to the test when Frech General Pellé, the supreme commander of the Czechoslovak armed forces since June 1, 1919,⁶² began a counter-offensive against the Hungarian Red Army in Slovakia on June 7, gradually pushing the Hungarian military units out of Czechoslovak territory. The Foch plan, however, was not endorsed by the United States, which did not want to be drawn into a conflict in central Europe, and which doubted the feasibility of a military campaign against Bolshevik Russia.⁶³ At any rate, Slovakia was now firmly in Czech hands.

The occupation of Subcarpathian Ruthenia was also justified on the grounds of the Bolshevik threat to the area. Following Beneš's plea to Pichon that the Allied powers should add Czechoslovakia in the event of intervention or war undertaken by the Allies or France,⁶⁴ and in conjunction with the proposed intervention in Russia by Czechoslovakia, the Allies approved Czechoslovak occupation of the western part of the province. The province was inhabited largely by Ukrainians (Ruthenians), whose representatives in the United States had agreed with Masaryk during the war that the area should be attached to the future Czechoslovak state. After the war, some groups of Carpatho-Ruthenians requested such an arrangement, and, in 1920, the whole province was added to Czechoslovakia by a special parliamentary statute on Subcarpathian Ruthenia.[65] Thus, for Beneš, the Bolshevik threat and the action of the Czechoslovak army in Russia served as a convenient rationalization of Czechoslovak territorial demands and objectives.[66] For Kramář, on the other hand, they provided the opportunity for the Czechs and Slovaks to carry out an unprecedented historical mission by liberating Russia—and thus the whole world—from Bolshevism.

At this point a word should be said about the relations between Kramář and Beneš, and their activities at the peace conference. Until January 16, 1919, negotiations and propaganda at Paris on behalf of Czechoslovakia were conducted by its foreign minister, Beneš, a tough bargainer hardened by his wartime experiences. After his arrival at Paris, Kramář, as prime minister of Czechoslovakia, became the official head of the Czechoslovak delegation. His outlook and attitudes there contrasted sharply with those of Beneš, as was noted by other participants at the conference.[67] Beneš, who had spent the war in western Europe, "have a very clear perception of the *quid pro quo* basis of the policy of the West." Also, when he solicited the Allies' approval of Czech occupation of the German-inhabited borderlands and of Slovakia, "he perceived the Allies' lack of interest in the affairs of Central Europe and their disinclination to intervene there."[68] He sensed the Allies' unwillingness to attach to Czechoslovakia territories that did not belong to the historical provinces and thus enlarge its already large national minorities. On the other hand, Kramář took a strongly nationalistic position, demanding a corridor to Yugoslavia (between Austria and Hungary), and Serb Lusatia, and clashing with the Poles over Teschen. Furthermore, he was very much concerned about Russia's absence from the peace conference.

There were several other differences between the two. Kramář was an "elder statesman" and "direct," while Beneš was "diplomatic," "sophisticated" and an "upstart." In addition to differences in age and temperament the two had different standards of intellectual honesty, ideologies, backgrounds, and wartime experiences. One additional reason for Kramář's difficulty at Paris was that he had expected too much, and that he believed that the Czechoslovak demands were reasonable and would be accepted by the Conference as a matter of course. One key to understanding Kramář's psychology, his high expectations, and his later conflict with Beneš is his meeting with Beneš at Geneva, where he arrived as the head of the delegation sent there by the Czech National Committee, toward the end of October 1918.

According to Kramář, at the Geneva Conference Beneš told the delegates from the homeland that the Allies, in appreciation of what the Czechoslovaks had done for the war effort abroad and at home, would give the Czechoslovak government a blank check[69] for its demands, all of which would be met by the peace conference. Kramář, the "elder statesman," could not conceive that the young Beneš would have told him something that was not quite true, and he took seriously this one of Beneš's many exaggerations. But the real situation at Paris was not what he had anticipated.

As Kramář said, he went to Paris "full of Geneva optimism, conscious of our credit for victory by breaking up and destroying the Austrian front and defending Siberia from German exploitation." He was also self-confident and "aware of the fact that we were then relatively the most orderly state in Central Europe."[70] He did not expect to find "horse trading" and "wheeler-dealing" at the conference. He was shocked when the great powers ignored the official Czechoslovak demand for a corridor to Yugoslavia and the addition of Lusatia to the new state. As a spokesman for one of the victorious powers, he "felt physically the pain of all that injustice" perpetrated on the Czechs,[71] when he had to give up many of the demands he had considered just and fair. He tended to blame for those setbacks those who had invoked the theory of "natural rights," in contrast to his theories of historical right and "state right," as the basis for their demand for Czech independence.[72] (Indeed, Germans from the Czech lands invoked the same "natural right of self-determination" that Masaryk and the Social Democrats had invoked on behalf of the Czechs before the war.)

Regardless of the validty of Kramář's conjectures and despite his disappointments, Czechoslovakia was able to secure more territory than many foreign observers believed it should have. Beneš was, indeed, willing to settle for less than Kramář's maximalist demands. Still, he was described by Lloyd George as "an impulsive, clever, but much less sagacious and more short-sighted politician who did not foresee that the more he grasped, the less he could retain."[73] Eventually, the British government accepted Beneš's argument for the need to preserve the unity of the Czech lands on geographical, strategic, and economic grounds. The British, like the French and Americans, granted the Czechs their historic frontiers. At its first meeting on February 27, the Commission of Czechoslovak Affairs unanimously agreed that "the frontier as defined by the political boundaries of Bohemia and Moravia of 1914, should be accepted in principle as the frontier of the Czechoslovak Republic, subject to such minor rectifications, additions or subtractions of territory as may be found desirable on the further investigation of particular points."[74] The unity of the Czech lands was preserved, despite German Austria's protests and the German leaders' vocal opposition. (As late as June 1, 1920, speaking on behalf of German deputies in the Czechoslovak parliament, Dr. Lodgman protested against the newly adopted constitution, which had been forced upon the Germans living in the historical lands by the Constituent Assembly, with which they had had nothing to do.[75] The German deputies also refused to take part in the election of the president of the state.)

In addition to the German problem, which continued to exist and reached its climax in Munich and the dismemberment of Czechoslovakia in the late 1930s, the new state had difficulties with some Slovaks who demanded autonomy for Slovakia. Although responsible Slovak leaders, including the highly respected Slovak patriot Father Andrej Hlinka, were principle architects of the October 30 declaration at Martin, the exact status of Slovakia within the new state had not been worked out by the government. On December 19, 1918, Hlinka restored (or founded anew) the Slovak People's party, whose program reflected Slovak nationalism and opposed the "centralism and liberalism" of the Prague government and its representative in Slovakia, Vavro Šrobár. In contrast to the "Czechoslovak" concept, Hlinka insisted that the Czechs and Slovaks were two distinct nations; therefore, the Slovaks had the right to self-government. Hlinka believed that the Pittsburgh Agreement of May 31, 1918, not the declaration of October 30, should be the basis for the status of Slovakia in Czechoslovakia. The Pittsburgh Agreement, signed

The New State   457

by Masaryk, stipulated that "Slovakia shall have its own administration, its own diet, and its own courts. The Slovak language shall be the official language in the schools, in government offices, and in public life generally."[76] Hlinka and his followers were convinced that the Pittsburgh Agreement was legally binding on the new state, since both the Czech delegates at the Geneva conference and the Revolutionary National Assembly had approved and ratified all agreements and undertakings made by Masaryk during his work abroad to achieve Czecho-Slovak independence. Masaryk, on the other hand, considered the Pittsburgh Agreement a local understanding between American Czechs and Slovaks.[77] Being unable to obtain redress of his grievance in Czechoslovakia, in August 1919, Hlinka and his closest associates decided to go to Paris and ask the peace conference to grant Slovakia autonomy on the basis of the Pittsburgh Agreement.

The Hlinka party traveled to Paris via Poland. In Warsaw the Slovaks had a private audience with Poland's chief of state, Józef Piłsudski. In Paris the Poles helped Hlinka to submit a memorandum dated September 20, 1919, to the secretary of the peace conference. The memorandum repudiated the "Czechoslovak thesis" of Masaryk, Beneš, and Vavro Šrobár, and requested minority status and "the greatest possible political autonomy" for the Slovaks.[78] "The Czechs and Slovaks are different nations," the memorandum said, and the Slovaks "wish to remain Slovaks forever."

Hlinka's effort at Paris failed, primarily for two reasons: (1) The memorandum could not be properly considered by the conference because it arrived late. The Treaty of St. Germain, which determined the structure of the succession states of Austria-Hungary, was signed on September 10, 1919. (2) The Czech delegation, most likely Beneš, tipped off the French police, who forced Hlinka and his associates to leave France on the grounds that their papers were not in order. After his return to Czechoslovakia, Father Hlinka was stripped of his parliamentary immunity, arrested, and imprisoned.[79]

It would go beyond the scope of this work to discuss in detail the reasons for Father Hlinka's disillusionment with the new state and the ensuing controversy, which has not yet been brought to its conclusion. It may be pointed out, however, that Hlinka had been chairman of the Slovak People's party since its establishment in 1913, and before that, in

1911, Hlinka had rejected the "progressivistic" views of Masaryk and warned against any attempt to implant them in Slovakia. In addition to the difference in their philosophies, Hlinka disagreed with Masaryk's interpretation of the Pittsburgh Agreement, which he discussed with him three times before 1922. The Czechoslovak president told Hlinka that the idea of Slovak autonomy has his sympathies, but that the agreement was valid only in America (sic).[80] Furthermore, Hlinka objected to the anti-Catholic campaign launched by some Czechs in Slovakia and to the policies of Vavro Šrobár. R. W. Seton-Watson, who investigated conditions in Slovakia after the war, wrote about his findings, "It seems almost incredible that any executive body for Slovak affairs should have been formed without his [Hlinka's] inclusion.... The rivalry of Šrobár and Hlinka, transferred from the petty platform of Ružomberok to the wide stages of Bratislava and of Prague, contributed as much as any single factor towards envenoming the situation in Slovakia."[81] Šrobár was doubtless appointed by Masaryk as minister for Slovakia because of his strong Czechophile orientation and his close ties with Masaryk, already established before the war. Father Hlinka's disillusionment grew as he observed Šrobár going about de-Magyarization: reorganizing the administration, the educational system, and especially the Catholic Church in Slovakia with the help of Czechs, while he was getting rid of any Slovaks who, rightly or wrongly, were suspected or accused of being Magyarophiles.[82]

While Hlinka was in prison, his party's periodical, *Slovák,* was banned, and *Slovenský denník* called for Hlinka's hanging. Šrobár publicly accused Hlinka of being Magyarophile and charged him with attempts to separate Slovakia from Czechoslovakia and attach it to Hungary. Scotus Viator (a pseudonyme of R. W. Seton-Waton) commented that anyone who tried to make Hlinka into a Magyarophile proved merely his own stupidity.[83] Hlinka had fought the Hungarian regime and its Magyarization policies for years before the war, and had in consequence spent thirty-three months in Hungarian prisons. Hlinka answered the charge that he had committed high treason against the Czechoslovak state by saying that if he were a traitor just becuase he had invoked the Pittsburgh Agreement, then the signatories of that agreement must also be traitors.[84]

The conflict between the centralists and the autonomists benefited the Social Democrats, who won in Slovakia more votes and more seats in the Czechoslovak National Assembly than any other party in 1920. The

Slovak People's party won double the number of seats it had held in the (Revolutionary/Constituent) National Assembly before the 1920 election. Šrobár lost his seat to a Social Democrat, Dr. Ivan Dérer. Ten days after the election Hlinka was released from prison. Although he was prevented from conducting a campaign by being held, illegally, in prison, he was freed by the Slovak people, who had elected him a deputy in the Czechoslovak National Assembly.[85]

Reporting on the arrest of Hlinka in his dispatch of October 16, 1919, Richard Crane, the U.S. minister at Prague, forwarded to the U.S. State Department a newspaper account of the arrest of Father Hlinka for alleged high treason. A copy of the dispatch of October 16, 1919, was transmitted to the American Commissioners to Negotiate Peace for their information. According to an article on "Arrest of Andrej Hlinka" (*Národní Listy,* October 14, 1919), an investigation was conducted against Hlinka "for high treason as perpetrated by him abroad and for inciting speeches at meetings held by his partisans last summer.... His confinement will prevent him from any further detrimental actions."[86]

Although Hlinka asked to be brought before a court, he was never tried, and was released from the prison at Mírov, Moravia, on April 18, 1920, after his constituents elected him to the Czechoslovak Chamber of Deputies (the lower house of the parliament). This was a rough beginning to the new political career of the leader of the Slovak People's party, who was convinced that the Czecho-Slovak Republic could not "become a center of order and peace in Central Europe except on condition of giving satisfaction to the legitimate aspirations of all the nations which compose it."[87]

The events in Slovakia were hardly encouraging to the Catholic 80 percent majority of people living there. However, Hlinka was a fair man who gave credit where credit was due; and on Kramář's seventy-fifth birthday, in 1935, Andrej Hlinka hailed Kramář as "an example of a selfless friend and defender" of the Slovaks from whom, and from whose Slavic policy, they expected the fulfillment of their natural rights. Hlinka was confident that Kramář would do his best to help the Slovaks achieve the "political autonomy promised to them at Pittsburgh, Cleveland and Petrograd," and that this autonomy would "strengthen the ties between the Historical Lands and Slovakia." Hlinka realized that "what was created by war, may be destroyed by war." But he did not want war; he was for peace, and he recognized the sanctity of the peace treaties that "guaranteed their rights" to all national minorities in Czechoslovakia.[88] Though constantly fighting for Slovak rights, Hlinka did not part with the Czechoslovak state; and he died before the Slovak state was established.

The Slovak problem was only one of the many that had been faced by the new state, and a very minor one for the Paris Peace Conference. Civil war was raging in Russia, and the peacemakers at Paris were discussing what to do about it. There were some Russian leaders in no official capacity at Paris; among them were the famous tsarist foreign minister Sazonov, the foreign minister in the First Provisional Government Miliukov, and the former revolutionary Boris Savinkov, a protégé of Maugham, to whom, reportedly, Klecanda had given 200,000 rubles on Masaryk's instructions.[89] At Paris Savinkov did not ask for foreign troops, believing that their presence would rather antagonize than assist Russia. He did ask, however, for active support from the Allies in money and supplies. According to Savinkov, in January 1919, the Bolsheviks had an army consisting of 400,000 men, which would rise to 600,000 by the spring; "but of these he thought only 50,000 or 60,000 were any good," Lloyd George tells us.[90] On the other side, "the anti-Bolsheviks forces he estimated at 200,000 men. His plan was to organize in Czechoslovakia and Poland an army of 200,000 men, composed of ex-Russian prisoners, Czech, Yugoslav and Polish volunteers and so forth, paid and equipped by the Allies." Savinkov was convinced that if such a force were deployed in a coordinated offensive on all fronts in Russia, the Bolshevik army would be smashed. Marshal Foch was impressed by the proposal, and at a meeting of the Council of Four, he "outlined a scheme for a vast attack on Soviet Russia by Finns, Estonians, Letts, Lithuanians, Poles, Czechs, Russians—in fact, all the peoples that lie along the fringe of Russia—all under Allied direction."[91] The project, however, was not fully endorsed by Marshal Pilsudski of Poland, who wanted to annex Galicia, inhabited mostly by Ukrainians and claimed by the Ukraine, to Poland.

Lloyd George opposed the Foch project on the grounds of its costs. On February 19, 1919, Lloyd George wrote to Philip Kerr of the American delegation about the French scheme to organize an army of Russian prisoners of war in Germany, who, "supported by Czecho-Slovaks and other odds and ends," would invade Russia. He suggested to Colonel House that before anything "of this kind is sanctioned the military should

The New State

be asked the costs." He was certain that neither France nor Great Britain would be able to finance the undertaking, and he was wondering whether the United States would bear the expense.[92]

At a January 1919, meeting of delegations from the British empire at Paris, Lloyd George brought up the question of intervention in Russia. William Morris Hughes of Australia agreed with Lord Reading that "Bolshevism knew no country," and pointed at Lockhard's report, according to which "the Bolsheviks had 213,000 troops in November 1919, but they had already 820,000 troops in January 1919." Hughes was convinced that an effectual intervention was not feasible. Therefore, the Allies should "keep Bolshevism inside Russia and apply economic pressures." He said, furthermore, that "Bolshevism must inevitably die if confined within the borders of Russia."[93] This was the first statement of the policy of containment, with which many people agreed, and many did not.

Lloyd George writes that one British cabinet member, Winston Churchill, was "an ardent advocate of plans for the overthrow of Bolshevism with the aid of Allied arms,"[94] but the prime minister pointed at how costly it would be to try to conquer Russia militarily. Yet the French military believed that military defeat of Bolshevism was both possible and desirable; otherwise, it would threaten the rest of Europe and the world. (In the long run it would be much costlier to contain Bolshevism than to defeat it militarily.) They found the principal Czech delegate, Prime Minister Kramář, very receptive to their ideas; in fact, the Czech delegate had a special interest in an Allied intervention of Russia, and had moreover, devised his own plan of intervention.

The conspicuous absence of Russia from the peace conference saddened the Neo-Slav Kramář, who believed that the new Czechoslovak state could not survive in the game of European power politics without the support in the international arena of a strong, national Russia. As long as Germany was prostrated, he believed, Czechoslovakia could play its envisioned pivotal role in Europe. But what would happen after Germany recuperated from the defeat? Kramář expected this to happen sooner or later; in fact, he foresaw that Germany would rise again in the near future. In this case Czechoslovakia would be too weak to cope with eighty million Germans; it needed a strong and dependable ally—national Russia. His experience at the Paris conference convinced him even more that Russia, without whose contribution the war could not have been won and without whose help the Czechoslovaks could not have attained their independence, had to be liberated from Bolshevism. Therefore, at Paris he began to organize a campaign for the liberation of Russia.[95] After some difficult negotiations, he obtained consent from the British and French governments to take definite steps in this direction. (In fact, the two governments had already been giving aid to the anti-Bolshevik forces, particularly Admiral Kolchak and General Denikin.) Although Britain and France agreed to supply military materials and make financial contributions to the anti-Bolshevik campaign, the two countries wanted Czechoslovakia to organize troops from among volunteers, especially Russian prisoners of war, and to assume responsibility for them. Yugoslavia's Prince Regent Alexander promised to send auxiliary corps of volunteers to Russia.

Kramář wrote about his plan to Prague, pointing out that Beneš and Štefánik supported it, and was dismayed to read in *Le Temps* of February 13, 1919, that Masaryk opposed any Czechoslovak participation in the intervention. Without consulting anyone, Masaryk granted an interview to a special correspondence of the Paris daily, in which he declared that intervention in Russia was "impossible now," and that the Czechoslovak army had "had enough of it" and "demands returning home." "After four and a half year long terrible war," said Masaryk, "the Allied states cannot demand from their soldiers to go to Russia to fight for an ill defined purpose...."[96]

The interview in *Le Temps* prompted Kramář to write a long letter to the president, expressing his disapproval of the latter's *modus operandi*. "It is not possible," Kramář wrote, "to have a responsible government, responsible Prime Minister, and an *irresponsible President* who *urbi et orbi*, in newspaper interviews, determines the direction of governmental policy...."[97] Kramář recalled Masaryk's statement at a meeting of the Czechoslovak ministerial council, according to which the president could have "saved Russia from Bolshevism" through the action of the Czechoslovak army. "It directly pierced my heart," wrote Kramář, "and I told myself that I would not want to carry your responsibility...." Kramář also reminded Masaryk that Josef Dürich, who was also in Russia during the Bolshevik revolution, had disagreed with Masaryk's conduct and his policy of neutrality toward the Bolsheviks, believing that the latter were not merely a Russian but also a European problem. Dürich was convinced that the Czechoslovak army could easily have defeated the Bolsheviks, and he wanted to launch a campaign against Masaryk on that issue.

The significance of defeating the Bolsheviks in 1917 or 1918 would have been tremendous, Kramář believed, since it would have kept Russia in the Allied fold and would have shortened the war. "How different our situation would be," wrote Kramář, "had you and ours saved Russia and the whole world. Now it is the second time when we could save Russia and deliver ourselves forever from the terrible danger of Russo-German alliance...." He "would not want to see" the day when people would say of Masaryk that he had "frustrated helping Russia for the second time."[98]

Three years later, speaking on the issue of intervention in Russia, Kramář said, "It wa really the only one moment in our whole history, so great that it will never come back again. As if destiny would place into our hands, for all our previous suffering, the possibility... to bring our nation to the highest level.... If Russia wre liberated with our help, we would have played the most prominent role in Slavdom and the others would envy us. But more than that—we would have liberated the whole world from Bolshevism, we wouldhave been allied with Russia forever, and we would have enjoyed our security forever."[99] As Kramář saw it, that was the call to greatness, this was Czechoslovakia's mission in European and world history. He was deeply disappointed when he found opposition where he had least expected it: at home.

For Kramář the struggle against Bolshevism was a matter of national interest and national survival, the logical culmination of the nationalistic program of the Czechoslovak army in Russia. He bitterly objected to invoking the slogan of non-involvement and non-intervention in domestic affairs whenever Bolsheviks were the issue, and disregarding it when a conflict arose between the Socialist Revolutionaries and Kolchak.[100] He understood the difficulty with which the Czechs were confronted in Siberia because of the bickering of Russian political factions, and their irritation over the incompetence and moral chaos in circles close to Kolchak. But all this was, Kramář believed, of only secondary importance in view of the worldwide importance of the mission with which destiny had entrusted the Czechs, which had no parallel in their whole history.

Kramář failed in his effort to organize help for Russia; and he was bitter about the "victory of ingratitude" to Russia in Czechoslovakia. His thesis was that only a new, democratic, national Russia could safeguard the Czechoslovak state against German revanchism and revisionism;[101] "the new Russia, national and Slavic, allied with Slavic states" would help to strengthen the European balance of power. It was the sole hope "not only for a lasting peace, but also for a peaceful and steady development of political and national life of all Slavic states."[102] His pro-Russian views and his concern with the Russian question alienated him from many of his countrymen, for whom short-range success was more important than the long-range consequences of the policies advanced by Beneš or those advocated by Kramář. To his great surprise, on July 8, 1919, Kramář was notified at Paris by a letter from President Masaryk that he had ceased to be prime minister, and that his successor would be the Social Democrat Vlastimil Tusar, a member of the largest political party, according to the results of the communal election of June 1919. Kramář was unceremoniously dismissed as prime minister, long before the parliamentary election was held, and everyone could see who had "the prerogative power" in the state. As one People's party deputy later put it, "the verdict of the Vienna court [i.e., his sentence to death] did not cuase him as much pain as this verdict did."[103] Masaryk's arbitrary decision reflected the latter's opposition to Kramář as a person as well as to his plan to rehabilitate Russia. The defeat of Bolshevism in Russia would have strengthened Kramář's position in the state and would have affected the orientation of the republic. In that case Masaryk's political concepts would have been challenged: he could not have sustained his position as a quasi-dictator or arbiter of all fundamental political issues during the formative years of the new state; he could not have become the "philosopher-king."

In Paris Kramář was also a member of the Commission for the League of Nations and took part in its deliberations. In his view, the league was destined to be an ineffective institution, because it lacked executive power, and because sanctions to be imposed by it would be decided upon only after a mutual consultation on what should be done by whom. Furthermore, a league without Russia and Germany was merely a torso. In addition, he was convinced that the League of Nations, at the very beginning of its existence, violated the moral principles on which it was based by passively looking on at the murder of more than one and a half million innocent Russians, at the Bolshevik's seizure of power and their negation of all principles of Christian civilization, and at their suppression, in the most brutal fashion, of all that mankind regarded as the natural rights and freedoms of nations.[104] For his views on the Russian situation he was denounced in Czechoslovakia by pro-Bolshevik agitators as "a useless trash," "a bloodthirsty capitalist," and even "a traitor."[105]

After signing the peace treaties, Kramář returned to Prague and prepared himself for a trip to Russia. At the beginning of October he went, via Istambul, to southern Russia, which was controlled by the Denikin army. At Rostov-on-the-Don he took part in discussions about the organization of the future Russian state, for which he had prepared a constitution.[106] Returning to Prague before Christman 1919, Kramář continued to be concerned with Russia and the future of the Czechoslovak state. As he put it, "we are too small to be able to determine our own destiny. We do not live on an island; we are surrounded by enemies.... We could have influence on questions of vital interest to us only through a larger unit and that unit is Slavdom."[107] Kramár believed that the western countries had their own interests, and that geography—the neighborhood of Germany—was stronger than all philosophizing. Beneš's and Masaryk's talk about democracy and their undue hopes in the League of Nations manifested self-deception and illusion on their part. Eventually, Kramář became the principal critic of the foreign policies of Beneš. According to Beneš and Masaryk, Bolshevism was a Russian internal affair, and the Czechoslovaks had no business getting involved there. This view became the policy of the Czechoslovak state.

CHAPTER SEVENTEEN

THOSE WHO FOUGHT IN RUSSIA AND SIBERIA

The saga of the Czechs and Slovaks who fought in Russia and Siberia has been told by several authors, who do not always agree on the reasons for the Czechoslovak's army uprising against the Bolsheviks,[1] and who often differ in their assessment of the significance of the anti-Bolshevik struggle in the genesis of Czechoslovakia. As has been indicated earlier, most of the Czech and Slovak prisoners of war in Russia—between three-fourths and two-thirds—did not participate in the independence movement's activities in Russia; they kept their oath of loyalty to the emperor of Austria-Hungary, though their motives for doing so varied. The number of those who died while fighting with the Austro-Hungarian armies was greater than the total number of those who volunteered for service in the Czechoslovak army in Russia, as the monuments built to honor them in the 1920s in Czechoslovak towns and villages testified. Yet the Czechoslovak army that fought in Russia and Siberia under the Allied flag could make a legitimate claim that, without it, Czechoslovak independence could not have been won. The members of this army were the last of the Czech and Slovak emigrés to return home. Some of them spent a year, some two years, in the protracted war in Siberia. Their first transport left Vladivostok in December 1919; the general staff reached Prague in June 1920; the last transport left in September 1920; and the evacuation was completed in November 1920.[2]

By late autum of 1918, the Czechs and Slovaks who were fighting the Bolsheviks were exposed to manifold pressures from within and without. They could no longer hold the line against the large number of troops brought against them, and they were forced to retreat. Intensified Bolshevik propaganda in their midst, as well as the absence of Allied troops on the battlefield, was demoralizing the troops. Just three days before the proclamation of Czechoslovak independence, on October 29, 1918, Colonel Josef Švec committed suicide when his troops refused to obey orders.

Colonel Švec left a note in which he spoke of an "infection" that was spreading rapidly in regiments, battalions, companies, and platoons. A demon—lack of confidence in oneself and one's own strength—was taking possession of many of the soldiers, who began to destroy the army's organization by refusing to obey all laws of order and discipline, and who were destroying the character and reputation of the Czechoslovak soldier. "I cannot live over that shame," the note said, "which had been inflicted upon our army by the reckless fanatics—demagogues who have destroyed in themselves and who are destroying in all of us what is most precious—honor."[3] The colonel's suicide was a concrete manifestation of the demoralization of some segments of the army because of Bolshevik agitation and the soldiers' gradual realization that, while they were sent to fight a numerically stronger enemy, assuming that Allied was forthcoming, the Allies were making no serious effort to forward to them badly needed troops, munitions, weapons, and supplies. Furthermore, when Austria-Hungary dropped out of the war, the soldiers believed that their mission had been completed, and they were eager to return home. After all, they had helped Masaryk to gain victory—the independent state had become a reality. Thus, when in November 1918, General Štefánik, now minister of war, and General Janin, now the commander of all non-Russian troops in eastern Russia and Siberia, arrived at the Czechoslovak army's headquarters, they noticed the low morale of the troops, whose usefulness as a fighting force was diminishing. Yet the army's action had made possible the establishment of Czechoslovakia, and the Legionnaires were hailed as heroes in their far-away home.

In contrast to the success of the "followers of Masaryk," who had succeeded by defying his instructions and breaking with his neutralist policy, neither the Czech and Slovak communists who joined the Soviet forces, nor the Czech and Slovak anti-communists who joined the anti-Bolshevik Russian volunteer armies, attained their goals. The Czechs who fought alongside the Whiles had to concede defeat as the civil war came to its end. The Czechoslovak communists in Russia were witnessing the advent of national revolutions and the emergence of new national states in central east Europe (above all, in Masaryk-led Czechoslovakia) and the failure of their strategy, which relied on the dawn of a socialist revolution in central Europe with the German proletariat at its helm. Yet the Czechoslovak communists remained optimistic, and returned home with the intention of promoting class struggle in the newly established state. They continued to hope that the October Revolution in Russia would influence the proletariat, temporarily "infected" by nationalism, and would thus affect events in both Germany and their homeland. As they believed, the bourgeois nationalist revolution would be followed by the socialist revolution; their task, they felt, was to destroy the bourgeois state and to establish a republic of soviets.

After August 1918, the Czechoslovak military unit that fought with the Volunteer Army had political representation at headquarters in the person of Josef Dürich, who continued to serve in that capacity even after the death of General Alexeev. On one occasion Alexeev told Dürich that the Russians had never expected such neutrality from the Czechs in the most critical hour for Russia. The general believed, and so did Dürich, that the situation could have been substantially different had the Czech army joined the Volunteer Army on the Don. (In December 1917, and several times later, Alexeev asked through Dürich, and also through Masaryk, that the Czechs join his forces.) Alexeev regretted that Masaryk was unwilling to bring the army to the Don and let it become the nucleus of the Russian national army that could have defeated the Bolsheviks when they were still very weak. The old general told Dürich sadly, "Look, when we could have such successes with merely 1,600 volunteers, where would we have been today had we had only one, but your Czech glorious brigade! Indeed, I know it best, for I was its godfather!" (His order of April 17, 1916, had established the Czech brigade.) Regretting that the Russians had been deserted by all, Alexeev remarked bitterly, "They have sold Slavdom, they have sold it."[4]

The Russian general, who was fond of the Czechs, was referring to the situation as it existed early in 1918 and to the relative importance of the Czechoslovak army corps during the civil war in Russia. When on March 15, 1918, Sovnarkom formally decided to let the Czechoslovak Legion leave Russia via Vladivostok, the Czechoslovak army numbered some 42,000 men. A few days later the Congress of Soviets ratified the Treaty of Brest-Litovsk, which obliged the Soviet government to demobilize the Russian army. Thus in April 1918, the Czechoslovak army corps was the only viable army in Russia and was growing. Since the Legion had been instructed to secure as many weapons as possible from the disintegrating Russian army, it was extremely well armed, as the amount of weapons it handed over to the Bolsheviks indicates. Up to April 4, 1918, the Legion turned over to the regional soviet at Penza 50,000 rifles, 5 million rounds of ammunition, 1,200 machine guns, 6,000 machine-gun belts (with bullets), 72 artillery guns, 3 airplanes, 197 baskets with ammunition, and equipment and horses).[5] In addition, the Legion saved a large quantity of war material abandoned around Bakhmach by the Bolshevik troops flying before the Germans, and handed it over to the Bolsheviks arleady at Kursk. Had it then joined the anti-Bolshevik forces rather than surrendering weapons to their enemies, the Bolsheviks might have been defeated. Only after the Czech revolt at the end of May 1918, did Trotsky begin to build a conscript army based on tough discipline. Furthermore, whereas the Legion had some 50,000 men in June 1918, the Volunteer Army of Denikin and Alexeev consisted of some nine thousand men and twenty-one guns in all."[6] It lacked money, arms, equipment, and ammunition.

At the time of the Czech revolt, according to the Soviet historian N. I. Shatagin, out of the 185,000 armed and 49,000 trained troops in the Red Army, only 17,039 could have been used directly at the front.[7] However, the number of Soviet troops (on paper), though poorly trained, poorly clad, and poorly equipped, increased to hundreds of thousands before the end of the year; and in late 1919 the Red Army numbered three million. Furthermore, before its encounter with the Czechs, the Red Army was militarily ineffective, because of poor training and poor discipline. Realizing this defect, Trotsky decided to use former tsarist officers to train the Red Army. By the end of 1918, over 20,000 former tsarist officers were serving in the Red Army, by June 1919, the figure had risen to 27,000; and between June 1918, and August 1920, some 48,000 former tsarist officers were enrolled. In addition to that, during

1918 alone, 128,000 former noncommissioned officers were called up, and many of them were made officers after enrollment.[8] Had a national Russian army been formed around the nucleus of the Czechoslovak army corps in March or April 1918, after Brest-Litovsk, these officers and noncommissioned officers of the defunct Russian army would most likely have joined the national Russian army, and would have fought the Bolsheviks, "allies" of the Central Powers, rather than the Czechoslovaks, the Poles, the Ukrainians, the Caucasian peoples, the Baltic peoples, the Finns, and the Whites. After Brest-Litovsk the Bolsheviks were unpopular even among the Russian socialists, Left SRs and Mensheviks. The Russian army was demobilized; the gangs of Red Guards were largely disorganized and their activity was not centrally coordinated. The neutralist policy toward the Bolsheviks meant, in fact, the recognition of the Lenin regime as the *de facto* government of Russia by Masaryk, who urged the Allies to adopt the same policy. Had the Legion broken with Masaryk's policy several months earlier, it could have become the nucleus of a strong national Russian army that could easily have defeated the Lenin government. In that case, the war might have been shortened and the history of Russia and the world might have been different.[9]

At Jekaterinodar (headquarters of the Volunteer Army) Dürich cooperated also with Václav Vondrák, who had refused to accept back his property from the hands of the Germans who had occupied Kiev, and who was rendering important services to the Whites. Before he left for home in December 1918, Dürich proclaimed the Czech battalion of the Volunteer Army a "perpetual" unit of the Russian army "in memory of brotherhood of Czech and Russian arms." General Denikin, who assumed the command of the Volunteer Army after the death of Alexeev, thanked Dürich for his "fruitful work on the field of Slavic mutuality, especially the Russo-Czech rapprochement." He regretted that the "dream of the Russian nation"—the liberation of western and southern Slavs from the foreign yoke by the Russians—had not come true and that "the Almighty Lord decided otherwise."[10] Dürich returned to his free homeland leaving behind a battlefield of fratricidal struggle in which, eventually, the Russia of his heart lost. At home he found a rather cool reception, even hostility on the part of some who came under the influence of anti-Dürich propaganda. The media were unfriendly to him: he was not able to defend his work for Kramář's proposed "Slavic Empire" in the newspapers, including *Národní Listy*. He published his book privately; the money that Kramář had given him in 1915, Dürich returned "to the proper places." In fact, Dürich had received 30,000 crowns from Kramář, Švehla, and Dr. Mattuš, and he returned to them 120,000 crowns, which, with his consent, Kramář and Švehla gave to Russian refugees.[11] Although he was accused by Masaryk and others of seeking his own profit, Dürich was the only one among the leading Czech exiles who practiced what the others were preaching, namely, that one should not be paid for work done for the nation. None of the triumvirate—Masaryk-Beneš-Štefánik— returned what he had received from others during the war.

As a consequence of constant vilifications, Dürich became a broken man. Only then did his son-in-law, writer Karel Horký, who defended Dürich's honor against false allegations, succeed in inducing Masaryk, the president of the republic, to state publicly that he had had political differences with Dürich but could not accuse him of doing anything dishonest. Even Kramář did not reopen the Dürich case in order to exonerate the deputy who had represented his views abroad probably because Kramář had signed the Geneva "Declaration of the Czecho-Slovak Deputies and the Delegates of the National Council of Prague" on October 31, 1918. At their meeting at Geneva Beneš had shrewdly claimed that the CSNC had received a "blank check" from the Entente powers, and he had asked the representatives of the home movement for independence for a blanket endorsement of all the CSNC's actions. Upon Beneš's request, the document had included a passage saying that its signatories approved "in their entirety of all the military and political actions of the National Czecho-Slovak Council, transformed into the Provisional Government of the Czecho-Slovak Countries, now functioning at Paris, as well as all the agreements made by it in the name of our nation with the Allied and Associated Governments. At the same time we express to it our thanks for the great services which it has rendered to the Nation."[12] Since Kramář, Klofáč, Staněk, Habrman, and Kalina had signed this unqualified approval of everything that the Paris council did before October 31, 1918, they culd not later question the propriety of anything that Beneš, Štefánik, and Masaryk had done before that date.

The other group of Czechs and Slovaks in Russia whose objectives did not materialize were the communists who supported the Bolsheviks, and, in turn, had their backing. Communists claim that more than 10,000

Czechs and Slovaks served in the Red Army at one time or another during the civil war.[13] That would imply that approximately 4 percent of the Czech and Slovak prisoners of war in Russia cooperated with the Bolsheviks. The establishment of the Czechoslovak state prompted the Soviets to try again, first to neutralize, and then to eliminate the Czechoslovak army as an instrument of intervention. Early in November 1918, Chicherin, the people's commissar of foreign affairs, sent a telegraphic message to the Czechoslovak government at Prague claiming that the Soviets were fighting only in defense of the revolution and proclaiming the willingness of the Soviet government to let the Czechoslovaks go home via Soviet Russia. The Soviet government, the message said, wished to enter into negotiations with the provisional Czechoslovak government about conditions for the departure of those Czechoslovaks who wanted to return to their homeland.[14] Although as late as October 29, 1918, Masaryk was still considering the possibility of making an arrangement with the Soviets in order to bring the troops home across their territory, he changed his mind and agreed with Beneš, Štefánik, and Kramář on the need to keep the troops in Siberia, issuing an order on November 14, 1918, directing the troops to continue to fight the Bolsheviks.[15] In his order to the troops Masaryk stated that their sacrifice would "strengthen the position of our nation at the peace conference."

While Chicherin, acting on behalf of the Soviet government, worked on the "high level" and called for negotiations with the Czechoslovak government, the Executive Committee of the Czechoslovak Communist Party in Russia (a section of the Russian Bolshevik party), working on the "low level," or, as Marxist-Leninists have called it, "from below," appealed to the Czechoslovaks in Russia who had not joined the Red Army to go home, and, following the example of the Russian Bolsheviks, to help the proletariat in the Czech lands to seize power. In a proclamation dated November 17, 1918, the Czechoslovak communist leaders in Russia called upon their "comrades" to be ready for their departure home and to enter "the ranks of the Czechoslovak sections of the Red Army which will be the foundation of the workers' army in Bohemia, Moravia and Slovakia."[16] Some of the Czechoslovak communists in Russia responded to these efforts to spread the revolution into central Europe and departed for their homeland.

Among these was the leader of the Czechoslovak communists in Russia, Alois Můna, who, after being instructed by Lenin on November 10 and 12, 1918, went to Czechoslovakia to propagandize for the aims of the Bolshevik Revolution and to agitate among Czech Social Democrats for the organization of a communist party.[17] In addition to their general objective, these agents of Lenin had a special mission in Czechoslovakia: they were to influence the socialist groups represented in the government to reject the Kramář proposal, and endorsed by Štefánik that the Czechoslovaks should lead the struggle against the Bolsheviks in Russia. Although they did not achieve their maximum objective—to bring about a communist-inspired revolution and capture of political power in the state—these Moscow-instructed Czech Bolsheviks did help create a climate of opinion in which it was possible for the majority in the Czechoslovak government to reject Kramář's plan for intervention in Russia.[18]

The dispatch of agitators and professional revolutionaries to Czechoslovakia decreased the number of Czechoslovak communists in Russia. When a conference of the Czechoslovak Communist Party in Russia was held in Moscow on March 2, 1919, the number of party members was given as 2,685. A large number of party members had left Soviet Russia earlier in the year, it was said, partly at their own request and partly because the party had decided to strength the forces working from within for the socialist revolutionary orientation of the Czechoslovak Social Democratic party, and thus prepared the ground for the revolution. The conference issued a political declaration calling upon the proletariat to seize power in Bohemia, and claiming that the existing Kramář-Masaryk government was merely a puppet of the capitalistic governments of the four powers and their stick exchanges. The manifesto ended with the slogan, "Long live government of the Soviets and the dictatorship of the proletariat in Bohemia! Glory to the Third International!"[19]

After the Moscow conference the larger part of the leadership of the Czechoslovak Communist Party in Russia moved to Kiev, where it decreed, in May 1919, the "Mobilization of Czechoslovak Communists." According to this "decree," the duty of all Czechoslovak communists was to place themselves at the disposal of the Red Army to fight the Whites. In June 1919, the same group issued a proclamation addressed to the "Czechoslovak proletariat" in the homeland, according to which "the day is not far off when also in France, Italy, Germany, in the Balkans and elsewhere will emerge workers' governments and governments of workers' Soviets." The proclamation ended, "Long live workers' world revolution! Long live Czech Soviet Republic!"[20]

As they were instructed, during 1919 and 1920, the Czechoslovak communists in Russia and Siberia continuously tried to demoralize the Czechoslovak army by propaganda and agitation until its departure for home. Some Czechoslovak communists in the Red Army units pursued the retreating Czechoslovaks to the Far East; the Fifth Red Army Corps, which was pursuing the Kolchak army via Omsk to Irkutsk, had a Czech, Jaroslav Hašek, among its political workers. Hašek headed the foreign section in the Fifth Army's staff which had been established at the beginning of December 1919, and whose purpose was to agitate among the nearly half a million former prisoners of war of German and Hungarian nationality. In addition, the Czech communists in the foreign section had a special task: to agitate among soldiers of the "intervention armies," including the Czechoslovak Legion, to demoralize them or to induce them to join the Red Army.[21]

After the armistice was signed with the Czechoslovak army in Siberia, the Czechoslovak communists were travelling westward, while the army went home via Japan. Before going home, the demobilized Czechoslovak members of the Red Army received instructions on how to work for the revolution. Some of them received political training in Moscow so that they could become more effective professional revolutionaries in Czechoslovakia.[22]

In April 1920, Bohumír Šmeral arrived in Moscow for consultations. In the same year another visitor from Czechoslovakia, Antonín Zápotocký, took part in the Second Congress of the Third International, and had, on this occasion, private conversations with Lenin.[23] Toward the end of 1920, the Czechoslovak communists in Russia completed their work and went home. After their arrival they gave speeches at hundreds of meetings of the Czechoslovak Social Democratic party, attempting to pull it into the communist fold; they failed to do so. However, after the collapse of the general strike in December 1920, they had a lion's share in founding the Communist Party of Czechoslovakia, a section of the Third International, in 1921.[24]

The mainstream of the Czechoslovak independence movement in Russia and Siberia, however, recognized the authority of the CSNC, and after its founding, that of the Czechoslovak government. But the leaders of that government differed on what should be done with the Czechoslovak troops in Russia and Siberia. On October 29, 1918, Masaryk wired Beneš about the need to request the return of Czechoslovak troops from Italy and France in the event of Austro-Hungarian capitulation, and also, "if possible, to initiate negotiations with Lenin about the release of our Russian army home."[25] Štefánik, in contrast, dispatched via Japan to the Czechoslovak army in Siberia in order to settle the problems that had arisen there, proceeded from the assumption that his task was to restore the morale of the troops and lead them to victory in their struggle with the Soviet forces.[26]

Štefánik, in his dual role as a French officer and a member of the CSNC, had a short by spectacular career. On June 20, 1918, when the French government decided to use the Czechoslovak Legion (officially part of the French armed forces) as the vanguard of the Allied intervention forces in Russia, Lieutenant Colonel (a temporary rank) Štefánik was notified by the French government that he had been promoted to brigadier general for the duration of his mission in the Czechoslovak army, in order that he might carry out effectively his mission as an aide to the commander of the Czechoslovak army, General Janin, and as a member of the CSNC.[27] Despite their close collaboration, Štefánik differed from Masaryk and Beneš, emotionally, politically, and philosophically, as Beneš noted in a letter to Masaryk dated July 28, 1918.[28] Beneš complained that Štefánik was extremely emotional, irritable, unpredictable, and unstable; that his concept of life and of everything else differed from his own and that this difference "at the end, inevitably, becomes manifest."

Although a French citizen, Štefánik accepted the appointment of minister of war in the provisional government of Czechoslovakia, and then in Kramář's, with the consent of the French government.[29] After the dissolution of the Russian branch of the CSNC on November 14, General Štefánik, as minister of war, became the chief administrative authority for the Czechoslovak forces in Siberia.[30] General Janin personally assumed command of the Czechoslovak army in Siberia in the second half of November 1918. On November 18, in agreement with the French and British governments, Admiral Kolchak carried out his "coup d'état," creating a new political climate in Siberia. His action was not popular among the Czechoslovaks, nor was Štefánik's abolishing the system of committees popular among those who had joined the army as a voluntary organization and who pointed at its revolutionary origin.[31]

In his speeches to the troops Štefánik attempted to improve their morale. In Omsk he declared that he would "rather die in Siberia," than to give up the struggle against the Bolsheviks, and that he would "force the Czechs to fight the Bolsheviks."[32] On December 2, 1918, he stated that the Czechoslovak army was an Allied expeditionary force, and that the Czechoslovak government would intervene in Russian domestic affairs as much as the governments of Britain and France did.[33] In his conversations with the troops he emphasized his conviction that the Czechoslovak republic "will need the Allies for a long time." He pointed out the importance of having "good relations especially with France."[34] While encouraging the Czechs to change their defeatist attitude and go onto the offensive, he coined the phrase "fighting our way [home] through Russia," before the offensive against Perm.[35] In the capture of Perm the Czech Legion reached the culmination of its campaign; shortly after it General Syrový, the commander in chief of the Legion, reported to Štefánik that in the opinion of the commanders of regiments and divisions, the Legion was no longer able to carry on fighting.[36] The Red Army was getting stronger and stronger; the Bolshevik agitation was lowering the morale of the Czech troops; and the French ministry of war sent new directives to Generals Janin and Štefánik toward the end of December 1918, according to which the Czechs should form merely "a defensive barrier on the Ural."[37] In January 1919, the Czech troops began to leave the Ural front and were replaced by White Russian military units.[38]

Believing that he had resolved the problems in the army, Štefánik left Siberia in January 1919. On January 25, before his departure for Europe, he sent a telegram to General Janin, whom he had named as the supreme commander of the Czechoslovak army in Siberia during his absence, urging him not to allow the departure of the Czechoslovak army across Bolshevik-held parts of European Russia, on the basis of an agreement negotiated with the Soviet government in Moscow by Prokop Maxa.[39] He also sent a telegram to the Czechoslovak government at Prague urging it "from the bottom of his heart" to make the fight against Bolshevism in all of its manifestations the overriding factor in its policy.[40] Štefánik's views, apparently, were not in accord with those of Beneš, who adjusted his public pronouncements to the wishes of the Entente powers, using the threats of Bolshevism and the Czechoslovak fight against the Bolsheviks as diplomatic weapons, but who was ambivalent about intervention.

Behind the policy decisions of the Czechoslovak government with respect to the Russian situation were not only rational considerations but also (as is usual in politics) irrational factors that were the products of personality clashes and personal animosities. As in the earlier case of Dürich, differences of opinion and personal jealousies evolved between Štefánik and Beneš. According to an intimate friend of Štefánik, Louise Weiss, editor of *L'Europe Nouvelle,* Štefánik's differences with Beneš became an obsession of the latter. Although Štefánik was extremely busy, he could enlighten her "within three minutes" about "this first grade Socialist, this paper revolutionary, this distorted diplomat." As soon as Štefánik left her office, Beneš came in and "for three hours expanded on 'this astronomer who thinks he is a soldier, this peasant who thinks he is an aristocrat, this politician who considers himself a genius, but who, in fact, is nothing but muddled up.'" Later, "when Štefánik returned from his expedition, he found Beneš more and more firmly established with some Government Offices with whom he was negotiating [in Štefánik's absence] and, in view of the circumstances, without informing Štefánik about it. Beneš could not witness without envy the aura surrounding Milan as a legendary hero."[41]

While political maneuvers were conducted behind the scenes, the Czechoslovak troops remained in Siberia and followed Masaryk's order of November 14, 1918, to stay there not to fight the Bolsheviks but in order to strengthen, by their sacrifice, the Czechoslovak position at the peace conference. Some soldiers and officers agreed with Kramář and Štefánik and tried to do their best to defeat the Bolsheviks; they were in the minority, however, and they cooperated with Kolchak.

Recognizing the qualities of General R. Gajda as a military strategist and leader, toward the end of 1918, Admiral Kolchak appointed him commander of the Russian Siberian army. The young Czech general prepared a plan for driving the Bolsheviks from the Ural region and for launching an offensive aimed at the capture of Moscow. Following a series of success by Gajda, some of the Russian generals became jealous of the "foreigner," resented his giving policy recommendations to the Kolchak government, and forced him to resign his post in June 1919. Gajda then departed for Vladivostok, where he was unsuccessful in an attempted coup against Kolchak, and eventually left for Czechoslovakia. The resignation of Gajda was the beginning of the decline of Kolchak's power in Siberia.[42]

Throughout 1919, Winston Churchill made strenuous efforts to bring help to the national Russian governments, believing that the Allies had a commitment to them. The help that was received by Denikin and Kolchak was very limited; and Churchill regretted that neither Japan nor the United States was willing to send a meaningful number of troops to Russia in 1918. He believed that in view of "the amazing exploits of the Czech Army Corps," a resolute effort by "a comparatively small number of trustworthy American or Japanese troops would have enabled Moscow to be occupied by National Russian and Allied forces even before the German collapse took place." In Churchill's opinion, "Divided counsel and cross-purposes among the Allies, American mistrust of Japan, and the personal opposition of President Wilson, reduced Allied intervention in Russia during the war to exactly the point where it did the utmost harm and gained the least advantage."[43]

Though Masaryk opposed Kramář's plan for intervention,[44] the Entente statesmen continued to discuss the Russian situation with Beneš, who was accommodating and seemingly not against a joint Allied action. From Paris, in the middle of June 1919, Beneš sent a message to the Czechoslovak Revolutionary National Assembly suggesting that "should there be an intervention, then it must be consistent one and till the end."[45] However, Beneš's commitments to the Allies were subject to the approval of the Prague government and the president. Masaryk's views were reflected in his statements to a delegation of Legionnaires who arrived from Siberia in March 1919, among whom was Janko Jesenský, who had been elected vice-president of the Russian branch of the CSNC at the Cheliabinsk congress. To the question what would happen to the Czechoslovak army in Siberia, Masaryk replied, "We will leave the army in Russia until the end of the peace negotiations and the signing of the peace [treaty]. Then we will negotiate its transit across central Russia with the Bolsheviks."[46] This contrasted with the view of Štefánik; the latter, however, died in May 1919.

On June 23, 1919, Beneš sent a telegram, followed by a letter, to Masaryk concerning his negotiations with the British minister of war, Winston Churchill, about the transportation of troops from Siberia. Churchill offered, in the name of the Allies, to bring the Czechoslovak troops home before the end of the year if his plan were accepted by the Czechoslovak government, in which case he promised to win endorsement of it by the peace conference. According to the Churchill plan, the Allies would bring the troops home, provided that 20,000 of them would travel via Vladivostok and the rest of them, 30,000, via Perm-Vyatka and Petrograd or Archangel. There was, however, one condition attached. If the Bolsheviks tried to prevent the establishment of junctions of the fronts Perm-Petrograd-Archangel by the Czechoslovak army, the army would have to fight its way through. The British had 30,000 men between Perm, the Baltic Sea, and the North Sea, and they were willing to strengthen their forces there if the Czechs would carry out the Churchill plan, i.e., if they were willing to fight the Bolsheviks. If the Czechoslovak government did not accept this proposal, it would take at least one and half years to bring the troops home, Beneš was told. If the Czechoslovak government did accept the plan, it should be carried out under the slogan, "The Czechs' way home," not as a help to Kolchak. Beneš was confident that this time the Allies meant business and that they would not provide ships for the Czechs if the latter did not take part in Churchill's plan, which, in any case, Beneš promised to keep secret.[47]

In the same communication Beneš expressed his satisfaction that Kramář's plan concerning Russian affairs had not been implemented becuase of political developments in Czechoslovakia. Had Kramář gone ahead with his plan, "it would have been necessary to replace him here [in Paris]," writes Beneš. But to do so "was no longer urgent now."[48] Beneš was referring to Kramář's plan of intervention, in which the then inactive Czechoslovak army in Siberia was assigned the task of mounting a westward offensive, west of the Ural mountains, and capturing Moscow. Beneš's remark indicates that he and Masaryk were prepared to sabotage that plan, should it become operational, by recalling Kramář from Paris; he would have been replaced as prime minister of Czechoslovakia. Another remark in the same letter indicates that Beneš had already by-passed Kramář and dealt in some matters with the western Allies behind Kramář's back.[49]

On July 5, 1919, Beneš sent a telegram to Pavlů at Omsk, notifying him that "during our negotiations on the repatriation of our army with the Allies the British recommended that a part of it should go to Archangel and the other one to Vladivostok. The [Czechoslovak] government is against taking any step that could endanger any part of the army; it would agree, however, if you would accept the plan as feasible and if the army itself would be prepared to fight its way to Archangel, even for the price of new fights with the Bolsheviks. Public opinion [in Czechoslovakia] ... is against intervention, but the will of the army will give the direction. Discuss the matter with Syrový and Janin, arrive at an agreement with them, and do not let yourself to be influenced by any other consideration except the attempt to get our army home as soon as possible."[50]

At this time the morale of the Czech troops was low—like that of any idling army exposed to systematic agitation by trained agitators. A mission sent to Siberia by the Czechoslovak government at Prague did not succeed in stimulating the patriotism of the troops, largely because it arrived too late, when the Kramář plan had already been defeated at home. The delegates left Prague on June 14, stopped at Paris for instructions from Prime Minister Kramář, and after their arrival in Siberia acquainted the troops with the Kramář message to them, urging them to launch an attack on Moscow and thus come home via Russia. The delegates assured Kolchak's representatives at Irkutsk that "the Czechoslovaks will not leave Siberia as long as their presence will be needed by Russia."[51] But the message expressing Kramář's view was delivered when he was no longer prime minister of Czechoslovakia; he was dismissed from that office by Masaryk on July 8, 1919.[52] In addition, the delegation brought also a message from the president in which the latter expressed a hope that the return of the troops was not merely a technical question of transportation home.[53] Subsequently, with Kramář out of office and Štefánik dead, the command of the army in Siberia received political directives from Beneš.

Replying to Beneš's telegram on July 16, Pavlů reported that though order had been restored in the army, he was certain that manifestations of discontent would come into the open again if no means of transportation home were provided soon. The most recent mutiny in the Czechoslovak army, said Pavlů, was a consequence of the internal troubles in Russia stemming from the Russian revolution; it was due to Bolshevik agitation. "The [White] Russians propose that we travel home either via Archangel or the South. Premier Kramář, reportedly, has no objection to it." But for psychological and military reasons, Pavlů doubted whether either course—fighting their way via Archangel or via the south, controlled by Denikin, was feasible. In his view, "today it would mean decomposition of the army."[54] Thus neither Kramář's plan nor Churchill's plan was implemented by the army.

Although Bolshevik propaganda was effective at home and in Siberia, it was, most importantly, the policy of the president that prevailed. Volunteers were not allowed to take part in the fight against the Bolsheviks, since even the leader of the delegation from home confirmed that the troops would stay in Siberia only until the signing of the peace treaties. Beneš's instructions were clear, though there were no ships in sight of Vladivostok. Early in October came a telegram from Paris in which Beneš instructed the command to concentrate the army in Vladivostok.[55] Implementation of this instruction would mean, as Generals Syrový and Janin realized, the collapse of the anti-Bolshevik front.

On October 20, 1919, under the impact of victories in the first phase of Denikin's offensive against Moscow from the south of Russia, Pavlů proposed to fight a way through for the Legion by deploying in the westward offensive the more courageous parts of the Czechoslovak army. He believed that the losses connected with such a military operation would not exceed those currently suffered while the army was inactive, but was under attack by Bolshevik guerrillas; and this course would also shorten the army's ordeal in Siberia. As he pointed out in his telegram to Beneš in Paris, the mounting of such a westward offensive would save time, money, and military materials and horses. Pavlů was particularly fond of the Legion's "12,000 excellent horses and the technically well equipped three divisions." Now Pavlů and General Syrový, the commander in chief, begged the government for a free hand for a possible westward drive in the current favorable circumstances, pointing out that only "the most courageous elements would take part in the action so that the risks involved would be minimal." Pavlů asked for a directive, emphasizing that this was a serious matter, not an adventure. He also repeated his request for the recall of Dr. Girsa, who refused any kind of cooperation with Kolchak and favored cooperation with the admiral's SR enemies.[56]

The Allied military in Siberia, especially General Knox, urged Pavlů, General Syrový, and the Czechoslovak soldiers to go to the front, to move westward and help their Russian cousins in their heroic efforts to overthrow the Bolsheviks. Knox pointed out that Great Britain was helping Generals Denikin and Yudenich (the latter commanded forces in the vicinity of Petrograd, threatening to capture that city), and that the Americans and Japanese should help Kolchak. Although he did as much as he could for Kolchak, Knox promised to help the Czechoslovak army in any possible way if the latter would join the forces of the Russian Siberian leader.[57]

But at this time, without waiting for the decision of the Allies, Beneš ordered the army to evacuate Siberia via Vladivostok and not to participate in the all-out anti-Bolshevik coordinateed action of the White armies of Kolchak, Denikin, and Yudenich.[58] Since the principal peace treaties had already been signed (the Treaty of Versailles in June and the Treaty of St. Germain in September 1919), and since on September 22 the president of the United States had approved an American loan of up to $12 million to the Czechoslovak government to cover the estimated cost of repatriating 50,000 Czechs,[59] Beneš and the government in Prague no longer had an interest in the Czech army's staying or fighting in Siberia and Russia. Although Pavlů and General Janin asked the government in Prague that the army be allowed to return home by land, their repeated requests were rejected.[60] In his message of October 28, 1919, Masaryk publicly proclaimed "I was and I am against intervention in Russia and Hungary. In difficult crises each nation must help itself, and Russia is undergoing a great and difficult crisis." The "philosopher-king" had spoken. Pavlů and Janin could not overrule him. Then General Syrový, invoking Beneš's order, began to carry out the evacuation.[61] Since the Russian Siberian army could not find replacements for the Czechoslovak army corps guarding the railway, its offensive failed. Indeed, the Czech behavior had a demoralizing effect on the Russian troops led by Kolchak. Those of the Czechs, represented by Dr. Girsa, who advocated negotiations with the Bolsheviks in order to return home, in so doing helped to undermine the Kolchak government, thus helping the Bolsheviks.[62]

According to Winston Churchill, Kolchak "was honest, loyal and incorruptible," but he had "no political experience and was devoit of those profound intuitions which have enabled men of equal virtue and character to steer their way through the shoals and storms of revolution. He was an intelligent, honorable, patriotic admiral."[63] A series of conflicts developed between Kolchak and the Czechs who were guarding the Siberian railway, and whose desire to go home was increasing. Kolchak made several unfavorable comments on the Czechoslovaks' unwillingness to go on fighting, which necessitated their withdrawal from the front. He also had some friction with General Janin, the commander of the non-Russian Allied forces. The Czechs on their part, did not approve of the Kolchak coup of November 18, 1918, and expressed their preference for other (largely socialist) political groups suppressed as a result of that event.[64] The ill feeling between Kolchak on one hand, and the Czechs and their supreme commander on the other, led to a series of events culminating in the arrest of Kolchak and his prime minister and their being turned over to a rival government of the "Political Centre" at Irkutsk by the Czechs to whom he had surrendered on January 4, 1920.

Toward the end of 1919, the Czechs knew that Kolchak, Denikin, and Yudenich had been defeated. As General Syrový stated in his letter of December 23, 1919, to the Entente representatives (published in *Československý Deník*), the collapse of the Russian state made it necessary for the Czechs to look after themselves.[65] By this time the Czechs' policy was never to fight except for their own security. The Czechoslovak army's unwillingness to fight did not win the sympathies of the Bolsheviks, but it did provoke an open hostility on the part of the anti-Bolshevik Russians, who began to call the Czechoslovaks cowards. A White Russian general, V. O. Kapell, whose troops—"Kapellovtsi"—had helped the Czechs to take Kazan and to capture the Russian gold reserves in the summer of 1918, challenged General Syrový to a duel. Also, Bolshevik propoganda exaggerated the looting and profiteering by the Czechoslovak soldiers, and their selfishness and cruelty, and many of the Siberian peasants began to call the Czechs *Czecho-svoloch* (Czech rubbish), and *Czecho-sobaki* (Czech dogs).[66] Paradoxically, a year earlier, the same Siberian population had hailed them as heroic liberators from the Bolshevik terror.

In January 1920, anti-Kolchak feeling in the Czech unit at Irkutsk, cultivated by certain Czech and Bolshevik propagandists, was running high. On January 14, acting upon orders from General Janin, two Czech officers handed Kolchak over to the Extraordinary Commission of the Political

Centre. The Extraordinary Commission (Cheka) conducted Kolchak's interrogation. Since its chairman was a Bolshevik, it continued the inquiry when Irkutsk became a part of the Soviet empire, following the Bolshevik Revolutionary Committee's (Revkom) replacement of the Political Centre on January 18, 1920. (The Social Democratic government in Irkutsk declared itself Bolshevik.) On the night of February 4- 5, 1920, the Revkom decided that Kolchak must not be recovered by the troops of Kapell and Vojtsekhovskii, who were approaching the city, and that he must be executed, subject to the approval of I. N. Smirnov at Fifth Red Army headquarters.[67] "It is a pity," wrote Churchill, "that the magnificent record of the Czechoslovak army corps has been marred by the surrender of Kolchak."[68]

In their attempt to appease the Bolsheviks during the protracted armistice negotiations, the Czech military did not permit the White Russian troops, commanded by General Vojtsekhovskii, to enter Irkutsk and rescue Kolchak from his captors. Subsequently Generals Janin and Syrový were held responsible for the admiral's fate. (For executing Beneš's evacuation orders Syrový was rewarded in Czechoslovakia by promotions and decorations. During the Munich crisis president Beneš appointed him prime minister of the government whose task was to carry out the capitulation. In 1947 Syrový was sentenced to twenty-five years in prison by the new "people's republic" headed by Beneš for alleged treason and collaboration with the Nazis. While in prison he had time to reflect upon his turbulent life, including the Kolchak incident.)

The Czechoslovak encounter with Bolsheviks in Siberia came rapidly to its end on February 7, 1920. On that day an armistice was signed by the two parties, the Bolsheviks represented by comrade Smirnov and the Czechs by Lieutenant Hub.[69] The conditions of the armistice blur the record of the Czechoslovak Siberian "Anabasis." Article 5 of the agreement stipulated that the Czechoslovaks would leave Admiral Kolchak at Irkutsk; Article 6 bound them to turn over the gold reserves of the tsarist Russian government to the Bolsheviks; and in Article 10 the Czechoslovaks agreed not to evacuate the army and property of Kolchak. The agrement left Kolchak in the hands of the Bolsheviks. On February 7, the day the agreement was signed, Kolchak and his prime minister were shot at Irkutsk. Kolchak's last words reportedly were, *"Spasibo vam Czecho-sobaki!"* ("Thank you, Czech dogs!")[70]

This was an inglorious end to the chapter that started with Štefánik's departure for Europe. The tsarist gold reserves had been taken by Colonel Švec's units before the evacuation of Kazan on September 10, 1918, and stored in eighteen railroad cars, which were turned over to the Bolsheviks on March 1, 1920. The conditions of the armistice were in grave contrast with the content of speeches delivered by Štefánik in November 1918, in which he urged the troops to remain "the invincible enemies of Bolshevism." In his address to the officers of the Slovak regiment on November 28, on the tasks of the Czechoslovak army after the attainment of independence, he declared, "Bolshevism is anarchy, Bolshevism in Russia threatens our state too. If normal conditions are not restored in Russia, sparks of anarchy will fly from Russia even to Bohemia. When someone's house is on fire, it would be wrong to wait until the fire comes close to our own home and ignites it; the fire has to be extinquished in time.... We have asked for help and we have received it.... Russia was among the first who helped us to get organized. Now our task is to help Russia. We cannot refuse to give this help. It would be un-grateful and un-Slavic, and, above all, it would be improvident because the existence of a strong, regenerated Russia is in our vital interest. We will certainly need her help in the future."[71]

Štefánik's words had a prophetic ring; however, Masaryk and some other men who assumed power in Czechoslovakia did not see it that way. It was not Štefánik's destiny to participate in the fight against Bolshevism that he had advocated so fervently. After his return to western Europe from Siberia, he left Rome by airplane for his native Slovakia. When the airplane was ready to land at the military airport close to Bratislava, it was, allegedly, brought down "by a Czecho [sic] anti-aircraft battery of Bratislava" on May 4, 1919.[72] Štefánik died in the debris of the plane. He was no longer able to influence in any way the course of Czechoslovak domestic and foreign policy.

Eventually, Štefánik was adopted by both the "Czechoslovak" centralists and the Slovak autonomists as their national hero. Some Slovak autonomists hinted that Štefánik's death was not accidental, as the above quotation from a Slovak writer indicates, and others blamed Masaryk and Beneš. While it is a matter of public record that Štefánik differed with Masaryk and Beneš on many issues, especially on the question of the Czechoslovak mission in Russia and Siberia, it has never been conclusively proven that his death was or was not accidental.[73]

Early in 1919, before Štefánik died, Masaryk and Beneš corresponded about Štefánik, who, with the consent of the French government, held the portfolio of minister of war in the Czechoslovak government, and they tried to find a new official position for him. As has been mentioned earlier, Beneš and Štefánik became rivals; the latter had aspired to become minister of foreign affairs, while the former actually received that office from Masaryk, who failed to ask Štefánik's advice or consent in this and other ministerial appointments. As minister of war, Štefánik was merely in charge of the Czechoslovak military operations in Siberia, while a separate ministry of national defense, headed by a prewar politician, Václav Klofáč, was established in Prague. The Masaryk-Beneš correspondence shows that the two planned to remove Štefánik from the government and give him a diplomatic assignment abroad, most likely in Rome.[74] Had this happened, one may speculate that—in view of Štefánik's explosive nature—he might have revealed the details of Masaryk's and Beneš's *modus operandi,* their secrets, and their work for the British and French governments during the war, which they carefully concealed. But the main significance of Štefánik's death was the reduction of the triumvirate exile leaders—Masaryk-Štefánik-Beneš—by one; the two who remained no longer had to cope with him, his political views, and the problems his impulsiveness might have created. There is no doubt, however, that the abrupt termination of Štefánik's life had a profound effect on the situation among those who fought in Russia and Siberia, whose last transport left Vladivostok in September 1920.

CHAPTER EIGHTEEN

REFLECTION, RECAPITULATION, AND AFTERMATH

One of the architects of the "New Europe," R. W. Seton-Watson, maintained that "there is a retributive justice which destroys great empires."[1] It would seem that a retributive justice destroyed both the Habsburg empire and the independence of Czechoslovakia. Seton-Watson suggests, furthermore, that "certain historical standards of truth exist;" and that "the historian who suppresses or perverts the truth will soon, rather than late, stand convicted before the bar of history."[2] Indeed, the truth will prevail at the end; and a scholar has the right and duty to search for truth. He has the right and duty to think, honor, and do what is true. Naturally, the age-old question, What is truth? may be asked. This writer has always believed that "a statement is true when it is in accord with the facts—with the realities, when the connections it asserts actually exist in the manner, place, and time in which it is asserted to exist. Our task is to discover relationships between things, and to hold truth, like goodness and beauty, as one of supreme values."[3]

The capital problem of a historian is that of "omission and selection," writes Seton-Watson, "whose "only fundamental rule is never conscientiously to suppress facts; and to find the right line between omission and suppression must depend on the sound judgment or the honesty of the individual writer."[4] However, even an honest writer who exercises sound judgment may still be charged with lack of objectivity by those whose bias or pride prevent them from seeing things the way they are. Undoubtedly, there will be those who will not be pleased that this book mentions the criticism of Masaryk by the Czech historian, Pekař; that it quotes Masaryk's statement that the sending of Voska to Steed in August 1918, was "the beginning;" that it documents Masaryk's connections with the British intelligence service and the British financing of Voska's intelligence network in the United States, Russia, and elsewhere; that it points out that some of Masaryk's statements were not true; that it shows how it was possible for Masaryk, who in 1914 had been so discredited by the Šviha affair that most leading Czech politicians did not want to speak with him, to return from abroad in 1918 ad the president of the new state.[5] Since all these and other facts and events were related to the genesis of Czechoslovakia, they had to be discussed in this work.

The achievement of Czechoslovak independence resulted from a series of historical accidents that were exploited by the leaders of the independence movement at home and abroad. In the final phase of the war the exile leaders received full support from the Czech political leaders at home and thus could claim to speak for the nation. The Czechoslovak independence movement was rising and falling with the great international events; it was strengthened by some and weakened by others, as Beneš had observed during the war.[6] He and the other members of the independence movement abroad were fully aware of the importance of the home front, and the exile movement never separated diplomatic-political work from the military exploits of its armed forces. Thus, those who fought for Czechoslovak independence at home and abroad realized the interdependence of work at home, on the militay fronts, and abroad.

Because of his tragic death in May 1919, Štefánik was not able to shape the destinies of the Czechoslovak state, as Masaryk and Beneš were. Despite their unity of aims during the war, the two leaders differed in their fundamental outlooks. Before the war Masaryk was a "realist" in politics; for Beneš "realism" was "non-political, without life, dry, doctrinaire, sometimes trivial, and in its essence non-revolutionary and non-radical."[7] Beneš cooperated closely with radical elements and was close to the Social Democratic party, being a contributor to *Právo lidu,* a paper published by the party, which had offered him a position as an editor. Masaryk was a middle-class politician. In his *Social Question,* Masaryk saw revolution as a sign of "weakness and imperfection." For his revolution was "political superstition," "political and social mysticism and mythus." He described the revolutionary as a gambler who plays with life, "a superstitious man, political fetishist who believes in social and political miracles. He believes in accident and is convinced that 2 x 2 = 5 or 4, depending on how it suits him. He is convinced of his geniality and greatness, he pretends to be a hero. Revolutionary is an aristocrat, absolutist and tyrant, though he goes into struggle with the slogan of equality and brotherhood." Yet Masaryk himself became a revolutionary, credited "lucky accidents" (among which he specifically recalled the Siberian "Anabasis") for his success, and admitted making "tactical mistakes" and improvising in his diplomatic activity.[8] Beneš, on the other hand, boasted that the main reason for the wartime success of the movement for independence was that he "always pursued scientific politics" and that he consistently applied his philosophy and scientific method to politics.[9]

Despite the differences in their outlook and ages, Masaryk and Beneš had much in common. Both tended to identify political illusions with realism and sobriety, as evidenced by Masaryk's letter to Chicherin and Beneš's belief in the magic of the League of Nations and his trusting Stalin. They saw reality through their own eyes only, never looking at themselves and at situations through alien eyes, thus becoming self-centered and self-righteous, and applying in concrete situations "the sacred law of selfishness." For both of them the Czech question was the problem of a small nation living between east and west, not that of a political nation whose history and traditions tied it to central Europe. (In World War I, Masaryk and Beneš strove to make the future state into a western-oriented political entity; during World War II, Beneš brought Czechoslovakia into the eastern, Soviet-dominated orbit.) Also, both Masaryk and Beneš represented the trend in modern politics characterized by the political manipulation of human relations, in which the atmosphere of irrationality is artificially created by those who are technically rational.

Before the war Masaryk's "new politics" made no headway in Czech politics; he was rather isolated, constantly bickering with other politicians —sometimes with National Socials, sometimes with Social Democrats, sometimes with both—and almost always with Kramář and the Catholics. The war offered an unusual opportunity for his kind of manipulation of the masses, since it created an artificial atmosphere of hysteria, fear, and hope in which propaganda and manipulation techniques became effective; the words and actions of Masaryk (and Beneš) were not analyzed by their competitors as they normally would have been in peacetime. Before the war the Czechs lived, fundamentally, by the principles embodied in their Christian culture and tradition. They were tolerant, and the intolerant attitude and semi-religious (or pseudo-religious) zeal of Masaryk's politics was alien to them; so were Masaryk's (and also Beneš's) fundamental conceptions of man and history, nature and time, being and truth. The maxim that permeated Masaryk's and Beneš's political practices could have never originated in Bohemia: "In politics you may even make alliance with the devil to achieve your goals, but you must be certain that you will outwit him, not that he will outwit you." As it happened, Masaryk died before Czechoslovakia collapsed. Beneš, however, as former British Prime Minister Clement R. Atlee noted, "put far too much confidence in his own cleverness" in his dealings both with the Germans and later with the Russians; and "did not seem to realize how long a spoon was needed to sup with the devil."[10]

Masaryk's religion was likewise foreign to the vast majority of Czechs and Slovaks before the war, as was his tendency to move from one extreme to another. His preoccupation with religion led him to believe that the Czech and Russian questions were religious questions.[11] Masaryk contended that the revolutionary movements in Russia before World War I were, in substance, religious movements. During the years 1906-07 he closely followed religious developments in Russia, and ascribed great importance to them. However, when he was in Russia in 1917, he paid no attention to the religious ferment in the country, though it was more manifest than ever. If Masaryk overemphasized the religious issue before the war, he left it out of his concerns in 1917. This indicates that religion was for him merely a means of influencing the masses to prop up a particular program and advance his own political objectives.

Though Masaryk originally intended to establish a new church rather than to initiate a new political group, the Realist party, the ideology of that party reflected his own philosophy and religion. It proved to be an inadequate instrument for changing the outlook and attitudes of the vast majority of the Czechs before the war. But after the war, while he was president of the state, he could and did mold the intelligentsia and the younger generation in accordance with his own image.

The hazards of any attempt at categorizing Masaryk have been mentioned earlier in this work. However, to this writer Masaryk appears to be a Gnostic turned politician whose spiritual great-grandfather was Plato. He belongs to a long line of Gnostics, basic to whose diversified teachings are dualism and the antagonism between matter and spirit. (In his first presidential message to the Revolutionary National Assembly, delivered on December 22, 1918, Masaryk described World War I as a struggle in which "the spirit won over the matter.") The Gnostic, because of his "inner vision," believes himself to be above all civil society and its laws, as well as independent of an hierarchical church that teaches religious truth and moral virtues; and he regards himself as the supremely qualified teacher of truths about God and His creation. Masaryk was one of the *illuminati* who have believed themselves to have a special insight into truth—one of those who had made their private conscience the supreme court of truth.

In his theoretical writings Masaryk subordinated politics to ethics; as a politician, he separate the two completely. The highest moral values, such as defense of truth, were not Masaryk's highest political values, as his war time political method amply demonstrates. Though he never spelled out his theories clearly, and though the gap between his moralizing and his political method is quite obvious, it may be argued that the real Masaryk was a combination of the theoretician and the propagandist-politician. Already in his *Czech Question* he hinted at the real Masaryk when he asked, "Why must Hus die and Wiclif not?... was his death really necessary and inevitable? Why could Luther live?"[12] According to Masaryk, the Czechs have a tendency toward martyrdom, reflecting the passivity of their character. But Masaryk was an activist, a political animal for whom nothing succeeds like success. To succeed by whatever method, regardless of professed ethics and objective truth, seems to have been the ultimate aim of this charistmatic leader, whose characteristics were so different from those that he—not quite accurately—ascribed to the Czechs. (Incidentially, Masaryk's stereotype of the Czech as martyr diametrically opposes another Czech stereotype, the good soldier Schweik.)

In his criticism of "Masaryk's Czech Philosophy"[13] the prominent Czech historian Josef Pekař noted that Masaryk was an agitator rather than a scholar, and that his ambition, zeal, anti-Catholic feelings, and proselytizing efforts impaired his ability to see the structure of reality. His pamphlet "In the Struggle for Religion" (1904) relfects his Gnosticism or even atheism. Masaryk writes, "Jesus required faith from the pious, but we no longer believe and we cannot, and we will not, believe, because we have come to understand that to believe in god always means to believe man, another one or oneself." Though he said in his "American Lectures," delivered in 1902, that every man should be his own pope,[14] he himself became the pope of the "Masaryk sect"—a fringe group before the war. After the war, when he became president of Czechoslovakia, this sect became a whole church; now, protected by the Law for the Protection of the Republic, adopted in 1923, he exercised a strong influence on the whole nation. Opportunists jumped on his bandwagon, trying to outdo the prewar "sectarians" in adulation of "papa Masaryk." To question, not merely the faith and morals, but even the methods, theories, writings, and politics of the "national pope" became a tabu, a sacrilege, to those of the "Masaryk democrats" who uncritically promoted the Masaryk mythology.

After the war Masaryk and Beneš had their admirers and enemies in Czechoslovakia and elsewhere. They both knew the value of favorable publicity and they saw to it that they got plenty of it at home and abroad. Their critics, however, blamed them for the "Balkanization of Central Europe" that brought economic misery and the curse of "organic nationalism" on the peoples living in the area, and that paved the way for Hitler's expansionism in World War II. During the period between the two wars the followers of Masaryk in Czechoslovakia, the "Masaryk democrats," professed proudly the philosophy of their idol, the "philosopher statesman," while other people in the wings, both right and left, as well as the centrist People's parties, Czech and Slovak, and the German, Polish, and Hungarian minorities did not share their enthusiasm for "papa Masaryk."

Wenzel Jaksch, a German Social Democrat, suggested that Masaryk's political philosophy was not genuine in the sense that "a philosophy is the consistent application of a set of principles." He described it as "a mélange of truths, falsehoods, and contradictions, a doctrine of pure expediency wearing the cloak of democratic ethics and concocted to meet the specific needs of Greater Czech *Machtpolitik*. The result was the propagation of a congeries of political errors which have corrupted the thinking of two generations."[15]

Fourteen years after succeeding in his efforts to bring about Czechoslovak independence, Charles Pergler, the leader of the Czech political action in the United States during World War I, declared at a large public meeting at Chicago that the Masaryk-Beneš regime in Czechoslovakia did not practice the rule of law as it was prescribed by the Czechoslovak constitution, that the rights of individuals who displeased Beneš were not respected, and that censorship there was much worse than it had been in Austria-Hungary during the reactionary and absolutist regime of Bach. The "Realist" clique was raging there, Pergler said. This time, however, it had the power of the state at its disposal, something it had lacked before the war. Furthermore, paragraph eleven of the Law for the Protection of the Republic, dealing with the president of the republic, prohibited criticism of the president and made inadmissible as a defense proof of truth of any such accusation in a court of law; the president was virtually above the law. The deeds and philosophy of the president could not be questioned. A priest-poet and writer, Jakub Deml, was prosecuted for criticism of a philosophical pronouncement that Masaryk, then a private citizen of Austria-Hungary, had made before the war. In 1932 Pergler himself, a native born Czech and the first Czechoslovak minister to Japan, was deprived of his seat in the Czechoslovak parliament and was barred from Czechoslovakia on the pretext that he was not a Czechoslovak citizen.[16] The denial of his right of citizenship violated article six of the peace treaty with Czechoslovakia (1919) and the Czechoslovak constitution of 1920.

Pergler also deplored the treatment accorded to the Slovaks. In 1929 Masaryk went so far as to claim that the Pittsburgh Agreement was a forgery and that it "was meant for America and American conditions," —as if Slovak autonomy in Czechoslovakia could ever be applicable to the United States. In May 1918, Masaryk needed the financial, political, and moral support of Slovaks in America; therefore, he drafted and signed the agreement. On November 12, 1918, the Revolutionary National Assembly formally ratified all commitments that had been made by Masaryk and he signed a calligraphic copy of the Pittsburgh Agreement on November 14, 1918, the day he was elected president of the Czechoslovak republic.[17] (This was his second signing of the document.) Implicit in the name of the republic, Czecho-Slovakia, was the idea of a dual republic; this spelling was used in all documents presented by the Czecho-Slovak delegation at the Paris Peace Conference.

In 1920, however, the situation was different: Czechoslovakia existed as a recognized independent state, with a constitution providing for a unitary form of government. Masaryk no longer needed the Slovaks in America. He and his associates believed that the Slovaks in Slovakia could be subdued with the help and collaboration of the Czechophile Vavro Šrobár and some other Protestant politicians, and through stern policies pursued by the centralist government in Prague. The Slovak Populists, however, protested the reduction of Slovakia to a province (or a "Czech colony") of the state dominated by the Czechs and their Czechophile Slovak friends. In 1922, 1930, and 1938, they submitted to the Czechoslovak National Assembly bills calling for Slovak autonomy and based on the Pittsburgh Agreement. Upon their insistance, Law No. 299, of November 19, 1938,[18] which brought the First Republic to its end and ushered in the federalized "Second" Czecho-Slovak Republic, explicitly recognized that "in the Pittsburgh Agreement and other similar agreements and declarations of domestic and international relevance the Czechoslovak nation was granted entire autonomy." The law stated, furthermore, that "the Czecho-Slovak Republic originated in the convergent and sovereign will of the two nations endowed with equal rights."[19]

Unfortunately, giving the Slovaks their due came too late—too late for the Czecho-Slovak state. As Nicholas Murray Butler, president of Columbia University, put it, "had the Republic of Czecho-Slovakia at the time of its organization in 1919 been based upon the cantonal system, its history . . . might have been very different and far happier."[20] Already in 1919 and early in 1920 Kramář bitterly denounced the mistakes made by the Prague government in Slovakia and Sub-Carpatho-Russia (Ruthenia), blaming the weakness of the administration and its socialistic tendencies, which he claimed were Bolshevik-inspired. As for the Slovaks, they had many reasons for disliking the Czechs. Many of the Czechs who had been sent to Slovakia by the Prague government were corrupt, incompetent, and arrogant. Also, the Czech soldiers, specially those of the Twenty-Eighth Regiment, behaved very badly, descrating shrines and churches, and treating Church-going Slovaks with contempt.[21] Masaryk did not want to recognize the injustices perpetrated by the new state against the Slovaks, nor did he admit to being inconsistent in demanding the right of self-determination for the Czechs but denying it to the Slovaks and the minorities of Germans, Hungarians, and Ruthenians living in Czechoslovakia.

But his principal critic in Czechoslovakia, Kramář, reproached Masaryk most for the inconsistency of his treatment of Russia.

Kramář pointed out that Masaryk had written a work published after the war, that "the Tsarist Sodom and Gomorrah had to be eradicated by fire and brimstone."[22] Yet the same Masaryk assigned Constantinople and the Straits to tsarist Russia in his memorandum for Secretary Grey of the British Foreign Office, dated April 6, 1915, and submitted to him at the beginning of May 1915. (See chapter 4 above.) At that time Masaryk stated that "a Bohemian republic" was advocated merely "by a few radical politicians," and he projected Bohemia as "a monarchical state" in which a "Russian dynasty in any form would be the most popular one. In any case, the Czech politicians wish to establish the Kingdom of Bohemia in complete accord with Russia. Wishes and intentions of Russia will be of determining influence."[23] One year later, in his "Message to the Czechs and Slovaks in Russia"of April 6, 1916,[24] he wrote, "Your colony in Russia has a special place among other colonies—you are the only people who live in a Slavic state, in the state of determining importance." Masaryk emphasized that "since we expect so much from Russia for our liberation, it is, therefore, extremely important that you have a correct attitude toward the Russian political world." Masaryk then reported himself "to the Russian representatives abroad first and foremost," and he "asked them for brotherly help." The reader may recall that, despite the warnings that Masaryk had received from his friends in Russia, he wrote an article for a paper published by Minister of the Interior Protopopov, the gravedigger of Russia, as Kramář called him, just a few weeks before the fall of the monarchy in Russia. Yet Dürich was expelled from the CSNC for doing exactly what Masaryk urged the Czechs and Slovaks in Russia to do and what he himself, ostensibly, did: for taking "the correct attitude toward the Russian political world." After the war Kramář was denounced for taking that kind of attitude toward Russia. Kramář resented it and claimed that there was no difference between what he did after the war and what Masaryk wrote to the Czechs in Russia in 1916.[25]

There was, however, one great difference between Masaryk and Kramář: whatever Kramář said about Russia, he said with strong conviction, while for Masaryk, being pro-Russian was merely a tactic. Kramář never learned about Masaryk's connections with British intelligence; or, if he did, he could not prove anything, since the matter remained secret. Štefánik had had the evidence; but Štefánik was dead. Kramář was an honest man who made no charges he could not prove; Beneš and Masaryk, who had no moral scruples whenever their own political interests were involved, had an unfair advantage over him. As it happened, Kramář's concept of the state foreign policy orientation was rejected and Masaryk's concept prevailed. Štefánik, being no longer any threat to anyone alive, became a national hero. It was, however, Beneš's destiny to become the most controversial person of the three who were credited by many with winning Czechoslovak independence. As president of the state, he decided to capitulate in the fall of 1938, and during and after World War II he led Czechoslovakia into the Soviet orbit.

But no matter what one thinks of any one of the three, Masaryk, Beneš, and Štefánik took upon themselves a gigantic task and struggled against great odds when they attempted to destroy an almost four-hundred-year-old monarchy and a viable economic and political unit in central Europe, long taken for granted and considered a bulwark against Russia and Germany. It was, indeed, the Czech nineteenth-century historian, František Palacký, who said that "if Austria had not existed, it would have been necessary to invet her."[26] Long after the Ottoman Turkish threat (mentioned in Masaryk's memorandum to the U.S. secretary of state on August 31, 1918) was gone, the existence of Austria-Hungary was taken for granted even by Masaryk and Beneš. In his dissertation, published as a book at Paris in 1908, Beneš wrote, "People have often spoken of a dismemberment of Austria. I do not believe in it at all. The historic and economic bonds among the Austrian nations are too strong to make such a dismemberment possible. The introduction of universal suffrage and the democratization of Austria, particularly in Bohemia, prepare the soil for national reconciliation."[27] In 1909, Masaryk, too, saw no better alternative to Austria-Hungary, and he continued to believe in its inevitability till the arrival of the war.[28]

After the war Beneš recalled that, when he arrived in Paris in 1915, he had presented his views on the need to destroy Austria-Hungary before a group of French journalists in the presence of a member of parliament, who, after Beneš's speech, told the journalists, "He is a nice boy, but he is crazy."[29] According to the general climate of opinion at that time, the idea of dismembering Austria-Hungary was insane. And yet Austria-Hungary collapsed at the end of the war.

Needless to say, the origins of World War I were not related to the national aspirations of the Czechs and Slovaks, but to the national interests of the powers involved in it. It was important for France to defeat Germany, as it had been for Prussia to defeat France in 1870-71. Contary to the tracts written by Masaryk and his followers, the war was no programmatic and ideological world revolution. It was not caused by the Czechoslovak problem or by the problems of any other small nations within Austria-Hungary. It is true that tsarist Russia planned to establish a Czechoslovak state in 1916, but it collapsed long before the end of the war; and until the summer of 1918 the western Allies were willing to preserve Austria-Hungary in one form or another. Masaryk's claim that the "program of the Allies was, in substance, program for the reorganization of Eastern Europe," and that "dismemberment of Austria-Hungary . . . [was] the main war aim,"[30] cannot be substantiated. The great powers recognized the existence and the national aspirations of the small nations in central and eastern Europe only when they came to believe that it was in their own interests to do so. It is quite usual that wars bring about the collapse of some states and give rise to others, but only a person who is unable or unwilling to see the structure of reality would argue that the great powers went to war in order to liberate the Czechs, Slovaks, Poles, Serbs, etc.

One may argue that Austria's doom was already sealed in 1914, as did Czernin, an embittered man and an apologist for himself, who wrote after the war that the empire had to die anyway. He regretted only that the country, by entering the war, "chose the most terrible manner" of death.[31] But, the empire would not have had to die, had it reformed itself in time. The true gravedigger of the empire, Francis Joseph, lived too long, failed to solve the nationality problem in Austria-Hungary, and brought the country into a war that developed into a worldwide conflict. His successor, Charles, was confronted with a difficult situation, since an attempt a federalization during the war would in all likelihood have encountered violent German and Hungarian opposition. According to Czernin, the nationality problem in the empire could have been solved during the war only with powerful help from outside[32] — with the help of the Allies. Indeed, Emperor Charles attempted to obtain such help when he contacted the Allies and made them a peace offer. The Sixtus affair, however, terminated the negotiations for either a separate or a general peace. When

President Wilson approved Lansing's recommendation "to declare without reservation for an independent Poland, an independent Bohemia and an independent Southern Slav State, and a return of the Rumanians and Italians to their natural allegiance,"[33] "Austria-Hungary as a great European power was doomed."[34]

The British recognition on August 9, 1918, of the Czechoslovak army and the CSNC as "the present trustee of the future Czechoslovak government"[35] was still short of an Allied commitment to dismember Austria-Hungary and the sanctioning of an independent Czechoslovak state, but it did undoubtedly lead to these developments later on. Henry Wickham Steed stated the decisive factor in the British decision to recognize the CSNC in his introduction to Masaryk's book, *The Making of a State:* "Thanks to his army in Siberia and to the Czechoslovak Legions simultaneously organized in France and Italy, Masaryk and his devoted helpers, Beneš and Štefánik, won formal recognition for their people as belligerent Allies."[36] While the recognition of the belligerency of the Czechoslovaks still did not imply the recognition of an independent political entity, most historians—communist, anti-communist, Czech, Russian, British, and American—agree that the recognition of the Masaryk-led committee as a provisional government of the future Czechoslovak state was related to the Czechoslovak anti-Bolshevik uprising in Russia in May 1918, and the fight with the Bolsheviks that followed it.[37] In Masaryk's own words, "the fact that we had an army and that, in Russia, it was the only political and military organization of any size, gave us importance; and, in the negotiations for our recognition, respect for our army was a weighty factor."[38]

According to Masaryk, the Czechoslovak army and its Siberian "Anabasis" provoked President Wilson's interest in the Czech question.[39] However, Masaryk's refusal to consent to the proposed deployment of the army in Russia and Siberia, at a time when the latter had already been fighting the Bolsheviks for a whole month, his embarrassing Lansing on June 25, and his other activities in the United States, discussed earlier, give us a clue to the reasons for the U.S. government's unwillingness to join the French and British governments in extending recognition to the CSNC.

Both the president and Lansing were very sympathetic to the Czech cause, and so were State Department officials and the American public.

Urging the U.S. government to supply weapons and other materials to the Czech army in August 1918, Breckinridge Long of the U.S. State Department pointed out that "the position of the Czecho-Slovak forces in Siberia, preventing Siberian supplies from going to Germany and preventing repatriation of German and Austrian prisoners of war," had a direct bearning upon "the campaign on the Western Front." He wrote in his memorandum that "the Czecho-Slovak soldiers in Siberia are saving the lives of American soldiers in France. The honor, as well as the interest of America is involved in their immediate relief...."[40] It was the Allied pressure on Wilson, and his recognition of the exigencies of military cooperation with the Czechoslovak army in Russia and Siberia, that led to the U.S. government's decision to recognize the CSNC. Thus, the factors that eventually compelled the American president to grant recognition to the CSNC were the performance of the Czechoslovak army in Russia and Siberia, and the resulting interest of the American public in the Czechoslovak cause.

The claims of communist historians notwithstanding, it cannot be demonstrated that the Bolshevik Revolution inspired the nation at home to follow the same course; and the idea of an independent Czechoslovak state was not original with the Bolsheviks—in fact, the tsarist government had endorsed it.[41] However, the Brest-Litovsk conference brought the issue of national self-determination to the attention of the oppressed nationalities of the Central Powers. Thus, in the "Epiphany Declaration" of January 6, 1918, the Czech deputies in Vienna, reacting to the slighting of the Czechs at Brest-Litovsk, demanded complete independence for the Czechoslovaks and the *"guaranteed participation and full freedom of defending their rights at the Peace Conference."*[42] By its willingness to deal with the Bolsheviks and entertain their proposals at Brest-Litovsk, the Austrian government created for itself a very grave domestic problem.

The Treaty of Brest-Litovsk was also an important factor in the development of the Allied anti-Bolshevik policy, as well as a seed of the future conflict between the Czechoslovak army and the Bolsheviks. Although at the time of its conclusion the treaty was hailed as a great Habsburg victory, in the long run it paved the way to the dismemberment of Austria-Hungary. While Austria-Hungary was able, as a consequence of the treaty, to disengage its military forces on the Eastern Front, the Danubian monarchy had to pay a high price. It recognized Lenin's Council of

People's Commissars as the government of Russia, with all the political and moral consequences and ramifications of that act, including the effect on the Poles[43] and the rapprochement of the Czech political leaders at home with the exiles. Recognition, it is true, "neutralized" Lenin's Russia in the war; however, the neutrality of Russia, which the Central Powers insisted must be observed to the letter, made the presence of armed Czechoslovak troops in Russia incompatible with the terms of the Brest-Litovsk Treaty, and hastened the arrival of the conflict that suddenly made the Czechoslovaks in Russia famous. Also, by signing the treaty the Bolsheviks placed themselves in the same camp of the enemies of the Allies and of the Czechoslovaks. This brought about the "emancipation" of the Czechoslovak army as an independent military force, both in the eyes of the Allied public and in fact. It was no longer possible to look upon the Czechs who took up arms against Austria-Hungary as a bunch of traitors who had broken their oath of allegiance to the Austro-Hungarian government, renounced their citizenship, and sworn new allegiance to the Russian tsar. Now their allegiance was no longer to the Russian government, but to the cause of Czechoslovak independence. As Churchill put it, "The Czech troops wre no longer mutineers nor traitors to the Habsburg Empire. They were the victorious soldiers and pioneers of Czechoslovakia."[44] Thus from traitors, as a segment of public opinion even in the Allied countries saw them, the Czechoslovaks became genuine patriots and nationalist heroes. The Bolsheviks acted as midwife in this birth of new heroes. The Czechoslovaks were enemies of the Allies' enemies, and of their Bolshevik "friends" or tools. This enmity, an important psychological factor, was a reason why Brest-Litovsk became the nemesis of Austria-Hungary, both in its internal affairs and in its relations with the Allied and Associated Powers.

Two Czech deputies in the Vienna parliament, an Agrarian, František Staněk, and a Social Democrat, Vlastimil Tusar, brought the disastrous consequences of the Peace of Brest-Litovsk for the Habsburg empire to the attention of Emperor Charles when they visited with him on June 26, 1918. On this occasion the two deputies attacked the foreign policy of Germany and the political agreement concluded by the emperor at Spaa on May 12, asserting that by virtue of the latter Austria-Hungary had ceased to be an independent state and had lost the ability to make her own decision on the issue of peace. Charles answered that the agreement

Reflection

concluded at Spaa was not as far-reaching as the two deputies has assumed, and that peace must be concluded. He added, however, that the enemy did not want to hear about peace and was considering plans for the partition of the empire. To this Tusar replied that the Peace of Brest-Litovsk was responsible for this regrettable situation, since, under its impact, the whole of Europe was against Austria. The emperor, looking very depressed, did not respond to this statement.[45]

The Austro-Hungarian government dug its own grave when it gave respectability to Lenin's Council of People's Commissars by recognizing the latter as the government of Russia. Commenting on the just-concluded "dishonest" Peace of Brest-Litovsk, Masaryk hastened to point out that Kaiser Wilhelm was willing to do business with Trotsky: "a legitimist monarch [deals] with a revolutionary who is, above all, a Jews, and who in his own army could not become even an officer."[46] Indeed, double standards are resented by many people; morality and moralizing are factors in both domestic and international politics. Whereas the Central Powers recognized the right to independence of some of the non-Russian peoples of the former Russian empire, e.g., the Ukrainians, they denied the same right to some of their subjects, e.g., the Czechs and Slovaks. Furthermore, if the Bolshevik regime was all right for Russia, why should a similar (or much better) regime in Germany or Austria be objectionable? The emperors of the central powers, selfish and improvident, sowed the wind and harvested the whirlwind.

The breakup of Austria-Hungary was sanctioned by the Allies before it actually occurred. Whether or not it was a wise decision is not a matter for consideration in this work, although one may understand or even agree with a noted American historian and diplomat, George F. Kennan, who "deplored the breakup of the Austro-Hungarian Empire," and who had "no sympathy for the fragmentation of sovereign power in the Danube basin to which the outcome of the First World War had led."[47] With the benefit of hindsight, one could make a case for the proposal made by Emperor Charles to federalize the empire (a proposal that came too late). The Czechoslovak army had, by taking a stand against the Bolsheviks in Russia, already achieved recognition of the exiles as the government of a future Czechoslovakia, though not of the state itself, and the exiles' views on the future of the Habsburg monarchy were accepted by the Allies. The Czechoslovak army's struggle with the Bolsheviks won Allied recognition of its belligerency, by shedding its blood on the steppes of Russia and the plains of Siberia. Although the number of those who died while fighting on behalf of the independence movement in Russia, Siberia, France, and Italy was relatively small (altogether 4,500 men),[48] Masaryk was correct when he said that "our freedom was truly bought with blood."[49]

Winning international recognition was a prerequisite for the establishment of Czechoslovakia. However, due credit must be given to the leaders of the independence movement at home, without whose support and cooperation the exile leaders could never have achieved their objectives. The Czechs had their elected representatives and spokesmen living in the empire during the war. Without their declaring independence and assuming power, all the work of the exile movement would have been of little consequence. It was the National Committee that used executive, legislative, administrative, and judicial powers *before* the frontiers of the state were defined; the state boundaries were discussed at the peace conference only *after* the revolutionary government sent troops to Slovakia and to the border regions inhabited predominantly by Germans. The peace conference was confronted with a series of *faits accomplis;* the new state could demonstrate the presence of all elements of statehood as required by international law: it had population, defined territory (as determined by the forces occupying it), and a government exercising effective control over that territory and able to enter diplomatic relations with other states. (Recognition had been extended to the government earlier.) Therefore, the revolution at home, its success, and the ability of the new government to rule, in addition to the previous commitments made by the British and French governments, were among the factors that helped the Czechoslovak delegate to obtain admission to the conference from the very beginning, and then to act with confidence. (Poland had some difficulty at the beginning of the conference, Yugoslavia [not Serbia] was admitted in June 1919, and Albania and some states on the Soviet Russian border did not gain official admission to the conference at all.) Had it not been for the existence of an effective Czechoslovak government determined to employ, and employing, the power of the state, the end of Austria-Hungary would not have been accepted as an accomplished fact by the conference's delegates (some of whom could not get over it for several months), and the issue of Czechoslovak existence (or nonexistence) would have been discussed by the great Allied powers without the Czechoslovak delegate's having a voice in that discussion. In recognition of the importance of the revolutionary act, October 28 has been celebrated as a national holiday—a national independence day—in Czechoslovakia.

Most likely, the main reason that the "official historians" either play down Kramář's role in the independence movement or ignore him altogether has been that his views on the situation in Russia in 1919 were not in accord with those of Masaryk, Beneš, the Social Democrats, and others. It is known that Masaryk's and Beneš's postwar foreign policy was based on Czechoslovakia's alliance with France. In his message to the Czechoslovak Revolutionary National Assembly in December 1918, Masaryk had clearly stated his pro-western orientation, which eventually became the orientation of the state. Describing the western powers as "non-militaristic democracies defending humanitarian ideals," he unequivocally proclaimed that the Czechs and Slovaks had stood from the beginning of the war on the side of the Allies and that "the destiny of our nation is directly and logically in union with the West and its modern democracy."[50]

Masaryk's rhetoric notwithstanding, the western Allies fought for their own interests rather than for "humanitarian ideals," and they agreed to the establishment of the Czechoslovak state only after they had concluded that the continuation of the Habsburg monarchy was no longer in their interest. When Austria-Hungary crumbled from within at the end of October 1918, the Allies were too busy with other matters and had no desire to struggle for her salvation in one form or another, or to fight for the establishment of a central European federation. In the meantime, the Czechs in Prague, the Hungarians in Budapest, the South Slavs in Zagreb, and the Austrian Germans in Vienna seized political power and thus confronted the victors with *faits accomplis*. The above quoted statement by Masaryk was used as a cue by those who eventually manufactured the "Wilsonian legend" and the theory that Czechslovak independence was a gift of the Allies. Indeed, Masaryk himself was more interested in personal aggrandizement than in "humanitarian ideals"; the reader may recall that in 1915 and 1916 Masaryk was proclaiming that the Czechs were Russophiles, that Russia was the most important country from the point of view of the Czechoslovak independence movement, and that a Romanov dynasty would be most popular in Bohemia. During the formative years of the new state, however, Masaryk and Beneš asserted that the Czech action abroad led by them during and after the war was based on an anticipation as far back as 1915 that Russia was out of the game as a great power and that the state would need the support of the other powers in order to attain its aspirations. The second important element in their policy statements was the claim that both of them had persistently refused to intervene in Russia or to use armed Czechoslovak forces against the Bolsheviks.

Kramář criticized Masaryk and Beneš for not pursuing the Czech struggle for independence to its end, but stopping just short of the conclusive blow that would have given security to Czechoslovakia and the world. From 1919 on, his view was that the end to be kept in sight was not the gaining of national independence, but the maintenance of it. In his public speeches as well as in private conversations Kramář emphasized that unless Russia was reconstituted as a democratic federal republic, the Czechoslovak state could not continue to exist. He was certain that the "Little Entente" would be ineffective against Bolshevik Russia; and that neither Yugoslavia nor Czechoslovakia could be made secure in the future without the reestablishment of a strong, Slavic Russia. The Czechs had an unprecedented opportunity "to rise to the pinnacle, to save Russia and gain her on behalf of Slav policy and to save the world from active and passive Bolsehvism. The time to do this was in 1917 when the Bolsheviks had just usurped power in Russia and were, according to their own recent confessions, very weak and without an army. Even two army units then could have accomplished wonders. Had the Czecho-Slovaks at the proper time supported the Russian patriots in saving their country from the heroes of Zimmerwald imported into Russia on the initiative of the German general staff, the Russian army which was never better equipped than in 1917, would have shorted the war by a year." Had the Czechs done so, "a rapprochement between Russia and Germany would have been prevented," and the Czechoslovak state would have been safe. Furthermore, "Bolshevism could never have properly been regarded as an internal Russian question because a social movement of that sort which gains possession of Russia represents a universal danger. Bolshevism is a world question and was so from the beginning." The Allies should have adopted Churchill's proposals, Kramář believed, and supported Denikin, Kolchak, and others. The only reason for the failure of the Allied intervention was the inadequacy of its implementation. "The Allies never intervened anywhere in

Russia, they supplied arms, provisions and funds, but even that inadequately." Since the defeat of the Whites, "instead of intervention in Russia, there is now the question of intervention of Russia in Europe."[51]

Kramář emphasized the importance of a free, national Russia for the survival of the new sovereign state. The liberation of Russia from Bolshevism not only was in the interest of the new state, but also constituted Czechslovakia's most important historical mission, for the following reasons: (1) Russia was needed in the European balance of power system to offset the weight of Germany and check the latter's attempts at revisionism and revanchism; (2) the defeat of Bolshevism in Russia would have meant the liberation of the whole world from the totalitarian menace; and (3) the services rendered by the Czechoslovaks to the Russians in the process of liberation would insure them an important place in history and would make possible (and probable) both the continuation of Czechoslovak influences in Russia and in the long run, the democratization of that country.[52] Kramář believed that the Czechs had, first, a moral obligation to Russia, without whose sacrifices the nation could not have attained its independence (he pointed at Russia's entry into the war in defense of a small Slavic state—Serbia—and its contributions, without which the Allies could not have won the war); and second, a vital interest in the existence of national, Slavic (in contrast to "non-Slavic," Bolshevik-International) Russia. The Czechs should not rely exclusively on the western powers, with whom they have no common boundary; they needed a powerful Slavic ally in order to survive. Because of these views, Kramář was ridiculed by many of his compatriots, some of whom called him "mentally imbalanced," and was dismissed by Masaryk as prime minister of Czechoslovakia. Later he came under political attack and found himself in political isolation on many occasions before his death in 1937. Fate arranged that his principal political rival in foreign affairs, Beneš, became president of the republic in 1935, and lived to see Munich and the dismemberment of Czechoslovakia.

Masaryk and Beneš knew the structural weaknesses of Austria-Hungary. But they perpetuted these defects by including too many minorities in the new Czechoslovak state, thus creating a miniature Austria-Hungary with all of the nationality problems and none of the economic and military advantages of the defunct empire. This situation was worsened by the unwillingness of Masaryk and Beneš to grant the Slovaks the autonomy promised to them in the Pittsburgh Agreement. Some two decades after the Paris Peace Conference Lloyd George stated that the British delegation at the conference had been misled by "deliberate falsifications"—an argument that was used to justify the revisionism of Neville Chamberlain and Lord Halifax during the Munich crisis. Nemesis presented her reckoning. From the conference held in 1919, the chain of events led to Munich, and from there to Teheran, Yalta, and Potsdam, and, eventually, to the events of 1948 and the Soviet invasion of Czechoslovakia in 1968. Since then Czechoslovakia has been an occupied territory. While for Masaryk and Beneš the Bolshevik regime in Russia and communism in general were a Russian internal affair, history has demonstrated that it has been a European and a worldwide problem.

The Czechs and Slovaks should learn a lesson from their history. In 1918 Masaryk and Beneš tried strenuously to make Czechoslovakia into an outpost of the west in central Europe; twenty years later France and Great Britain agreed to the dismantling of Czechoslovakia at Munich. Then Beneš tried the eastern, Soviet orientation in which Czechoslovakia was to be a bridge between East and West; instead, it was transformed into a Soviet bridgehead into Europe. By their geography and historical traditions the Czechs and Slovaks belong to the center of Europe, and they should try to make the best of it. When Soviet rule comes to its end—and this will happen one day—the Czechs and Slovaks should cooperate with the other small nations in the area and find a federal solution to the problem that is common to all of them: they are too weak to stand alone between the solid masses of Germans and Russians.

NOTES

Introduction

1. On the early history of the Czechs and Slovaks in the context of other peoples see three books by Francis Dvorník: *The Slavs: Their Early History and Civilization* (Boston: The American Academy, 1956); *The Making of Central and Eastern Europe* (London, 1949); and *The Slavs in European History and Civilization* (New Brunswick, N.J.: Rutgers University Press, 1962).

2. Victor S. Mamatey, *Rise of the Habsburge Empire, 1526-1815* (New York: Holt, Rinehart and Winston, 1971). See especially the "Bibliographical Note," pp. 161-166.

3. Among the historical writings are the following: František Palacký, *Geschichte Böhmens* (Prague, 1864-67), vols. I-V (Czech edition, *Dějiny českého národa* [Prague, 1908]); T. V. Bílek, *Dějiny konfiskací v Čechách po r. 1618* [History of the Confiscations in Bohemia After 1618] (Prague, 1882-1883), vol.s I-II; and K. Tieftrunk, *Odpor českých stavů proti Ferdinandovi I; léta 1547* [Resistance of Bohemian Estates to Ferdinand I; Year 1547] (Prague, 1872). See also Robert J. Kerner, *Bohemia in the Eighteenth Century* (New York, 1932).

4. For an excellent essay, see "Czech-Slovak Relations and the Student Organization Detvan, 1882-1914," in *Slovak Politics: Essays on Slovak History in Honour of Joseph M. Kirschbaum*, ed. Stanislav J. Kirschbaum (Cleveland, Ohio, and Rome, 1983).

Among the many books dealing with the history of the Czechs and Slovaks one may mention the following English language histories: Robert

William Seton-Watson, *A History of the Czechs and Slovaks* (London, 1943); Kamil Krofta, *A Short History of Czechoslovakia* (New York, 1934); S. Harrison Thomson, *Czechoslovakia in European History* (Princeton, N.J., 1943; 2nd ed., 1953); Joseph Kirschbaum, *Slovakia: Nation at the Crossroads of Central Europe* (New York: R. Speller, 1960); Jozef Lettrich, *History of Modern Slovakia* (New York: F. A. Praeger, 1955); and Gilbert L. Oddo, *Slovakia and Its People* (New York: R. Speller, 1960).

5. Peter Brock and Gordon Skilling, eds., *The Czech Renascence of the Nineteenth Century* (Toronto, 1970).

6. For details and analysis see Zdeněk Václav Tobolka, *Politické dějiny československého národa od r. 1848 až do dnešní doby* [Political History of the Czechoslovak Nation from 1848 till the Present Time] (Prague, 1932-1937, 4 vols. in 5), IV, 88ff.

7. Jaroslav Bidlo et al., *Slovanstvo. Obraz jeho minulosti a přítomnosti* [Slavdom. A Portrait of Its Past and Present] (Prague, 1912), pp. 150-151.

8. R. W. Seton-Watson, *The New Slovakia* (Prague, 1924), p. 14; Samuel Osuský, *Štefan: Služba národu* (Bratislava, 1938), cited in Branislav Štefánek, "Masaryk and Slovakia," in *T. G. Masaryk in Perspective: Comments and Criticism,* ed. Milíč Čapek and Karel Hrubý (New York, SVU Press, 1981), p. 205.

9. Details and documentation will be given in this work.

10. This claim by Masaryk has been disputed in Josef Kalvoda, "Masaryk in America in 1918," *Jahrbücher für Geschichte Osteuropas,* 27 (1979), pp. 85-99. Masaryk made the statement in all editions—Czech, English, and German—of his memoirs. See note 12 below.

11. František Kubka, *Mezi válkami. Masaryk a Beneš v mých vzpomínkách* [Between the Wars. Masaryk and Beneš in My Memories] (Prague, 1969), p. 54.

12. Masaryk and Beneš did not deny the importance of the home resistance, but they emphasized their own work abroad in order to increase their prestige and political influence in Czechoslovakia. Their uncritical admirers and flatterers exaggerated the importance of the struggle abroad and belittled that of the resistance at home. Most of these individuals were journalists by profession who assumed the role of "Castle historians" (the president of the state, Masaryk, lived in the Hradchin Castle), and they followed Masaryk's and Beneš's interpretations of the events. Despite some

inaccuracies contained in the memoirs written by the two men, they are indispensable sources of documentation in a work dealing with the birth of Czechoslovakia. See Dr. Edvard Beneš, *Světová válka a naše revoluce; vzpomínky a úvahy z bojů za svobodu národa* [World War and Our Revolution: Reminiscences and Reflections from the Time of Struggle for Freedom of the Nation] (Prague, 1927; vols. I and II; and 1928; vol. III). The third volume, containing documents, is extremely valuable. Henceforth this work will be cited as follows: Beneš, I (or II, or III). Masaryk's book, *Světová revoluce za války a ve válce 1914-1918* [World Revolution During the War and in the War, 1914-1918] (Prague, 1925), has been published in German and English translations, though the latter differs somewhat from the Czech original. See Thomas Garrigue Masaryk, *The Making of a State: memories and observations 1914-1918*. An English version arranged and prepared with an introduction by Henry Wickham Steed (New York, 1927). The inaccuracies, incorrect dates, inconsistencies, misstated facts, and interpretations in this book reflect upon the author, who was about seventy-five years old when his memories were published in Czech. In this work references will be made to the English version of the book by Masaryk rather than to its Czech language "original," unless the note says otherwise.

The "Castle historians'" version of the story—the "Masaryk legend"— was challenged by some journalists and politicians during the period between the two wars. Disputes over facts and their interpretations, as well as over whose contribution to winning independence was more important and more extensive, that of those who went abroad or that of those who remained at home, led to polemics published largely in newspapers and other periodicals. As examples of polemical books dealing with this subject, see Karel Kramář, *Kramářův soud nad Benešem. Spor Dr. K. Kramáře s ministrem zahraničních věcí Dr. E. Benešem. S předmluvou Jiřího Stříbrného* [Kramář's Judgment of Beneš. Conflict of Dr. K. Kramář with the Minister of Foreign Affairs, Dr. E. Beneš. Foreword by Jiří Stříbrný] (Prague, 1938); and Jiří Stříbrný, *TGM a 28. říjen* [T. G. M[asaryk] and the Twentieth-eighth of October] (Prague, 1938). There were also professional and respectable historians who did not attempt to pervert history. See, e.g., Jan Opočenský, *Konec Monarchie Rakousko-Uherské* [End of the Austro-Hungarian Monarchy] (Prague, 1928); and Tobolka, *Politické dějiny*, vol.s III and IV; Milada Paulová, *Dějiny Maffie* [The History of the Maffie] (Prague, 1937), vol. I.

13. Václav Kopecký, *ČSR a KSČ* [Czechoslovakia and the Communist Party of Czechoslovakia] (Prague, 1960), p. 9.

14. Jiří S. Hájek, *Wilsonovská legenda v dějinách Československé Republiky* [The Wilsonian Legend in the History of the Czechoslovak Republic] (Prague, 1953), p. 109. A collection of documents attempting to prove that "the victory of the October Revolution meant the beginning of the end of Austria-Hungary" was published in Prague. See the introduction by Jaroslav Křížek in Ludmila Otáhalová, *Souhrnná hlášení presidia pražského místodržitelství o protistátní, protirakouské a protiválečné činnosti v Čechách 1915-18* [Summary Reports of the Presidium of the Vice-Royalty in Prague on the Anti-State, Anti-Austrian and Anti-War Activity in Bohemia, 1915-1918] (Prague, 1957). The documens assembled here hardly prove the thesis. Strikes and general resentment were kept under control as long as the administration functioned. The failure of the socialist strike and the declaration of October 14, 1918, clearly demonstrate that the workers' movement, if there was any, was poorly organized. The leadership of the independence movement at home was firmly in the hands of the middle-class politicians with whom the "unorthodox" Social Democrats closely cooperated.

15. This thesis has been advanced by Czech communist historians, including Václav Král, who has asserted that it was not the activity of Masaryk, Beneš, and Štefánik that led to the establishment of an independent Czechoslovakia, but rather "the revolutionary working people at home and on the fronts who, having been inspired by the example of the Great October Socialist Revolution, buried the old, reactionary monarchy...." Václav Král, *O Masarykově a Benešově kontrarevoluční protisověské politice* [About Masaryk's and Beneš's Counter-Revolutionary and Anti-Soviet Politics] (Prague, 1953), p. 7.

16. Vavro Šrobár, an orthodox "Czechoslovak" and a colleague of Hodža in the Slovak Agrarian party, criticized the latter for his behavior in October 1918. According to Šrobár, Hodža wanted to be on the winning side no matter who won. While keeping contacts with certain Czech deputies in Vienna, he was also in touch with statemen in Budapest who supported an Austro-Hungarian federation. See Vavro Šrobár, *Oslobodené Slovensko* [Liberated Slovakia] (Prague, 1929), p. 96.

17. For an account of the formation and the end of the "bourgeois coalition" (black-green or gentlemen) see Duša Uhlíř, "Republikánská

strana ve vládě panské koalice" [The Republican party in the Government of the Gentlemen's Coalition], *Československý časopis historický* [The Czechoslovak Historical Gazette], XVII (1970), 195-233; and idem, "Konec vlády panské koalice a republikánská strana v roce 1929" [The End of the Rule of the Gentlemen's Coalition and the Republican Party in 1929], *Československý časopis historický*, XVII (1970), 551-591.

18. At this conference Georges Clemenceau, French premier, David Lloyd George, British prime minister, and Vittorio Orlando, Italian prime minister, approved of U.S. declaration of May 29, 1918, in which Robert Lansing, secretary of state, stated that "the nationalistic aspirations of the Czecho-Slovaks and Jugo-Slavs for freedom" had the earnest sympathy of the U.S. government. Lansing to Page, May 29, 1918, and Frazier to Lansing, June 4, 1918, U.S. Department of State, *Papers Relating to the Foreign Relations of the United States: The World War. 1918*, Supplement 1, vol. I, pp. 808-810. Henceforth this source will be cited as FRUS.

19. Vladimír Sís, ed., *Dr. Karel Kramář. Život–dílo–práce. Vůdce národa* [Dr. Karel Kramář. Life–Work–Labor. Leader of the Nation.] (Prague, 1936), p. 86.

20. For details see, for example, Rudolf Urban, *Tajné fondy III. sekce. Z archivu ministerstva zahraničí Republiky československé* [Secret Funds of the IIIrd Section of the Ministry of Foreign Affairs of the Czechoslovak Republic] (Prague, 1943).

Chapter One:
The Czechs and Slovaks and Their Leaders on the Eve of the War

1. Among the many English language books dealing with the Austro-Hungarian empire are Robert A. Kann, *The Multinational Empire, Nationalism and National Reform in the Habsburg Monarchy, 1848-1918*, 2 vols. (New York, 1950, reprinted 1964); and Arthur J. May, *The Habsburg Monarchy, 1867-1914* (Cambridge, Mass., 1951). For a detailed analysis of the attitudes of the Czech political parties before World War I, see Tobolka, *Politické dějiny*, III, passim.

2. František Bokes, *Dejiny Slovákov a Slovenska od nejstarších čias až po prítomnosť* [History of the Slovaks and Slovakia from Their Earliest Time up to the Present] (Bratislava, 1946), pp. 318-320 and 325-328. On Hodža see "Milan Hodža and the Politics of Power, 1907-1914," in *Slovak*

Politics, ed. Kirschbaum, pp. 42-62. On the religious situation see Ludvik Nemec, *Our Lady of Hostýn, Queen of the Marian Garden of the Czech, Moravian, Silesian and Slovak Madonnas* (New York, 1981); also a review of the book by Josef Kalvoda in *Nationalities Papers,* XI, No. 2 (Fall 1983), pp. 32-321.

3. Tobolka, *Politické dějiny,* III, Part 2, p. 560. On the 1911 election see pp. 557-562.

4. These and other statistics and detailed information are in Bidlo *et al., Slovanstvo,* pp. 150-151. An introduction to this monumental work (xv + 777 p.) was written by Dr. Karel Kramář. Incidentally, the vast majority of Jews in the Czech lands and the Slovak province of Hungary spoke German and Magyar respectively. Even in Prague, a city which by 1890 had become almost entirely Czech, the Jews formed the majority of the German-speaking population. The nationalistic Czechs and Slovaks saw the Jews as instruments of Germanization and Magyarization. Also, the Jewish peddlers and merchants who acted as moneylenders and exploited Czech and Slovak peasants provoked resentment among gentiles and Jews alike. The charging of exorbitant rates of interest, which forced peasants, and sometimes even gentlemen farmers, to sell at auction their property, and often purchased by these peddlers at cheap prices, together with the pro-German and pro-Magyar outlook of the Jews, created latent anti-Semitism in large segments of the two nations. For details see Hans Kohn, "Before 1918 in the Historic Lands," and Ruth Kestenberg-Gladstein, "The Jews Between Czechs and Germans in the Historical Lands, 1848-1918," in *The Jews of Czechoslovakia: Historical Studies and Surveys,* vol. I (Philadelphia: The Jewish Publication Society of America, 1968), pp. 12-20 and 21-71.

5. For details and historical background see Josef Kalousek, *České státní právo* [Bohemian State Right], 2nd ed. (Prague, 1892); and Josef Redlich, *Das österreichische Staats- und Reichsproblem,* 2 vols. (Leipzig, 1920-1926). For an analysis see Rudolf Wierer, "Das Böhmische Staatsrecht und der Ausgleichsversuch des Ministeriums Hohenwart-Schaffle," in *Bohemia,* Jahrbuch des Collegium Carolinum, Band 4 (Munich, 1963). See also Tobolka, *Politické dějiny,* vols. I and II, *passim;* Karel Mattuš, *Historické právo a národnost co základové státního zřízení říše Rakouské* [Historical Right and Nationality as Foundations of the State Structure of the Austrian Empire] (Prague, 1867).

6. Stanley B. Winters, "Kramář, Kaizl, and the Hegemony of the Young Czech Party," in *The Czech Renascence*, ed. Brock and Skilling.

7. Elizabeth Wiskemann, *Czechs and Germans: A Study of the Struggle in the Historic Provinces of Bohemia and Moravia* (London-New York-Toronto, 1938), pp. 46-47. In addition to Kramář, among the Realists who joined the Young Czech party in 1890 was also T. G. Masaryk, who, however, broke with the party in 1893. See Stanley B. Winters, "The Young Czech Party (1874-1914): An Appraisal," *Slavic Review*, XXVIII, No. 3 (1969), pp. 426-444. This is an English language comprehensive appraisal of the Young Czech party (with footnote references).

8. *Revue de Paris*, February 1, 1899; and *National Review*, October 1902. See also Sís, *Dr. Karel Kramář*, p. 92.

9. *National Review*, October 1902.

10. Johannes Lepsius, Albrecht Mendelssohn Bartholdy, and Friedrich Thimme, eds., *Die Grosse Politik der Europäischen Kabinette 1871-1914*, vol. 13 (Berlin, 1924), pp. 151-157 and 161-164.

11. *The Times* (London), October 2, 1902.

12. Ibid. Kramář was neither the first nor the only Czech who tried to influence the British public. A Bohemian aristocrat, Count Francis Lützow, who worked for several years at the Austro-Hungarian embassy in London, after leaving the diplomatic service published in London several articles and books between 1896 and 1914. In 1905 Lützow wrote an extensive article, "Bohemia and the Conflict Between Austria and Hungary," published in *The Westminster Gazette* (April 27, 1905), in which he sharply criticized the Dualism of 1867 as the basic cause of the political problems and nationalistic agitation in Austria-Hungary. He pointed out that the Czechs were fundamentally loyal to the Habsburgs, while many of the Austrian Germans openly agitated against the dynasty and advocated a close union with Germany. According to Lützow, "an autonomous Bohemian kingdom under Habsburg rule would ... be conducive to the peace of Europe and to the preservation of the equilibrium of the Continent."

13. Sís, *Dr. Karel Kramář*, pp. 38-40.

14. Ibid., p. 51.

15. Ibid., pp. 72, 87, and 93.

16. Ibid., pp. 153 and 156ff.

17. Ibid., p. 153.

18. Ibid., p. 156.

19. Ibid., p. 159.
20. Ibid., p. 161.
21. Ibid., p. 52.
22. Ibid., p. 163.
23. Ibid., pp. 158 and 162.
24. Ibid., pp. 64 and 76.
25. Ibid., p. 164; also Dr. Karel Kramář, *Pět přednášek o zahraniční politice* [Five Lectures on Foreign Policy] (Prague, 1922), p. 37.
26. Most books by Masaryk and large number of works about Masaryk are listed in the bibliography. Several will be cited below. The first biography of Masaryk was written by Jaromír Doležal, *Masarykova cesta životem*, 2 vols. (Brno, 1920-1921).
27. Zbyněk Zeman, *The Masaryks: The Making of Czechoslovakia* (London, 1976), p. 17. See also Willy Lorenz's essay on the Masaryks in his *Monolog über Böhmen* (Vienna, 1964); also "Wer war Thomas Garrigue Masaryk?" *Die Fürche*, September 14, 1957.
28. Jan Vrzalík, *Tomáše G. Masaryka původ a léta mladosti* [The Origin of Tomas G. Masaryk and His Young Years], unpublished manuscript. See also Willy Lorenz, "Wer war Thomas Garrigue Masaryk?" in *Festschrift für Otto von Habsburg sum fünfzigsten Geburtstag* (Vienna-Munich, 1965), pp. 109-114; and the original (unabridged) manuscript of the article.
29. Lorenz, *Festschrift*, p. 112.
30. Karel Čapek, *Hovory s T. G. Masarykem* (*President Masaryk Tells His Story*) (London, 1951; first published as a whole in 1936), p. 69.
31. *Masaryk a židovství* [Masaryk and Judaism], ed. Ernst Rychnovský in collaboration with Dr. O. Donath and Dr. F. Thieberger (Prague, 1931; published also in a German version under the title *Masaryk und das Judentum*, 1931), p. 247.
32. Čapek, *Hovory*, p. 72.
33. Ibid.
34. Ibid., p. 76.
35. The original manuscript was published in book form in 1881, in German, and its title, in translation, was *Suicide as a Social Mass Phenomenon of Modern Civilization;* its Czech version was published in Prague in 1926; in 1970 an English translation appeared under the title *Suicide and the Meaning of Civilization*, trans. by William B. Weist and Robert G.

Notes to Chapter One 515

Batson, with an introduction by Anthony Giddens (Chicago and London: The University of Chicago Press, 1970).
36. *Masaryk a židovství,* ed. Rychnovský, p. 144.
37. Ibid.
38. Ibid. According to Masaryk's first biographer, the amount of the inheritance from the Jewish student was 62,000 florins (gouldens). See Doležal, *Masarykova cesta životem,* I, p. 31.
39. See a book by one of the defenders of the *Rukopisy,* Vladimír Kopecký, *Plno záhad kolem Hanky* (Prague, 1969); also published in Switzerland, 1981. Kopecký was a curator in the National Museum, Prague. A list of defenders of the manuscripts is published in F[rancisco] C. Štěrba, *Rukopisný slovníček* [The Manuscripts' Little Dictionary] (Sao Paulo, 1967).
40. Doležal, *Masarykova cesta,* II, p. 170.
41. Eva Schmidt-Hartmann, *Thomas G. Masaryk's Realism: Origins of a Czech Political Concept* (München, 1984), p. 130.
42. *Čas,* March 6, 1900.
43. Jan Herben, *Deset let proti proudu* [Ten Years Against the Stream] (Prague, 1898), p. 92.
44. *Čas,* March 6, 1900.
45. Hartmann, *Thomas G. Masaryk's Realism,* p. 178.
46. Tomáš G. Masaryk, *Americké přednášky* [American Lectures], 2nd ed. (Prague, 1929), p. 133.
47. T. G. Masaryk, "Rukověť sociologie: podstata a methody sociologie" [Manual of Sociology: The Substance and Methods of Sociology], *Naše doba,* 8, (1901), 824.
48. G. G. Masaryk, *Otázka sociální. Základy marxismu sociologické a filosofické* [The Social Question. Sociological and Philosophical Foundations of Marxism] (Prague, 1898), p. 299.
49. T. G. Masaryk, *The Spirit of Russia,* ed. George Gibian; ed. and trans. Robert Bass (vol. III, New York: Barnes & Noble, 1967), p. 86.
50. Ibid.
51. T. G. Masaryk, *Česká otázka. Snahy a tužby národního obrození* [The Czech Question. Efforts and Aspirations of the National Renaissance] (Prague, 1895).
52. Masaryk, *Otázka sociální.*
53. Jan Herben, *Masarykova sekta a Gollova škola* [The Masaryk Sect

and the School of Goll] (Prague, 1912). Among the critics of Masaryk's religious and philosophical views were not merely seasoned philosophers and Catholic theologians, but also Protestant theologians. See, for example, Josef L. Hromádka, *Křesťanství a vědecké myšlení* [Christianity and Scientific Thinking] (Prague, 1922), pp. 7-8 and 30-31. Roman Szporluk, in *The Political Thought of Thomas G. Masaryk* (Boulder, Colo., 1981), writes that the overwhelming majority of the Czechs refused to follow "Masaryk's philosophical message" when it became "the official philosophy of Czechoslovakia," and that this refusal was "evidence of their political and cultural maturity rather than of their failure to heed the voice of a prophet" (p. 100). Space limitations preclude further discussion of this subject.

54. Masaryk, *The Making of a State*, p. 83. Despite the popular version of the story, Hilsner was neither charged with, or tried for, ritual murder; however, the charge of "ritual murder" appeared in public discussions of the case during the trial. Therefore, the Austrian supreme tribunal quashed the death sentence and ordered a new trial at another location in a different court district. In the second trial, Hilsner was convicted of taking part in the murder of a young girl, and sentenced to life imprisonment. Ritual murder was never mentioned in the second trial; in the first trial the phrase "ritual murder" was used in the courtroom only by the attorney for Hilsner in his attempt to get his client acquitted. The law recognized murder but not "ritual murder." Details of the case and parts of a transcript of the courtroom testimony are in *Masaryk a židovství*, ed. Rychnovský, pp. 151-241.

55. *Masaryk a židovství*, ed. Rychnovský, p. 320.
56. Masaryk, *The Making of a State*, p. 236.
57. Ibid., pp. 83 and 236-237.
58. Ivan Herben, "Dvakrát 28. říjen" [Twice 28th of October], in *Padesát let* [Fifty Years], published by *Naše Hlasy* [Our Voices] (Toronto, 1968), pp. 99-106. Masaryk's records are in the Masaryk Archive (MA), VII/15a. In his *Světová revoluce* (1925) Masaryk writes, on p. 279, "And particularly in America the Hilsner affair, I would say, paid off at this time."
59. T. G. Masaryk, *Otázka sociální. Základy marxismu filosofické a sociologické*, 5th (3rd Czech) ed. (Prague, 1946), vol. II, pp. 306-307. Masaryk wrote his *Nová Evropa. Stanovisko slovanské* [The New Europe.

Notes to Chapter One 517

Slavic Standpoint] in 1918 and parts of the work were published in that year; the book came out in Prague in 1920.

60. "People called me an incorrigible pacifist and idealist," writes Masaryk in *The Making of a State*, p. 1; yet he rejected Tolstoy's doctrine of nonresistance, and held that "we must resist evil always and in everything" (p. 59).

61. Milan Machovec, *Tomáš G. Masaryk* (Prague, 1968), p. 161.

62. Čapek, *Hovory*, III, 189 and *Masarykův sborník*, III, 97, quoted in Machovec, *Masaryk*, p. 46. The phrase, "I did not understand myself," Masaryk also used in 1919 in an effort to explain away a statement that he had made in the 1880s when he wondered "whether the struggle for the preservation of our nationality is worth the sacrifices," and whether, for cultural reasons, "it would not be more advantageous" for the Czech people "to join a great cultural nation and thus release the energies, now wasted by struggle for the maintenance of the nationality, for a positive cultural work" that would be more beneficial and that would broaden the people's horizons. Karel Kramář, *Paměti* [Memoirs] (Prague, 1938), p. 93. Masaryk used the same phrase, "I did not understand myself," and admitted that he had made many mistakes, including "especially... antagonizing people," in a letter to Josef Gruber, editor of Albín Bráf, *Život a dílo* [Life and Work] (Vol. I, *Memoirs*, Prague, 1922). The letter, dated June 6, 1919, is published in the above work in the introductory remarks of the editor. Bráf, an outstanding economist, was one of those who were sharply critical of Masaryk's methods. Bráf cites a joke reflecting on Masaryk's attitude: "God knows everything, the German Emperor (William II), knows everything better, but Masaryk knows everything best." (p. 27).

63. Machovec, *Masaryk*, p. 47. On the Pekař-Masaryk controversy see *Český časopis historický*, VI (1900), pp. 142-156; *Česká Mysl*, 1910, pp. 117-137; Josef Pekař, *Smysl českých dějin* [The Meaning of Czech History] (Prague, 1929); and Jan Slavík, *Pekař contra Masaryk* (Prague, 1929). On Masaryk's "determinism" see his *Suicide and the Meaning of Civilization*, p. 225.

64. Josef Pekař, "Notices," *Český časopis historický*, XVIII (1912), pp. 130-136.

65. Ibid.

66. Ibid., pp. 170-208.

67. Wenzel Jaksch, *Europe's Road to Potsdam*, trans. and ed. Kurt Glaser (New York-London, 1963), p. 131; see also Karel Pichlík, *Zahraniční odboj, 1914-1918, bez legend* [Resistance Abroad, 1914-1918, Without Legends] (Prague, 1968), p. 26.

68. May, *The Habsburg Monarchy*, p. 427.

69. Tobolka, *Politické dějiny*, III, part 2, p. 560; on the 1911 election see pp. 557-562.

70. The charge that Šviha was in the service of the police was published first in *Národní Listy* (March 4, 1914); and one of the results of the affair was bitter hostility between Masaryk and Kramář, who were not even on speaking terms. Communication between them was resumed through Beneš only when Masaryk was in exile in 1915. Details of the incident are in Czech contemporary newspapers (March-May 1914); for summaries see Milada Paulová, *Dějiny Maffie* [The History of the Maffie] (Prague, 1937), vol. I, pp. 70-76; and Tobolka, *Politické dějiny*, III, pp. 611ff.

71. Among the staunchest critics of Masaryk and *Čas* were the Social Democrats. They published in book form the whole transcript of the trial with commentaries. See *Zrádce dr. Karel Šviha před porotou* [The Traitor, Dr. Karel Šviha, Before the Jury] (Prague, 1914).

72. Svetozár Hurban Vajanský, *Complete Works* (Turčiansky Sv. Martin, 1912), vol. XI, pp. 280-281, quoted in Joseph A Mikus, *Slovakia. A Political History: 1918-1950* (Miwaukee, 1963), p. xxxii.

73. See Edita Bosak, "Czech-Slovak Relations," in *Slovak Politics*, ed. Kirschbaum, pp. 6-42; and, in the same source, the essay by Susan Mikula on Milan Hodža, pp. 42-67. There are, of course, many Slovak-language sources on the situation in Slovakia and Czech-Slovak relations before World War I.

Chapter Two:
The Russian and British Connections

1. See, for example, documentation in Paul Vyšný, *Neo-Slavism and the Czechs, 1898-1914* (Cambridge, 1977).

2. Paulová, *Maffie*, pp. 34-38; and Milada Paulová, *Tajný výbor [Maffie] a spolupráce s Jihoslovany v letech 1916-1918* [The Secret Committee Maffie and Collaboration with the Yugoslavs during the Years 1916-1918] (Prague, 1968), p. 10. See also Tobolka, *Politické dějiny*, III, pp. 631ff.

Notes to Chapter Two 519

3. A. Popov, "Chekho-slovatskii vopros i tsarskaia diplomatiia," *Krasnyi Arkhiv* (Moscow), XXXIII (1929), p. 5. Paulová, *Maffie*, pp. 38-39; also Pichlík, *Zahraniční odboj*, p. 29.

4. Karel Kramář, *Na obranu slovanské politiky* [In Defense of Slavic Policy] (Prague, 1926), pp. 62-63. See also Sergei D. Sazonov, *Fateful Years, 1909-1916* (London, 1928), pp. 273-274.

5. Kramář, *Na obranu*, p. 63.

6. The text of the constitution is in Paulová, *Maffie*, vol. I, Appendix, pp. 635-640.

7. Ibid., pp. 56 and 305; also *Dr. Karel Kramář*, ed. Sís, p. 95; and Pichlík, *Zahraniční odboj*, p. 32.

8. See *Národní osvobození*, June 24 and July 5, 1934.

9. Paulová, *Maffie*, p. 49; cf. also Pichlík, *Zahraniční odboj*, p. 32.

10. Jaroslav Werstadt, "The Czechoslovak State Idea in the Revolution of Liberation during the World War," in *Die Tschechoslowakische Republik* (Prague, 1937), vol. I, p. 133; also *Dr. Karel Kramář*, ed. Sís, p. 95.

11. Masaryk, *The Making of a State*, p. 6. Masaryk was referring to a message that he had received from H. W. Steed, a British journalist and intelligence officer. See Paulová, *Maffie*, pp. 163-164.

12. Beneš, I, p. 43. For a systematic survey of the attitudes of all Czech political parties, as well as those of the Slovaks, toward the question of war and independence, see Tobolka, *Politické dějiny*, IV, pp. 88ff.

13. For details see Robert W. Seton-Watson, *Masaryk in England* (Cambridge, 1943), pp. 35-36.

14. On the Kramář group see Paulová, *Maffie*, p. 151; and *Tajný výbor*, pp. 13ff; also Tobolka, *Politické dějiny*, IV, p. 53; and *Dr. Karel Kramář*, ed. Sís, p. 99.

15. Sazonov, *Fateful Years*, p. 275. note.

16. Sir Eyre Crowe: From Memorandum on the Present State of British Relations with France and Germany, January 1, 1907, *British Documents on the Origins of the War, 1914-1918*, ed. G. P. Gooch and Harold Temperley, vol. III (London, 1928), pp. 402-403.

17. Public Record Office, Foreign Affairs, 371/2162, August 5, 1914. (Hereafter cited as FO 371.) See also Harry Hanak, "The Government, the Foreign Office and Austria-Hungary, 1914-1918," *Slavonic and East European Review*, 47 (1969), 163.

18. *Naše doba* (August 1914); excerpts of Masaryk's analysis were also published in *Čas*, the daily of his party.

19. Masaryk, *The Making of a State*, pp. xi and 5-6. On the molding of British public opinion and diplomatic policy by H. W. Steed and Robert W. Seton-Watson before and during the war see Arthur J. May, "R. W. Seton-Watson and British Anti-Habsburg Sentiment," *The American Slavic and East European Review*, XX (February 1961), pp. 40-54.

20. Hugh and Christopher Seton-Watson, *The Making of a New Europe: R. W. Seton-Watson and the Last Years of Austria-Hungary* (Seattle, 1981), p. 108.

21. Seton-Watson met Masaryk for the first time in July 1907; he is mistaken, his son points out, when he writes that he first met Masaryk in 1910, "in company of his friend and Maecenas, Charles R. Crane...." See Hugh and Christopher Seton-Watson, *The Making of a New Europe*, pp. 52 and 55. Seton-Watson made the erroneous statement in *Masaryk in England* (1943), p. 35. On Steed's contacts with Masaryk see Henry Wickham Steed, *Through Thirty Years, 1892-1922* (Parts I and II, New York, 1924), passim.

22. Details in "Paměti kapitána Em. V. Vosky" [Memoirs of Captain Emanuel V. Voska], published in serialized form in *Jas* (vols. VII, VIII, IX, and X, 1933, 1934, 1935, and 1936, esp. Nos. 16, 17, 19 [1933], and 27 [1934]. Also cf. Masaryk, pp. 259-262; Paulová, *Maffie*, pp. 160-165; Steed, *Through Thirty Years*, I, p. 316, and II, pp. 45-48. See also Robert W. Seton-Watson, *Masaryk in England* (Cambridge, 1943); and Peter Schuster, *Henry Wickham Steed und die Habsburgermonarchie* (Wien-Kol-Graz, 1970), especially pp. 84ff. On Voska's not quite accurate and reliable English account of his maneuvering in America and Europe see Emanuel Victor Voska and Will Irwin, *Spy and Counter-Spy* (London, 1941). The transmitting of hard intelligence data to the British constituted treason, as Masaryk fully realized. He himself writes that for what he has done before leaving Austria-Hungary in December 1914, "the gallows would be certain." See Masaryk, *Světová revoluce*, p. 18; also the German edition, *Die Welt-Revolution* (Berlin, 1927), p. 9.

23. Steed, *Through Thirty Years*, II, pp. 43 and 45; and Voska, "Paměti," *Jas* (1933, No. 18).

24. A Jewish editor, Oskar Stein, who had fought for Šviha along with Masaryk, arranged for the latter's meeting with the diector of police at Prague, for whom Šviha had worked, in August 1914; and he claims credit for Masaryk's ability to travel abroad. See *Masaryk a židovství*, ed. Rychnovský, p. 332, and the facsimile of Masaryk's letter on p. 333. See

also Masaryk, *The Making of a State,* pp. 6-7; and Beneš, III, p. 227. Masaryk's passport was issued on September 17, 1914.

An old Czech historian who still lived in Prague in the early 1970s was convinced that the Austro-Hungarian government had let Masaryk travel abroad on the understanding (or assumption) that he would bring back information to the government in Vienna and that he acted as an informer. (Masaryk, indeed, talked to Austrian officials before going abroad.) When Masaryk proved to be working for the British government (or being used by it) rather than for the Austrian government, he was charged with treason; and for the same reason Prime Minister Czernin called him "wretched Masaryk" in early 1918. How the British saw Masaryk is indicated in the "Memorandum of conversation between Professor T. G. Masaryk and R. W. Seton-Watson, at Rotterdam, on October 24-25, 1914," submitted as "confidential" to the Foreign Office, in which Seton-Watson three times refers to Masaryk as an "informant" (FO 371/1900/67456). The Czech historian mentioned above was aware that there was no documentation for his contention (which was, incidentally, voiced by many other people), because the incriminating material was allegedly removed from the Vienna offices and archives by people working for Masaryk. Indeed, as soon as the armistice was arranged for in early November 1918, Voska and members of his intelligence unit went to Vienna and "carried off three loads of Austrian archives to Prague" where "twenty scholars, historians and clerks rummaged through them." See Voska and Irwin, *Spy and Counter-Spy,* p. 297. In February 1919, Voska's people illegally brought private papers of the Habsburg family to Prague. In order to avoid a possible search of the two motor vehicles by border guards, they crossed the Austrian border at a speed exceeding 100 km per hour and caused a border shooting incident. See Voska, "Paměti," *Jas,* X, No. 9 (1936).

25. Masaryk, *The Making of a State,* p. 8. Also, Pichlík, *Zahraniční odboj,* p. 100. Charles R. Crane, a self-educated man and the heir to a considerable fortune, met Masaryk for the first time in 1896. Before his trip to Russia and central Europe, his intimate friend, William R. Harper, president of the University of Chicago, urged Crane to contact Professor Masaryk, who was known as an opponent of Pan-Slavism, in Prague. During his conversation with Masaryk, Crane mentioned his business interests. In 1902 Crane brought Masaryk to lecture at the University of Chicago. His lectures were followed by those given by Professor Paul

Miliukov of the University of Moscow and Maxim Kovalevsky, a Russian sociologist; this series of lectures led to the establishment of the School of Slavonic Studies at the university.

It is well known that the British worked with native "natural leaders" in order to influence the policies of other countries from within. They succeeded in penetrating Hindu, Buddhist, Moslem, and other countries. In Russia the British were seen as rivals and were suspect; they therefore preferred to use the United States as a base for penetration of the Slavic world.

Masaryk had been on intimate terms with Charles R. Crane since 1904-1905, according to *The National Cyclopedia of American Biography* (Vol. XXX, 1943), p. 221; according to Masaryk, he had been intimate with Crane since 1901. See Masaryk, *The Making of a State,* p. 224. Masaryk passed intelligence data on to Steed; he received monetary payments from an American millionaire. At the beginning of the war Steed also acted as an intermediary between Masaryk and Crane. Incidentally, Steed had already secretly received information relating to Austria from Masaryk before the war, when he had been stationed in Vienna. See Steed, *Through Thirty Years,* I, pp. 367-368.

Crane and Masaryk had maintained close contacts ever since Masaryk's visit to Chicago in 1902. When Masaryk's son, Jan, became a rebellious adolescent, ill fitting into the intellectual environment of his father's world, he went to the United States, where he spent several years before World War I. During part of that time he worked in the Crane factory in Bridgeport, Connecticut. He suffered a nervous breakdown there and the Crane family took care of him and placed him in a sanatorium. Jan's mother came to the United States to help her son after the latter's breakdown, and she also turned to Mrs. Crane for support.

Among other things, Crane was involved in American politics. After he switched from the Republican to the Democratic party, he became a friend and supporter of Woodrow Wilson and contributed heavily to his presidential campaign in 1912. After Wilson became president, Crane was a frequent guest in the White House and a member of the president's circle of close friends. Crane did not accept Wilson's offer of the post of ambassador to Russia, but he remained an unofficial advisor to the president on Russian affairs. Crane was, no doubt, a very important connection for Masaryk, and so was Steed.

Notes to Chapter Two 523

Copies of some of the documents that were obtained for Masaryk in Vienna are deposited in the Masaryk Archive (MA), "Válka" [War] I/11. On Crane and his activities see his "Memoirs" and the Crane Papers, Russian and East European Archives, Columbia University, and the Harper Papers deposited at the University of Chicago. Samuel Harper, son of William R. Harper (President of Univ. of Chicago), was one of the scholars supported by Crane. The latter agreed to fund a position in Russian studies at the University of Chicago for Harper, subject to several conditions, among which were the following: Harper was to divide his time each year equally between the university and travel in Russia, and, on occasion, he was to discuss Russian affairs with various economic and political leaders in the United States. In March 1918, as an expert on Russia, Harper received an appointment in the Department of State; he became an active proponent of intervention in Russia and was the author of several position papers relating to Russia. Harper's most famous involvement in the policymaking process was his role in the committee that accepted as genuine the forgeries known as "the Sisson documents."

26. Voska, "Paměti," *Jas* (1933, Nos. 19 and 20). Masaryk was fully aware of the treasonable nature of his activity. Before going to Holland, he asked his friends at Prague to warn him by sending an agreed password to Rotterdam *poste restante,* should it not be safe for him to return home. Complete communications and Masaryk's own records are in MA, "Válka," I; and MA, "Rakousko-Češi," II. See also Karel Pichlík, "První projekt samostatného Československa z podzimu 1914" [The First Project of an Independent Czechoslovakia from the Fall of 1914], *Histoire a vojenství* (1966, No. 3), pp. 357-407.

27. MA, "Válka," I/1. See also Pichlík, "První projekt," p. 399.

28. MA, "Válka," I/11; Voska, "Paměti," *Jas* (1933, No. 20).

29. The memorandum is printed in Seton-Watson, *Masaryk in England,* pp. 40-47; see also the same source, pp. 20, 38-39, and 49-51; also Masaryk, *The Making of a State,* pp. 7-8; Beneš, III, pp. 227-236 (Czech translation of the memorandum); and Beneš, III, p. 4 (Seton-Watson's proposal of a state based on ethnography). Details on propaganda and espionage activity in Emil Filla, *Hlídka české Maffie v Holandsku* [Outpost of the Czech Maffie in Holland] (Prague, 1934); Voska, "Paměti," *Jas* (1933-1936); and Voska and Irwin, *Spy and Counter-Spy,* passim.

30. Beneš, I, pp. 40ff. At that time Masaryk saw Beneš as a member of his "subterranean organization, and a Social Democrat" Masaryk, *The Making of a State,* p. 49.

31. Theodor Syllaba, *T. G. Masaryk a revoluce v Rusku* [T. G. Masaryk and the Revolution in Russia] (Prague, 1959), p. 118. See also Max Ronge, *Kriegs- und Industrie-Spionage. Zwölf Jahre Kunschaftsdienst* (Zürich-Leipzig-Vienna, 1930), pp. 201-202 and 211. Masaryk customarily made notes on conversations with influential people. According to his notes on his visit with Thun, he told the viceroy that although he also had Slavic and Russian sympathies, his book was prohibited in Russia. "I will not be now in Prague for tsarism and the tsarist police," said Masaryk. See Doležal, *Masarykova cesta,* I, p. 63. Masaryk travelled to Vienna to talk to Austrian government officials, and, at the same time, to get confidential material, including copies of documents from the ministry of the interior made by a Czech employee in the ministry. (Doležal, *Masarykova cesta,* I, p. 65.) Among the works on espionage are those by one of the spies: Jan Hajšman, *O špionáži, špioni, špionky, špiclové...* [On Espionage, Spies, Female Spies, Snoopers...] (Prague, 1928) and *Česká Maffie* (2 vols., Prague, 1932, 1935).

32. In a letter that eventually fell into the hands of the police, Masaryk wrote to his wife: "Right now, on March 15 [1915] I have been warned not to return home." This warning must have come from Steed. Although he came out publicly against Austria-Hungary on July 6, a warrant for his arrest was not issued until August 4, and his house was searched only on August 30, 1915. See Doležal, *Masarykova cesta,* pp. 67 and 74. Masaryk's professorial salary was mailed to him abroad.

33. Masaryk, *The Making of a State,* p. 15; Beneš, I, pp. 66-67 and 39.

34. The name *Maffie* was borrowed from the Sicilian organization; however, this secret committee consisted of respectable middle-class politicians, not gangsters. For details, see Paulová, *Tajný výbor, pp. 13ff.;* and Beneš, I, pp. 40ff.

35. Pichlík, *Zahraniční odboj,* p. 107; also Masaryk, pp. 9 and 41-42; and see also Beneš, I, pp. 31ff.

36. Beneš, III, pp. 17-21 and 22-28.

37. Tobolka, *Politické dějiny,* IV, p. 148; see also Josef Dürich, *V českých službách. Vypsání mého pobytu za hranicemi 1915-1918* [In the Service of the Czech Nation. A Narrative of May Stay Abroad, 1915-1918] (Klášter nad Jizerou, 1921), p. 13; henceforth cited as "Dürich." Dürich's daughter, married to a writer, Karel Horký, lived with her husband

Notes to Chapter Two 525

and an unmarried sister in Spain. On the pretext of visiting his daughters in Spain and bringing them back home, Dürich was able to obtain a passport. Before he left his homeland, Dürich received 30,000 crowns from Kramář with the request that he give from that sum 10,000 crowns to Professor Masaryk in Switzerland. Masaryk, however, declined that money saying that he expected financial contributions to arrive from America. Dürich, p. 15.
38. Pichlík, *Zahraniční odboj,* pp. 115-116.
39. Martínek, "Jak jsme to dělali," in *Padesát let (Naše Hlasy,* Toronto, 1968).
40. Ibid.
41. Unpublished memoirs of František Kopecký, the mail clerk in the Austrian consulate in New York, whom Voska in *Spy and Counter-Spy* identifies only under his code name "Zeno," calling him "our most valuable agent." In 1937 publication of the memoirs was prohibited by the Czechoslovak ministry of foreign affairs on the grounds that it would worsen the relations between Czechoslovkia and Great Britain. Kopecký documents how Voska was cheating his employer, the British intelligence service. A copy of the memoirs is in *Vojenský historický archiv* (Military Historical Archive) at Prague. Voska's correspondence with Masaryk, Steed, and Captain (later Admiral) Guy Gaunt (the British naval attaché in charge of British naval intelligence in the United States), and other documentary evidence, are in *Jas,* vols. VII, VIII, and IX.
42. Masaryk to Voska, quoted in Voska's "Paměti," *Jas* (1933, No. 52). Details in *Jas,* 1933, Nos. 28 and 29; and 1934, Nos. 1 and 2. Masaryk's letter to Crane of February 3, 1915, is in the Charles R. Crane Papers; Masaryk's letter to Voska of February 19, 1915, was published in *Masarykův sborník,* ed. V. K. Škrach (Prague, 1925), pp. 269-272.
43. Paulová, *Maffie,* I, pp. 580-588, and II, pp. 43-44. See also Pichlík, *Zahraniční odboj,* pp. 147-148.
44. MA, VII/2. The passport's number was 766; British visas were issued on September 22, 1915; and Masaryk left for England on September 24.
45. Robert W. Seton-Watson, *The Future of Bohemia* (London, 1915), p. 31. See also Robert W. Seton-Watson, "The Origins of the School of Slavonic Studies," *The Slavonic and East European Review,* XVII, No. 50 (1939), pp. 360-372. All the following direct quotations and information

are from this highly informative article. See also Arthur J. May, "Seton-Watson and the Treaty of London," *Journal of Modern History* (March 1957), p. 45.
    46.   MA, VI/15a. Telegram of October 5, 1915, with notes from the meeting in Masaryk's handwriting.
    47.   MA, VII/60b. A letter from Voska to Masaryk, mailed from New York on October 29, 1915. Voska writes that he hopes that Masaryk had received "a report" that he had sent on Steed's address, and that he continues to work in the same direction.
    48.   Hugh and Christopher Seton-Watson, *The Making of a New Europe*, p. 154.
    49.   MA, VII/15. A letter from Seton-Watson to Masaryk, dated December 5, 1915. Also MA, VII/15a, Masaryk's own records.
    50.   MA, VII/15a; see also Masaryk, *The Making of a State*, p. 338. Masaryk writes that he knew Wiseman in England. There is also a Masaryk file in the Wiseman Papers (Colonel E. M. House Collection), Yale University.
    51.   MA, VII/15a; and MA, VII/32; a letter from Principal Burrows to Masaryk, dated December 23, 1915. Also Masaryk's record of December 31, 1915, MA, VII/15a.
    52.   MA, I/11. Voska's letter to Masaryk, February 8, 1916. See also Masaryk's letter to Voska, dated December 9, 1915, quoted in Václav Král, "Americké plány na světovládu a Masarykův první odboj" [American Plans for World Domination and Masaryk's First Struggle for Independence], *Historie a vojenství* (1953, No. 2). Before World War I Robert F. Young (nephew of Lord Bryce) resided in the United States, ostensibly to study Slavic peoples, particularly the Czechs, in this country. He, however, kept in touch with many non-Slavic individuals, one of whom was Charles R. Crane; the latter, in turn, had connections with the "kingmakers" in American politics. (As has been mentioned above, Crane made the largest single financial contribution to the election campaign of Woodrow Wilson in 1912, and he played an active role in that campaign.) In the fall of 1916, Seton-Watson provided a link between Masaryk and the British Intelligence service during R. F. Young's absence in Switzerland. After the war, Young went to Prague with the British legation as temporary first secretary. See Hugh and Christopher Seton-Watson, *The Making of a New Europe*, p. 154. Voska would meet Young again in October-November 1917, in

Notes to Chapter Two 527

England, and in June 1918, in France. (This time Voska would be a captain in the U.S. Intelligence Service.) See Voska's "Memoirs," *Jas* (1935, Nos. 23 and 43).
53. MacDonogh to Burrows, February 12, 1916; and Burrows to Masaryk, February 29, 1916. MA, VII/32.
54. Ibid.
55. Details in Voska, "Memoirs," *Jas* (1934, No. 49).
56. MA, VII/50. Masaryk's record of the meetings in the War Office, March 24, 1916.
57. MA, III/1; and MA, II/4 (Gaunt's letter to Voska). Voska published a facsimile of the letter in his "Memoirs," *Jas* (1934, No. 49).
58. Seton-Watson to Masaryk, May 6, 1916, MA, VII/15a.
59. Seton-Watson to Masaryk, May 6, 1916, MA, VII/15a. See also Wiseman to Murray, June 8, 1918, Wiseman Papers, General No. 1. Wiseman writes as follows: "I want to introduce you to Captain E. V. Voska, of the United States Intelligence Service. Captain Voska is the Chief organizer of the Bohemian National Alliance in this country, and has done most valuable work for the Cause, and especially good work for the British. *I have worked closely with him for two years* [emphasis added], and can assure you that he is in every way reliable and worthy of your confidence. He will explain to you his mission, and I shall be glad if you will help him in any way that you can." The Voska papers are in *Vojenský historický archiv*. Voska claimed that his organization consisted of sixty-eight people (eighty four, in *Spy and Counter-Spy*) for whom it received payments. In his unpublished memoirs, however, Voska's chief agent "Zeno" (Kopecký) challenges this claim as an exaggeration designed for the purpose of getting more funds from the British military intelligence.
60. W. B. Fowler, *British-American Relations, 1917-1918: The Role of Sir William Wiseman* (Princeton, 1969); David Wise and Thomas B. Ross, *The Espionage Establishment* (New York, 1967); Sir Samuel Hoare, *The Fourth Seal* (London, 1930); Sir Guy Gaunt, *The Yield of the Years* (London, 1940); Sir Arthur Willert, *Road to Safety: A study in Anglo-American relations*, with a preface by Charles Seymour (London, 1952; also New York, 1953). As told by Willert, the story of Voska and Masaryk (pp. 23-30) belongs to the category of fairy-tales. See also Richard Deacon, *A History of the British Secret Service* (New York, 1969).
61. František Šindelář, *Z boje za svobodu otčiny* [From the Struggle for Freedom of the Fatherland] (Chicago, 1924), p. 135.

Chapter Three:
The Emergence of the Independence Movement

1. *Dokumenty našeho osvobození* [Documents on Our Liberation], ed. Cyril Merhout (Prague, 1919), p. 14. Details in Dr. V. Vondrák, *Z doby bojů a samostatnost Československého vojska* [From the Time of Struggle for the Independence of the Czechoslovak Army] (Prague, 1925); František Šteidler, *Československé hnutí na Rusi* [The Czechoslovak Movement in Russia] (Prague, 1922); also Jindřich Veselý, *Češi a Slováci v revolučním Rusku 1917-1920* [Czechs and Slovaks in Revolutionary Russia, 1917-1920] (Prague, 1954), pp. 13-15; and Otakar Vaněk *Čechoslováci v Rusku* [Czechoslovaks in Russia] (Prague, 1919).

2. The memorandum is printed in Beneš, III, pp. 554-555; it was originally published in *Čechoslovan,* Kiev, August 25, 1914. See also Šteidler, *Československé hnutí,* p. 7.

3. In addition to the sources mentioned in note 1 above, there is an extensive Czech literature on the *Družina* written largely by its former members. See Jaroslav Čižmář, *V řadách české družiny a československé brigady* [In the Ranks of the Czech *Družina* and the Czechoslovak Brigade] (Brno, 1925); Emil Dostál, *Svatý Václav patronem čsl. odboje na Rusi* [St. Wenceslas as Patron of the Czechoslovak Resistance in Russia] (Prague, 1929), and *Katolíci v zahraničních bojích o československou samostatnost. Úvahy, doklady a vzpomínky z let 1914-1920* [The Catholics in the Struggles Abroad for the Attainment of Czechoslovak Independence. Reflections, Documents and Memories from the Years 1914-1920] (Brno, 1928); Alois Navrátil, *Katolicism a úcta svatovaclavská v čsl. legích* [Catholicism and the Saint Wenceslas Cult in the Czechoslovak Legions] (Přerov, 1930); Alois Navrátil and Josef Krejčí, *Tradice cyrilometodějská v československém odboji. Sborník dokladů v vzpomínek* [The St. Cyril and Methodius Tradition in the Czechoslovak Resistance. Collection of Documents and Memories] (Přerov, 1936); Vladimír Lazarevský, *Rusko a československé znovuzrození* [Russia and the Rebirth of Czechoslovakia] (Prague, 1927); *Vondrák contra Masaryk* (Bohemia, No. 1 Köln, 1958); Alois Navrátil, *Svatý Václav a Čsl. legie* [Saint Wenceslas and the Czechoslovak Legions] (Přerov, 1929); Vojtěch Prášek, *Česká družina* [The Czech *Družina*] (Prague, 1934). See also Victor M. Fic, *Revolutionary War for Independence and the Russian Question: Czechoslovak Army*

Notes to Chapter Three 529

in Russia 1914-1918 (New Delhi, India, 1977), pp. 5-7. There are also many articles on the same subject.

4. Among the members of the delegation received by the tsar on September 17, 1914, were Otakar Červený (Kiev) and Jiří Klecanda (Petrograd), who had been mentioned above, Svatopluk Koníček, an enthusiastic Czech tsarophile and owner of an advertising agency in Moscow, and Josef Orzagh, part owner of a department store in Warsaw and brother of Jan Orzahg, a Slovak leader at Warsaw who cooperated with the Czechs in Russia. See Beneš, III, p. 555; and L'udovít Holotík, Štefánikovská legenda a vznik ČSR, 2nd ed. (Bratislava, 1960), p. 106.

5. Cited from Čechoslovan (Kiev) in Dostál, Svatý Václav, pp. 28-29. Also, Nikolaj Alexandrovič Chodorovič, Odbojové hnutí a československé vojsko v Rusku (1914-1917) [The Resistance Movement and the Czechoslovak Army in Russia (194-1917)], trans. (from Russian) by Jiří Tret'jakov (Prague, 1928), p. 24.

6. These activities are described by many writers, including one of the emissaries, Vladimír Vaněk, in his extensive work Moje válečná odysea. Osudy starodružiníka ve čtyřech dílech [My Wartime Odyssey. Destines of a Member of the Old Družina in Four Parts] (Prague, 1925).

7. Josef Kudela, Přehled vývoje čsl. revolučního hnutí na Rusi do odchodu čsl. armádního sboru z Ukrajiny [Review of the Development of the Czechoslovak Revolutionary Movement in Russia Until the Departure of the Czechoslovak Army Corps from the Ukraine] (Prague, 1923), p. 18.

8. Ibid.

9. Peter P. Yurchak, The Slovaks. Their History and Traditions (Whiting, Ind., 1946), p. 251; Pichlík, Zahraniční odboj, p. 58; see also Tobolka, Politické dějiny, IV, pp. 112ff.

10. Kudela, Přehled, pp. 37-40; Pichlík, Zahraniční odboj, pp. 194-195; for more details see František Zuman, Osvobozenecká legenda [The Liberation Legend], 2 vols. (Prague, 1922), I, pp. 126-129.

11. Kudela, Přehled, p. 45.

12. Karel Kramář, "M. Kramar et la politique slave," Le Monde Slave, No. 11 (November 1926), p. 294.

13. Sergei D. Sazonov, Fateful Years, 1909-1916 (London, 1928), pp. 273-274.

14. Ibid., p. 275, note.

15. Izvestiia Ministerstva Inostrannykh Del (St. Petersburg), No. 6 (1914), p. 3. See also Beneš, III, p. 553.

16. Ibid.

17. Josef Kudela, "Ruské letáky u nás na počátku války" [Russian Leaflets at the Beginning of the War], *Naše revoluce,* VI (1929-1930).

18. Paléologue to Delcassé, September 14, 1914, in *Mezhdunarodnye otnosheniia v epokhu imperializma,* Series III (Moscow, 1931-38), VI, Part 1, pp. 247-248; hereafter cited as MOEI. Also F. A. Golder, ed., *Documents of Russian History, 1914-1917* (New York, 1927), p. 57.

19. MOEI, VI, Part 1, pp. 247-248; Golder, *Documents of Russian History,* p. 57.

20. FO 371/2163, 244, Buchanan to Grey, August 7, 1914, and 371/2164, 210, August 10, 1914. See also Hanak, "The Government...", 161-197.

21. FO 371/2164, 487, August 9, 1914, and 371/2163, 17, August 9, 1914.

22. FO 371/2241, 4404, January 7, 1915. See also Hanak, "The Government...", p. 166.

23. D. Lloyd George, *The Truth about the Peace Treaties,* 2 vols. (London, 1938), I, p. 39.

24. Pichlík, *Zahraniční odboj,* p. 59. Among the writings on the Czech and Slovak colonies abroad and their participation in the struggle for independence are Vojta Beneš, *Československá Amerika v odboji* [Czechoslovak America in the Resistance] (Prague, 1931); and *Masarykovo dílo v Americe* [Masaryk's Work in America] (Prague, 1925); Thomáš Čapek, *The Czechs (Bohemians) in America: A Study of Their National, Cultural, Political, Social, Economic and Religious Life* (Boston-New York, 1920); Konstantin Čulen, *Dejiny Slovákov v Amerike* [History of the Slovaks in America] 2 vols. (Bratislava, 1942); idem, *Pittsburghská Dohoda* [The Pittsburgh Agreement] (Bratislava, 1937); Kenneth Dexter Miller, *The Czecho-Slovaks in America* (New York, 1922); Vladimír Nosek, *Anglie a náš boj za samostatnost* [England and Our Fight for Independence] (Prague, 1926); Charles Pergler, *America in the Struggle for Czechoslovak Independence* (Philadelphia, 1926); and *Politická bilance československé Ameriky* [Political Balance-Sheet of the Czechoslovak America] (Prague, 1920); Karol Sidor, *Slováci v zahraničnom odboji* [Slovaks in the Resistance Abroad] (Bratislava, 1929); and Václav Vojtěch, *Česká kolonie pařížská v našem odboji* [The Czech Paris Colony in Our Resistance], *Naše revoluce,* IV (1926-1927).

Notes to Chapter Three 531

25. In addition to the above sources, see Josef Martínek, "Jak jsme to dělali v Americe" [How Did We Do It in America] in *Pradesát let. Soubor vzpomínek a úvah o Masarykově republice* [Fifty Years. Collection of Memories and Reminiscences on Masaryk's Republic] (*Naše Hlasy*, Canada, 1968), pp. 53-59; and Šindelář, *Z boje za svobodu otčiny*.

26. Čulen, *Pittsburghská Dohoda*, p. 78; see also Yurchak, *The Slovaks*, p. 210; and Victor S. Mamatey, *The United States and East Central Europe, 1914-1918: A Study in Wilsonian Diplomacy and Propaganda* (Princeton, 1957), p. 130.

27. Vojtěch, *Česká kolonie;* and Tobolka, *Politické dějiny*, IV, pp. 118ff.

28. Jaroslav Werstadt, ed., "K životopisu a veřejné činnosti Svatopluka Koníčka-Horského" [On Biography and Public Activity of Svatopluk Koníček-Horský], *Naše revoluce*, IX (1933). See also Pichlík, *Zahraniční odboj*, pp. 75ff.

29. Pichlík, *Zahraniční odboj*, pp. 75ff. Details in Lev Sychrava, *Revoluční hnutí ve Švýcarech, Francii a Anglii* [The Revolutionary Movement in Switzerland, France and England] (Prague, 1924).

30. Details on the persecution of Czechs are in Tobolka, *Politické dějiny*, IV, pp. 66-81. See also Paulová, *Tajný výbor*, p. 12. In addition to the books by Paulová, domestic resistance is discussed in a great number of articles and books, including the following: Jaroslav Durich, *Okamžiky z válečných let* [Moments from the War Years] (Prague, 1924); Antonín Hajn, *Česká politika za války* [The Czech Politics During the War] (Prague, 1924); Jan Hajšman, *Česká Maffie* [Czech Maffie] (Prague, 1932) and *Maffie v rozmachu* [Maffie at Its Height] (Prague, 1933); Josef Pekař, *K českému boji státoprávnímu za války* [On the Czech State-Rights Struggle During the War] (Prague, 1930); František Soukup, *28. říjen 1918. Předpoklady a vývoj našeho odboje domácího v československé revoluci za státní samostatnost národa* [The 28th of October 1918. The Assumptions and Development of Our Resistance at Home During the Czechoslovak Revolution Struggling for the State Independence of Our Nation], 2 vols. (Prague, 1928); and Zdeněk Václav Tobolka, *Česká politika za světové války* [Czech Politics During the World War] (Prague, 1922).

31. Dr. Karel Kramář, ed. Sís, pp. 97-98; and Tobolka, *Politické dějiny*, IV, p. 50.

32. Paulová, *Tajný výbor*, p. 12.

33. Tobolka, *Politické dějiny,* IV, p. 52. The same book (pp. 51-57) contains a detailed description of positions and attitudes of Czech and Slovak political parties at the beginning of the war.
34. Ibid., pp. 177-178.
35. See Juriga's work quoted in L'udovít Holotík, *Štefánikovská legenda a vznik ČSR* [The Štefánik Legend and the Genesis of Czechoslovakia], 2nd rev. ed. (Bratislava, 1960), p. 86.
36. Tobolka, *Politické dějiny,* IV, p. 57.
37. Ibid., p. 59. Klofáč fell into a trap set for him by the police, who used a female agent provocateur.
38. Kudela, "Ruské letáky," *Naše revoluce,* VI (1929-30).
39. Karel Pichlík, Vlastimil Vávra, and Jaroslav Křížek, *Červenobílá a rudá* [Red-White and Red] (Prague, 1957), pp. 40-43.
40. Ibid., pp. 34-37.
41. Dr. *Karel Kramář,* ed. Sís, pp. 102-103; and Paulová, *Tajný výbor,* pp. 20-22.

Chapter Four:
The Organization of the Czech Independence Movement by Émigrés Abroad, and Setbacks at Home

1. Lev Sychrava, "Jak jsem se dostal za hranice" [How Did I Get Abroad], *Národní Osvobození* (Prague, 1926, Nos. 191, 194, 199, and 205). Also Pichlík, *Zahraniční odboj,* pp. 90-91.
2. Beneš, I, p. 62. For Sychrava's own account of his activities abroad see Lev Sychrava, "Několik vzpomínek ze Švýcar" [A Few Memories from Switzerland] in Edvard Beneš, *Sborník vzpomínek na T. G. Masaryka* [A Symposium of Memories of T. G. Masaryk] (Prague, 1930); Lev Sychrava, *Československé revoluční hnutí na evropském západě* [Czechoslovak Revolutionary Movement in Western Europe] (Prague, 1923); and Lev Sychrava and Jaroslav Werstadt, *Československý odboj* [The Czechoslovak Resistance] (Prague, 1923).
3. Hugh and Christopher Seton-Watson, *The Making of a New Europe,* pp. 173 and 199.
4. For the complete memorandum see Seton-Watson, *Masaryk in England,* pp. 116-136; and/or Beneš, III, pp. 237-267. See also Paulová, *Tajný výbor,* p. 22. Because of some exaggerations in it, Hugh and Christopher Seton-Watson call it the work of a "political propagandist" (*The Making of a New Europe,* p. 124).

Notes to Chapter Four   533

5. Seton-Watson, *Masaryk in England* and/or Beneš, III, p. 255. The memorandum also stated that a "republic is favored only by a few radical politicians." Masaryk apparently did not consider himself to be one of them at this time.

6. Beneš, I, p. 111.
7. FO 371/2241, 53297, May 3, 1915; Hanak, "The Government," p. 166.
8. Pichlík, *Zahraniční odboj*, p. 126.
9. *Karel Kramář a Slovanstvo* [Karel Kramář and Slavdom], ed. S. G. Puškarev and V. P. Šapilovský (Prague, 1937), p. 44.
10. Beneš, I, pp. 70-79; and Tobolka, *Politické dějiny*, pp. 66-81.
11. Ibid.
12. Čulen, *Pittsburghská Dohoda*, p. 78; Yurchak, *The Slovaks*, p. 210; and Mamatey, *The United States and East-Central Europe*, p. 130.
13. Paulová, *Tajný výbor*, pp. 31-32.
14. Ibid., p. 32.
15. *Dr. Karel Kramář*, ed. Sís, pp. 121-123.
16. Ibid., pp. 118-131.
17. Ibid., pp. 120-121. See also Seton-Watson, *Masaryk in England*, pp. 35-36 and 84-88.
18. *Dr. Karel Kramář*, ed. Sís, pp. 122-124.
19. Ibid., p. 125.
20. Ibid., pp. 126-128.
21. Ibid., p. 128.
22. Beneš, III, pp. 3-9.
23. See Seton-Watson's article on the origins of the School of Slavonic and East European Studies in *The Slavonic and East European Review* (London), XVII, 50 (1939), pp. 360-371.
24. Martínek, "Jak jsme to dělali," in *Padesát let*, p. 54; Pichlík, *Zahraniční odboj*, p. 136.
25. Pichlík, *Zahraniční odboj*, p. 141.
26. Ibid., p. 142.
27. For details see Dr. František Iška, *V zájmu národa—ve službách lidskosti. Soubor článků psaných za války proti lživlasteneckému fanatismu, v Iškově "Vesmíru"* [In the Interest of the Nation—In the Service of Humanity. Collection of Articles Written During the War Against Mendacious-Patriotic Fanaticism, in Iška's *Vesmír*] (Chicago, 1917). See also the unpublished memoirs of František Kopecký, deposited in *Vojenský*

historický archiv, Prague, which devoted one chapter to the case of *Vesmír* and described how the former mail clerk at the Austrian consulate general in New York participated in the fradulent campaign against Iška. Voska's framing of Iška is corroborated by Josef Martínek, a member of the Voska group in the United States, in "Conversations with Josef Martínek," by Zdeněk Hruban, published in serialized form in *Americké Listy* in April 1979.

Like many other émigrés, Masaryk was used as a potential weapon of war. For a scholarly study of the subject see Kenneth T. Calder, *Britain and the Origins of the New Europe, 1914-1918* (Cambridge, London, Melbourne, New York, 1976). As part of their propaganda the British distributed a pamphlet called *"Austrian Terrorism in Bohemia,* With an Introduction by Professor T. G. Masaryk, Czech Member of the Austrian Parliament and President of the Czech National Committee for Foreign Affairs" (n.d. [1916]). This pamphlet contains some exaggerations, for instance, that the emperor ordered "wholesale hanging and shooting" (p. 19), and that by May 1916, "the death sentences of civilians pronounced in Austria since the beginning of the War already exceeded the terrific number 4,000; 965 of the victims were Czechs. A large proportion of the condemned were women. The total of soldiers executed already amounts to several thousands" (p. 23). Four Czech civilians were executed in 1914-1915 for activities that included distributing Russian propaganda leaflets. No woman was condemned to death. When the new emperor granted amnesty to political offenders, fewer than 1,000 Czechs, including those sentenced to death, were released. See Tobolka, *Politické dějiny,* IV, p. 256.

28. Čulen, *Pittsburghská Dohoda,* p. 78; Mamatey, *The United States,* p. 130; also Štefan Osuský, "How Czechoslovakia Was Born," address prepared for the Slovak World Congress, Toronto, Canada, June 17-19, 1971. This writer received a copy of the address by the courtesy of Mrs. Pavla Osuská.

29. Beneš, I, p. 96. See also Steed, *Through Thirty Years,* II, p. 129.

30. Beneš, I, pp. 104ff. The most recent pro-Štefánik biography has been Jan Juříček, *M. R. Štefánik. Životopisný náčrt* [M. R. Štefánik. Biographical Sketch] (Bratislava, 1969).

31. On Štefánik, see *Štefánik,* ed. Š. Osuský, B. Pavlů, and J. Bartůšek, 2 vols. (Prague, 1938); Rostislav Rajchl, *Štefánik, Voják a Diplomat* [Štefánik, Soldier and Diplomat] (Prague, 1948); Maurice Janin, *Milan Rastislav Štefanik* (Prague, 1932); and Holotík, *Štefánikovská legenda.*

Notes to Chapter Four 535

32. Masaryk, *The Making of a State*, p. 51.
33. Seton-Watson, *Masaryk in England*, p. 133; Beneš, III, pp. 237-256.
34. On "mas conversion" to Orthodoxy see *Denník plukovníka Švece*, p. 234; Chodorovič, *Odbojové hnutí*, p. 116.
35. The declaration was published in *La Nation Tchèque*, vol. I, pp. 215-218. For an English translation see Čestmír Ješina, ed., *The Birth of Czechoslovakia* (Washington, D.C., 1968), pp. 1A-4. See also Beneš, I, pp. 184-186; Dürich, p. 18; and Masaryk, *The Making of a State*, pp. 78-79.
36. Masaryk, *The Making of a State*, p. 51; Pichlík, *Zahraniční odboj*, pp. 184 and 187.
37. Beneš, pp. 295-296.
38. Ibid., pp. 173-176.
39. Masaryk, *The Making of a State*, p. 96. According to Beneš, Briand told Masaryk that the French were sympathetic to the Czech cause and that they "will do everything so that the Czechs will become independent." Beneš, I, p. 110.
40. Beneš, III, pp. 237-256.
41. Masaryk, *The Making of a State*, p. 96; and Beneš, I, p. 109.
42. Seton-Watson, *Masaryk in England*, pp. 88-96.
43. Dürich, p. 50. See also Beneš, III, p. 78. Although later during the war the London office of the council used the term Czecho-Slovak National Council (or National Czecho-Slovak Council), its accuracy may be questioned. In his postwar writtings in Czech Beneš used the name *Československá národní rada;* yet in French it was *Conseil National des Pays Tchèques* ("Czech Lands"), a term advocated by the Slovak Štefánik, according to Beneš, I, p. 117. In view of the total ignorance of Slovak matters in Allied countries, Štefánik did not want to complicate the political struggle by bringing the Slovak question into it. He was afraid that the Slovak problems would not be understood and that they might be used against the whole independence movement by its enemies. Slovakia was a northern part of Hungary; it had belonged to the Crown of St. Stephen for some thousand years. It was never a part of the Crown of St. Wenceslas, and the independence movement invoked the state right of the Czech lands to independence, not the right of self-determination of nations.
44. Masaryk, *The Making of a State*, p. 131.
45. Ibid., p. 223.

46. *Dokumenty,* ed. Merhout, pp. 30-33.

47. Dürich, p. 16. As Dürich pointed out, money from the American collections went into the hands of Masaryk, who used it as he saw fit. Yet Dürich's name was used when these collections were made; e.g., for several weeks in 1916 Czech-American newspapers carried advertisements asking for contributions for a "Christmas collection for Masaryk and Dürich." The amounts of money collected were considerable (see below).

Czech newspapers published at home could not prove that some of the money that Masaryk was receiving came from foreign intelligence sources, but they charged him with being in foreign employ. *Národní Listy* of January 5, 1917, called Masaryk and his agents "liars and deceivers who are concerned only with their material interests." *Čech* of January 21, 1917, attacked Masaryk for his advocacy of partitioning Austria-Hungary and claimed that Thomas Garrigue "expects a greater profit from this partitioning than when he was taking 1,000 pieces of silver in the fatherland. Otherwise he has remained loyal to his original name: Masařík [butcher]. He slaughters and quarters at least by his tongue and pen." On March 25, 1916, the police instructed all Czech dailies to print an article under the title "In Foreign Service," saying that Masaryk and his comrades, "for a few pieces of silver, are committing the worst crime of all times: high treason."

The amounts of money received by Masaryk were substantial. The first contribution that arrived from the U.S.—a check for $1,000 payable to his wife—Masaryk received in Prague through Voska in October 1914; the second, $3,000, in Rotterdam; and the third, $1,250, during his visit to Geneva, from which he did not return home. Since Masaryk was not short of funds, he could accommodate his supporters, who, in turn, were loyal to him. His demands on the Czechs in America were increasing; they were met largely by income from bazaars. The bazaar held in New York netted $22,000, in Cleveland, $30,000, in Chicago, $400,000, in small Cedar Rapids, Iowa, $25,000, in Texas $54,000, and in Omaha $70,000. Furthermore, the "national tax" declared by the Bohemian National Alliance netted hundreds of thousands of dollars. See Josef Martínek, "Jak jsme to dělali," in *Padesát let,* pp. 53-54. Šindelář gives somewhat different figures; e.g., the bazaar in Chicago netted $50,000, in Omaha $65,000, and in Texas $40,000. See Šindelář, *Z boje za svobodu otčiny,* p. 136.

48. For Masaryk's version of the origin of the "Dürich affair" see pp.

Notes to Chapter Four 537

76-79 of his book; and for Dürich's see the work by Dürich cited above.
49. Beneš, I, p. 66. Later Beneš doubted Dürich's suitability; cf. pp. 184-186.
50. Pichlík, *Zahraniční odboj*, p. 191.
51. Ibid.
52. Dürich, pp. 27-29; also Beneš, I, p. 183. According to Beneš, (I, p. 185), Lokhvicky told him that Dürich should not be sent to Russia because he was not suitable for the task, and that Masaryk should go there instead.
53. Beneš, III, p. 563. According to Veselý, *Češi a Slováci*, the number of troops was 2,000.
54. Pichlík, *Zahraniční odboj*, p. 193; František Zuman, *Osvobozenecká legenda* [The Liberation Legend], 2 vols. (Prague, 1922), I, p. 146. Although the tsar consented, there were difficulties with the government. Vondrák told the tsar that he recognized Masaryk as the leader of the movement.
55. Beneš, III, p. 565.
56. Kudela, *Přehled*, pp. 37-40; Zuman, *Osvobozenecká legenda*, I, pp. 126-127. For an official Russian government view of the event see Papoušek, *Carské Rusko*, pp. 127-129.
57. Tobolka, *Politické dějiny*, IV, p. 179.
58. The memorandum is printed in Beneš, III, pp. 566-572; and Papoušek, *Carské Rusko*, pp. 73-77.
59. Ibid.
60. Ibid., p. 571 and p. 76, respectively.
61. Dürich, p. 31. Cf. also Beneš, III, p. 586; and Pichlík, *Zahraniční odboj*, p. 195.
62. Beneš, III, p. 586.
63. Ibid., p. 579; and Karel Kramář, *Na obranu slovanské politiky* [In Defense of the Slavic Policy] (Prague, 1926), pp. 57-59. Also Tobolka, *Politické dějiny*, IV, pp. 177-178.
64. Beneš writes that the council was established in February 1916. See Beneš, I, p. 117. Masaryk states that Beneš used, in his capacity as secretary general, the name "The National Council of Czech Countries." (Masaryk, p. 79.) Osuský says that, when he arrived in Paris and met Beneš in the latter's office in the summer of 1916, he noticed that the name of the organization established in February 1916, was "Czech

National Council." He protested, saying that this was not acceptable to the Slovaks in America. Beneš therefore contacted Dürich, Štefánik, and Košík, all of whom were in Russia at that time, and they agreed to change the name to "National Council of Czech Countries." The change of name was still not satisfactory to Osuský, who told Beneš that the name of the organization was about the same as before. Only after their conversation, according to Osuský, did Beneš agree to change the name to "National Czecho-Slovak Council"; and this became the official name of the organization, "such as it was recorded at the Peace Conference." Štefan Osuský, "How Czechoslovakia Was Born." This change of name, with all of its programmatic implications, could have taken place only late in the summer of 1916, because Košík and Štefánik departed for Russia on July 28, 1916. See Tobolka, *Politické dějiny*, IV, p. 170; and Pichlík, *Zahraniční odboj*, p. 200.

65. Dürich, p. 30.
66. Holotík, *Štefánikovská legenda*, pp. 362-363. French documents relevant to Štefánik's activity during World War I are printed in French and in a Czech translation on pp. 346ff.
67. Ibid., pp. 364-370.
68. Ibid.
69. Ibid., p. 164.
70. Janin, *Moje účast*, pp. 17 and 22. Also Holotík, *Štefánikovská legenda*, p. 164.
71. Holotík, *Štefánikovská legenda*, pp. 370-372.
72. Ibid., p. 374.
73. Supplement to the protocol about the conference with Professor Masaryk by the delegates from Kiev, Beneš, III, pp. 580-587.
74. Holotík, *Štefánikovská legenda*, p. 145.
75. Papoušek, *Carské Rusko*, p. 110.
76. Janin, *Moje účast*, p. 12; Holotík, *Štefánikovská legenda*, p. 145.
77. The whole document is in Papoušek, *Carské Rusko*, pp. 97-98. See also Pichlík, *Zahraniční odboj*, p. 202.
78. Papoušek, *Carské Rusko*, pp. 97-98, and Pichlík, *Zahraniční odboj*, p. 202.
79. Pichlík, *Zahraniční odboj*, p. 202; and Tobolka, *Politické dějiny*, IV, pp. 113 and 177ff.
80. Papoušek, *Carské Rusko*, p. 184; also Tobolka, *Politické dějiny*, IV, p. 179.

Notes to Chapter Four 539

81. Papoušek, *Carské Rusko,* p. 184.
82. Tobolka, *Politické dějiny,* IV, p. 181.
83. Papoušek, *Carské Rusko,* p. 95.
84. Ibid., p. 96. Masaryk told his former colleague from the Vienna parliament, Ante Trumbić, when they met in Rome in December 1914, that if Bohemia became an independent state, it would have a king from the British ruling house. See Pichlík, *Zahraniční odboj,* p. 107. See also Beneš, I, p. 29.
85. Papoušek, *Carské Rusko,* pp. 101-102.
86. Dürich, p. 35.
87. Papoušek, *Carské Rusko,* p. 118.
88. Ibid., pp. 104-105.
89. Ibid.
90. Beneš, III, pp. 587-589. Also Papoušek, *Carské Rusko,* pp. 109-11; and *Dokumenty,* ed. Merhout, pp. 33-35.
91. Beneš, III, p. 271. The declaration was published in Czech newspapers, e.g., *Národní politika,* November 19, 1916. In the summer of 1915, Social Democrats František Soukup and Gustav Habrman decided, definitely, against going into exile, and soon afterwards all contacts between Social Democrats at home and the independence movement abroad were terminated. In America a socialist, Charles Pergler, a member of Voska's secret organization, was disappointed with the leader of the Social Democratic party, B. Šmeral, and his opposition to the idea of an independent Czechoslovak state. See Pichlík, *Zahraniční odboj,* pp. 148 and 178ff. Details in Tobolka, *Politické dějiny,* IV, pp. 186-208.
92. See Emil Strauss, *Die Enstehung der Tschechoslowakischen Republik* (Prague, 1934), p. 140.
93. The whole document is in Beneš, III, p. 287. For background and analysis see Tobolka, *Politické dějiny,* IV, pp. 216ff.
94. Kramář, *Pět přednášek,* p. 63.
95. A list of some of Osuský's articles is in Nosek, *Anglie a náš boj,* pp. 51-55; Beneš, III, pp. 272-279; Beneš, I, p. 123. Masaryk, pp. 51 and 280ff passim; Pichlík, *Zahraniční odboj,* pp. 208-211; and Harry Hanak, "Th. G. Masaryk's Journalistic Activity in England during the First World War," *The Slavonic and East European Review,* XLII, No. 98 (December 1963), pp. 184-189; and Harry Hanak, "The New Europe, 1916-20," *The Slavonic and East European Review,* XXXIX, No. 93 (June 1961), pp. 369-399.

96. André Chéradame, *Le plan pangermaniste démasqué* (Paris, 1916). Also, by the same author: *La question d'Orient. La Macedonnie. La cheminde fer de Bagdad* (Paris, 1915); *The Pan-German Plot Unmasked: Berlin's Formidable Peace-Traps of "the Drawn War"* (New York, 1917); *Pan-Germany, the Disease and Cure* (Boston, 1917); and *The Essentials of an Enduring Victory* (New York, 1918).
97. Seton-Watson, *Masaryk in England*, pp. 35-36 and 84-88.
98. Robert W. Seton-Watson, "The Reorganization of Europe," *New Europe*, November 9, 1916.

Chapter Five:
Plans for the Future of Central Europe, and the Struggle for Control of the Independence Movement

1. *The Times*, September 25, 1914; Harry Hanak, "The Government, the Foreign Office and Austria-Hungary, 1914-1918," *The Slavonic and East European Review* (London), (1969), 161-197.
2. David Lloyd George, *Memoirs of the Peace Conference*, 2 vols. (New Haven, 1939), II, pp. 501-502.
3. Ibid., p. 502.
4. Tobolka, *Politické dějiny*, IV, pp. 106ff.
5. Paulová, *Maffie*, I, pp. 151-155; Tobolka, *Politické dějiny*, IV, pp. 92-94.
6. Robert W. Seton-Watson, *What is at Stake in the War* (London, 1915).
7. Ibid., pp. 65-70.
8. May, "Seton-Watson and the Treaty of London," p. 45; Harry Hanak, *Great Britain and Austria-Hungary During the First World War. A Study in the Formation of Public Opinion* (London, 1962), p. 100; and Seton-Watson, *Masaryk in England*, p. 62.
9. A. Popov, "Chekho-slovackii vopros i tcarskaia diplomatsiia v 1914-1917 gg," *Krasnyi arkhiv* (vol. 33), pp. 27-29; Holotík, *Štefánikovská legenda*, p. 149; also Papoušek, *Carské Rusko*, p. 75.
10. F. Naumann, *Central Europe* (New York, 1917). For details see Theodor Heuss, *Friedrich Naumann* (Stuttgart, 1937); Henry Cord Meyer, *Mitteleuropa in German Thought and Action, 1815-1945* (The Hague, 1955); also Jaksch, *Europe's Road to Potsdam*, pp. 150-152 and 156.

Notes to Chapter Five   541

11. Popov, "Chekho-slovackii vopros," pp. 27-29; and Holotík, *Štefánikovská legenda,* p. 149. Svatkovsky maintained close contacts with emigrés from Austria-Hungary and had his informers within the empire. Early in 1915, when Beneš visited Masaryk in Switzerland, Svatkovsky asked the visitor from Prague to urge Kramář to go to Russia. After Beneš became an exile, Svatkovsky met with him frequently. See Beneš, I, pp. 33-39; 51; 60; 62; 64; 75; 82; 99; 126; 184; 233-236; 287; 294; 414-417; 439; II, 98 and 157.

12. Popov, "Chekho-slovackii vopros," p. 29; and Holotík, *Štefánikovská legenda,* p. 150.

14. MA, VII/15a; Pichlík, *Zahraniční odboj,* p. 261; the phrase "the most important CZECH secret Society in America" was used by Sir William Wiseman. See report under File "R," "Russia," Wiseman General, No. 1, WWP.

15. "Memorandum of M. Priklonsky on the Czechoslovak Question" in Papoušek, *Carské Rusko,* pp. 73-77.

16. FO Cab. 17/160, August 29, 1916; Hanak, "The Government," p. 170.

17. Most of the memoranda are in FO Cab. 17/160, August 7, 1917; the Foreign Office's memorandum is printed in Lloyd George, *Memoirs of the Peace Conference,* pp. 11-23; several other memoranda are in H. H. Asquith, *Memories and Reflections* vols. I and II, London, 1928), and David Lloyd George, *War Memoirs* (6 vols., London and Boston, 1933-1936).

18. Lloyd George, *Memoirs of the Peace Conference,* p. 11. For the Foreign Office memorandum see pp. 11-23.

19. Ibid., p. 11.

20. Ibid., p. 23.

21. Asquith, *Memories,* vol. II, p. 142.

22. FO Cab. 42/22, November 14, 1916; Hanak, "The Government," p. 171.

23. The memoranda were copied at the Stavka by Jaroslav Papoušek, who was Masaryk's secretary while the latter resided in Russia in 1917-1918. They are printed in a Czech translation in Papoušek, *Carské Rusko,* pp. 120-144 and 147-155. For a French translation of the documents see "La Russie tsariste et la question tchechoslovaque," *Le Monde Slave,* No. 1 (November 1924), pp. 123-138; and No. 2 (Decmeber 1924), pp. 294-300.

The documents will be quoted *ex extenso*, because they have never been published in English, except for a few excerpts in Merritt Abrash, "War Aims Toward Austria-Hungary," in Alexander Dallin, ed., *Russian Diplomacy and Eastern Europe, 1914-1917* (New York, 1963), pp. 100-114. The following pages merely recapitulate the content of these three documents; therefore, notes are not used. All the direct quotations are translations from the memoranda as printed in Papoušek, *Carské Rusko*.

24. Vladimír Sís, to whom Kramář gave a power of attorney to represent him in his contacts with Allied diplomats at Sophia, was receiving instructions from his brother František Sís. Either because he misunderstood the instructions, or because he was influenced by the Balkan environment and his own awareness of the views held by the Allied diplomats and their home offices, in the spring of 1915, Sís submitted to all Allied representatives a memorandum calling for the establishment of an independent state. Thus the programs of the *Maffie* (Kramář) and Masaryk were the same on the issue of state independence. In "Independent Bohemia," submitted to the Allied governments in May 1915, Masaryk asked for the "reestablishment of Bohemia as an independent state"; the memorandum submitted by Sís called for the "restoration of the Czech state." See Paulová, *Maffie*, I, pp. 414-421.

25. According to Beneš, Masaryk hoped that the rule of a British prince would bring about the establishment of a parliamentary government, based on the British model, in Bohemia and the latter's complete attachment to the west. Beneš, I, p. 29.

26. Lloyd George, *Memoirs of the Peace Conference*, vol. I, p. 28, and vol. II, p. 495.

27. Wiseman to Auchincloss, January 26, 1918, WWP, "Propaganda and Intelligence. Czecho-Cum-Pole Scheme."

28. Papoušek, *Carské Rusko*, pp. 94ff, 100ff, the three memoranda quoted above, 155ff, 157ff, and 182-186.

29. Wiseman to Auchincloss, January 26, 1918, WWP.

30. Details in Rajchl, *Štefánik*, pp. 90ff; Holotík, *Štefánikovská legenda*, pp. 158ff; for Masaryk's version of the conflict see Masaryk, pp. 87-79 and 155; and for Dürich's version see Dürich, pp. 36ff.

31. The whole document is in Dürich, pp. 37-38, and Beneš, III, pp. 589-591. See also Tobolka, *Politické dějiny*, IV, pp. 177ff.

32. Dürich, p. 37.

Notes to Chapter Five   543

33. Holotík, *Štefánikovská legenda*, pp. 160-161.
34. Janin, *Moje účast*, p. 20; Holotík, *Štefánikovská legenda*, p. 161.
35. Pichlík, *Zahraniční odboj*, p. 213.
36. Ján Kvasnička, *Československé légie v Rusku 1917-1920* [Czechoslovak Legions in Russia, 1917-1920] (Bratislava, 1963), p. 21. Kvasnička's book is based largely on archival materials in Czechoslovakia and the Soviet Union.
37. Papoušek, *Carské Rusko*, p. 111.
38. Ibid., p. 110; and Holotík, *Štefánikovská legenda*, p. 159. For more information on the secret society organized by Voska in Russia and the "Masaryk agents" see the memoirs of Voska (*Jas*, 1933) and *Čechoslováci ve válce a revoluci* [Czechoslovaks in War and Revolution] (Moscow, 1919), pp. 71-77 and 102. A "Club of Collaborators" in Kiev, a group of Czech officers who organized the recruiting of prisoners of war for the Czech *Družina* (Legion), cooperated closely with this secret society. The liaison between the club and the Petrograd group headed by Jiří Klecanda, Bohumil Čermák, and Bohdan Pavlů was historian Jaroslav Papoušek. For details see a work by one who took part in the events: Jan Šeba, *Rusko a Malá dohoda v politice světové* [Russia and the Little Entente in World Politics] (Prague, 1936), pp. 354-362.
39. Papoušek, *Carské Rusko*, pp. 109-116.
40. Ibid., p. 114.
41. Ibid., p. 116.
42. Holotík, *Štefánikovská legenda*, p. 383.
43. Ibid., p. 166; also Pichlík, *Zahraniční odboj*, p. 71.
44. Dürich, p. 39.
45. Tobolka, *Politické dějiny*, IV, p. 181.
46. Ibid.
47. Holotík, *Štefánikovská legenda*, p. 383.
48. Pichlík, *Zahraniční odboj*, p. 225.
49. Ibid., p. 227.
50. Ibid., p. 229.
51. Kvasnićka, *Československé légie*, p. 27.
52. Ibid., p. 26.
53. Text of the document is in Dürich, pp. 41-43; and Papoušek, *Carské Rusko*, pp. 169-171.
54. Ibid. Also Beneš, III, pp. 606-609.

55. Dürich, p. 46.
56. Ibid.
57. Ibid., p. 47.
58. Ibid.
59. Ibid., p. 48.
60. Ibid., pp. 52-53.
61. Pichlík, *Zahraniční odboj*, p. 231.
62. Donald W. Treadgold, *Twentieth Century Russia* (Chicago, 1959), pp. 118-119.
63. Dürich, pp. 63-64. A photocopy of the whole article in Russian, as it was translated from Masaryk's German manuscript, is attached to the book by Syllaba, *Masaryk a revoluce v Rusku.*
64. Pichlík, *Zahraniční odboj*, pp. 229-230. See also Masaryk, p. 119.
65. Dürich, p. 63.
66. Pichlík, *Zahraniční odboj*, p. 232.
67. Ibid.
68. Beneš, I, pp. 275-276; Dürich, p. 48; and Tobolka, *Politické dějiny*, IV, p. 183.
69. Ferdinand Písecký, *Moje poznámky o pobytu dra Štefánika v Petrohradě od 17. do 31. ledna 1917* [My Notes on the Stay of Dr. Štefánik at Petrograd from January 17 till January 30, 1917]; Holotík, *Štefánikovská legenda*, p. 170.
70. Janin, *Moje účast*, pp. 39-40; Holotík, *Štefánikovská legenda*, p. 170.
71. Masaryk, *Světová revoluce*, pp. 305-307. "Report of Rotenberg," May 1917, WWP. See also Irwin and Voska, *Spy and Counter-Spy*, pp. 196 and 198.
72. Holotík, *Štefánikovská legenda*, p. 170.
73. Colonel House Diary, entry of January 15, 1917. E. M. House Collection.
74. Papoušek, *Carské Rusko*, pp. 168-169; Masaryk *Světová revoluce*, p. 117.
75. Holotík, *Štefánikovská legenda*, p. 171; Beneš, III, p. 599. The position of the Dürich council was similar to that of the several exile organizations established by émigrés from east central Europe after 1948, including the Council for a Free Czechoslovakia, which were subsidized for years by the U.S. government through the C.I.A. These councils were

not elected. Also for some twenty years the C.I.A. controlled and financed Radio Free Europe and Radio Liberty, which were staffed largely by refugees from the Soviet bloc countries. See "Congress Is Asked to End Financing of Radio by C.I.A.," *New York Times,* May 24, 1971.
76. Dürich, p. 48.
77. Tobolka, *Politické dějiny,* p. 183.
78. Dürich, p. 49.
79. Beneš, I, p. 130; and III, pp. 606-607.
80. Pichlík, *Zahraniční odboj,* p. 234.
81. Papoušek, *Carské Rusko,* p. 179.
82. Ibid., p. 180.
83. Tobolka, *Politické dějiny,* IV, p. 183.
84. Dürich, p. 50.
85. Pichlík, *Zahraniční odboj,* p. 191.
86. Beneš, I, p. 66.
87. Dürich, p. 56.
88. Sharp to Lansing, October 22, 1918, FRUS, 1918, Supp. 1, WW, I, pp. 854-855.
89. Dürich, pp. 15-16.
90. Ibid., p. 59.
91. Papoušek, *Carské Rusko,* pp. 180-181; Dürich, p. 51; Beneš, III, p. 608.
92. The names of these people are given in Papoušek, *Carské Rusko,* p. 180, which, however, does not mention Voska's intelligence network in Russia.
93. Ibid., p. 181.
94. Tobolka, *Politické dějiny,* IV, p. 302.
95. Holotík, *Štefánikovská legenda,* p. 173.
96. Ibid., p. 173; *Dokumenty,* ed. Merhout, pp. 41-43 (Štefánik's proclamation); Dr. Josef Kudela, *Profesor Masaryk a československé vojsko na Rusi* [Professor Masaryk and the Czechoslovak Army in Russia] (Prague, 1923), p. 42. This book contains documents on Masaryk's relationship with the Czechoslovak independence movement in Russia. Other documents are printed in Prokop Maxa and Jaroslav Papoušek, *Masarykovy řeči a projevy za války* [Masaryk's Speeches and Addresses During the War] (vols. I and II, Prague, 1920); and Jaroslav Papoušek, *Masaryk a revoluční armáda* [Masaryk and the Revolutionary Army] (Prague, 1922).

97. Tobolka, *Politické dějiny*, IV, p. 184.
98. Papoušek, *Carské Rusko*, pp. 182-86.
99. Tobolka, *Politické dějiny*, p. 184.
100. Masaryk, p. 79.
101. Dürich, pp. 67-68.
102. Ibid., pp. 69-70.
103. Ibid., p. 70.
104. Ibid., p. 72.
105. Masaryk, p. 83, and pp. 236-237; see also *Masaryk a židovství* [Masaryk and Judaism], ed. Dr. E.Rychnovský (Prague, 1931).
106. *Dokumenty*, ed. Merhout, pp. 39-40. Pichlík, *Zahraniční odboj*, pp. 237-38.
107. Masaryk, pp. 79 and 285; Jaroslav Kratochvíl, *Cesta revoluce* [The Way of Revolution] (Prague, 1928), p. 32.
108. *Deník plukovníka Švece*, p. 234.
109. Pichlík, *Zahraniční odboj*, p. 253.
110. The resolution of the congress is in *Dokumenty*, ed. Merhout, pp. 44-47; see also Masaryk, *The Making of a State*, p. 79; Beneš, I, p. 331; Tobolka, *Politické dějiny*, IV, pp. 184-185; Pichlík, *Zahraniční odboj*, p. 240; and Šeba, *Rusko a Malá Dohoda*, pp. 390-391. In April 1917, L. Tuček resigned from all political activity. Dürich, however, was unwilling to give up. In mid-April 1917, he arrived in Kiev along with Crkal and distributed there a leaflet addressed to the "Czech Public." Dürich was barred from the congress. Paradoxically, those who most decried the Dürich council as unrepresentative and undemocratic, now used both undemocratic and unfair methods in order to gain control of the independence movement. See Dürich, pp. 73-74 and 54-60.
111. Jaroslav Křížek, *Jaroslav Hašek v revolučním Rusku* (Prague, 1957), pp. 92-101.
112. Tobolka, *Politické dějiny*, IV, pp. 185-186.
113. Beneš, III, pp. 615-616.
114. *Rech'*, No. 70, March 23, 1917, quoted in *The Russian Provisional Government*, ed. Robert Paul Browder and Alexander Kerensky (Stanford, Calif.: Stanford Univ. Press, 1961), II, p. 1044.
115. *La Nation Tchèque*, II (1923), pp. 366-367, quoted in Syllaba, *Masaryk a revoluce v Rusku*, p. 132.
116. Masaryk, *The Making of a State*, p. 351.

Notes to Chapter Six 547

117. Archiv Vojenského historickeho ústavu, FMV/2; Holotík, *Štefánikovská legenda,* p. 175; National Archives, Department of State File 861.00/1579 Di and 861.00/1601; Antonín Svatopluk Kalina, *Krví a železem dobyto československé samostatnosti* [Czechoslovak Independence Was Won by Blood and Iron] (Prague, 1939), p. 295; also "The Inquiry" (Colonel House Papers), Reports, W. Somerset Maugham, December 7, 1917, Polk Drawer 73.

Chapter Six:
The Spring and Early Summer of 1917, At Home and Abroad

1. Graf Arthur Polzer-Hoditz, *Kaiser Karl* (Vienna, 1928), p. 168. For the emperor's biography see Gordon Brock-Shepherd, *The Last Habsburg* (New York: Weybright and Talley, 1968).
2. Hanak, *Great Britain and Austria-Hungary,* pp. 206ff.
3. Hanak, "The Government," p. 172.
4. *Official Statements of War Aims and Peace Proposals, December 1916 to November 1918,* ed. James Brown Scott (Washington, 1921), pp. 2f. See also Beneš, III, p. 271.
5. FO 371/3134, "Emperor Karl's Letter to Prince Sixte, Proceedings in Regard to a Separate Peace with Austria," p. 1 (a memorandum written by Colonel Sir Maurice Hankey, secretary to the Committee of Imperial Defense and secretary to the War Cabinet, May, 1918); Hanak, "The Government," p. 171.
6. Page to Lansing, February 20, 1917, FRUS, WW, 1917, Supplement, pp. 55ff; and Lansing to Penfield, February 22, 1917, pp. 57ff.
7. Cab. 24/6, G. T., 43, February 12, 1917, and February 17, 1917, Lord Hardinge's minute; Hanak, "The Government," p. 174.
8. National Archives, Department of State File 763.72/5163 1/2; also U.S. Department of State, *The Lansing Papers,* II, pp. 19-32.
9. Hanak, "The Government," p. 184.
10. Ibid., p. 174.
11. National Archives, Department of State File 763.72/5163 1/2; also *The Lansing Papers,* II, pp. 19-32.
12. National Archives, Department of State File 763.5163 1/2; also *The Lansing Papers,* II, pp. 19-32. Also, Cab. 21/77, p. 16, April 28, 1917; Hanak, "The Government," p. 175.

13. See Beneš's memorandum to the French ministry of foreign affairs of December 29, 1916, in Beneš, III, pp. 272ff.
14. Ibid., pp. 279ff and 287ff. The document printed here was entitled: "Presidium of the Alliance of Czech Deputies at Vienna to the Minister of Foreign Affairs, Count Otakar Czernin: The Second Rejection of the Declaration of the Four Powers Alliance for the Liberation of Czechoslovaks from the Foreign Yoke in the Reply to Wilson's Inquiry about the Aims of the War." The first rejection is printed in Beneš, III, pp. 284-286. Both documents were signed by F. Staněk, B. Šmeral, and F. Maštálka. For details see Tobolka, *Politické dějiny*, IV, pp. 216-224.
15. Beneš, II, pp. 552-555.
16. Ibid., I, pp. 249-250.
17. Masaryk, *The Making of a State*, p. 128.
18. Beneš, III, pp. 107-109.
19. Ibid., pp. 117-120.
20. Tobolka, *Politické dějiny*, IV, pp. 223ff; *Dr. Karel Kramář*, ed. Sís, pp. 137-138; and Pichlík, *Zahraniční odboj*, pp. 221-223.
21. Paulová, *Tajný výbor*, pp. 150-151.
22. For a complete text of the memorandum see Otakar Czernin, *Im Weltkriege* (Berlin-Vienna, 1919), pp. 198-204.
23. Paulová, *Tajný výbor*, p. 151; Beneš, I, p. 313.
24. Tobolka, *Politické dějiny*, IV, pp. 230ff; Beneš, I, p. 313.
25. Paulová, *Tajný výbor*, p. 158.
26. Beneš, I, p. 442.
27. Paulová, *Tajný výbor*, p. 159.
28. For documents on Prince Sixtus of Bourbon-Parma and the Armand-Revertera secret negotiations see *Austria's Peace Offer, 1916-1917*, ed. G. de Mantayer (London, 1921).
29. Paulová, *Tajný výbor*, pp. 186-187.
30. Beneš, III, p. 113.
31. Ibid.
32. Ibid., p. 291. Details on its background in Paulová, *Tajný výbor*, pp. 188ff; and Tobolka, *Politické dějiny*, IV, pp. 229ff.
33. Beneš, III, p. 291.
34. Ibid.
35. Ibid.
36. Tobolka, *Politické dějiny*, p. 247.

37. Pichlík, *Zahraniční odboj*, p. 222.
38. Ibid. Also Tobolka, *Politické dějiny*, IV, pp. 223-247.
39. Tobolka, *Politické dějiny*, IV, pp. 297ff.
40. Beneš, III, p. 618.
41. There are numerous books on Lenin and the history of the Russian revolution; among them are a small volume of text and documents by J. S. Curtis, *Russian Revolutions of 1917* (Princeton, N.J., 1957); W. H. Chamberlin, *Russian Revolution*, 1917-1921, 2nd ed., 2 vols. (New York, 1952); Richard E. Pipes, *Formation of the Soviet Union* (Cambridge, Mass., 1954); J. S. Reshetar, *The Ukrainian Revolution, 1917-1920, A Study of Nationalism* (Princeton, N.J., 1952).
42. *Masaryk a revoluční armáda. Masarykovy projevy k legiím a o legiích v zahraniční revoluci* [Masaryk and the Revolutionary Army. Masaryk's Address to the Legion and About the Legion During the Revolution Abroad], ed. Jaroslav Papoušek (Prague, 1922), pp. 41ff. Henceforth cited as *Masaryk a revoluční armáda*.
43. Prof. T. O. Masaryk, *Nachala socialisticheskavo obshchestva*, I., *Revolutsia ili evoliutsia?, S.-Pb.* 1906. *Ot komiteta partii "svobodomysliashchikh," str.* V. (p. 5.)
44. Details of Masaryk's propagandizing are given in Syllaba, *Masaryk a revoluce v Rusku*, pp. 144-203, passim.
45. Report of W. Somerset Maugham, December 7, 1917. Polk Drawer 73, E. M. House Collection (Yale University).
46. *Za Svobodu* [For Freedom], ed. Rudolf Medek *et al.* (4 vols., Prague, 1926-29), II, p. 321.
47. *Masaryk a revoluční armáda*, p. 42.
48. Tobolka, *Politické dějiny*, IV, p. 302; Kalina, *Krví a železem*, p. 156.
49. Vladimír Richter, "Zborovským hrdinům," *Národ* (Chicago), July 8, 1972. Details in Dostál, *Svatý Václav* and *Katolíci;* Navrátil, *Katolicism* and *Svatý Václav;* and Navrátil and Krejčí, *Tradice cyrilometodějská.*
50. Tobolka, *Politické dějiny*, IV, p. 302.
51. Zuman, *Osvobozenecká legenda*, II, p. 79. Cited from *Čechoslovan* (Kiev), April 11 (March 29), 1917. Kerensky, minister of justice in the First Provisional Government, told Vondrák, "I cannot be enthusiastic about that kind of fight carried on by your compatriots in their resistance

to their government. Alas, they had a constitution, they could have declared a revolution while they were still at home.... What did they gain by joining a state which is much worse...?"
    52. *Za Svobodu,* II, pp. 312 and 516; and *Masaryk a revoluční armáda,* pp. 138-139.
    53. Masaryk, p. 161; Holotík, *Štefánikovská legenda,* p. 175.
    54. The battle of Zborov became a legend, and there is an extensive literature on the event. See, among others, Vladimír Klecanda, *Bitva u Zborova* [The Battle of Zborov] (Prague, 1927); Josef Kudela, *U Zborova a po Zborovu* [At Zborov and After Zborov], in *Vojensko-historicky sborník,* vol. I (1933), pp. 120-130; Ludvík Lotocký, *Vídeň–Skobelovo–Zborov* [Vienna–Skobelovo-Zborov] (Brno, 1926); and Jaroslav Papoušek, *Zborov* (Prague, 1921).
    55. Veselý, *Češi a Slováci,* p. 32. Details are in Klecanda, *Bitva u Zborova,* pp. 57 and 122f.
    56. Tobolka, *Politické dějiny,* IV, p. 304.
    57. Ibid., p. 302.
    58. Pichlík, *Zahraniční odboj,* pp. 248-249.
    59. Ibid., p. 291.
    60. Masaryk, pp. 165-167; Beneš, III, pp. 626-629.
    61. *Masaryk a revoluční armáda,* p. 105; Beneš, III, p. 586.
    62. Tobolka, *Politické dějiny,* IV, p. 259. At the same conference Masaryk named two foes of the Czechoslovak independence movement; international capitalism and the Vatican. See Pichlík, *Zahraniční odboj,* p. 255.
    63. FO 371/3134; *War Memoirs,* IV, pp. 1983-2035; Hanak, The Government," p. 178.
    64. Cab. 24/35, G.T., 2976, December 10, 1917; Hanak, "The Government," p. 181.
    65. Hanak, "The Government," p. 181.
    66. Jaroslav Papoušek, *Masaryk a naše revoluční hnutí v Rusku* [Masaryk and Our Revolutionary Movement in Russia] (Prague, 1925), p. 28.
    67. Pichlík, *Zahraniční odboj,* p. 255.
    68. *Masaryk a revoluční armáda,* pp. 95-100.
    69. Syllaba, *Masaryk a revoluce v Rusku,* p. 170.

Notes to Chapter Seven 551

Chapter Seven:
Peace Overtures, Propaganda, and the Building of the Czechoslovak Army

1. On the secret Austro-Allied negotiations and on the Allies' willingness to preserve Austria-Hungary until the summer of 1918, see Prince Sixte de Bourbon, *L'offre de paix séparéé de l'Autriche* (Paris, 1920); David Lloyd George, *War Memoirs* (London, 1934), IV, pp. 1909ff; and Edmund Glaise von Horstenau, *The Collapse of Austro-Hungarian Empire* (London and Toronto, 1930), pp. 51ff. See also *Austria's Peace Offer, 1916-1917*, ed. Mantayer.
2. Wiseman, "Russia" [May 15, 1917], WWP 112; House Diary, May 15, 1917.
3. "Report to Rotenberg," File "R," May 15, 1917, WWP (Wiseman General No. 1).
4. Wiseman, "Russian Affairs," May 26, 1917, WWP 112; also Wiseman to Drummond, memorandum of May 23, 1917, Private Secretary Archives, 1917-1924, A. J. Balfour, FO 800/197; W. B. Fowler, *British-American Relations, 1917-1918: The Role of Sir William Wiseman* (Princeton, N.J.: Princeton University Press, 1969), p. 112; and Voska and Irwin, *Spy and Counter-Spy*, pp. 212-213.
5. Wiseman, "Russia" [n.d., probably early in June 1917], WWP 112.
6. Wiseman, "Russia," May 26, 1917, WWP 112.
7. Private Secretary Archives, 1917-1924, A. J. Balfour, FO 800/197; Fowler, *British-American Relations*, p. 113.
8. Wiseman to Drummond, June 16, 1917, WWP 42; Wiseman to Drummond, June 20, 1917, WWP 42; Drummond to Wiseman, June 26, 1917, WWP 42; Drummond's minute on Wiseman's cable of June 20, 1917, Private Secretary Archives, 1917-1924, A. J. Balfour, FO 800/197; Fowler, *British-American Relations*, p. 113.
9. Wiseman to Drummond, June 20, 1917, WWP 24; Lansing to Wilson, June 8, 1917, National Archives, State Department file 861.00/423-1/2A; Polk to McAdoo, July 16, 1917, Polk Papers.
10. Wiseman, "Committee, of Slav Origin, for Russia," June 30, 1917, WWP, File "S."
11. Ibid.
12. *Carské Rusko*, ed. Papoušek, p. 157.

13. Veselý, Češi a Slováci, p. 19.
14. Holotík, Štefánikovská legenda, p. 173. Tobolka, Politické dějiny, p. 302, gives different, but only partial figures.
15. Veselý, Češi a Slováci, p. 31.
16. Wiseman, "Russian Matters," July 12, 1917, WWP 112.
17. Wiseman, Code names for the Maugham-Voska expedition, July 19, 1917, WWP, File "B."
18. Irwin and Voska, Spy and Counter-Spy, p. 187.
19. Receipts from Voska for $1,200 and $2,800 of July 16 and 21, 1917, respectively, in WWP 112.
20. W. Somerset Maugham, The Summing Up (London, 1938), pp. 203-204.
21. W. Somerset Maugham, Reports, December 7, 1917, WWP, Polk Drawer 73.
22. Ibid.
23. Irwin and Voska, Spy and Counter-Spy, pp. 191 and 194; Voska, "Memoirs," Jas (1935, Nos. 7 and 10); also Masaryk, Světová revoluce, p. 160; and Šeba, Rusko a Malá dohoda, pp. 381-382.
24. Irwin and Voska, Spy and Counter-Spy, p. 191.
25. Ibid., p. 198.
26. Ibid.
27. Report of Alois B. Koukol to the Bohemian National Alliance, Chicago, Ill., dated New York, March 20, 1918, WWP 114.
28. WWP 102.
29. Report of Alois B. Koukol to the Bohemian National Alliance, March 20, 1918, WWP 114.
30. Holotík, Štefánikovská legenda, p. 183. While in the United States, Štefánik addressed several meetings attended by his countrymen. Dürich's daughter, the wife of the writer Karel Horký, came to one of these meetings with a horsewhip, intending to make a scene and to beat the general up for slandering her father. When Štefánik learned about the presence of Dürich's daughter, he abruptly left the hall through the back door. Subsequently, she published a leaflet describing the incident and denouncing the general.
31. Tobolka, Politické dějiny, p. 294; Beneš (I, p. 347) gives the figure 2,500.
32. Martínek, "Jak jsme to dělali," in Padesát let, p. 54. Martínek

Notes to Chapter Seven 553

gives the same figure on volunteers for service in the French armed forces as Tobolka does.
33. Masaryk, *The Making of a State,* p. 166; and Beneš, I, pp. 349-351.
34. Beneš, II, pp. 36-74.
35. Ibid.
36. Pichlík, *Zahraniční odboj,* p. 262; details in Rajchl, *Štefánik,* pp. 129ff; and Juríček, *M. R. Štefánik,* pp. 126ff.
37. Beneš, I, pp. 374-388. Space limitation does not allow giving more attention to Italy. The most detailed study on the Czech and Slovak prisoners of war in Italy and the formation of the Czechoslovak army in Italy is Jindřich Kretší, *Vznik a vývoj československé legie v Italii* [The Origin and Development of the Czechoslovak Legion in Italy] (Prague, 1928). Another lengthy work is František Hlaváček, *Dr. Edvard Beneš a Italie za světové války* [Dr. Edvard Beneš and Italy During the World War] (Prague, 1936). On the activity of First Lieutenant "Testolini" Hlaváček's alias in the Italian army, see also the symposium *František Hlaváček* (Prague, 1927) and articles in *La Nazione* (Florence), May 23, 1973, and *La Stampa* (Turin), May 22, 1973. A shorter study is Miroslav Lokay, *Československá Legie v Italii* [The Czechoslovak Legion in Italy] (New York, 1970).
38. Beneš, III, pp. 307-309.
39. *Masaryk a revoluční armáda,* pp. 108-117; Masaryk, pp. 167-169; Beneš, III, pp. 626-629.
40. Report dated September 1 [1917]. OS.14 NS, WWP 112. See also Wiseman, "Summary of Reports received from Agent in Petrograd, under date of September 11," HP 20:45; Maugham to Wiseman, September 14, 1917, WWP 112; Wiseman to Drummond, September 24, 1917, WWP 42. See also the fictionalized account of Maugham's escapade in Petrograd in *Ashenden, or the British Agent* (New York, 1927), pp. 293-295.
41. Maugham's report of September 1, 1917, WWP 112.
42. Fowler, *British-American Relations,* p. 116.
43. *The Russian Provisional Government,* ed. Browder and Kerensky, III, pp. 1625-1627.
44. Wiseman, "Intelligence & Propaganda Work in Russia July to December 1917," January 19, 1918, WWP 113; Private Secretary Archives, 1917-1924, A. J. Balfour, FO 800/197; see also Maugham, *The Summing Up,* p. 205; and Fowler, *British-American Relations,* p. 117.

45. *Istoriya diplomatii,* ed. V. P. Potemkin (Moscow, 1945), II, p. 302.
46. Pichlík, *Zahraniční odboj,* pp. 266-267; see also Klecanda, *Bitva u Zborova,* p. 122.
47. František Koza, "Jak uprchl gen. Kornilov z rakouského zajetí" [How General Kornilov Escaped from Austrian Captivity] and Josef Laube on the same subject in *Domov za války* [Home During the War], ed. Alois Žípek (Prague, 1929), pp. 64-73. See also Nikolaj Alexandrovič Chodorović, *Odbojové hnutí a československé vojsko v Rusku (1914-1917)* [The Resistance Movement and the Czechoslovak Army in Russia (1914-1917)], trans. (from Russian) Jiří Třeťjakov (Prague, 1928), pp. 118-191.
48. *Masaryk a revoluční armáda,* pp. 63-64; see also Kvasnička, *Československé légie,* p. 42.
49. V. Sidorin, *Ruské armádní velitelství a Zborov* [The Russian Army Command and Zborov] (Prague, 1937), p. 31.
50. Zuman, *Osvobozenecká legenda,* II, p. 125.
51. V. Najbrt, *Rozlet a rozlom sibiřského bratrství* [The Launching and the Breakup of the Siberian Brotherhood] (Prague, n.d.), p. 23.
52. Wiseman, "Russia" [May 15, 1917], WWP, 112.
53. *Masaryk a revoluční armáda,* p. 42; also pp. 115 and 116.
54. *Čechoslovák,* September 15, 1917.
55. *Československý voják,* October 11, 1917.
56. Ibid.
57. Beneš, III, pp. 626-629.
58. *Masaryk a revoluční armáda,* pp. 117-120.
59. Masaryk, *The Making of a State,* p. 186; see also K. J. Vopička, *Taje Balkánu* (Prague, 1927), p. 149.
60. Masaryk, *The Making of a State,* p. 187; Syllaba, *Masaryk a revoluce v Rusku,* p. 188.
61. Masaryk, *The Making of a State,* p. 186; and Syllaba, *Masaryk a revoluce v Rusku,* p. 188. During his journey to Romania, Masaryk's adjutant was Jan Šeba; the latter writes how, under various pretexts, Masaryk refused to bring the army to the Romanian front. See Šeba, *Rusko a Malá dohoda,* pp. 415-416.
62. Beneš, III, pp. 316-317.

Notes to Chapter Eight 555

Chapter Eight:
The Bolshevik Revolution

1. There is an abundant literature on the Bolshevik Revolution. (1) Among the documentary collections are FRUS, 1918, Russia, 3 vols.; FRUS, *The Lansing Papers, 1914-1920,* 2 vols.; *Dekrety sovetskoi vlasti,* Vol. I, October 25, 1917-March 16, 1918 (Moscow, 1957); *Dokumenty vneshnei politiki SSSR,* vols. I and II (Moscow, 1959). See also French documents relating to the Czechoslovak Legion in Russia in Vlastimil Vávra, *Klamná cesta. Příprava a vznik protisovětského vystoupení čs. legií* [The False Way. Preparations for and Origins of the Anti-Soviet Uprising of the Czechoslovak Legion] (Prague, 1958); and Vlastimil Vávra, "Podíl francouzské politiky na vzniku protisovětského vysoupení čs. legií v Rusku" [The Role Played by French Politics in the Origins of the Anti-Soviet Uprising of the Czechoslovak Legion in Russia], *Historie a vojenství* (Prague, 1964), No. 3, pp. 479-498. (2) Among the memoirs relevant to the revolution are D. R. Francis, *Russia from the American Embassy* (New York, 1921); Sir George Buchanan, *My Mission to Russia and Other Diplomatic Memories,* 2 vols. (London, 1923); Joseph Noulens, *Mon Ambassade en Russie Sovietique, 1917-1919,* 2 vols. (Paris, 1922); Sir Arthur Knox, *With the Russian Army, 1914-1917* (London, 1921); R. B. Lockhart, *Memoirs of a British Agent* (London, 1932); J. Sadoul, *Notes sur la Révolution bolchévique* (Paris, 1919). (3) Among interpretations of the events are George F. Kennan, *Soviet-American Relations, 1917-1920,* 2 vols. (London, 1958); Richard H. Ullman, *Anglo-Soviet Relations, 1917-1920: Intervention and War* (Princeton, 1960); and *Istoriia diplomatii,* ed. V. P. Potemkin, vol. II (Moscow 1945).

2. Tobolka, *Politické dějiny,* IV, p. 309.
3. Documentation is cited in Kvasnička, *Československé légie v Rusku,* p. 59.
4. *Masaryk a revoluční armáda,* pp. 142-152, 169, and 183.
5. Irwin and Voska, *Spy and Counter-Spy,* p. 198.
6. *Čechoslovák,* July 3, 1917; *Masaryk a revoluční armáda,* p. 56.
7. *Čechoslovák,* June 23, 1917; Pichlík, *Zahraniční odboj,* pp. 248-249.
8. *Boj o směr vývoje československého státu* [Struggle for the Direction of Development of the Czechoslovak State], ed. A. Kocman, V. Pletka,

J. Radimský, M. Trantírek, and L. Urbánková (Prague, 1965), I, p. 69. Also *Staroslovan,* Nos. 9 and 10, 1921, cited in Zuman, *Osvobozenecká legenda,* II, pp. 115-116.

9. *Documents of Russian History,* ed. Golder, pp. 646-648; *The Russian Provisional Government,* ed. Browder and Kerensky, II, pp. 1128-1130.

10. Text in *The Russian Provisional Government,* ed. Browder and Kerensky, II, pp. 1152-1159; a photocopy of the article is attached to Syllaba, *Masaryk a revoluce v Rusku,*

11. *Masaryk a revoluční armáda,* pp. 79, 90, 97, 118, and 162.

12. *Čas,* May 18, 1909. On January 9, 1913, at a conference of workers of his political party, he declared, "I would like to formulate the Austrian problem for Austria and for us Czechs as follows: If a German can be Austrian, why could not a Slav, let us say a Serb, be Austrian? We all want equality and equal rights, we all want freedom in Austria, and then we will have no reason to leave Austria in the foreseeable future." *Čas,* No. 8, 1913. Klofáč, who had been arrested in 1914, was elected chairman of the Club of the Czech Deputies at Vienna upon his return from prison, and *The Times* (London) expressed its delight on June 2, 1917; see also *Daily Chronicle,* June 4, 1917. The amnesty for Kramář and his subsequent release from prison was noticed by virtually all leading newspapers.

13. A photocopy of the entire article is attached to Syllaba, *Masaryk a revoluce v Rusku,* with a Czech translation and a Marxist analysis of the article on pp. 200-205.

14. Memorandum of T. G. Masaryk to Secretary of State Lansing, "The Situation in Russia and the Military Help of the Allies and the United States, August 28, 1918," Department of State File 763.72/11171-1/2.

15. Masaryk's memorandum to Chicherin, FRUS, 1918, Russia, II, pp. 224-226.

16. Ibid.

17. Masaryk's Tokyo memorandum, April 10, 1918, in Masaryk, *The Making of a State,* pp. 201-205.

18. *Masaryk a revoluční armáda,* pp. 104-105.

19. Ibid., p. 119.

20. Ibid., p. 148.

21. Beneš, III, p. 629.

Notes to Chapter Eight 557

22. *Masaryk a revoluční armáda*, p. 142.
23. Dürich, pp. 77-78; Švec, pp. 278-286; Pichlík, *Zahraniční odboj*, p. 297.
24. Pichlík, *Zahraniční odboj*, p. 339.
25. Ibid., p. 298.
26. Ibid.; Kvasnička, *Československé légie v Rusku*, p. 61; Veselý, *Češi a Slováci*, pp. 59-60; and Masaryk, p. 190.
27. Dürich, pp. 77-78.
28. Ibid., p. 78.
29. Ibid.; Pichlík, *Zahraniční odboj*, p. 299; Syllaba, *Masaryk a revoluce v Rusku*, p. 218.
30. *Masaryk a revoluční armáda*, pp. 141ff.
31. Ibid., pp. 142-144.
32. On the "Kiev incident" see *Za svobodu*, III, pp. 597-615; and *Borba za vlast Sovetov na Kieevshchine* (Kiev, 1957), pp. 378-379. See also Richard Pipes, *The Formation of the Soviet Union* (Cambridge, Mass., 1954), pp. 118ff.
33. Dürich, p. 78.
34. Pichlík, *Zahraniční odboj*, pp. 300-301; Veselý, *Češi a Slováci*, p. 64.
35. Pichlík, *Zahraniční odboj*, p. 314.
36. British Foreign Office Memorandum of November 12, 1917, cited in Ullman, *Anglo-Soviet Relations*, p. 3; S. Melgunov, *Kak bolsheviki zakhvatili vlast* (Paris, 1953), p. 184; Noulens, *Mon Ambassade en Russie Sovietique*, p. 128.
37. FO Milner, Box AE-2, Memorandum of November 19, 1917; J. F. N. Bradley, "The Allies and Russia in the Light of French Archives (7 November 1917-15 March 1918)," *Soviet Studies*, XVI, No. 2 (October 1964), p. 173.
38. Ullman, *Anglo-Soviet Relations*, p. 42; see also Fowler, *British-American Relations*, pp. 117-118.
39. Kratochvíl, *Cesta revoluce*, pp. 34 and 31-32. See also K. J. Vopička, *Taje Balkánu* [Mysteries of the Balkans] (Prague, 1927), pp. 142, 151, and 158. Vopička was U.S. minister to the Romanian government at Jassy.
40. A memorandum of November 19, 1917, WWP 112; Fowler, *British-American Relations*, pp. 117-118. Also Colonel House Diary, November 20, 1917; and Auchincloss Diary, November 20. 1917.

41. Hankey Memorandum, quoted in Ullman, *Anglo-Soviet Relations*, p. 46.
42. Ibid.
43. Masaryk, *The Making of a State*, pp. 220-222. See also The Secretary of State to President Wilson and Draft Telegram to the Ambassador in Great Britain (Page), United States Department of State, FRUS, *The Lansing Papers, 1914-1920*, 2 vols. (Washington, 1939-1940), II, pp. 343-346, hereafter cited as *Lansing Papers*.
44. Dürich, pp. 79 and 84.
45. Ibid., p. 84.
46. Ibid.
47. Telegram of General Janin and Bohdan Pavlů to the Czechoslovak government, Omsk, January 23, 1919 (sent through French diplomatic channels); French original and a Czech translation in Holotík, *Štefánikovská legenda*, pp. 496-497.
48. Kvasnička, *Československé légie*, pp. 66-67; Chodorović, *Odbojové hnutí*, pp. 124,, 123, and 218; Šteidler, *Československé hnutí*, pp. 23 and 42; Zuman, *Osvobozenecká legenda*, I, pp. 50 and 114; Navrátil, *Sv. Václav a československé legie*, pp. 5-6; Žampach, *Katolíci v zahraničních bojích*, p. 40; Blažej Ráček, *Československé dějiny* [Czechoslovak History] (Prague, 1929), p. 636.
49. *Masaryk a revoluční armáda*, p. 193.
50. Ibid., p. 212.
51. Ibid., pp. 142-154; T. G. Masaryk, "Naše situace" [Our Situation], *Československý voják*, December 6 (Nov. 23), 1917; *Za svobodu*, II, pp. 622ff; Syllaba, *Masaryk a revoluce v Rusku*, pp. 210ff; and Pichlík, *Zahraniční odboj*, pp. 307-308.
52. Masaryk, *The Making of a State*, p. 185.
53. Kudela, *Profesor Masaryk a čs. vojsko na Rusi*, p. 136; Syllaba, *Masaryk a revoluce v Rusku*, pp. 212-215; and Pichlík, *Zahraniční odboj*, p. 307.
54. Ibid.; *Za svobodu*, II, pp. 627-628.
55. Details in Pipes, *The Formation of the Soviet Union*, pp. 119ff.
56. Michael Hrushevsky, *A History of the Ukraine* (New Haven, 1941), pp. 530-536.
57. Ibid., pp. 536-540. For Masaryk's account of the events see *Masaryk a revoluční armáda*, pp. 193-203.

58. Winston Churchill, *The World Crisis, 1918-1928. The Aftermath* (New York, 1929), pp. 81-82.

59. Ibid., p. 167. For the text of the convention see Louis Fischer, *The Soviets in World Affairs: A History of the Relations Between the Soviet Union and the Rest of the World, 1917-1929* (London, 1930; 2nd ed., Princeton, 1951), vol. I, p. 836.

60. Masaryk, p. 189; see also Veselý, *Češi a Slováci*, p. 64.

61. Kudela, *Profesor Masaryk a československé vojsko na Rusi*, pp. 159-160.

62. Kratochvíl, *Cesta revoluce*, p. 32; see also F. Popov, *Checho-slovackii miatezh i samarskaiia uchredilka* (Samara, 1932), p. 25; and Vopička, *Taje Balkánu*, p. 149.

63. For details see diplomatic communications in FRUS, 1917, 2, II, pp. 344, 457-458, 459-470, 471, 473; and FRUS, 1918, p. 751. See also Kalina, *Krví a železem*, pp. 110-114.

64. Bradley, "The Allies and Russia," *Soviet Studies*, p. 182.

65. Jusserand to Lansing, January 16, 1918, FRUS, 1918, p. 751; Kalina, *Krví a železem*, p. 113.

66. Kalina, *Krví a železem*, pp. 112-114; Bradley, "The Allies and Russia," *Soviet Studies*, p. 182; and Masaryk, *The Making of a State*, pp. 220-222.

67. Beneš, III, pp. 631-632.

68. Pichlík, *Zahraniční odboj*, p. 312.

69. *Masaryk a revoluční armáda*, pp. 195-196.

70. Vávra, *Klamná cesta*, pp. 110-115.

71. Kudela, *Profesor Masaryk a československé vojsko na Rusi*, p. 166; also Beneš, III, pp. 631-632; and Syllaba, *Masaryk a revoluce v Rusku*, p. 219.

72. *Masaryk a revoluční armáda*, p. 197.

73. Ibid.

74. Ibid., p. 200.

75. Ibid., p. 197.

76. Ibid., p. 198.

77. Ibid., pp. 199-200.

Chapter Nine:
The Czech Bolshevik Attempt to Control the Army Corps,
the Retreat from the Ukraine, and the Peace of Brest-Litovsk

1. T. G. Masaryk, "The Situation in Russia and the Military Help of the Allies and the United States, August 28, 1918, a memorandum addressed to U.S. Secretary of State Lansing; National Archives, Department of State File 763.72/11171-1/2, p. 15; Kvasnička, *Československé légie v Rusku*, pp. 79-82; Vávra, *Klamná cesta*, pp. 112-113 and 119; and Holotík, *Štefánikovská legenda*, p. 176.
2. Kvasnička, *Československé légie v Rusku*, p. 321.
3. Ibid.
4. *Svoboda*, October 19, 1917, quoted in Veselý, *Češi a Slováci*, p. 46. The newspaper's political orientation was indicated in an editorial published in the first issue: "The Russian revolution is the beginning of the great socialist and proletarian revolution that will continue in the rest of the world..." (p. 49). See also Jindřich Veselý, *O vzniku a založení KSČ* [On the Origins and Founding of the Communist Party of Czechoslovakia] (Prague, 1953), pp. 50-51.
5. Pichlík, *Zahraniční odboj*, p. 315.
6. Veselý, *Češi a Slováci*, p. 50; and Veselý, *O vzniku a založení KSČ*, pp. 50-51.
7. Ibid., pp. 53 and 51 respectively.
8. Veselý, *Češi a Slováci*, pp. 51-54; the resolutions of the conference are printed on pp. 201-204.
9. Ibid., p. 50.
10. Ibid., pp. 80-81; see also p. 49.
11. Ibid., pp. 78-80.
12. Kudela, *Professor Masaryk a čs. vojsko na Rusi*, p. 166; see also *Masaryk a revoluční armáda*, p. 155.
13. Masaryk, *The Making of a State*, p. 177; and Beneš, III, pp. 632-633.
14. Beneš, III, p. 633.
15. *Masaryk a revoluční armáda*, p. 193.
16. Ibid., p. 200.
17. Pichlík, *Zahraniční odboj*, p. 329.
18. *Masaryk a revoluční armáda*, pp. 187-193.
19. Šteidler, *Československé hnutí na Rusi*, p. 55.

Notes to Chapter Nine 561

20. Vávra, *Klamná cesta*, p. 128-129; Masaryk, *Světová revoluce*, p. 217.
21. Pichlík, *Zahraniční odboj*, p. 335.
22. Ibid., p. 337; see also Veselý, *Češi a Slováci*, pp. 84-85; and Veselý, *O vzniku*, pp. 52-53.
23. Masaryk, pp. 176-177; Veselý, *Češi a Slováci*, p. 86; and *Masaryk a revoluční armáda*, p. 200.
24. Veselý, *O vzniku*, p. 52.
25. Ibid., p. 54.
26. *Masaryk a revoluční armáda*, p. 201.
27. Ibid., p. 202.
28. W. Somerset Maugham, *A Writer's Notebook* (New York, 1949), p. 185; Wiseman's memorandum dated November 19, 1917, WWP 112.
29. *Dokumenty o protilidové a protinárodní politice T. G. Masaryka* [Documents on the Anti-People's and Anti-National Policy of T. G. Masaryk], ed. František Nečásek, Jan Pachta, and Eva Raisová (Prague, 1953), p. 13.
30. Ibid., pp. 13-14 and 15-20; also Louis Fischer, *Soviets dans les Affaires Mondiales* (Paris, 1933), p. 95; Šeba, *Rusko a Malá Dohoda*, p. 445; Masaryk, *Světová revoluce*, pp. 234-235; and General A. Denikine, *The White Army*, trans. Catherine Zvegintzov (Gulf Breeze, Florida, 1973), p. 138.
31. Veselý, *O vzniku a založení KSČ*, pp. 61-62. Masaryk writes that he had great difficulty in changing the £80,000 he had received from the British. See Masaryk, *The Making of a State*, p. 197.
32. Ministère de la Guerre, *Russie*, Niesse to War Minister, February 18, 1918; J. F. N. Bradley, "The Allies and the Czech Revolt against the Bolsheviks in 1918," *The Slavonic and East European Review*, XLIII, No. 101 (June 1965), pp. 275-292; Masaryk, *Světová revoluce*, p. 233; F. Šíp, *Několik kapitol o hospodářství naší sibiřské armády* (Prague, 1926), pp. 68ff; Kvasnička, *Československé légie v Rusku*, pp. 79-80.
33. Masaryk, *Světová revoluce*, p. 235.
34. *Masaryk a revoluční armáda*, pp. 202-208.
35. Beneš, III, p. 625.
36. *Masaryk a revoluční armáda*, p. 208.
37. For French documents on Štefánik's mission in Italy, see Holotík, *Štefánikovská legenda*, pp. 442-456; see also Beneš, III, pp. 337-339.

38. See *František Hlaváček* (a symposium).
39. John W. Wheeler-Bennet, *Brest-Litovsk, the Forgotten Peace, March 1918* (London, 1938), text of the treaty, pp. 403ff. The book discusses in great detail the peace negotiations.

Chapter Ten:
The Home Front, Congresses in Rome and Prague, and the Increasing Importance of the Army Abroad

1. Tobolka, *Politické dějiny*, IV, p. 258.
2. Soukup, *28. Říjen 1918*, I, pp. 442 and 467. For details see Paulová, *Tajný výbor*, pp. 275ff. See also Polzer-Hoditz, *Kaiser Karl*, pp. 303ff.
3. Victor Mamatey, "The Union of Czech Political Parties in the Reichsrat, 1916-1918," in *The Habsburg Empire in World War I*, ed. R. A. Kann, B. K. Király, and P. S. Fichtner. East European Monographs No. 23 (Boulder, Colo., 1977), pp. 20-22.
4. Paulová, *Tajný výbor*, p. 317; details in Tobolka, *Politické dějiny*, IV, pp. 271ff.
5. The document is in Beneš, III, pp. 318-321; for details see Paulová, *Tajný výbor*, pp. 372-390; and Tobolka, *Politické dějiny*, IV, pp. 313ff.
6. Wheeler-Bennet, *Brest-Litovsk, the Forgotten Peace*, p. 121; and *Offical Statements of War Aims*, ed. Scott, p. 221.
7. Details in Tobolka, *Politické dějiny*, IV, pp. 313ff.
8. "The Imperial and Royal Minister of Foreign Affairs, Count Czernin: Address to a Delegation of the Council of Vienna, April 2, 1918," FRUS, Supp. 1, WW, I, pp. 194-195; also *Official Statements of War Aims*, ed. Scott, pp. 298ff.
9. Masaryk, *The Making of a State*, p. 217.
10. Tobolka, *Politické dějiny*, IV, pp. 322ff. Austria-Hungary's economic breakdown is discussed in Gustav Gratz and Richard Schüller, *Der Wirtschaftliche Zusammenbruch Österreich-Ungarns* (Vienna, 1930).
11. Paulová, *Tajný výbor*, p. 420.
12. Ibid.
13. Beneš, III, p. 664.
14. Paulová, *Tajný výbor*, p. 428.

Notes to Chapter Ten 563

15. Complete text in Beneš, III, pp. 327-329; and Soukup, *28. říjen 1918*, II, pp. 656-658. Details in Soukup, pp. 655-656; and Paulová, *Tajný výbor*, pp. 429-434.
16. Paulová, *Tajný výbor*, p. 434.
17. Polzer-Hoditz, *Kaiser Karl*, p. 559.
18. For details and background of the U.S. declaration of war on Austria-Hungary see Mamatey, *The United States and East-Central Europe, 1914-1918*, p. 160. This book is a study of Wilsonian diplomacy and propaganda as related to east central Europe during the years 1914-1918.
19. *The Times* (London), January 7, 1918.
20. For a complete text of Lloyd George's speech of January 5, 1918, see his *War Memoirs*, V, or FRUS, 1918, supp. 1, I, pp. 4-12. For a complete text of the January 8, 1918, "Fourteen Points" speech of President Wilson, see FRUS, 1918, supp. 1, I, pp. 12-17, or Lloyd George, *Memoirs of the Peace Conference*, I, pp. 37-38. Details of the secret negotiations between Austria-Hungary and the Allies are in Glaise-Horstenau, *Die Katastrophe*, pp. 85ff; and Lloyd George, *War Memoirs*, pp. 246ff.
21. Details in Hanak, *Great Britain and Austria-Hungary During the First World War*, pp. 238ff.
22. Masaryk's memorandum of July 20, 1918, FRUS, Supp. 1, WW, I, p. 818.
23. Tobolka, *Politické dějiny*, IV, p. 25.
24. Details in Beneš, II, pp. 9-34; the decree was published in *Journal Officiel de la République Francaise*, December 19, 1917, p. 10379; a translation is in *The Birth of Czechoslovakia*, ed. Ješina, p. 20.
25. Pichlík, *Zahraniční odboj*, p. 358.
26. On the situation in Italy and the negotiations about the establishment of a Czechoslovak army there see Beneš, II, pp. 38ff; Holotík, *Štefánikovská legenda*, pp. 191-212; and František Bednařík, *V Boj! Obrázková kronika čs. revolučního hnutí v Italii* [Forward to Struggle! A Chronicle of the Czechoslovak Revolutionary Movement in Italy in Pictures] (Prague, 1927).
27. Details in Kretší, *Vznik a vývoj československé legie v Italii*, pp. 135-147.
28. For citations of government documentary materials see Holotík, *Štefánikovská legenda*, pp. 203ff, with compete texts of French documents on pp. 448-455.

29. *The Birth of Czechoslovakia*, ed. Ješina, p. 25; on the congress see Beneš, II, pp. 105ff; Tobolka, *Politické dějiny*, IV, pp. 355ff.
30. For the specific demands contained in the confidential resolutions addressed to the Allied governments see Page (Rome) to Lansing, April 12, 1918, FRUS, 1918, Supp. 1, I, pp. 796-797.
31. Beneš, III, pp. 337-339; see also Page to Lansing, May 7, 1918, FRUS, 1918, Supp. 1, I, pp. 802-803; and Page to Wilson, May 7, 1918, *The Lansing Papers*, II, pp. 122-123.
32. Beneš, II, p. 72; also Tobolka, *Politické dějiny*, pp. 355ff.
33. Polzer-Hoditz, *Kaiser Karl*, pp. 376 and 559. Details in Robert A. Kann, *Die Sixtusaffäre* (Vienna, 1966).
34. Robert Lansing, *War Memoirs of Robert Lansing, Secretary of State* (New York, 1935), p. 266; on the Sixtus affair see pp. 264 and 265-266.
35. Ibid., p. 263.
36. Ibid., p. 266.
37. Ibid.
38. Ibid., pp. 266-267.
39. Glaise-Horstenau, *Die Katastrophe*, p. 130; also *Official Statements of War Aims*, ed. Scott, p. 320.
40. Page to Lansing and Page to Wilson, *The Lansing Papers*, II, pp. 122ff.
41. Beneš, III, pp. 154f.
42. Paulová, *Tajný výbor*, p. 456.
43. For detailed discussions of the events at Prague see Paulová, *Tajný výbor*, pp. 454-465, and Tobolka, *Politické dějiny*, pp. 358ff.
44. Sís, *Dr. Karel Kramář*, p. 147.
45. Ibid., p. 148.
46. Stovall to Lansing, FRUS, Supp. 1. WW, I, pp. 806-807.
47. Frazier to Lansing, ibid., pp. 807-808.
48. *Nation*, March 23, 1918.
49. For details of the arguments and counterarguments in the British press see Hanak, *Great Britain and Austria-Hungary*, pp. 255-261.
50. Beneš, III, pp. 342-357.
51. Pichlík, *Zahraniční odboj*, p. 370.
52. Beneš, II, pp. 208-209 and 212-214.
53. Ibid., p. 211.

54. Kalina, *Krví a železem*, p. 190.
55. Beneš, III, pp. 162-164.
56. Ibid., p. 164.
57. Ibid., pp. 144-146.

Chapter Eleven:
Masaryk's Journey to America

1. Memorandum on the Proposed Japanese Military Expedition into Siberia, March 18, 1918, Lansing Papers; Lansing's confidential communication to U.S. embassies at London and Paris of February 13, 1918; and Francis to Lansing, March 9, 1918, 861.00/1264, Breckinridge Long Papers. Lansing's Desk Diaries evidence the U.S. government preoccupation with the question of Japanese intervention in Siberia; excerpts from the Breckinridge Long Diary pertaining to the events in Siberia between January 10 and November 6, 1918, are contained in *Siberia*, Breckinridge Long Papers. For the British view see Winston S. Churchill, *The World Crisis. The Aftermath* (London, 1921), pp. 89-90; and Ullman, *Anglo-Soviet Relations*, pp. 128-130.
2. Milner Papers, Box B (New College, Oxford), quoted in J. F. N. Bradley, "The Allies and the Czech Revolt against the Bolsheviks in 1918," *The Slavonic and East European Review*, XLIII, No. 1 (June 1965), p. 280; Foch to Lavergne, March 21, 1918, in Vávra, "Francouzské dokumenty," p. 479. The documents published by Vávra came from the archives of the Czechoslovak ministry of foreign affairs; the French ministry of war kept Beneš informed on developments that might affect the Czechoslovaks in Russia; and Beneš published some of these documents himself.
3. Foch to Lavergne, March 21, 1918, quoted in Vávra, "Francouzské dokumenty," p. 479; Bradley, "The Allies," p. 281.
4. Panouse to War Minister, April 1, 1918; Ministère de la Guerre, *Angleterre*, Panouse to War Minister, April 2, 1918; Vávra, "Francouzské dokumenty," p. 482; Bradley, "The Allies," pp. 283-284; Ullman, *Anglo-Soviet Relations*, pp. 153-155; Beneš, III, pp. 636-637.
5. Vávra, "Francouzské dokumenty," p. 482; Bradley, "The Allies," p. 284.
6. French Consul at Vladivostok to Quai d'Orsay, April 6, 1918; Vávra, "Francouzské dokumenty," p. 482; Bradley, "The Allies," p. 286.

7. Dr. František Šteidler, *Naše vystoupení v Rusku r. 1918* [Our Rising in Russia in 1918] (Prague, 1923), p. 74.
8. Ibid.
9. Clemenceau to Panouse, April 7, 1918; Vávra, "Francouzské dokumenty," p. 483-484; Bradley, "The Allies," p. 276.
10. Lavergne to War Minister, April 9, 1918; Vávra, "Francouzské dokumenty," p. 484; Bradley, "The Allies," p. 287.
11. Milner–Folder 33, General Spears to War Office, April 16, 1918; Bradley, "The Allies," p. 287.
12. Ibid.
13. Sharp to Lansing, April 22, 1918, FRUS, 1918, pp. 149-150.
14. War Minister to Lavergne, April 26, 1918; Vávra, "Francouzské dokumenty," p. 486; Bradley, "The Allies," p. 288.
15. Lansing to Morris, March 29, 1918, FRUS, Russia, II, p. 92.
16. Jusserand to Lansing, March 24, 1918, FRUS, 1918, p. 132.
17. C. K. Cumming and W. W. Pettit, *Russian-American Relations* (New York, 1920), p. 119, cited in Kalina, *Krví a železem*, p. 164.
18. Francis to Lansing, April 2, 1918, FRUS, Russia, I, p. 491.
19. Morris to Lansing, April 13, 1918, FRUS, 1918, Russia, II, p. 122.
20. Ibid.
21. Masaryk, *The Making of a State*, pp. 201-205; the same memorandum was sent to the British Foreign Office; see Seton-Watson, *Masaryk in England*, pp. 108-112.
22. Beneš, II, pp. 186-187.
23. Ibid., p. 187.
24. Kalina, *Krví a železem*, p. 193; Zuman, *Osvobozenecká legenda*, II, 115ff; Lazarevský, *Rusko a československé znovuzrození*, p. 148; *Vondrák contra Masaryk*, passim.
25. Beneš, II, p. 180; also Pichlík, *Zahraniční odboj*, p. 380.
26. Beneš, II, p. 181.
27. Memorandum of May 9, 1918, "Slavs of Austria-Hungary," Lansing to Wilson, August 21, 1918, enclosures, National Archives, Department of State File. Kalina, *Krví a železem*, pp. 130-131; Victor S. Mamatey, "(Documents) The United States Recognition of the Czechoslovak National Council of Paris (September 3, 1918)," *Journal of Central European Affairs*, XIII, No. 1 (April, 1953), pp. 47-60.

Notes to Chapter Eleven 567

28. Šindelář, *Z boje za svobodu*, pp. 58-64, 135, and 70-78.
29. Details in Karel Pergler, *Amerika a československá nezávislost* [America and Czechoslovak Independence] (Prague, 1926); and Karel Pergler, *America in the Struggle for Czechoslovak Independence* (Philadelphia, 1926).
30. Wiseman, "Propaganda and Intelligence-Czecho-Slav-Cum-Pole Scheme," n.d., WWP.
31. Ibid.
32. Wiseman to Auchincloss, January 26, 1918, WWP.
33. Irwin and Voska, *Spy and Counter-Spy*, p. 5.
34. Wiseman to Murray, June 8, 1918, Wiseman, General, WWP.
35. Hugh and Christopher Seton-Watson, *The Making of a New Europe*, pp. 184 and 199; for details see Steed, *Through Thirty Years*, II, pp. 185-216; Campbell Stuart, *The Secrets of Crewe House* (London, 1920); Reginald Pound and Geoffrey Harmsworth, *Northcliffe* (London, 1959), pp. 656-667; and *Jas* X, (1934, No. 42; and IX, 1935, Nos. 22, 23, and 25).
36. Čulen, *Pittsburghská Dohoda*, p. 177; the whole document is in Beneš, III, pp. 365-366; Mikuš, *Slovakia*, pp. 331-332; and Lettrich, *Modern Slovakia*, pp. 289-290. See also Mamatey, *The United States and East Central Europe*, p. 283.
37. Masaryk, *The Making of a State*, pp. 220-221. Masaryk is mistaken when he writes that he signed the document on June 30, 1918.
38. Čulen, *Pittsburghská Dohoda*, p. 413; Tobolka, *Politické dějiny*, IV, p. 296; Sidor, *Slováci v zahraničním odboji*, pp. 243-245; Sidor, *Andrej Hlinka* (Bratislava, 1934), p. 495; Yurchak, *The Slovaks*, p. 208; and Mamatey, *The United States*, pp. 283ff. See also Juraj Kramer, *Slovenské autonomistické hnutie v rokoch 1918-1929* [The Slovak Autonomist Movement During the Years 1918-1929] (Bratislava, 1962), pp. 35-48; and Joseph Kirschbaum, "The Pittsburgh Pact: Its Significance in Slovak Politics," *Bulletin of the Slovak National Council Abroad* (Middletown, Pa., June 1958); Victor S. Mamatey, "The Czecho-Slovak Agreement of Pittsburgh (May 30, 1918) Revisited," *Kosmas*, II, No. 2 (Winter 1983).
39. Beneš, II, p. 182; Ullman, *Anglo-Soviet Relations*, p. 152. Details in Vávra, "Francouzské dokumenty."
40. Beneš, II, p. 183.

41. Lansing to Sharp, April 22, 1918, FRUS, Russia, II, p. 130. See also Lansing Desk Diaries, entry of April 22, 1918; and Breckinridge Long Papers, Diaries, April 22, 1918.
42. Supreme War Council, Fifth Session, National Archives; Ullman, *Anglo-Soviet Relations,* p. 155.
43. Beneš, II, pp. 190-191; Ullman, *Anglo-Soviet Relations,* pp. 153-154.
44. Pichlík, *Zahraniční odboj,* p. 381.
45. Milner—Folder 33. L. S. Amery, Note on a Conversation with Dr. Beneš, May 14, 1918; Bradley, "The Allies," p. 291.
46. *Masaryk a revoluční armáda,* pp. 207-208; Pichlík, *Zahraniční odboj,* p. 382.
47. Pichon to Jusserand, April 30, 1918; Jusserand to Pichon, May 11, 12, and 13, 1918, quoted in John Bradley, "La France, la Russie et l'indépendance tchécoslovaque, 1918," *Revue d'histoire moderne et contemporaine,* XVIII (April-June 1971), pp. 189-202.
48. Seton-Watson, *Masaryk in England,* pp. 107-112; and Voska, "Paměti," *Jas* (IX, 1935, No. 33).
49. Charles Crane to Tumulty, May 8, 1918; Memorandum for the President (from Tumulty), May 9, 1918; Richard Crane to Tumulty, May 11, 1918; Richard Crane to Wilson, May 11, 1918. Wilson Papers, Series 4.
50. Ruggles to Department of War, May 10, 1918, FRUS, 1918, Russia, I, p. 158; and Kalina, *Krví a železem,* pp. 172-173.
51. Page to Lansing, May 7, 1918, FRUS, Supp. 1, WW, I, pp. 803.
52. Stovall to Lansing, May 13, 1918, National Archives, Department of State File 763.72119/1668; Kalina, *Krví a železem,* pp. 296-297.
53. Breckinridge Long, "Memorandum of Conversation Had with Professor Masaryk to-day," May 16, 1918, Breckinridge Long Papers, Library of Congress.
54. Ibid; Kalina, *Krví a železem,* pp. 296-297.
55. Memorandum for the Secretary of State, Breckinridge Long Papers, Siberia, May 21, 1918; Kalina, *Krví a železem,* pp. 297-298.
56. Stovall to Lansing, May 23, 1918, FRUS, Supp. 1, WW, I, pp. 808-809.
57. Kalina, *Krví a železem,* pp. 299-300.
58. Lansing to Page, May 29, 1918, FRUS, Supp. 1, WW, I, pp. 808-809.

59. FRUS, Supp. 1, WW, I, pp. 809-810.
60. Masaryk lists the people in the United States who were helpful to him on pp. 235-236 of his memoirs.
61. Breckinridge Long to Secretary of the Treasury, William G. McAdoo, April 17 and 20, 1918, National Archives, Department of State File 861.00/1579 Di and 861.00/1601; in Czech, in Kalina, *Krví a železem*, Annexes Nos. 11 and 12, p. 295.
62. *The New York Times*, May 27, 1918; detailed discussion of the American press articles related to the Czechoslovak independence movement in Kalina, *Krví a železem*, pp. 176ff, passim.
63. Details in Kalina, *Krví a železem*, pp. 182-183.
64. Ibid. According to Lansing Desk Diaries, entry of June 3, 1918, "Masaryk talked about the advantage of getting the army to the West."
65. Kalina, *Krví a železem*, p. 164.
66. Beneš, II, pp. 229-230.
67. Lansing, *War Memoirs*, pp. 267-269.
68. Page to Lansing, May 29, 1918, National Archives, Department of State File 861.00/2106; Kalina, *Krví a železem*, p. 303.
69. Breckinridge Long, Memorandum of Conversation with the Russian Ambassador, June 7, 1918, National Archives, Department of State File 861.00/2008; Kalina, *Krví a železem*, pp. 301-302.
70. Memorandum of the British Embassy to the State Department, June 7, 1918 (received June 8), National Archives, Department of State File 763/72/10279; Kalina, *Krví a železem*, pp. 302-303.
71. Kalina, *Krví a železem*, reproduction of the cartoon, p. 184; see also p. 219.
72. *Washington Post*, June 16, 1918.
73. Memorandum on Intervention in Russia, June 12, 1918, Confidential Memoranda, Lansing Papers.
74. FRUS, 1918, Russia I, p. 383, and note 1; Breckinridge Long Papers, Diary, February 23, 1918.
75. Kalina, *Krví a železem*, p. 255.
76. Masaryk, *The Making of a State*, p. 298.
77. Ibid., p. 274ff. See also Kalina, *Krví a železem*, pp. 256-261; Mamatey, *The United States and East-Central Europe*, pp. 284-286; and *Dokumenty o protilidové a protinárodní politice T. G. Masaryka*, ed., Nečásek *et al.*, p. 21.

78. Ibid. (Kalina, p. 260; Mamatey, p. 286; *Dokumenty,* ed. Nečásek *et al.,* pp. 21-22.

79. Facsimile of Masaryk's record of the audience with Wilson, June 19, 1918, in *Dokumenty,* ed. Nečásek *et al.,* Annex No. 5. Masaryk's own handwritten notes and typewritten notes about the meeting with the president are in Masaryk Archive (MA), sec. 11, part 6. The typewritten notes are also in Richard Crane Papers, Georgetown University.

Masaryk was in daily contact with the two Cranes while he was in Washington, D.C. The elder Crane arranged for Masaryk the audience with President Wilson. (Incidentally, Crane's daughter married Jan Masaryk after the war, but the marriage ended in divorce. After the Munich events in 1938, Richard Crane shot and killed himself.)

80. Masaryk's unwillingness to commit the army in Russia as "the nucleus" of the Allied forces displeased the British, who had hoped for and in a great measure counted upon it as early as May 20. He certainly was not helpful to the British efforts to "get the U.S. into line." See FO 371/3135/06597, Cecil minutes, May 20, 1918.

81. Report dated September 1 [1917], OS 14 NS, WWP 112. Masaryk suggested that "Japanese intervention might be paid for . . . by the cession of a part of Manchuria . . . ." He thought that "Russia would be willing to cede to China some part of Central Asia . . . ."

82. Masaryk's handwritten notes, MA, sec. II, part 6.

83. Auchincloss Diary, June 19, 1918. See also Fowler, *British-American Relations,* p. 181.

84. Wiseman, memorandum dated March 11, 1918, WWP 113; and Wiseman to Drummond, May 30, 1918 (CXP 627, 628, 629), WWP 129. The cablegram of May 30, 1918, is reprinted in Fowler, *British-American Relations,* pp. 271-275.

85. Memorandum of June 5, 1918, submitted by Thomas L. Chadbourne, Clarence M. Woolsey, and John Foster Dulles, "Papers on Russia," 55, in Auchincloss Papers.

86. Auchincloss Diary, June 13, 1918. Auchincloss's diary contains a copy of the letter, which is also in *The Lansing Papers,* II, pp. 362-363. See also Fowler, *British-American Relations,* pp. 181-183.

87. Auchincloss Diary, June 13, 1918.

88. Beneš, II, p. 187; Pichlík, *Zahraniční odboj,* p. 383; Kalina, *Krví a železem,* p. 193.

Notes to Chapter Twelve 571

89. Lev Borský, *Z civilního generálního štábu* [From the Civilian General Staff] (Prague, 1924), pp. 130-131.
90. The whole letter is reproduced in Holotík, *Štefánikovská legenda,* p. 460.

Chapter Twelve:
The Origins of the Conflict Between the Czechoslovak Army and the Bolsheviks

1. For the Communist counter-argument see Pichlík *et al., Červenobílá a rudá,* pp. 206-216; and Karel Pichlík, *Vzpoury navrátilců z ruského zajetí na jaře* 1918 [Rebellions of the Returnees from Captivity in Russia in the Spring of 1918] (Prague, 1964). To "prove" a "direct" influence of the Bolshevik Revolution on the Czech independence movement at home, the Czechoslovak historians quote the only armed Czech rebellion that took place in May 1918, when the Seventh Infantry Regiment of Pilsen, stationed at Rumburk, mutinied. The ringleaders of his mutiny were former prisoners of war in Russia, released under the Brest-Litovsk Treaty, who had come under Bolshevik influence while in Russia. See Jan Fiala, *Rumburská vzpoura* [The Rumburk Rebellion] (Prague, 1953); and an eyewitness account by one participant, František Pála, *Vzpoura rumburská* [The Rebellion at Rumburk] (Pilsen, 1920).
2. On the Bolsheviks' receiving money from the imperial German government before and after the Bolshevik Revolution, see Z. A. B. Zeman and W. B. Scharlau, *The Merchant of Revolution: The Life of Alexander Israel Helphand (Parvus) 1867-1924)* (London, 1965), esp. pp. 225-26, 231, and 235-36; and *The Provisional Government 1917,* ed. Browder and Kerensky.
3. Masaryk, *The Making of a State,* p. 189; Kratochvíl, *Cesta revoluce,* p. 29; see also David Footman, *Civil War in Russia* (New York, 1961), p. 53.
4. Veselý, *O vzniku a založení KSČ,* pp. 51-53; Veselý, *Češi a Slováci,* p. 82. With the permission of the Bolshevik government, a separate Czech Red Guard detachment was organized by Alois Můna and Arno Hais in February 1918. See Tobolka, *Politické dějiny,* IV, p. 310.
5. Memorandum of the Foreign Office for the War Office, March 21, 1918, and reply of the War Office to the Foreign Office, April 1, 1918;

Panouse to War Ministry, April 1, 1918, and Panouse to War Minister, April 2, 1918; Vávra, "Francouzské dokumenty," p. 482; Bradley, "The Allies," p. 286.

6. Milner–Box B, Lockhart to Foreign Office, February 25, March 2, March 12, March 21, and March 31, 1918; Bradley, "The Allies," p. 285.

7. Ullman, *Anglo-Soviet Relations,* pp. 52, 53, and 161-167; Churchill, *The Aftermath,* p. 82. On p. 83 Churchill states: "Every effort was made by the British to obtain a formal invitation [to intervene against Germany] from the Bolshevik leaders. This would have been all important in overcoming the reluctance of the United States."

8. Ullman, ibid., p. 122. Detailed studies on the Allied intervention are those of Kennan, *Soviet-American Relations;* Ullman, *Anglo-Soviet Relations;* James William Morley, *The Japanese Thrust into Siberia, 1918* (New York, 1957); John Albert White, *The Siberian Intervention* (Princeton, 1950); George A. Brinkley, *Allied Intervention in South Russia, 1917-1921* (Notre Dame, Ind., 1966); John Swettenham, *Allied Intervention in Russia, 1918-1919* (London, 1967); John Bradley, *Allied Intervention in Russia* (London, 1968); and a few others.

9. Memorandum of the British Embassy to the Department of State, January 28, 1918, FRUS, 1918, Russia, II, p. 38; Kalina, *Krví a železem,* p. 94.

10. Francis to Lansing, February 19, 1918, FRUS, 1918, Russia, II, p. 49; Kalina, *Krví a železem,* p. 101.

11. Details in Jiří Čermák, *Boje pod Bachmačem a ústup z Ukrainy, r. 1918* [Fighting at Bakhmach and Retreat from the Ukraine, 1918] (Prague, 1923); Václav Cháb, *Bachmač* (Prague, 1948); and *Od Zborova k Bachmači* [From Zborov to Bakhmach] (Prague, 1938).

12. Kvasnička, *Československé légie v Rusku,* p. 95.

13. "Report of Captain Vladimír S. Hurban, of the Czechoslovak Army, August 6, 1918," "The Inquiry," Box 14, Folder 270, WWP 270; the same report is also in the Hoover Collection.

14. M. Klante, *Von der Wolga zum Amur* (Berlin, 1931), pp. 130-132; General L. Krejčí, "U Bachmače," in *Brno v boji za svobodu* [Brno in the Struggle for Freedom] (Brno, 1937), pp. 146-150; and Generál Ruských Legií Radola Gajda, *Moje paměti; československá anabase; zpět na Urál proti Bolševikům–Admirál Kolčak* [My Memoirs: the Czechoslovak

Anabasis; Back to Ural Against the Bolsheviks—Admiral Kolchack] (Prague, 1920), p. 16.

15. Panouse to War Minister, April 1, 1918; Ministère de la Guerre, *Angleterre,* Panouse to War Minister, April 2, 1918; Vávra, "Francouzské dokumenty," p. 482; Bradley, "The Allies," p. 284. Also Beneš, II, p. 181.

16. Beneš, II, p. 181; Tobolka, *Politické dějiny,* IV, p. 32.

17. *Istoricheskii arkhiv,* 1956, I, p. 140, cited in Kvasnička, *Československé légie v Rusku,* p. 98.

18. Ibid., pp. 78-79.

19. Janin, *Moje účast,* p. 87.

20. Ministère de la Guerre, *Russie,* Niesse to War Minister, February 18, 1918; Bradley, "The Allies," p. 278; Masaryk, *Světová revoluce,* p. 233; Šíp, *Několik kapitol,* pp. 68ff; Kvasnička, *Československé légie v Rusku,* pp. 79-80.

21. Masaryk, *Světová revoluce,* p. 235.

22. Kratochvíl, *Cesta revoluce,* pp. 38ff.

23. Karel Zmrhal, *Armáda ducha druhé míle* [The Army with the Spirit of the Second Mile] (Prague, 1920), p. 15; Beneš, III, p. 635.

24. Zmrhal, ibid., pp. 15-16; Beneš, III, p. 635.

25. Kratochvíl, *Cesta revoluce,* pp. 40-43; Vávra, *Klamná cesta,* p. 144.

26. V. Maksakov and A. Turunov, eds., *Khronika grazhdanskoi voiny v Sibiri 1917-1918,* quoted in *Intervention, Civil War, and Communism in Russia, April-December 1918,* ed. James Bunyan (Baltimore, 1936), p. 80.

27. Zmrhal, *Armáda ducha druhé míle,* p. 22. This sources contains many documents.

28. Beneš, III, pp. 636-637.

29. Ibid., II, p. 179.

30. Zmrhal, *Armáda ducha druhé míle,* pp. 16-19; Kratochvíl, *Cesta revoluce,* p. 42; Beneš, III, pp. 635-636. On the importance of Penza and the Czech Bolsheviks' agitation see Jaroslav Křížek, *Penza—slavná bojová tradice čs. rudoarmějců* [Penza—the Glorious Martial Tradition of the Czechoslovak Red Army Men] (Prague, 1956; same author, *Čeští a slovenští rudoarmějci v sovětském Rusku 1917-20* [Czech and Slovak Red Army Men in Soviet Russia, 1917-20] (Prague, 1955); and Rudolf Pitra, *Z Penzy do Ufy. Zápisky bratra Pitry* [From Penza to Ufa. Notes of Brother Pitra] (Prague, 1923).

31. Za Svobodu, III, p. 15; Čeněk Hruška, *Velká říjnová socialistická revoluce a naše národní svoboda* [The Great October Socialist Revolution and Our National Liberation] (Prague, 1950), pp. 70-71; and Veselý, *O vzniku*, pp. 58-59.
32. Holotík, *Štefánikovská legenda*, p. 497.
33. Masaryk, *The Making of a State*, pp. 111-112.
34. Dürich, *V českých službách*, p. 72.
35. Ibid., p. 86.
36. Pichlík, *Zahraniční odboj*, p. 395.
37. Dürich, *V českých službách*, p. 90.
38. Ibid., p. 91.
39. Churchill, *The World Crisis. The Aftermath*, p. 61.
40. Veselý, *Češi a Slováci*, pp. 89 and 97.
41. *Průkopník*'s subtitle was "Organ of the Czechoslovak Social-Democrats (Communist-Internationalists)." The quotations are from Veselý, *Češi a Slováci*, pp. 96-97; see also pp. 99-101.
42. Ibid., pp. 92 and 102; and Pichlík, *Zahraniční odboj*, pp. 396-397. See also Footman, *Civil War in Russia*, p. 90.
43. Pichlík, *Zahraniční odboj*, p. 397. According to Beneš, the Czechoslovak communists bore the main responsibility for the Czechoslovak army's conflict with the Soviet government. They campaigned against the departure of the troops via Archangel by claiming that Germans would eventually sink the ships going to France. Beneš, II, p. 196.
44. Zmrhal, *Armáda ducha druhé míle*, pp. 23-24; Křížek, *Penza*, pp. 119-127.
45. Pichlík, *Zahraniční odboj*, p. 395.
46. Kratochvíl, *Cesta revoluce*, pp. 59-61.
47. Ibid.
48. Beneš, III, pp. 642-643. The stopping of the trains was intentional; it made it easier for the Czechoslovak communists to conduct propaganda among the troops.
49. Veselý, *Češi a Slováci*, pp. 92-94.
50. Ibid., pp. 87-89 and Veselý, *O vzniku*, pp. 54-55.
51. Ivan Völgyes, *The Hungarian Soviet Republic, 1919: An Evaluation and a Bibliography* (Stanford, 1970), p. 6.
52. Syllaba, *Masaryk a revoluce v Rusku*, p. 193; Veselý, *O vzniku*, p. 55.

Notes to Chapter Twelve 575

53. "Appeal to the Czecho-Slovak Social Democrats in Russia," Průkopník, April 4, 1918, reprinted in Veselý, Češi a Slováci, pp. 207-208. The appeal stated that "with the Russian revolution we shall either win or fall. Therefore, it is necessary that our people know the Russian language...."
54. Ullman, Anglo-Soviet Relations, pp. 153-155; Beneš, III, pp. 636-637.
55. Beneš, III, pp. 638-639.
56. Ullman, Anglo-Soviet Relations, pp. 154-156.
57. Sims to the Secretary of Navy, June 3, 1918, FRUS, 1918, Russia, II, p. 488; also Francis to Lansing, June 15, 1918, FRUS, 1918, Russia, II, pp. 213-214; details in Charles C. M. Maynard, *The Murmansk Venture* (London, 1929), pp. 11ff; Ullman, Anglo-Soviet Relations, pp. 172-175 and 178-180; and Footman, *Civil War in Russia*, pp. 167ff.
58. Lord Robert Cecil to Clemenceau, May 18, 1918, quoted in Ullman, Anglo-Soviet Relations, p. 170; Beneš, II, pp. 208-209; also pp. 212-214.
59. Documentary citations in Kvasnička, *Československé légie v Rusku*, p. 95; for Gajda's account of his activities see him memoirs, *Moje paměti;* for a Communist version of the origin of the conflict see Veselý, Češi a Slováci, pp. 120-123; and for a detailed account of the armed conflict by a foreign observer see the report of the U.S. consul at Omsk, Alfred R. Thomson, to the secretary of state, July 4, 1918, with enclosed documents. FRUS, 1918, Russia, II, pp. 248-260.
60. See Facsimile of *Československá rudá armáda*, Veselý, Češi a Slováci, pp. 96-97; also Pichlík, *Zahraniční odboj*, p. 403.
61. Veselý, Češi a Slováci, p. 104, and Pichlík, *Zahraniční odboj*, p. 415. See also *Kapitoly z dějin vzájemných vztahů národů ČSR a SSSR; Sborník prací* [Chapters from the History of Mutual Relations of the Nations of Czechoslovakia and the Soviet Union; Collection of Works], ed. Václav Čejchan (Prague, 1958), II, p. 26.
62. Šteidler, *Naše vystoupení na Rusi*, pp. 31-32.
63. Beneš, II, pp. 256-257.
64. Jaroslav Papoušek, *Proč došlo k bojům legií s Bolševiky?* [Why Did the Legions Clash with the Bolsheviks?] (Prague, 1928), pp. 21 and 42. Czechoslovak communists were supported by the Soviet government and Soviet officials from the very beginning. Even Masaryk noticed that

"Moscow was influenced by the treacherous conduct of some Czechs who had joined the Bolsheviks;" and he pointed out that the French Captain Sadoul, who later joined the Bolsheviks, "saw quite clearly that the Bolshevik Government in Moscow... unjustly attributed reactionary tendencies to our army" (Masaryk, *The Making of a State*, p. 279).
65. FRUS, 1918, Russia, II, p. 249; Kalina, *Krví a železem*, p. 213.
66. Papoušek, *Proč došlo*, p. 52; Beneš, II, p. 198; Kalina, *Krví a železem*, p. 213.
67. Kratochvíl, *Cesta revoluce*, pp. 79-80.
68. The foregoing narrative is based on Chapter VI, "Left-Wing Social Democrats Established Czecho-Slovak Communist Party in Russia," in Veselý, *Češi a Slováci*, pp. 90-112; for the resolutions of the congress, see pp. 211-213. For an analysis of the congress see Pichlík, *Zahraniční odboj*, pp. 410-420. See also Ferdinand Peroutka, *Budování státu* [The Building of the State], 4 vols. (Prague, 1933-36), I, pp. 561ff; and Paul Reimann, *Geschichte der Kommunistischen Partei der Tschechoslovakei* (Hamburg-Berlin, 1931), pp. 68-77.
69. Šteidler, *Naše vystoupení*, pp. 38-39; Kalina, *Krví a železem*, p. 216; Veselý, *Češi a Slováci*, p. 120.
70. Kratochvíl, *Cesta revoluce*, p. 80; Beneš, III, p. 647.
71. Kratochvíl, *Cesta revoluce*, p. 81.
72. Beneš, III, pp. 647-648.
73. *Za Svobodu*, p. 195.
74. Gajda, *Moje paměti*, pp. 24-25.
75. Pichlík, *Zahraniční odboj*, p. 409.
76. Gajda, *Moje paměti*, p. 23; also Beneš, II, pp. 198-199.
77. *Za Svobodu*, III, p. 249.
78. Zmrhal, *Armáda ducha druhé míle*, pp. 46-47.
79. Vladimír Lazarevský, *Rusko a československé znovuzrození* [Russia and the Czechoslovak Rebirth] (Prague, 1927), pp. 122-123; Kalina, *Krví a železem*, p. 217.
80. Lazarevský, *Rusko a československé znovuzrození*, pp. 122-123. Similar views have been held by Vondrák, Dürich, Zuman, Kalina, and others. "Masaryk clearly overestimated the strength of the Bolsheviks because the conflict of the Czechoslovaks with them, which started at the end of May, showed that they could have been defeated had a march against Moscow and Petrograd been ordered in January-March 1918,"

Notes to Chapter Thirteen 577

writes a follower of Masaryk, Victor M. Fic, in *Revolutionary War for Independence and the Russian Question. Czechoslovak Army in Russia 1914-1918* (New Delhi, India: Abhinav Publications, 1977), p. 204. In 1920, in his pamphlet *O bolševictví* [About Bolshevism], Masaryk wrote that after the Bolshevik Revolution Russia was falling apart. In that situation "any organized power had to succeed. The best proof of it are our legions; fifty thousand men... even against the will of the Bolsheviks succeeded later to reach Siberia and to hold the line several thousand versts long for more than two years." *Cesta demokracie* [The Way of Democracy] (Prague, 1933), pp. 369-370.

Chapter Thirteen:
The Czechoslovak Resistance to the Bolsheviks, and the Decision to Intervene

1. Among the several studies dealing with the subject matter of this chapter are Victor M. Fic, *The Bolsheviks and the Czechoslovak Legion* (New Delhi, 1978); same author, *The Intervention and Civil War in Russia* (New Delhi, 1981); and Geburg Thunig-Nittner, *Die Tschechoslowakische Legion in Russland. Ihre Geschichte und Bedeutung bei der Enstehung der 1. Tschechoslowakischen Republik.* (Wiesbaden, 1970). See also Josef Kalvoda, "Czech and Slovak Prisoners of War in Russia During the War and Revolution," in *Essays on World War I: Origins and Prisoners of War,* ed. Samuel R. Williamson, Jr., and Peter Pastor (New York, 1983), pp. 215-238.

2. Zmrhal, *Armáda ducha druhé míle,* pp. 60-61. Unless the notes state otherwise, the following account of the armed conflict is based on the following sources: a detailed report by A. R. Thomson, U.S. consul at Omsk, Thomson to Lansing, July 4, 1918, FRUS, 1918, Russia, II, pp. 248-260; Papoušek, *Proč došlo k bojům;* Gajda, *Moje paměti;* Pichlík, *Zahraniční odboj;* Veselý, *Češi a Slováci;* and several reports by U.S. diplomats in Russia, Siberia, and China as specified in notes.

3. Report on clashes between Czechs and Austro-German prisoners of war and good offices of American and French consuls, by the U.S. Consul General Ernest L. Harris to the Secretary of State, Irkutsk, June 2, 1918, FRUS, 1918, Russia, II, pp. 184-186.

4. Beneš, III, pp. 649-650.

5. FRUS, 1918, Russia, II, p. 131.

6. Veselý, Češi a Slováci, pp. 89-91.
7. Zmrhal, Armáda ducha druhé míle, p. 61.
8. Kalina, Krví a železem, pp. 219ff; Pichlík, Zahraniční odboj, p. 425.
9. Kalina, Krví a železem, p. 213. Veselý writes, "The White Guardist elements were helping the Czechs... they supplied plans, maps and reports on the situations and strength of the enemy." Veselý, Češi a Slováci, p. 120. Extensive documentation on the Czechoslovaks' excellent intelligence can be found in Zmrhal, Armáda ducha druhé míle. Zmrhal published unabbreviated telegraphic messages, including their code numbers, sent by government officials from Moscow and Siberia to all regional soviets and Siberian soviets, communications between soviets in Siberia and the Volga region, etc.
10. Minutes of meetings of the executive committee at Cheliabinsk, June 4 and 6, 1918, in Holotík, Štefánikovská legenda, pp. 462-465.
11. Gajda, Moje paměti, p. 24.
12. Ibid.
13. Noulens to Lavergne, Beneš, III, p. 651.
14. Francis to Lansing, May 21, 1918, FRUS, 1918, Russia, II, p. 183.
15. Beneš, III, pp. 652-653.
16. Francis to Lansing, June 3, 1918, FRUS, 1918, Russia, II, p. 188.
17. Lansing to Francis, June 4, 1918, ibid., I, p. 519.
18. Lansing to Francis, June 4, 1918, FRUS, 1918, Russia, II, p. 189.
19. Reinsch to Lansing, June 5, 1918, FRUS, 1918, Russia, II, p. 189.
20. Za svobodu, III, p. 293.
21. Francis to Lansing, June 7, 1918, FRUS, 1918, Russia, II, p. 195.
22. Izvestia, No. 119, June 12, 1918, p. 3; also Poole to Lansing, June 11, 1918, FRUS, 1918, Russia, II, p. 203.
23. Beneš, III, pp. 657-659; also Yu. Kliuchnikov i A. Sabanin, Mezhdunarodnaia politika noveishego vremeni v dogovorakh, notakh i deklaratsiiakh (Moscow), II, pp. 144-146.
24. Šteidler, Naše vystoupení, p. 65; Kvasnička, Československé légie v Rusku, p. 108.
25. Pichlík, Zahraniční odboj, p. 429.
26. Reinsch to Lansing, Peking, June 13, 1918, FRUS, 1918, Russia, II, pp. 206-207.

27. Francis to Lansing, June 14, 1918, FRUS, 1918, Russia, II, pp. 211-212.
28. Francis to Lansing, Vologda, June 15, 1918, ibid., pp. 213-214.
29. The French Ambassador, Jusserand, to the Secretary of State, June 15, 1918, FRUS, Supp. 1, WW, I, pp. 813-814.
30. Beneš, II, pp. 249-250; Kalina, *Krví a železem,* p. 221; Pichlík, *Zahraniční odboj,* p. 430.
31. Pichlík, *Zahraniční odboj,* p. 430. Veselý, *Češi a Slováci,* pp. 133-134.
32. Francis to Lansing, June 22, 1918, FRUS, 1918, Russia, II, pp. 220-223.
33. A Detailed Military Argument With Regard to Allied Intervention in Siberia, British War Office, June 19, 1918, P.A.R. C., Siberian Records, A-88, File 2, Folder 17; John Swettenham, *Allied Intervention in Russia, 1918-1919* (London, 1967), pp. 110-112.
34. Ibid.
35. Ibid.
36. Ibid.
37. Ibid.
38. Beneš, II, pp. 249-250.
39. Holotík, *Štefánikovská legenda,* pp. 465-466.
40. *Izvestia,* No. 140, July 13, 1918. Chicherin protested against this message. In his reply to the protest, the French ambassador, Noulens, stated that Guinet had not been authorized to make the announcement.
41. Caldwell to Lansing, Vladivostok, June 29, 1918, FRUS, 1918, Russia, II, p. 235, and pp. 226 and 271; and Ullman, *Anglo-Soviet Relations,* p. 213.
42. Caldwell to Lansing, June 29, 1918, FRUS, Russia, II, p. 235.
43. Gajda, *Moje paměti,* p. 83.
44. Konrad H. Jarausch, "Cooperation or Intervention? Kurt Riezler and the Failure of German *Ostpolitik,* 1918," *Slavic Review,* 31, No. 2 (June 1972), pp. 381-398.
45. Ibid., p. 384. Eyewitness accounts of the Fifth All-Russian Congress of Soviets are in Lockhart, *Memoirs,* pp. 291ff; Sadoul, *Notes,* pp. 393ff; and M. Philips Price, *Die russische Revolution* (Hamburg, 1921), pp. 406ff.
46. V. I. Lenin, *Collected Works,* vol. 27, February-July 1918 (Moscow, 1965), p. 466.

47. Wiseman to Drummond, May 30, 1918, WWP; see also Wiseman to Drummond, June 14, 1918, WWP.

48. Wilson to Lansing, June 19, 1918, National Archives, Department of State File 861.00/2148 1/2; the request to which Wilson was referring is in Poole to Lansing, June 12, 1918, FRUS, 1918, Russia, II, pp. 205-206. On Wilson's interest in and attempts to aid liberal-national Russia, see N. Gordon Levin, Jr., *Woodrow Wilson and World Politics* (New York, 1968), pp. 96-108.

49. Lansing to Wilson, June 23, 1918, FRUS, *The Lansing Papers, 1914-1920*, 2 vols. (Washington, 1939, 1940), II, p. 364, hereafter cited as *Lansing Papers;* and Lansing to Caldwell, June 25, 1918, FRUS, 1918, Russia, II, p. 224.

50. Lansing Desk Diaries, entry of June 25, 1918.

51. Pichlík, *Zahraniční odboj,* p. 431. On Wilson's idea of sending missions to Vladivostok and Murmansk see Wiseman to Drummond, May 30, 1918, WWP. The idea was discussed between Wilson and Lansing, and the latter stated it very clearly in his confidential memorandum for the president of June 12, 1918, quoted here in chapter 11, note 73. In his reply to Lansing, the president mentions his plan involving the Czechs. See Wilson to Lansing, June 17, 1918, *The Lansing Papers,* II, p. 363. It should be noted that Masaryk's public pronouncements did not differ from the views expressed to Lansing. For example, in an interview with a *New York Times* reporter, Masaryk recommended that the Allies and the United States assist Russia in rebuilding her economic and administrative life. He doubted the value of military intervention, and he was quoted as saying that whoever would aid Russia must be on good terms with the Bolshevik government. Masaryk believed that the recovery of Russia was essential, and he stressed that "you can't work against the Government." "Masaryk Urges Help for Russia," *The New York Times,* May 27, 1918.

52. Kalina, *Krví a železem,* p. 269; Mamatey, *The United States and East-Central Europe,* pp. 298ff.

53. FRUS, 1918, Russia, II, pp. 224-226.

54. Ibid.

55. Ibid., pp. 226-227.

56. Beneš, II, pp. 254 and 252.

57. Ibid., p. 255.

58. Ibid., III, p. 175.

Notes to Chapter Thirteen 581

59. Holotík, *Štefánikovská legenda*, pp. 438-440.
60. Commander in Chief, Asiatic Squadron at Vladivostok, to Secretary of Navy, June 29, 1918, Woodrow Wilson Papers (WWP).
61. Miles to Lansing, July 1, 1918, WWP.
62. Lansing Desk Diaries, July 3, 1918.
63. Frazier to Lansing, Paris, July 2, 1918, FRUS, 1918, Russia, II, pp. 241-246.
64. Ibid.
65. Ibid.
66. Memorandum on the Siberian Situation, July 4, 1918, Confidential Memoranda, Lansing Papers (Library of Congress).
67. The bracketed paragraph is printed in the document of July 6, 1918, FRUS, 1918, Russia, II, pp. 262-263; it does not appear in the handwritten "Memorandum of a Conference at the White House in Reference to the Siberian Situation, July 6, 1918," Lansing Papers.
68. Dr. František Šteidler, *Československé hnutí na Rusi* [The Czechoslovak Movement in Russia] (Prague, 1921), p. 69; also Beneš, III, p. 663.
69. Masaryk, *The Making of a State*, p. 281; Holotík, *Štefánikovská legenda*, pp. 465-466.
70. Pichlík, *Zahraniční odboj*, p. 433.
71. Harris to Lansing, July 29, 1918, FRUS, 1918, Russia, II, pp. 308-314.
72. Ibid.
73. Masaryk to Polk (Acting Secretary of State), July 20, 1918, FRUS, Supp. 1, WW, I, p. 818. The enclosure was marked "confidential" and was not printed in FRUS. See National Archives, Department of State Files 763.71/10884.
74. Memorandum for the British, French, and Italian Embassies and the Chinese Legation, July 26, 1918, Breckinridge Long Papers, Siberia, 1918. See also memorandum of conversation with Mr. Sookine, formerly of the Russian Embassy, June 26, 1918, Breckinridge Long Papers, Siberia, 1918.
75. Baruch to Wilson, September 16, 1918, and Wilson to Baruch, September 17, 1918, Woodrow Wilson Papers; and memorandum of conversation with Professor Masaryk, September 17, 1918, Breckinridge Long Papers.

76. *Masaryk a revoluční armáda,* pp. 213-214.
77. Ibid., pp. 215-216.
78. Ibid., pp. 213-216; also Beneš, III, pp. 665-666.
79. Ibid.
80. *Masaryk a revoluční armáda,* p. 215.
81. Footman, *Civil War,* p. 100.
82. *Trotsky's Diary in Exile, 1935* (Cambridge, Mass., 1953), p. 81.
83. Pichlík, *Zahraniční odboj,* p. 435.
84. Veselý, *Češi a Slováci,* p. 129.
85. Ibid., p. 130.

Chapter Fourteen:
The Quest for Recognition, the Fight with the Bolsheviks, and the Limited Extent of Allied Help

1. Beneš, II, pp. 201-202.
2. Ibid., pp. 205-220.
3. Ibid., III, pp. 174-177. See also memorandum of the British embassy to the State Department, June 7, 1918, FRUS, 1918, Supp. 1, WW, I, pp. 810ff.
4. Balfour to Reading, June 5, 1918, "Czecho-Slovak National Council," WWP (William Wiseman Papers).
5. Ibid.
6. Jusserand to Lansing, June 15, 1918, FRUS, 1918, Supp. 1, WW, I, pp. 813-814.
7. Lansing to Sharp, June 18, 1918, FRUS, Supp. 1, WW, I, p. 814.
8. Sharp to Lansing, June 22, 1918, ibid., pp. 814-815.
9. Lansing to Wilson, August 21, 1918, Department of State Files; in Czech in Kalina, *Krví a železem,* p. 131; for details see Victor S. Mamatey, "Documents: The United States Recognition of the Czechoslovak National Council in Paris, September 3, 1918," *The Journal of Central European Affairs,* XIII (April 1953), pp. 47-60. Henceforth cited as "Documents."
10. Wilson to Lansing, June 17, 1918, *The Lansing Papers,* vol. II, p. 363. See also Mamatey, *The United States in East-Central Europe,* pp. 300-311.
11. Lansing, *War Memoirs,* pp. 269-271.
12. Department of State Files 860f.01/17; see also Kalina, *Krví a železem,* p. 311.

13. See P[hillips] to Putney, July 5, 1918, Department of State Files 860f.01/17; and Lansing Desk Diaries, June 29, 1918. See also two letters Lansing to Wilson, June 29, 1918, Lansing Papers (Library of Congress).
14. Francis to Lansing, June 22, 1918, Department of State Files 861.00/2094; also Kalina, *Krví a železem*, p. 310.
15. Pichlík, *Zahraniční odboj*, p. 431.
16. Lansing to Wilson, June 29, 1918, The Wilson Papers; FRUS, 1918, Russia, II, pp. 230-231; see also Mamatey, "Documents."
17. Kalina, *Krví a železem*, pp. 273-276.
18. Ibid.; Masaryk, *The Making of a State*, p. 272; see also Mamatey, *The United States*, p. 287.
19. Lansing to Page, May 29, 1918, FRUS, 1918, Supp. 1, WW, I, pp. 808-809.
20. Ibid., pp. 815-816.
21. Lansing to Wilson, June 29, 1918, Department of State Files 860f.01/17.
22. Lansing to Wilson, June 29, 1918, Woodrow Wilson Papers.
23. Lansing Desk Diaries, June 29, 1918.
24. Beneš, II, pp. 229-230.
25. Ibid., III, pp. 385-389.
26. Jusserand to Lansing, June 29, 1918, FRUS, 1918, Supp. 1, WW, I, pp. 816-817.
27. Holotík, *Štefánikovská legenda*, p. 465.
28. Beneš, III, pp. 174-177.
29. FO 371/3135, 127473, July 22, 1918; Hanak, "The Government, the Foreign Office and Austria-Hungary," p. 193.
30. Ibid.
31. Beneš, II, pp. 235-236.
32. Ibid., III, pp. 398-404; also II, pp. 268-283 on negotiations with Balfour.
33. Ibid., III, pp. 398-404. Also Milner Papers, Box 118, Amery to Milner, August 1, 1918; and Hanak, "The Government, the Foreign Office," p. 193.
34. Beneš, II, p. 273.
35. Ibid., p. 241. In his message to Dr. Šámal of July 8, 1918, Beneš reported that 120,000 men belonged to the Czechoslovak armed forces. In his book he claims that at the time he sent the message he had no exact

information on the number of troops in Siberia, and that at that time the actual total number of Czechoslovak troops in all Allied countries approached 80,000.

36. Sharp to Lansing, Paris, July 11, 1918, FRUS, 1918, Supp. 1, WW, I, pp. 818-826.
37. Masaryk, p. 276.
38. Gajda, *Moje paměti,* p. 178.
39. Beneš, III, p. 143.
40. Paulová, *Tajný výbor,* pp. 512-517.
41. Beneš, III, pp. 396-398.
42. Ibid., pp. 174-177.
43. Holotík, *Štefánikovská legenda,* pp. 459-461.
44. Ibid.
45. Beneš, III, pp. 174-177.
46. The Balfour Declaration of August 9, 1918, ibid., II, p. 283; also Masaryk, pp. 287-288.
47. Ibid., II, p. 283.
48. FO 371/3136, 152102, September 5, 1918; Hanak, "The Government, the Foreign Office," p. 194.
49. Steed, *Through Thirty Years,* II, p. 232.
50. Agreement Between the British Government and the Czecho-Slovak National Council, London, September 3, 1918, FRUS, 1918, Supp. 1, WW, I, pp. 844-845.
51. Masaryk, p. 272; Wilson to Lansing, July 4, 1918, The Wilson Papers; Kalina, *Krví a železem,* Annexes Nos. 49 and 53. The document of August 31, 1918, is in National Archives, Department of State Files 763.72/11172-1/2; also in Beneš, III, pp. 419-436.
52. *The Lansing Papers,* II, pp. 139-141; see also Mamatey, "Documents."
53. Lansing to Wilson, August 21, 1918, enclosures, Department of State Files; also Mamatey, "Documents."
54. Lansing to Wilson, August 21, 1918, Department of State Files; Mamety, "Documents."
55. *The Lansing Papers,* II, p. 141; also Mamatey, "Documents."
56. Woolsey to Lansing, August 23, 1918, Department of State Files; Mamatey, "Documents."
57. Lansing Desk Diaries, August 23, 1918; also Mamatey, "Documents."

Notes to Chapter Fourteen 585

58. Masaryk, p. 172; Mamatey, "Documents."
59. Memorandum on the Recognition of the Czecho-Slovaks as a Nationality, August 23, 1918, Private Memoranda, Lansing Papers; also Mamatey, "Documents."
60. Memorandum on Probability of Peace Proposals by Central Powers, August 25, 1918, Private and Confidential Memoranda, Lansing Papers.
61. Ibid.
62. Lansing Desk Diaries, August 30, 1918; also Mamatey, "Documents."
63. Elected were seven socialists, seven members of the bourgeois parties, and two Slovaks. See Kratochvíl, *Cesta revoluce* (1922), p. 194. Also Janko Jesenský, *Cestou k slobode. Úryvky z denníka 1914-1918* [Following the Way Toward Freedom. Excerpts from Diary, 1914-1918] (Bratislava, 1961), p. 167; and Pichlík, *Zahraniční odboj,* p. 436.
64. Members of the Czecho-Slovak National Council at Vladivostok to Masaryk, July 31, 1918, FRUS, 1918, Russia, II, pp. 319-320. Copies of the "Report of Capt. Vlad. S. Hurban, of the Czechoslovak Army, August 6, 1918" are in the William Wiseman Papers and in the special collection at the Hoover Institution. The telegram of August 10, 1918, from the Hurban archive, is quoted in Vávra, *Klamná cesta,* p. 233. It is possible that Masaryk attempted to take credit for the sending of 100,000 Russian rifles that had been authorized by the U.S. War Department, consigned to Admiral Knight at Vladivostok, on July 11, 1918. See Phillips Papers, entry of July 11, 1918. On President Wilson's granting a credit of $7,000,000 "from the funds at his personal disposal," see Masaryk, *The Making of a State,* p. 277.
65. *Official Bulletin,* August 5, 1918; the communiqué was also printed in the daily press.
66. See FRUS, 1918, Russia, II, pp. 309-314, 342, and 346-348.
67. Memorandum of the Secretary of State on Siberian Policy after Conference with the President, August 20, 1918, FRUS, 1918, Russia, II, p. 351.
68. Lansing Diaries, August 23 and 25, 1918; see also Mamatey, "Documents," *Journal of Central European Affairs,* XII (April 1953), p. 53.
69. Pergler, *America in the Struggle for Czechoslovak Independence,* p. 50; portions of the memorandum are published on pp. 50-56.

70. National Archives, Department of State File 763.72/1171-1/2 (a secret document).

71. On October 28, 1919, in his message to the nation and the troops in Siberia, Masaryk publicly repudiated what he had said in the confidential memorandum of August 28, 1918. He declared: "I was and I am against intervention in Russia and Hungary. In difficult crises each nation must help itself...." See *Boj o směr vývoje československého státu* [The Struggle for the Direction of the Development of the Czechoslovak State], ed. A. Kocman, V. Pletka, et al., 2 vols. (Prague, 1965 and 1969), II, p. 88; also Pavel Fink, *Bílý admirál. Profil Kolčakovštiny...* [The White Admiral. A Profile of Kolchakovshtina...], 3rd ed. (Brno, 1929), p. 6. Masaryk's pronouncement had a prophetic ring, but the Czechs did not recall it in either 1938 or 1968.

72. In the covering letter Masaryk writes that he is submitting the document as "additions and explanations" to what he had discussed with Secretary Lansing. He hopes that a second memorandum will be ready on the next day. It is apparent that he is referring here to the conference with Lansing on August 25, and to the document submitted to the secretary on August 31, 1918.

73. Auchincloss Diary, July 8 and 9, 1918. See also Memorandum of the Secretary of State on a Conference at the White House in Reference to the Siberian Situation, July 6, 1918, FRUS, 1918, Russia, II, pp. 262ff.

74. Confidential memorandum on the Japanese role in the intervention in Siberia, October 15, 1918, WWP 118.

75. *Dokumenty,* ed. Nečásek, *et al.,* p. 2. Following his audience with Wilson, Masaryk went to the British embassy and reported that he heard suspicions of the British frequently expressed in the State Department and even by the president himself. Barclay (chargé in Washington) to Balfour, September 13, 1918, and Hohler (commercial attaché, Washington) to Drummond, September 13, 1918, Balfour Papers, 49748, British Museum, cited in Fowler, *British-American Relations,* pp. 193-194.

76. Department of State Files 763.72/1172-1/2 (a secret document).

77. It is easy to understand why this piece of propaganda, in which Masaryk used the "big lie technique," was declared "classified-secret," by the Czechoslovak government after the war and, therefore, was not accessible to researchers. In his effort to "prove" that *"The Dismemberment*

of *Austria-Hungary is one of the foremost Objects of the War and Peace,*" as Masaryk emphasized in the memorandum, the Czech leader made many unfounded claims. For example, he states that the Czecho-Slovak National Council was founded in 1915 with the complete sanction of the leading Czech political parties. The truth of the matter is that a declaration of the Czech [sic] Committee Abroad of November 14, 1915, was signed by only two (out of more than one hundred) Czech deputies to the Vienna parliament, Masaryk and Dürich, in addition to representatives of the Czech and Slovak colonies abroad, who telegraphed their consent to having their names placed on the declaration. At that time Kramář was in prison and the vast majority of Czech and Slovak deputies endorsed statements of loyalty to the empire. The Czech *Družina* was organized by the Czech colony and the tsarist military in Russia, not by the then nonexistent Czecho-Slovak National Council. The military unit was transformed into a brigade by order of General Alexeev, chief of staff of the Russian army, on April 17, 1916, that is, more than a year before Masaryk came to Russia. The Czech [sic] National Council was established by an agreement between Masaryk and Dürich in February 1916, not in 1915 as Masaryk claims. The statutes, bylaws and constitution of the Czecho-Slovak National Council, which may be found in the National Archives, and part of which have been published in *The Birth of Czechoslovakia,* ed. Čestmír Ješina (Washington, D.C., 1968), pp. 5-7, were fabricated in October 1918. Masaryk claims, without any documentation, that the pope called Emperor Francis Joseph "the bloody sovereign," and a few pages later he asserts that "Rome is working for the Habsburgs." He also asserts that Francis Joseph ordered the execution "of some 30 to 60 thousand persons." This figure had been used by Masaryk before on several occasions: sometimes it was "from 30,000 to 40,000"; and in his telegram to President Wilson in December 1917, Masaryk claimed that the 40,000 to 60,000 people who were executed were "all civilians." While in the fall of 1914 the military government ordered executions of probably as many as 1,000 people in Galicia, the exact number of soldiers and civilians executed throughout the whole empire is not known. It is known, however, that four Czechs were executed between November 1914, and May 1915, for alleged treason. See *The Birth of Czechoslovakia,* ed. Ješina, p. iv. In her letter to this writer, Dr. Anna Coerth, Archivoberrat, Österreichisches Staatsarchiv, Vienna, August 22, 1972, gave the figure of 1,000, though there are no exact statistics available. In her view, there is no doubt that Masaryk exaggerated in his propaganda during the war the number of executions throughout Austria-Hungary. Furthermore, of the 750,000 Czechs who served in the Austro-Hungarian army, only a small fraction surrendered voluntarily to the enemy, and of those captured an even smaller number took part in the "peculiar revolution" of Masaryk. The behavior of Masaryk's son was more "typical" of the Czech soldiers' attitude than that of the "Czechoslovak soldier" described by Masaryk. Jan Masaryk, son of the man who became the "Enemy Number One" of the empire, had no difficulty serving in the Austro-Hungarian army throughout the war, as documented by the following data furnished by the Austrian State Archives (War Archives), under reference number 19.147/155:

> Johann Masaryk—born, 1886; year of conscription, 1914; joined Transportation Division No. 8 as a wartime volunteer; appointed effective August 1, 1915, to cadet in the reserve, effective August 1, 1916 to 2nd Lieutenant in the reserve, and effective November 1, 1918 to 1st Lieutenant in the reserve. According to a recommendation for reward of the 34th Infantry Division (Division Transportation Command), dated April 5, 1917, he was in the field from June 1, 1915, to the date of recommendation and beyond, and was decorated with the Silver Bravery Medal, second class.

See Jaksch, *Europe's Road to Potsdam,* p. 133.

History has already refuted the contentions of Masaryk that with the disappearance of the Turkish danger, "Austria has lost her *raison d'etre,*" that the Czechoslovak state would be an "effective barrier against Germany," and that the "Slovak language is an archaic dialect of the Czech," not to mention the apparent error that Slovakia is "the southern part of the nation."

    78. *The Lansing Papers,* II, pp. 144-145; Mamatey, "Documents."
    79. Lansing to Morris, September 3, 1918, FRUS, 1918, Supp. 1, WW, I, pp. 824-825; also Mamatey, "Documents."
    80. Beneš, II, pp. 295-296.
    81. Ibid., III, pp. 455-463.
    82. Ibid., II, p. 352.

Notes to Chapter Fourteen 589

83. Masaryk to Wilson, September 7, 1918, Woodrow Wilson Papers.
84. Vasil Škrachl, "Masaryk a Wilson," *Národní Osvobozeni,* March 6, 1932.
85. Pergler, *America in the Struggle,* p. 56.
86. Beneš, III, p. 666; Masaryk, pp. 276-277.
87. Janin, *Moje účast,* pp. 102-103.
88. Österreichischer Staatsarchiv-Kriegsarchiv, Wien (KAW), 25-1/9; Militärkazlei Seiner Majestät von 1918 (MKSM v. 1918); Armeeoberkommando, Operationsabteilung von 1918 (AOK.Op. Abt. v. 1918), Nr. 119. 083, enclosure 17; see also Karel Pichlík, *Vzpoury navrátilců z ruského zajetí na jaře 1918* [Rebellions of Returnees from Russian Captivity in the Spring of 1918] (Prague, 1964), p. 23; and same author, *Československé osvobozenecké hnutí 1914-1918 a vznik ČSR* [Czechoslovak Liberation Movement 1914-1918 and the Genesis of Czechoslovakia] (Prague, 1968), p. 68.
89. Tobolka, *Politické dějiny,* IV, p. 328.
90. K. Teringl, *Desátá rota pod Kazaní* [The Tenth Company Below Kazan] (Prague, 1935), diaries and notes of soldiers who fought in the Volga region; also A. P. Stepanov, *Beloie delo* (Berlin, 1926), I, pp. 92-94; Bradley, "The Czechoslovak Revolt Against the Bolsheviks," *Soviet Studies,* pp. 148-149.
91. Šteidler, *Naše vystoupení,* p. 77.
92. Harris to Lansing, Irkutsk, September 2, 1918, FRUS, 1918, Russia, II, p. 364; and September 4, 1918, p. 365.
93. Lansing to MacMurray, September 5, 1918, FRUS, 1918, Russia, II, p. 369.
94. Harris to Lansing, September 7, 1918, FRUS, 1918, Russia, II, p. 369.
95. Ibid., pp. 369-370.
96. Ibid., September 10, 1918, pp. 374-375.
97. Teringl, *Desáta rota,* p. 252; Isaac Deutscher, *The Prophet Armed* (London, 1954), pp. 414-422.
98. L. Trotsky, *Kak vooruzhalas revolutsiia* [How the Revolution Armed Itself], 5 vols. (Moscow, 1923-1925), I, p. 249.
99. Caldwell to Lansing, September 12, 1918; and MacMurray to Lansing, September 13, 1918, FRUS, 1918, Russia, II, pp. 377 and 379.

100. MacMurray to Lansing, September 13, 1918, FRUS, 1918, Russia, II, pp. 379-380.
101. Harris to Lansing, September 15, 1918, ibid., pp. 381-382.
102. Ibid.
103. Caldwell to Lansing, Vladivostok, September 16, 1918, ibid., pp. 383-394.
104. Memorandum of the Third Assistant Secretary of State, Long, on the visit of the Russian Ambassador, Washington, September 17, 1918, ibid., p. 384.
105. Morris to Lansing, Vladivostok, September 23, 1918, ibid., pp. 387-390.
106. Ibid.
107. Lansing to Morris, Washington, September 26, 1918, ibid., pp. 392-394.
108. Lansing to Wilson, September 9, 1918, *Lansing Papers*, II, pp. 381-382.
109. Ibid., pp. 386-387; see also FRUS, 1918, Russia, II, pp. 387-390.
110. Phillips Papers, entries of September 20, 21, and 28; and Wilson to Masaryk, September 16, 1918, Woodrow Wilson Papers.
111. Lansing to Masaryk, September 27, 1918, National Archives, Department of State File 861.00/2887a.
112. Balfour to Barclay, October 2, 1918, FRUS, 1918, Russia, II, p. 404; and Balfour to Barclay (No. 6001), October 2, 1918, WWP 118.
113. "Gen. Knox Says Allies Should Go to the Urals," *New York Times*, October 16, 1918.
114. "Some Notes on the Memorandum of September 27th, 1918," September 29, 1918, WWP 118.
115. Ibid., p. 7.
116. Thomson to Lansing, Irkutsk, n.d. [Received September 30, 1918], FRUS, 1918, Russia, II, p. 398.
117. Lansing to Harris, October 9, 1918, ibid., pp. 410-411.
118. Jameson to Lansing, Chelyabinsk, October 10, 1918 [Received October 22, 1918], ibid., p. 441.
119. Morris to Lansing, Tokyo, October 27, 1918, ibid., p. 418. See also Ullman, *Anglo-Soviet Relations*, pp. 265-266.

Notes to Chapter Fifteen   591

Chapter Fifteen:
The Declaration of Independence

1. Beneš, III, pp. 174-177 and 191-197.
2. Ibid., II, pp. 321-322.
3. Ibid., p. 323.
4. Ibid., III, pp. 464-465.
5. Ibid.
6. Ibid., II, p. 358; and III, pp. 205-209.
7. Ibid., II, pp. 361-362.
8. Ibid., pp. 363-365.
9. Ibid.; and Sharp to Lansing, Paris, October 16, 1918, FRUS, Supp. 1, WW, I, pp. 846-847.
10. Beneš, III, pp. 205-209.
11. Soukup, *28. říjen 1918,* II, pp. 780ff.
12. *La Question de l'Adriatique,* ed. Paul Henri Michel (Paris, 1938), Doc. No. 266, cited in Mamatey, *The United States and East-Central Europe,* p. 323.
13. *La Question Polonaise pendant la Guerre mondiale,* ed. Stanislav Filaśiewicz (Paris, 1918), Document No. 266, quoted in Mamatey, *The United States and East-Central Europe,* p. 323.
14. Tobolka, *Politické dějiny,* IV, p. 383; see also Beneš, II, p. 392.
15. *Neues Pester Journal,* October 15, 1918; *Enemy Press Supplement,* October 31, 1918; also *The Times* (London), October 18, 1918, p. 6, column 2. Dr. Soukup condemned the action of the Socialist Council. See Tobolka, *Politické dějiny,* IV, p. 382.
16. Beneš, II, p. 392.
17. On the drafting of the Czechoslovak Declaration of Independence and the identity of its "Fathers," see J. B. Kozák, *T. G. Masaryk a vznik Washingtonské deklarace v říjnu 1918* [T. G. Masaryk and the Genesis of the Washington Declaration in October 1918] (Prague, 1968); see also Mamatey, *The United States and East-Central Europe,* pp. 331-332.
18. The complete document is in Kramář, *Řeči a projevy,* pp. 89-92.
19. Excerpts from the secret agreement, containing the essence of its first three articles, were attached to the letter of Charles Pergler, Masaryk's representative in Washington, D.C., to William Phillips, assistant secretary of state, dated October 15, 1918. National Archives, Department of State File 860f.01/4.

20. Kramář, *Řeči a projevy*, p. 101.
21. FRUS, Supp. 1, WW, I, pp. 846ff.
22. Ibid., pp. 367-368; see also Mamatey, *The United States and East-Central Europe*, pp. 328-329.
23. Tobolka, *Politické dějiny*, pp. 41-42; Karl F. Nowak, *Collapse of Central Europe* (London, 1924), p. 268; and Mamatey, *The United States and East-Central Europe*, p. 335.
24. On the effect of the manifesto on the army see Karl Friedrich Nowak, *Chaos* (Munich, 1923), pp. 10ff. See also Harry R. Rudin, *Armistice 1918* (New Haven, 1944).
25. Rudin, *Armistice*, pp. 304ff; Tobolka, *Politické dějiny*, IV, p. 42; Opočenský, *Konec monarchie Rakousko-Uherské*, p. 65; Mamatey, *The United States and East-Central Europe*, p. 341; Kann, *The Multinational Empire*, pp. 279-285; and Friedrich Wieser, *Osterreichs Ende* (Berlin, 1919), p. 264.
26. Lansing to Ekengren, October 19, 1918, FRUS, Supp. 1, WW, I, p. 368. See also Stovall to Lansing, September 19, 1918, National Archives, Department of State File, quoted in Mamatey, *The United States and East-Central Europe*, p. 322.
27. Masaryk, p. 394.
28. The whole document is printed in FRUS, Supp. 1, WW, I, pp. 847-851.
29. Holotík, *Štefánikovská legenda*, pp. 480-488.
30. It would seem that Masaryk attempted to create a vested interest for the United States in establishing a new state by requesting financial support for a government that he would head. However, on October 19, Lansing inquired who had authorized Masaryk to contract loans on behalf of the then yet nonexistent Czechoslovak state, and Beneš informed the U.S. ambassador in Paris that the Czecho-Slovak National Council had been founded in February 1916, that the constitution and federal laws of the council had been adopted on February 6, 1916, and that the powers of Professor Masaryk, president of the council, had been established by a decree of February 10, 1916. Beneš fabricated those documents, as it is clear from the fact that the second deputy in exile, Dürich, never learned of their existence, and that his activity in Russia, for which he was expelled from the council, was fully compatible with the spirit and the letter of the council statutes that Beneš forwarded to Washington, D.C.

Since Lansing was a lawyer by profession, it probably occurred to him that the documents might be spurious. Therefore, on October 25, 1918, the U.S. secretary of state requested that the U.S. ambassador in Paris forward authenticated copies of the original documents that had been submitted by Beneš, especially "the decree or other proceeding quoted making Masaryk President of the Council." See FRUS, 1918, Supp. 1, pp. 855-856. See also Sharp to Lansing, October 22, 1918; Lansing to Sharp, October 25, 1918; Sharp to Lansing, October 28, 1918, FRUS, 1918, Supp. 1, pp. 854-865.

Although Masaryk became president of the council by making an agreement with Dürich, the latter's vice-presidency was not even recognized in the decree that Beneš fabricated. However, the documents, not authenticated by anyone, arrived in Washington, D.C., only *after* the National Council in Prague declared state independence on October 28, 1918. See eight enclosures to dispatch No. 6731 from Paris (Sharp to Lansing), October 28, 1918, in National Archives. Beneš, who had a mania for documents, never published the spurious documents and, therefore, Dürich could not expose them as forgeries.

31. Lansing to Sharp, October 19, 1918, FRUS, Supp. 1, WW, I, pp. 851-852. See also the White House Memorandum, October 16, 1918, Woodrow Wilson Papers.

32. Mamatey, *The United States and East-Central Europe*, p. 343. The original of the declaration is in the Woodrow Wilson Papers; see also Masaryk to Wilson, November 1, 1918; Wilson to Masaryk, November 5, 1918; and Masaryk to Wilson, November 7, 1918, Woodrow Wilson Papers.

33. Paulová, *Tajný výbor*, p. 533; Tobolka, *Politické dějiny*, IV, p. 385.

34. Tobolka, *Politické dějiny*, p. 395; Mamatey, *The United States*, p. 343; see also Herbert Miller, "What Woodrow Wilson and America Meant to Czechoslovakia," in *Czechoslovakia*, ed. Robert Kerner (Berkeley, 1945), pp. 80-82; Glaise-Horstenau, *Die Katastrophe*, pp. 260ff, 306ff, and 323ff; Count Michael Karolyi, *Fighting the World, The Struggle for Freedom* (New York, 1925), pp. 390-391; and Count Michael Karolyi, *Memoirs, Faith Without Illusion* (London, 1956), pp. 105ff.

35. Details in Tobolka, *Politické dějiny*, IV, pp. 395-399; and Beneš, II, pp. 381-400.

36. The proclamation was published in all Czech newspapers, e.g.,

České slovo, October 29, 1918. See also Soukup, 28. říjen 1918, II, pp. 1006ff.

37. Published in Prague's newspapers, e.g., České slovo, Prager Tagblatt, and Národní Listy, October 29, 1918; see also Beneš, II, pp. 430-432.

38. Karol A. Medvecký, Slovenský prevrat [Slovak Revolution], 4 vols. (Trnava, 1930-1931), III, p. 347.

39. František Bokes, Dejiny Slovenska a Slovákov [History of Slovakia and the Slovaks] (Bratislava, 1946), pp. 360-361.

40. Ibid., pp. 361-362.

41. Ibid., 363; Medvecký, III, pp. 364-365.

42. Beneš, II, pp. 438-440; Lettrich, History of Modern Slovakia, pp. 288-289.

43. Beneš, III, pp. 492-494; also National Archives, Department of State File, Enclosure 2, Dispatch No. 6768.

44. FO 371/3136, 142344, August 17, 1918, and 148362, August 29, 1918; see also FO 371/3134, 184693, November 7, 1918; Hanák, "Great Britain and Austria-Hungary," The Slavonic and East European Review, 47 (1969), pp. 194-197.

45. Tobolka, Politické dějiny, IV, p. 38. There are two general works on the "new diplomacy" by Arno J. Mayer: Political Origins of the New Diplomacy, 1917-1918 (New Haven, 1959, and New York, 1970); and Politics and Diplomacy of Peacemaking: Containment and Counterrevolution at Versailles, 1918-1919 (New York, 1967 and 1969).

46. Beneš, II, p. 450.

47. Ibid., p. 515.

48. 54 Agrarians, 49 Social Democrats, 40 National Democrats, 28 Czech Socialists, 24 Catholics, 4 Centralist Socialists, 1 Moravian Artisan, and 40 Slovaks. Beneš, II, p. 476.

49. Ibid., p. 477; details in Opočenský, Konec monarchie, pp. 214ff.

50. Karol Sidor, Slovenská politika na pôde pražského snemu, 1918-1938 [The Slovak Politics in the Parliament of Prague, 1918-1938] (Bratislava, 1943), p. 36.

51. Dokumenty, ed. Merhout, pp. 212-230.

52. Masaryk liked to brag about himself and take credit for work done by others. For example, on St. Wenceslas's day in 1920, the sixth anniversary of the swearing in of the old Družina, Masaryk declared in his

Notes to Chapter Sixteen 595

oration to its surviving members, "When I came abroad, I realized that my diplomatic struggle would be futile if it could not lean on an armed resistance of my own nation and, therefore, I urged you to get organized." See Lazarevský, *Rusko a československé znovuzrození,* p. 127. The fact is that Masaryk had nothing to do with organizing the *Družina.* He learned about its existence only after it was established and sent to the front.

53. Memorandum on the Recognition of the Czecho-Slovaks as a Nationality, August 23, 1918, The Lansing Papers (Division of Manuscripts, Library of Congress).

54. Ibid.

Chapter Sixteen:
The New State and the Paris Peace Conference

1. Sís, *Dr. Karel Kramář,* p. 219.
2. Peroutka, *Budování státu,* p. 159; Wiskemann, *Czechs and Germans,* p. 81; and M. Čihák, M. Klír, and J. Koudelková, *Dějiny ČSR a KSČ v letech 1918-1923* [A History of Czechoslovakia and the Communist Party of Czechoslovakia During the Years 1918-1923] (Prague, 1967), p. 60.
3. Peroutka, *Budování státu,* p. 159.
4. Rudolf Bechyně, *Pero mi zůstalo, 1938-1945* [Pen Has Been Left in May Possession, 1938-1945] (Prague, 1947), pp. 161 and 23-24.
5. Jaksch, *Europe's Road to Potsdam,* pp. 170-171.
6. Ekengren to Lansing, November 21, 1918, FRUS, PPC, 1919, II, pp. 377-378.
7. Memorandum, Swedish Legation to the Department of State, December 13, 1918, FRUS, PPC, 1919, II, p. 379.
8. House Collection, Box 30, 144; Czechoslovakia; miscellaneous papers.
9. *Dokumenty,* ed. Nečásek *et al.,* pp. 38-40.
10. Ibid., pp. 43-45.
11. Masaryk, *Nová Evropa,* pp. 205-224.
12. Beneš, III, p. 500.
13. Alena Gajanová, *ČSR a středoevropská politika velmocí 1918-1938* [Czechoslovakia and Politics of Great Powers in Central Europe, 1918-1938] (Prague, 1967), p. 18. For the text of the agreement between

Clemenceau and Beneš of January 20, 1919, see *Boj o směr vývoje*, ed. Kocman *et al.*, I, pp. 47-48.

14. Beneš, III, p. 488. Beneš also wrote that "the Czechs must occupy militarily Slovakia, because Bolshevism threatens Hungary most... and it could spread also to Yugoslavia and Italian territories" (p. 497).

15. *O československé zahraniční politice v letech 1918-1939* [On Czechoslovak Foreign Policy During the Years 1918-1939], ed Vladimír Soják (Prague, 1956), p. 43.

16. See: Delegation Propaganda: Czechoslovak Republic. Documents Presented at the Paris Peace Conference, 1919, Hoover War Collection, Hoover War Library, The Hoover Institution on Peace, War, and Revolution. The first part of the documentary material was entitled: "The Czecho-Slovaks. Their History and Civilization.–Their Struggles and Their Work.–Their Role in the World."

17. Ibid., *Mémoire*, No. 2, pp. 1-2.
18. Ibid., Part I, p. 10.
19. Ibid., *Mémoire*, No. 2, p. 8.
20. Ibid., pp. 9-10.
21. Ibid., p. 21.
22. Ibid., p. 30.
23. Ibid., p. 39.
24. Ibid., *Mémoire*, No. 7.
25. Ibid., *Mémoire*, No. 3, p. 4.
26. Ibid., p. 16.
27. Ibid., p. 18.
28. Ibid., *Mémoire*, No. 5, pp. 25-30.
29. Ibid., *Mémoire*, No. 6, p. 13. See also National Council of Uhro-Rusins to Wilson, November 15, 1918, Woodrow Wilson Papers.

30. Herbert Hoover, *The Ordeal of Woodrow Wilson*, 4th ed. (New York, 1948), p. 213.

31. Minutes of the Council of Ten, February 5, 1919, *Paris Peace Conference* (PPC), III, p. 878.

32. Eduard Beneš, *Eduard Beneš in His Own Words: Threescore Years as a Statesman, Builder and Philosopher* (New York, 1944), pp. 14-15.

33. American Commission to Negotiate Peace, Memorandum of a Conference with Dr. Edouard Beneš, Foreign Minister of the Czecho-Slovak State, Major Douglas Johnson to Colonel E. M. House, February 7,

1919, E. M. House Collection. The truth of the matter was that considering what the Czechs accomplished, their losses were very small. From June 1 to November 15, 1918, the total number of Czech troops engaged in the campaign amounted to 49,709 soldies and 1,600 officers. The actual battling forces were 23,499; and the actual losses amounted to 1,161 men and 64 officers killed in action, 220 dead of wounds, 3,888 wounded, 362 missing, and 3,161 seriously ill. "The statistics have been prepared by Czech General Staff and are reliable," reported U.S. Consul Harris from Ekaterinburg, adding that "reports of there being fifteen to twenty thousand killed" were spread abroad in order to obtain sympathy and Allied help. In fact, Czech troops everywhere in Russia were better fed and clothed than Russian troops. Harris regretted that assistance and moral support had not been given to the Russian troops in the same spirit as they had been given to the Czechs. Harris to Lansing, December 10, 1918, FRUS, 1918, Russia, II, pp. 458-460.

34. Memorandum of a Conference with... Beneš, February 7, 1919.
35. *Eduard Beneš in His Own Words*, pp. 94 and 97.
36. Minutes of the Council of Ten, PPC, pp. 879ff.
37. See Delegation Propaganda: Czechoslovak Republic, *Mémoire* No. III.
38. Lloyd George, *Memoirs of the Peace Conference*, II, pp. 608-609.
39. Wiskemann, *Czechs and Germans*, p. 88.
40. Čihák *et al.*, *Dějiny ČSR a KSČ*, p. 47.
41. Lloyd George, *Memoirs of the Peace Conference*, II, p. 608.
42. Swedish Minister Ekengren to Lansing, November 16, 1918, FRUS, PPC, 1919, II, p. 189. For a "Diplomatic History of the Boundaries of Czechoslovakia, 1914-1920" see Perman, *The Shaping of the Czechoslovak State;* see also the chapter on Czechoslovakia in Piotr S. Wandycz, *France and Her Eastern Allies, 1919-1925* (Minneapolis, 1962).
43. Beneš, III, p. 505.
44. Article four of the armistice with Austria-Hungary stipulated that "the armies of the Associated Powers shall occupy such strategic points in Austria-Hungary at such times as they may deem necessary to enable them to conduct military operations or to maintain order." The whole document is in Rudin, *Armistice,* pp. 406-409. See also Supreme War Council, Resolutions, VIII Session, Fourth Meeting, November 4, 1918, Bliss Papers.

45. Čihák et al., *Dějiny ČSR a KSČ*, p. 60. For a German version of the struggle see Oskar Lukas, *4. Marz 1919* (Karlsbad, 1939), p. 20 et passim; and Hans Krebs, *Kampf in Böhmen* (Berlin, 1935), p. 104.

46. Military Convention Between the Allies and Hungary, signed at Belgrade, November 13, 1918, FRUS, PPC, 191, II, pp. 183-185. See also Bohdan Krizman, "The Belgrade Armistice 13 November 1918," *The Slavic and East European Review*, 48 (1970), pp. 67-87; the text of the document is on pp. 85-87.

47. Kramář, *Řeči a projevy*, pp. 22-26; see also Sís, *Dr. Karel Kramář*, pp. 203-204.

48. Robert W. Seton-Watson, "Louis Eisenmann," *The Slavic and East European Review*, No. 16, 46 (1937), pp. 193-196.

49. Among the books dealing with Slovakia's becoming a part of Czechoslovakia are the following: Václav Chaloupecký, *Zápas o Slovensko 1918* [The Struggle for Slovakia, 1918] (Prague, 1930); Fedor Houdek, *Oslobodenie Slovenska* [Liberation of Slovakia] (Bratislava, 1929); Karol Medvecký, *Slovenský prevrat* [The Slovak Revolution], 4 vols. (Bratislava, 1930-1931); and Vavro Šrobár, *Oslobodené Slovensko* [Liberated Slovakia], 2 vols. (Prague, 1928). There is a voluminous Hungarian literature on the Hungarian Soviet Republic. Among the English language books dealing with the subject are G. E. R. Gedye, *The Revolver Republic* (London, 1930); Albert Kaas and Fedor de Lazarovics, *Bolshevism in Hungary* (London, 1931); H. C. Smitt, *The Hungarian Revolution* (London, 1919); and Rudolf L. Tőkés, *Béla Kun and the Hungarian Soviet Republic* (New York, 1967). See also Völgyes, *The Hungarian Soviet Republic 1919, An Evaluation and a Bibliography*.

50. V. Kholodovsky, "Toward the Lenin Centenary: Socialist Community—A Retrospect," *New Times* (Moscow), No. 30 (July 30, 1969), p. 7.

51. Ibid.

52. Ibid.

53. V. Semyonov, "An Historian Looks Back: The Slovak Republic of Soviets," *New Times* (Moscow), No. 25 (June 25, 1969), p. 22.

54. Ibid. For more details on the Slovak Soviet Republic see Martin Vietor, *Slovenská sovietská republika* [The Slovak Soviet Republic] (Bratislava, 1955); Václav Král, *Intervenční válka čs. buržoazie proti maďarské sovětské republice r. 1919* [The War of Intervention of the

Czechoslovak Bourgeoisie against the Hungarian Soviet Republic in 1919] (Prague, 1954); and Peter A. Toma, "Slovak Soviet Republic of 1919," *American Slavic and East European Review*, XVI (April 1958), pp. 203-215.
55. Semyonov, "An Historian Looks Back," *New Times*.
56. Čihák *et al.*, *Dějiny ČSR a KSČ*, p. 76.
57. Report of Lieutenant R. C. Foster to A. C. Coolidge, FRUS, PPC, 1919, XII, p. 320.
58. Čihák *et al.*, *Dějiny ČSR a KSČ*, p. 67.
59. Perman, *The Shaping of the Czechoslovak State*, p. 81.
60. Jiří S. Hájek, *Wilsonovská legenda v dějinách ČSR* [The Wilsonian Legend in the History of Czechoslovakia] (Prague, 1953), p. 134. See also *O československé zahraniční politice*, ed. Soják, p. 46.
61. Gajanová, *ČSR a středoevropská politika*, p. 34. See also Alfred D. Low, *The Soviet Hungarian Republic and the Paris Peace Conference*, Translations of the American Philosophical Society (Philadelphia, 1963), pp. 46-47.
62. Gajanová, *ČSR a středoevropská politika*, p. 38.
63. Ibid., p. 34.
64. *O československé zahraniční politice*, ed. Soják, p. 48.
65. Čihák *et al.*, *Dějiny ČSR a KSČ*, p. 50.
66. See notes 32, 33, and 35 above.
67. Harold Nicolson, *Peacemaking 1919* (New York, 1933), pp. 239-240.
68. Perman, *The Shaping of the Czechoslovak State*, p. 125.
69. Sís, *Dr. Karel Kramář*, p. 216.
70. Ibid., p. 219.
71. Ibid., p. 220.
72. Ibid.
73. Lloyd George, *Memoirs of the Peace Conference*, II, p. 612.
74. David Hunter Miller, *My Diary at the Conference of Paris* (New York, 1925), XVII, pp. 88-89.
75. Wiskemann, *Czechs and Germans*, p. 112. On the German-Austrian attitude toward the Sudeten Germans see David F. Strong, *Austria, October 1918-March 1919* (New York, 1939), pp. 165-173.
76. Lettrich, *History of Modern Slovakia*, pp. 289-290; Mikuš, *Slovakia*, pp. 331-332; and Beneš, III, pp. 365-366.

77. Masaryk, p. 220.
78. The whole document is in Mikuš, *Slovakia*, pp. 331-340.
79. František Jehlička, *Father Hlinka's Struggle for Slovak Freedom* (London, 1938), pp. 31-32; and Stephen Bonsal, *Suitors and Supplicants: The Little Nations at Versailles* (New York, 1946), pp. 158 and 163. See also Čulen, *Pittsburghská Dohoda;* Karol Sidor, *Andrej Hlinka, 1864-1926* (Bratislava, 1934); and Juraj Kramer, *Slovenské autonomistické hnutie v rokoch 1918-1929* [The Slovak Autonomist Movement During the Years 1918-1929] (Bratislava, 1962), pp. 35-48.
80. Dr. L. C. Fagula, *Andrej Hlinka* (Bratislava, 1943), pp. 51, 53, and 93.
81. Robert W. Seton-Watson, *The New Slovakia* (Prague, 1924), pp. 40-41.
82. C. A. Macartney, *Hungary and Her Successors* (New York, 1937), pp. 112-118; see also Mamatey, *The United States and East-Central Europe*, p. 283.
83. Fagula, *Andrej Hlinka*, p. 65.
84. Ibid., p. 70.
85. Ibid., p. 78.
86. Crane to the Secretary of State, October 16, 191, National Archives, Department of State File 860F.00/34.
87. Mikuš, *Slovakia*, p. 346.
88. Vladimír Sís, *Dr. Karel Kramář. Život a dílo. Skizza* [Dr. Karel Kramář. Life and Work. Skizza] (Prague, 1930), p. 136.
89. *Dokumenty*, ed. Nečásek *et al.*, pp. 13-20.
90. Lloyd George, *Memoirs of the Peace Conference*, I, p. 242.
91. Ibid.
92. Ibid., pp. 246-247.
93. Ibid., p. 229.
94. Ibid., p. 378.
95. Sís, *Dr. Karel Kramář*, pp. 167-168; and Peroutka, *Budování státu*, II, pp. 1318-1330.
96. *Boj o směr vývoje,* ed. Kocman *et al.*, I, p. 361.
97. Ibid., pp. 68-70.
98. Ibid.
99. Sís, *Dr. Karel Kramář*, p. 168; and Kramář, *Pět přednášek*, p. 90.

Notes to Chapter Seventeen   601

100. Sís, *Dr. Karel Kramář*, p. 169. Some of the leaders of the Czech Legion in Siberia were anti-Kolchak and favored the socialist groups.
101. Ibid., pp. 250-251.
102. Ibid., p. 171.
103. Ibid., pp. 229-230.
104. Ibid., pp. 221 and 224.
105. Ibid., p. 224.
106. Ibid., p. 170. The whole document is in Dr. Karel Kramář, *Ruská krise* [The Russian Crisis] (Prague, 1921), pp. 507-520.
107. Kramář, *Pět přednášek*, p. 108.

Chapter Seventeen:
Those Who Fought in Russia and Siberia

1. The various interpretations are found in some of the sources cited previously, for example Bradley, "The Allies," Šteidler, Zmrhal, Kvasnička, Vávra, Veselý, Holotík, Fic (two books), František Polák, *Sibiřská anabase čsl. legií* [The Siberian Anabasis of the Czechoslovak Legions] (New York, 1961); Zuman, Lazarevsky, and many others.
2. Šteidler, *Československé hnutí*, p. 114. According to Šteidler, altogether 67,750 persons were evacuated from Siberia, of whom 56,459 were soldiers. Among the latter, however, some were Russians who had joined the Czechoslovak army earlier and who had no other place to go, and conscripts from among the prisoners of war in Siberia whose domicile was in Czechoslovakia.
3. *Deník plukovníka Švece*, pp. 338-339; see also Konstantin W. Sakharov, *Das weisse Sibirien* (Munich, 1925), pp. 27-28; Josef Kudela, *Aksakovská tragedie (Plukovník Švec)* [The Aksakov Tragedy (Colonel Švec)] (Brno, 1932); and Ferdinand Pražský, *Dějiny pěšího pluku 10 Jana Sladkého Koziny* [History of the Tenth Infantry Regiment of Jan Sladký Kozina] (Brno, 1927).
4. Dürich, *V českých službách*, p. 93.
5. *Pravda*, No. 65, April 6, 1918.
6. Denikine, *The White Army*, p. 158.
7. N. I. Shatagin, *Organizaciia i stroiitelstvo Sovietskoi armii v 1918-1920 gg.* (Moscow, 1954), p. 63, cited in Vávra, *Klamná cesta*, p. 219n.
8. Footman, *Civil War*, pp. 83, 158, and 161.

9. Lazarevský, *Rusko a československé znovuzrození*, pp. 122ff.
10. Dürich, *V českých službách*, pp. 99-100.
11. Kramář, *Pět přednášek*, p. 64.
12. Beneš, III, pp. 492-495; and Karel Horký, *Masaryk redivivus?* (Prague, 1926), p. 23.
13. Syllaba, T. G. *Masaryk a revoluce v Rusku*, p. 193; and Veselý, *O vzniku*, p. 55.
14. Veselý, *Češi a Slováci*, p. 137.
15. *Masaryk a revoluční armáda*, pp. 224-226.
16. Veselý, *Češi a Slováci*, p. 136; and *Boj o směr vývoje*, ed. Kocman et al., I, pp. 250-252.
17. Peroutka, *Budování státu*, p. 563. For a personal account of one of the Czech Bolsheviks in Russia who was a political commissar in the Red Army and who returned, clandestinely, to Czechoslovakia to carry out the assignments for which he was trained in Russia, see Čeněk Hruška, *Cesta k revoluci. Vzpomínky generálporučíka Čeňka Hrušky z let 1914-1919* [The Road to Revolution. Memories of Lieutenant-General Čeňek Hruška on the Years 1914-1919] (Prague, 1965).
18. Hruška, *Cesta k revoluci*, pp. 26-264.
19. Veselý, *Češi a Slováci*, pp. 147-149.
20. Ibid., p. 230.
21. For details and documentation see Kvasnička, *Československé légie v Rusku*, p. 219-318. See also Křížek, *Jaroslav Hašek*, pp. 235-293.
22. Veselý, *Češi a Slováci*, p. 179; Hruška, *Cesta k revoluci*, pp. 232-264.
23. Veselý, *Češi a Slováci*, pp. 180-181.
24. Ibid., p. 184.
25. Pichlík, *Zahraniční odboj*, p. 464.
26. Holotík, *Štefánikovská legenda*, pp. 291-293.
27. Ibid., p. 458.
28. Ibid., p. 460.
29. Ibid., pp. 509-510; and p. 241.
30. Masaryk, *The Making of a State*, p. 312.
31. Veselý, *Češi a Slováci*, p. 155; Kvasnička, *Československé légie*, pp. 162-168; and Holotík, *Štefánikovská legenda*, pp. 252-253.
32. Kratochvíl, *Cesta revoluce*, p. 295; Holotík, *Štefánikovská legenda*, p. 246.

Notes to Chapter Seventeen 603

33. Holotík, *Štefánikovská legenda*, p. 247.
34. J. Řepka, *II. sjezd československého vojska na Rusi* [The Second Congress of the Czechoslovak Army in Russia] (Prague, 1928), p. 72.
35. Janin, *Moje účast*, p. 181; Holotík, *Štefánikovská legenda*, p. 250.
36. Holotík, *Štefánikovská legenda*, p. 251.
37. Jindřich Skácel, *Československá armáda v Rusku a Kolčak* [The Czechoslovak Army in Russia and Kolchak] (Prague, 1926, pp. 132-133.
38. *Československý denník*, January 17, 1919; Holotík, *Štefánikovská legenda*, p. 252.
39. Holotík, *Štefánikovská legenda*, pp. 297 and 257.
40. Ibid., p. 257.
41. Louise Weiss, *Mémoires d'une Européenne*, quoted in Osuský's paper.
42. On Kolchak and the war in Siberia see John F. N. Bradley, *La légion tchécoslovaque en Russie 1914-1920* (Paris, 1965); G. Gins, *Sibir, Soyuzniki in Kolchak* [Peking, 1921); L. Grondijs, *Le Cas Koltchak* (Leyden, 1949); General M. Janin, *Ma mission en Sibérie 1918-20* (Paris, 1933); Margarete Klante, *Von der Wolga zum Amur* (Berlin, 1931); S. P. Melgunov, *Tragediya Admirala Kolchaka*, 3 vols. (Belgrade, 1930-1931); P. S. Parfenov, *Borba za Dalni Vostok* (Moscow, 1928), and *Grazhdanskaya Voina v Sibiri* (Moscow, 1924); Sakharov, *Das weisse Sibirien;* G. Semenov, *O sebe* (Harbin, 1938); Elena Varneck and H. H. Fisher, *The Testimony of Kolchak and Other Siberian Materials* (Stanford, 1935); Fink, *Bílý admirál;* Skácel, *Československá armáda* (the list is not exhaustive).
43. Churchill, *The Aftermath*, p. 285.
44. For details and documents see *Boj o směr vývoje*, ed. Kocman *et al.*, vol. I, pp. 67-71 and 361-364; Kramář, *Kramářův soud nad Benešem*, pp. 95-96; and T. G. Masaryk, *Cesta demokracie* [The Way of Democracy] (Prague, 1933), I, pp. 81-83.
45. Document cited in Kvasnička, *Československé légie*, p. 237.
46. Janko Jesenský, *Cestou k slobode; úryvky z denika 1914-18* [The Road to Freedom; Excerpts from Diary, 1914-1918] (Turčianský Sv. Martin, 1933 and Bratislava, 1968), pp. 220-221.
47. On Churchill's plan and Beneš's attitude toward it, see the memorandum by Winston Churchill, and Beneš to Lloyd George, June 23, 1919,

FRUS, PPC, 1919, vol. VI, pp. 684-686 and 708-709. The texts of the telegram and the letter of June 23, 1919 (Beneš to Masaryk) are in *Dokumenty*, ed. Nečásek *et al.*, pp. 49-52.
48. *Dokumenty*, ed. Nečásek *et al.*, p. 51.
49. Ibid., p. 52.
50. Kvasnička, *Československé légie*, p. 238.
51. Ibid., pp. 252-253.
52. Sís, *Dr. Karel Kramář. Skizza*, p. 301.
53. Skácel, *Československá armáda*, p. 234.
54. Kvasnička, *Československé légie*, pp. 239-240. In his report from Omsk, dated July 30, 1919, Ambassador Morris informed Lansing that "the Czech army is not in a position to proceed to the front or to continue the permanent guard of the railway, and will have to be evacuated gradually via Vladivostok." In view of the low morale of the troops, it was generally believed that "they will not fight their way to Archangel or to the Black Sea, irrespective of whether such will be the decision of the Czech Government or whether British troops would be maintained at Archangel to secure the junction." Morris to Lansing, July 30, 1919, Breckinridge Long Papers, Siberia, 1919.
55. Skácel, *Československá armáda*, pp. 235 and 240.
56. Kvasnićka, *Československá légie*, p. 269. See also Kratochvíl, *Cesta revoluce* (1922), p. 581; and Šeba, *Rusko a malá Dohoda*, pp. 472-473.
57. Kvasnička, *Československé légie*, p. 269.
58. Šeba, *Rusko a Malá Dohoda*, p. 473.
59. The Acting Secretary of State to the Commission to Negotiate Peace, September 22, 1919, FRUS, Russia, 1919, p. 298 (also pp. 299-301).
60. Kratochvíl, *Cesta revoluce* (1922), pp. 497 and 635; also *Národní Listy*, November 5, 1919. On the strenuous efforts of Pavlů and the several army officers not to abandon their positions, to return via land, and not to cause the collapse of the front, see Skácel, *Československá armáda*, pp. 274ff.
61. Šeba, *Rusko a Malá Dohoda*, p. 473; details in Skácel, pp. 250ff.
According to the judgment of Ambassador Morris, Kolchak was "an honest and courageous man of very limited experience in public affairs, of narrow views and small administrative ability . . . . His intentions are good,

but he seems to have had no appreciation, until recently, of the political and economic dangers which threaten the Government. He has no military knowledge or experience." The admiral was under the influence of "earnest men" who were honest but inefficient. His prospects therefore were dim. Morris to Lansing, August 4, 1919, Breckinridge Long Papers, Siberia, 1919.

62. The Secretary of State to the Commission to Negotiate Peace, November 22, 1919; The Chargé in China (Tenney) to the Secretary of State, November 25, 1919; The Chargé in China (Tenney) to the Secretary of State, December 18, 1919; and The Chargé (Tenney) to the Secretary of State, undated, received December 30, 1919, FRUS, 1919, Russia, pp. 314-315, 226-227, 230-231, and 235-236. Also Skácel, *Československá armáda*, pp. 250ff. Despite the offer by the Kolchak government to meet all Czechoslovak conditions, the evacuation was carried out, causing the collapse of the front. Details in Skácel, *Československá armáda*, pp. 282ff.

63. Footman, *Civil War*, p. 217.
64. Ibid., p. 226.
65. Kvasnička, *Československé légie*, p. 259; also Kratochvíl, *Cesta revoluce*, pp. 634ff.
66. Churchill, *The Aftermath*, pp. 258-260; and Footman, *Civil War*, p. 241.
67. Churchill, *The Aftermath*, p. 260.
68. Footman, *Civil War*, p. 242.
69. The text of the armistice agreement is in Kratochvíl, *Cesta revoluce*, pp. 653-656; and Skácel, *Československá armáda v Rusku a Kolčak*, pp. 372-373. See also V. Olivová, *Československo-sovětské vztahy v letech 1918-1922* [Czechoslovak-Soviet Relations during the Years 1918-1922] (Prague, 1957), pp. 107-109 and 475-479.
70. *Boj o směr vývoje*, ed. Kocman *et al.*, I, p. 27.
71. Mikuš, *Slovakia*, p. 15.
72. For details see Holotík, *Štefánikovská legenda*, pp. 266-276; also Král, *Intervenční válka*, p. 236; and Šeba, *Rusko a Malá Dohoda*, pp. 461-463.
73. Holotík, *Štefánikovská legenda*, pp. 269-271.

Chapter Eighteen:
Reflection, Recapitulation, and Aftermath

1. Robert W. Seton-Watson, *The Historian as a Political Force in Central Europe* (London, 1922), pp. 34-35.
2. Ibid.
3. Josef Kalvoda, "Academic Freedom in the Age of Conflict" (The Search for Truth), *Vital Speeches of the Day,* XXIX, No. 17 (June 15, 1963), pp. 526-531.
4. Seton-Watson, *The Historian as a Political Force,* p. 35.
5. "States are preserved by the ideals from which they had originated" is a dictum of Masaryk; it raises the questions: what were the ideals from which Czechoslovakia originated? Was that origin in the program of the State Rights party? Was it in Kramář's program for a Czech state affiliated with the Slavic Federation? Was it in Masaryk's *Independent Bohemia?* Was it in the Legion's decision to defy Masaryk, rise against the Soviets, and fight its way through to Vladivostok? According to Masaryk, the sending of Voska to Steed, early in the war, with intelligence data and a request for instructions was "the beginning."

As has been noted in this work, at that juncture of the war the architects of the "New Europe" saw an independent Bohemia as an alternative to a Russian-dominated Bohemia, and Masaryk was encouraged to endorse the idea of national independence at a time when Russian entry into Bohemia seemed to be imminent. Masaryk's "British connection" seems to be the "simple explanation" for the conflict between his and his followers' activities during the early stages of the war, and what the Czech leader had stood for before the war, a conflict incomprehensible to the free-thinking Czech-American publisher of *Vesmír,* Dr. Iška, who hoped that one day someone would discover an explanation.

After he called for a parliamentary inquiry on how government members (including Beneš) had acquired their properties, Charles Pergler was expelled from the parliament and from Czechoslovakia in 1932. The real reason for his expulsion from his native country might have been a fear that such an inquiry could have led to startling discoveries, exposing British intelligerence operations and the source of Masaryk's great fortune.

According to "The Last Will and Testament" written by Masaryk on April 15, 1917, before leaving for Russia, he had a debt in Prague and about

Notes to Chapter Eighteen 607

1,400 pounds of sterling in a London bank for his daughters Alice and Olga; he also had two other accounts from the "American Fund" amounting to over 16,000 pounds. Yet in 1932 he gave more that 10,000,000 crowns to the "Foundation of T. G. Masaryk." See Jaroslav Pecháček, *Masaryk, Beneš, Hrad* [Masaryk, Beneš, Castle] (München, 1984), pp. 81-82 and 166-173. Earlier, in March 1923, Masaryk gave 2,050,000 crowns to each member of his family—his wife Charlotte, son Jan, and daughters Alice and Olga, 1,025,000 crowns to Beneš, and the same amount to the latter's wife, for a total of 10,250,000 crowns. When in 1926 Beneš revealed receiving two million crowns gift from Masaryk, Count Clary, nephew of the Duke of Portland, told Jan Masaryk, then the Czechoslovak Minister in London, that the event was commented upon in England as follows: "I wonder if Beneš is the only one whom the President bought for himself." *Dokumenty,* ed. Nečásek *et al.,* p. 111. In 1923 Masaryk gave 500,000 crowns to a young journalist, Ferdinand Peroutka, for launching a new periodical *Přítomnost.* See Julius Firt, *Knihy a osudy* [Books and Fates] (Köln, 1972), p. 48; also Julius Firt, "Die 'Burg' und die Zeitschrift Přítomnost," in *Die "Burg." Einflussreiche politische Kräfte um Masaryk und Beneš,* ed. Karl Bosl, vol. II (München-Wien, 1974), pp. 111-126.

Beneš paid tens of millions of crowns in subsidies to foreign periodicals, journalists and other individuals from the secret funds of the Czechoslovak foreign ministry. For details see Rudolf Urban, *Tajné fondy III. sekce. Z archivu ministerstva zahraničí Republiky česko-slovenské.* [The Secret Funds of the III. Section. From the Archive of the Ministry of Foreign Affairs of the Czechoslovak Republic] (Prague, 1943). Among others, Urban lists amounts of money that Beneš sent to the Czechoslovak Minister in Paris, Štefan Osuský; they correspond to those this writer has found in the Osuský Papers. For example, in 1922, Beneš sent to Osuský for propaganda 401,600 frs., in 1927 already 746,000 frs. (of which 200,000 were paid to the Russian historian Miliukov). In 1938 the total amount sent by Beneš to France amounted to 3,346,533.95 crowns of which Osuský received two million. From the 2,476,788 frs. that Osuský received, he paid out 1,560,910 frs. In one year Henry Wickham Steed received £10,000 in subsidies for his periodical *Review of Reviews.* In 1935 a publishing house in Prague, Orbis, received from Beneš one million crowns. These are just a few examples of the many payments made by Beneš from the secret funds of "his" ministry.

By a strange twist of fate the career of Voska, Masaryk's messenger to Steed and later his intelligence chief, ended in a communist prison camp in Czechoslovakia. The octogenarian Voska was imprisoned for an alleged involvement in the affair of Rudolf Slánský, the one-time secretary general of the Communist party of Czechoslovakia, who was executed in 1952.

6. Beneš, I, p. vii.
7. Ibid., p. 8.
8. Masaryk, *The Making of a State*, pp. 30 and 316; and Masaryk, *Otázka sociální*, II, pp. 300-301.
9. Beneš, I, pp. vii and 10.
10. Clement Richard Attlee, *As It Happened* (New York, 1954), pp. 131-132.
11. Masaryk, *Česká otázka;* see also chapter 1 above, notes 63-64 and Syllaba, *Masaryk a revoluce v Rusku*, pp. 12ff.
12. Masaryk, *Česká otázka*, p. 255.
13. See chapter 1, notes 63-66.
14. Tomáš G. Masaryk, *Americké přednášky* (Prague, 1924), p. 51; and *V boji o náboženství* (Prague, 1904), p. 43.
15. Jaksch, *Europe's Road to Potsdam*, p. 126.
16. *Do roka a do dne! Řeč Dra. Karla Perglera na veřejné schůzi Čechů a Slováků v Chicagu 18. září 1932* [Before One Year and One Day is Over! Address Delivered by Dr. Karel Pergler at a Public Meeting of Czechs and Slovaks in Chicago] (Chicago, 1932). Also *Treaty Series, 1919*, pp. 129-140.
17. Čulen, *Pittsburghská Dohoda*, pp. 413ff; Slovak Catholic Federation of America, *The Slovaks and the Pittsburgh Pact* (Chicago, 1934), pp. 36-39; Fragula, *Andrej Hlinka*, pp. 51, 53, and 93; Sidor, *Andrej Hlinka*, p. 495.
18. Sidor, *Slovenská politika*, pp. 186-187 and 169.
19. Mikuš, *Slovakia*, p. 70.
20. Nicholas Murray Butler, *Why War?* (New York, 1940), p. 20.
21. Crane to the Secretary of State, February 11, 1920, National Archives, Department of State File 860F.00/71.
22. The quotation is from Masaryk, *The Making of a State*, p. 140; Kramář, *Na obranu Slovanské politiky*, pp. 57-59.
23. Ibid.; see also Seton-Watson, *Masaryk in England*, pp. 116-136; and Beneš, III, pp. 237-256.

Notes to Chapter Eighteen

24. The whole document is in *Dokumenty*, ed. Merhout, pp. 30-33.
25. Kramář, *Na obranu Slovanské politiky*, p. 57.
26. Masaryk, *The Making of a State*, p. 61.
27. Eduard Beneš, *Le problème autrichien et la question tschèque* (Paris, 1908), p. 307.
28. Details in chapter 1.
29. Beneš, I, p. 143.
30. Masaryk, *Nová Evropa*, pp. 109-114.
31. Czernin, *Im Weltkriege*, p. 41; for details, see pp. 40ff.
32. Ibid., p. 259.
33. Lansing, *Memoirs*, pp. 269-271.
34. Ibid., p. 271.
35. Beneš, III, p. 415, and II, p. 283.
36. Masaryk, p. xiv.
37. Among the historians have been those quoted in this work, e.g., Holotík, Kvasnička, Křížek, Kalina, Hanák, Fowler, Footman, Bradley, etc.
38. Masaryk, *The Making of a State*, pp. 368 and 191.
39. Ibid., p. 276.
40. Memorandum, Relief of Czecho-Slovak Forces in Siberia, n.d., with attachments on availability of military supplies to the Czecho-Slovaks, dated August 19 and 29, 1918, Breckinridge Long Papers, Siberia, 1918. See also Perman, *The Shaping of the Czechoslovak State*, p. 41.
41. Papoušek, *Carské Rusko*, pp. 147-155; 180-181.
42. Beneš, III, pp. 318-321.
43. Hans Roos, *A History of Modern Poland* (New York, 1966), pp. 33-34.
44. Churchill, *The Aftermath*, p. 256.
45. Paulová, *Tajný výbor*, pp. 471-472.
46. Masaryk, *Nová Evropa*, p. 130.
47. George F. Kennan, *Memoirs, 1925-1950* (Boston-Toronto, 1967), p. 94.
48. Masaryk, *The Making of a State*, p. 288.
49. Ibid., p. 369.
50. Čihák, et al., *Dějiny ČSR*, p. 55; *Dokumenty*, ed. Merhout, pp. 212ff.
51. The U.S. Legation at Prague (Crane) to the Secretary of State,

February 15, 1920, and February 8, 1921, National Archives, Department of State File 860F.00/75 and 860F.00/156.
  52. Sís, *Dr. Karel Kramář*, pp. 170, 168, 171, and 250.

Kramář worried about the future of his country, deplored Masaryk's attitudes toward the Catholics and the Slovaks, and did his best to make the two groups into loyal supporters of the state. He succeeded in reconciling the conflicting positions of Catholics and so-called freethinkers on the issue of state holidays honoring Jan Hus and Sts. Cyril and Methodius; and he gained the confidence of Andrej Hlinka and the Slovaks by working out a compromise. As they did in the cases of General Gajda and Jiří Stříbrný (one of the "men of the twenty-eighth of October"), Masaryk and Beneš plotted against Kramář. In a letter to Beneš (August 23, 1926), Masaryk expressed his view that the party of Kramář had to be "finished off for good." (See Pecháček, *Masaryk, Beneš, Hrad,* p. 41.) Yet Kramář was not silenced and continued to voice his forebodings, exhortations, and warnings until his death. On issues of foreign policy and national defense, however, his voice was that of one crying in the wilderness.

On May 29, 1937, at Kramář's coffin, Prime Minister Milan Hodža declared, "In our nation's heart, next to the victorious fighter, an honorable place has always belonged to the martyr." (See *Odkaz a pravda Dr. Karla Kramáře* [The Legacy of Dr. Karel Kramář], ed. Vladimír Sís (Prague, 1939), p. 8; also pp. 126-128.) Kramář combined both the fighter and the martyr. As a fighter, he led the nation to independence—to October 28, 1918—while his adversaries brought it to the capitulation of September 30, 1938.

BIBLIOGRAPHY

DOCUMENTS AND PRIVATE PAPERS

Allied and Associated Powers. *The Treaties of Peace 1919-1923*. With an Introduction by Colonel Lawrence Martin, Library of Congress. New York: Carnegie Endownment for International Peace, 1924, 2 vols.

Gordon Auchincloss Diary and Papers, Sterling Memorial Library, Yale University.

Austria. Haus-, Hof- und Staatsarchiv, Vienna. Kriegsarchiv: Armeeoberkommando Operationsabteilung, 1914-1918; Armeeoberkommando, Evidenzbüro, 1915-1917; Korpskommando (Militärkommando Prag), 1914-1918; Kriegsüberwachunsamt, 1915-1918; K.u.k. Kriegsministerium, Präsidialakten, 1915-1918; Militärkanzlei Seiner Majestät, 1914-1918; Deutsch-Österreichisches Staatsamt für Heerwesen, 1918-1920.

Bednařík, František, ed., *Československé vojsko v Italii ve světle současných zpráv* [Czechoslovak Army in Italy in the Light of Current Reports], Prague, *Naše revoluce*, vol. VIII, 1932.

———, *General M. R. Štefánik v Italii. Řada dokumentů*. [General M. R. Štefánik in Italy. Several Documents], Prague, *Naše revoluce*, vol. X, 1934.

———, *K činnosti československých výzvědných oddílu na italské frontě* [About the Activities of the Czechoslovak Patrol Units on the Italian Front], Prague, *Naše revoluce*, vol. IX, 1935.

———, *Několik dokumentů ke vzniku italské legie* [A Few Documents on the Emergence of the Italian Legion], Prague, *Naše revoluce*, vol. I, 1923.

Bednařík, F., V. Beneš, J. Borovička, and F. Lakomý, eds., *Dokumenty o revoluční činnosti Štefánikovy* [Documents About Revolutionary Activity of Štefánik], Prague, *Naše revoluce*, vol. II, 1924.

Beneš, Eduard, ed., *Světová válka a naše revoluce. Dokumenty* [World War and Our Revolution. Documents]. Vol. III, Prague: Orbis, 1928, xx, 686 pp.

Tasker H. Bliss Papers. Manuscripts Division, Library of Congress.

Crane, Charles R. The Crane Papers, Butler Library, Columbia University.

Crane, Richard. The Richard Crane Papers, Manuscript Division, Georgetown University.

Cumming, C. K., and W. W. Pettit, eds., *Russian-American Relations, 1917-1920*. Documents and Papers. New York, 1920.

Czechoslovak Republic. Ministerstvo zahraničních věcí [Ministry of Foreign Affairs] *Archiv diplomatických dokumentů československých.* [Archive of Czechoslovak Diplomatic Documents] Prague: Orbis, 1927-28. 2 vols.

————, Národní Shromáždění, [National Assembly]. *Těsnopisecké zprávy o schůzích Národního shromáždění, 14 XI, 1918 - 15, IV, 1920* [Stenographic Reports of Sessions of the National Assembly, 11-14-1918 through 4-15-1920], Prague: Politika, 1919-20. 4 vols.

————, ————, *Tisky k těsnopiseckým zprávám o schůzích Národního shromáždění, 14 XI, 1918 - 15. VI, 1920* [Accompanying Documents to the Stenographic Reports . . .], Prague, 1919-20. 10 vols.

————, Předsednictví Národního Shromáždění [Presidium of the National Assembly]. *Národní shromáždění československé v prvním roce republiky* [Czechoslovak National Assembly During the First Year of the Republic]. Prague: Státní nakladatelství, 1919. 300 pp.

————, Masarykův archiv, Prague. Vojenský historický archiv, Prague. Archiv Národního muzea, Prague.

Delegation Propaganda: Czechoslovakia. Delegation to the Paris Peace Conference. Memoires. Nos. I-XI, Hoover Library, Stanford University. 13 vols.

France. Ministère de la Guerre, section historique, Paris.
Diplomatické dokumenty o československém státu [Diplomatic Documents About the Czechoslovak State]. Paris, 1918.

Great Britain. Foreign Office. *Documents on British Foreign Policy 1919-1939*. Edited by E. L. Woodward and Rohan Bulter. First Series, 1919-30. London: H. M. Stationery Office, 1947-52. 4 vols.

Bibliography

———, ———. *British and Foreign State Papers.* 1917-1920. London: H. M. Stationery Office, 1921-23. Vols. CXI-CXIII.

———. General Staff. War Office. *Daily Review of the Foriegn Press.* Enemy Press Supplements. 1916-1919. 2 vols.

———. House of Commons. *Treaty between the principal Allied and Associated Powers and Czecho-Slovakia.* Signed at Saint-Germain-enlaye, September 10, 191. Treaty Series, 1919, no. 20. London: H. M. Stationery Office, 1919, pp. 129-40.

———, ———. *Treaty between the principal Allied and Associated Powers and Poland, Roumania, the Serb-Croat-Slovene state and the Czecho-Slovak state relative to certain frontiers of these states.* Signed at Sevres, August 10, 1920. Treaty Series, 1921, no. 20. London: H. M. Stationery Office, 1921. pp. 281-88.

———. The War Cabinet. *Report 1917-1918.* London: H. M. Stationery Office, 1919. 2 vols., maps.

———. Public Record Office. Cabinet, 1914-1918.

———. Public Record Office. Foreign Office, 1914-1919.

———. The Milner Papers, Oxford.

Golder, Frank Alfred, ed. *Documents of Russian History, 1914-1917.* Translated by Emanuel Aronsberg. New York: 1927.

Gwyn, Stephen, ed. *Documents of Russian History, 1914-1917.* New York: 1927.

Samuel N. Harper Papers, University of Chicago.

George D. Herron Papers, Hoover Library, Stanford University.

E. M. House Papers. E. M. House Collection, Sterling Memorial Library, Yale University.

Kocman, A., V. Pletka, J. Radimský, M. Trantírek, and L. Urbánková, eds., *Boj o směr vývoje československého státu,* 1 [Struggle for the Direction of Development of the Czechoslovak State], 2 vols. Prague, 1965-69.

Kudela, Josef, ed., *Deník plukovníka Švece* [Diary of Colonel Švec], Prague, 1921.

———, *Masaryk v OČSNR na Rusi* [Masaryk in the Branch of the Czecho-Slovak National Council in Russia], *Naše revoluce,* vols. VII-VIII, 1931-32.

———, *Petrohradský sjezd a druhé slyšení u cara Nikolaje II. Soubor dokumentů a vzpomínek.* [Petrograd Congress and the Second Audience with Tsar Nicholas II. Collection of Documents and Memories], Prague, *Naše revoluce,* vol. X, 1934.

——, *Zpráva plnomocníka OČSNR v Samaře a Ufě* [Report of the Plenipotentiary of the Branch of the Czecho-Slovak National Council in Russia in Samara and Ufa], Prague, *Naše revoluce,* vol. XI, 1936.

Robert Lansing Confidential Memoranda, Manuscript Division, Library of Congress.

Robert Lansing Desk Diaries, Manuscript Division, Library of Congress.

Robert Lansing Papers, Manuscript Division, Library of Congress.

Breckinridge Long Papers, Manuscript Division, Library of Congress.

Breckinridge Long Papers, Diary; and *Siberia,* Excerpts from Long's Diary, January 10-November 6, 1918.

Masaryk a revoluční armáda; Masarykovy projevy k legiím a o legiích v zahraniční revoluci [Masaryk and the Revolutionary Army; Masaryk's Speeches to the Legions and About Legions During the Revolution Abroad], Prague, 1921.

Masarykova práce, Sborník ze spisů, řečí a projevů... [Masaryk's Work, Selection of Speeches and Addresses...], Prague, 1930.

Masarykovy projevy a řeči za války [Masaryk's Addresses and Speeches During the War], I-II, Prague, 1919-1920.

Merhout, Cyril, ed. *Dokumenty našeho osvobození* [Documents on Our Liberation], Prague: 1919.

National Archives, Department of State Files, 1917-1924, Washington, D.C.

Nečásek, František, Jan Pachta and Eva Raisová, eds. *Dokumenty o protilidové a protinárodní politice T. G. Masaryka* [Documents Relating to Anti-People and Anti-National Policy of T. G. Masaryk], Prague, 1953.

Nečásek, František, and Jan Pachta, eds. *Dokumenty o protisovětských piklech československe reakce. Z archivního materiálu o kontrarevoluční činnosti Masaryka a Beneše v letech 1917-1924* [Documents Relating to Anti-Soviet Conspiracy of the Czechoslovak Reactionaries. From the Archival Materials on the Counter-Revolutionary Activity of Masaryk and Beneš, 1917-1924], Prague, 1954.

Otáhalová, Libuše, ed., *Souhrnná hlášení presidia pražského místodržitelství o protistátní, protirakouské a protiválečné, činnosti v Čechách 1915-1918* [Comprehensive Reports of the Presidium of the Viceroyalty at Prague on the Anti-State, Anti-Austrian and Anti-War Activity in Bohemia, 1915-1918], Prague, 1957.

Pamětní spis o československé otázce. Vydáni českého výpomocného spolku v Petrohradě 1914. [The Memorial Script on the Czech Question]. Prague, *Naše revoluce,* vol. I, 1923.

Popoušek, Jaroslav, ed., *Důvěrné memorandum o československé otázce. Elaborát ruského ministerstva zahraničních věcí ze září 1916* [Confidential Memorandum on the Czechoslovak Question. Analysis by the Russian Ministry of Foreign Affairs of September, 1916], Prague, *Naše revoluce,* vol. II, 1924.

――――. *Carské Rusko a naše osvobození* [Tsarist Russia and Our Liberation]. Prague, 1927.

――――, *Masarykovo memorandum o československém vojsku a zajatcích ze dne 3. III. 1918* [Masaryk's Memorandum on the Czechoslovak Army and Prisoners of War of March 3, 1918], Prague, *Masarykův sborník,* vol. II, 1926-1927.

William Phillips Papers. Harvard University.

Frank L. Polk Papers. E. M. House Collection, Sterling Memorial Library, Yale University.

Scott, James Brown, ed. *Official Statements of War Aims and Peace Proposals, December 1916 to November 1918.* Washington, 1921.

Soukup, František, *28 říjen 1918* [28th of October, 1918]. 2 vols. Prague, 1928.

Soviet Union. *Dokumenty vneshnei politiki SSSR* [Document of the Foreign Policy of the U.S.S.R.]. Vols. I and II (November 7, 1917—December 31, 1918; and January 1919—June 30, 1920). Moscow, 1957 and 1958.

Tobolka, Zdeněk, ed., *Obžalovací spis proti Václavu Klofáčovi a Rudolfu Giuniovi pro zločin velezrady dle par. 58c tr. z.* [Bill of Indictment against Václav Klofáč and Rudolf Giuniov for the Crime of High Treason according to Article 58c of the Penal Code], Prague, 1919.

――――, *Proces dr. Kramáře a jeho přátel, I-V* [Trial of Dr. Kramář and His Friends], Prague, 1918-1920.

United States of America. Department of State. *Papers Relating to the Foreign Relations of the United States.* The Lansing Papers, 1914-1920. Washington: U.S. Government Printing Office, 1939-40. 2 vols.

――――. ――――. *Papers Relating to the Foreign Relations of the United States.* 1917. Washington: U.S. Government Printing Office, 1926. 1242 pp.

———. ———. *Papers Relating to the Foreign Relations of the United States.* 1917. Supplement I, The World War. Washington: U.S. Government Printing Office, 1931. 708pp.

———. ———. *Papers Relating to the Foreign Relations of the United States.* 1917. Supplement 2, The World War. Washington: U.S. Government Printing Office, 1932. Vol. I, 796pp.

———. ———. *Papers Relating to the Foreign Relations of the United States.* 1918. Supplement I, The World War. Washington: U.S. Government Printing Office, 1933. Vol. I, 914pp.

———. ———. *Papers Relating to the Foreign Relations of the United States.* 1918. Supplement 2, The World War. Washington: U.S. Government Printing Office, 1933. 862pp.

———. ———. *Papers Relating to the Foreign Relations of the United States.* 1918. Russia. Washington: U.S. Government Printing Office, 1931-32. 3 vols.

———. ———. *Papers Relating to the Foreign Relations of the United States.* 1919. Washington: U.S. Government Printing Office, 1934, 2 vols.

———. ———. *Papers Relating to the Foreign Relations of the United States.* 1919. Paris Peace Conference. Washington: U.S. Government Printing Office, 1942-47. 13 vols.

———. ———. *Papers Relating to the Foreign Relations of the United States.* 1919. Russia. Washington: U.S. Government Printing Office, 1937. 807pp.

———. ———. *Papers Relating to the Foreign Relations of the United States.* 1920. Washington: U.S. Government Printing Office, 1935-36. Vol. I, 861pp. Vol. III, 823pp.

Vávra, V. ed., *Francouzské dokumenty k přípravě protisovětského vystoupení čs. legií* [French Documents on the Preparation of the Anti-Soviet Action by the Czechoslovak Legions], Prague, *Historie a vojenství,* 1963/3.

Werstadt, Jaroslav, ed. *Hrdinové a věřící* [Heroes and Believers], Prague, 1928.

———, *K politice poslance dr. Bohumíra Šmerala, vůdce české sociální demokracie v prvních letech války* [On Politics of Deputy Dr. Bohumír Šmeral, Leader of Czech Social Democracy During the First Years of the War], Prague, *Naše revoluce,* vol. IX, 1933.

Bibliography 617

———, *K revoluční činnosti M. R. Štefánika* [On Revolutionary Activity of M. R. Štefánik], Prague, *Naše revoluce,* vol. VI, 1929-30.
———, *K úloze Karla Kramáře v našem odboji. Soubor dokumentů a projevů* [On the Role of Karel Kramář in Our Resistance. Collection of Documents and Speeches], Prague, *Naše revoluce,* vol. XIV, 1938.
———, *K životopisu a veřejné činnosti Svatopluka Koníčka-Horského* [On the Biography and Public Activity of Svatopluk Koníček-Horský], Prague, *Naše revoluce,* vol. IX, 1933.
William Wiseman Papers. E. M. House Collection, Sterling Memorial Library, Yale University.
The Arthur Willert Papers, Sterling Memorial Library, Yale University.
Woodrow Wilson Papers. Manuscripts Division, Library of Congress.
Zapletal, Florian, ed. *Album velezrádců. Velezrádné rejdy Čechů za hranicemi* [Album of High Traitors. Treasonous Tricks of Czechs Abroad], Prague, 1919.

MEMOIRS AND REMINISCENCES

Beneš, Edvard, "Milan Rostislav Štefánik," *Naše revoluce,* vol. II, 1924.
———, *Několik setkání s T. G. Masarykem, Sborník vzpomínek na T. G. Masaryka* [A Few Meetings with T. G. Masaryk, Collection of Memories on T. G. Masaryk], Prague, 1930.
———. *Světová válka a naše revoluce,* vzpomínky a úvahy z bojů za svobodu národa [World War and Our Revolution, Reminiscences and Reflections from the Time of Struggle for the Freedom of the Nation], Prague, 1927. 2 vols.
Beneš, Vojta. *Tottenham Court Road. Sborník vzpomínek...* Prague, 1930.
———. *Vojáci zapomenuté fronty* [Soldiers of the Forgotten Front], Prague, 1923.
Bělehrádek, František. *Z mafiánských a jiných vzpomínek* [From the Maffian and Other Reminiscences], *Naše revoluce,* vol. VI, 1929-1930.
Borský, Lev. *Z civilního generálního štábu* [From the Civilian General Staff], Prague, 1924.
———. *Znovudobytí samostatnosti* [The Regaining of Independence], Prague, 1928.

Ček, Stanislav. *Z bouří a zmatku* [From the Storms and Confusions], *Sborník vzpomínek*... Prague, 1930.

Červinka, General M. *Až kam* [Up to Where.], Prague, 1923.

Císař, Jaroslav. *Masarykova America, Masaryk-Osvoboditel* [Masaryk's America, Masaryk-Liberator], Prague, 1920.

Denikine, Anton. *The White Army,* Coral Breeze, Florida, 1973.

Dürich, Josef. *V českých službách,* vypsáni mého pobytu za hranicemi, 1915-1918 [In the Czech Service; description of my sojourn abroad, 1915-1918]. Klášter nad Jizerou, 1921.

Dyk, Viktor. *Vzpomínky a komentáře* [Memories and Commentaries], Prague, 1927. 2 vols.

―――. *O národní stát* [For a National State], 1917-1919, Prague, 1933.

Eisenmann, Louis. *Masaryk a Denis* [Masaryk and Denis]. *Masarykův sborník,* Prague, vol. VI, 1930-1931.

Fierlinger, Zdeněk. *T. G. Masaryk a vojáci naší revoluce* [T. G. Masaryk and the Soldiers of Our Revolution]. *Sborník vzpomínek*... Prague, 1930.

―――. *Vzpomínka na T. G. Masaryka, T. G. M. Jak jsme ho viděli* [Reminiscence on T. G. Masaryk. T. G. Masaryk. How We Saw Him]. Prague, 1947.

Filla, Emil. *Hlídka české Maffie v Holandsku* [Outpost of the Czech Maffie in Holland]. Prague, 1934.

Forman, Josef. *Záhadná aféra české tiskové kanceláře v Londýně za války* [The Mysterious Affair of the Czech Press Office in London During the War], *Naše revoluce,* vol. X, 1934.

Gajda, Generál Ruských Legií R. *Moje paměti;* československá anabase; zpět na Urál proti Bolševikům―Admirál Kolčak [My Memoirs; the Czechoslovak Annabasis; Back to Ural against the Bolsheviks―Admiral Kolchak]. Prague, 1920.

Getting, Milan. *V rušnom roku 1918 v New Yorku* [In the Busy Year 1918 in New York], *Sborník vzpomínek*... Prague, 1930.

Habrman, Gustav. *Mé vzpomínky za války* [My Memories from the Time of War]. Prague, 1928.

Hajšman, Jan. *Česká Maffie.* Vzpomínky na odboj doma [Czech Maffie. Reminiscences on the Home Resistance]. Prague, 1934.

―――. *Maffie v rozmachu* [Maffie in Its Growth]. Prague, 1933.

Herben, Jan. *Kniha vzpomínek* [Book of Memories]. Prague, 1933.

Hlaváč, Bedřich. *Masaryk a Rakousko* [Masaryk and Austria], *Masarykův sborník*, vol. VI, 1930-1931.

Hlaváček, František. *Činnost dr. Beneše za války v Italii a moje spolupráce s ním* [Activity of Dr. Beneš in Italy during the War and My Collaboration with Him]. *Naše revoluce*, vol. XII, 1936.

Hruban, Mořic. *Z časů nedlouho zašlých* [Out of Recent Times]. Rome-Los Angeles, 1967.

Hryhorijiv, N. *Autorita prof. T. G. Masaryka na Ukraině* [The Authority of Professor T. G. Masaryk in the Ukraine], *Naše revoluce*, vol. XII, 1936.

Janin, Maurice. *O vedení a vůdcích československé revoluce za hranicemi* [About the Leadership and the Leaders of the Czechoslovak Revolution Abroad], *Naše revoluce*, vol. XII, 1936.

———. *Moje účast* [My Participation]. Prague, 1926.

———. *Úvahy o Dürichově misi* [Reflections on the Dürich Mission]. *Naše revoluce*, vol. XIII, 1937.

Kozák, J. B. *European Review, Sborník vzpomínek...*, Prague, 1930.

Kramář, Karel. *Paměti Dr. Karla Kramáře* [Memoirs of Dr. Karel Kramář]. Prague, 1938.

Kudela, Josef. *S naším vojskem na Rusi* [With Our Army in Russia]. Prague, n.d. 2 vols.

Kvapil, Jaroslav. *O čem vím* [What I Know]. Prague, 1928.

———. *Projev českých spisovatelů r. 1917* [Address of the Czech Writers in 1917]. Prague, 1924.

Lansing, Robert. *War Memoirs.* Indianopolis: Bobbs-Merrill, 1935.

Lavička, Josef. *Švýcarské vzpomínky z válečných let* [Reminiscences on Switzerland from the War Years]. *Naše revoluce*, vol. X, 1934.

Linhart, Josef. *Z počátku našeho odboje ve Švýcarsku* [On the Beginnings of Our Resistance in Switzerland]. *Sborník vzpomínek...*, Prague, 1930.

Machar, J. S. *Vídeňské profily* [Vienna Profiles]. Prague, 1919.

Masaryk, T. G. *The Making of a State;* memories and observations, 1914-1918. An English version arranged and prepared with an introduction by Henry Wickham Steed. New York: F. A. Stokes, 1927.

———. *Světová Revoluce za války a ve válce 1914-1918* [World Revolution During the War and in the War, 1914-1918]. Prague, 1925.

Maxa, Prokop. *T. G. Masaryk a štockholmská konference* [T. G. Masaryk and the Conference at Stockholm], *Sborník vzpomínek...*, Prague, 1930.

Medek, Rudolf. *Pouť do Československa. Válečné paměti a vzpomínky z let 1914-1920* [Pilgrimage to Czechoslovakia. War-Time Memories and Reminiscences from the Years 1914-1920]. Prague, n.d. 4 vols.

Mezi Prahou a Švýcary. *Vzpomínky revolučních poslů (L. V. Facka, J. Lavičky, L. Linhartové, E. Bernarda, A. Kopřivové)* [Between Prague and Switzerland. Reminiscences of Revolutionary Couriers...]. *Naše revoluce,* vol. V, 1927-1928.

Miljukov, P. N. *Čemu mně naučil Masaryk* [What I Have Learned from Masaryk]. *Sborník vzpomínek...,* Prague, 1930.

Miller, David Hunter. *My Diary at the Conference of Paris.* New York, 1924-26, 12 vols.

Nosek, Vladimír. *Anglie a náš boj za samostatnost* [England and Our Struggle for Independence]. Prague, 1926.

―――. *Dvě kapitoly z naší revoluční propagandy v Anglii* [Two Chapters from Our Revolutionary Propaganda in England]. *Naše revoluce,* vol. V, 1927-1928.

Osuský, Štefan. "How Czechoslovakia Was Born." Address delivered at Slovak World Congress in Toronto, Canada, June 17-19, 1971.

Papoušek, Jaroslav. *Masaryk v Rusku; Masaryk-Osvoboditel* [Masaryk in Russia; Masaryk-Liberator]. Prague, 1920.

Pavlů, Bohdan. *O založení Národní rady československé v Paříži* [On the Establishment of the Czechoslovak National Council at Paris]. *Naše revoluce,* vol. XII, 1936.

Pergler, Karel. *Amerika a československá nezávislost* [America and the Czechoslovak Independence]. Prague, 1926.

―――. *Politická bilance československé Ameriky* [The Political Balance-Sheet of the Czechoslovak America]. Prague, 1920.

―――. *Z americké fronty našeho osvobozeneckého boje* [From the American Front of Our Liberation Struggle]. Prague, *Naše revoluce,* vol. II, 1924.

Plesinger, Božinov Miroslav. *U T. G. Masaryka v Ženevě* [With T. G. Masaryk at Geneva]. Prague, *Naše revoluce,* vol. XI, 1935.

Rašín, Ladislav. *Paměti dr. Aloise Rašína* [Memoirs of Dr. Alois Rašín]. Prague, 1929.

Seton-Watson, R. W. *Masaryk exulant* [Masaryk as Emigree]. Prague, *Masarykův sborník,* vol. V, 1930-1931.

Bibliography 621

———. *Moje první setkání s presidentem Masarykem* [My First Encounter with President Masaryk]. Prague, *Lidové noviny*, March 7, 1935.

Steed, Wickham H. *President Masaryk*, Prague, *Masarykův sborník*, vol. V, 1930-1931.

———. *Třicet let novinářem* [Thirty Years as Journalist], Prague, 1924, 2 vols.

Sychrava, Lev. *Několik vzpomík ze Švýcarska* [A Few Memories from Switzerland], Prague, *Sborník vzpomínek na T. G. Masaryka*, 1930.

Ščepichin, A. A. *Za generálem Čečkem.* (Ze vzpomínek ruského důstojníka) [Following General Čeček (From Reminiscences of a Russian Officer)]. Prague, *Naše revoluce*, vol. VI, 1929-1930.

Šícha, Miroslav. *Můj cestovní pas ve službách českého odboje* [My Passport in the Service of the Czech Resistance], Prague, *Naše revoluce*, vol. XII, 1936.

Šeba, Jan. *Masaryk v nejtěžších dobách svého života* [Masaryk in the Most Difficult Times of His Life]. *Sborník vzpomínek...*, Prague, 1930.

Šrobár, Vavro. *Oslobodené Slovensko, Paměti z rokov 1918-1920* [Liberated Slovakia, Memories of the Years 1918-1920]. 2 vols. Prague, 1928.

Šulhyn, Alexander. *Masryk a Ukraina za světové války* [Masaryk and the Ukraine During the World War]. Prague, *Masarykův sborník*, vol. VI, 1930-1931.

Vaněk, Vladimír. *Moje válečná odysea* [My Wartime Odysei]. Prague, 1925.

Vondrák, Dr. Vácslav. *Z doby bojů o samostatnost Československa* [From the Time of Struggle for Czechoslovak Independence]. Prague, 1925.

Vopička, Karel J. *Taje Balkánu; Sedm roků diplomatova života v bouřlivém centru Evropy* [The Secrets of the Balkans; Seven Years of a Diplomat's Life in the Turbulent Centre of Europe]. Prague, 1927.

Voska, Emanuel V. *Z účasti zaoceánského emigranta v československém odboji* [From the Participation of an Trans-Atlantic Emigrant in the Czechoslovak Resistance]. Prague, *Naše revoluce*, vol. I, 1923.

———. "Paměti kapitána Em. V. Vosky" [Memoirs of Captain Emanuel V. Voska], Prague, *Jas*, vols. VII, VIII, IX; 1933, 1934, 1935.

BIBLIOGRAPHIES, BOOKS, PAMPHLETS AND ARTICLES

An active and Responsible Czechoslovak Statesman (pseud.). *Germany and*

Czechoslovakia. Part II. Czechoslovakia at the Peace Conference and the Present German-Czechoslovak Discussion. Prague, 1937.

Almond, Nina and Fisher, H. H. Special Collections in the Hoover Library on War, Revolution and Peace. Stanford, Calif., 1940.

Almond, Nina and Lutz, Ralph Haswell. An Introduction to a Bibliography of the Paris Peace Conference. Stanford, Calif., 1935.

Baerlein, Henry. The March of the Seventy Thousand. London, 1926.

Bartůšek, Josef. Přehled dosavadních publikací a zpráv o M. R. Štefánikovi, Prague, Naše revoluce, vol. I, 1923.

Baumgart, Winfried. Deutsche Ostpolitik 1918. Von Brest-Litovsk bis zum Ende des Ersten Weltkrieges. Vienna-Munich, 1966.

Bednařík, František. Masaryk a Italie za války. Prague, Naše revoluce, vol. VIII, 1932.

Beneš, Eduard. Bohemia's Case for Independence. With introduction by Henry Wickham Steed. London, 1917.

―――. Détruisez l'Autriche-Hongrie! Le martyre des Tchécho-Slovaques à travers l'histoire. Paris, 1916.

―――. K budoucímu míru [The Future Peace] [Translated from French]. Prague, 1919.

―――. Masarykovo pojetí idey národní a problémy jednoty československé [Masaryk's Interpretation of the National Idea and Problems of Czechoslovak Unity]. Bratislava, 1935.

―――. Pět let zahraniční politiky československé [Five Years of Czechoslovak Foreign Policy]. Prague, 1924.

―――. Zničte Rakousko-Uhersko! [Destroy Austria-Hungary!]. Prague, 1920.

Beneš, Eduard, and Kramář, Karel. Československá zahraniční politika. Dvě řeči pronesené v Národním shromáždění dne 30. září 1919 [Czechoslovak Foreign Policy. Two Speeches Made in the National Assembly, September 30, 1919]. Prague, 1919.

Beneš, Vojta. Československá Amerika v odboji, I, Od června 1914 do srpna 1915 [Czechoslovak America in Resistance, I, From June 1914 to August 1915]. Prague, 1931.

―――. Economic Strength of the Czechoslovak Lands. 2nd ed. Chicago: Bohemian National Alliance of America, 1918.

―――. Masarykovo dílo v Americe [Masaryk's Work in America]. Prague, 1923.

Bibliography 623

Bokes, František. *Dejiny Slovenska a Slovakov od najstarších čias až po oslobodenie* [History of Slovakia and the Slovaks from the Earliest Times until the Liberation]. Bratislava, 1946.

Bonsal, Stephen. *Suitors and Supplicants: The Little Nations at Versailles.* New York, 1946.

Bradley, John. *Allied Intervention in Russia.* London, 1968.

Bradley, J. F. N. "The Allies and the Czech Revolt against the Bolsheviks in 1918," *The Slavonic and East European Review.* Vol. XLIII, No. 101, June 1965.

―――. "The Allies and Russia in the Light of French Archives (7 November 1917–15 March 1918)," *Soviet Studies.* Vol. XVI, No. 2, October 1964.

―――. "The Czechoslovak Revolt against the Bolsheviks." *Soviet Studies.* Vol. XV, No. 2, October 1963.

―――. *La légion tchécoslovaque en Russie 1914-1920.* Paris, 1965.

Brändström, Elsa. *Unter Kriegsgefangene in Russland und Sibirien 1914-20.* Berlin, 1922.

Briggs, Mitchell Pirie. *George D. Herron and the European Settlement.* Stanford, 1932.

Brock, Peter, and Gordon Skilling, eds. *The Czech Renascence of the Nineteenth Century.* Toronto, 1970.

Brož, Josef A. *České desaveau noty Spojenců ze dne 10. ledna 1917 a jeho ohlas ve francouzském tisku* [Czech Disavowal of the Allied Note of January 10, 1917, and Its Reflections in the French Press]. Prague, *Naše revoluce,* vol. XII, 1937.

Bunyan, James. *Intervention, Civil War, and Communism in Russia, April-December 1918.* Documents and Materials. Baltimore: John Hopkins Press, 1936.

Burian von Rajecz, Stephan. *Drei Jahre aus der Zeit meiner Amtsführung im Weltkriege.* Berlin, 1923.

Calder, Kenneth J. *Britain and the Origins of the New Europe 1914-1918.* Cambridge, 1976.

Čapek, Karel. *Hovory s T. G. Masarykem* [Conversations with T. G. Masaryk]. Prague, 1938.

Čapek, Milíč, and Karel Hrubý, eds. *T. G. Masaryk in Perspective.* Comments and Criticism. New York, 1981.

Čapek, Tomáš. *Origins of the Czechoslovak State.* New York: Revell Press, 1926.

A Catalogue of the Paris Peace Conference Delegation Propaganda in the Hoover War Library. Hoover War Library, Bibliographical Series I. Stanford, Calif.: Stanford University Press, 1926.

Cecil, Robert. *All the Way*. London, 1949.

――――. *A Great Experiment*. An autobiography. New York: Oxford University Press, 1941.

Ček, Stanislav. "Ot Penzy do Urala. Doklad," *Voliia Rossii*, VII-IX, 1928.

Čechoslováci ve válce a v revoluci [Czechoslovaks in War and Revolution]. Moscow, 1918.

Čermák, Jiří. *Boje pod Bachmačem a ústup z Ukrajiny. R. 1918* [Fights at Bakhmatch and the Retreat from the Ukraine. Year 1918]. Prague, 1923.

Červinka, Jaroslav. *Cestou našeho odboje. Příspěvek k historii vývoje formací československého vojska na Rusi v roce 1914-1918* [The Way of Our Resistance. A Contribution to the History of the Development of Formations of the Czechoslovak Army in Russia in 1914-1918]. Prague, 1920.

Česká Státoprávní Demokracie [Czech State Rights Democratic Party]. *Česká deklarace ze dne 22. srpna 1868* [Czech Declaration of August 22, 1868]. Prague, 1918.

Česká strana pokroková [Czech Progressive Party]. *Program české strany pokrokové*. Schválen třetím valným sjezdem strany, konaným v Praze 6. a 7. ledna 1912 [Program of the Czech Progressive Party, approved by the third general assembly, held in Prague, January 6th and 7th, 1912]. Prague, 1912.

Chaloupecký, Václav. *Zápas o Slovensko, 1918* [The Struggle for Slovakia]. Prague, 1930.

Chmelař, Josef. *The German Problem in Czechoslovakia*. Prague, 1936.

――――. *National Minorities in Central Europe*. Prague, 1937.

――――. *Polská menšina v Československé republice* [Polish Minority in Czechoslovak Republic. *Národnostní otázky*, No. 6, Prague, 1935.

Chodorovič, Nikolaj Alexandrovič, *Odbojové hnutí a československé vojsko v Rusku 1914-1917* [The Liberation Movement and the Czechoslovak Army in Russia, 1914-1917]. Prague, 1928.

Churchill, Winston S. *The Aftermath*. New York: Charles Scribner's Sons, 1929.

———. *The Unknown War*. New York: Charles Scribner's Sons, 1931.
———. *The World Crisis*. Vols. I-III. New York: Charles Scribner's Sons, 1923-29.
Čihák, M., M. Klír and J. Koudelková. *Dějiny ČSR a KSČ v letech 1918-1923* [History of Czechoslovakia and the Communist Party of Czechoslovakia during the Years 1918-1923]. Prague, 1967.
Clemenceau, Georges Eugene Benjamin. *Discours de Guerre*. Paris, 1934.
———. *The Grandeur and Misery of Victory*. New York: Harcourt Brace, 1930.
Conseil National de la Russie Carpathique. *Memorandum du Conseil National de la Russie Carpathique*. Sanok, Galicia, Decembre 1918. Paris, n.p. 1918.
Čulen, Konštantín. *Pittsburghská Dohoda* [The Pittsburgh Agreement]. Bratislava, 1937.
Czako, Istvan. *How the Hungarian Problem was Created?* Budapest, 1934.
Czech National Alliance in Great Britain. *Austrian Terrorism in Bohemia*. With an introduction by Professor T. G. Masaryk. [London], 1916.
Czernin von und zu Chudenitz, Ottokar Theobald Otto Maria. *Im Weltkriege*. Berlin and Vienna, 1919.
Denis, Ernest. *Čechy po Bílé Hoře* [Bohemia After the Battle of White Mountain]. Poznámky a překlad Jindřicha Vančury. Prague, 1921.
———. *Otázka Rakouska; Slováci* [The Question of Austria; the Slovaks]. Prague, 1919.
———. *La question d'Autriche*, Les Slovaques. Paris, 1917.
———. *Válka, příčiny přímé a vzdálené* [The War: Its Direct and Long-Range Causes]. Prague, 1919.
———. *Vzkříšení Čech* [The Resurrection of Bohemia]. Prague, 1919.
Dillon, E. J. *Inside Story of the Peace Conference*. New York: Harper, 1920.
Dolanský, Julius. *Masaryk a Rusko předrevoluční* [Masaryk and Pre-Revolutionary Russia]. Prague, 1959.
Doležal, Jaromír. *Masarykova cesta životem* [Masaryk's Way Through Life]. Brno, 1920. 2 vols.
Doležal, Josef. *Politická cesta českého katolicismu 1918-1928* [Political Road of The Czech Catholicism, 1918-1928]. Prague, 1929.
Dostál, Emil. *Svatý Václav patronem čsl. odboje na Rusi* [Saint Wenceslas as Patron of the Czechoslovak Resistance in Russia]. Prague, 1929.

Dupuy, Richard Ernest. *Perish by the Sword: the Czechoslovakian Anabasis and our Supporting Campaign in North Russia and Siberia 1918-20.* Harrisburg, 1939.
Durich, Jaroslav. *Okamžiky z válečných let* [Moments from the War Years]. Prague, 1924.
Dvorský, Viktor. *Území českého národa* [Territory of the Czech Nation]. Prague, 1918.
Eisenmann, Louis. *Edouard Beneš.* Geneva, 1921.
———. *The Problem of Minorities* (an article). New York: Carnegie Endowment for International Peace, 1926.
———. *La Tchécoslovaquie.* Paris, 1921.
Fagula, Dr. L. G. *Andrej Hlinka.* Bratislava, 1943.
Fic, Victor M. *The Bolsheviks and the Czechoslovak Legion.* Origin of Their Armed Conflict, March to May 1918. New Delhi (India), 1978.
———. *Revolutionary War for Independence and the Russian Question.* Czechoslovak Army in Russia 1914-1918. New Delhi (India), 1977.
Fink, Pavel. *Bílý Admirál: Profil Kolčakovštiny* [The White Admiral: A Profile of Kolchakovshtina]. 3rd ed., Brno, 1929.
Fischer, Louis. *The Soviets in World Affairs,* a history of the relations between the Soviet Union and the rest of the world, 1917-1929. Princeton, N.J.: Princeton University Press, 1951. 2 vols.
Fleming, Peter. *The Fate of Admiral Kolchak.* London, 1963.
Footmann, David. *Civil War in Russia.* New York, 1961.
———. *Kolchak—The Last Phase in Civil War in Russia.* London, 1961.
Fowler, W. B. *British-American Relations, 1917-1918.* The Role of Sir William Wiseman. Princeton, N.J., 1969.
Glaise-Horstenau, Edmund von. *Die Katastrophe. Die Zertrummerung Osterreich-Ungarns und das Werden der Nachfolgerstaaten.* Leipzig, 1929.
Glaser, Kurt. *Czecho-Slovakia: A Critical History.* Caldwell, Idaho, 1961.
Graham, Malborne Watson. *New Governments of Central Europe.* New York, 1924.
Graves, Sidney C. *America's Siberian Adventure.* New York, 1931.
Gromada, Thaddeus V. "Pilsudski and the Slovak Autonomists," *Slavic Review,* vol. 28, No. 3, September 1969.
Grew, Joseph C. *Turbulent Era,* a diplomatic record of forty years, 1904-1945. Edited by Walter Johnson. New York: Houghton Mifflin, 1952, 2 vols.

Hájek, Hanuš J. *T. G. Masaryk Revisited: A Critical Assessment*. Boulder, Colo., 1983.

Hájek, J. S. *Wilsonovská legenda v dějinách ČSR* [The Wilsonian Legend in the History of the Czechoslovak Republic]. Prague, 1953.

Hajn, Alois. *Dr. Edvard Beneš a jeho životní dílo* [Dr. Edvard Beneš and His Life's Work]. Prague, 1935.

———. *O českých stranách politických* [About Czech Political Parties]. Prague, 1921.

Hajn, Antonín. *Česká politika za války* [Czech Politics during the War]. Prague, 1924.

Hajšman, Jan. *Česká Maffie, vzpomínky na odboj doma* [The Czech Maffie. Memories of the Resistance Movement at Home]. Prague, 1932-35. 2 vols.

Hanak, Harry. *Great Britain and Austria-Hungary during the First World War. A Study in the Formation of the Public Opinion*. London, 1962.

———. "The Government, the Foriegn Office and Austria-Hungary, 1914-1918," *The Slavonic and East European Review*. Vol. 47, 1969.

———. "The New Europe, 1916-20," *The Slavonic and East European Review*. Vol. 39, No. 93, June 1961.

———. "Marginalia–T. G. Masaryk's Journalistic Activity in England during the First World War," *The Slavonic and East European Review*. Vol. 42, No. 98, December 1963.

Hartl, Antonín, ed. *Bibliografie prací Dra Edvarda Beneše* [Bibliography of Works of Dr. Edvard Beneš]. Prague, 1925.

———. *Masaryk, realisté a Viktor Dyk* [Masaryk, the Realists and Victor Dyk]. Prague, *Naše revoluce*, vol. VII, 1931.

Hatalák, Petr. *Jak vznikla myšlenka připojit Podkarpatskou Rus k Československu* [The Genesis of the Idea to Annex Carpatho-Russia to Czechoslovakia]. Ungern, *Podkarpatské hlasy*, Nos. 192/203, 1935.

Heidler, Jan. *České politické strany v Čechách, na Moravě a ve Slezku* [Czech Political Parties in Bohemia, Moravia and Silesia]. Prague, 1914.

———. *"1917" Projevy českých spisovatelů* [1917–Statements of Czech Writers]. Prague, 1921.

Herben, Jan. *Deset let proti proudu* [Ten Years against the Stream]. Prague, 1898.

Hlaváček, František. *Dr. Edward Beneš a Itálie za světové války* [Dr. Edvard Beneš and Italy During the World War]. Prague, 1936.

František Hlaváček (a symposium). Prague, 1927.

Hoch, Karel. *Alois Rašín. Jeho život, dílo a doba* [Alois Rašín. His Life, Work and Time]. Prague, 1934.

Hodža, Milan F. *Federation in Central Europe,* reflections and reminiscences. London, 1942.

Hofbauer, Josef. *Der Kampf um Deutschböhmen.* Leipzig, 1919.

Holotík, Ľudevít. *Štefánikovská legenda a vznik ČSR* [The Štefánik Legend and the Emergence of Czechoslovakia]. Bratislava, 1958.

Hora, Alois. *Podkarpatská Rus* [Carpatho-Russia]. Prague, 1919.

Horký, Karel. *Vlast* (Práce z doby světové války) [Fatherland (Work from the Time of World War)]. Klášter nad Jizerou, 1923.

———. *Masaryk Redivivus?* Prague, 1926.

Hruška, Čeněk. *Cesta k revoluci. Vzpomínky generálporučíka Č. H. z let 1914-1919* [The Road to Revolution. Recollections of Lieutenant-General Čeněk Hruška from the Years 1914-1919]. Prague, 1965.

Hrušovský, F. *Slovensko v dejinách Strednej Európy* [Slovakia in the History of Central Europe]. Turčiansky Sv. Martin, 1939.

Hudec, J. *Ruská revoluce* [The Russian Revolution]. 2 vols. Prague, 1920.

Hoyt, Edwin P. *The Army without a Country.* New York, 1967.

Husa, Václav. *Dějiny Československa* [History of Czechoslovakia]. Prague, 1962.

Jaksch, Wenzel. *Europe's Road to Potsdam.* Translated and edited by Kurt Glaser. New York, 1963.

Janin, Maurice. *Milan Rastislav Štefánik.* Prague, 1932.

Jaszi, Oscar. *The Dissolution of the Habsburg Monarchy.* Chicago: Chicago University Press, 1929.

Jehliczka, Franz Rudolf. *André Hlinka à la Conference de la Paix de Paris; le véritable Hlinka.* Geneva, 1938.

———. *Father Hlinka's Struggle for Slovak Freedom.* London, 1938.

Jelínek, František /Pechar/ Melichar. *Stručné dějiny čsl. legií* [A Short History of the Czechoslovak Legions]. Prague, 1936.

Jesenský, Janko. *Cestou k slobode; úryvky z deníka 1914-18* [The Road to Freedom; Excerpts from Diary, 1914-18]. Turčiansky Sv. Martin, 1933, and Bratislava, 1968.

Juríček, Ján. *M. R. Štefánik. Životopisný náčrt* [M. R. Štefánik. Biographical Sketch]. Bratislava, 1969.

Kalina, Antonín Svatopluk. *Krví a železem dobyto československé samo-*

statnosti [Czechoslovak Independence was Won by Blood and Iron]. Prague, 1938.

Kalvoda, Josef. *Czechoslovakia's Role in Soviet Strategy*. Washington, D.C. 1978.

―――――. "Masaryk in America in 1918," *Jahrbücher für Geschichte Osteuropas*. Vol. 27, No. 1, 1979.

―――――. "Czech and Slovak Prisoners of War in Russia During the War and Revolution" in *Essays on World War I: Origins and Prisoners of War*. Ed. by Samuel R. Williamson, Jr., and Peter Pastor. New York, 1983.

―――――. "The Czechoslovak-Hungarian Dispute" in *War and Society in East Central Europe. Vol. VI. Essays on World War I: Total War and Peacemaking. A Case Study of Trianon*. Ed. by Bela K. Kiraly, Peter Pastor, and Ivan Sanders. New York, 1982.

―――――. "National Minorities in Czechoslovakia, 1919-1980" in *Eastern European National Minorities, 1919-1980. A Handbook*. Ed. by Stephan M. Horak. Littleton, Colorado, 1985.

―――――. "The Origins of the Czechoslovak Army, 1914-1919" in *War and Society in East Central Europe. Vol. XIX. East Central European Society in World War I*. Ed. by Bela K. Kiraly and Nandor Dreisziger. New York, 1985.

―――――. "General Alois Podhajský" in *War and Society in East Central Europe. Vol. XXV. Civilian and Military Leaders from the 18th to the 20th Century*. Ed. by Bela K. Kiraly and Albert A. Nofi. New York, 1986.

Kann, Robert A. *The Multinational Empire*. 2 vols. New York, 1950.

―――――. *Die Sixtusaffäre*. Vienna, 1966.

Kann, Robert A., Béla K. Király, and Paul S. Fichtner, eds. *The Habsburg Empire in World War I*. New York, 1978.

Kárník, Zdeněk. *Socialisté na rozcestí: Habsburk, Masaryk, či Šmeral?* [Socialists at the Crossroad: Habsburg, Masaryk or Šmeral?]. Prague, 1968.

Karžanský, Nikolaj. *Rusko a čsl. legie* [Russia and the Czechoslovak Legion]. Prague, 1919.

Katolíci v zahraničních bojích o československou samostatnost. Úvahy, doklady a vzpomínky z let 1914-1920 [Catholics in the Struggles for Czechoslovak Independence Abroad. Reflections, Documents and Memories from the Years 1914-1920]. Brno, 1928.

Kirschbaum, Jozef. *Slovakia: Nation at the Crossroads of Central Europe.* New York, 1960.

Kirschbaum, Stanislav J., ed. *Slovak Politics. Essays on Slovak History in Honour of Joseph M. Kirschbaum.* Cleveland and Rome, 1983.

Klante, Margarete. *Von der Wolga zum Amur* (Die tschechische Legion und der Burgerkrieg). Berlin-Konigsberg, 1931.

Klecanda, Vladimír. *Bitva u Zborova* [The Battle of Zborov]. Prague, 1927.

———. *Operace československého vojska na Rusi v letech 1917-1920* [Operations of the Czechoslovak Army in Russia during the Years 1917-1920]. Prague, 1921.

———. *Slovenský Zborov* [The Slovak Zborov]. Prague, 1934.

Klimov, J. M. *K úloze čs. legionářů v občanské válce v Rusku* [On the Role of the Czechoslovak Legionaires in the Civil War in Russia]. Prague, 1952.

Koudelka, Jaroslav. *Sociální demokracie v československé revoluci* [The Social Democratic Party in the Czechoslovak Revolution]. Pilsen, 1920.

Koutek, Jaroslav. *Přehled dějin ČSR v letech 1918-20* [A Review of History of Czechoslovakia during the Years 1918-20]. Prague, 1957.

Koutský, Miroslav. *Několik armádních problémů* [A Few Problems in the Army]. Prague, 1923.

Kozák, J. T. G. *Masaryk a vznik Washingtonské deklarace v říjnu 1918* [T. G. Masaryk and the Genesis of the Washington Declaration in October 1918]. Prague, 1968.

Král, Václav. *Masaryk, Beneš a osvobozenecká legionářská legenda* [Masaryk, Beneš and the Legionnaires' Legend of Liberation]. Prague, *Historie a vojenství,* 1952/1.

———. *Masaryk ve službách amerického imperialismu* [Masaryk in the Service of American Imperialism]. Prague, *Historie a vojenství,* 1953/3.

———. *O Masarykově a Benešově kontrarevoluční protisovětské politice* [About Masaryk's and Beneš's Counter-Revolutionary and Anti-Soviet Politics]. Prague, 1953.

———. *Plány amerických imperialistů na světovládu a Masarykův první odboj* [Plans of American Imperialists for World Domination and Masaryk's First Resistance Struggle]. Prague, *Historie a vojenství,* 1953/2.

Kramář, Karel. *Anmerkungen zur böhmischen Politik.* Vienna, 1906.

Bibliography

———. *Das böhmische Staatsrecht*. Vienna, 1896.

———. *Der Hochverratsprozess gegen dr. Kramář und Genossen*. Vienna, 1918-1919.

———. *Kramářův soud nad Benešem*. Spor Dr. K. Kramáře s ministrem zahraničních věcí Dr. E. Benešem. [Kramář's Judgment of Beneš. Conflict of Dr. K. Kramář with the Minister of Foreign Affairs Dr. E. Beneš]. S. předmluvou Jiřího Stříbrného [Foreword by Jiří Stříbrný]. Prague, 1938.

———. *Na obranu Slovanské politiky* [In Defense of the Slavic Policy]. Prague, 1926.

———. *Pět přednášek o zahraniční politice* [Five Lectures on Foreign Policy]. Prague, 1922.

———. *Řeči a projevy* [Speeches and Addresses]. Edited by František Stašek and J. R. Marek. Prague, 1935.

———. *Ruská krise* [The Russian Crisis]. Prague, 1921.

———. *Les Tchèques et la Russie*. Paris, 1920.

Kramer, Juraj. *Slovenské autonomistické hnutie v rokoch 1918-1929* [The Sloval Autonomist Movement During the Years 1918-1929]. Bratislava, 1962.

Kratochvíl, Jaroslav. *Cesta revoluce* [The Way of the Revolution]. Prague, 1922 and 1928.

Kretší Jindřich. *Vznik a vývoj československé legie v Italii* [The Origin and Development of the Czechoslovak Legion in Italy]. Prague, 1928.

Křížek, Jaroslav. *Jaroslav Hašek v revolučním Rusku* [Jaroslav Hašek in Revolutionary Russia]. Prague, 1957.

———. *K boji čs. levice o čs. legie v Rusku počátkem r. 1918* [On the Struggle of the Czech Left for the [Control of] Czechoslovak Legions in Russia at the Beginning of the Year 1918]. Prague, *Historie a vojenství*, 1964/6.

———. *Levicové hnutí Čechů a Slováků v Rusku v letech 1917-1920. Ke vzniku ČSR* [The Left-Wing Movement of Czechs and Slovaks in Russia during the Years 1917-1920. On the Origin of Czechoslovakia]. Prague, 1958.

———. *Penza. Slavná bojová tradice čs. rudoarmějců* [Penza. The Glorious Fighting Tradition of the Czechoslovak Red Army Men]. Prague, 1956.

———. *Protisovětské vystoupení čs. legií a změna vztahu Dohody k čs.*

zahraničnímu odboji v roce 1918 [The Anti-Soviet Uprising of the Czechoslovak Legions and the Change in Attitude on the Part of the Entente toward the Czechoslovak Resistance Abroad in 1918]. Prague, *Historie a vojenství,* 1966/1.

———. *První ozbrojené vystoupení čs. legií proti sovětské moci 11. —13. listopadu 1917* [The First Military Action of the Czechoslovak Legions Against the Soviet Power, November 11-13, 1917]. Prague, *Historie a vojenství,* 1955/3.

———. *T. G. Masaryk a vystoupení čs. legií na jaře 1918* [T. G. Masaryk and the Uprising of the Czechoslovak Legions in the Spring of 1918]. Prague, *Československý časopis historický,* 1966/5.

Křížek, Jurij. *Česká buržoazní politika a "česká otázka" v letech 1900-1914* [Czech Bourgeois Policy and the "Czech Question" during the Years 1900-1914]. Prague, *Československý časopis historický,* 1958/4.

———. *"Česká otázka" v buržoazní politice na počátku první světové války* ["Czech Question" in the Bourgeois Policy at the Beginning of the First World War]. Prague, *Československý časopis historický,* 1959/4.

———. *Říjnová revoluce a česká společnost* [The October Revolution and the Czech Society]. Prague, 1967.

Krofta, Kamil. *A Short History of Czechoslovakia.* New York: R. M. McBride, 1934.

———. *Byli jsme za Rakouska . . .* úvahy historické a politické [We Existed under Austria . . . historical and political reflections]. Prague, 1936.

———. *Čechové a Slováci před svým státním sjednocením* [Czechs and Slovaks Before Their Unification in One State]. Prague, 1932.

———. *Čechy a Rakousko v minulosti* [Bohemia and Austria in the Past]. Prague, 1909.

———. *Malé dějiny československé* [Short History of Czechoslovakia]. Prague, 1931.

———. *Národnostní vývoj zemí československých* [Nationality Development of the Czechoslovak Lands]. Prague, 1934.

———. *Němci v Československém státě* [Germans in the Czechoslovak State]. *Národnostní otázky,* No. 8. Prague, 1937.

———. *The Substance of Hungarian Revisionism.* Prague, 1934.

———. *Zahraniční politika československa a její kořeny* [Czechoslovak Foreign Policy and Its Roots]. Prague, 1937.

Kudela, Josef. *Druhý sjezd čs. vojska na Rusi.* (Oficialní historie) [The Second Congress of the Czechoslovak Army in Russia. (Official History)]. Prague, *Naše revoluce,* vol. X, 1934.
———. *28. říjen v ruských legiích* [28th of October in Russian Legions]. Prague, *Naše revoluce,* vol. VI, 1929-1930.
———. *Jubilejní oslavy Husovy v Moskvě v roce 1915* [Anniversary Celebrations of Huss in Moscow in 1915]. Prague, *Naše revoluce,* vol. V, 1927-1928.
———. *Katolíci v odboji a o odboji.* (Přehled a rozbor literatury) [Catholics in the Resistance and about the Resistance, (Overview and Analysis of the Literature)]. Prague, *Naše revoluce,* vol. XI, 1935.
———. *Přehled vývoje čsl. revolučního hnutí na Rusi do odchodu čsl. armádního sboru z Ukrainy* [Review of the Development of the Czechoslovak Revolutionary Movement in Russia until the Departure of the Czechoslovak Army Corps from the Ukraine]. Prague, 1923.
———. *Profesor Masaryk a československé vojsko na Rusi* [Professor Masaryk and the Czechoslovak Army in Russia]. Prague, 1923.
———. *Ruské letáky u nás na počátku války* [Russian Leaflets at Home at the Beginning of the War]. Prague, *Naše revoluce,* vol. VI, 1929-1930.
Kulhánek, František. *Boj o Kladsko* [Struggle for the Region of Kladsko]. Prague, 1946.
Kvasnička, Ján. *Československé légie v Rusku 1917-1920* [Czechoslovak Legions in Russia, 1917-1920]. Bratislava, 1963.
Kybal, Vlastimil. *Les Origines diplomatiques de l'État tchécoslovaque.* Sources et documents tchecoslovaques, No. 11. Prague, 1929.
Lane, Franklin Knight. *The Letters of Franklin K. Lane.* Edited by Anne W. Lane and Louise H. Wall. Boston and New York: Houghton Mifflin, 1924.
Lansing, Robert. *The Big Four and Others of the Peace Conference.* New York: Houghton Mifflin, 1921.
Laun, Rudolf von. *Czecho-Slovak Claims on German Territory.* 3rd ed. The Hague, 1919.
Lazarevský, Vladimír. *Rusko a československé znovuzrození* [Russia and the Rebirth of Czechoslovakia] Transl. from Russian by Jaroslav Hauc. Prague, 1927.
Lazarevskii, Vladimír. *Rossiia i Chekhoslovatskoe Vozrozhdenie.* Ocherki chesko-russkich otnoshenii 1914-1918. Berlin, 1927.

Leppmann, Wolfgang. *Ruský konzulát v Praze.* Kapitola k carské politice v Čechách před světovou válkou [Russian Consulate at Prague. A Chapter on the Tsarist Policy in Bohemia before the World War]. Prague, *Naše revoluce,* vol. XIII, 1937.

Lettrich, Jozef. *History of Modern Slovakia.* New York, 1955.

Lev, Vojtěch. *Brána na východ* (Karpatské Rus) [Gateway to the East (Carpatho-Russia). Prague, 1920.

Lloyd George, David. *Memoirs of the Peace Conference.* 2 vols. New Haven, 1939.

———. *War Memoirs.* 6 vols. London, 1936.

Lodgman von Auen, Rudolph, ed. *Deutschböhmen.* Berlin, 1919.

———. *Le droit de libre disposition pour la Bohème Allemande,* discours de Rudolph Lodgman von Auen, chef due comité exécutif de la diete de la Bohème Allemande, devant l'assemblée de la diète lors de sa session à Vienne, le 28 decembre 1918. Vienna 1919.

Macartney, Carlie Aylmer. *The Danube Basin.* Oxford Pamphlet on World Affairs, No. 10. Oxford: Clarendon Press, 1939.

———. *Hungary and Her Successors:* The Treaty of Trianon and Its Consequences 1919-1937. London, New York: Oxford University Press, 1937.

———. *National States and National Minorities.* London: Oxford University Press. H. Milford, 1934.

———. *Problems of the Danube Basin.* Cambridge: Cambridge University Press, 1942.

Machovec, Milan. *Tomáš G. Masaryk.* Prague, 1968.

Magocsi, Paul Robert. *The Shaping of a National Identity: Subcarpathian Rus', 1848-1948.* Cambridge, MA, 1978.

Malý, J. *Z historie demácího odboje za války. K státoprávnímu prohlášení poslance A. Kaliny z 30. května 1917* [From the History of Home Struggle During the War. On the State-Right Declaration of Deputy A. Kalina of May 30, 1917]. Prague, 1927.

Mamatey, Victor S. *The United States and East-Central Europe, 1914-1918.* Princeton, N.J.: Princeton University Press, 1957.

———. "(Documents) The United States Recognition of the Czechoslovak National Council of Paris (September 3, 1918)," *Journal of Central European Affairs.* Vol. XIII, No. 1, April 1953.

Masaryk, Thomas Garrigue. *At the Eleventh Hour.* A memorandum on the military situation. London, 1916.

Bibliography 635

———. *Austrian Terrorism in Bohemia*. With an Introduction by Professor T. G. Masaryk, Czech Member of the Austrian Parliament and President of the Czech National Committee for Foreign Affairs. The Czech National Alliance in Great Britain [1916].

———. *Cesta Demokracie,* soubor projevů za republiky [The Road of Democracy, collection of speeches]. Prague, 1933-1934. 2 vols.

———. *Česká otázka.* Snahy a tužby národního obrození [The Czech Question. Efforts and Aspirations of National Renaissance]. 2nd ed. Prague, 1908.

———. *Karel Havlíček;* snahy a tužby politického probuzení [Karel Havlíček; Efforts and Aspirations of Political Awakening]. Prague, 1896.

———. *Masaryk a revoluční armáda* [Masaryk and the Revolutionary Army]. Prague, 1922.

———. *Masarykova čítánka* [Masaryk's Reader]. Edited by K. J. Obrátil. Brno, 1920.

———. *The New Europe: The Slav Standpoint.* London, 1918.

———. *Nová Evropa;* stanovisko slovanské [The New Europe, the Slavic Standpoint]. Prague, 1920.

———. *Palackého idea národa českého* (1898) [Palacky's Idea of the Czech Nation]. Prague, 1926.

———. *The Problem of Small Nations in the European Crisis;* inaugural lecture at the University of London, King's College. London, 1916.

———. *The Slavs among the Nations.* London, 1916.

———. *O bolševismu* [About Bolshevism]. Prague, 1921.

———. *Los von Rom,* an address, Boston, 1902.

———. *Přednášky profesora Th. G. Masaryka* [Lectures of Professor T. G. Masaryk]. Chicago, 1907; also: *Americké přednášky* [American Lectures]. Prague, 1929.

———. *Otázka sociální: Základy marxismu filosofické a sociologické.* [The Social Question. Filosophical and Sociological Foundations of Marxism]. Prague, 1898.

———. *Právo přirozené a historické* [Natural and Historical Right]. Prague, 1900.

———. *Russland und Europa.* Studien über die geistigen Strömugen in Russland. Erste Folge. Zur russischen Geschichts- und Religionsphilosophie. Sociologische Skizzen. Jena, 1913. 2 vols.; in English: *The*

Spirit of Russia. Studies in History, Literature and Philosophy. London-New York, 1919; 3rd vol. was published in London (1961) and New York (1967); in Czech: *Rusko a Europa,* Prague, 1921.

———. *Der Selbstmord also sociale Massenerscheinung der modernen Civilisation.* Vienna, 1881.

———. *Suicide and the Meaning of Civilization.* Translated by William B. Weist and Robert G. Bateson. Chicago-London, 1970.

———. *V boji o náboženství* [In the Struggle for Religion]. Prague, 1927.

May, Arthur J. *The Habsburg Monarchy, 1867-1914.* Cambridge, Mass., 1951.

———. "R. W. Seton-Watson and British Anti-Hapsburg Sentiment," *The American Slavic and East European Review.* Vol. XX, No. 1, February 1961.

Mayer, Arno J. *Political Origins of the New Diplomacy, 1917-1918.* New York, 1970.

———. *Politics and Diplomacy of Peacemaking.* Containment and Counterrevolution at Versailles, 1918-1919. New York, 1967.

Medek, Rudolf. *The Czechoslovak Anabasis Across Russia and Siberia.* London, 1929.

Medek, Rudolf, Otakar Vaněček and Václav Holeček, eds., *Za Svobodu. Obrázková kronika Čsl. revolučního hnutí na Rusi* [Towards Freedom. Illustrated Chronicle of the Czechoslovak Revolutionary Army in Russia, 1914-1920]. Prague, 1925-1929. 4 vols.

Medvecký, Karol A. *Slovenský prevrat* [The Slovak Revolution]. Bratislava, 1930-1931. 4 vols.

Mikuš, Joseph A. *Slovakia. A Political History: 1918-1950.* Milwaukee: The Marquette University Press, 1963.

Molisch, Paul. *Die Sudetendeutsche Freiheitsbewegung in den Jahren 1918-1919.* Vienna, 1932.

Mordacq, Jean Jules Henri. *Le Ministere Clemenceau,* journal d'un temoin. Paris, 1930-1931. 4 vols.

Mowrer, Paul Scott. *Balkanized Europe.* New York: Dutton, 1921.

Mrázek, Jaroslav. *Woodrow Wilson a americké uzání československé Národní Rady za vládu de facto* [Woodrow Wilson and American Recognition of the Czechoslovak National Council as a *de facto* Government]. Prague, 1933.

Navrátil, Alois. *Katolicism a úcta svatováclavská v čsl. legiích* [Catholicism and the Cult of St. Wenceslas in the Czechoslovak Legions]. Přerov, 1930.

――――. *Společnou prací k 28. říjnu* [Through Joint Effort to 28th of October]. Přerov, 1934.

――――. *Svatý Václav a čsl. legie* [St. Wenceslas and the Czechoslovak Legions]. Přerov, 1929.

Najbrt, Václav. *Od Zborova k Bachmači* [From Zborov to Bakhmach]. Prague, 1928.

――――. *Rozlet a rozlom sibiřského bratrstva* [The Rise and Downfall of the Siberian Brotherhood]. Brno, 1936.

Nečas, Jaromír. *Upřímné slovo o stycích česko-ukrajinských* [A Frank Word about the Czech-Ukrainian Relations]. Česká series č. 3. Kijev, Prague, 1919.

Nejedlý, Zdeněk. *Dr. Kramář, rozbor politického zjevu* [Dr. Kramář, an Analysis of a Political Phenomenon]. Prague, 1920.

――――. *T. G. Masaryk.* Prague, 1930-1937. 4 vols.

Nicolson, Harold George. *Peacemaking 1919.* Being Reminiscence of the Paris Peace Conference. Boston: Houfton, 1933.

Nosek, Vladimír. *Anglie a náš boj za samostatnost* [England and our Fight for Independence]. Prague, 1926.

――――. *Great Britain and the Czecho-Slovaks.* Prague, 1919.

――――. *Independent Bohemia: An Account of the Czechoslovak Struggle for Liberty.* London and Toronto, 1918.

Noulens, Joseph. *Mon Ambassade en Russie Soviétique 1917-1919.* Paris, 1933.

Novotný, J. O. *Vzkříšení samostatnosti československé,* kronika let 1914-18 [Resurrection of Czechoslovak Independence, Chronology of the Years 1914-18]. Prague, 1932. 2 vols.

Nowak, Karl Friedrich. *Chaos.* Munich, 1923.

――――. *Versailles.* Berlin, 1927.

――――. *Der Weg zur Katastrophe.* Berlin, 1919.

Nowak, Robert. *Der kunstliche Staat,* Ostprobleme der Tschecho-Slowakei Geleitwort von Professor K. Haushofer. Berlin, 1938.

Odložilík, Otakar. *Nástin československých dějin* [Outline of Czechoslovak History]. Prague, 1946.

――――. *T.G.M.–nástin života a díla* [T.G.M.–Outline of His Life and Work]. Chicago, 1950.

Olivová-Pávová, Věra. *Československo-sovětské vztahy v letech 1918-1922* [Czechoslovak-Soviet Relations in 1918-1922]. Prague, 1957.

Opočenský, Jan. *The Collapse of the Austro-Hungarian Monarchy and the Rise of the Czechoslovakian State.* Prague, 1928.

———. *Cesta českých politiků do Švýcar v říjnu r. 1918* [Journey of the Czech Politicians to Switzerland in October 1918]. Prague, *Naše revoluce,* vol. IV, 1926-1927.

———. *Čtrnáctý říjen 1918* [October 14th 1918]. Prague, *Naše revoluce,* vol. III, 1925-1926.

———. *Konec Monarchie Rakousko-Uherské* [End of the Austro-Hungarian Monarchy]. Prague, 1928.

———. *Vznik národních států v říjnu 1918* [Birth of the National States in October 1918]. Prague, 1927.

Osuský, Štefan. *G. D. Herron, dôverník Wilsonov počas vojny* [G. D. Herron, Wilson's Confidant During the War]. Brno, 1925.

———. *O česko-slovenském poměru a osvobozenském programu zahraničních Slováků v československém odboji za světové války* [The Czecho-Slovak Relations and the Liberation Program of Slovaks in Exile in the Czechoslovak Resistance Movement during the World War]. Prague, 1936.

Papoušek, Jaroslav. *Carské Rusko a naše osvobození* [Tsarist Russia and Our Liberation]. Prague, 1927.

———. *Carské Rusko a náš boj o samostatnost. Revoluční Rusko a československé legie. Konflikt československých legií se sověty* [Tsarist Russia and Our Struggle for Independence. Revolutionary Russia and the Czechoslovak Legions. Conflict of the Czechoslovak Legions with the Soviets]. Prague, *Naše revoluce,* vol. VIII, 1932.

———. *Kritické poznámky o počátcích revoluční akce na Rusi* [Critical Remarks on the Beginnings of the Revolutionary Action in Russia]. Prague, *Naše revoluce,* vol. V, 1927-1928.

———. *Masarykovy projevy a řeči za války* [Masaryk's Statements and Speeches during the War]. Prague, 1936. 2 vols.

Paulová, Milada. *Balkánské války a český lid* [Balkan Wars and the Czech People]. Prague, 1962.

———. *Dějiny Maffie,* odboj Čechů a Jihoslovanů za světové války, 1914-1918 [History of the Maffie, Resistance of Czechs and Yugoslavs during the World War, 1914-1918]. Prague, 1937. 2 vols.

———. *Jihoslovanský odboj a česká Maffie* [Yugoslav Resistance and the Czech Maffie]. Prague, 1928.

———. *Kongres potlačených národností Rakouska-Uherska v Římě r. 1918.* [Congress of Oppressed Nationalities of Austria-Hungary in Rome in 1918]. Prague, 1926.

———. *Tajný výbor [Maffie] a spolupráce s Jihoslovany v letech 1916-1918* [The Secret Committee [Maffie] and Collaboration with the Yugoslavs during the Years 1916-1918]. Prague, 1968.

Pekař, Josef. *K českému boji státoprávnímu za války* [The Struggle for Czech State Rights during the War]. Prague, 1930.

———. *Světová válka; stati o jejím vzniku a jejích osudech* [World War; Essays on Its Origins and Its Development]. Prague, 1921.

———. "Masarykova česká filosofie" [Masaryk's Czech Philosophy], *Český časopis historický.* Vol. XVIII, 1912.

———. "Zprávy" [News]. *Český časopis historický.* Vol. XVIII, 1912.

———. *Dějiny československé* [Czechoslovak History]. Prague, 1921.

Pergler, Karel. *Amerika a československá nezávislost* [America and Czechoslovak Independence]. Prague, 1926.

———. *America in the Struggle for Czechoslovak Independence.* Philadelphia: Dorrance, 1926.

———. *Za národní stát* [For a National State]. Prague, 1923.

———. *Slovo k legiím. O Americe. O nás pro nás* [A Word to the Legions. About America. About Us for Us]. Prague, 1920.

Perman, Dagmar. *The Shaping of Czechoslovak State.* Diplomatic History of the Boundaries of Czechoslovakia 1914-1920. Leiden, 1962.

Peroutka, Ferdinand. *Budování státu* [The Building of a State]. 4 vols. Prague, 1933-36.

———. *Kdo nás osvobodil?* [Who Has Liberated Us?]. Prague, 1927.

Peters, Gustav. *Der neue Herr von Böhmen.* Eine Untersuchung der politischen Zukunft der Tschechoslowakei. Berlin, 1927.

Petrš, Josef. *K historii intendanční služby čs. armády na Rusi* [On the History of the Intendant Service of the Czechoslovak Army in Russia]. Prague, 1926.

Pfaff, Ivan, and Vladimír Závodský, *Tradice česko-ruských vztahů v dějinách.* (Projevy a doklady) [The Tradition of Czech-Russian Relations in History. (Addresses and Documents)]. Prague, 1957.

Pfitzner, Josef. *Sudetendeutsche Geschichte.* Reichenberg, 1937.

———. *Tschechischer Geschichtsmythos.* Der Kietwart H. 4. Vienna, 1938.

Pichlík, Karel. *Bojovali proti válce* [They Fought Against the War]. Prague, 1953.

———. *Čeští vojáci proti válce (1914-1915)* [Czech Soldiers Against the War (1914-1915)]. Prague, 1961.

———. *První projekt samostatného Československa z podzimu 1914* [The First Project of Independent Czechoslovakia of Fall 1914]. Prague, *Historie a vojenství,* 1963/3.

———. *K otázce navrátilců z ruského zajetí* [On the Question of Those Who Returned from Russian Captivity]. Prague, *Historie a vojenství,* 1962/1.

———. *První světová válka a "česká otázka"* [The First World War and the Czech Question]. Prague, *Historie a vojenství,* 1964/3.

———. *Vzpoury navratilců z ruského zajetí na jaře 1918* [Rebellions of the Returnees from Russian Captivity in the Spring of 1918]. Prague, 1964.

———. *Zahraniční odboj 1914-1918 bez legend* [Resistance Abroad, 1914-1918, Without Legends]. Prague, 1968.

Písecký, Ferdinand. *M. R. Štefánik v mém deníku* [M. R. Štefánik in My Diary]. Bratislava, 1934.

———. *Světem za svobodu. Osudy československého legionáře* [Through the World for Freedom. Fate of a Czechoslovak Legionaire]. Prague, 1920.

Pleský, Metoděj. *Bratr Generál* [Brother General]. Prague, 1931.

Polák, František. *Sibiřská anabase čsl. legií* [The Sibirian Anabasis of the Czechoslovak Legions]. New York, 1961.

———. *Masarykovy legie v boji proti sovětům* [Masaryk's Legions in Struggle against the Soviets]. New York, 1957.

Polák, Josef. *Peněžnictví v ruských legiích* [Financing of the Russian Legions]. Prague, 1924.

Polzer-Hoditz, Arthur Graf. *Kaiser Karl.* Aus der Geheimmappe seines Kabinettchefs. Zurich-Leipzig-Vienna, 1929.

———. *The Emperor Karl.* New York, 1938.

Pomaizl, Karel. *Vznik ČSR 1918. Problém vědecké marxistické interpretace* [The Emergence of Czechoslovakia in 1918. The Problem of Scientific Marxist Interpretation]. Prague, 1965.

Bibliography 641

Popov, Fedor G. *Checho-slovackii miatezh i samarskaia uchredilka.* Moscow, 1937.
Prášek, Vojtěch. *Česká družina* [The Czech Družina]. Prague, 1934.
Pražský, Ferdinand. *Dějiny pěšího pluku 10 Jana Sladkého Koziny* [History of the Infantry Regiment No. 10—Jan Sladký Kozina]. Brno, 1927.
Přikryl Bohumil. *Sibířské drama* [The Siberian Drama]. Prague, 1929.
Procházka, František. *Názory Dr. Beneše o federalisaci Rakousko-Uherska v letech 1908-1916-1917* [Opinions of Dr. Beneš about Federalization of Austria-Hungary in 1908, 1916 and 1917]. Letovice, 1925.
Puškarev, S. G. and V. P. Šapilovský, eds. *Karel Kramář a Slovanstvo* [Charles Kramář and Slavdom]. Prague, 1937.
Rajchl, Rostislav. *Štefánik, Voják a Diplomat* [Štefánik, Soldier and Diplomat]. Prague, 1948.
Rašín, Ladislav. *Vznik a uznání československého státu* [The Genesis and the Recognition of the Czechoslovak State]. Prague, 1926.
Reiman, Pavel et. al. *Dějiny komunistické strany Československa* [The History of the Communist Party of Czechoslovakia]. Prague, 1961.
Repke, Jan. *II. sjezd československého vojska na Rusi: Události a dokumenty* [The Second Congress of the Czechoslovak Army in Russia: Events and Documents]. Prague, 1928.
Rudin, Harry Rudolph. *Armistice, 1918.* New Haven: Yale University Press, 1944.
Rychnovský, Ernst. ed. *Masaryk a židovství* [Masaryk and Judaism] (also in German, *Masaryk und das Judentum*). Prague, 1931.
Sakharov, Konstantin V. *Die verratene Armee.* Berlin, 1939.
———. *Cheshskie legiony v Sibiri.* Riga, 1930.
———. *Das weisse Sibirien.* Munich, 1925.
Schlesinger, Rudolf. *Federalism in Central and Eastern Europe.* London, 1945.
Schmidt-Hartmann, Eva. *Thomas G. Masaryk's Realism: Origins of a Czech Political Concept.* Munich, 1984.
Šeba, Jan. *Rusko a Malá dohoda v politice světové* [Russia and the Little Entente in World Politics]. Prague, 1936.
Seton-Watson, Hugh and Christopher. *The Making of a New Europe. R. W. Seton-Watson and the last years of Austria-Hungary.* Seattle, 1981.
Seton-Watson, Robert William. *A History of the Czechs and Slovaks.* London, 1943.

———. *Masaryk in England.* Cambridge, 1943.
———. (ed.) *The New Europe.* A weekly review of foreign politics. October 1916-October 1920. London, vols. I-XVII.
———. *The New Slovakia.* Prague, 1924.
———. *The Future of Bohemia.* London, 1915.
———. "The Origins of the School of Slavonic Studies," *The Slavonic and East European Review.* Vol. XVII, No. 50, 1939.
Seymour, Charles. *The Intimate Papers of Colonel House.* 4 vols. New York, 1926-28.
———. *Geography, Justice, and Politics at the Paris Conference of 1919.* New York, 1951.
Shagatin, N. I. *Organizatsiia i stroitelstvo Sovetskoi Armii v period innostrannoi voennoi interventsii i grazhdanskoi voiny 1918-1920 gg.* [Organization of the Soviet Army during Foreign Intervention and Civil War, 1918-1920]. Moscow, 1954.
Sidor, Karol. *Biography of Monsignor Andrej Hlinka.* Bratislava, 1934.
———. *Slováci v zahraničnom odboji* [The Slovaks in Their Resistance Abroad]. Bratislava, 1928.
———. *Slovenská politika na pôde pražského snemu, 1918-1938* [The Slovak Politics in the Parliament of Prague, 1918-1938]. Bratislava, 1943.
Sidorin, V. *Ruské armádní velitelství a Zborov* [The Russian Army Command and Zborov]. Prague, 1937.
Šindelář, František. *Z boje za svobodu otčiny* [From the Struggle for Freeing the Fatherland]. Chicago, 1924.
Šíp, František. *Několik kapitol o hospodářství naší sibiřské armády—v odpověď na Bílou Sibiř generála Sacharova* [A Few Chapters on Economy of Our Siberian Army—in Reply to White Siberia by General Sakharov]. Prague, 1926.
Sís, Vladimír. ed. *Dr. Karel Kramář. Život-dílo-práce. Vůdce národa* [Dr. Karel Kramář. Life-Work-Labor. Leader of the Nation]. Prague, Vol. I, 1936; Vol. II, 1937.
———. *Karel Kramář. Život a dílo. Skizza* [Karel Kramář. Life and Work. Skizza]. Prague, 1930.
———. *Odkaz a pravda Dr. Karla Kramáře* [The Legacy and Truth of Dr. Karel Kramář]. Prague, 1939.
Skácel, Jindřich. *Československá armáda v Rusku a Kolčak.* (Protibol-

ševický boj v roce 1918-20) [The Czechoslovak Army in Russia and Kolchak, (The Anti-Bolshevik Struggle in 1918-20)]. Prague, 1926.
———. *S generálem Syrovým v Sibiři* [With General Syrový in Siberia]. Prague, 1923.
Šmeral, Bohumír. *Historické práce 1908-1940* [Historical Works, 1908-1940]. Prague, 1961.
———. *Chekho-Slovaki i esery*. Moscow, 1922.
Smirnov, I. N. *Borba za Ural i Sibir*. Moscow, 1926.
Soukenka, Jan. *Karel Kramář, 1914-1918*. Prague, 1931.
Spahn, Martin, and Konstantin V. Sakharov. *Die Wahrheit uber die tschechischen Legionen im Weissen Sibirien*. Berlin, 1932.
Steed, Henry Wickham. *The Fifth Arm*. London, 1940.
———. *The Habsburg Monarchy*. New York: Charles Scribner's Sons, 1913.
———. *A Programme for Peace*. Chicago, 1917.
———. *Through Thirty Years, 1892-1922*. Garden City: Doubleday, 1924. 2 vols.
Štefánik, M. R. *Štefánik*. Ed. by Š. Osuský, B. Pavlů and J. Bartůšek. Prague, 1938. 2 vols.
Stloukal, Karel. *Československý stát v představách T. G. Masaryka za války* [The Czechoslovak State as Projected by T. G. Masaryk during the War]. Prague, 1930.
Strauss, Emil. *Die Enstehung der Tschechoslowakischen Republik*. Prague, 1934.
Stříbrný, Jiří. *TGM a 28. říjen* [T. G. Masaryk and 28 of October]. Prague, 1938.
Sychrava, Lev and Linhart, Josef. *6. červenec 1915 a vznik Československé republiky* [July 6th, 1915 and the Birth of the Czechoslovak Republic]. Prague, 1935.
Sychrava, Lev and Werstadt, Jaroslav. *Československý odboj* [Czechoslovak Resistance]. Prague, 1923.
Syllaba, Theodor. *T. G. Masaryk a revoluce v Rusku* [T. G. Masaryk and the Revolution in Russia]. Prague, 1959.
Šantrůček, B. *Masaryk a Klofáč*. Prague, 1938.
Šteidler, František. *Československé hnutí na Rusi* [Czechoslovak Movement in Russia]. Prague, 1922.
———. *Naše vystoupení v Rusku r. 1918* [Our Rising in Russia in 1918]. Prague, 1923.

———. *O naše vystoupení v Rusku v r. 1918* [On Our Rising in Russia in 1918]. Prague, *Naše revoluce,* vol. II, 1924.

Szporluk, Roman O. *The Political Thought of Thomas G. Masaryk.* Boulder, Colo., 1981.

Thomson, Samuel Harrison. *Czechoslovakia in European History.* Princeton, N.J.: Princeton University Press, 1943.

Thunig-Nittner, Geburg von. *Die Tschechoslowakische Legion in Russland. Ihre Geschichte und Bedeutung bei der Enstehung der 1. Tschechoslovakischen Republik.* Wiesbaden, 1970.

Tobolka, Zdeněk Václav. *Česká politika* [Czech Politics]. Prague, 1906-1913. 5 vols.

———. *Politické dějiny československého národa od r. 1848 až do nešní doby* [Political History of the Czechoslovak Nation from 1848 till the Present Time]. Prague, 1932-1937. 4 vols.

———. *Politika* [Politics]. Prague, 1923-1925. 3 vols.

Tompkins, Pauline. *American-Russian Relations in the Far East.* New York: Macmillan, 1949.

Urban, Otto. *Bohumír Šmeral a František Modráček jako představitelé dvou ideologických linií v české sociální demokracii před první světovou válkou* [Bohumír Šmeral and František Modráček as Representatives of Two Ideological Lines in the Czech Social Democratic Party before the First World War]. Prague, *Československý časopis historický,* 1963/4.

Urban, Rudolf. *Die tschechoslowakische Hussitische Kirche.* Marburg/Lahn, 1973.

———. *Tajné fondy III. sekce. Z archivu ministerstva zahraničí Republiky československé* [Secret Funds of the Third Section. From the Archives of the Czechoslovak Ministry of Foreign Affairs]. Prague, 1943.

Vávra, Vlastimil. *Americký imperialismus v pozadí čs. intervence na Sibiři* [American Imperialism in the Background of the Czechoslovak Intervention in Siberia]. Prague, *Historie a vojenství,* 1954/4.

———. *Klamná cesta. Příprava a vznik protisovětského vystoupení čs. legií* [The Wrong Way. Preparation and Origins of the Anti-Soviet Uprising of the Czechoslovak Legions]. Prague, 1958.

———. *K počátkům intervence čs. legií v Rusku (léto 1918)* [The Beginnings of the Intervention by the Czechoslovak Legions in Russia (summer 1918)]. Prague, *Historie a vojenství,* 1959/4.

Bibliography

———. *Podíl francouzské politiky na vzniku protisovětského vystoupení čs. legií v Rusku* [Contribution of the French Policy to the Origins of the Anti-Soviet Uprising of the Czechoslovak Legions in Russia]. Prague, *Historie a vojenství*, 1964/3.

———. *Příprava protisovětské intervence na severu Ruska v r. 1918* [Preparation of Anti-Soviet Intervention in the Russian North in 1918]. Prague, *Historie a vojenství*, 1963/1.

———. *Z Masarykovy kontrarevoluční činnosti v Rusku* [From Masaryk's Counterrevolutionary Activity in Russia]. Prague, *Historie a vojenství*, 1954/1.

Veselý, Jindřich. *Češi a Slováci v revolučním Rusku 1917-1920* [Czechs and Slovaks in Revolutionary Russia, 1917-1920]. Prague, 1954.

———. *O vznik a založení KSČ* [On Genesis and Founding of the Communist Party of Czechoslovakia]. Prague, 1952.

———. *Vznik a character předmnichovského Československa* [The Genesis and Character of the Pre-Munich Czechoslovakia]. Prague, 1958.

Vlasák, František. *Zpráva plnomocníka OČSNR v Samaře a Ufě* [Report of the Plenipotentiary of the Russian Branch of the Czecho-Slovak National Council at Samara and Ufa]. Brno, 1935.

Vlasák, Rudolf. *Ve víru* [In Whirlwind]. 2 vols. Prague, 1933.

———. *Vojáci republiky* [Soldiers of the Republic]. 2 vols. Prague, 1936.

Vlasta, Ladislav. *Legionáři socialisté v Rusku v revoluci* [The Socialist Legionaires in Russia and in Revolution]. Prague, 1922.

Vojtěch, Václav. *Česká kolonie pařížská v našem odboji* [Czech Colony in Paris in Our Resistance]. Prague, *Naše revoluce*, vol. IV, 1926-1927.

Vondráček, Felix John. *The Foreign Policy of Czechoslovakia, 1918-1935.* New York: Columbia University Press, 1937.

Vondrák contra Masaryk. Bohemia, No. 1. Köln, 1958.

Voska, Emanuel Victor and Irwin, William Henry. *Spy and Counterspy.* New York: Doubleday, 1940.

Vyšný, Paul. *Neo-Slavism and the Czechs 1898-1914.* Cambridge, 1977.

Weiss, Louise. *La République Tchéco-Slovaque.* Paris, 1919.

Werstadt, Jaroslav. *Československý odboj* [Czechoslovak Resistance]. Prague, 1923.

———. *Den osvobození* [The Day of Liberation]. Prague, 1923.

―――. *Drama osvobození 1914-1918.* Ideje, postavy a akty [The Drama of Liberation 1914-1918. Ideas, Personages and Actions]. Prague, 1948.

―――. *Masarykova a Kramářova cesta k samostatnosti* [Masaryk's and Kramář's Roads to Independence]. Prague, 1948.

―――. *O filosofii českých dějin, Palacký-Masaryk-Pekař* [Philosophy of Czech History, Palacký-Masaryk-Pekař]. Prague, 1937.

―――. *Od "České otázky" k "Nové Evropě",* linie politického vývoje Masarykova [From the "Czech Question" to "New Europe," the Direction of Masaryk's Political Development]. Prague, 1920.

―――. *K úloze Karla Kramáře v našem odboji; soubor dokumentů a projevů* [On the Role of Karel Kramář in Our Resistance Movement; Collection of Documents and Speeches]. Prague, *Naše revoluce,* vol. XIV, 1938.

―――. *Masarykův a Seton-Watsonův prvý projekt samostatných Čech* [Masaryk's and Seton-Watson's First Plan of Independent Bohemia]. Prague, *Naše revoluce,* vol. IV, 1926.

―――. *O Masarykovo osvoboditelství* [Masaryk Liberator]. Prague, *Naše revoluce,* vol. XIII, 1937.

―――. *Politické plány české Maffie v prvním roce války* [Political Plans of Czech Maffie during the First Year of the War]. Prague, *Naše revoluce,* vol. VI, 1930.

―――. *Spiklenecká dvojhra Masarykova a Benešova z léta a podzimu roku 1915* [Conspiratory Duo of Masaryk and Beneš in Summer and Fall of 1915]. Prague, *Naše revoluce,* vol. XII, 1936.

―――. *Ve jménu Husově pro svobodu národa* [In the Name of Huss for Freedom of the Nation]. Prague, 1935.

―――. ed. *Dr. Edvard Beneš, spoluzakladatel nové svobody a tvůrce zahraniční politiky československé.* Sborník statí [Dr. Edvard Beneš, Co-Founder of New Freedom and Author of Czechoslovak Foreign Policy. Collection of Essays]. Prague, 1924.

White, John Albert. *The Siberian Intervention.* Princeton, N.J.: Princeton University Press, 1950.

Wichtl, Friedrich. *Dr. Karl Kramarsch, der Anstifter des Weltkrieges.* Munich and Vienna, 1918.

Williamson, Samuel R. and Peter Pastor, eds. *Essays on World War I: Origins and Prisoners of War.* New York, 1982.

Winters, Stanley B. "The Young Czech Party (1874-1914); An Appraisal," *Slavic Review,* Vol. 28, No. 3, September 1969.

Bibliography 647

Wiskemann, Elizabeth. *Czechs and Germans.* London-New York, 1938.
Wotawa, A. ed. *Unser Friede! Flugblatter fur Deutschosterreichs Recht.* Vienna, 1919.
Woytko, M. G. *Slovakia's Road to Statehood.* Whiting, Ind., 1957.
Die Wunde Europas. Das Schicksal der Tschechoslowakei. Unter Mitwirkung von Rudolf Fischer u. W. Wucher hrsg. von Friedrich Heiss. Berlin, 1938.
Yurchak, P. *The Slovaks.* Whiting, Ind., 1946.
Založení komunistické strany československé. Sborník dokumentů ke vzniku a založení KSČ (1917-1924) [The Founding of the Communist Party of Czechoslovakia. Collection of Documents on the Genesis and Founding of the Communist Party of Czechoslovakia (1917-1924)]. Prague, n.d. (1954).
Zeman, Zbyněk A. B. *The Break-Up of the Habsburg Empire 1914-18.* A Study in National and Social Revolution. Oxford, 1961.
———. *The Masaryks.* The Making of Czechoslovakia. London, 1976.
Zmrhal, Karel. *Armáda ducha druhé míle* [The Army with the Spirit of the Second Mile]. Prague, 1922.
———. *O samosprávu a demokracii v sibiřské armádě* [For Selfrule and Democracy in the Siberian Army]. Prague, 1923.
———. *Vláda sovětů a Čechoslováci* [The Soviet Rule and the Czechoslovaks]. Prague, 1919.
Zuman, František. *Osvobozenecká legenda* [The Legend of Liberation]. 2 vols. Prague, 1922.
———. *Osudné rozhodování. Vzpomínka na převratovou dobu v Rusku* [The Fateful Decision-Making. Memories of the Russian Revolution]. Prague, 1927.

PERIODICALS

Bohemia, 1916, 1917, 1918
Bohemian Review, 1917, 1918
Bulletin de la Colonie tcheque de France, 1915, 1916, 1917, 1918
Čechoslovackaia krasnaia armia [Czechoslovak Red Army], 1918
Čechoslovan [Czecho-Slav], 1916, 1917, 1918
Čechoslovák [Czechoslovak], 1915, 1916, 1917, 1918
Česka demokracie, 1917, 1918
České slovo [Czech Word], 1914, 1918
Český časopis historický, 1900-1914

Československá rudá armáda [Czechoslovak Red Army], 1918
Československá samostatnost [Czechoslovak Independence], 1915, 1916, 1917, 1918
Československý bulletin [Czechoslovak Bulletin], 1918
Československý časopis historický [Czechoslovak Historical Periodical], 1960-1970
Československý deník [Czechoslovak Daily], 1917, 1918
Československý voják [Czechoslovak Soldier], 1917, 1918
L'Independance tchèque, 1915
Masarykův sborník [Symposium on Masaryk], 1930-1931
Národ [The Nation], 1918
Národ [The Nation] (Chicago), 1967-1972
Národní listy [National Leaves], 1913, 1914, 1918
Národní osvobození
Národní politika [National Politics], 1914-1918
La Nation tchèque, 1915, 1916, 1917, 1918
Naše doba
Naše revoluce [Our Revolution], 1924-1937
The New Europe, 1916, 1917, 1918
Pochodeň [Torch], 1918
Poděbradka (Chicago), 1917, 1918
Prager Tagblatt
Pravda, 1918
Právo lidu [Right of the People], 1913, 1914, 1918
Průkopník [Pioneer], 1918
Průkopník svobody [Pioneer of Freedom], 1918
Revoluce, 1917
Rudé právo
Samostatnost [Independence], 1914
Slovenské hlasy [Slovak Voices], 1917, 1918
Svoboda [Freedom], 1917, 1918
Věstník odbočky ČSNR [Bulletin of the branch of the Czecho-Slovak National Council], 1918
Večer
Venkov
Vesmír (Chicago), 1914-1918
Vídeňský deník

INDEX

Adrianoff, Professor, 192
Agrarian party (Agrarians), 11, 32, 50, 101, 103, 107, 123, 387
Alba, General (French), 356
Alexander, Prince Regent, 462
Alexeev, General Mikhail V., establishes Czech brigade, 94, 587n; and Dürich, 102; favors building Czech army, 105, 106, 150; 123, 135, 148; asks Czechs to go to the Don, 220, 221, 229, 230; cooperation with rejected by Masaryk, 232, 291; 277, 305, 310, 316, 408, 414; tells Dürich that Russians had been deserted by all, 468, 470
Alliance of Brethren (*Jednota bratská*), 22
Alliance of Czech (later Czech-Slovak) Associations in Russia (ACSAR), 62, 63, 64, 65, 87, 90, 93-95, 100-101, 103, 105, 121-124, 135-136, 140, 142, 151-152, 154-156
All-Russian Provisional Government, established at Ufa, 409
All-Russian Union of Co-operative Societies, 360
Alsace-Lorraine, 168, 170
American Declaration of Independence, 433
Amett, Cardinal (France), 153
Amfiteatrov, Alexander V., 143
"Anabasis," 484, 489, 498

Anglican Church, 104
Anglo-French convention, December 23, 1917, 229, 231
Antonov-Ovseyenko, V., 310; thanks the Czech corps for leaving arms in Russia, 311
April Theses (Lenin's), 168
Aralov, P. V., 310, 329; telegrams of 329-330, 335; 333, 336
Archangel, 225, 286, 324
Armia i flot, 219
Armistice in Siberia, 484; conditions of, 484
"Arnold," code name for Ven Svarc, 186
Asquith, Herbert Henry, 110, 160
Atlee, Clement R., on Beneš, 490
Auchincloss, Gordon, 282, 300; letter on Siberian situation for Lansing, 301
Aurora, 208
Austrian National Provisional Assembly, 436

Baerenreither, Josef M., 39
Baird, Major John, 54
Baker, Newton Diehl, 360
Bakhmach, railroad junction, "battle of," 273, 307-309
Balfour, Arthur James, 158, 161; Balfour mission, 58; memorandum of, 161; 267; receives Beneš, 268; responds to Beneš's memoranda, 269; and recognition of CSNC, 378, 384, 388, 389

Balutis, B. K., 183
Baráček, Pavel, 149
Baruch, Bernard, 373
Bechyně, Rudolf, 436, 437
Belgrade, Armistice of, 449
Bém, J., 356
Benedict XV, Pope, peace note, 180
Beneš, Eduard (Edvard, Edouard), and Masaryk, 5, 6, 8, 9, 47, 92, 102, 107, 115, 120, 159, 162, 165, 338; and Šmeral, 48: member of *Maffie,* 49: arrives in exile, 78-79: and Štefánik, 84, 85, 98, 138, 147, 155, 535n, 475-477, 485, 486; as seen socialist in Russia, 88: secretary general of Czech (Czecho-Slovak) National Council, 89, 97, 535n; and Dürich, 98, 141, 144, 148, 149, 152, 153: and *Maffie,* 163, 168; and Czechoslovak army in France, 196, 197, 198, 259; messages home, 254; and Congress of Oppressed Nationalities in Rome, 261, 264-265; negotiates in England, 264; and the May 1918 Congress at Prague, 266-267; negotiates with Balfour, 268-269; asked by Cecil to leave some troops in Russia, 269; and Balfour's willingness to recognize CSNC, 269; message proposing establishment of provisional government, 269-270; and reaction to Masaryk's Tokyo memorandum, 279; and the army in Russia, 285-287, 302, 312, 356; to Masaryk on intervention in Russia, 302-303; approves Cecil's request to leave some troops in Russia, 325; agrees to use the army in intervention, 364. 365; negotiates with Orlando, 377; asks for French recognition, 377-378; receives French recognition, 379, 383, 388; message left to *Maffie* denying Czech involvement in intervention, 387; requests British recognition, 383-385; on Foreign Office's reluctance to recognize CSNC, 388; receives British recognition, 389; obtains Japanese recognition, 403; and Italian recognition, 403-404; and establishment of provisional government, 417-419; and declaration of independence, 425; meets delegates from home in Geneva, 428; and the Geneva decalration, 431, 471; invited to Versailles, 431-432, 435; as principal negotiator, 437; and instructions from Masaryk, 438-439; asks National Committee to approve bringing French military-political mission to Prague, 440; on danger of Bolshevism in Vienna. 441; presents territorial claims at Paris Peace Conference, 441-447; and Doctor's Day and Seymour and Major Douglas Johnson, 443-444; promises that Czecho-Slovakia's regime will resemble that of Switzerland, 445; rejects, plebiscite, 447; and Slovakia, 448; compared and contrasted with Kramář, 454-456; as described by Lloyd George, 456; claims made at Geneva, 471; and intervention in Russia, 478; and Churchill's plan for intervention, 478-480; instructs the army to go to Vladivostok, 481; orders evacuation of the army, 482; and Syrový, 484-485; compared and

Index

contrasted with Masaryk, 488-489; political practices, 490, 492; on Austria-Hungary before the war, 496; Kramář's criticism of, 504-505; and his concept's failure, 506; exaggerates strength of Czechoslovak armed forces, 583-584n; fabricates documents forwarded to Washington, 592-593n; and subsidies to foreign periodicals, journalists and other individuals, 607n; plots with Masaryk against Kramář and others, 610n
Beneš, František, 218, 237, 240
Beneš, Josef, 325
Beneš, Vojta, 79, 108, 152
"Bennet", code name for Rev. Koukol, 186
Berthelot, General Henri M., 137, 205, 230; urges intervention in Russia, 296
Beseda, 103
Bethman-Hollweg, Theobald von, on struggle of Germans and Slavs, 36
Birzhevie Vedomosti, 81, 103, 169, 170, 171
Black Hand, 156
Black Hundreds, 148
Bobrinsky, Count Vladimir Alexeev, 138
Bogoslovskii, General, 406
Bohemian Brethren, 27
Bohemian National Alliance in the United States, 51, 57, 69, 79, 82, 83, 103, 132, 182-184; and Cleveland Agreement, 70, 79, 83; sends letter to Wilson, 258; 279-281; and Pittsburgh Agreement, 283-284
Bohemian Review, 82
Bolshevism (Bolsheviks), 207, 219, 250,; and Dürich, 216-218, 222, 314, 315, 462, 463, 468-470; Czechs' conflict with and resistance to, 304ff. 339ff, 476-483; armistice with, 484; and Beneš: 364, danger of in Vienna, 441; and Teschen, 453; 387, 443-444, 478; Russian problem, 506; and Kramář, 454, 461-454, 477-479, 481, 504-505; and Masaryk: 175, 211, 216, 217, 222, 227, 228, 232, 233, 239; believes in possibility of doing business with, 241; 242, 243, 245; advises Allies their recognition, 276, 293; on causes of the conflict with, 359, 363, 576; on their weakness, 577n; believes negotiations with them not possible, 397; urges intervention against, 397-398; opposes intervention, 462, 482; sees it as Russian problem, 506; and Štefánik, 473, 476, 477, 485; in Hungary, 450-453
Bordes, Captain (French), 405
Borský, Lev, 33; disapproves Masaryk's policy, 302; acredited to represent provisional government in Italy, 419
Bosnia-Herzegovina, 16
Bráf, Albín, quoted on Masaryk, 317n
Brandeis, Louis D., 23, 413
Brentano, Franz, 19
Best-Litovsk, Armistice of, 228; negotiations at, 231, 241, 252, 253, 299; Peace of, 236, 255; Treaty of, 250, 255, 256, 290, 309, 314, 322, 323, 358, 469, 470, 499; effect of on Austria-Hungary, 499-501; return of prisoners of war, 405
Briand, Aristide, 55, 88, 92, 98, 278

British War Office, memorandum on Japanese occupation of Trans-Siberian Railway, 307; memoranda on Czechoslovak army in Russia, 309; consideration of alternative use of Czech troops, 324; need for intervention, 356
Brusilov, General Alexis, 177, 199
Buchanan, Sir George W., 67
Burcev (Burtseff), Vladimir, 143, 188, 192
Bureau of Propoganda (Bolshevik), 194
Burrows, Ronald, 47, 53, 54, 55, 56, 58; and the "Slovanic School", 53-54
Butler, Nicholas Murray, 494

Caldwell, John K. (U.S. Consul at Vladivostok), urges aid to Czechs, 407-408
Caporetto, Battle of, 206
Carpatho-Russia (Ruthenia), 47
"Carpathorussions", 438
Carson, Sir Edward, 188; Voska's report to, 188-191; 283
Čas, 20, 21, 31
"Castle" Historians, 508-509n
Catholics (Czech) in the United States. See the National Alliance of Czech Catholics.
Catholic parties, 12, 22, 49, 72, 76, 103, 167, 197, 387, 489
Čeček, Stanislav, 244, 334, 339, 342, 346, 353; receives order to defend Volga front, 368; issue historic order to Czech troops, 369, 375, 376, 406
Čech, quoted on Masaryk, 536n
Čechoslovák, 87, 90, 102, 103, 139, 142, 144, 155, 176, 203, 218; and Kornilov, 203, 439
Čechoslovan, 156, 222, 227, 549n

Cecil, Lord Robert, 161, 268, 293; proposes Beneš to keep Czechoslovak troops in Russia, 269; and British recognition of CSNC, 388, 389, 390
Čeřenský, Czech army officer, 220
Čermák, Bohumil, 87, 90, 121, 135, 151, 188, 248; arrested in Moscow, 329; sings order to disarm, 330, 543n
Červený, Otakar V., 60
Červinka, General Jaroslav, 106, 142, 150, 175, 204
Česká demokracie, 164, 167
Československá samostatnost, 75, 89, 144
Československá rudá armáda, 326, 330
Československý deník, 227, 240, 243, 326, 327, 328, 336, 345, 346, 352, 353, 483
Československý voják, 204; on Kornilov, 204
Český časopis historický, 25-27
Chamberlain, Austen, 161
Chamberlain, Neville, 506
Charles I, Emperor of Austria, 159, 177, 180, 206, 251, 257; interested in peace, 257; and "Sixtus affair", 263, 264, 265, 267; attempts saving his empire, 497, 498; amnesties political prisoners, including Kramář and Rašín. 159, 210, 251-252; and agreement at Spaa, 264, 500-501; meets delegates of Czech Alliance (Union), 420; meets with Klofáč, 427; and Beneš, 432; on Spaa agreement and Brest-Litovsk Peace, 500-501
Charles IV (I), King of Bohemia and Holy Roman Emperor, 2
Chelčický, Peter, 27

Index

Cheliabinsk "incident", 327-328
Cheradame, André, 108, 113, 114, 119, 124
Chernov, Victor M., 218, 347
Chicago Herald Examiner, 296
Chicherin, George V., 321, 351; Masaryk's memorandum for, 362-363, 372, 489; offers Prague government transit of Czechoslovak army for return home, 472
Churchill, Winston, S., on Bolesheviks, 316, 317; comments on intervention, 478; plan for intervention, 479, 481, 504; on Kolchak, 482-483; on Kolchak's surrender, 484
Clemenceau, Georges, 80, 206; sings agreement regarding Czechoslovak army in France, 259; imbroglio with Czernin and revelation of the "Sixtus letter", 259; receives participants in Rome Congress, 262, 264, 265; wnts Japan to bring Czechs from Vladivostok to France, 275; resists British pressure for sending the troops to Archangel, 286; and Masaryk, 298; attends meeting presided over by House, 431
Clementel, French minister of trade, 93
Clerk, Sir Geroge R., 47, 76, 77
Cleveland Agreement, 70, 79, 83
Club of Collaborators, 543n; *or* Club of Confidants, 156
Coerth, Anna, on number of persons executed in Galicia, 587-588n
"Cole", code name for Trotsky, 187
Comenius, Amos, 210

Committee of Imperial Defense, 117
"Committee, of Slav Origin, for Russia" (Committee of American Citizens of Slav Origin), 184, 186
Communist Party of Czechoslovakia, 331, 333; founding of, 474. *See* also Czechoslovak Communist Party
Congress of Oppressed Nationalities of Austria Hungary in Rome, 156, 260, 261, 268, 289
Consituent Assembly (Russian), election of, 228, 230, 370, 409
Consitution of the Slavic Empire, 37
Cossacks, 190, 191, 229, 230; enter Irkutsk, 369
Council of Four (Paris Peace Conference), 460
Council of People's Commissars, 226, 313, 340, 351, 407, 499-501
Cramme, Mme de, 192
Crane, Charles R., 44, 45, 51, 183, 281; recommends Masaryk to Wilson, 288, 298, 521-523n; 526n; 570n
Crane, Richard, 288, 289, 298; dinner in his house attended by Masaryk, 289-291; on Masaryk's audience with Wilson, 300, 560n
Crkal, Viluš, 71, 93, 96, 102, 138-140, 217, 546n
Crowe, Sir Eyre, 41, 43
Crown of St. Wenceslas. *See* St. Wneceslas Crown
Cummings, Sir Mansfield, 57
Czech Alliance. *See* Czech Union and Union of Czech Deputies
Czech Commitee Abroad, declaration of November 14, 1915, 86, 87

Czech Committe in Moscow, 90
Czech National Committee (Prague), 4, 5, established, proclaims loyalty to empire and dynasty, 107; restored (established), 386, 387, 388, 418, 420; Imperial Manifesto, 425; declares Czecho-Slovak independence and assumes executive powers, 428, 430; and the Geneva declaration, 431; Deutschböhmen and Sudetenland attempt to negotiate with, 436-437; and Beneš, 440; and *faits accomplis,* 502
Czecho-Slovak National Council (Paris) (CSNC), proclaims independence, 5; establishment and name of, 89, 535n, 537-538n; composition of, 97-98; sends Dürich to Russia, 96-98; sends Štefánik to Russia, 100, 106; Dürich recognized representative of in Russia, 106, 123, 133; and Štefánik's actions in Russia, 134, 135, 137, 147-149; and Dürich, 141, 142, 147-149; and Russian government, 145; and Dürich's expulsion from, 137, 147-148, 150, 152, 153, 495; and its Russian branch, 155; *(See* also CSNC, Its Russian branch.) and authority of its three members (Masaryk, Beneš, Štefánik), 156; and its army, 175; and Voska, 190; and Koukol, 191; and recruitment of troops in U.S., 196; and establishment of army in France and Italy, 197-198, 249, 260, 262; makes army in Russia part of army in France, 231-232; and decision to leave the Ukraine, 245; Balfour considers recognition of, 269, 296; Bohemian National Alliance and National Alliance of Czech Catholics submit to its leadership, 280; its American branch establsihed, 281; and British government's reluctance to recognize, 309, 324, 388; Masaryk's efforts for U.S. recognition of, 370; U.S. declines to recognize, 370-372; and Beneš's claims, 377; recognized by France, 383; recognized by Great Britain, 389, 498; recognized by United States, 390, 402; agreement with Great Britain, 390; Lansing on British recognition of, 494; recognized by Italy, 404; concludes secret agreement with France, 421; France recognized territorial claims of, 421, 422; transformed into provisional government, 417-419; nature of the recognitions, 390, 403; Masaryk requests U.S. recognition as *de facto* co-belligerent government, 425; and Beneš's claims, 279, 471; and Štefánik, 475; reasons for recognition of, 499
CSNC, Its Russian branch, formation, 155; Masaryk in charge of its propoganda commission, 169; Masaryk's use of, 177; official organ of, 203, 227; and Masaryk's neutrality policy, 213, 214, 217; makes army in Russia part of army in France, 231, 232; and Czech socialists, 237, 238; rejects views held by Bolesheviks, 240; maintains neutrality in Kiev, 241; urged by Masaryk to prevent return of prisoners of war home, 242; and Red Guards, 243; and dissatisfaction of soldiers, 244; orders Legion to leave Ukraine, 245;

Index

and Masaryk's instructions to, 247; and financing the army, 248; refuses participation in proposed intervention, 285, 288; urged by Klecanda not to disarm troops, 213; and Dürich, 315, 316; dissentions within on neutrality policy, 320; conflict with the army increasing, 321, 322; and the Allied proposals to send troops to Archangel, 324; and agreement with Siberian cooperatives, 325; confiscation of Moscow's offices, 326; tries to calm alarmed soldiers, 327; its leaders, Maxa and Čermák, negotiate with Boleshevisk, arested in Moscow, 329; Maxa and Čcermák order army to disarm and complete split with the latter, 330; coup d'etat by Czechslovak Communists, 330 333; defied by soldiers and officers, complete break with neutrality policy, 334, 335, 336, 339, 340, 344, 345, 347; dissolved by Council of People's Commissars, 351; new leaders urge Allies to assist Czechs, 357; cooperates with Allies, 363; new leaders elected, 394; decrees mobilization of all citizens of the future state, 405; urges formation of All-Russian government, 409; urges Allies save Volga front, 415; dissolved by Štefánik, 475
Czechoslavic Alliance, 95
Czechoslovak army in France, establishment of, 206
Czechoslovak Communist Party (Communists) in Russia, 305; congress in Moscow, 330-334; orders mobilization of Czechslovak Communists, 473-474

Czechoslovak National Assembly, 459. *See* also Revolutionary (Constituent) National Assembly
Czechoslovak National Council in Petrograd, formation, 140-143; members of, 142; relations with the Paris Council, 147-155; Russian government's approval and support of, 145-147; and Štefánik, 144-151; disolution of, 152
Czecho-Slovak Press Office (in Russia), 140
Czechoslovak Revolutionary Council of Workers and Soldiers, formation, 245; collapse of, 246; former members of, 322
Czechoslovak Revolutionary (Constituent) National Assembly, not elected, 141; members of, 432, 433; elects Masaryk president of state, 432; Masaryk's first message to, 433, 491, 503; Beneš's message to, 478
Czechoslovak section of the People's Commissariat of Nationalities, 325
Czech Paris Bureau, 149
Czech Question, The, 22, 23, 491
Czech-Slav Press Bureau (in the United States), 70
Czech State Right Democracy, 252, 387
Czech Union (Union of Czech Deputies, Czech Alliance), formation, 106; members and officers of, 107; disavows Masaryk-led independence movement, 162-163; adopts new Czech demands, 165; new leadership of, 252; demands for Czech representation at Brest-Litovsk rejected by Czernin, 253; issues resolution denouncing Vienna government, 418; and Staněk's support of CSNC,

419; representatives of meet with Charles, 220
Czernin, Count Ottokar, 159, 160, 180; at Brest-Litovsk, 252-253; denounces Masaryk, 254-256; address of April 2, 1918, 267; imroglio with Clemenceau over "Sixtus letter", 262-263; resigns, 256; comments on end of Austria-Hungary, 497

Daszynski, Ignacy, 255, 420
David, Josef, 356
"Davis", code name for Lenin, 187
Daxner, Francis, 87
"Decree on Peace" (Lenin's), 219
Dědina, František, 216, 217
Dělnické listy, 186, 187
Deml, Jakub, 493
Denikin, General Anton, I., 199, 207, 226, 291, 465, 478; offensive against Moscow, 481. 482, 483, 504
Denis, Ernest, 1, 45, 70, 71, 80, 84, 108
Dérer, Ivan, 459
Deutschböhmen, 436; provisional government of protests to Wilson, 437
Dieterichs, General M.K., 244, 309, 310, 312, 314, 335, 340, 348, 368, 374, 406, 407
Dimitriev, General Radko, 63
Dmowski, Roman, 15, 16, 388
Donath, Oskar, 19
Drummond, Sir Eric, 161, 178
Družina, 40, 62, 63, 67, 81, 90, 94, 108, 121, 149, 153, 587n
Dukhonin, General Nicholas, N., 204, 224, 226
Dula, Matúš, 430
Duma (Russian), 157

Dürich, Josef, arrives in exile, 50, 51, 77, 79, 84, 524n; waits for invitation to go to Russia, 85; and Masaryk 85, 86, 90, 91, 471; signs declaration for "Czech Committee Abroad", 86, 87; selected to represent indpendence movement in Russia, 88; agrees to Masaryk's request to form Czech National Council, 89; and Beneš, 89, 92, 96, 97; and French government, 93, goes to Russia, 96, 97, 98; arrives in Petrograd, 101; deals with Russian government, 101-107; and Russian government, 114, 115, 123, 132-156; and "Kievan Pact", 133, 134, 136, 138; and Štefánik, 133-138, 144-150; expelled from CSNC, 137, 147, 148, 150, 152, 153, 495; head of Czechslovak National Council in Petrograd, 140-143, 145-151; and dissolution of the council, 152; attacked by Štefánik, Beneš, Masaryk and others, 152-155, 176; and the Kiev incident, 215- 217, 222; joins anti-Boleshevik forces, 222, 304, 314, 315; goes to Gelenjik, 315-316; in Volunteer Army headquarters, 468-470; on money collections in America, 536n; defended by his daughter, 552n; returns home, 470, 471; defended by Karel Horký, 471
Dzieduszycky, Count, 16

Edinstvo, 169, 210, 211
Eisemann, Louis, 84, 450
Emerson, Colonel, 291
Epiphany Declaration of January 6, 1918, 252-254, 281, 499
European Federation of Socialist Republics, 317, 332

European Review, 39
Evangelical Church, 28
Extraordinary Commission of the Political Centre (Itkutsk), 483-484

Federation of the Foreign Groups of the Russian Communist Party, 323
Fic, Victor M., quoted on Masaryk's overestimating Bolsheviks' strength, 576-577n
Fiedler, 420
Fifth All-Russian Congress of Soviets, 359, 369
Fisher, Louis, 69, 82, 87
Foch, Marshal Ferdinand, 300, 448
Foreman, J., 108
Four Power Alliance, 133
France, established Czechoslovak army, 206, 258, 259; recognizes CSNC as *de facto* provisional government, 353; recognizes provisional government, 421; concludes secret agreement with CSNC (Beneš), 421
Franz-Joseph (Francis Joseph) I, Emperor of Austria, death of, 79, 159, 497, 587n
Franchet d'Esperey, General Louis, asks Austria to withdraw army from Slovakia, 437; and Belgrade armistice agreement, 449
Francis, David R., proposes sending two U.S. divisions to Russia, 201; on Czech prisoners of war, 276, 291; favors intervention, 349, 350, 353, 354; on Soviet order to disarm Czechoslovaks, 351
Frazier, ARthur, A., 266-267
Freissler, Robert, 436
Fremdenblatt, 164

French Declaration of the Rights of Man and Citizen, 433
French Foreign Legion, 196
Furtenburg, 189

Gajda, Radola (Rudolph Gejdl), 65, 244; and contingency plans, 325; member of Temporary Executive Committee, 334; warned not take any action, 336; takes Novonikolaevsk, 337; involved in planning anti-Bolshevik action, 339, 340; fights Bolsheviks, 343, 344, 346, 348, 352; Harris reports on his troops taking Irkutsk, 369-370; on how independence was regained, 386-387; 406, 407; urges Allied aid, 410, 411; appointed commander of Russian Siberian army, 477; attempts coup, 478; departs from Siberia, 478; plotted against by Masaryk and Beneš, 610n
Gajer, Lieutenant, 244
Galicia, 66, 67; number of people executed in, 587n
Garrigue, Charlotte, 18
Gaunt, (Captain, later Admiral) Guy, 56, 57
Gauvain, Auguste, 108
Geneva, Masaryk comes out publicly against Austria-Hungary, 85; Beneš meets with delegates from Prague, 427, 428, 431, 471
German Social Democratic party, organizes a demonstration, 448
Gerovsky, Alexander, 103, 104, 105, 114, 132, 138
Girsa, Václav, 348, 481, 482
Glabinski, Stanislav, 255
Goll, Jaroslav, 25, 26, 30, 31
Grawes, General William S., suggests going with troops to Omsk,

410-411; U.S. government rejects his suggestion, 411-412
GReater Moravian Empire, 2
Grey, Sir Edward, 68, 76, 495
Grenard, French consul in Moscow, 248
Grew Joseph, 290
Grigoriev, Nicholas, 214
Guchkov, Alexander I., 173, 185
Guinet, Major Alfred, 336, 345, 347, 353, 356; notifies Czechs about Allied intervention, 357, 405
Gurka, General V., 135

Haberman, Gustav, 50, 252, 427, 431, 471, 539n
Habsburg dynasty (monarchy), 3, 17
Hais, Arno, 214, 239, 245, 325
Halifax, Lord, 506
Hankey, Colonel Sir Maurice, 117
Hardinge, Lord, 161
Harper, Samuel, 523n
Harper, William R., 523n
Harris, E.L., U.S. consul at Irkutsk, reports on Gajda's taking the city, 369-370; urges aiding Czechs, 406-408; gives number of Czech troops involved in Siberian campaign, 597n
Hašek, Jaroslav, 7, 156, 222, 240; writes on "Why Going to France?", 317-318; with Fifth Red Army in Siberia, 474
Herben, Jan, 21, 26, 30, 31
Herder, Johann W., 27
Hintze, Admiral von, 359
Hlasists, 3
Hlaváček, František, 250
Hlinka, Father Andrej, 8, 34; and Masaryk, 284; on relations of Slovaks with Magyars, 429;

432; leader of Slovak People's party, 456-460; at Paris, 457; and Pittsburgh Agreement, 284, 456-458; on Kramář, 459; and Kramář, 610n
Hodža, Milan, 8, 11, 34; uelogy of Kramář, 610n
Hoffman, General Max, 226
Holeček, Josef, 105
Holy Sea, 280
Hoover, Herbert, 301
Horký, Karel, 108, 471, 524n, 552n
Horodyski, Jan, 221
House, Colonel Edward Mandel, 58, 146, 181, 183; head of "Inquiry", 183, 184; and Wiseman, 58, 146, 184, 282, 300; Voska's report to, 189-191; and Balfour, 221, 289, 301; Masaryk on, 438; at Paris Peace Conference, 460
Houska, Václav, 204, 348
Hruban, Mořic, 107, 420
Hrushevsky, Michael, 217
Hub, Lieutenant, signs armistice with Bolsheviks, 484
Hudec, Josef, 164, 168
Hughes, William Morris, 461
Hungarian Red Army, 451
Hurban-Vajanský, Svetozár, 284
Hurban, Vladimír S., 140, 149, 194; and report to Masaryk, 308; about Dürich to Masaryk, 315-316; sent to Washington, 394-395
Huss (Hus), Jan (John), 85, 210, 223; regiment of, 224; holiday of, 610n
"Hussite Cross", 223
Hussite Division, 224
Hussite revolution (Hussites), 28, 29, 318

Index 659

Hussite Wars, 2

Illiador, anti-German Russian monk, 183
Imperial manifesto on federalization of Austria, October 16, 1918, 422, 501
Inquiry, 183, 283
Inter-Allied Committee in Petrograd, 187; its Second Mureau, 188
Iška, František, 83, 606n
Izvestia, 209, 219
Izvolsky, Alexander P., 89, 153

Jackl, František, 71
Jaksch, Wenzel, on Masaryk's philosophy, 492
Jameson, U.S. consul for special duty in Russia and Siberia, reports Czechoslovaks hold U.S. government solely responsible for Allied failure to aid them on Volga front, 416
Janík, F., 245
Janin, General Maurice, chief of French military mission in Russia, 99, 100, 101, 134, 150; condemns Maxa for his handling situation in Kiev, 223; commander of Czechslovak army in France, 259, 302, 356, 385, 404, 414; arrives in Siberia, 467; in Siberia, 475-476, 480, 482, 483; blamed for Kolchak's fate, 484
Janoušek, Antonín, 451
Japan Advertiser, 314
Jastrebov, N.J., 81, 169
Jaszi, Oscar, 39
Jesenský, Janko, 394, 478
Jews, in Czech lands, 19, 512n; Orthodox and Zionists, 23; Masaryk acknowledges support of, 154
Ježek, J., 356

Jirásek, Alois, 256
Joffre, Marshal Joseph, 98, 99, 100
Johnson, Grand Duke, 78
Joseph II, Emperor of Austria, 28
Juriga, Father Ferdiš (Ferdinand), supports Austro-Hungarian monarchy, 72; demands right of self-determination for Slovaks, 429-430
Jusserand, J.J., 275, 298

Kadlec, Eduard, at Bakhmach, 307, 315; prepares contingency plans, 325; fights Bolesheviks, 337, 343, 352
Kaizl, Josef, 12
Kaledin, General A.M., 191, 216, 220, 221, 226, 231, 239
expects arrival of Russian, 75; released from prison, becomes vice-chairman of Czech Union, 252, 253, 256n; becomes member of National Committee, 387, meets with Emperor Charles, 427; meets with Beneš and signs Geneva declaration, 431, 470; minister of national defense, 486
Knox, General Alfred V.F., 273, 411, 414; urges Czechs to go to front, 482
Kolchak, Admiral Aleksandr V., 463; and November 1918 coup, 475, 483; appoints Gajda commander of Russian Siberian army, 477; forces Gajda's resignation, 478, 479-482; Churchill's characterization of, 482-483; as characterized by Morris, 604-605n; his surrender and death, 483-484
Kolomenski, General, 216
Komárek, Captain, 244
Komuch, 376
Koníöek, Karel, 245, 247

Koníček, Svatopluk, alias Štěpán-Horský (Koníček-Horský), 40, 70, 71, 82, 90, 95, 96, 101, 102, 113, 121, 142, 152, 217, 304
Kopecký František (Francis), 54, 87, 104
Kopecký, František, Austrian consulate clerk, Voska's agent "Zeno", 525n, 527n, 533n
Körber, E. von, 48
Kornilov (Korniloff), General Lavr G., 175, 188, 199; and the crisis, 201, 203; and his escape from Austrian captivity, 202; likes Czechs, 202-203; and Masaryk, 201-203 opposes Bolesheviks, 226, 230, 231, 239, 277, 305, 316,
"Kornilov affair", 207, 208, 214, 215, 220
Kornilovci, 202, 214
Korošec, Anton, 256, 419
Košík, Gustav, 83
Koudelka, Oldřich, 247, 322, 342
Kovalevsky, Maxim, 522n
Koukol, Reverend A.B., in Russia, 188; reports on mission in Russia, 191-196
Koza (Koza-Permský), F., 333
Kalina, Antonín, 33, 49, 50, 167, 427; signs Geneva declaration, 431, 471
Kalina, Antonín Svatopluk, 299, 381
Kamkov, Left SR, 359
Kapell, General V.O., challenges Syrový to duel, 483
"Kapellovtsi", 483, 484
Karolyi, Count Michael, 178, 448, 449
Kavćić, Dr., 387
Kennan, George F., 501
Kepl, Rudolf, 40, 82

Kerensky, Alexander F., collapse of his regime, 110, 189; disapproves of recruitment for Czech army, 173, 174, 549-550n: changes his attitude after the battle of Zborov, 175, 185; and Maughma, 201, 204; releases Bolesheviks and proclaims republic, 207; sees enemy on the right, 208
Kerr, Philip, 460
"Kievan Pact", 106, 133, 134-138
Kievskaiia Mysl, 171
Kirilenko, Commissar in Russian army in Kiev, 214
Kirsanov Resolution, 320-321
Kitchener, Lord Herbert, 42, 43
Klecanda, Jiří, writes "The Memorial Script on the Czechoslovak Question", 61; sympathizes with Masaryk, 121, 135, 139, 543; secretary of the Russian branch of CSNC, 155, 177; cooperates with Allied agents in Russia, 188; appointed Masaryk's representatives with the army corps, 204; opposed by Kievan Social Democrats, 240; negotiates in Moscow, 310, 311, 312; opposes disarming troops, 313; gives Savinkov 200,000 rubles, 460; dies in Omsk, 310, 313
Klecanda, Václav, 142
Klecanda Vladimír, 202; and Kornilov, 202-203
Knoflíček, Karel, 218, 237, 240; chief of Czechoslovak section of the People's Commissariat of Nationalities, 325
Klofáć, Václav, offers Sazonov to organize spy nettwork for Russia, 35, 36, 38, 39; arest of, 73; 454-456; and Hlinka, 459; favors

Index

intervention, 445; and plan for intervention in Russia, 461-464, 478, 479, 481; dismissed as prime minister by Masaryk, 464; on League of Nations, 464; on Boleshevik regime in Russia, 504, 505; worries about future of his country, 610; Hodža's eulogy of, 610n
Krasnov, General P.N., 226
Kropotkin, Prince Peter, 143
Krylenki, Ensign Nicholas V., 218
Kudela, Josef, 336, 345, 346
Kühlmann, Richard von, 358
Kuhn, Loeb & Co., New York, 59
Kulturkampf, 19
Kun, Béla, 323, 450, 451, 453
Kupka, František, 87
Kurayev, V. V., 312, 342
Kvapil, Jaroslav, 166
Kwiecinski, General, 214, 215, 217, 222
Kysela, Josef, 204, 356

Lammasch, Heinrich, 427
La Nation tcheque, 76, 77, 97
Langer, František, 176, 209, 352
Lansdowne, Lord Henry, 117
Lansing, Robert, 5; seeks to separate Austria from Germany, 161; on proposed Japanese intervention, 272, 273, 286; and memorandum on "Slavs of Austria-Hungary", 279-280; and oppressed nationalities in Austria-Hungary, 292, 295; receives Masaryk, 292-295; on intervention in Russia, 296, 297; on non-recognition of the Bolsheviks, 298; and his plan concerning Russia, 299; recommends establishment of commission for Russia, 301; considers intervention in Russia, 350; asks Wilson to help Czechoslovak army in Siberia, 360, 361; meets with Masaryk on June 25, 1918, 361-363, 498; receives communications from Siberia concerning Czechs, 364, 365; memoranda for and on July 1, 1918, White House conference, 366-368; and June 24 memorandum on Austria-Hungary, 379-380; advises Wilson against recognizing CSNC, 381-382; recommends recognition of CSNC as *de facto* "Revolutionary Government", 391; on problems with Král, František, supports Dörich, 102; member of D?rich's National Council, 142; abducted and prevented from attending ACSAR's congress in Kiev, 155; *Revoluce* protests his treatment, 177; organizes Czech unit in Volunteer Army on the Don, 218. 228, 230, 304, 306
Král, Václav, communist historian quoted, 510n, 526n
Kramář, Karel, leader of independence movement at home, 6-8; Czech leader in Vienna, leader of the Young Czech party, 12-17, 22; comments on Russian foreign policy, 36; and his political concepts, 22, 37-38, 124; drafts Constitution of Slavic Empire, 37-38; and Neo-Slavism, 15, 16, 36, 39; and his contacts abroad, 39, 40, 52, 53, 108, 111, 112, 542n; and British concept of balance of power, 41; leader of *Maffie,* 49-50; and Dürich, 50, 80, 525n; sees war struggle between Germandom

and Slavdom, 71-72; arrested, 74, 78; trial of, 79; sentenced to death, 79-80; and foreign reaction to death sentence, 80-81; amnestied by Emperor Charles, 159, 163, 164, 210, 251, 556n; becomes leader of independence movement at home, 167, 252, 332, 384; chairman of Czech State-Right Democracy, 252; and the April 13, 1918 manifestation, 256; and they May 1918 congress of oppressed nationalities in Prague, 265-266; becomes president of Revolutionary Committee, 266; head of Czech National Committee at Prague, 386-387; first Czecho-Slovak prime minister, 422, 447, 454; demands formation of independent state, 425; heads delegation of National Committee at Geneve conference with Beneš, 427; signs Geneva declaration, 431, 471; and Slovaks and struggle for Slovakia, 429, 448-453; at Paris Peace Conference, 435, Peace Conference, 447; and intervention in Russia, 460, 461; comments on Paris Peace Conference, 506
Lockhart, Bruce, H., 273, 306
Lodgman von Auen, Rudolph, 436, 456
Lokhvicky, General, 93
London Czech Committee, 54
Long, Breckenridge, memorandum re Masaryk, 290-291; and non-recognition of Bolesheviks, 298; on conversation with Masaryk, 373; on significance of Czech action in Siberia, 499
"Long", code name for Štefánik, 187

Lusatia, Serb (Sorb), 37, 61
Lützow, Count Francis, 513n
Lvov, Prince George E., 151, 168

McDough, General Sir George, 55, 56, 58, 274
McLaren, Lt. Commander, 194

Machovec, Milan, on Masaryk, 24-25
Maffie, formation and members of, 49, 436; sends Dürich abroad, 50; and intelligence activity, 54, 387; views of, 76-78, 542n; and Masaryk and Dürich, 79, 91, 92, 106; and Beneš, 49, 163, 165; and congress in Prague, 265-266
Mamatey, Albert P., 87; and Pittsburgh Agreement, 284-285
Mamatey, Victor S., 299
Mamontov, M.P., proclaims Masaryk "dictator", 155; confirmed by Masaryk as "Czechoslovak Colonel", 178-179; sends troops to Kiev, 214; dismissed from Czechoslovak army by Masaryk, 216
Manifesto of the Czech Writers, 166-167
March, General Peyton C., Willing and able to procure weapons for Czechs in Russia and Siberia, 365, 371; opposes intervention, 367, 413
"Marcus", code name for Masaryk, 187
Markov, General (Russian), 199, 413
Markovic, Ivan (Jan), 139, 140, recognition, 392-394; and the August 28 and 31 memoranda from Masaryk, 396-401; and U.S. recognition of CSNC, 402; recommends aiding Czechs on Volga

front, 412; and rejection of his recommendation, 411-412; and Masaryk's declaration of independence, 423; comments on British double-standards, 433-434; and communication on morale of Czech army, 604n
Lavergne, General, French military attaché in Moscow, comments on Czechs going to France, 274; on Trotsky's order, 320, 324, 345, 349, 350; receives directives to prepare for intervention, 356, 363
Law for the Protection of the Republic, 492, 493
Lay, Julius, 290
League of Nations, 464, 489
Lebedev, V.I., 374
Leger, Louis, 80
Lenin, V.I., 6, 181, 187, 209, 218, 219, 228, 230, 235, 248; and Brest-Bitovsk Treaty, 250, 278; and Lansing's attitude toward his regime, 298, 304, 306, 307, agreement on transferring Czech army to France, 312; confers with Czech Communists, 333; and intervention, 349; and Germans, 358-359; and Czech-Bolshevik conflict, 359; and Masaryk, 363, 475; urges defeat of Czechs on Volga front, 376; endorses Kun's appeal, 451; meets Šmeral, 474; and effects of his regime's recognition on Austria, 499-501
L'Entente, 171
L'Europe Nouvelle, 477
Le Temps, 462
Libuše, wife of the founder of Premyslide dynasty, 265
Lietuva, 183

L'Independance tscheque, 71
Little Entente, 504
"Little Russians", 438
Lloyd George, David, 115, 160, 201; war aims speech, 257-258; pays tribute to Czechoslovak army, 389, 404, 407; at Paris CSNC, 155; on February Revolution (telegram to Miliukov), 157; and telegram to Rodzianko, 157; arrives in Russia under name Thomas George Marsden, 158; as British propogandist in Russia, 168-172, 178-179; and Maugham's statement on original purpose of going to Russia, 171; on being Russophile, 172; and recruitment of prisoners of war, 175-176; proclaimed president and dictator by Mamontov, 189; on building army in Russia, 198-199; and Maugham, 199-201; and agreement for transferring 30,000 troops to France, 200, 249; on Kornilov crisis, 201-203; and establishment of army corps, 204-205; goes to Jassy, 205; and Boleshevik Revolution, 207-234; protests against Soviets' instructions, 209-210; and events in Kiev, 214-216; dismiss Mamontov, 216; and neutrality in Russian internal affairs, 208, 212-216, 244; rejects cooperation with Volunteer Army on the Don, 220, 230-232; and Hussite orientation of army, 223-224; and Muraviev, 241; on Czech Bolesheviks, 239; and Bolesheviks, 227-228, 233-234, 241-243, 246; last speech before leaving Russia, 247; and Savinkov, 248; last manifesto issued

Marsden, Thomas George, alias of T.G. Masaryk, 158, 181, 293
Martínek, Josef (Joseph), 186, 534n; in Russia, 193; on money collected for Masaryk in America, 536n
Masaryk, Alice, 52, 432
Masaryk, Jan (John, Johann), 522n; married Crane's daughter, 570n; served in Austrian army, 588n
Masaryk, Olga (Masaryk-Halík), 108, 258
Masaryk, Tomáš (Thomas) Garrigue, Czechoslovakia's first president, 1; Realist party deputy, 4, 12; leads exile movement, 5; and "Masaryk legend", 5-6; and other theories of origins of Czechoslovakia, 6-9; background and pre-war activities, 17-32; characterized by Machovec, 22-25; Pekař's criticism of, 38, 39; and Voska, 42, 43, 45, 51, 52; and "Šviha affair", 33, 44; meeting with Seton-Watson in Holland, 46-47; and Austrian officials, 48; third trip abroad, 48, 49; decides to stay abroad, 48; and Crane, 44, 45, 51, 52; and collections in America, 51, 536n; arrives in London, 53; and British intelligence operations, 51-59; and "Independent Bohemia", 76-77; and trial of National Social party deputies, 79; accepts lectureship at King's College, 82, 84, 112; comes out publicly against Austria-Hungary in Geneva (July 6, 1915), 85; and Dürich Czech National Council, 89; president of Czecho-Slovak National Council, 97; disavowed by Czech Union, 107; increases propoganda abroad, 108-109; and Russian government, 113-115, 118-130; and Wiseman, 54-57, 131-132, 414, 438; and conflict within independence movement in Russia, 132-156; and *Ruskaia Volia* (Protopopov's newspaper), "Delenda est Austria", 143-144; and establishment of Russian branch of in Russia, 249; appoints Klecanda and Maxa plenipotentiaries in Russia, 249; publicly denounced by Czernin, 255, 256; and Irish independence movement, 258; on sending Japanese troops to Russia, 200, 271, 300, 397, 401; Tokyo memorandum for Wilson, 275-278; amd reaction to it, 279, 360; and Pittsburgh Agreement, 283-285; not received by Wilson, despite Crane's recommendations, 288; in Richard Crane's home, 289-291; received by Lansing, 292-294; advocates recognition of Bolesheviks, 293-297; received by Wilson, 289-300, 360; and Hurban's report, 308; approves Maxa's actions in Russia, 314; and revolt against his neutrality policy 338; meeting with Lansing (June 25), 361-363; memorandum for Chicherin, 362-363; requests U.S. recognition, 370-372; visits with Long, 373; July 21 message to troops, 374; new efforts for U.S. recognition, 390-392, 396; August 28 and 31 for Lansing, 396-402, 586-588n; received by Wilson the second time, 404; notified on U.S. decision regarding Volga front, 411, 413-414; analyzes the decision, 414-415; and establishment of provisional government,

417-419; and declaration of independence, 422-425; requests U.S. recognition of CSNC as *de facto* co-belligerent government, 425; at meeting of Mid-European Democratic Union, 426; signs declaration and accompanying letter to Wilson, 426-427; elected president of Czechoslovakia, 432; first message to Revolutionary National Assembly, 433, 491, 493, 503; instructions for Beneš, 437-439; and intervention in Russia, 396-399, 462-463, 582, 586n; dismisses Kramář as prime minister, 464; and purpose of army in Siberia, 478; on intervention in Russia and Hungary, 482, 586n; and Štefánik's death, 485-486; compared and contrasted with Beneš, 488-489; on revolution, 488-489; and political practices, 490-492; and his religion, 492; and Slovaks, 494; criticized by Kramář, 495-496, 504-505; on causes and aims of World War, 497; on price of independence, 502; failure of his concept, 506; and Austrian press, 536n; on Czechs in Austria, 556n; on Boleshevism, 397-399, 576n, 580n; likes to brag about himself, 594-595n; and his financial situation, 606-607n; plots against Kramář and his party, 610n

Maštálka, Jindřich, G., 107
Mattuš, Karel, 50, 107, 471
Maugham, W. Somerset, 171, 186, 187; meets Voska in Russia, 188; 193; and Masaryk in Petrograd, 199; on situation in Russia, 201, 220, 221, 460

Maxa, Prokop, appointed Masaryk's representative in army, 204; and Kiev events, 241-217; criticized for decisions made, 223, 240, 240, 244; appointed Masaryk's plenitpotentiary for military matters, 249; negotiates with Bolesheviks, 311, 312, 313, 314, 315, 316; agrees to surrender arms, 312-313; arrested in Moscow, 329, 334; orders troops to disarm, 330; deposed by soldiers, 335, 336; revolt against his policy, 338; and leaflets to troops, 334-345; negotiates departure of troops with Soviets, 476
Medek, Rudolph, 204, 240
Medvecý, Karol, 430
Mensheviks, 168, 218, 343
Mid-European Democratic Union, declaration of, 426-427
Mihailović, Ljubo, 49, 292, 362
Miles, Basil, 290, 291, 361, 365
Miliukov, Paul N., 39, 151, 156-158, 168, 173, 192, 220, 239 395, 460, 521-522n, 607n
Milner, Alfred, 268, 286
Mirbach, Count Wilhelm von, 341, 359
Miscarea, 171
Mitteleuropa, 113
Modráček, František, 164, 168
Montagu, Edwin S., 115
Moravian Empire, 2
Morgan J.P. & Co., 184
Morning Post, 125
Morris, Roland S., 275, 276, 289; on Kolchak, 604-605n
Mrňák, František, 202
Müller, V., 144
Můna, Alois, 214, 238, 239, 333
Muraviev, Michael A., 233, 241

Murmansk, 225

Namier, Lewis, 80, 364
Národ, 164, 167
Národní Listy, 39, 71, 107, 107, 459, 471; on Šviha affair, 518n; on Masaryk, 536n
Nation (London), 267
National Alliance of Bohemian Catholics, 69, 280; and Pittsburgh Agreement, 283-284
National Council (Paris), 71, 82
National Review, 13
National Social party (National Socials), 11, 33, 35, 45, 46, 49, 73, 75, 79, 101, 103, 107, 168, 237, 387, 420, 489
National Socialist party, 8
National Theatre, 265
Naumann, Friedrich, 113
Němec, Antonín, 436
Němeček, Captain, 218, 228, 230, 304, 306
Neo-Slavism, 13, 15, 16, 39, 86
Neratov, 132
New Europe, 56, 109, 157, 162
New Statesman, The, 80
New York Herald, 296
New York Herald Tribune, 295
New York Times, 293, 295, 296, 298, 389, 403; Masaryk quoted in, 508n
Nicholas II, tsar, rudered, 375
Nikolaevich, Grand Duke Nicholas, 66, 70
Northcliffe, Lord, 283
Noulens, Joseph, 275, 349
Nosek, Vladimír, 108, 258
Nová Europa (New Europe), 439
Novák, J., 69
Novotný, František, 239

October Revolution, 6, 7, 9, 304, 468, 510n

Old Czech party, 12, 50, 101, 103, 387
Order of St. Vladimir, 148
Orel, 173
Orlando, Vittorio E., 206, 260-262, 431
Orszag, Josef, 63
Orthodox Church (Orthodoxy), 85, 154, 155, 173
Osuský, ü

Orthodox Church (Orthodoxy), 85, 154, 155, 173
Osuský, Štefan (Stephen), 69, 83, 108, 134, 196, 419, 607n, on CSNC, 537-538n

Page, Thomas Nelson, 264, 289
Paget, Sir Ralph, memoranda on war aims, 115-117
Palacký, František, 15, 29, 72, 496
Paleologue, Maurice, 67
Pan-Germanism (Pan-Germanists), 13, 36, 72, 113
Pankhurst, Madame, 188
Pan-Slavism, 13, 15, 90, 95
Papoušek, Jaroslav, 147, 153n
Paris Czech Press Bureau, 108
Paris, General, 309, 411
Parvus (Hoelflund), 193
Patejdl, Josef, 394
Pavelić, Ante, 256
Pavlů, Bohdan, 73, 87, 90, 103, 121, 135, 147, 151, 188; and Kornilov, 203-204; condemns Maxa for decision made in Kiev, 223; against disarming troops, 312; chairman of Temporary Executive Committee, 334, 336, 341, 346, 352; elected vice-president of Russian branch of CSNC, 394; reports to Harris on lack of arms, 408; urges formation of

All-Russian government, 409; represents provisional government in Russia, 419; on state of army in Siberia, 480-481; on westward offensive, 481 482
Pekař, Josef, on "Masaryk's Czech Philosophy", 25-32; 488, 491
Pellé, General Maurice, 450
Penížek, Josef, 19
People's Commissariat of Nationalities, 351
People's party, 464
Pergler, Charles, 69, 82, 87, 197, 279, 539n, 281, 283; represents CSNC in United States, 418; acredited to U.S. government, 419; first Czecho-Slovak minister to Japan, 493; denounces Masaryk and Beneš, 493; expelled from Czechoslovakia, 606n
Phillips, William, recommends recognition of CSNC jointly with British and French governments, 361, 380-381, 390-391; recommends aiding Czechs on Volga front, 413
Piccione, General Luigi, 450
Pichon, Stephen, 80, 265, 287; recognizes CSNC, 383, 384, 388, 422; rejects plebiscite proposed by Austria, 437
Pilsidski, Jozef, 457, 460
Písecký, Ferdinand, 135
Pittsburgh Agreement, 283-285, 456, 458, 493, 494
Plato (Platonic), 17, 22, 290, 291, 491
Plekhanov, 143, 191, 210, 211
Plesinger, Miroslav, 89, 258
Pochodeň, 240, 243, 245, 246, 325
Pokrovsky, Nicolai N., 147, 148
Political Centre (Irkutsk), 483

Political Intelligence Department, 178
Political parties (Czech and Slovak), 4, 8, 11, 12, 32-34. See also individual political parties
Poole, General Sir Fredrick C., 324
Posse (Posse-Brázda), Amelie, 192
Pravda (Boleshevik), 219
Právo Lidu, 167, 488
Priklonsku, M., 95, 101, 115, 132, 148, 151, 152, 153; memoranda on future settlement in Europe, 117-131
Progressive, bloc of, 12, 45, 102, 107
Progressive State Rights party, 4, 12, 33, 45, 46, 49, 50, 101, 103, 107
Protopopov, A.D., 143, 152, 153, 495
Provisional Constitution of Czecho-Slovak Republic, 432
Provisional German Austrian Nationally Assembly, 423
Provisional Government (Russia), 152, 168, 169, 185, 224, 307
Provisional Government of Siberia, 337, 343, 344, 346, 352
Průkopník, 317, 319, 322, 323, 326, 330; merges with *Svoboda*, 333
Průkopník Svobody, 248, 333
Pučálka, M., 121
Putney, Albert H., on "Slavs of Austria-Hungary", 279-280, 379; on Bohemia, 391

Raczkowski, V.K., 183
Radek, Karl, 189, 193, 219
Rašín, Alois, 6, member of Maffie, 49; arrest of, 78, trial of, 79; sentenced to death, 80, 81;

pardoned by Emperor, 159, 210, 251; author of Epiphany Declaration, 252; and Seliger, 436
Rasputin, 143
Reading, Lord, 58, 378, 461
Realist party, 4, 12, 22, 104, 107, 387, 490
Rech' (*Rietch*), 169, 170, 192
Red Army, 309, 313, 323, 329, 331, 333, 341, 345, 474 (Czechoslovak), 318, 322, 325, 326, 333, 342, 343, 469
Red Cross, 300, 361
Red Guards, 233, 306, 308, 309, 313, 326, 327, 331, 338, 340, 341, 345, 351, 358, 360, 369, 370, 412, (Hungarian) 450
Redlich, Josef, 17
Reinsch, Paul, S., 350
Rejman, Zdeněk, 63, 96
Republic of Plato, 290
Revkom, 484
Revoluce, 156, 307
Revolutionary (Constituent) National Assembly, 141, 422, 425, 427; elects Masaryk president, 432; composition of, 432-433, 433, 491, 493, 503, 456; *See* also Czechoslovak Revolutionary (Constituent) National Assembly
Revue de Paris, 13, 14
Ribot, Alexander, 177
Richter, František, 204, 340, 341, 346, 356, 394
Robertson, Sir Williams, 55
Robins, Raymond, 273, 276
Rodzianko, M.V. 157, 395
Romania mare, 171
Rome Congress of Oppressed Nationalities. *See* Congress of Oppressed Nationalities
Root, Elihu, mission in Russia, 188
Rosen, Baron, 192
Royard, Major (French), 356

Rukopisy, 20
Russkia Vedomosti, 169; Masaryk's telegram printed in, 209-210
Ruskaia Volia, 192; Masaryk's article "Delenda est Austria" printed in, 143
Russkoye Slovo, 192
Russo-Slovak L'Štúr Society, 34, 64, 90, 95, 134, 139, 142

Sadlucki (Sadlutsky), 328, 334
Sts. Cyril and Methodius, 27; regiment of, 173; regiment's change of name, 223-224; holiday of 610n
St. Germain, Treaty of, 457, 482
St. Stephens's Crown (Crown of St. Stephen), 72, 422, 535n
St. Wenceslas, 62; regiment of, 175; regiment's change of name, 224; 535
St. Wenceslas Crown (Crown of St. Wenceslas), 2, 47, 61, 62, 125, 128, 167, 421
Sabbath, Adolph J., 83, 298, 379
Sadoul, Captain Jacques, 306, 576n
Šámal, Přemysl, 49, 50, 51, 78, 163
Savinkov (Savinkoff), Boris V., 191, 221, 248, 460
Savjolov, Chamberlaim, 64
Sazonov, Sergei, 35, 36, 41, 47, 61, 65, 67, 85, 101m 106, 460
Scheiner, Josef, 36, 49, 50, 51, 75, 78, 163
Scotus Viator (R.W. Seton-Watson), 458
Seignobos, Charles, 108
Seliger, Josef, 436, 437
Shatagin, N.I., 469
Semenov, Ataman Gregorii, 274, 291, 321

Seton-Watson, Robert W., 39, 42; meets Masaryk in Holland, 46-47; and Masaryk, 48, 52, 53, 54, 55, 56, 57, 58, 76, 439; and Dürich, 104; and *New Europe,* 109; and propoganda, 132, 283; works in Political Intelligence Department, 178; comments on Masaryk's Tokyo memorandum, 288; and Slovakia, 458; on history, 487
Shcherbachev, General Dimitri G., 205, 226, 228
Shokorov, General V.N., 204, 213, 214, 244, 335, 336, 356
Sidor, Karol, 432
Sidorin, V., 202
Sinn Fein, 258; Sinnfeinists (Czech), 267
Šíp, František, 248, 249
Sís. František, 39, 52, 53, 542n
Sís, Vladimír, 39, 40, 111, 112, 542n
Sisson documents, 523n
Sixtus of Bourbon-Parma, Prince, 165, 177, 180; "affair" of, 262-264, 497
Skoták, A., 322, 342
Slovanic Emigration Institute, 186
Slav Press Bureau, 82, 184, 189; Petrograd branch of, 187, 192
Slovák, 458
Slovak League of America, 69, 79, 87, 139, 182, 280, 281; and Cleveland Agreement, 70, 79, 83; and Pittsburgh Agreement, 283-285
Slovak National Council, 4, 429; formally established and declaration of, 430
Slovak People's party (Slovak Populists), 8, 456, 457, 459, 494
Slovak Soviet Republic (Slovak Republic of Soviets), 451, 452

Slovenský denník, 458
Slovak National party, 4, 72
Šmeral, Bohumír, 47, 48, 72, 78, 107, 167, 539n; in Moscow, 474
Smetana Hall, 256
Smetánka, J.F., 82
Smirnov, I.N., 484
"Smith", code name for Joseph Martínek, 187
Smitt, O. 142
Social Democratic party (Social Democrats), 4, 11, 12, 17, 22, 32, 39, 44, 47, 49, 50, 69, 72, 78, 103, 107, 119, 120, 167, 168, 331, 333, 387, 455, 458, 459, 464, 473, 474, 489, 503, 510n
Social Democrats (Czech) in Russia, 212, 214, 219, 237, 238, 240, 245-247, 304, 317, 331
Socialist Council (Czech), 420
Socialist International, 44
Socialist party (American), 69
Socialist Revolutionaries (SRs), 168, 218, 277, 310, 325, 343, 369, 374, 376, 463, 470, 481
Socialists (Russian), 218, 470
Social Question, The, 22, 23
Sokol, 36, 69, 75, 78, 173, 251; in U.S., 69
Sokoloff, Nicholas, 192
Sonnino, Baron Sidney, 197
Sorokin, Pitirin, 192
Soukup, František, 252, 387, 420, 436, 539n
Soviets, Soviets, of Workers' and Soldiers' Deputies, 152, 168, 173, 174
Sovnarkom, 310, 312, 358, 469
Spaa, agreement of, 264, 500-501
Špaček, J. 348
Šrobár, Vavro, 11, 84, 166, 432, 449, 457, 458, 459, 494; on Hodza, 510n

Štafl, Ivan, 93, 96, 102, 134, 135, 136, 137
Stalin, Joseph V., 310, 311, 312,
Staněk, František, 107, 253, 419, 420; signs Geneva declaration, 431, 471; on consequences of Brest-Litovsk peace, 500
State Rights party. *See* Progressive State Rights party
Steed, Henry Wickham, 14, 39; and Masaryk, 42-48, 51, 52, 54, 58, 59, 84, 169, 439, 522n, 524n; and propoganda, 108, 109, 283; and Beneš, 268, 607n; on meaning of "trustee", 390; on British recognition of CSNC, 498
Štefánek, Anton, 73
Štefánik, Milan, R., 5, 6; biographical data, 84-85; and Dürich, 98, 101, 133-138, 144-151; and French government, 98-101, 259, 287; goes to Russia, 100-101, 106; and Russian government, 123, 136, 137, 174; and Maxa, 223; mission in United States, 196-197; and Masaryk, 279, 302, 333, 364, 365; minister of war in provisional government, 419, 475; arrives in Siberia, 467; in Siberia, 475-477; on Boleshevism, 485; and Dürich's daughter, 535n; and Beneš, 535n, 477, 496; death of, 478, 485, 488
Šteidler, František, 601n
Štěpánek, Vítězslav, 33, 40, 82, 96, 101, 108, 140, 217
Štern, E., 93, 135, 148, 153, 154
Stevens (American Railway Mission), 291
Štíbner, V., 144

Stilip, Frank, 194
Stránsky, Adolf, 107, 252
Stříbrny, Jiří, 8, 164, 610n
Štrimpl, L., 84
Štrombach, Jaroslav, 318, 342
Štúr, L'udovít, 3, 284
Stürmer, M., 101
Subcarpathian Ruthenia (Carpatho-Ruthenians), 453-454
Sub-Carpatho Russia (Ruthenia), 494
Sudetenland, 436
Sumenson, Mme., 192
Supreme War Council (Paris), 178, 229, 247, 286, 287, 353, 404-405; urges intervention in Russia, 365-366
Švarc, Ven, 186, 188, 193
Svatkovsky, Vsevolod, 37, 40, 49, 84, 114, 149
Švec, Josef, 343, 467, 485
Švehla, Antonín, 50, 166, 387, 471
Šviha, Karel, 33; "Šviha affair", 33, 44, 48, 488
Švihovský, V., 142
Svoboda, 228, 238, 239, 243, 245, 246, 317, 322, 325, 326; merges with *Průkopník*, 333
Sychrava, Lev, 75, 82, 84, 149, 196, 419
Sýkora, Jan, 54, 87
Synek, Jan, 247, 322, 333
Syrový, Jan, 224, 339, 404, 406; querry to Allies re Volga front, 409; report to Štefánik, 476; on westward offensive, 481; carries out evacuation, 482; challenged to duel, 483; held responsible for Kolchak's fate, 484
Szporluk, Roman, quoted on Masaryk's "philisophical message", 516n

Index

Taborites, 29, 318
Tabouis, General (French), 230, 247
Tardieu, Andre, 108
Temporary Executive Commitee (TEC), 334-336, 339, 345-347; on why Czechs had taken to arms, 350-351; and Guinet, 356; and Masaryk, 363
Teschen, Duchy of, 452, 453, 454
Third International, 331, 332, 473, 474
Thirty Years War, 2
Thomas, Albert, agreement on transfer of Czech and Slovak troops to France, 249
Thun-Hohenstein, Count Franz von, 46, 48, 524n
Times (London), 14, 42, 80, 108, 169, 389, 556n
Tobolka, Zdeněk, Václav, 107
Tolstoy, Leo N., 168, 170
Treaty of Berlin (1878), 16
Treaty of London (1915), 111
Trotsky, Leo (Leon Bronstein), 187, 189, 207, 209, 218, 219, 274, 285, 306, 320, 324, 329, 338; requests leaving Czech troops in Russia, 312-314; decides to dismantle army corps, 329-330; and order of May 25, 1918, 337, 342, 347-349; on execution of tsar's family, 375; and victory statement, 407; and building disciplined army, 469-470; Masaryk's comment on, 501
Trubeckoj, Prince Eugene N., 248
Tuček, Louis, (Lois), 40, 63, 90, 94
Turčiansky Sv. Martin, 4, 429, 430
Tusar, Vlastimil, 420, 464; on consequences of Brest-Litovsk peace, 500-501
Tyrrell, Sir William, memoranda on war aims, 115-117

Udržal, František, 32
Ukrainian Central Council (Rada), 214, 217, 222, 226, 229
"Ukrainians" (Ruthenians), 438
Union of Czech Deputies. *See* Czech Union
Utro Rosiji

Vajanský, Svetozár Hurban, 11, 34, 284
Vančcura, J., 25, 26, 27, 31
Vandervelde, Emile, 39
Vaněk, Vladimír, 96, 108, 149
Vaníček, Václav, 247, 322, 342
Vav[k, 28
Vatican, 178
Vecherniie, Vremiia, 169, 171
Veöe
Vecherniie, Vremiia, 169, 171
Večerník, 164, 166
Venkov, 164
Verge, Major Arsene, 344
Versailles, Treaty of, 482
Veselý, Antonín, 71, 87
Vesmír, 83, 533-534n, 606n
"Victor", code name for Voska, 186
Vienna parliament, 4, 104, 166
Vinogradov, Paul, 47, 144
Vojtsekhovskii, Sergei, 244, 334, 339, 346, 356, 368, 406; commands White Russian troops, 484
Volf, J., 106
Volia Naroda, 192
Volnost, 169
Volunteer Army (Russian), 213, 230, 232, 248, 304, 306, 312, 375, 408, 468, 470

Vondrák, Vácslav, 43, 60, 62; elected president of ASCAR, 64; secures tsar's approval for release Czech and Slovak prisoners of war, 94; and Masaryk, 96; signs Kievan Pact, 106; and Russian government, 121-123, 549n; and Dürich, 135, 139, 470; recognizes Masaryk's leadership of independence movement abroad, 151

Voska, Emanuel Victor, sent to Steed by Masaryk, 42, 43, 488; heads Masaryk's "private" intelligence, 45-46, 51, 52, 54-56; and Wiseman, 56, 57, 58, 59, 131, 132, 145, 149, 182, 236; signs declaration of "Czech Committee Abroad", 87; silences Iška, 83; on mission in Russia, 182-195, 543; and propoganda scheme (report) for Carlson and House, 188-191; believes Czechs could have taken and held Petrograd, 208; and Masaryk, 288, 438, 488. 521n; proposes propoganda scheme, 281-282; in U.S. intelligence service, 282, 283; works for "Inquiry" in Europe, 439, 527; imprisoned, 508n

Vortuba, František, 73

Vrbenský, Bohumil, 164

"Warring Co.", code name for Russian government, 187

War Trade Board, on appointing Russian commissioner and commission, 301

Washington Post, 287, 295, 296, 298

Washington Sunday Star, 296

Weiss, Louise, on Beneš, and Štefánik, 477

Werkerle, Alexander, 422

White Guards, 407

White Mountain, battle of, 48

Whyte, Fredrick, 56

Wilhelm II (William II), Emperor of Germany, 164, 264, 358, 432, 501

Williams, Roger, H., 52

"Wilsonian legend", 503

Wilson, (Mrs.) Edith Bolling, 301

Wilson, Woodrow, 5, 131, 160; joint reply of Allies to, 131, 160, 178; and declaration of war on Austria-Hungary, 180, 227; and Fourteen Points, 226, 257, 258; and Masaryk's Tokyo memorandum, 276-278; meets Masaryk, 298-300, 379, 404; on sending civil commission to Russia, 301, 360, 361; refuses aiding Czechs on Volga front, 368, 411-412; refuses to recognize CSNC, 377-378; grants recognition and meets Masaryk in White House, 404; and note of October 18, 1918, 423, 425, 428, 439

Wiseman, Sir William, and Masaryk, 54, 56, 414, 438; in United States, 56-58, 59, and Voska, 56-59, 131, 132, 145, 182-188, 191, 281, 282, 283, 439, 527n; and House, 58, 146; and Maugham, 171, 186, 187, 201; and Auchincloss: recommends Voska for intelligence and propoganda work, 282; receives Masaryk's "Notes" on U.S. decision re Volga front, 414-415; and Murray (on Voska) 527n

Woolsey, Lester H., 392, 394

Wright, Butler J., 289, 290, 294

Yastrebov, Professor (University of Petrograd), 192
Young Czech party (Young Czechs), 11, 13, 22, 37, 38, 39, 40, 49, 78, 101, 103, 107, 167, 252
Y.M.C.A., 300, 361
Young, Robert F., 55, 56, 283, 526n
Yundenich, General Nikolai, N., 482, 483
Yugoslav, Committee in London, 145
Yugoslav National Council in Zagreb, 419

Zajíček, Captain, 316
Západocký, Antonín, 474
Závada, Bohuslav, 356
Zborov, 73, 185, 308, battle of, 174-175
Zhilinski, General, 35
Zionists, 23, 154
Zíval, G.A., 217
Žižka, Jan (John), regiment of, 224; leader of radical Hussites, 318
Zlámal, Rev. Oldřich, 69, 280